Heinemann **PSYCHOLOGY A2** *for OCR*

Heinemann

PSYCHOLOGY A2

for OCR

Karen Legge Philippe Harari
Linda Sherry Sally Gadsdon

Heinemann

Inspiring generations

Heinemann Educational Publishers
Halley Court, Jordan Hill, Oxford OX2 8EJ
Part of Harcourt Education

Heinemann is the registered trademark of
Harcourt Education Limited

Introduction; Chapters 1, 2, 3, 6 © Karen Legge and Philippe Harari; Chapter 4 © Linda Sherry;
Chapter 5 © Sally Gadsdon 2005

First published 2005

08 07 06 05
10 9 8 7 6 5 4 3 2 1

British Library Cataloguing in Publication Data is available
from the British Library on request.

ISBN 0 435 806 718

Typeset and illustrated by ↗ Tek-Art, Croydon, Surrey
Original illustrations © Harcourt Education Limited
Printed by CPI Bath Press
Picture research by Sally Cole

Acknowledgements
Every effort has been made to contact copyright holders of material reproduced in this book. Any omissions will be
rectified in subsequent printings if notice is given to the publishers.
The publishers would like to thank the following for permission to reproduce photographs:
Action Plus/Glyn Kirk p.111; AKG p.179; Alamy A Room with Views p.209; Brandeis University Libraries p.27;
Corbis p.20; Harcourt Education/Liz Edison p.98; Photofusion pp.58, 8; Photofusion/Paula Solloway p.310;
Popperfoto pp.179, 238; Beatrix Potter, copyright Frederick Warne & Co 1902, 2002 p.64; Press Association/DPA p.85;
Press Association p.298; Rex Features pp.72, 179, 315; Rex Features/Sipa Press pp.90, 240, 314; Rex Features/Nils
Jorgensen p.240; Science Photo Library/Hank Morgan p.117; Albert Bandura, Stanford University p.19; The
Wellcome Trust p.278
The publishers would like to thank the following for permission to reproduce artwork:
American Psychological Association pp.162, 306: Copyright © 1964 and 1994 respectively by the American
Psychological Association. Adapted with permission; Harcourt Inc p.220; Hodder Headline p.268; Home Office
p.287; John Wiley and Sons Ltd p.316

CD ROM Interactive material
Attribution © Victoria Richings; Classical conditioning © Hilary McQueen; Nature/Nurture © Victoria Richings.

CD ROM Text acknowledgements
British Crime Survey extracts (*Crime and ethnicity, Crime and gender, Public Expectations and Perceptions of
Policing, Interviewing eyewitnesses, Children's Testimony*) Crown Copyright material is reproduced under Class
License Number C01W0000141 with the permission of the Controller of HMSO and the Queen's Printer for
Scotland; *Why Sunshine is good for you* 17/4/03, Michael Hanlon © Daily Mail; *Upside down map* 13/06/97 ©
Daily Mail, Adapted and reprinted from *Leadership and decision making* by Victor H. Vroom and Phillip W. Yetton,
by permission of the University of Pittsburgh Press, © 1973 by University of Pittsburgh Press; *Diagnostic Criteria for
Posttraumatic Stress Disorder*. Reprinted with permission from the Diagnostic and Statistical Manual of Mental
Disorders © 2000. American Psychiatric Association; Eysenck's Model of Personality reproduced with permission
from the HJ Eysenck memorial fund © Eysenck; *Keep your distance* 14/9/99, The Guardian © Oliver Burkeman;
Coping in a crisis 22/3/03, The Guardian © Karen Hainsworth; *World Cup Control, Asian Style* 13/7/01, The
Guardian © J Watts; Job Description Index. The Measurement of Satisfaction in work and retirement, Chicago and
McNally © JDI Office, Bowling Green State University; McGill-Melzack pain questionnaire (1975) © R Melzack;
Loaded! Why Supermarkets are getting richer and richer ©Andrew Purvis, 25/1/04, The Observer.

CONTENTS

CD-ROM contents

Education

Additional key studies
Measurement scales
Theoretical approaches
Real life applications
Links
Sample exam questions

Health

Additional key studies
Measurement scales
Theoretical approaches
Real life applications
Links
Sample exam questions

Organisations

Additional key studies
Measurement scales
Theoretical approaches
Real life applications
Links
Sample exam questions

Environment

Additional key studies
Thcorctical approaches
Real life applications
Links
Sample exam questions

Crime

Additional key studies
Measurement scales
Theoretical approaches
Real life applications
Links
Sample exam questions

Sport

Psychology and sport
Links
Sample exam questions

INTRODUCTION

ABOUT THIS BOOK

This textbook contains all the information you need to fulfil the requirements of the OCR A2 Psychology specification. It covers the six specialist choice modules that make up the OCR A2 specification in Psychology. To complete the A2 qualification, candidates take any two of these modules. Each of these modules looks at how psychology can be applied in a practical setting:

- **2544 Psychology and education**
- **2545 Psychology and health**
- **2546 Psychology and organisations**
- **2547 Psychology and environment**
- **2548 Psychology and sport** (on the CD-ROM)
- **2549 Psychology and crime.**

There is also a section in this book that gives full coverage of how to tackle **Module 2543, the Psychology research report,** which is examined by completing two pieces of coursework. One of these involves you designing and carrying out a piece of practical research, and the other requires you to write a structured essay showing how psychology can be related to everyday life.

In each chapter of the book, the subsections of the specification are covered in the right amount of detail and depth to help you understand the material without giving too much extra evidence. There is additional material on the CD-ROM if you are particularly interested in a topic, or need additional information for a specific idea on your coursework.

FEATURES OF THIS BOOK

- Each chapter of this book covers one module of the OCR A2 Psychology syllabus. The sections and sub-sections contained within each chapter correspond to the OCR specification.
- Each chapter contains a number of **key studies**. These are up-to-date pieces of research, which are explained in detail.
- At the end of each of the eight sections in a chapter there are sample Section A questions to use for exam practice. Section B questions (which are always based on the eight section headings for each module) can be found on the CD-ROM (see below).
- Throughout the book, there are **margin boxes** that provide additional information. Some of these are directly relevant to essay writing and the exams, and some of them help explain concepts or theories in more detail. The margin boxes have the following headings:
  - **Evaluation issue:** these boxes contain specific points of evaluation concerning a study or a theory. They can be used in preparing answers to essay questions.
  - **Key definition:** these boxes contain clear and concise definitions/explanations of key psychological concepts used in the text.
  - **For consideration:** these boxes ask questions, and can be used to make you think about an issue. They may also be used to prompt discussion or an activity.

- **Exam hint:** these boxes provide useful tips for answering exam questions.
- **CD-ROM:** these boxes direct you to additional material on the CD-ROM.

• This book is accompanied by a CD-ROM containing the following material:

- **Additional key studies:** detailed descriptions of research that could be used as alternatives to the key studies described in the book.
- **Measurement scales:** copies of the psychometric tests mentioned in the book, with scoring procedures. These can be used to understand the test and its application, and some of them can also be used in coursework.
- **Theoretical approaches:** descriptions of underlying psychological theories mentioned in the book; these are presented on the CD-ROM in more detail than is required by the OCR specification but may be of interest.
- **Real life applications:** detailed cases of how psychological theories are applied in the real world.
- **Interactive activities:** activities to help understanding.
- **Links:** a list of useful and up-to-date Internet links is provided.
- **References:** a comprehensive list of every publication cited in the book.
- **Sample exam questions:** these include copies of all the Section A sample exam questions presented in the book and also Section B sample exam questions, the latter of which carry the bulk of exam marks.
- **Exam guidance:** in addition to the 'exam hints' margin boxes throughout the book, and the questions at the end of each section, the CD-ROM contains advice on how to answer Section A and Section B exam questions.

CHAPTER 1 | PSYCHOLOGY RESEARCH REPORT

CHAPTER 1: INTRODUCTION

This module involves two pieces of coursework:

- One piece of coursework is a practical project in which you must carry out your own piece of research and write it up. This is the same kind of research that you carried out in AS Psychology in the Psychological Investigations module, but you have to write up your practical project more fully in this A2 module.
- The other piece of coursework is an assignment in which you have to evaluate a source (usually an article from a magazine or newspaper), in a psychological context.

This module carries the same number of marks as the two other specialist choice modules.

THE PRACTICAL PROJECT

The practical project involves carrying out an investigation

You can use a number of methods to carry out your research, including an experiment, a correlation, an observation, a content analysis or a survey or questionnaire. The mark scheme tends to favour the use of statistical testing, as it is easier to pick up marks in the results section if you have carried out a statistical test.

The practical project involves carrying out an investigation in which you:
• decide on a research question
• write your aims and/or hypotheses that you will test
• choose a method to carry out this investigation
• operationalise the variables and design the study
• collect and analyse the data
• evaluate your investigation.

The research is written up into a report that must not exceed 1400 words. This does not include the references or appendices and tables.

It is very important for any psychological research to be ethical, and OCR requires candidates to fill out a proposal form. This will be sent to the exam board by your teacher before you can start collecting your data.

WRITING UP YOUR COURSEWORK REPORT

Abstract

This is a brief summary of the aims, nature and findings of your study. It should include the aim of the study and how it was carried out. It should also include a brief description of what was expected, and what was found (including a brief summary of the inferential statistics, if used, to support the findings). This section should be concise.

Background

This section is a review of some relevant and appropriate research studies or theories that relate to your investigation. You only need to refer to one or two studies (if you are using a lot of detail one is enough, but two often cover what you need to say more appropriately). You should show how the background research is related to your own study, and how your study leads on from this.

Hypotheses

Write your hypotheses (both the research/experimental and the null) as clearly as possible, and operationalise them. Indicate whether your research hypotheses are one or two tailed.

Methodology

Anything that you refer to here, for example a copy of standardised instructions, a questionnaire or any other relevant materials must be referenced and put in the appendix. This section is divided into four parts:
• Design: describe the type of study (the design), for example whether it is independent or repeated measures, and the operationalisation of any concepts.

- Materials: provide details of all the materials that you used in conducting the study, for example how you adapted existing tests for your own use, or how you decided which questions to ask, and refer to standardised instructions that you wrote (see Appendices below).
- Sampling/participants: it is good practice to describe your parent population, and how you recruited your sample from this population. Name and describe the sampling techniques, and give details of the participants, for example, how many there were, their ages, where they were located, the numbers of males and females (and any other details that may be relevant to your study, such as their occupation).
- Procedure: this should be thorough and detailed, and give an account of exactly how the study was conducted. Describe the method, including precise details of what happened in each condition. Describe any controls, such as how you minimised the effect of any confounding variables, and the use of standardised instructions (and make reference to a copy in the appendix). Include details of how you measured what the participants did (and make reference to a copy in the appendix).

Results

Your results section should include:
- a clearly labelled summary table of your results (you should refer to a copy of the raw data in the appendix)
- clearly labelled graphs, pie charts, etc.
- a brief discussion of the results to suggest what they appear to show (from the graphs and summary table)
- the results of your statistical tests, including a statement of significance (refer to a copy of the workings in the appendix).

Discussion

In this section you should evaluate the methods you have used to conduct your study, for example the design, the procedure, location, controls and ethics. For each evaluative comment (positive or negative) that you make, you should discuss the effect that this had on your study, and how possible improvements or changes would affect the results. You should also relate your findings to the background section, and discuss how your research challenges or supports the theory/studies. You should also say how you might extend your research, what further research might be interesting?

References

List alphabetically by author's last name all of the studies you have referred to in your report, and all of the articles and books you used. You must use the conventional format for citing references:
- For studies or articles you have read about in other books the format is as follows:
  Name, date, title of study or article, book it is in, place and date of publication.
- For books the format is as follows:
  Name, date, title, place of publication, publisher.

Appendices

Include items such as questionnaires, a blank answer sheet, word lists, standardised instructions, raw data and workings of statistical tests. These are important evidence of your planning and work, but would make the text too bulky. Your appendices should be clearly labelled, and be referenced in the text of your report.

1.2 THE ASSIGNMENT

The assignment involves the use of an article, which you will evaluate in a psychological context. You will select a source, in discussion with your teacher, and then write about it, in the form of a structured essay. The assignment should not exceed 1000 words.

FINDING A SOURCE

You can use a newspaper or magazine article, or an advert or public information leaflet. The Internet can be a good source of articles (especially newspaper sites). The source should be current (i.e. within the last year) especially if it is a newspaper report.

You should try to find a source that interests you, since you have to write about it and research the background information.

You will be expected to find a source that has some link to issues that could be related to psychology. Your article has to have psychological assumptions in it.

IDENTIFYING ASSUMPTIONS IN THE SOURCE

This can be the hardest part of the exercise because your source should have three clear assumptions in it, and it is very difficult to write about ambiguous or complicated assumptions.

An assumption is a statement or description in a source that can be linked to a psychological theory or idea. Some examples are given below:
- If you were reading an article about a person who was driven to hit their child for some reason, and the discussion of events in the article mentioned that the person had been hit by their own parent, then the underlying assumption might be **social learning theory** (Bandura), since the article is suggesting that the adult hit the child because they were possibly imitating their own parents.
- If you were reading an article about juggling work and home life, and the person in the article described lots of minor irritations in their day, then this could be linked to the **measurement of stress using daily hassles** (Kanner).

Usually a 'rule of thumb' is that for an assumption to be meaningful, there has to be an explanation of the behaviour, not just a mention of the behaviour. For example, if a newspaper report mentions the fact that a young person was sent to a young offender institution because they committed arson, this is not an assumption on its own. However, if the article mentions the fact that the young person set fire to the building because they were encouraged to do so by a group of friends, then this can be related to peer pressure.

When you have found a suitable article you have to research existing psychological studies or theories that are related to your article. Also, you must check that there is adequate and clear background information.

WRITING ABOUT THE SOURCE

The structured questions that you will answer include the following:
- What are the underlying psychological assumptions or the issues raised by the source? (What psychological concepts, theories or issues does the source refer or relate to?)
- Describe and relate some psychological evidence to the source (at least one piece for each assumption).
- How can psychological theory be used to intervene in the issues raised in the source? (You might make some suggestions based on psychological theories and evidence, and suggest what effects these interventions will have.)

You will also be awarded marks for your overall writing style, spelling, etc. and the inclusion of a list of references.

There is a style of writing the sections of this assignment that ensures that you adhere to the mark scheme, and makes the layout of your assignment clear and easy to follow (for the examiner).

In section a) you should:
- identify each assumption
- for each assumption, show how it relates to the source and give a short quote to show you understand this
- briefly refer to the psychological study, theory or issue to which this relates.

In section b) you should:
- describe the evidence you have referred to in section a) for each assumption
- show how each piece of evidence relates to the source for each assumption.

In section c) you should:
- describe a suggestion for each assumption that could improve the situation you describe in the other sections. This suggestion should have some connection to a psychological study or theory/idea if possible
- explain the effect of each suggestion on the situation and evaluate it.

REFERENCES

List alphabetically by author's last name all of the studies you have referred to in your assignment, and all of the articles and books you used. You must use the conventional format for citing references:
- For studies or articles you have read about in other books the format is as follows:
  Name, date, title of study or article, book it is in, place and date of publication.
- For books the format is as follows:
  Name, date, title, place of publication, publisher.

When submitting the assignment you must hand the source in with the assignment.

CHAPTER 2 | PSYCHOLOGY AND EDUCATION

CHAPTER 2: INTRODUCTION

Everything teachers do in the classroom reflects their personal beliefs in some way or other. These beliefs cover a wide range of questions related to education, for example, determining the most effective way of imparting knowledge and skills to students, motivating students and dealing with disruptive students. A question as apparently simple as how best to lay out the desks in a classroom depends on beliefs about how students learn and about what kind of relationship should exist between students and teachers, and these beliefs in turn depend on beliefs about basic human nature. Perhaps the most important belief of all is about the fundamental purpose of education. Is it to train people to do specific jobs, to create good citizens, or to lead people to intellectual or spiritual enlightenment?

Educationalists' beliefs about education arise out of their personal experience, their own education, the books they have read and so on. Different teachers hold widely different views, and this is reflected in their classroom practice. The role of educational psychology is to examine different views about learning and to establish theories so that educational practice can be built on a valid theoretical foundation. Most psychologists use the scientific method to establish theories, i.e. they collect data and test this empirical evidence against hypotheses in order to confirm or contradict it. Once psychologists have established theories, this can then lead to practice. However, as in other areas of psychology, there are many different theories, each with their own supporters, and this leads to a wide variety of educational practice.

In his book *Psychology for Teachers*, Fontana (1995) sets out a number of practical hints and tips for teachers which he feels represent best educational practice:

- Interest the class: a class that is absorbed in its work will not want to cause problems; teachers need to provide work that is relevant, interesting and enjoyable to students.
- Avoid personal mannerisms: unusual mannerisms of speech and dress can seem irritating or comic to students.
- Be fair: be consistent, make the punishment match the offence.
- Be humorous: be prepared to introduce humour into teaching material, to laugh at yourself, and to laugh with the class (but not at the expense of other students).
- Avoid unnecessary threats: threats are not a particularly good way of controlling students, but issuing threats and then failing to carry them out can seriously undermine the teacher's position.
- Be punctual: in order to set a good example, and also so that the class does not get out of hand before you set foot in the classroom.
- Avoid anger: if you lose your temper in the classroom, you may say things you regret later. Students may take advantage of your loss of self-control.
- Avoid over-familiarity: be friendly, but not too familiar as this confuses students who know that the teacher represents school authority.
- Offer opportunities for responsibility: offering students responsibility shows them that they have the teacher's confidence and also helps them to take some responsibility for what happens in the classroom.

- Focus attention: it is more effective to ask a student by name to be quiet, rather than to address the class as a whole; another advantage of learning your students' names as quickly as possible is that it demonstrates your interest in them as individuals.
- Avoid humiliating students: this can not only harm the 'victims', but also turn the rest of the class against the teacher.
- Be alert: try to know what is happening at all times in every part of the classroom.
- Use positive language: explain to students what you want them to do, rather than what they should not do.
- Be confident: teaching involves quite a lot of bluff on the part of the teacher; teachers with a hesitant or tentative manner give students the impression that they are expecting trouble.
- Be well-organised: a well-organised lesson is less likely to be disrupted by misbehaviour than one in which the worksheets contain mistakes or the video recorder does not work.
- Show that you like your students: teachers who are able to convey messages of sympathy, understanding and a personal delight in the job of teaching students tend to have fewer behavioural problems to deal with in the classroom.

This chapter looks at how these and other suggestions about being a 'good' teacher are related to psychological research and theory.

2.1 PERSPECTIVES ON LEARNING

EVALUATION ISSUES

THEORETICAL APPROACH

Traditional behaviourists are not interested in what is going on in people's minds. Instead, they try to establish laws that link environmental stimuli with specific actions; their aim is to describe, predict and control behaviour. This can be compared or contrasted to other approaches.

CD-ROM

- For a description of the theory of classical conditioning, see Education: Theoretical approaches: Classical conditioning.
- For a description of Watson and Rayner's classic study on investigating classical conditioning in human beings, see Education: Additional key studies: Watson and Rayner (1920).

This section describes two fundamentally different approaches to education: one based on behaviourist theory (section 2.1.1) and the other on humanist theory (section 2.1.2). It also examines the contribution that cognitive psychologists have made to educational theory (section 2.1.3).

2.1.1 BEHAVIOURIST APPLICATIONS TO LEARNING

Early psychologists often studied mental processes using a process of introspection, looking inside their own minds to describe and analyse their conscious experience. However, at the beginning of the twentieth century behaviourist psychologists began to criticise the idea that psychology was about the study of inner consciousness. Behaviourists disapproved of introspection on the grounds that it was subjective and could not be replicated; they accepted that the mind existed, but argued that it was impossible to observe it scientifically. Behaviour, on the other hand, could be observed and was therefore considered the only legitimate subject matter for scientific psychology.

Behaviourists believe that organisms behave in particular ways as a result of adapting to their environment; behavioural adaptation is learned by making associations. In this section, we will describe three different ways in which people learn behaviour through the process of association: classical conditioning, operant conditioning and social learning. We will also discuss the implications of these three theories for education.

Classical conditioning

Classical conditioning is a process by which people learn to associate automatic responses with specific stimuli. In their classic studies, Ivan Pavlov trained dogs to associate salivating with the sound of a bell and John Watson trained a small boy to associate fear with a pet white rat.

The implications of classical conditioning for teaching are less important than those of the other two behaviourist theories (described in the text that follows), but there is a need for teachers to try to make sure that students associate only pleasant emotional responses with educational situations. For example, classical conditioning may explain why some students develop school phobia. If a student is bullied at school, then they may learn to associate school with fear. This learned response could persist after the bullies have stopped, or even if the student moves to another school. A student may develop a seemingly irrational dislike of a particular subject that continues throughout his or her school career following an unpleasant experience, such as a teacher humiliating him/her in front of the class. It is not unusual for teachers to punish students, for example, by giving them extra work to do, staying behind in detention and writing an essay. If this happens several times, the student may associate writing essays with the negative emotions felt as a result of receiving the punishment.

The implication is that schools should be happy places in which students experience positive emotions. This means that, as far as possible, teachers should avoid punishment, though punishment is an important component of the second behaviourist theory, operant conditioning.

EVALUATION ISSUES

DETERMINISM/REDUCTIONISM

The theory of classical conditioning can be said to be:
- determinist, i.e. it believes that human behaviour can be predicted from past experiences
- reductionist, i.e. it explains human behaviour in simplistic ways.

Operant conditioning

In operant conditioning, organisms learn to behave in certain ways through a process of trial and error. If past behaviour is reinforced (i.e. the individual associates a positive outcome with that behaviour) then the behaviour will be repeated.

In educational settings, there are various types of reinforcers (or rewards) that can be used to encourage students to behave in particular ways. For example, reinforcement can either be **extrinsic** or **intrinsic**. Extrinsic reinforcement (i.e. coming from other people) can either be **social** or **material**. The following text explains these distinctions, and also the difference between **positive reinforcement** and **negative reinforcement**, and between **continuous reinforcement** and **partial reinforcement**.

- **Extrinsic reinforcement** is presented to an individual by other people, either deliberately (for example, by offering a child a financial reward to do a chore) or inadvertently (by talking to a child when she misbehaves without realising that you are actually rewarding the child with the attention she craves).
- **Intrinsic reinforcement** comes from within the individual, for example, the feeling of satisfaction a student may have when he hands in work on time and thereby feels in control of his own studies. Behaviourists tend to focus on extrinsic, rather than intrinsic reinforcement, because it is observable and can be manipulated in order to change other people's behaviour.

Extrinsic reinforcement can be either social or material. **Social reinforcement** in the classroom would include the praise and approval of the teacher, or even just being given more attention. This may be given directly to students (for example, the teacher saying 'Well done'), or by using signs such as ticks, gold stars and so on. **Material reinforcement** consists of more concrete rewards, such as treats or money, being allowed to play a computer game or being given tokens that can be cashed in at a later date for a material reward. Hall (1989) suggests that material rewards only work because of the social reinforcement that is given at the same time. In a token economy, for example, tokens are given to students in order to reward them for specific actions. These tokens can be cashed in for material rewards. However, if the teacher says 'Well done' as she hands over the token, then the child is also receiving social reinforcement and it is this, rather than the token itself, that may be motivating behavioural change.

The examples given above are all **positive reinforcement** because they consist of giving the student something that they value (that is, a 'reward'). The other way to reinforce behaviour is to remove punishment or the threat of punishment (that is, a 'relief'). For example, allowing a student to leave detention early because she has been good is a **negative reinforcement**.

As well as reinforcing certain 'good' behaviour, the teacher can also discourage students from acting in ways that he disapproves of by punishing 'bad' behaviour. **Punishment** can consist of withdrawing rewards or imposing something unpleasant on the student.

Types of punishment used in schools include the following:
- Reprimands: these can range from being shouted at by a teacher in front of the class to a look of mild disapproval.
- Exclusion: students can be made to sit in a corner or on a table by themselves, asked to stand outside the door or sent to a special

CD-ROM

For a description of the theory of operant conditioning, see Education: Theoretical approaches: Operant conditioning.

EVALUATION ISSUES

EFFECTIVENESS

There may be situations in which the intrinsic benefits of a behaviour are not immediately apparent, and extrinsic reinforcement is needed in order to get the child to behave in a particular way. However, if that behaviour has no intrinsic reward at all, then the reinforcement is less likely to be effective in the long term; the behaviour is likely to stop very quickly once the extrinsic rewards are withdrawn (extinction). For example, if you give students money in order to get them to do their homework, they will stop when the money is withdrawn unless they also receive a sense of internal satisfaction from it.

CD-ROM

Token economies are often used in schools as a way of getting students to behave in certain ways. For an example of the use of a token economy in a school setting, see Education: Real life applications: Token economies.

EVALUATION ISSUES

EFFECTIVENESS

It may seem that material rewards, such as money or toys, would be more valued by students than social rewards such as approval, and would therefore be more effective in modifying behaviour. However, social reinforcement is commonly used in classrooms, and there is a great deal of evidence to indicate that it is, in fact, more effective than offering material rewards.

supervised room. Students can be temporarily suspended or permanently expelled.
• Unpleasant activities: teachers give students extra work or lines to write, make them pick up litter or clean desks and so on.
• Withdrawal of benefits: some schools have point systems and students can be 'fined' for misbehaving. Also, students can have their break times withdrawn (detention) or be stopped from taking part in pleasurable activities.
• Corporal punishment: shaking or hitting students is now against the law in schools in the UK, but it used to be commonplace.

Once a teacher has decided that she wishes to change the behaviour of her students using operant conditioning techniques, she has to establish a schedule of reinforcement.

Continuous reinforcement means that a reward is given every single time the child exhibits the 'correct' response. This means that the child will learn the behaviour very quickly. However, this is balanced out by a fast rate of extinction; when the rewards are stopped, the child very quickly ends the behaviour. In **partial reinforcement** rewards are not given every single time, but every second or third time, or even at random intervals in response to the correct behaviour. Here, the rate of learning is much slower, but so is the rate of extinction.

In practice, formal reinforcement schedules often use a combination of continuous and partial reinforcement, by starting with rewarding every correct behaviour so that learning takes place quickly, then expecting more and more instances of the behaviour before offering the reward so that the child comes to depend less on the reinforcement.

It is very important for teachers to be consistent in the way they reinforce behaviour. Students who are faced with moody and unpredictable teachers become confused about which behaviours get rewarded and which get punished. One reaction to this is for the students to become sullen and passive, reluctant to make contributions to lessons in case they get into trouble. Another way in which teachers can misuse reinforcement is to punish one student for the actions of another. Inconsistent schedules of reinforcement are sometimes referred to as **arbitrary control** and, in the classroom, this may initially be an effective way for the teacher to dominate the classroom and make students listen quietly, but it can make students resentful and hostile and harm their education in the long term.

Social learning

In operant conditioning, organisms learn to behave in specific ways by trial and error. This theory ignores certain human mental processes. For example, if a teacher says to a student 'If you don't stop running about I'll send you outside', then the student may modify his behaviour without even trying out the alternatives. Albert Bandura (1977) recognised the importance of cognitive processes and combined these with operant conditioning theory to come up with the idea that learning occurs mainly through observation and imitation. By observing others, not only do we learn how to do things, but also we can predict the likely consequences of our actions. Bandura suggests that people are motivated to imitate others either because they perceive them as **role models** or because they see them being rewarded or punished for their behaviour (**vicarious reinforcement**).

Observational learning in the classroom can occur in a number of ways:
• **Modelling:** the most efficient way to get students to learn how to carry out a complicated procedure is to demonstrate it. For example, a

KEY STUDY

Influence of models' reinforcement contingencies on the acquisition of imitative responses
Bandura (1965)

Aim: To show that children will imitate a model to a greater extent if the model is rewarded for his (or her) behaviour than if he is punished or if there are no consequences.

Sample: 33 boys and 33 girls from Stanford University Nursery School.

Method: The children were individually shown a television programme that depicted a model attacking a Bobo doll for about 5 minutes. (A Bobo doll is an inflatable figure with a heavy base; when knocked over, it swings back into an upright position.) For one-third of the children, the programme ended with the model being rewarded by another adult who came into the room, gave the model sweets and soft drinks, and praised him for being a 'strong champion'. The second group of children saw an ending in which the second adult comes in and shakes his finger at the model, saying: 'Hey there, you big bully. You quit picking on that clown. I won't tolerate it.' He then spanks the model with a rolled-up magazine. The third group saw the model beating up the Bobo doll, but with no consequences at all; no other adult came into the room. Immediately after watching the film, the children were put into another room containing a Bobo doll and observed by two judges through a one-way mirror.

Results: At first, children in the model-punished condition showed significantly less aggressive imitation than children in the model-rewarded and the no consequences groups. When the children were then offered a reward of fruit juice and colouring books for reproducing the acts of the model, they all showed high levels of imitation and there was no difference between the three conditions.

Conclusions: As the children in all three conditions could be induced to imitate the aggressive acts by being offered reinforcers, Bandura concluded that they had all learned the behaviour by observing the model. However, prior to being offered these inducements, the fact that the children in the model-punished condition showed less imitation supports the notion of vicarious reinforcement, that is, children are more likely to imitate behaviour if they see the model being rewarded and less likely if they see the model being punished.

Albert Bandura's Bobo doll experiment

💿 CD-ROM

For a description of the theory of social learning, see Education: Theoretical approaches: Social learning.

⚖ EVALUATION ISSUES

THEORETICAL APPROACHES

Social learning theory can be compared to other behaviourist theories or contrasted with humanist and cognitivist approaches.

chemistry teacher will show the class how to carry out a specific experiment before they try it themselves; a maths teacher will sit next to a student and do a sum before setting the student similar examples.

- **Facilitation**: one way of encouraging students to carry out a task that they may be uncertain about is to let them see someone else doing it first. For example, in a swimming lesson some of the students may be too frightened to jump off the diving board. Seeing someone else of their own age doing it may make it easy for them to do it as well, not because they have learned how to jump off the diving board by observing their classmate, but because they have been given the confidence to try.
- **Inhibition**: students can be discouraged from certain behaviours by observing the negative consequences applied to others. For example, if a student is punished in front of the class, then others may be reluctant to act in the same way. However, the humiliation suffered by the student being publicly punished has to be taken into account before using this technique in the classroom.

Carl Rogers pioneered a humanist approach to psychotherapy and to education

- **Disinhibition**: students may be encouraged to act in certain ways because they see others being rewarded for those actions. For example, if a student misbehaves in class and, despite being told off by the teacher, gains approval from other students in the class, then others may choose to misbehave in order to gain the same social reward.

2.1.2 HUMANIST APPLICATIONS TO LEARNING

Much of psychology is concerned with discovering general laws that govern human behaviour, in other words, in finding out the ways in which human beings are the same as each other. Humanist psychologists, in contrast, are more interested in what makes us individual and unique. Humanist psychology is based around the idea of a unique 'self' and, as we shall see, humanists have a very different concept of human nature from behaviourists. This is reflected in very different ideas about education.

Carl Rogers

Carl Rogers (1902–87) was a key figure in the development of humanist psychology. As a psychotherapist he introduced the concept of **client-centred therapy** and applied the same principles in his description of **student-centred education**.

CD-ROM

For a more detailed description of Rogers' work, see Education: Theoretical approaches: Carl Rogers and Education: Real life applications: Implications of Rogerian Theory.

EVALUATION ISSUES

METHODOLOGY/REDUCTIONISM

Rogers has no actual scientific evidence for his theories; they simply consist of assertions that Rogers says are self-evident from interviews he conducted. This lack of scientific evidence, however, does not necessarily mean that Rogers' beliefs are false; humanists argue that it is not possible to explain human beings using the scientific method without reducing people to the equivalent of machines or animals that do not have self-consciousness. The debate between humanism and behaviourism is not simply an argument about which theory of human nature is correct, it is also an argument about the methods used to support the theories.

KEY STUDY

Client-centred therapy
Rogers (1951)

In his book, Rogers (1951) describes a set of propositions that form the basic assumptions of humanistic psychology:

- **Phenomenology**: phenomenological theory states that individuals see the world in their own unique way and therefore have their own internal reality. This implies that there is no such thing as external reality; the real world consists of what people perceive it to be, and different people may perceive the world very differently. Furthermore, people behave in ways that reflect their own sense of reality.
- **Self-actualisation**: humanist psychologists believe that we are motivated by an innate drive towards self-actualisation. At a basic level, this involves survival, getting food to eat, protecting ourselves from threats and so on. We share these basic drives with other animals but, as human beings, we are motivated in a unique way; we want to become 'better people'. Self-actualisation means fulfilling our human potential, becoming all that we are capable of being. A self-actualised person is autonomous and free, healthy, competent and creative.
- **The concept of self**: we construct a subjective view of what we are like based on our interaction with the world. Our experiences of failure and success, what other people tell us about ourselves, how other people treat us, our beliefs and values all contribute to our concept of self. We then react to our environment in ways that reflect our self-concept. For example, a child from a poor background who is mistreated by her parents and bullied by other students at school is likely to feel more worthless and incompetent than another child brought up in a privileged culture, surrounded by loving friends and family. As a result, the second child will behave in very different ways to the first child.
- **Psychological health**: according to Rogers, psychological tension is created when there is a discrepancy between the perceived self (what

the client thinks he is actually like) and the ideal self (what the client would wish to be like). A clear example of this is a person with an eating disorder who believes that he is much fatter than he wants to be. Psychologically, a person in whom such a discrepancy exists may feel that he is not acting like himself, that is, not 'being the real me'.

The implications of Rogers' propositions for teaching include the following:
- **Phenomenology**: the teacher must recognise that every student sees the world in a unique way, and that the best way to understand students is to try to see things from their point of view as much as possible. It is important to listen to students and to take seriously what they say.
- **Self-actualisation**: the teacher must recognise that students' true nature is to want to better themselves; the motivation to learn comes from within. Human beings are born with a natural curiosity, a desire to find out about the world around them; the role of the humanist teacher is to facilitate this journey of self-discovery.
- **The concept of self**: the teacher needs to recognise that some students, due to their upbringing and life experiences, may have a very poor self-concept, and that their behaviour needs to be interpreted with this in mind. For example, a child may become a bully because she has developed very low self-esteem as a result of being bullied or abused herself. Bullying others is one (inappropriate) way that such students use to feel more worthwhile or more powerful.
- **Psychological health**: the teacher can also help to reduce the discrepancy between the perceived self and the ideal self. In order not to further damage students' self-concept, the humanist teacher must treat students with respect and not, for example, inflict humiliating punishments on them. Humanist education also lays great stress on actually improving students' self-esteem, by providing them with experiences of success, by making the students feel cared for and by giving them positive feedback. If a student does something 'wrong' then teachers should criticise the behaviour and not the child.

Student-centred education

The key features of a humanist, student-centred school include the following:
- **Teachers are learning facilitators**: humanist teachers assume that students have an inner motivation to learn and do not need to be forced to study. This inner motivation expresses itself in a natural curiosity about the world that can be stifled if the teacher imposes a curriculum on students. Students are better off finding out information for themselves rather than being told 'the facts' by a didactic instructor. Humanist teachers favour discovery learning, as opposed to reception learning, and see as their role to provide resources that will allow students to discover the answers for themselves and help students develop the skills needed to make the most effective use of those resources.
- **Teachers must be sensitive, caring, genuine and empathetic**: Rogers (1961) stresses the importance of the teacher's 'real-ness'; he believed that learning is improved if the teacher expresses her true feelings in the classroom and becomes a real person in the relationship with her students. This means that it is acceptable for teachers to show their enthusiasm, boredom, anger, insecurity and so on in the classroom.

However, learning is also improved if the teacher actually feels positive and caring towards students. It is important for the humanist teacher to like students, and to value and respect them. It is also important for the teacher to be prepared to see things from the student's point of view and to empathise with the student. In order to achieve all of this, the teacher needs to be a caring person, in touch with her own feelings and willing to engage in honest interpersonal communication with students.

- **Development of positive self-concepts in students**: Because our behaviour and state of mind is so dependent on our self-concept, it is very important for the humanist teacher to foster positive self-concepts in students. This means enhancing students' self-esteem by, for example, trying to provide them with meaningful experiences of success. Succeeding at a very easy task will not improve a student's self-esteem, but asking students to undertake tasks that are too difficult for them will simply make them feel like failures. Students need to be treated as individuals and have work set at the right level for them.

Another way of improving self-esteem is to show students how much they are valued and to give them a sense of empowerment, that is, to make students feel they have some measure of control over their own education.

Humanist teachers should avoid anything that actually reduces a student's self-esteem, such as unjustified or negative criticism, public humiliation and so on. Clearly, negative messages can come from other students as well as from teachers, so it is important to help students develop socially and personally, and learn not to be unpleasant to each other. The humanist would try to achieve this not, for example, by punishing the playground bully so that he does not do it again, but by helping the bully understand why he feels so hostile towards other students, and by facilitating general class discussions on the issue of bullying.

- **Students take part in decisions**: If students are to feel empowered in school, then they need to be involved in all sorts of decisions about what goes on in the classroom. For example, decisions about what to learn (the curriculum), how to learn it, the timetable, how to deal with discipline problems and so on need to be made democratically, involving all the students, rather than be imposed by a teacher who feels he knows best.
- **Against performance-orientated, test-dominated approach**: Rogers (1961) argues that traditional methods of assessing student achievement are artificial and reductionist; they can only measure certain aspects of education (for example, acquisition of information or specific skills). Other aspects of education, such as learning to care for other people, gaining insight about yourself, developing positive values and so on are impossible to measure but are, for the humanist, just as important, if not more so.

2.1.3 COGNITIVE APPLICATIONS TO LEARNING

Cognitive psychology, the study of mental processes such as perception, memory, decision-making and so on, has some very direct applications to education. Cognitive approaches to education focus on the way in which students learn by acquiring and organising knowledge. They look at the way in which students' mental skills and abilities change over time, and the impact this has on the strategies they use to learn. Many cognitive psychologists are interested in specific processes such as memory and forgetting; others are interested in broader themes such as the acquisition and use of language.

The text that follows focuses on two theorists – Vygotsky and Piaget – whose work is very important in shaping the way we think about cognitive development in the classroom.

Lev Vygotsky (1896–1934)

Much of Vygotsky's work was published in the English language after his death, and was based on research he carried out at the Herzen Pedagogical Institute in Lenigrad in the 1920s and 1930s.

Vygotsky was interested in the way in which children become aware of their own thought processes. He argued that children learn to speak without really thinking about it, but that in order to learn to write, it is necessary to reflect on the mental processes involved (i.e. to engage in **metacognition**). It is this abstract nature of written language that tells us why children's ability to write is less developed than their ability to speak. As Vygotsky argues 'Writing requires deliberate analytical action on the part of the child. In speaking, he [sic] is hardly conscious of the sounds he pronounces and quite unconscious of the mental operations he performs' (1983, p. 265).

Vygotsky was also interested in the way in which children learn and use knowledge they pick up from the culture of which they are a part. One of the main ways in which they do this is from other people, for example, their teachers, parents and peers. One of Vygotsky's most important and influential ideas that leads on from this is that children's levels of development should be measured not only in terms of what they can do on their own (the **zone of actual development**), but also in terms of what they can achieve with some assistance (the **zone of proximal development**).

Radziszewska and Rogoff (1988; cited in Hetherington and Park, 1999) asked children to plan a shopping trip in order to buy certain things and also to make the most economical journey (by not retracing their route, and by visiting certain shops and not others). In one condition a group of 9-year-olds were paired with children of their own age, and in the other condition a different group were paired with one of their parents. The results of the study showed that the children planning with the parent made better and more efficient plans than the children planning with another child. As Vygotsky suggested, children benefited from the assistance of an adult and the transmission of knowledge in this particular way.

He showed this idea by giving children harder tasks than they could achieve on their own, then giving them a little help, e.g. by using a leading question or assisting in the early stages of the problem-solving exercise. He discovered that individual children achieved at quite different levels using this type of co-operative task. Some had larger zones of proximal development than others, and these children, he argued, would do better in school.

Jean Piaget (1896–1980)

Piaget started his academic life as a biologist, and his later understanding of cognitive development was greatly influenced by this early work. He saw cognitive development as a way of organising and adapting to the external environment, in much the same way as any biological organism adapts to its environment.

Piaget's research techniques were controversial when he started his research. At a time when most of psychology concerned itself with rigorous control and hypothesis testing, Piaget's work was mostly observational,

CD-ROM

For a more detailed discussion of Vygotsky's theories see Education: Theoretical approaches: Lev Vygotsky.

EVALUATION ISSUES

EFFECTIVENESS

The implication of Vygotsky's theories for effective classroom practice is that, first, the teacher is very important in the process of the transmission of knowledge. This means teachers must take great care that the knowledge they impart is accurate and useful to the child. Secondly, Vygotsky suggests that students need teaching that stretches them; if students are not taught in this way they cannot use their zone of proximal development and therefore are not able to reach their true potential and teaching is not effective.

CD-ROM

For a more detailed discussion of Piaget's theories see Education: Theoretical approaches: Jean Piaget.

although it was very systematic. He asked students questions, then analysed their answers in detail.

In his book, Piaget describes the four basic concepts he uses to explain how cognitive development occurs:

- **Schemata**: these can be defined as categories that the individual uses to organise the world. Piaget describes the mind as having structures in much the same way as the body does, and these structures (schemata) adapt and change as the child grows and develops. A young child will have fewer schemata than an older child or adult. Piaget argues that these schemata are 'constructed' by the child. As the child grows their ability to differentiate between objects and experiences grows with them, and they learn to make more sense of the world and all that happens by categorising these experiences in more complicated and sophisticated ways.

- **Assimilation**: this is the cognitive process by which people are able to integrate new information into existing schemata. The schemata do not change, but they may grow to take in new information.

- **Accommodation**: this describes the way in which schemata have to adapt when faced with information that cannot easily be assimilated. For example, if a child with relatively few schemata with which to explain the world is faced with information that does not fit in to existing schemata, she has to accommodate the information in some way. In order to do this the child can either create a new schema to accommodate the information, or she can change or revise an existing schema to do the same thing.

Accommodation accounts for development (a qualitative change) and assimilation accounts for growth (a quantitative change); together these processes account for intellectual adaptation and the development of intellectual structures.

- **Equilibration**: this is the process that regulates assimilation and accommodation. These two processes must be balanced if the child is to develop cognitively in a 'normal' way. Not being able to assimilate information causes disequilibrium. This is put right by the process of accommodation through which the child regains equilibrium. Piaget believed that disequilibrium (as a state of imbalance) is a motivating force for children to either assimilate or accommodate new information.

It is through the process of assimilation and accommodation that the environment is organised and structured. Schemata are the products of this organisation.

EVALUATION ISSUES

METHODOLOGY

Piaget partly developed his theories by interviewing hundreds of children and then drawing his own conclusions from the material he collected. Even though there were numerous empirical aspects to his work, some would argue that his approach was not wholly scientific. Psychologists who prefer a more 'scientific' approach would question conclusions arising out of studies that did not involve controlled variables.

Piaget looked at the way in which children develop cognitively, and how their ability to assimilate and accommodate new information might affect the learning process. Some of the work for which Piaget is most famous concerns the developmental stages of children. Piaget identified four main stages through which children pass in their cognitive development, and he argued that these stages influence what they are ready to learn; if they are not ready then children will not be able to learn with understanding.

Piaget's work has had very far-reaching implications for educational practice and policy. The curriculum has to be designed with students' cognitive ability in mind. For example the curriculum should:

- provide physical and mental activity
- provide optimal difficulty; to enable students to both assimilate and accommodate new information
- understand the limitations of students' thought processes and be able to assess their readiness to learn new ideas
- provide opportunities for students to engage in social interaction with their peers and teachers.

Both Piaget and Vygotsky are **constructivists,** i.e. they both see knowledge as a construction although they disagree on the way in which the knowledge is constructed. Piaget has been accused of ignoring the importance of social and cultural factors affecting the development of knowledge, whereas Vygotsky was particularly interested in this. Piaget believed that children construct their own knowledge, based on assimilation and accommodation, whereas Vygotsky believed that children construct knowledge that is transmitted more directly from those with whom they interact. Piaget saw the role of the teacher as one in which they should stimulate and support the child, whereas for Vygotsky the teacher acted as a model for the child.

SECTION A EXAM QUESTIONS

a Describe one humanist application to learning. [6]
b Contrast humanist applications to learning with either behaviourist *or* cognitive applications to learning. [10]

a Describe one cognitive application to education. [6]
b Evaluate the effectiveness of cognitive applications to education. [10]

FOR CONSIDERATION

Kegan (1994) argues that 'People grow best where they continuously experience an ingenious blend of support and challenge … Environments which are weighted too heavily in the direction of challenge (cognitive demands too high) without adequate support are toxic … Those weighted too heavily in the direction of support without adequate challenge (cognitive demands two low) are ultimately boring …'
- Throughout the course of your education, have your teachers always hit the optimum level of cognitive demands, or have you found some of your lessons either 'toxic' or 'boring'?

EXAM HINTS

This section of the syllabus concerns *applications* of behaviourist, humanist and cognitive theories to education. It is not enough to describe the theories in isolation; they should be related to educational practice.

CD-ROM

For Section B sample exam questions see Education: Sample exam questions.

2.2 MOTIVATION AND EDUCATIONAL PERFORMANCE

Motivation consists of the forces or pressures, whether internal or external, that make us behave in certain ways. In education, students need to feel motivated in order to achieve success in their studies. Some students are very highly motivated; they enjoy studying and are keen to do well and, as a result, are more likely to put a lot of effort into their work and to attempt difficult tasks. Other students do not enjoy learning, are much less confident of their ability to succeed, are much more afraid of failing and so are less likely to attempt work that may be challenging. The strategies a particular teacher employs in the classroom are linked to his view of what motivates human beings in general.

In developing theories of motivation, psychologists are trying to discover what it is that initiates, encourages or prevents human behaviour. This source of behaviour could come from within the person or from the environment.

2.2.1 DEFINITIONS, TYPES AND THEORIES OF MOTIVATION

Psychologists in the past have come up with many different theories of motivation, for example:
- instinct theory
- drive theory
- psychological hedonism
- arousal theory.

These historical theories of motivation are described in detail on the CD-ROM. This section examines current behaviourist, humanist and cognitive theories of motivation.

Behaviourist approach to motivation

The theory of psychological hedonism (see above) suggests that people behave in ways that give them pleasure and avoid pain. Behaviourists are not interested in the concepts of pleasure and pain, because these are internal feelings, and therefore not susceptible to objective observation and measurement. Instead, behaviourists simply define the concept of reinforcement as an outcome that increases the probability of particular behaviours occurring. For example, if experience shows that praising a student for working hard makes it more likely that he will work hard in future, then we know that students can be motivated by praise, and any thoughts or emotions the student may experience are irrelevant.

The behaviourist position is that students are motivated to learn as a result of external reinforcement. In order for reinforcement to be effective in motivating students, it is important to follow these principles:
- the learner must be aware of exactly what behaviour she is being rewarded for
- the reward must be given as soon after the behaviour is performed as possible
- rewards must be offered in a consistent manner
- the teacher should start off by giving frequent rewards (continuous reinforcement), then gradually reduce them (partial reinforcement)

CD-ROM

For a description of instinct theory, drive theory, psychological hedonism and arousal theory, see Education: Theoretical approaches: Historical theories of motivation.

EVALUATION ISSUES

THEORETICAL APPROACH

The behaviourist theories of operant conditioning and social learning (see pages 17–21) both suggest that people are motivated by external reinforcement. In operant conditioning, individuals have been reinforced for certain behaviours in the past, and have learned to repeat them in contrast to social learning, in which individuals see other people gain reinforcement and imitate their behaviour.

- the teacher must not be over-generous in offering rewards; this can actually lower motivation
- the teacher should make sure that every student in the class is able to earn a reward at some time.

Humanist approach to motivation

The behaviourist notion that behaviour can be modified or controlled by manipulating the extrinsic rewards offered to a child has been criticised by some psychologists as mechanistic and dehumanising. Humanist psychologists, in particular, stress the importance of intrinsic rewards. For example, if a student completes an essay on time and is praised by the teacher, he is receiving extrinsic reinforcement. On the other hand, if the student feels a sense of achievement and satisfaction at having completed his work, then this constitutes intrinsic reinforcement.

Abraham Maslow (1908–70), an important humanist psychologist, took a pragmatic approach to human motivation. He did not attempt to answer the question about where human motivation comes from; he simply described what he thought human beings are motivated by. He developed a hierarchy of needs based on his experience as a psychotherapist and psychologist; these needs form a hierarchy because they start off with the basic survival needs that humans share with other animals, then move up towards more sophisticated needs that are unique to human beings. (See page 184.)

Maslow referred to the first four levels of needs as deficiency needs because, if these needs are not satisfied in an individual, then she is physically or psychologically deficient, that is, unable to survive and live more or less happily. The next three levels of needs are growth needs, and it is these that motivate us to learn and study. Maslow argues that the lower level needs must be satisfied before the person can concentrate on higher level needs.

The key difference between behaviourist and humanist theories of motivation is that the former are entirely based on the extrinsic reinforcement and the latter also include intrinsic motivation. In fact, all of Maslow's higher level growth needs are intrinsic in nature. Humanists argue that growth needs are the ones that motivate students in education whereas behaviourists would deny the very existence of internal growth needs. Furthermore, humanists would argue that, attempting to motivate students to learn by giving them extrinsic motivation actually undermines their intrinsic motivation. The key study by Lepper and Green (1975) clearly illustrates this process.

EVALUATION ISSUES

REDUCTIONISM

Behaviourist theories of motivation are reductionist as they ignore mental processes and argue that motivation arises entirely as a result of external reinforcement. In contrast humanist theories of motivation recognise the role of external motivation, but argue that human beings are also intrinsically motivated to discover more about the world and therefore want to take part in education for its own sake.

Abraham Maslow developed a hierarchy of needs relating to human motivation

? FOR CONSIDERATION

It is very hard to persuade a student to learn about poetry in class if he is not getting enough to eat or feels physically threatened every time he goes home. However, once the more basic needs are satisfied, then motivation comes from within. This is the philosophy of Summerhill School where students are free to choose whether to go to lessons or not. Teachers at Summerhill do not consider it necessary to provide incentives (or punishments) in order to encourage students to attend classes; they argue that when given complete freedom to choose what to do, students will want to attend lessons because of their intrinsic need for knowledge and understanding.
- Would you have liked to attend a school in which lessons were voluntary?

KEY STUDY

Turning play into work: effects of adult surveillance and extrinsic rewards on children's intrinsic motivation
Lepper and Greene (1975)

Aim: To measure the effects on children's motivation of extrinsic reinforcement and surveillance by adults.

Sample: 80 4- and 5-year-olds from a nursery school located on Stanford University campus.

Method: The children were taken individually into a room containing a table holding a set of puzzles, a television camera and a set of attractive toys hidden by a cloth screen. One group of children were shown the toys and told they could play with them if they worked hard on the

puzzles (extrinsic reinforcement); the other group were not shown the toys. In both conditions, the experimenter left the room and returned after the child had completed six puzzles. All the children were told they had done a good job with the puzzles and were allowed to play with the toys for ten minutes, but it was made clear to the first group that this was a reward for having done so well on the puzzles. The second group were offered the toys in a non-contingent manner, that is, the reward was not linked to a specific behaviour; they were told that the toys just happened to be there and that they could play with them if they wanted to. Two weeks later, the puzzles were set out in the children's classrooms alongside other activities that would normally be there. The children were observed by two people from behind a one-way mirror.

Results: Significantly fewer of the children who had been offered the toys as a reward for doing the puzzles chose to play with the puzzles two weeks later (70 per cent versus 92 per cent).

Conclusions: The children who expected a reward for doing the puzzles were less likely to play with them when no reward was offered. On the other hand, the children who were not initially offered a reward to do the puzzles may have derived satisfaction and enjoyment from them, and were more likely to choose to do them again. It seems, for this study, that offering children extrinsic reinforcement for an activity can actually undermine the intrinsic satisfaction they derive from that activity.

EVALUATION ISSUES

EFFECTIVENESS

Humanists would suggest that intrinsic motivation and satisfaction is more effective than using extrinsic reinforcement in the form of rewards.

Cognitive approach to motivation

Cognitive psychologists argue that people make conscious decisions to behave in certain ways rather than simply responding to external reinforcement (the behaviourist approach) or to internal needs (the humanist approach). Cognitive psychologists attempt to describe how and why we decide to do things; part of this is to explore the links between the decision-making process and our attitudes, that is, our opinions and our values. The text that follows looks at how one type of attitude – **self-efficacy** – is linked to motivation, and the following section (2.2.2) describes two linked cognitive theories of motivation, **attribution theory** and **learned helplessness.**

Our perception of our own competence or ability to succeed is referred to as **self-efficacy.** Clearly, high levels of self-efficacy are likely to be linked to greater motivation; students who feel more confident that they can succeed are more likely to undertake tasks and will show greater perseverance at them. Bandura (1986) describes four different influences that can affect self-efficacy:

- **Enactive influences:** this refers to the individual's past experiences of success and failure. Someone who is used to being successful will feel more confident about succeeding in future. It is therefore important for teachers to provide their students with experiences of success, by making sure the tasks they are set are easy enough for the student to stand a good chance of success, but not so easy that the student feels no sense of achievement.
- **Vicarious influences:** this consists of comparing oneself with others and judging our own competence accordingly. This means that teachers should be careful about reading out marks in class or creating academic competition in the classroom, as this could make some students feel less competent.
- **Persuasory influences:** Bandura suggests that an individual's self-efficacy can be enhanced by other people persuading her to undertake the task

EVALUATION ISSUES

ETHICS

One of the major criticisms expressed when Standardised Assessment Tasks (SATs) were first introduced into primary schools was that for every child who performs above average there is another who performs below average. This second child's sense of self-efficacy will suffer if public comparisons in test results are made, and this can be seen to be unethical and also harmful to the child's education.

in question. If a student is reluctant to tell a story in front of other students through lack of confidence, the teacher could make her feel more able to carry out this task successfully by providing reassurance and encouragement.

- **Emotive influences**: Bandura suggests that over-anxiety may lead an individual to feel that he is not capable of succeeding at a specific task. Teachers need to make sure that students are aroused enough to feel motivated, but not so aroused that they feel that they cannot manage.

2.2.2 ATTRIBUTION THEORY AND LEARNED HELPLESSNESS

Attribution theory

People make attributions (that is, find explanations for behaviour) in several different ways. First, attributions can be **internal** (due to the individual's personality or intentions) or **external** (due to the situation an individual is in, the environment, other people or even chance). Second, attributions can be **unstable** (that is, temporary) or **stable** (that is, permanent). If a student does well in a test, for example, a stable internal attribution would be 'I am clever', whereas a stable external attribution would be 'These tests are always easy'. An unstable internal attribution might be 'I revised really hard for this test', whereas an unstable external attribution would be 'I did well because I was lucky'. Third, attributions can be **global** (applying to other situations) or **specific** (only applying to that specific situation). If a student fails a maths test, then an internal, stable and global attribution would be 'I failed because I am hopeless at everything, including maths'.

Students who tend to attribute failure at academic tasks to internal stable causes (that is, lack of ability or aptitude) are less likely to persevere with their work than students who attribute failure to internal unstable causes (that is, lack of effort). The student who attributes her lateness for lessons externally (for example, 'It wasn't my fault if I slept in') will be less likely to do something about the problem than the student who accepts responsibility for being late. The student who attributes success internally ('I succeeded because I am good at it, or I tried hard') is more likely to attempt similar tasks in future, especially if they attributed their success globally ('I could succeed at anything if I try hard enough'). On the other hand, the student who feels that his success is due to external causes ('I was lucky') may feel less motivated in the future. Clearly, then, attributional style is linked to the extent to which people persevere with their learning, and also with the degree to which they are prepared to take risks in the future.

Most attempts to change students' attributions in order to improve motivation have aimed to shift attribution from external to internal, so that students feel they are more in control of the outcomes of their own behaviour. In other words, they take responsibility for their own learning and, as a result, put more effort into their studies. Teachers can try to do this by talking to students and trying to convince them that they are responsible for what happens to them, but it is important that students' actual experiences in school reinforce this. For example, work set by the teacher has to be of a level such that a student can succeed if she puts the effort in (repeated failure may make a student feel that she could not succeed even if she tried really hard), but not so easy as to make the student feel that anyone could have succeeded. Students must not be placed in situations in which they can blame their success or failure on chance.

CD-ROM

See Education: Theoretical approaches: Attribution.

KEY DEFINITIONS

Each of us has a specific **attributional style**; in other words, we have a tendency to attribute behaviour in certain ways and to make specific types of attributional errors. For example, over-confident people tend to attribute success to internal, stable and global reasons ('I did well in my biology test because I am brilliant at everything'), and they attribute failure in an external unstable and specific way ('I failed my biology test because it contained questions that we had not been told to revise').

EVALUATION ISSUES

REDUCTIONISM

Cognitive theories of motivation are less reductionist than behaviourist ones, because they recognise that motivation in human beings does not just arise out of a learned response to a specific stimulus, but also involves complicated thought processes.

EVALUATION ISSUES

EFFECTIVENESS

Another way of effectively encouraging students to attribute success to internal, stable causes (and thereby increase motivation) is to teach them specific skills that will enable them to succeed. These metacognitive strategies will make students realise they can do something specific to help themselves become more effective learners, and this will increase their sense of personal control and hence their motivation.

Learned helplessness

Seligman and Maier (1967) exposed dogs to unavoidable electric shocks. When they allowed the dogs to escape the shocks, the dogs did not do so. The dogs had learned that they had no control over what happens to them; Seligman called this phenomenon **learned helplessness** and defined it as 'the interference with instrumental responding following inescapable aversive events'. The key study by Hirohito and Seligman (1975) described below suggests that if people learn that they are helpless in a particular situation, this can make them feel less empowered in general.

> **KEY STUDY**
>
> *Generality of learned helplessness in man*
> Hirohito and Seligman (1975)
>
> **Aim:** To investigate whether learned helplessness in human beings only impairs performance in situations similar to the original experience, or whether it impairs a broad range of behaviour.
>
> **Sample:** 96 undergraduates (51 men, 45 women) from the University of Pennsylvania who responded to an advertisement offering them $2 to take part in a study on 'noise pollution'.
>
> **Method:** The participants were divided into three groups and presented with a series of loud tones and a keypad. After a while, the tones stopped. Group 1 were told that there was a way of stopping the tones (by pressing a series of buttons) but were afterwards told that they had failed to do so and that the tones had stopped anyway; Group 2 were also told they could stop the noise, and were afterwards told that they succeeded; Group 3 acted as a control and just listened to the noise. Afterwards, all participants were played a loud noise and told that they had to discover a way of stopping it; they were timed to see how long it took them to discover the technique.
>
> In the second part of the experiment, the researchers gave participants a puzzle to do, and told one group that the puzzle was unsolvable the second group that it could be solved, and the third group nothing at all. All three groups were then presented with the loud noise and timed to find out how long it took them to work out how to stop it.
>
> Both parts of the experiment were repeated, but instead of having to stop a loud noise, all participants were given a set of anagrams to solve.
>
> **Results:** In both parts of the experiment, the experimenters tried to create learned helplessness in the first group, either by telling them that they had not stopped the tones, or that the puzzle they were given was unsolvable. They found that these participants took longer to find a way of stopping the loud noise and also took longer to solve the anagrams. This shows that not only does creating the impression of failure in a specific task mean that the individual then performs less well on that task in future, but also performs less well on other tasks.
>
> **Conclusions:** An experience of failure or inescapability in one context can induce learned helplessness in different contexts. This suggests that learned helplessness is an induced 'trait', i.e. a general pattern of behaviour that has been learned from past experience.

Seligman is suggesting that certain childhood experiences (being made to feel powerless or stupid, for example) can lead to an individual 'learning' that they are helpless, i.e. that whatever they do, things will not improve.

Learned helplessness is very de-motivating and can lead to feelings of apathy and depression.

Learned helplessness can arise out of experiencing an inconsistent schedule of reinforcement as a child. If parents punish and reward a child arbitrarily (i.e. not as a direct result of the child's 'good' or 'bad' behaviour) then the child learns that whatever he does makes no difference to the outcome.

2.2.3 IMPROVING MOTIVATION

The strategies an individual teacher uses to motivate students will depend on the particular theory of motivation he believes in.

- **Behaviourist** teachers believe that students are motivated to learn and study by external reinforcement and will therefore try to increase such motivation. They may offer actual rewards in the classroom, whether material or social, or may stress to students the material benefits of learning (e.g. the gaining of qualifications that can lead to later employment). They will publicly reward students who work hard, attempting to motivate others through vicarious reinforcement. They will make sure that the schedules of reinforcement they adopt in the classroom are effective and consistent.
- **Humanist** teachers, on the other hand, will avoid external reinforcement on the grounds that it motivates students to learn for the wrong reasons. They will try to ensure that the basic needs described by Maslow are satisfied so that the students' internal motivation to learn can come through. Above all, they will do what they can to foster high self-awareness and self-esteem in their students.
- **Cognitive** teachers will attempt to reduce learned helplessness by making sure that rewards and punishments are not given arbitrarily, by modifying students' attributional styles and by improving self-efficacy. In order to achieve this last goal, they will provide students with experiences of success and try to avoid situations in which students can compare themselves unfavourably to others, and they will do what they can to encourage students to believe in their own abilities.

The strategies to improve motivation used by behaviourist, humanist and cognitive teachers overlap with each other. For example, humanists will try to foster high self-esteem so that students feel able to focus on the higher growth needs that provide a motivation to study, and teachers with a more cognitive approach will do the same, but because they want to increase perceived self-efficacy. Behaviourists will try to make their reinforcement schedules consistent in order to be more effective, and cognitive teachers will do this in order to avoid learned helplessness.

The impact of teacher behaviour on the motivation of students was dramatically illustrated in the key study by Rosenthal and Jacobson (1968), described below. Teacher expectations of students is a key factor in their motivation and achievement. If teachers have high expectations then somehow this makes it more likely that their students will indeed do well. This process is called the **self-fulfilling prophecy**; teachers can motivate students by having high expectations of them (but not too high, or else the student will fail to meet the expectations and may lose their sense of self-efficacy). Conversely, they may de-motivate students by not expecting enough of them. Rosenthal and Jacobson's (1968) study demonstrates the self-fulfilling prophecy in a dramatic way.

EVALUATION ISSUES

THEORETICAL APPROACH

An individual with a high level of learned helplessness is also likely to have a tendency to adopt external attributions, to have low self-efficacy and to have low self-esteem.

EXAM HINTS

In describing strategies for improving students' motivation, it is a good idea to link each suggestion with the theory of motivation to which it relates.

EVALUATION ISSUES

ETHICS

Humanists criticise the behaviourist approach to motivation on the grounds that it is manipulative and undermines students' internal motivation. On the other hand, behaviourists criticise humanists on the grounds that their approach can result in students being left to make their own decisions, and these might not be the 'best' ones for the students themselves.

FOR CONSIDERATION

Consider the strategies that your own teachers (past and present) have used to motivate students.
- Have these strategies been predominantly behaviourist, humanist or cognitive?
- Which strategies have been most effective?
- What do you think is the best way of motivating people to learn?

CD-ROM

For an application of the self-fulfilling prophecy to educational practice see Education: Real life applications: Predicting exam grades.

VALIDITY

It must be noted that Rosenthal and Jacobson's (1968) study is controversial; some psychologists have since failed to replicate its results, and have criticised the findings as lacking validity, while others claim they have confirmed Rosenthal and Jacobson's conclusions.

KEY STUDY

Teacher expectations for the disadvantaged
Rosenthal and Jacobson (1968)

Aim: To demonstrate that teacher expectation can influence students' achievement.

Sample: The study was carried out in Oak School, an elementary (primary) school in a working class area of San Francisco. The school consisted of six year groups, each split into three streamed classes.

Method: The teachers were initially told that the purpose of the study was to validate a new psychometric test designed to predict academic blooming (that is, the extent to which students would improve intellectually). The test was entitled the 'Test of Inflected Acquisition', and teachers were told that it would be sent back to Harvard University for scoring and for the data to be processed. In fact, the students were given a standard intelligence test. Five students were chosen at random from each class, and the teachers were told informally that these students had scored highly in the test and were therefore really going to improve academically during the coming year. Over the next year, the students were given the same intelligence test three more times. The teachers were also asked to describe the classroom behaviour of all their students.

Results:

- The intelligence test scores of the students who had been named as potential 'bloomers' improved significantly more than those of the other students.
- The self-fulfilling prophecy effect was stronger for the younger students.
- The students who had been designated as 'bloomers' were rated by teachers as more curious, more interesting and happier than the other students.
- Out of the students who had not been designated as bloomers, those who showed a greater improvement in IQ were actually rated less favourably by the teachers.
- The students who received the worst behaviour ratings from teachers were those in the lower sets who had not been designated as 'bloomers' but who had improved most.

Conclusions: Rosenthal and Jacobson concluded that teacher expectation does have an effect on student achievement. They also said that students who break teacher expectations, even if they do better than expected, are seen by teachers as less well-adjusted, particularly if they are from a below-average ability set.

SECTION A EXAM QUESTIONS

a Describe one theory of motivation in education. [6]
b Evaluate theories of motivation in education. [10]

a Outline how attribution theory affects educational motivation. [6]
b Contrast this theory with one or more other theories of educational motivation. [10]

a Describe how learned helplessness affects educational motivation. [6]
b Evaluate learned helplessness as an explanation of educational motivation. [10]

CD-ROM

For Section B sample exam questions see Education: Sample exam questions.

LEARNING AND TEACHING STYLES

2.3

The previous two sections of this chapter describe the different theoretical approaches to education, and how these can affect how teachers behave in the classroom. This section examines different teaching styles in more detail, but also looks at how different students prefer to be taught in different ways.

2.3.1 DEFINITIONS, THEORIES AND MEASUREMENT OF LEARNING AND TEACHING STYLES

Learning styles

It is widely recognised that every individual student has certain preferences in the way they like to learn. These preferences can cover a whole range of aspects. Griggs and Dunn (1995) identify 21 of these, grouped into five categories:

- **environmental learning style**: sound, temperature, classroom layout and light
- **emotional learning style**: sense of responsibility for studying, preference for structure in lessons, persistence and motivation
- **sociological learning style**: preference for learning alone or in groups, whether peer-oriented or authority oriented
- **physiological learning style**: best time of day for studying, preference for eating or drinking during studying, need to move around during lessons, information may be better understood if presented in visual or auditory form
- **psychological learning style**: lateral v linear thinkers, preference for competition or co-operation.

Curry (cited in Claxton and Murrell, 1987) suggests that an individual's learning style, which he describes as **instructional preference** (how the individual prefers to learn), is an aspect of his or her personality and can be thought of as representing the outer layer of an onion. Instructional preference is dependent on the middle layer of the onion, which represents the ways in which the individual prefers to process information (**information processing style**). This, in turn, is dependent on the inner layer of the onion; the **cognitive personality style**. So someone whose learning style is 'activist' (see Honey and Mumford, 1992, below) has a cognitive personality style that is flexible, open-minded and impulsive. Their information processing style is such that they tend to think laterally rather than sequentially; they welcome new information but tend to get bored with implementation and longer-term consolidation. The instructional preference of such a student would involve group-work and unstructured activities; they would dislike passive learning situations such as lectures or reading alone. Curry further suggests that the inner layers of the onion are more difficult to change than the outer ones, so that although an individual's cognitive personality style is relatively fixed, it is possible for him to learn to enjoy different types of lessons.

Researchers have identified three applications of learning styles measurement:

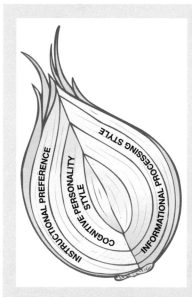

Curry's 'onion' model of learning styles

Consider the subjects you have really enjoyed studying at school, and those that you have enjoyed less.
- Was it the case that you did not enjoy studying certain subjects so much because the way the subject was taught did not match up with your learning style?
- Do you think that all Psychology students have a similar learning style?

- by identifying someone's learning style, it is possible to match them to the course or to the teacher that they would prefer, thereby improving learning outcomes
- by identifying weaknesses in someone's learning style, they can be given advice about how to become a more effective student
- if there is a mis-match between a student's learning style, and the way that they are being taught, then either the learning style or the teaching style needs to be modified.

An early instrument for measuring learning styles was designed by Kolb (1976) who argued that the learning process consists of a series of stages and that individuals seem to prefer some parts of the learning cycle over others. He developed the **Learning Style Inventory (LSI)** to identify an individual's preference for a particular stage of the cycle. As a psychometric test, however, the LSI has been much criticised: it has been found to have low internal reliability (i.e. results on certain parts of the Inventory are inconsistent with those on other sections), low test-retest reliability (i.e. individuals tend to come out with different scores if they do the test again after a while) and low construct validity (i.e. the theory upon which the test is based is questionable).

Honey and Mumford (1986) designed an alternative instrument called the **Learning Styles Questionnaire (LSQ)** that they claimed was superior to the LSI as it focuses on observable behaviour and has greater face validity. One of the criticisms of the learning style approach to education is that there are currently dozens of different learning styles measuring instruments with no clear evidence to suggest that any of them are 'better' than the others, and there is also little research that shows that the learning styles approach actually improves educational attainment.

For a copy of Honey and Mumford's Learning Styles Questionnaire see Education: Measurement scales: LSQ.

KEY STUDY

The manual of learning styles
Honey and Mumford (1992)

In their book, Honey and Mumford present the LSQ, a scoring system for it and an interpretation of the results.

The LSQ consists of 40 statements which the respondent has to tick or cross depending on whether he mostly agrees or disagrees with it. Examples of statements are:
- I quite like taking risks
- I don't often take things for granted
- I like to check things out for myself
- Usually I talk more than I listen.

The questionnaire leads to four separate scores, each referring to an archetypal learning style. An individual's learning style is determined by looking at the combination of the four scores. According to Honey and Mumford, learners can be:
- **Activists**: flexible and open-minded and happy to be exposed to new situations; they are unlikely to resist change. On the other hand, they tend to take unnecessary risks and rush into action without sufficient preparation. They tend to hog the limelight and they get bored with implementation or consolidation. They prefer to learn in unstructured activities and like group-work, role-play and games. They do not like lectures, reading alone or structured teaching approaches.

- **Pragmatists**: keen to test things in practice; they are practical, down to earth and realistic and they tend to get straight to the point. On the other hand, they are not interested in theory or basic principles and reject anything without an obvious application. They prefer to learn by carrying out practical activities, on their own or in groups, and do not like theoretical lectures or discussion that explores concepts.
- **Reflectors**: careful, thorough, thoughtful and methodical. They are good at listening to others and rarely jump to conclusions. On the other hand, they tend to hold back from direct participation and are slow to make up their minds. They are not assertive and can be over-cautious. They prefer activities which enable them to observe and think things over; they like lectures, group discussions, and tasks which involve the collection and analysis of data.
- **Theorists**: logical thinkers, rational and objective. They have a disciplined approach and are good at asking probing questions. On the other hand, they are not good at lateral thinking and have a low tolerance for uncertainty, disorder and ambiguity. They prefer well-prepared and precise lectures and demonstrations, and do not like unstructured activities or group-work, especially if it involves exploring feelings and emotions.

EVALUATION ISSUES

EFFECTIVENESS

Teachers can deal with a range of learning styles effectively by individualising the way they teach. However this would not suit students who do not like to work individually. If there is a serious mis-match between a student's learning style and the way they are being taught, then they will learn less effectively, so teachers need to try very hard to vary their teaching style in order to please all students some of the time.

Teaching styles

Teaching style is a term that refers to the way that teachers attempt to educate their students; it describes how the teacher actually behaves in the classroom. Each teacher has her own teaching style. This section examines the work of two educational theorists: Jerome Bruner and David Ausubel, who have two very different approaches to teaching methods. Bruner's theories are associated with what is known as **discovery learning**, and Ausubel's theories are associated with what is known as **expository teaching** or **reception learning**. Although both these psychologists work from a cognitive perspective it could be argued that humanist approaches to teaching and learning underpin the ideas of Bruner, while Ausubel might be recognised as more behaviourist in his approach to teaching styles.

Jerome Bruner (1915–)

Bruner's ideas have a lot in common with those of Piaget. Piaget states that we learn through interacting with the environment, and that through this interaction we assimilate and accommodate new information. By doing this learners construct their own knowledge. Bruner (1961) states that learning is an information-processing activity, by which students try to understand their environment. According to Bruner, students do this by organising and categorising information using what he calls a coding system. He believes that the most effective way to develop a coding system is to discover it rather than being told it by the teacher, hence the term 'discovery learning', which he uses to describe this learning method.

According to Bruner, a good teacher will help students to discover the relationships between different bits of information for themselves. The teacher should give students access to the information they need, but without organising it for them. The students themselves will then organise and sort the information, learning in the process what the teacher wants them to know. Bruner believes that when students are presented with material that is too highly structured they become too dependent on others, whereas if they are allowed to discover things for themselves, they will remember the information longer and be able to apply it to 'real life' situations.

EVALUATION ISSUES

EFFECTIVENESS

One of the problems with co-operative learning is that although it is thought to raise self-esteem and enhance communication skills, it relies on each member of the group making a significant contribution. If one member of the group does not co-operate effectively, there might be an unfair burden of work on the other members. Moreover, the student who is less involved will gain little from this type of activity. Assessment of co-operative learning has to be individual, so that each member of the group is assessed on the basis of their own participation in order to make it effective.

The role of the teacher is what Bruner refers to as a mediator. The teacher must not direct the student too much, but needs to give enough guidance to enable the student to have the means to learn. Bruner also advocates the use of a **spiral curriculum**, in which ideas are repeatedly presented over a period of time, in a simple form at first, then in more complex ways as the student gets older and is able to understand more sophisticated concepts.

Discovery learning can be done by students on their own, but in practice it is often done in groups. Co-operative learning is when students are put into small groups to work together, and the success of the group depends on all the members working together for a common goal. This type of approach encourages interpersonal skills and positive self-esteem, and often a group of people working together can achieve much more than each working individually, on their own or in competition with the others

David Ausubel (1918–)

Expository teaching (sometimes referred to as direct explanation teaching) is the name given to the type of approach that Ausubel believes is the most effective. What is interesting about this approach is that although it is often presented as completely teacher-led, Ausubel (1960) actually argues that it is constructivist because the student is not a passive recipient of information, but actively learns from it. The outcome of expository teaching is reception learning. The student receives the information from the teacher, rather than discovering it for themselves.

Ausubel (1977) discusses what he calls meaningful learning; not all reception learning is meaningful. For learning to be meaningful Ausubel argues that the teacher must explain how new knowledge can be integrated into existing knowledge; relationships between pieces of knowledge and prior learning must be made explicit. Ausubel argues that most teaching and learning in the classroom is expository and receptive, not least because discovery learning is very time consuming by comparison. Ausubel also argues that there is no conclusive evidence to suggest that discovery learning is better than reception learning.

Ausubel suggests presenting material in certain ways to make it meaningful. One example is to use what he calls **advance organisers**. This is a term used to describe the way in which the teacher should start the lesson by presenting concepts to the students to focus their attention on the relationship between the lesson content and prior learning. Ausubel describes two different types of advance organisers: expository and comparative. An expository organiser is a descriptor of relevant concepts (in other words, the concepts being exposed to the learner). A comparative organiser is a presentation of how the knowledge about to be learned compares to, and fits in with, existing knowledge.

There are no measurement scales specifically designed to assess the way individuals prefer to teach, but this can be described qualitatively for any specific individual. It is likely that a person's teaching style is closely related to the way that they themselves prefer to learn, so by measuring a teacher's learning style, using one of the inventories mentioned above, it may be possible to draw valid conclusions about their teaching style.

2.3.2 INDIVIDUAL DIFFERENCES IN LEARNING STYLES

A person's learning style is an aspect of their personality and therefore develops in the same way as personality does. There is, of course, much debate among psychologists about exactly how personality develops, how

EVALUATION ISSUES

USEFULNESS

Ausubel argues that reception learning is more useful because it is efficient in providing the relevant information. Bruner argues that discovery learning reflects the way that students learn about the world naturally and that, although students may go down blind alleys and sometimes get things wrong, it is more useful because they learn more from the process. Most teachers use a combination of the two techniques, but the strict demands of exam specifications makes discovery learning much harder to implement.

CD-ROM

Cognitive apprenticeship are an approach that offer both the expository teaching of the expert and the discovery of the beginner, and appear to combine the ideas of both Bruner and Ausubel. See Education: Real life applications: Cognitive apprenticeships.

FOR CONSIDERATION

Consider whether you take part in discovery learning or reception learning in the subjects you are currently studying.
- What are the advantages and disadvantages of each approach?
- Which teaching style do you prefer?

much of it is due to genetic inheritance and how much to life experiences, how easy it is to modify, etc. This section briefly looks at whether certain groups of people have learning styles in common by describing two key studies, one on ethnicity and one on gender.

KEY STUDY

Hispanic-American students and learning style
Griggs and Dunn (1996)

Aim: To review the research on the learning styles of Hispanic-American students.

Sample and Method: In this study, Griggs and Dunn do not do any actual research themselves but review a number of other studies.

Results:
- Mexican-Americans preferred cool temperatures and formal classroom design.
- Mexican-Americans prefer a higher degree of structure in lessons to other students.
- African-American students showed the most preference for group-work, followed by Mexican-Americans, and finally by white students.
- Puerto-Rican students did not like working in the early morning.
- White students prefer to eat snacks and to move around while learning, compared to the other groups.
- Hispanic females tended to make more internal attributions than other students, whereas Hispanic males tended to make more external attributions.

Conclusions: Griggs and Dunn suggest that ethnic differences in learning styles are entirely the result of cultural differences between ethnic groups. Although they point to the danger of assuming that all members of a particular ethnic group are identical, they suggest that teachers need to take into account these differences in educational preferences in order not to disadvantage students from ethnic minorities.

EVALUATION ISSUES

GENERALISABILITY

Boaler's (1997) findings cannot be generalised to other cultural groups as the sample was ethnically homogenous. Similarly, Griggs and Dunn focused on a specific ethnic group, but their aim was to investigate general differences in learning style between this group and another. Both studies seem to draw valid conclusions that have useful implications for schools.

KEY STUDY

Reclaiming school mathematics: the girls fight back
Boaler (1997)

Aim: To investigate the underachievement of girls in mathematics.

Sample: This is a case study of two secondary schools located within mainly white, working class areas. The schools were very similar in terms of their students, but had very different approaches to the teaching of mathematics. Amber Hill School was very authoritarian and traditional; students in classes would be sitting quietly in rows, watching the board or listening to the teacher. Phoenix Park School was much more humanist in its approach; students were given independence and choice and expected to be responsible for their own studying. Phoenix Park adopted a **discovery learning** approach, whereas Amber Hill used **reception learning**.

Method: The study took place over three years and data consisted of test results in mathematics, lesson observations, structured and unstructured interviews with teachers and students and student questionnaires.

Results: Students did not enjoy mathematics at Amber Hill, but this disaffection seemed to affect girls much more than boys; their results were

EVALUATION ISSUES

EFFECTIVENESS

Most secondary school or sixth form teachers would argue that they are under a great deal of pressure to work their way through the specification in plenty of time to prepare students for the exams, and therefore cannot afford to spend a lot of time helping young people become better students. On the other hand, it may be that by spending this time in the first place, students will then learn more quickly and efficiently making the learning process more effective. However, some educationalists would argue that the curriculum in the UK is too full anyway.

EVALUATION ISSUES

USEFULNESS

In order to teach students the best ways of writing essays, it is probably more useful to do this in the context of a specific subject, rather than, say, in a tutorial lesson. In contrast a stand-alone programme is taught in isolation on the assumption that the skills and knowledge gained can be applied to all subjects being studied, thereby saving having to repeat the learning in all the different subjects being studied, for example revision techniques.

significantly poorer than those of the boys. One year 11 boy interviewed at Amber Hill said: 'I don't mind working out of textbooks, because you can get ahead of everyone else', whereas for the girls, understanding the work was much more important than getting a lot of work done. At Phoenix Park, students worked on co-operative projects at all times, and this approach seemed to suit the girls much better; they enjoyed maths more, were more confident about it, and gained better results.

Conclusions: This is one of the first studies to find significant gender-based differences in learning style. The traditional, expository teaching based, authoritarian, highly structured and competitive approach seems to suit boys much more than it does girls, at least in mathematics.

2.3.3 IMPROVING LEARNING EFFECTIVENESS

The two sections on learning and teaching styles above suggest that one way of improving the learning effectiveness of a student is to make sure that there is not too much of a mis-match between that student's learning style and the teaching styles with which he is presented. This section looks at study skills and metacognitive strategies as ways of improving learning effectiveness, and concludes with a summary of the work of Robert Gagné, whose theory of learning outcomes is aimed at helping teachers provide their students with a more effective learning experience.

Study skills

Study skills are generally taught to students within their curriculum subjects, and include being taught how to write essays, how to take and organise notes, how to revise for exams and so on. The following activities will improve a student's time management:

- set aside times and places to work
- set priorities
- break large tasks down
- do not set yourself too much
- work on one thing at a time
- check your progress often.

Metacognitive strategies

Reuven Feuerstein did a great deal of work with students with learning disabilities and was very critical of intelligence tests that measure what a child can do in a fixed period of time. He argued that a more useful measure of intelligence would be a measure of the capacity to benefit from future experience, and that by teaching a child specific cognitive processes, this capacity could be increased. Feuerstein (1979) devised a stand-alone programme aimed at students of all levels designed to teach metacognitive strategies. Through a series of paper and pencil exercises, **Feuerstein's Instrumental Enrichment (FIE)** programme teaches students to learn how to:

- understand what they are supposed to do
- understand why they are doing a task
- appreciate that a task has value outside the classroom
- be aware of what they can do and when they need help
- develop skills of self-reflection and awareness of inner thoughts and feelings.

Robert Gagné (1916–2002)

Robert Gagné was a cognitive psychologist interested in what are called learning outcomes. He looked at these as the end product of the students' learning and argued that the teacher must first identify the desired learning outcomes in order to plan the way in which students will achieve them.

KEY STUDY

Conditions of learning
Gagné (1985)

In his book, Gagné describes what he considers to be the five types of learning outcomes:

- **Verbal learning** refers to the ability to name objects, places and understand the meaning of words. It is important to understand that students have to learn things in a certain order, as they need to assimilate new information on the basis of information they have previously acquired.
- Gagné describes different types of **intellectual skills** that students need to learn. For example, discrimination learning involves the child being able to understand the difference between things. Concept learning involves students being able to understand that objects can be grouped together. Defined concepts (such as prejudice or happiness) are more abstract and can only be understood with reference to other concepts. The most difficult intellectual skills a student will learn are rules. Students often know the rules of grammar, but do not apply them to their own writing or speech, for example.
- Gagné describes the need for students to be taught to use **cognitive strategies** in order to learn.
- **Motor skills** refer to accurate movements that students develop (e.g. writing). Alongside the other skills a child learns, Gagné highlights the need to learn motor skills in a classroom setting.
- Gagné takes a behaviourist view of the way in which school can influence the development of **attitudes**. He recognises that attitudes are affected by reinforcement and argues that teachers should be aware of the need to encourage students so that their experience of school is a good one. Additionally, Gagné argues that students' attitudes are also likely to be affected indirectly through imitation (of their teachers and peers, for example).

The implication of Gagné's theories is that a teacher must plan his delivery of the curriculum very carefully, so that teacher and student both understand the nature and purpose of the learning strategy. Perhaps more important than the work of individual teachers in this respect is the need to plan the whole curriculum and the order in which it is taught. In common with many other cognitive psychologists, Gagné was interested in the hierarchy of learning. For example, a child cannot learn how to group numbers or shapes in sequences or patterns (concept learning) before she has learned the names of all the objects she is grouping (verbal learning).

SECTION A EXAM QUESTIONS

a   Describe one specific teaching style. [6]
b   Discuss the effectiveness of different teaching styles. [10]

a   Describe one study about individual differences in learning styles. [6]
b   Discuss the usefulness of research into individual differences in learning styles. [10]

a   Describe one theory of learning styles. [6]
b   Discuss the problems of measuring learning styles. [10]

KEY DEFINITIONS

Metacognition involves reflecting upon the thinking process itself. The FIE programme teaches metacognitive strategies to students, meaning that it gets students to think about how they learn, and to develop new and more effective strategies for learning.

CD-ROM

- For an example of a stand-alone activity aimed at improving sixth form students' time management see Education: Real life applications: Time management.
- For examples of Feuerstein's exercises aimed at teaching metacognitive strategies, see Education: Links.

FOR CONSIDERATION

Consider how you have been taught study skills or metacognitive strategies.
- Was it embedded in your subject teaching or as a stand-alone programme?
- Was there enough of it?
- Was it effective?

CD-ROM

For Section B sample exam questions see Education: Sample exam questions.

DISRUPTIVE BEHAVIOUR IN SCHOOL

Problem behaviour in the classroom is generally defined as behaviour that is dangerous, offensive or disruptive, and many teachers describe dealing with such behaviour as the most difficult and stressful aspect of their work. Problem behaviour lies along a spectrum ranging from mild, everyday 'naughtiness' to extremely dangerous or disruptive behaviour.

Students who frequently display such extreme behaviour and who persistently fail to respond to corrective strategies employed by teachers are labelled as having emotional or behavioural difficulties (EBD). Such students are often excluded from mainstream schools and may be temporarily sent to local behavioural support units or for more long-term treatment to special EBD schools. The official statistics for the 1998–99 academic year published by the Department for Education and Skills (DfES) reveal that 10 438 students were excluded from school (including 1366 from primary schools). Include (a charity campaigning for the re-integration of excluded students), estimates that around two-thirds of excluded students never return to mainstream education.

2.4.1 TYPES, EXPLANATIONS AND EFFECTS OF DISRUPTIVE BEHAVIOURS

Disruptive behaviour in schools takes many forms and the text that follows focuses on two specific types of behaviour: conduct disorder and bullying (there is a discussion of a third type of disruptive behaviour – school refusal – on the CD-ROM). Section 2.4.2 looks at a fourth type of disruptive behaviour, attention deficit hyperactivity disorder (ADHD). These are all forms of behaviour that would be considered problematic by teachers and that often lead to students being excluded from school.

Conduct disorder

This is sometimes referred to as **delinquency** and consists of behaviour that is especially antisocial, such as lying, stealing, vandalism and violence. Many students act in these ways from time to time, but students with conduct disorders do so persistently, and this can make them very difficult to manage in the classroom. There is a range of possible causes for conduct disorder:

- **Adolescent rebellion**: there is evidence that the physical changes that occur during adolescence can make young people's moods particularly labile (changeable). Also, many adolescents feel that society, and parents in particular, treat them like children when they feel they belong to the grown-up world. Furthermore, adolescence is a time when people try out different patterns of behaviour and experiment with attitudes and personalities before establishing a more stable adult identity.
- **Genetic/biological causes**: a disproportionate number of students excluded from schools for conduct disorder have special educational needs, and these are often linked to genetic factors or birth complications (for example, cerebral palsy, dyslexia, hearing impairment and poor memory). Furthermore, some medical conditions, for instance, asthma, epilepsy and allergies, have been linked to

CD-ROM

For a discussion of the different explanations of why students truant, see Education: Real life applications: School refusal.

EXAM HINTS

ADHD is discussed in the next section, but it can be used in essays as an example of a specific type of disruptive behaviour.

conduct disorder. It is also possible that conduct disorder is linked to hereditary personality traits, but research in this area has been inconclusive so far.

- **Poor discipline at home**: students of parents who are extremely lax are more likely to show conduct disorder, but then so are students of over-strict parents, or parents who use physical punishment or show a lack of affection or attention, another type of discipline regime.
- **Economic and social deprivation**: there is a strong correlation between child delinquency and poverty. However, the reasons for this are not clear. For example, students of single mothers are more likely to be convicted for crimes. Is this because these students have no fathers to provide moral guidance, or rather because single parent families tend to be less well off? Are working class students more likely to display conduct disorders because of a clash between the school ethos (which is likely to represent more middle class values) and the home environment? Or does being poor simply make it harder to be a good student?

Bullying

School bullying can take many different forms and is very prevalent in schools. Bullying can be physical, such as hitting, pushing, pinching or stealing money. It can also be psychological, for example, teasing, name-calling, whispering, tale-telling and deliberately excluding people.

A significant proportion of students are involved in bullying, either as victims or perpetrators, and the effects of bullying can be serious. Victims of bullying may suffer a loss of self-esteem (Kidscape 1999), which can have an adverse effect on their lives in many different ways, or they can simply be put off school and education in general. Bullies themselves, apart from running the risk of getting into trouble at school, are three times more likely to become involved with the criminal justice system later in life (Olwdeus (1989; cited in Rubin and Heppler).

All schools recognise the need to deal with bullies, and they use a wide range of strategies to ensure that incidents of bullying or harassment are reported, that perpetrators are dealt with effectively and that victims are given adequate support. The nature of these strategies will depend on the ethos of the school and the attitudes of the individual teachers concerned.

KEY STUDY

Long-term effects of bullying
Kidscape Survey (1999)

Aim: Kidscape children's charity conducted the first ever retrospective survey of adults to discover the effects of being bullied at school.

Sample: 1044 adults, some of whom volunteered as a result of television appeals and magazine adverts, and others who were approached in the street and asked to participate. 828 had been bullied at school (70 per cent of this group was female) and 216 had not been bullied (49 per cent female).

Method: Respondents were given a questionnaire consisting of 16 set questions, with a space for more open responses (a significant majority of

---

⚖ EVALUATION ISSUES

THEORETICAL APPROACH

Psychologists have identified different ways in which parents discipline their children, but perhaps the most damaging type of discipline regime is an inconsistent one; this can lead to the child having a confused notion of 'right' and 'wrong', and can also lead to learned helplessness.

💿 CD-ROM

For a description of how psychologists have classified different parenting styles, see Education: Real life applications: Parental discipline.

⚖ EVALUATION ISSUES

REDUCTIONISM

There is a tendency to blame individual students for their antisocial behaviour in the classroom, but there is a great deal of evidence to suggest that a number of factors can cause this and that teacher behaviour is also an important factor in generating or preventing conduct disorder. Teachers have a tendency to attribute student behaviour externally and to ignore the way their own behaviour, or the school ethos, contributes to the way students behave.

❓ FOR CONSIDERATION

School bullying is very widespread; in a typical class of sixth-formers, almost all will, at some time in their school career, have been the victim of bullying, the perpetrator of bullying or both. Consider your own experience of bullying (as a victim, a perpetrator or a witness).
- Why do students bully each other?
- What effect does bullying have on the victim?
- What is the best way of dealing with bullies?

bullying victims added several pages of details). The non-bullied respondents acted as a control group.

Results: Being bullied at school lowered victims' self-esteem as adults, reduced their ability to make friends and to succeed in education, in work and in social relationships. Nearly half (46 per cent) of those who were bullied contemplated suicide (compared with 7 per cent of those who were not bullied). Most victims reported still feeling angry and bitter about the bullying they had received as students and most said that they had received no help at the time and that telling adults either made no difference or made matters worse.

Conclusions: Being bullied as a child is likely to have a dramatic, negative, knock-on effect throughout life.

2.4.2 CAUSES AND EFFECTS OF ATTENTION DEFICIT HYPERACTIVITY DISORDER (ADHD)

Causes of ADHD

In the key study below, Dr Nykos Myttas describes the symptoms and possible causes of ADHD.

KEY STUDY

Understanding and recognising ADHD
Myttas (2001)

Symptoms: children with ADHD have a very short attention span and cannot concentrate on a task for any length of time. They are either easily distracted, or hyper-focused, and they lose their train of thought easily. They daydream, lose things, forget instructions and avoid tasks that demand attention or concentration. They have a poor sense of time and priorities. They are moody and get very easily bored; they are full of energy and are very restless and fidgety and have trouble getting to sleep. They are impulsive and have difficulty waiting their turn. In class, they shout out, they disrupt others and they rush through their work making careless mistakes. They misjudge social situations; they are domineering and loud and they cannot take 'no' for an answer. In order to receive a clinical diagnosis of ADHD, the symptoms must have had an early onset (around 4-years-old) and must have been present for more than 6 months. It is estimated that 6–8 per cent of students in the UK suffer from ADHD; three times as many boys as girls are diagnosed with the condition but there is no social, economic or ethnic bias.

Causes: Most psychologists believe that ADHD is caused by neurobiological malfunctioning: although environmental factors can influence the course of the disorder, they do not bring it about. The prevailing theory is that children with ADHD have difficulties in impulse suppression; they respond to all impulses, being unable to exclude those that are unnecessary for the situation. Rather than failing to pay attention, they try to pay attention to everything and cannot choose what is most important at the time. There is strong evidence of a genetic predisposition to ADHD, and it seems that children with the condition do not grow out of it, although early treatment is very effective in reducing complications such as antisocial behaviour, substance mis-use and poor academic and social functioning.

EVALUATION ISSUES

EFFECTIVENESS/ETHICS

Ritalin can be very effective in dealing with the symptoms of ADHD, much more so than psychological treatments. Some people argue that it is unethical to control a child's behaviour with a drug they believe to be potentially harmful and addictive simply because that behaviour makes life more difficult for the child's teachers and parents. On the other hand, the child's behaviour may be interfering with their own learning as well, and by controlling the behaviour with Ritalin, the child benefits in the end.

Children with ADHD appear to be very highly over-aroused, and it is possible that this is a chronic condition caused by physiological factors, such as allergic reactions to food additives, for example. Another explanation could be that these children are actually under-aroused and therefore constantly have to seek stimulation from the environment in order to prevent themselves becoming bored; this could account for the inability to concentrate on one thing for more than a few seconds, and the constant rushing around that is typical in children with ADHD. This last theory is supported by the fact that ADHD is often successfully treated with a drug called Ritalin, an amphetamine that increases psychological and physiological arousal, and, contrary to what might be expected, calms ADHD students down.

Effects of ADHD

Children with ADHD can find learning very difficult as the behavioural symptoms of the condition are not conducive to good learning. They can be very disruptive to their own learning as well as to that of their classmates. ADHD behaviour is generally perceived as being 'naughty' and so children with ADHD are much more likely to get into trouble at school. (See Mytass' study (2001) on the previous page for a discussion of the effects of ADHD in the classroom.)

2.4.3 CORRECTIVE AND PREVENTIVE STRATEGIES

Children with emotional or behavioural difficulties can be difficult to deal with, but low level 'naughtiness' can also be very disruptive in the classroom; teachers spend a great deal of time and effort attempting to 'control' their students. Humanist teachers argue that it is precisely these efforts to control students that encourage them to behave inappropriately. In his book on Summerhill School, the school's founder, AS Neill, says 'Neurosis begins with parental discipline, which is the very opposite of parental love. You cannot have a good humanity by treating it with hate and punishment and suppression. The only way is the way of love. A loving environment, without parental discipline, will take care of most of the troubles of childhood' (Neill, 1960).

However, all teachers, including Neill, would agree that individual freedom should not extend to the freedom to hurt other people, and that it is necessary to maintain a classroom environment in which students can learn effectively. Teachers must take into account the needs and rights of individual students, but also those of the rest of the class.

Classroom management, therefore, has two functions: the facilitation of learning and the prevention and correction of misbehaviours. Teachers with different perspectives disagree how to fulfil these two functions, and even how to define them: 'learning' and 'misbehaviour' mean very different things to different people. The text that follows examines behaviourist, cognitive and humanist techniques of classroom management.

Behaviour modification

Behaviour modification is a set of behaviourist techniques based on operant conditioning and used to eliminate or change behaviour considered unacceptable by the teacher. In the **ABC model** of behaviour modification, behaviour is changed by manipulating either the antecedents or the consequences; behaviourists do not question the root causes of behaviour or examine internal mental processes, but are content simply to change behaviour from 'bad' to 'good'.

CD-ROM

For a discussion of the use of Ritalin to treat students with ADHD see Education: Real life applications: Wonder drug or playground curse?

FOR CONSIDERATION

- Have you ever met anyone who was diagnosed as having ADHD?
- What was their behaviour like and how did it affect the other children in the class?
- How did the teachers try to deal with the problem?

The most common way in which 'bad' behaviour is reinforced in the classroom is by attention, either from the teacher or from other students, and it is often the case that a particular child will prefer negative attention (for example, being told off) to no attention. Other ways in which bad behaviour can be rewarded are, for example, by being sent out of the classroom (some students might find this a relief) or by receiving recognition and admiration from other students.

- Can you think of specific examples where 'bad' behaviour was reinforced by teachers?

In the ABC model of behaviour modification:

- **antecedents** are the conditions that apply immediately prior to the behaviour in question, and that may trigger, or even directly cause, the behaviour. If it is possible to change the antecedents of unwanted behaviour, then it could be prevented from occurring in the first place
- **behaviour** is what the teacher wishes to change or eliminate
- **consequences** are the outcomes of the behaviour for the students concerned. The theory of operant conditioning suggests that students will only continue to behave in certain ways if they receive reinforcement for doing so. It is therefore important to make sure that students are reinforced for desired behaviour, and not reinforced for undesired behaviour.

Changing the antecedents of behaviour is not, strictly speaking, an aspect of operant conditioning because this theory focuses entirely on the consequences of actions. However, this has become an important aspect of modern behavioural technique; for example, if a certain child seems to become aggressive in class every time she is asked to hand out worksheets, then the behaviourist teacher is content to avoid asking that child to perform that particular task (as long as it stops the child becoming aggressive) and is not overly concerned with the reasons behind the aggression.

There are several ways in which teachers can influence the consequences of behaviour in order to modify it:

- They can make sure that students do not receive reinforcement for 'bad' behaviour. This usually consists of ignoring students when they are naughty and making sure that students are not deriving any other hidden benefit from punishment, such as admiration of fellow students.
- They can reward students for 'good' behaviour by offering extrinsic reinforcers, whether social or material.
- They can punish students for 'bad' behaviour: apart from a few extreme humanist schools, some form of punishment or sanction takes place in every classroom in the world. However, punishment draws attention to unwanted behaviour, it is accompanied by negative emotional side-effects (such as anger, resentment and low self-esteem), and it can damage the relationship between student and teacher. Also, punishment often suppresses behaviour rather than eliminating it; students develop strategies for avoiding punishment rather than learning that the behaviour that instigated the punishment is wrong. Finally, punished students receive a clear object lesson that strength and power are effective ways of getting other people to do what you want.

When behaviour modification is used in a clinical setting, psychologists observe and record the behaviour in question, as well as the antecedents and consequences. They will design a systematic programme for altering the antecedents or consequences and will measure the behaviour before and after the intervention in order to ascertain its effectiveness. When behaviour modification occurs in the classroom, it is rarely this systematic; a teacher with 30 or more students simply cannot make detailed observations of a single child. However, teachers do apply behaviour modification in a more ad hoc manner, and it can be a very effective technique for making students behave differently.

It is possible to use behaviour modification without punishing students, by ignoring undesired behaviour, and reinforcing desired behaviour. However, bad behaviour can sometimes be very difficult to ignore, especially if it is causing serious disruption to the class or putting other people in danger. In extreme cases, the child rarely, or never, exhibits wanted behaviour and so the teacher is unable to provide appropriate reinforcement. A technique for dealing with such a situation is to use **non-contingent reinforcement**. This is a recently developed technique in which the child is systematically rewarded at fixed time intervals, whether she has displayed the required behaviour or not. This works because it creates a flooding effect in which the child learns that reinforcement does not only come when she behaves badly. After a time, the reinforcement is slightly delayed when the child displays the unwanted behaviour; the programme then resembles traditional operant conditioning more closely.

Cognitive behaviour therapy

The criticism that cognitive psychologists make about the traditional behaviourist approach to classroom control is that it takes no account of the child's thought processes.

Cognitive behaviour therapy (CBT) is based on the assumption that students' behaviour in the classroom relates to their interpretations of events and not, as traditional behaviourists would argue, simply to the events themselves. Our interpretation of events is linked to our beliefs about ourselves and about the world around us; if these beliefs are irrational or deluded, then our behaviour is flawed. For example, if a child thinks that everybody in the class hates him or her, then he may become hostile and aggressive. Cognitive therapies attempt to challenge irrational beliefs by, for example, reminding such a child of interactions with classmates in which it was clear that they did not hate him.

Teachers use informal cognitive behaviour therapy all the time in the classroom, in the sense that they constantly challenge students' opinions and beliefs, and try to persuade them to accept certain values. More formal programmes are very time consuming and beyond the scope of most teachers. A specific example of a cognitive programme was described by Meichenbaum and Goodman (1971).

KEY STUDY

Training impulsive students to talk to themselves: a means of developing self-control
Meichenbaum and Goodman (1971)

Aim: To demonstrate the effectiveness of a cognitive behavioural intervention (self-instructional training) in treating impulsive and hyperactive students.

Sample: Fifteen students placed in a special education classroom because of behavioural problems (hyperactivity and poor self-control).

Method: The students were split into three groups of five. The first group (SI) received the self-instructional treatment, the second (attention-control) did not receive any treatment but were given an equivalent amount of attention, and the third (assessment-control) received no treatment or attention and were used to establish a baseline. The self-instructional training programme consisted of four hours and 30 minutes spread over two weeks, during which the following procedures were carried out:
* the researcher performed a task while talking through it out loud; the child observed

For a discussion about whether children with severe behavioural difficulties should be kept within mainstream schools see Education: Real life applications: Social inclusion: pupil support.

 **EVALUATION ISSUES**

EFFECTIVENESS

Meichenbaum and Goodman's study (1971) shows the effectiveness of self in structural training.

EVALUATION ISSUES

ETHICS

Behaviourist techniques for managing classroom behaviour can be criticised on ethical grounds because they are manipulative and can lower the self-esteem of students. In comparison humanist techniques are criticised because they allow students to choose to behave in ways that could be harmful to their own education or to that of their fellow classmates. The debate is between whether it is right to give students freedom and allow them to make their own mistakes in the hope that they will do the best thing in the end, or whether to control their behaviour in their own best interests.

- the child performed the same task while the researcher gave instructions out loud
- the child performed the task, speaking self-instructions out loud
- the child performed the task, whispering self-instructions
- the child performed the task by thinking the self-instructions to herself

The SI group were instructed in this way to perform a range of sensory-motor and problem-solving tasks.

Results: The SI group performed significantly better on the tasks than the students in the two control groups (immediately and when they were re-assessed three weeks later). There was no observable improvement in classroom behaviour or in teacher ratings of behaviour for these students.

Conclusions: Meichenbaum and Goodman concluded that a cognitive self-instructional programme that teaches students to talk to themselves can help impulsive or hyperactive students to concentrate on their work and that this, eventually, will have beneficial effects on their classroom behaviour.

The humanist approach to classroom management

In general, the humanist approach to classroom management is preventative rather than corrective. In other words, the humanist teacher will try to promote an ethos in the classroom that will make it easier for students to behave in ways that are conducive to learning. For example, by valuing and respecting students, by refusing to mistreat or oppress them, and by allowing them freedom of action and expression, the humanist hopes that the students' natural goodness and curiosity will shine through. In this way, students will not only be keen to engage in education for its own sake, but will also treat each other, and the teachers, with love and respect.

This is not to say that humanists do not have strategies to deal with behaviour problems in the classroom, but these strategies tend to be much more democratic than those employed by behaviourist teachers. Webster (1968; cited in LeFrançois, 1997), for example, describes a set of procedures by which democratic order can be maintained in the classroom:

- Teachers must make sure that all the students understand what the rules are and the reasons for their existence.
- The first violation of a rule should lead to a warning, a discussion of alternative ways of behaving and clarification of the consequences of repeated infractions.
- Teachers should endeavour to discover the underlying causes of misbehaviour.
- Whenever possible, teachers should address students in private regarding their misbehaviour.
- Sarcasm, ridicule and other forms of discipline that lead to public humiliation should be avoided.
- Teachers should apologise when they make mistakes.
- The punishment should fit the crime; minor misbehaviours should not bring about harsh punishment.
- Extra class work and assignments, tests and other school-related activities should never be used as a form of punishment.

These principles are put into practice at Summerhill School; AS Neill (1960) describes it as a self-governing school in which all punishment for social offences is settled by vote at weekly school meetings. All students and staff have an equal say in deciding what the school rules should be and what to do if anyone breaks them. Few schools are this democratic, but similar principles can be used in 'ordinary' schools to a certain degree. Even within a particular school, some teachers will act in a more democratic way than others.

SECTION A EXAM QUESTIONS

a Describe one strategy for correcting disruptive behaviour. [6]
b Evaluate strategies for correcting disruptive behaviour. [10]

a Describe one study of a preventive strategy for disruptive behaviour. [6]
b Discuss the strengths of preventive strategies for disruptive behaviour. [10]

CD-ROM

- For a description of Summerhill School, see Education: Real life applications: Summerhill School.
- Humanist techniques of classroom management are sometimes referred to as conflict management or pro-social programmes. For a specific example of such a programme see Education: Additional key studies: Moreno and Torrego (1999).

CD-ROM

For Section B sample exam questions see Education: Sample exam questions.

2.5 DESIGN AND LAYOUT OF EDUCATIONAL ENVIRONMENTS

Environmental psychologists have carried out a great deal of research to discover how the classroom setting can facilitate or hinder learning, but there is a recognition that there is no universal answer to this question. A particular classroom layout, for example, may suit a specific teaching style and different subjects are best taught in different types of classroom. The text that follows first discusses classroom layout (that is, the way the tables are placed and what is put on the walls), then considers briefly other environmental factors such as noise, temperature, light and colour.

2.5.1 PHYSICAL FEATURES OF LEARNING ENVIRONMENTS

Layout of desks

Traditionally designed classrooms have the desks laid out in rows, with the teacher's desk at the front of the classroom, sometimes on a raised platform. This is an efficient way of filling a room as less space is wasted between desks. Also, the students are all facing the teacher, rather than each other, and they can all see the board at the front of the room. This design is suited to authoritarian, didactic teaching and still exists in many schools today.

There is contradictory evidence as to the best way of setting out desks in a classroom. Wheldall et al. (1981) concluded that students pay more attention in class (referred to as 'on-task' behaviour) when seated in rows as opposed to clusters, whereas Rosenfield et al. (1985) found the opposite; desks arranged in circles and, to a lesser extent, in clusters, during classroom discussion can facilitate interaction as well as diminish off-task behaviour.

These findings seem contradictory but, apart from the fact that each of them has certain methodological problems and that different teachers will define 'on-task' and 'off-task' behaviour quite differently, together they reinforce the notion that the most effective classroom layout depends on the type of lesson being taught and the style of the teacher. For example, if a teacher is trying to encourage students to take part in discovery, then an open classroom arrangement, in which students are free to move about, use available resources and work together in groups, may be most suitable. On the other hand, for didactic teaching, sitting the students in rows is probably the best way of keeping their attention. Finally, if the teacher wishes to hold a class discussion, the advantage of putting desks in a circle is that every student can see and interact with every other. A recent attempt to resolve contradictions within previous research into classroom layout was made by Hastings and Chantrey Wood (2002).

Layout of wall displays

Another aspect of classroom layout, apart from the way the desks are arranged, is how much and what kinds of material are put on the walls.

KEY STUDY

Reorganising primary classroom learning
Hastings and Chantrey Wood (2002)

UK primary classrooms are known and admired throughout the world for their physical organisation, i.e. students sitting in groups. Group seating is meant to support co-operative learning and small group teaching, but recent observational research seems to indicate that these kinds of teaching and learning strategies do not actually feature very highly in UK primary classrooms. The large majority of lessons are taken up either with the teacher talking to the whole class at once, or else talking to students one at a time; even though students tend to sit in groups, most of their work is done individually. Group seating makes both these types of teaching significantly more difficult for most students and dramatically so for some, than do other seating arrangements.

Hastings and Chantry Wood conclude that seating arrangements have very strong effects on interaction between students and teachers, and among students, and on the degree to which students pay attention to their work or to the teacher. They do not argue that all primary schools should be rearranged so that the desks are in rows or in a circle, but that classrooms should be built to be flexible, so that the teachers can vary the students' seating and working environment to match the demands of the activities taking place. They describe one school in which the desks are on wheels and the students are drilled to change the classroom from one layout to another in a couple of minutes. They conclude from this observation that this is a practical and effective solution to the problem of how to lay out the desks in a classroom.

Creekmore (1987; cited in Gifford, 1997) argues that each classroom should contain three different types of walls:

- **Acquisition wall:** this should be placed at the front of the room and should hold the blackboard/whiteboard and the class notice-board. Only material relating to educational concepts that are new or that students are struggling with should be placed on this wall.
- **Maintenance walls:** these should be at the sides of the room, and should help students review and understand more fully material with which they are already familiar.
- **Dynamic wall:** this should be at the back of the room and should contain students' work, temporary notices, holiday decorations and so on.

Creekmore's (1987) rationale is that this distribution of different learning materials around the classroom enables students to focus their attention without interference.

A second issue relating to wall displays is how much to include. The humanist teacher would argue that complex and informative wall displays create a rich environment that facilitates the process of discovery learning. Furthermore, presenting students' work on the walls can have a positive effect on self-esteem (as long as this is done in a non-competitive way) and can help students work co-operatively. More didactic teachers, on the other hand, may consider complex wall displays to be distracting to students and therefore make it more difficult for them to concentrate on their studies. There is little research that compares sparse wall displays with more complex ones, but as with the question of desk layout, it seems likely that the best way of decorating classroom walls depends on the style of the teacher and the subject being taught in that classroom.

FOR CONSIDERATION

As you have progressed through the education system, you will have experienced a number of different classroom layouts.
- Have you noticed differences in layouts depending on the age of the students or the subjects being taught?
- What is your favourite classroom layout?

Whereas layout of classrooms has been shown to have an effect on students' 'on-task' behaviour, other aspects of the classroom environment can have an effect on the students' feelings and on their cognitive performance.

Noise

Some teachers may assume that noise in the classroom hinders learning and may spend a lot of effort attempting to keep noise levels low so that students can concentrate better. However, the relationship between noise in the classroom and students' performance is not straightforward. For example, different students react to noise in different ways depending on individual characteristics such as gender, motivation, personality, ability and so on. Noise can have an adverse effect on performance on certain types of task and actually enhance performance on others. Different types of noise can have different effects. Finally, noise has a different effect if it occurs during the learning of material or during the task performance. There has been a great deal of research on the effects of noise on performance as the examples that follow show.

- Bronzaft (1981): measured the reading ability of students in a New York School was measured and found it to be significantly lower for those who had classrooms on the side of the building facing a noisy train line. One year after rubber sound-reducing materials were installed on the train line, this difference had disappeared.

- Christie and Glickman (1980): gave elementary school students were given visual puzzles to do in noisy and in quiet conditions. Overall, there was no difference in performance between the conditions, but the boys did significantly better when it was noisy, and the girls did better when it was quiet.

- Zentall (1983): showed that noisy rock music actually helped hyperactive students to be less disruptive and verbally aggressive, but made autistic students more passive and repetitive in their actions than usual. (See also chapter 5, section 5.1.2 for a discussion of the negative effects of noise on performance.)

KEY STUDY

The effects of noise on the attainments and cognitive performance of primary school children
Shield and Dockrell (2003)

Aim: This paper consists of a summary of various pieces of research carried out by the authors to investigate the effects of chronic noise on children's attainment.

Sample and method: In one study, measures of noise were taken in primary schools from three London Boroughs and correlated with KS1 and KS2 SATs results. In a second study, children and teachers were given questionnaires asking them about their perceptions of noise. In a third, study groups of children were exposed to more or less noise and asked to perform specific cognitive tasks.

Results:
- In every school, average noise levels outside the classrooms exceeded World Health Organisation guidelines.

- By far the greatest source of noise was from within the classrooms themselves.
- There was a significant negative correlation between SATs results and noise levels.
- Children were very sensitive to noise and were annoyed by specific sound sources.
- Teachers reported that children were disturbed and distracted by noise, but did not have any strategies for dealing with the problem.
- Performance on verbal and non-verbal cognitive tasks was significantly worse in children exposed to noise simulating classroom 'babble'.

Conclusions: Children in London primary schools are exposed to higher levels of noise than is recommended and this has an adverse effect on their performance in SATs and in specific cognitive tasks. Children are well aware of their noisy environments and experience feelings of annoyance at specific sound sources.

There are several reasons why noise may have an adverse effect on the learning process. It may interfere with communication between students and teacher or among students. It may interfere with cognitive processes such as memory or problem-solving. Finally, it may cause stress or lower students' sense of personal control.

Temperature

In most schools, climate is well controlled, but classrooms can be too hot in summer (or even in winter if the heating is high and there is little ventilation), or too cold or damp. An interesting aspect of research in this area is that it is not always the case that the climate that makes students most comfortable is the one at which they perform at an optimal level. Students perform better in arithmetic or general intelligence tests and at language tasks when the temperature is slightly lower than they normally find comfortable, and when humidity is low and air circulation high. In PE lessons, higher temperatures are associated with lower performance and fitness. Students in hot climates perform better if the classrooms are air-conditioned. In general, it seems that cooler and less humid classrooms are better for learning but, again, it is likely that individual students perform better in climates they prefer or are more used to. (See section 5.2.2 for a discussion of the effects of temperature on educational performance.)

Light and colour

There are several questions to consider in determining the best kind of lighting to have in a classroom. Most classrooms in the UK use fluorescent lighting, but is daylight, or at least artificial lighting that simulates daylight, better? What is the effect on students of light reflecting off surfaces in the classroom? What is the optimum intensity of light, and is this the same for everyone or does each individual perform better at the level of brightness that he prefers? Linked to the issue of lighting is that of colour. Most primary school classrooms contain bright colours, whereas secondary classrooms tend to be painted in more pastel shades. Does the colour of the walls actually make any difference to the learning process?

There have been several research studies aimed at answering these kinds of questions, and below is a summary of some of the findings:
- Students and teachers tend to prefer 'ordinary' light bulbs to fluorescent lighting, but fluorescent lights are much cheaper and have not been

FOR CONSIDERATION

- If you could design your ideal classroom, what would it be like?

EVALUATION ISSUES

USEFULNESS

The research into classroom environments is useful in helping teachers design good classrooms, however an obstacle to creating the perfect classroom environment is cost. It does not cost anything to rearrange the desks (although a flexible system in which the desks can be arranged into different layouts may well be more expensive), but building soundproof windows and walls is expensive, as is providing fully controllable and effective heating/air conditioning, etc.

shown to affect either the performance or the health of students in any significant way.

- Although a minimum of light intensity is required for students to see what they are doing, the human eye is very adaptable to different lighting levels and there is little evidence of an overall association between intensity of illumination (within the range found in classrooms in practice) and performance, although it may be the case that specific students prefer certain levels of lighting and work best when they are provided in their classrooms.
- There is little evidence that the colour of the walls in a classroom affects performance or mental state to any significant degree. Many people believe that emotional arousal can be affected by colour; for example, red is supposed to make people more angry and blue more calm. Research has failed to discover any changes in physiological arousal as a result of working in differently coloured rooms, but it may be that a red room makes those in it feel more excitable or angry, or a blue room calmer and more passive, simply because we think it should do. Of course, it may be that students work better in rooms that are painted in their own favourite colour, but this is an individual preference and does not lead to any generalisations about the 'best' colour to paint a classroom. (See section 5.2.2 for further discussion of light and educational performance.)

2.5.3 CREATING BETTER ENVIRONMENTAL CONDITIONS FOR LEARNING

The evidence described above suggests that an ideal classroom environment for learning could be created by:
- having flexible seating and desk arrangements, so that these can be made to match the style of teaching and the activity
- making sure that the layout of the walls matches the teaching style
- keeping the classroom quiet by not building schools near railway lines or major roads, or under flight paths, by installing effective sound insulation (e.g. double glazing) to cut out external noise, and by installing carpets, curtains, etc. to absorb as much internal noise as possible
- allowing students and teachers to determine the colours in which the classroom is painted and to control the levels of light and heat in the classroom.

The key study by Sommer and Olsen (1980) described below, describes a successful attempt to design and implement an alternative classroom at the University of California.

KEY STUDY

The soft classroom
Sommer and Olsen (1980)

A paper by Sommer and Olsen (1980) describes a successful attempt to design and implement an alternative classroom at the University of California. Previous classrooms were very traditional, with the chairs arranged in straight rows facing the front of the room, or around a large rectangular table in the smaller seminar rooms. Students rated these rooms as cold, impersonal, bare and ugly. Furthermore, little student interaction occurred in the classrooms. Even in the seminar rooms, student comments only took up about six minutes of a one-hour session; the rest of the time was taken up by the teacher. In the lecture rooms, there was no interaction among students (except for whispering between students sitting next to each other); it was as if the desks being in rows gave the message to the students that all interaction should be between student and teacher, and not among students.

At first, Sommer and Olsen attempted to improve the classrooms by bringing in plants, putting up posters and mobiles and even painting a mural. These small changes were well received but when they attempted to put the desks in a large circle instead of in rows, the students moved them back before the class started. At this point, the researchers asked for permission from the university to redesign one of the classrooms completely and received a modest grant to pay for the changes. During the next month, they carried out an extensive survey of staff and students to discover opinions about lighting, furniture and so on. During the summer of 1974, the classroom was remodelled. It started off with 30 chairs with attached writing surfaces facing two large tables and a teacher's chair at the front of the room. This was replaced with sofas and cushions around the edges of the room, a small blackboard and a multicoloured carpet. Lighting could be controlled using a dimmer switch, wooden panels were used to break up the rectangular shape of the room, and decorative coat hooks and mobiles were put up.

The researchers were worried that the new classroom would be vandalised or misused in some way, and posted observers to keep an eye on it and to record people's reactions. Students and staff were very positive about the room and students participated to a much greater degree in lessons (about three times as much as when the desks were in rows). They also moved about the room during lessons. The fact that there was no focal point where the teacher should stand meant that he could also move around, creating a more informal, democratic environment.

Some classes were not suited to the room because they were too large or required specialist equipment. Also, the researchers had trouble persuading site staff to maintain the room properly. There was no equipment available for vacuuming the carpet and, interestingly, the male site staff considered jobs such as vacuuming, rearranging sofa cushions and watering plants as 'women's work', whereas they were much more willing to carry out traditional jobs such as fastening rows of chairs together or polishing tiled floors with heavy machines.

The creation of a 'soft classroom' may not seem particularly revolutionary nowadays, but Sommer and Olsen felt they were breaking new ground in classroom design. They considered their experiment a success in that the new classroom was much preferred by the large majority of students and staff, and that it did a great deal to encourage student participation in lessons.

EVALUATION ISSUES

METHODOLOGY

Sommer and Olsen's (1980) study is a case study and it is therefore difficult to generalise its findings too far. However, as in all case studies, the researchers were trying to demonstrate that a specific possibility existed, and they seem to have done this effectively.

FOR CONSIDERATION

Consider the 'soft classroom' designed by Sommer and Olsen (1980).
- How 'soft' are your classrooms?
- What do you think would be the effect of making them 'softer'?

SECTION A EXAM QUESTIONS

a   Describe one study of layout of educational environments. [6]
b   Evaluate the usefulness of research into educational environments. [10]

a   Describe one study of the effect of classroom design on performance. [6]
b   Discuss the weakness of research into classroom design. [10]

a   Describe one study of the effect of classroom design on feelings. [6]
b   Discuss the problems of investigating the effect of classroom design on feelings. [10]

CD-ROM

For Section B sample exam questions see Education: Sample exam questions.

2.6 ASSESSING EDUCATIONAL PERFORMANCE

The text that follows looks at the various types of assessment that are used within the education system. Teaching and learning relies on assessment, not just to judge performance but also to understand how students learn and to diagnose what they need. It is almost impossible not to assess, and there are many ways in which teachers try to assess progress. These range from observing to standardised testing.

⚖ EVALUATION ISSUES

USEFULNESS

Some educational psychologists are critical of the so-called 'test and tell' approach, in which psychologists administer psychometric tests to children, and then write reports. They argue that, often, all that these tests do is confirm a problem that parents and teachers are already aware of, without pointing the way to a solution and are therefore not very useful.

🔑 KEY DEFINITIONS

Exams and school tests measure educational achievement.
Psychometric tests, on the other hand, measure students' ability and potential, i.e. they measure what students are like rather than what they have learned to do.

2.6.1 TYPES AND LIMITATIONS OF PSYCHOMETRIC TESTS

Psychometric tests are designed to provide numerical measures of psychological functioning. They can measure cognitive and other mental abilities, such as intelligence, creativity, linguistic ability, etc. and can also be used to measure different aspects of personality. Perhaps their widest use in modern society is as a recruitment tool, but they are also used within the education system by educational psychologists. They can be helpful in the diagnosis of learning difficulties or to identify personality factors that may have a link to disruptive behaviour. Psychometric tests that are currently used in schools include the following:

- Weschler Intelligence Scale (WISC III): this is the IQ test used by most educational psychologists.
- British Ability Scales (BAS II): some psychologists prefer this test to the WISC because it measures general cognitive ability, which they argue is a wider and more useful measure than IQ.
- Teacher Report Form: a scale that identifies groups of behaviours that occur together to form syndromes, such as conduct disorder, Tourette's syndrome, etc.
- Connors Rating School: a test used to help diagnose ADHD.
- B-G Self-esteem Inventory: a measure of self-esteem.
- WORD: a test that uses elements of the WISC to measure reading, comprehension and spelling.
- British Picture Vocabulary Scale (BPVS II): measures receptive and expressive language skills.

Designing a psychometric test

Psychometric tests are designed by psychologists and sold for other people to use. In order to design an effective test for use in education, it must satisfy certain conditions:

- A psychometric test must measure something **useful**, i.e. it must aim to measure some mental feature that is relevant to education and also that is relatively constant. For example, a test that measures mood may be useful in a clinical setting, but will not tell teachers anything very useful about a child. However, a test that measures an enduring aspect of personality that may underlie changes in mood, such as self-efficacy, is potentially much more helpful.
- A psychometric test needs to be **standardised** in order for any conclusions to be drawn from its results. If a test is designed to measure intelligence, then a score of 130 on that test has no meaning unless **norms** have been previously established for that test. This involves presenting the test to a large, representative sample (most commercial

tests have been standardised using samples a few thousand strong) and establishing a probability distribution for the population. This enables psychologists to conclude that an IQ of 130 is not just above average but lies in the top 2.5 per cent of the population (IQ scores follow a normal distribution with a mean of 100 and a standard deviation of 15). Psychometric test scores usually have to be adjusted for age; a 30 year-old has to get a higher raw score that a 13 year-old in order to end up with the same IQ score, for example. This adjustment is done using tables contained within a handbook sold alongside the test materials.

- A psychometric test must be **reliable** and **valid**. These conditions apply to all forms of assessment and are discussed in Section 2.6.3.

Tests designed to measure intelligence are probably the most commonly used psychometric test in education and the key study by Alpay (2003) sets out the limitations and the value of IQ testing.

KEY STUDY

What do we stand to learn about an individual whose intelligence is measured by an IQ test?
Alpay (2003)

All IQ tests make assumptions about the nature of intelligence and there are ongoing debates about whether intelligence is a single entity or covers a broad spectrum of abilities. There is also controversy concerning the degree to which intelligence is innate. However, it is widely accepted that modern standardised tests do not measure all abilities, such as creativity, practical sense and social sensitivity. The fact that these tests (such as the Weschler Scale) correlate well with school achievement is no surprise as this itself primarily focuses on the logical-mathematical and linguistic abilities emphasised by IQ tests. The widespread use of these tests has created a culture in which other abilities (or intelligences) are not equally valued.

Other criticisms of the way IQ tests have been used in research are listed below:

- Differences in IQ scores between different nationalities have been attributed to differences in intelligence, whereas it is more likely that this represents differences in culture and schooling.
- Test differences have been attributed to innate factors, ignoring the possibility that they may arise from early environmental differences. For example, whereas black students tend to score lower than white students, there are no such differences between white students and black students adopted or fostered by white guardians; this implies that ethnic differences in IQ scores are a result of upbringing and not genetics.
- No overall gender differences have been found, but the differences between males and females have been attributed to physiological causes instead of environmental ones.
- IQ tests are given outside the context of normal human behaviour, and this may favour certain types of people. Even Raven's Progressive Matrices, which rely on abstract visual reasoning and reduce bias associated with prior knowledge, are not reflective of the experience-based intelligence which is required in everyday life.
- The concept of an IQ test gives little recognition to Vygotsky's ideas of a zone of proximal development in learning (see page 23). Furthermore, as Piaget noted, it is not the number of correct answers that matters, but the reasoning behind them, and IQ tests take little account of this.

Given all these criticisms, what does an IQ test tell us about an individual? If the abilities for a particular task can be clearly defined, and social, motivational and other personal characteristics are not relevant, then it may be possible to design a test that measures an individual's ability to do the task; however, this is not a situation that is likely come up very often. Other benefits of IQ testing may be to assess specific aspects of an individual's abilities to help with further development of these abilities. Similarly, where IQ tests give low scores, this may help identify an individual's learning difficulties and any special educational provision that would help them.

2.6.2 TYPES OF PERFORMANCE ASSESSMENT AT DIFFERENT AGES

There are now many more forms of assessment than there used to be. In the 1960s, for example, there were very few formal assessment procedures in place. There was the eleven-plus exam, which was used in what is now Year 6. This IQ test was used to determine which kind of secondary school a child should progress to. There were also O and A levels, which were usually taken at age 16 and 18 respectively. Then there were university exams for about 7 per cent of all 21-year-olds. In the year 2000 there are now SATs for 7, 11 and 14-year-olds. There are GCSEs at age 16, and AS and A2 exams at age 17 and 18. There are also Applied GCSEs, AVCE, GNVQ and Key Skills qualifications. At degree level, 35 per cent of all 21-year-olds will take final examinations (Child, 1997). The emphasis is now on standardised testing to assess students' performance, and it is seen as necessary information for teachers, students and parents, as well as being used for government league tables.

Purposes of assessment

Assessment of students' educational achievement can serve four distinct purposes:
- **Formative assessment** gives an indication of the stage that a student is at, in order that a teacher can plan the curriculum effectively. Formative assessment can be carried out before a task or stage has begun (sometimes referred to as pre-task assessment), or used once a course of work is underway to check progress and development, and to give feedback to students.
- **Diagnostic assessment** is used to discover any problems that a student might have, for example, a specific learning difficulty. For the most part this is carried out alongside formative assessment, within this stage of a child's educational career (although problems sometimes get overlooked or misdiagnosed).
- **Summative assessment** is concerned with judging the overall achievement of a student and to measure the outcomes of learning. For example, SATs, GCSEs and A level exams are summative. These are not only used to judge overall achievement and to give qualifications, but are also sometimes used to predict future performance.
- **Evaluative assessment** is concerned with evaluating the whole performance of a class or school, often in relation to other classes or schools in order to check their performance against others. Examples of evaluative assessments are inspection reports and government league tables based on exam performance at, for example, A level or using SATs results.

⚖ EVALUATION ISSUES

ETHNOCENTRISM

Some forms of assessment are ethnocentric and favour certain groups in the population; it is very hard to design completely 'culture-free' tests.

Formative and diagnostic assessment are used to help teachers tailor educational provision to the needs of individual students. Summative and evaluative assessment are used to judge how well students, teachers and schools are doing.

Types of assessment

Quantitative assessment (i.e. assessment that provides numerical data) is referred to as **measurement** and includes tests and exams with results given as marks, percentages or grades, attendance and punctuality figures and grades given for 'effort' on reports. The other type of assessment, **evaluation**, is qualitative and consists of written or spoken reports that comment on the meaning of the student's educational achievement.

One of the problems with quantitative measurement in education is that this form of assessment can only work to measure numerical outcomes, and there are many aspects of educational provision that are not numerical. For example, measurement can tell a teacher how well a student performed in a maths test, but cannot describe whether the student's sense of self-efficacy in maths has been increased by their educational experience. One of the dangers of over-using measurement techniques is **reification**, a process in which a numerical measure is used as a means of assessing a particular outcome and the assumption is then made that the outcome consists wholly of that numerical measure. For example, the results of SATs tests are currently used to compare schools in league tables, but SATs results only provide a small part of the picture. Reification in this context is when people begin to assume that because SATs scores are the only numerical information we have about how schools are performing, they tell us all we need to know.

In order to make sense of educational measurements, an individual student's score on a test has to be compared to something. There are two ways of doing this:

- **Criterion-referenced** measurement is based on a set standard against which a student's work is measured. The criteria for achievement are set out in a mark scheme, for example, for a piece of coursework or an exam.
- **Norm-referenced** measurement compares students with each other. This means that students might be ranked according to their performance or, in the case of diagnostic tests, their performance might be measured against a norm for students of their age or ability.

These two types of referencing are useful for different purposes of assessment. Formative assessment may be both criterion-referenced and norm-referenced. Diagnostic assessment is likely to be norm-referenced. For example, the British Ability Scale, used to measure cognitive ability in a number of ways, was norm-referenced on 3000 students when it was first designed and is checked every two years with a group of 1500 students. Summative assessment is usually criterion-referenced, but can also be norm-referenced.

A-level marks used to be norm-referenced; fixed percentages of candidates received each grade, so getting a grade A meant that you were in the top 15 per cent for that cohort. In the 1980s this was considered unfair because it only allowed a fixed proportion of candidates to succeed at each level and the system was changed to a criterion-referenced one, in which candidates achieved a certain grade because the standard of their work met the fixed criteria. A consequence of this change meant that results in A levels improved over the years amidst reports that the exams were getting

EVALUATION ISSUES

ETHICS

Diagnostic and formative testing can be very helpful to the teacher and the student, but there are sometimes problems with the way in which a teacher may subsequently stereotype the student (and also with the way the student may stereotype themselves). Summative assessment is necessary in modern society because so much depends on an individual's educational qualifications, but end-of-course tests put a great deal of pressure on students and, arguably, do not reflect real-life situations. Some people argue that such tests are unethical.

EVALUATION ISSUES

RELIABILITY/REDUCTIONISM

Measurement has the advantage of, arguably, being more objective and therefore more reliable than evaluation. The numerical data it provides can be used to compare students and schools with each other and issue qualifications. On the other hand, it is reductionist, as it attempts to describe educational achievement using a set of numbers.

KEY DEFINITIONS

Reification is when a particular outcome is defined in terms of how it is being measured. For example, IQ tests are a way of measuring certain aspects of intelligence. Reification occurs when it is assumed that intelligence is the same as IQ. It is clear that IQ tests simply measure how good someone is at doing IQ tests, but Harvard Psychologist EG Boring reified IQ tests when he wrote in 1923 '...intelligence is what intelligence tests test'.

Exams are a form of quantitative assessment

easier. In 2002 the Government imposed limits on the numbers of students who should receive good grades (in order to restore the credibility of A levels) but this attempt to introduce norm-referencing by the back door led to a scandal that resulted in the resignation of the Secretary of State for Education.

KEY STUDY

Criterion-referenced assessment as a guide to learning – the importance of progression and reliability
Green (2002)

The author of this study works in the research department of an examination board, and her paper consists of a discussion of criterion-referenced assessment. She starts by saying that the aim of criterion-referencing is to '… focus on individual, differentiated assessment. By moving away from norm-referencing, to a system which describes what students know, understand and can do, assessments can be used to provide feedback and inform future teaching and learning needs'.

In order for criterion-referenced assessment to work, it is necessary to define 'success' at a given level, by describing the types and range of performance that students at that level should be able to demonstrate. Green stresses how important it is that performance scales be age independent, so that they can be used to assess a student's progression, and not just their achievement at one particular moment in time. A major difficulty of assessment occurs when levels of performance require interpretation and human judgement; if assessment is more subjective, then it is less reliable. For 'true' criterion-referencing, we should not accept criteria that allow for a range of interpretations. However, such criteria would be too numerous, narrow and unmanageable. Green argues that in order to reconcile the demands of rigorous assessment and the problems of subjective evaluations, it is necessary to create a shared understanding of subjective evaluations of performance and of progression in the curriculum. In other words, it is better to stick to evaluation, rather than use numerical measurement, but attempt to establish comparability of standards through the professional judgements of a community of experts.

Examples of assessment

The table below lists a whole range of possible sources of assessment data, some written and some not, and describe their strengths and weaknesses.

Types of assessment

Method	Strengths	Weaknesses
Tests/exams	Can be targeted to ask specific questions; objective	Exam situations can be threatening and do not reflect real life; often only one 'correct' answer
Essays	Open-ended; allows individuality; useful for formative assessment	Marking can be subjective; poor coverage of whole course
Samples of work	Rooted in everyday teaching; useful for formative assessment	Difficult for poor writers; one bad piece of work can have major effect

Method	Strengths	Weaknesses
Self-assessment	High student ownership; allows students to express things that teachers could not observe or assess otherwise	Irrelevant for national curriculum assessment; problem for inarticulate writers; can lead to institutional responses only
Observation	High ecological validity; assess students in a real life context	Time-consuming; can be subjective
Interviews	Can be very detailed; enables freedom of response	Time-consuming; student may feel inhibited
Presentations	Useful for poor writers; captures factors that written assessment misses; motivating	Can be threatening; difficult to isolate an individual's contribution; favours students with high self-esteem

2.6.3 IMPLICATIONS OF ASSESSMENT AND CATEGORISATION

One of the most important issues is how to make assessment as constructive and objective as possible. Assessment is often seen as competitive and results in success or failure, rather than being a record of a person's strengths and developments. Students learn the meaning of assessment at an early age; for example, after the age of eight, students become aware of the difference between trying to do something and actually achieving it; and they become aware of competition when they see the difference between their own performance and that of others. The problems of this awareness are that some students who find it easy to do well might stop making the effort and, in particular, those who see themselves 'failing' in relation to their peers might stop trying altogether.

Students expect their work to be assessed by their teachers, but this can have both positive and negative consequences, as it can motivate them to work well or it can make them worry too much about the assessment and not enough about the actual task. The same can also be said of teachers, who sometimes have to focus on the exam the students will take at the expense of broadening the curriculum. The study by Black and Wiliam (1998) describes how assessment can be used to help or hinder the educational process.

? FOR CONSIDERATION

• What do you think would be the best way to assess how well a student is doing on an A-Level Psychology course?

KEY STUDY

Assessment and classroom learning
Black and Wiliam (1998)

This review article looks at the effects of formative assessment and argues that overall standards rise if assessment is used to identify students' learning needs. The authors looked at 600 research studies from all over the world, involving more than 10 000 learners. These studies were carried out at all levels of the curriculum and across a range of very different subjects. The studies show that assessment that diagnoses students' difficulties and that provides specific and constructive feedback, leads to an improvement in learning. In a Portuguese study of 246 students with 25 teachers, students were given learning objectives and assessment criteria by their teachers, then asked to rate their own performance on a daily basis. The study showed that students in the experimental group progressed twice as fast as those in the control group.

Black and Wiliam conclude that it is the quality of the feedback given by teachers that is one of the most crucial factors if formative assessment is to be a success. Their survey indicates that there are five factors that are crucial for success, and five that are detrimental.

Factors crucial for success include:
- regular classroom testing (to improve learning and teaching, not for competitive use)
- clear, meaningful feedback
- the active involvement of all the students
- careful attention to the levels of self-esteem and motivation of each student
- self-assessment by the students (both in groups and with the teacher).

Factors limiting success include:
- tests that are superficial and encourage learning by rote
- failure of teachers to review testing procedures with each other
- over-emphasis on marks and grades at the expense of meaningful advice
- too much emphasis on competition between students (instead of focusing on personal improvement)
- feedback, testing and record-keeping, which is for managerial purposes rather than learning purposes.

The problem that the authors identify in the UK is that although formative assessment is recognised as important, the education system is very much geared towards summative assessment (SATs, GCSEs and A levels, for example).

EVALUATION ISSUES

METHODOLOGY/VALIDITY

Black and Wiliam (1998) did not carry out their own research but reviewed studies done by other people. The fact that they considered so many studies, and from all over the world, adds validity to their conclusions.

EVALUATION ISSUES

RELIABILITY

Inter-rater reliability is an important requirement for any test, but it is not always easy to achieve, especially in subjects in which the mark scheme is open to interpretation. Teachers and exam boards spend a great deal of time engaged in a process called moderation, in which different examiners mark the same papers and compare results in order to achieve maximum consistency. Despite these efforts, there is often a tolerance of several percentage points between different examiners.

Reliability and validity in assessment

It is very important that assessment is both reliable and valid if it is to be effective and useful. One of the major concerns that students have is whether assessment (in whatever form) is fair. There are several forms of **reliability** that are useful in the context of the need for consistent assessment:
- **Test-retest reliability** means that if a student took the same test twice she should get the same result (excluding the possibility of a practice effect).
- **Split-half reliability** looks for internal consistency within the measurement tool. If the test is divided in half, and both halves are measuring the same thing, then the scores on the two halves should be similar.
- **Alternate forms reliability** looks for consistency between two different forms of the same test.
- **Inter-rater reliability** means that if two different people mark the same exam, they should come up with the same result.

As with reliability, there are several types of **validity**:
- **Face validity** means that a test looks on the surface as though it measures what it intends to. This type of validity is perhaps more important for the student, who needs to be reassured by looking at a test that it is appropriate.
- **Content validity**: a test that does not measure the knowledge and/or skills that relate directly to the content of the course the student has been studying cannot be very useful.

- **Predictive validity** represents the degree to which a test is a measure of the student's future performance. An interesting (and perhaps puzzling) finding is that GCSE results are better at predicting success at higher education than A level results.
- **Concurrent validity** is when the results from two different assessment tools give the same measurement of performance.

When criticism is levelled at exam boards, it is generally that the tests they produce are not reliable or not valid; clearly an assessment tool that is either unreliable, unvalid, or both is useless, and has the potential to damage individual students and the credibility of the education system as a whole.

SECTION A EXAM QUESTIONS

a   Describe one type of educational assessment. [6]
b   Evaluate the strengths of educational assessment. [10]

a   Describe one study of the implications of educational assessment. [6]
b   Evaluate research into the implications of educational assessment. [10]

CD-ROM

For Section B sample exam questions see Education: Sample exam questions.

2.7 INDIVIDUAL DIFFERENCES IN EDUCATIONAL PERFORMANCE

CD-ROM

For a detailed discussion of the relationship between educational achievement and social class, see Education: Real life applications: Educational achievement and social class.

EXAM HINTS

'Cultural diversity' could refer to either ethnicity or social class; neither issue is specifically named in the OCR syllabus, so you can write about either, or both. However, 'gender' is specifically mentioned, so questions could be asked on this. (See CD-ROM box above for information on social class.)

FOR CONSIDERATION

* In your experience, do girls do better than boys at school? If so, why do you think this is?

Not all students do equally well in the school environment, and a great deal of research has been carried out into the reasons why this might be so. There are differences in the performance of boys compared to girls. There are also differences in the performance of students of different social classes within our society, as well as between the performance of different ethnic groups. This section examines the relationships between educational achievement, gender and ethnicity.

2.7.1 CULTURAL DIVERSITY AND GENDER ISSUES

Gender

Gender differences in educational attainment are interesting because they are not static. For many years boys outperformed girls (especially in exam results) at most levels of the educational system, but in recent years the balance has shifted in favour of girls. Girls now outperform boys in virtually all subjects at each key stage up to and including A level. In 2003, 7-year-old girls did better than boys by 11 per cent in reading and 16 per cent in writing. At 11 years, girls did better in the writing element of English by 17 per cent and were still leading by 13 per cent at age 14. At GCSE 6 per cent of girls got an A*, compared to 4 per cent of boys; 62 per cent of girls achieved grade A to C, whereas only 54 per cent of boys did this well. Girls also performed significantly better at A level.

Ethnicity

Since the 1970s there has been a lot of interest in the educational achievements of different ethnic groups, and many studies show that students from the main ethnic minority groups tend to do less well in education than white students, even after controlling for social class (e.g. Smith and Tomlinson, 1989). Recent studies suggest that although black students have lower attainment than white students, some ethnic minority groups actually perform better than their white peers; Afro-Caribbean students do particularly badly, whereas Asian students do well at school. To complicate matters even further, one study (Arnot et al., 1999) shows that white girls outperform white boys (see previous section), whereas the opposite is true for Black and Asian boys and girls.

> **KEY STUDY**
>
> *Ethnic and gender differences in educational achievement and implications for school improvement strategies*
> **Demie (2001)**
>
> **Aim:** To discover differences in educational attainment relating to gender and ethnicity.
>
> **Sample:** This paper is a case study using data from 1998 tests (2340 students at KS1, 2267 at KS2 and 1225 at GCSE). The data were collected from schools in the London Borough of Lambeth.

Method: As well as looking at test results, Demie asked schools to provide the following information:
- whether the students qualified for free school meals (a measure of social deprivation)
- ethnic group
- fluency in English (from stage 1 – beginner, to stage 4 – fluent).

Results:
- The schools studied by Demie contained three main ethnic groups: English/Scottish/Welsh, Caribbean and African. On average, the English/Scottish/Welsh group performed better than the other two.
- African students performed better than Caribbean students at each key stage, and better than Pakistani, Vietnamese, Irish and English/Scottish/Welsh at KS1, but not at KS2 and GCSE.
- Caribbean students had the lowest attainment of any group, but they did perform better than Bangladeshi students at KS1 and KS2, although Bangladeshi students did better at GCSE (perhaps because they had become more fluent in English by that stage).
- Chinese, Indian and Vietnamese students were the highest performing ethnic groups of all. Caribbean, African and Portuguese students are the main underachieving ethnic groups.
- Overall, girls performed better than boys at every key stage and for each ethnic group (with the exception that Bangladeshi boys did better than girls at KS2).
- By the end of GCSE, girls were outperforming boys in all subjects, but at KS1 and KS2, boys of all ethnic groups were tending to do better at maths and sciences.

Conclusions: Students from different ethnic groups show differences in educational attainment at the end of each key stage. Fluency in English is a key factor in educational attainment, and once the disadvantage of language is overcome, it is possible for an ethnic group to catch up with other groups who have outperformed them at the early stages of education. Gender is strongly associated with achievement, regardless of ethnic background with girls outperforming boys at KS1, KS2 and GCSE.

2.7.2 EXPLANATIONS FOR DIFFERENTIAL EDUCATIONAL PERFORMANCE

Gender

The influence of biological differences

Some theorists argue that there are biological differences between boys and girls that can explain the different levels of attainment between them in school. For example, it is thought that girls mature earlier than boys and this may account for some of the reasons why girls do better than boys in school up to the age of about 11. Gray and Buffrey (1971) argue that girls and boys develop different aptitudes after the age of 2, based on the dominance of different hemispheres of the brain, which explains why boys show a greater aptitude for spatial and mathematical tasks in primary school (associated with the right hemisphere) and girls show a greater aptitude for verbal reasoning tasks (associated with the left hemisphere).

The influence of the environment

Environmental differences can be looked at in terms of socialisation within the home, and the influence of peers and the media on gender differences.

By the time girls and boys go to school at the age of 4 their experiences at home and with their peers will have shaped their attitudes to gender roles

⚖ EVALUATION ISSUES

GENERALISABILITY

Demie's (2001) study was carried out on one London borough; it may not be possible to generalise the findings to other parts of the world, or even to other parts of London.

⚖ EVALUATION ISSUES

NATURE/NURTURE

There are so many possible reasons for the differences in performance, that biological evidence, whatever it may be, is inconclusive. It cannot be denied that there are biological differences between boys and girls, but whether these can account for differences in their educational performance is another question. It is just as likely that the way in which children are socialised might have an influence. Hyde et al. (1990), who examined more than 100 research studies of gender difference, have shown that any gender differences in spatial, mathematical and reasoning tasks are very small. They also show that these small differences have been decreasing over the last two decades; suggesting that socialisation must at least play a part.

Parental expectations, and the ways in which girls and boys are socialised by their parents, may have a considerable influence on their behaviour in the classroom. Some research suggests that parents still have different expectations of boys and girls, and that these stereotyped expectations may affect their children. For example, Lummis and Stevenson (1990) showed that parents expected their daughters to be good at reading and their sons to be good at maths.

• Does your own experience support Lummis and Stevenson's (1990) findings?

Peter Rabbit: a typical boy?

 CD-ROM

For a discussion of whether educationalists should be worrying about boys' performance at school, see Education: Real life applications: Boys' underachievement? Not the real question.

to a considerable degree. Pilcher (1999) argues that 'doing gender', as she calls it, is learned from toys, books, clothing and television. She states that: '[G]irls and boys enter the formal education system looking and behaving in "gender-appropriate" ways and with their own firmly held expectations and understandings about the differences between girls and women on the one hand and boys and men on the other' (1999, p. 17).

Yee and Eccles (1988; cited by Golombok and Fivush, 1994) asked parents to answer questions on their children's ability in maths. There were no gender differences in the ability of the children; however, the mothers of girls thought their daughters were less able at maths than the mothers of boys. The mothers also thought that their daughters had to work harder than their sons to achieve good grades in maths, and fathers also showed the same attitudes. Yee and Eccles argue that this is important because they suggest that girls are learning (from their parents) to make different attributions for their achievements. Girls are learning that their success is due to hard work, whereas boys are learning that their success is due to their own ability. This means that girls are more likely to be motivated to work hard in the future.

The influence of school

There are many studies that argue that one of the most important factors in explaining the differential achievement of girls and boys is the attitudes and expectations of teachers. Clarricoates (1987) shows the ways in which teachers' expectations of students in primary schools follow gender-stereotyped patterns; boys were thought to be more interesting to teach than girls, and girls were expected to conform and be less disruptive than boys. Although many teachers today try to practise anti-sexist education, there is still evidence to suggest that many still stereotype using gender as the criteria for doing so. An HMI report in 1990 cited by Trowler (1996) reports a teacher saying to a class in a biology lesson that involved dissection, 'Now which of you boys will do the cutting?' and 'Girls, let me know if you feel sick' (1996, p. 187).

The curriculum itself is still seen to favour boys. Early research by Lobban (1974) suggested that primary school reading material was stereotyped, in other words, boys were portrayed as heroes in active roles, and girls in the same text books were more often portrayed in domestic situations. Although this study is dated, more recent studies (such as Best, 1993) show that there are still twice as many male characters in pre-school children's books. Female characters are still portrayed in domestic roles (75 per cent), whereas 81 per cent of male characters are portrayed in roles outside the home. Bradshaw et al. (1995) have shown that although computer software now often represents characters as neither feminine nor masculine, children more often attributed a male identity to the characters than a female one.

In spite of all the evidence that most aspects of both the home and school environment are disadvantageous to girls, they are in fact doing better than boys in almost all areas of the curriculum. As we have already noted, girls have always thrived (at least academically) when compared to boys, in the primary school environment. The current trend, however, is that girls are performing better than boys in the secondary school and A level environment. Some researchers argue that although this is an overall improvement in the performance of girls, it still only represents a partial change. Girls are now performing as well as boys in some subjects, and slightly better in others. Stereotyping of subject choice is still a problem, and the difference in the performance of male and female students is marginal. For example, girls are more likely to take and pass A levels than boys, but boys obtain higher grades overall (Pilcher, 1999); and males go on to earn, on average, 50 per cent more than females. It could therefore be argued that the concern over what is often labelled the current underachievement of boys is a 'moral panic'.

One explanation for the underachievement of boys is that schools are perceived by students as 'female' environments. Most primary school teachers are women and many of the values promoted in schools (co-operation, conscientiousness, compliance, reliability, etc.) may be seen by boys as 'girly' values. A Freudian explanation is that just as boys are trying to establish their gender identity by modelling themselves on their fathers, they are sent to primary school to be taught (in most cases) by female figures of authority. They assert their masculinity by rejecting female authority and thereby harming their educational achievement. Whether this is the true explanation or not, most teachers would accept that girls are more conscientious students on the whole and that this may well account for their higher attainments at school.

Ethnicity

The influence of biological differences

In the USA, Jensen and Eysenk, as late as the 1970s, were still subscribing to the view that black people had lower innate intelligence (measured using IQ tests) than the white population. They suggested that statistical evidence showed that black people scored 10 to 15 points lower on IQ tests than white people. Nowadays, practically all psychologists would attribute these findings to environmental rather than biological differences.

The influence of the environment

There is a history to racism in our own society that cannot be ignored as a factor that has shaped the experience of people from ethnic minorities within the education system. One of the places to start looking at contemporary racism in this society is in the post-war period of immigration in the 1940s and 1950s. By the late 1950s there was a growing resistance to this immigration among some members of the white population; and in 1958 a series of riots, sparked by attacks on people from ethnic minorities, caused policy makers to look to schools to change attitudes.

Prior to this it was assumed that black people would assimilate into UK society by accepting and learning UK values and traditions. In the mid-1960s, however, Roy Jenkins, the (then) Home Secretary, made a speech that was seen to influence this assimilationist policy towards a more integrationist phase. The outcome of this was the development of multicultural education (Kirby et al., 1997).

Multicultural education worked on the assumption that the curriculum might be perceived as Eurocentric. Multicultural education was supposed to combat the underachievement of people from ethnic minorities by making the curriculum reflect the experiences and cultures of all students, not just the white population. The problem, however, was that it was seen by many as condescending and had little impact on the real issue of achievement.

A cultural factor that may create problems within the education system concerns communication between teachers and their students. Bennett (1993) identifies five aspects of ethnicity that are potential sources of student-teacher misunderstanding:
- **Verbal communication**: problems with verbal communication can occur for students for whom English is a second language.

- **Non-verbal communication**: some forms of communication, such as eye contact, are used in different ways by different cultures, and these signals can be misinterpreted. In some Native American and Asian cultures it is not appropriate to hold eye contact with someone in authority; looking down or away might be misconstrued as disinterest or ignorance by a teacher who did not understand this.
- **Time orientation**: Mainstream American culture is very time orientated. Time is highly valued and the education system is geared towards appropriate time management. Groups in the population, such as Hispanic Americans and Native Americans, whose cultures do not stress this sense of urgency are disadvantaged in an education system that does.
- **Competition and individualism**: Many classroom activities and the system of examinations in schools reward competitive and individualistic behaviour. Bennett argues that Mexican Americans, for example, are more likely to be taught co-operative values at home, which do not fit in with the ethos of their education.
- **Types of knowledge and learning**: Bennett found that different ethnic groups within the American population prefer different learning styles, depending on their own cultural influences.

The influence of school

Gilroy (1990) argues that the education system sees ethnicity as a white and black issue, and ignores other ethnic groups. He sees this as what he calls essentialist (defining something on the basis of a set of essential characteristics) and reductionist (reducing the problem to one single cause). Gilroy talks about the 'cultural politics of difference', and others like him argue that there are many different forms of identity that need to be considered, including, for example, class, religion and gender.

Much of the research into racism and issues surrounding the status of ethnic minority groups within the education system is inevitably qualitative; studies are often carried out using observational techniques and interviews.

KEY STUDY

Early education: multiracial primary school classrooms
Wright (1992)

Aim: To investigate the nature of racism in 'multiracial' primary schools.

Sample: Wright studied four multiracial inner-city primary schools and observed a total of 970 children and 57 staff.

Method: Wright carried out classroom observations and informal interviews of teachers, support staff and the parents of children. Wright also looked at the test results of three of the four schools.

Results: In spite of the commitment of the staff to equality of educational opportunity, Wright found considerable discrimination in the classroom. In all the classes, Asian girls were 'invisible' to their teachers, who stereotyped them in terms of their expectations of the girls' traditions and customs. Wright found that the isolation felt by these girls was exacerbated by other children, who picked up on the attitudes of the teachers. Wright also found that teachers' expectations of Afro-Caribbean children were also stereotyped, but in different ways. Wright found that teachers expected Afro-Caribbean boys in particular to be disruptive, and punished them more harshly than white boys exhibiting the same behaviour.

Conclusions: Wright argues that young children will be affected by their early experiences of racism within the school environment. Not only did children suffer from the racism of their teachers and fellow classmates, but also, when topics relating to ethnic minority concerns were raised by the teachers (looking at religious festivals, for example), the teachers often mispronounced words or names, embarrassing black children and causing white students to laugh. Wright argues that, unintentionally, the teacher helps to make this knowledge seem exotic, unimportant and difficult.

Many other studies also show that teachers hold stereotypical views of black students. Figueroa (1991) shows how this affects the educational opportunities and experiences of black students in the following ways:

- through inappropriate assessment, i.e. using assessment tools that are culturally biased
- through misplacement, i.e. by being put in lower streams than test results suggest, on the basis of teacher expectations
- through channelling, for example the over-representation of Afro-Caribbean students in sport rather than mainstream academic subjects.

Although many studies have been outlined here that show the reasons why children from some ethnic minorities are disadvantaged within the system, more recent research focuses on the broader implications of racism and students' experience of it. Some feminist researchers (such as Mirza) are interested in 'deconstructing the myth of black educational underachievement'. Mirza (cited in Kirby et al., 1997) argues that there is actually a movement away from the underachievement of ethnic minority students (particularly girls). Statistics show that in post-16 education, 56 per cent of students from ethnic minority backgrounds stay in the education system, compared to 37 per cent of white students. In new universities, black students, and particularly female students, are over-represented in relation to their respective population sizes. In new universities, people of Caribbean origin were over-represented by 43 per cent, Asians by 162 per cent and Africans by 223 per cent. For Mirza it is possible that '... doing well can become a radical strategy. An act of social transformation' (1997, p. 263).

2.7.3 STRATEGIES FOR IMPROVING EDUCATIONAL PERFORMANCE

The explanations for cultural and gender-related differences in educational performance described in the previous section have been classified under three broad headings: biological explanations, the influence of society and the influence of school.

If differences in performance are largely biological then there is not much that teachers can do about them, and it could be argued that we should accept biological differences as the way things 'should' be. However, there is very little evidence indeed to suggest that differences relating to gender, ethnicity and class have any significant biological components. To ignore differences in performance on the grounds that there is nothing that can be done could be seen as condoning inequality and discrimination.

When it comes to social influences, some teachers would argue that changing society is not what education is about; the aim is to teach young people to make their way within society and that there is not much that can be done within a classroom to make the outside world less racist. Other teachers would disagree, and argue that changing society is exactly what education is all about. In either event, teachers can help students understand the way society is, and this can help individuals deal with injustice and inequality a little better.

The strategies adopted by schools to redress inequalities in educational performance will depend on the accepted explanations for those inequalities:

- If the reason that girls perform better at school is because they tend to attribute their success to hard work rather than natural ability, and are therefore more strongly motivated to work hard, then it may be possible to encourage boys to modify their attributions.
- If boys are demotivated by perceiving schools as 'female' environments, than this perception could be changed. One obvious way of achieving this would be to have as many male primary school teachers as female. Currently, the large majority of primary school teachers are female (although the majority of primary school head teachers are male) and the government could launch a campaign to recruit more men to the profession.

The obvious way to deal with the underachievement of black students is to stop racist behaviour in schools. This is easier said than done, but all schools have equal opportunities policies and many have staff specially appointed to co-ordinate anti-racist initiatives such as staff training, systems to deal with racist bullying, review of teaching materials in order to avoid the use of ethnocentric textbooks and worksheets, etc.

A second strategy to address the underachievement of students from ethnic minorities stems directly from the research carried out by Demie (2001). The findings of Demie's research confirm that there is a strong relationship between fluency in English and the achievement of bilingual students; performance levels of ethnic minority students increase as fluency in English increases. Some language support for bilingual students is currently provided using additional government funding (the Ethnic Minority Achievement Grant) and this could be increased and extended to cover numeracy. Demie also notes in her paper the strategies already being adopted by schools in Lambeth; monitoring and target-setting, new teaching methods, parental involvement, role modelling/mentoring and staff training.

❓ FOR CONSIDERATION

- Are you aware of any initiatives, in the schools you have attended, to address the underachievement of specific groups of students?

SECTION A EXAM QUESTIONS

a Describe one study of cultural differences in educational performance. [6]
b Discuss problems of researching cultural differences in educational performance. [10]

a Describe one explanation for gender differences in educational performance. [6]
b Discuss the validity of explanations for gender differences in educational performance. [10]

a Describe one strategy for improving educational performance. [6]
b Discuss the strengths of one strategy for improving educational performance. [10]

💿 CD-ROM

For Section B sample exam questions see Education: Sample exam questions.

SPECIAL EDUCATIONAL NEEDS

2.8

A humanist educationalist might argue that there are no such things as **special educational needs** because all students are unique and should be treated by their teachers as individuals. However, there is a general recognition within education that some students do have educational needs that lie outside the 'normal' range. In its broadest sense, the term 'special needs' can be applied to any student who requires some sort of special educational treatment as a result of being 'unusual' in one or more of the following areas:

- **social-emotional**: students with ADHD, autism and so on
- **physical**: students with sensory deficits (visual or hearing impairments), cerebral palsy, epilepsy, etc. or students who have particular physical talents (e.g. sporting ability)
- **intellectual**: students with learning difficulties or gifted students.

Social-emotional and physical difficulties can have a lasting impact on an individual's education, but these kinds of problem tend to be diagnosed and treated by professionals working outside the educational system (for example, clinical psychologists), although specialist educational units do exist for students with such difficulties. This section focuses on intellectual special needs, i.e. learning difficulties and giftedness.

CD-ROM

For a historical review of special needs education in the UK, see Education: Real life applications: A history of special education.

2.8.1 DEFINITIONS, TYPES AND ASSESSMENT OF SPECIAL EDUCATIONAL NEEDS

Learning difficulties

The term **learning difficulty** is used to define a number of conditions. Historically, the various terms used to describe different degrees of learning difficulty (mild, moderate, severe and profound) were related to specific IQ levels. This approach tended to label individuals, and to ignore their actual abilities and difficulties. More recently, there is a recognition that all students can have difficulties with their learning, but that certain students have difficulties that require special help. Students with learning difficulties are generally categorised as follows:

- **Moderate learning difficulty (MLD)**: students who can be taught in mainstream schools with some learning support.
- **Severe learning difficulty (SLD)**: students who require a much higher degree of specialist support, usually within special units or schools.
- **Profound and multiple learning difficulty (PMLD)**: students with very serious intellectual difficulties, combined with sensory and other physical impairments.

There is also a category for students with difficulties that are not related to general impairments in intellectual ability:

- **Specific learning difficulty (SPLD)**: these refer to conditions such as dyslexia and dyscalcula.

The 2001 Code of Practice (SEN and Disability Act 2001) describes a graduated three-stage approach to identifying students with learning difficulties:

It is useful to a child with SEN to receive a statement from the LEA. It means that she will receive extra support; without a statement, the LEA will not provide funds. In marginal cases of learning difficulty, it can be hard to get a child statemented, and parents often have a long fight to achieve this.

CD-ROM

See Education: Real life applications: IEP.

KEY DEFINITIONS

An HMI report (1992; cited in Child, 1997) on the education of **gifted students** states 'The majority of educationalists working in this field accept criteria which include general intellectual ability, specific aptitude in one or more subjects, creative or productive thinking, leadership qualities, ability in creative or performing arts and psychomotor ability. The term 'very able' is intended to refer broadly to the top 5 per cent of the ability range in any of these areas, while the term 'exceptionally able' refers to that tiny minority 'functioning several years beyond their age group'.

FOR CONSIDERATION

Some people argue that the education system in the UK is not very good at identifying gifted students and that such students often do not get the special help they need.

- Do you agree with this point of view?

1 **Early years/school action:** the first step is for the teacher of a child, or for the school Special Educational Needs Co-ordinator (SENCO), to recognise that a particular child has special needs. The teacher and the SENCO together provide interventions that are additional to or different from those provided as part of the school's normal curriculum. In most cases an Individual Education Plan (IEP) will be drawn up to monitor the level of difficulty experienced by the child and to see if the school's interventions are helping.

2 **Early years/school action plus:** if the SENCO feels that the IEP is not working, he, in consultation with parents, will seek advice and support from outside specialists, such as an educational psychologist. A new IEP is devised containing additional or different interventions to those tried in Stage 1.

3 **Statemented provision:** if it is still felt that the child is not making appropriate progress, the school applies to the LEA for statutory assessment of the child, in order to obtain extra resources and help. If the child receives an SEN statement from the local education authority (LEA), then there are mandatory requirements and extra funding for the school to provide special help for the child (for example, annual review of needs and learning support assistants (LSA) in the classroom).

Giftedness

There is no single agreed definition of giftedness, although there do seem to be common characteristics between the various definitions that psychologists have come up with. For example, Shore and Kanevsky (1993) say that a gifted learner has:

- an exceptional memory and knowledge base
- very good metacognitive abilities
- a very quick response to test questions
- a clear understanding of problems; understanding what is missing and what is irrelevant
- an awareness of how to use knowledge effectively
- flexibility
- a preference for complexity in problem-solving tasks.

Renzulli, Reis and Smith (1981; cited in LeFrançois, 1997) argue that giftedness can be defined by three characteristics:

- high ability (high achievement or high IQ)
- high creativity
- high commitment.

The main way of formally recognising giftedness is to measure the performance of gifted students in relation to norm-referenced measures of ability. Some education authorities use checklists that list the main characteristics of gifted students (Child, 1997). One of the problems with the process of testing potentially gifted students is that the types of tests available may not be able to test their individual abilities adequately. Another problem is that parental attitude and cultural background may be

KEY STUDY

Gifted students: their identification and development in a social context
Freeman (1979)

Aim: To examine the relationship between high IQ and the environment in which the child grows up and is educated.

Sample: Freeman used three groups of 70 students: the target sample was students whose parents had joined the National Association for Gifted students (NAGC). The matched control sample was made up of students in the same school classes as the original sample, who got the same score on the Raven's Progressive Matrices test (a culture-fair measure of intellectual aptitude). The random control sample consisted of other students chosen at random from the school.

Method: The students in the target and matched control samples were assessed using the Raven's test. All the students selected were then tested using intelligence, personality, creativity and music ability tests. The students and their parents were all interviewed.

Results: The matched control group who scored the same on the Raven's test as the target group, scored lower on the general ability tests. Mothers of the target students tended to have reached higher-level occupations and put greater pressure on their children than the control groups; they complained more about their children's schooling. However, Freeman found no differences between the groups on physical and emotional development or personality profiles.

Conclusions: Freeman concluded that students with parents who considered them to be gifted would score more highly on general ability tests, but not on the culture-fair Raven's test. Therefore, using only general IQ measures to identify gifted students would miss those from poor educational environments; it is important to use a measure that identifies all gifted students, regardless of social background.

a factor in whether a child performs well on tests for giftedness, and this may lead to under-identification of working class students (see Freeman, 1979).

2.8.2 CAUSES AND EFFECTS OF DYSLEXIA

Dyslexia is a specific learning disability linked to persistent problems with reading and spelling. 'Word blindness' was first identified at the start of the twentieth century, and was believed to be caused by inherited brain dysfunction. Dyslexia is currently defined as a failure to read or write at an appropriate level, despite having been taught; dyslexia is not seen as being necessarily related to general abilities such as intelligence.

Students with dyslexia are likely to display the following symptoms:
- significant discrepancy between intelligence and written performance
- spelling is erratic and inconsistent; handwriting is poor
- problems with ordering things sequentially
- problems with sentence structure and punctuation
- easily mis-reads and mis-copies, and loses place easily when reading
- finds it hard to follow verbal instructions, and is easily distracted
- gets confused between left and right
- finds it hard to remember facts, new terminology, names, etc.

On the other hand, they are also likely to:
- be highly aware of their environment and remember details that others do not
- think quickly, in pictures rather than words
- be highly imaginative, intuitive and insightful
- think holistically.

EVALUATION ISSUES

ETHICS

Labelling some students as 'gifted' could be damaging. Students labelled as gifted may find themselves isolated by other students. However, it is important to recognise each child's individual needs, and to fail to provide a gifted child with special educational provision on the grounds that it could make other students feel inferior could lead to the gifted child becoming bored and disillusioned at school, and this could lead to behavioural difficulties. Either of these points could be considered unethical.

KEY DEFINITIONS

In 1999, the Division of Educational and Clinical Psychology which is part of the British Psychological Society, defined **dyslexia** as '... evident when accurate and fluent word reading and/or spelling develops very incompletely or with great difficulty. This focuses on literacy learning at the "word level" and implies that the problem is severe and persistent despite appropriate learning opportunities. It provides the basis for a staged process of assessment through teaching.'

 CD-ROM

For a copy of a screening test for dyslexia, see Education: Measurement scales: Dyslexia checklist.

Harrison Ford – a famous actor who has dyslexia

⚖ EVALUATION ISSUES

NATURE/NURTURE

The debate about whether dyslexia is caused by environmental or genetic factors has been going on for some time and both theories have implications for parents. If the cause is primarily environmental, then parents are made to feel that they may have been inadequate in their child-rearing. If the cause is primarily genetic, then parents may feel helpless in improving their child's reading and writing.

✎ EXAM HINTS

The OCR specification refers to 'one specific learning difficulty or disability'. We have chosen to write about dyslexia. However, in the exam you can refer to any specific learning difficulty.

❓ FOR CONSIDERATION

It is possible that many students for whom English is not their first language, and who are also dyslexic, are not being diagnosed because their problems are put down to their difficulty with English. These students are missing out on vital support, as they may also be having difficulty with their first language as a result of their dyslexia. Other students fail to get diagnosed as dyslexic for other reasons.
• Do you know of anyone who was diagnosed with dyslexia late in their school career?
• What effect do you think this had on them?

Somewhere between 4 and 5 per cent of the population of the UK are estimated to have severe dyslexia; this represents about 375 000 students in the UK with dyslexia, and a total of 2 million people who are severely affected. A further 6 per cent are thought to have mild difficulties with reading and writing. Recent research seems to show that as many girls as boys have dyslexia, but that three times as many boys receive additional teaching because of their dyslexia (Brooks, 1997).

There is general agreement among psychologists that dyslexia is linked to neurological anomalies, but the cause of these anomalies is not yet clear, and there is debate about whether they are congenital, or arise out of early experience. People with dyslexia seem to have atypical asymmetry in the planum temporale (in Wernicke's area), which appears to be directly associated with phonological coding deficits which may underlie reading problems. They also have been found to have deficits in the magnocellular pathway which is involved in visual attentional processes. However, research with musicians and taxi-drivers has shown that practising a skill at a high level can actually alter the size and functioning of parts of the brain, so these brain differences in people with dyslexia may arise as a result of the dyslexia, and not be the cause of it.

DeFries and Alarcon (1996) found that the concordance rate for identical twins (70 per cent) was higher than that for non-identical twins (40 per cent). This implies that dyslexia is hereditary but this finding could be partly explained by the fact that identical twins tend to be treated more like each other than non-identical twins. Coles (2000) examined a range of studies such as this and found that some studies claiming to show genetic causes for dyslexia were subsequently 'corrected' for incorrect data and found to show no effects at all, while others gave contradictory and inconclusive findings. He concludes that dyslexia is more likely to be caused by early experiences which affect phonological awareness, rather than underlying genetic problems. However, there is no convincing evidence that links specific early experiences to literacy problems in later life.

So, whether children are born with dyslexia is unknown, but the fact that people with dyslexia do seem to have brain abnormalities suggests that it is a condition that is less susceptible to psychological treatment than ones which do not have any physiological factors involved. However, there are many ways in which parents and teachers can help students with dyslexia cope with their difficulties, and there are many high-achievers in society with severe dyslexia.

2.8.3 STRATEGIES FOR EDUCATING CHILDREN WITH SPECIAL EDUCATIONAL NEEDS

Children with learning difficulties

The key debate in the education of children with SEN is whether it is better to teach them in mainstream schools or in special schools or units. There is certainly a trend towards inclusion both within the UK and internationally at the present time. The UNESCO Salemanca World Statement on Special Needs Education calls on governments to adopt the principle of inclusive education, enrolling all students in regular schools unless there are compelling reasons for doing otherwise (cited in Hornby, 1999, p. 52). Public policy in the UK supports the inclusion of as many SEN students as possible in mainstream schools.

Many theorists believe that inclusive education for students with SEN should be thought of as a 'right', whereas others believe that it may mean that the teaching of SEN students becomes less effective. Marston (1996) found that students who were taken out of classes and taught in special groups for some activities did better than those who received support in mainstream classes.

One of the criticisms of full inclusion is that it focuses on the process of the education rather than the outcome, and on the curriculum of mainstream education rather than the curriculum of SEN (Hornby, 1999). Another problem is that inclusion is much more expensive than segregation, because specialist support has to be provided in many different locations, rather than concentrated in a small number of special schools. If specific teacher skills are required to deal with certain students, then it is easier (and cheaper) to train a few teachers and concentrate them in specialist units, but this is not necessarily better in educational terms. The attitudes and skills of teachers are fundamentally important, and there is a need to combat negative attitudes from inexperienced and untrained staff.

Some studies have focused on the attitudes of SEN students and their parents to inclusive education. Kidd and Hornby (1993) carried out a survey in which they questioned 29 sets of parents of students who had 'moderate' learning difficulties. These students had been transferred from special schools into mainstream schools. Kidd and Hornby found that 65 per cent of the parents and 76 per cent of the students were 'satisfied' with the transfer. However, they found that there was a difference in how happy the parents were depending on what kind of inclusion the students experienced. 47 per cent of parents of students included in mainstream classes were happy, compared to 92 per cent of parents of students placed in units in mainstream schools (Hornby, 1999).

The trend towards inclusion is growing, but there is still a 'substantial proportion' of students in segregated units, and there is still some way to go before there is enough evidence about the outcomes of inclusion to draw valid conclusions.

Children with dyslexia

Techniques for supporting dyslexic learners include:
- using colours that people with dyslexia find easier to read
- using metaphors and analogy to promote understanding
- giving the whole picture first, and explaining what is expected in advance
- using demonstrations rather than just words
- allowing dyslexic students to use appropriate technology
- recognising the difficulties that dyslexic students have, and not attributing them to poor motivation, laziness, etc.

On the other hand, teachers with dyslexic students in their classes should avoid:
- dictation or extensive note-taking
- asking dyslexic students to read out loud, or singling them out to answer a question in class
- putting time pressure on students, or expecting accurate reading.

Gifted children

The education system in the UK has been much criticised, by OFSTED and others, for ignoring the needs of gifted students, and it is true that much more energy and money is put into this aspect of education in the USA.

🔑 KEY DEFINITIONS

Integration or **inclusion** means teaching students with SEN within mainstream schools, in the same classes as other students, with additional support if required. **Segregation** is when students with SEN are taught in special schools, tailored to meet their specific needs. A half-way position between the two is to have special units located within a mainstream school, so that the students with SEN can have lessons both in ordinary classes and in the special unit.

💿 CD-ROM

For an article about inclusion and segregation, see Education: Real life applications: Inclusive education is a 'human right'.

⚖️ EVALUATION ISSUES

EFFECTIVENESS

If a student with SEN is taught within a mainstream class, he might need extra attention from the teacher, or may be disruptive or difficult in the class, and this could harm other students' education. However, it can be argued that the other students in the class benefit a great deal from working with students with special needs and that inclusive education helps to remove stereotypes and ignorance. It is also argued that students with SEN are themselves better off in segregated classrooms as this allows LEAs to concentrate its specialist teachers and resources in one place. The objection to this is that the disadvantage of keeping students with certain difficulties together is that it makes it harder for them to integrate fully into society once they leave school.

❓ FOR CONSIDERATION

Consider the strategies that are in place in your current educational institution for educating students with special needs.
- In your opinion, is the provision adequate?
- If not, how could it be improved?

KEY DEFINITIONS

Acceleration happens when a student goes through the education system much more quickly than his or her peers, and is able to work alongside older students.

Enrichment involves keeping gifted students within their year groups and providing them with a curriculum that is modified to suit their special needs.

CD-ROM

For a description of the difficulties faced by gifted students at school, see Education: Real life applications: Problems for gifted students.

EVALUATION ISSUES

ETHICS

One of the problems with acceleration is the way in which a student is inevitably isolated from his peers, with serious social and psychological consequences. In contrast, enrichment programmes involve very mixed ability teaching, and this can cause difficulties in the classroom.

The key debate in this field is whether it is better to teach gifted students through a strategy of **acceleration** or **enrichment**.

There are different ways in which acceleration can happen. For example, a child might enter school early or, more likely, once she is in school, miss a year and go into the year above. Gifted students often take exams early, and sometimes, though rarely, students go on to university at a much younger age than normal. The media occasionally report on these exceptional cases. One example in the UK is the case of Ruth Lawrence, whose A levels enabled her to go to St Hughs College, Oxford at the age of 12. She received her BA two years later and her PhD when she was 17 (Child, 1997).

Enrichment means that students are not usually separated from their peers, but that they are given exercises and resources to help them to reach their potential. They may be separated for some lessons or they might simply have access to materials that they can use that are different to those provided for other students.

Many of the strategies that are used with gifted students are also beneficial to other students and are examples of good practice in teaching. For instance, using individualised teaching plans is good for all students. It is also important for all students to be measured against their own potential, and not always measured against other students. Using this type of measurement, it does not matter if the students are gifted or not, as they are striving to do better than themselves. There is also the non-academic curriculum to be considered; school is a social as well as an academic place where students learn more than what is in the curriculum. All students, gifted or not, benefit from the social relationships they develop in school and the support and encouragement of their teachers and peers, both within and outside the classroom.

It is possible to segregate gifted students and provide special schools or classrooms for them (this is an extension of the streaming that currently occurs in most mainstream secondary schools). In 2002, England's first Gifted and Talented Academy was set up at Warwick University at a cost of £20 million. A talent search was instigated to find the 100 brightest students to attend a three-week summer school. More than one third (39 per cent) of the students were identified as 'non-white' British, the gender split was even and only six students came from private schools. Although the first year was funded by the Government, this kind of initiative is likely to come at a price to parents and the concern is that only middle class parents will be able to afford the fee.

KEY STUDY

Ability grouping in English secondary schools: effects on attainment in English, mathematics and science
Ireson, Hallam, Hack, Clark and Plewis (2002)

Aim: To examine the effects of mixed ability and setting on secondary school students' attainments and their self-concepts.

Sample: A cohort of students from 45 comprehensive schools were followed from year 9 to year 11; some of the schools put students in sets and others used mixed ability teaching.

Method: GCSE results were controlled for gender, social disadvantage and prior attainment at Key Stages 1 and 2. Schools that set were compared with those that did not set.

Results: Teaching students in sets had no significant impact on attainment in English, mathematics and science. With respect to self-concepts, unsurprisingly students with higher attainments had more positive self-concepts, as did boys. Interestingly, students in higher sets seemed to have more negative self-concepts than students with similar levels of attainment, but who were taught in mixed ability classes.

Conclusions: In terms of academic attainment, there is no benefit to setting students or to teaching them in mixed ability groups, but some students had their self-concepts damaged by being put into higher sets (perhaps because this meant that they were no longer near the top of the class).

EVALUATION ISSUES

EFFECTIVENESS

The study by Ireson et al. (2002) is not necessarily an effective way of improving attainment, and may actually harm students' self-concepts.

SECTION A EXAM QUESTIONS

a Describe one way of assessing special educational needs. [6]
b Evaluate ways of assessing special educational needs. [10]

a Describe one cause of a specific learning difficulty or disability. [6]
b Evaluate causes of a specific learning difficulty of disability. [10]

a Describe one strategy for educating children with special needs. [6]
b Evaluate the effectiveness for educating children with special educational needs. [10]

CD-ROM

For Section B sample exam questions see Education: Sample exam questions.

CHAPTER **3** | PSYCHOLOGY AND HEALTH

CHAPTER 3: INTRODUCTION

KEY DEFINITIONS

The word **'health'** is derived from the same root as **'whole'**, reflecting the traditional idea that a healthy person is someone who exists in a state of equilibrium of mind, body and spirit. When this equilibrium is disturbed, then the health of the individual is impaired. This traditional idea of health underpins so-called 'alternative medicine'. A central aspect of this traditional view is that healthiness is seen as a positive characteristic that an individual can possess to a greater or lesser degree. However, the concept of 'equilibrium of mind, body and spirit' is considered by many people as too vague, and the growth of professional medicine, which started about 200 years ago, resulted in changes in this attitude to health.

EVALUATION ISSUES

REDUCTIONISM

The medical model of health is reductionist as it tends to restrict its focus to the specific area of the body that is 'malfunctioning'. It is very much built around the concept of biological normality, that is, a person is healthy if his or her body is in 'normal' working order. In only considering the absence of disease or injury as a definition of health and ignoring positive characteristics, such as fitness or peace of mind, the medical model offers an incomplete picture; two individuals, both completely free of disease or injury at a particular moment in time, cannot be considered to be equally healthy.

CD-ROM

For a description of different models of health see Health: Theoretical approaches: Biopsychosocial model of health and Health: Theoretical approaches: The medical model of health.

The great contradiction of health is that there is a universal recognition of the importance and value of good health, but at the same time we often show an apparent disregard for our own health and that of others. We live in an unhealthy world in which environmental damage, oppression and inequality, sickness and despair are prevalent. For many of us, goals such as material wealth, pleasure-seeking, power and influence and the search for knowledge seem very important, and the value of good health only becomes truly apparent when we fall ill.

As well as these contradictions, the area of health also contains many controversies. People do not agree on how to improve health, or even on what good health actually consists of. As a result, the task of improving health in our society needs to be a multi-disciplinary one. Advances in medical science are very important, but so are psychological treatments, public health initiatives, health education and health promotion programmes, and political changes aimed at reducing poverty, deprivation and conflict. Science, education, politics, philosophy and spiritual teaching can all contribute to a healthier world.

Up until the end of the eighteenth century, health was perceived as a state positively characterised by certain qualities such as vigour, suppleness or fluidity. These qualities were lost or reduced as a result of illness, and the role of medicine was to restore them. As medicine came to be seen as more of a science, doctors established what the 'normal' functioning of the body should consist of and developed techniques aimed at bringing it back into normal working order. Doctors became less interested in whether patients *felt* unwell, but focused on biological abnormalities, i.e. diseases or injuries that could be observed objectively. As the biological mechanisms of human physiology became better understood by scientists, people started to perceive the body as a 'soft machine', operating according to the laws of physics. According to the **medical model of health**, healthiness occurs when the machine is in good working order.

In 1946, the World Health Organisation wrote in its constitution that 'Health is … a state of complete physical, mental and social well-being and … not merely the absence of disease and infirmity.' This **biopsychosocial** approach to health is holistic because it is interested in the interaction between the biological, psychological and social systems described above, and it challenges the medical model in that it defines health as a positive state of well-being. It recognises that no system exists in isolation and that an intervention at one level can have knock-on effects at other levels. For example, a certain psychological treatment such as cognitive therapy for stress may have an effect on a person's biological systems (for example, fewer headaches) and also on the social systems (for example, better family relationships).

This chapter presents a review of health psychology from a biopsychosocial perspective and introduces the reader to ways in which the study of psychology can be used to improve the state of people's health.

Health psychology has five main goals:

1 To prevent illness by developing an understanding of how mental states can influence health behaviour. In other words, if we wish to stop

people doing things that are bad for their health, we have to understand why they do those things in the first place.

2 To promote good health, because health psychologists see health as being more than just the absence of disease, they are interested in actively promoting well-being.

3 To help with the treatment of illness: despite preventive measures, people do fall ill, and health psychologists have a role in developing treatments that take psychological aspects into account.

4 To investigate the psychological factors that correlate with illness: this is a vital aspect of the work of health psychologists. It involves carrying out research to find out which specific mental states are linked to which physical diseases.

5 To improve the health care system and health policy: the knowledge gained by health psychologists, and their general approach to health and illness, can inform the people who run health care systems and help them to provide a more effective service.

CD-ROM

For a description of the historical development of health psychology see Health: Theoretical approaches: The relationship between mind and body and Health: Real life applications: The role of health psychology.

3.1 LIFESTYLES AND HEALTH BEHAVIOUR

KEY DEFINITIONS

Pitts defines **preventive health behaviours** as 'behaviours undertaken by people to enhance or maintain their health' (1996, p. 3).

This section starts by defining the concept of health-enhancing behaviour. It then goes on to describe the different theories that attempt to explain why some people lead healthier lives than others.

3.1.1 DETERMINANTS OF HEALTH-ENHANCING BEHAVIOURS

The notion that an individual's health can be improved by a change in behaviour is based on the assumption that certain specific behaviours or lifestyles are better for health than others. This seems a safe assumption; it is clear that certain behaviours, such as smoking tobacco for example, can lead directly to specific medical conditions. It is also generally accepted that overall lifestyle can affect health; a person who leads a hectic, stressful life is more likely to develop high blood pressure or coronary heart disease, for example. Specific behaviours can increase or reduce the risk of becoming ill in the first place, but individual behaviour can also affect the chances of recovery from disease or injury. For example, recognising the early signs of an illness and seeking medical help is a behaviour that promotes health.

Genetic theories

It is possible for genetic disposition towards a particular condition to have an indirect impact on health preventive behaviour. For example, a woman whose mother and grandmother had breast cancer may be more likely to examine her own breasts for lumps because she feels that she is more susceptible to the disease than average.

Is it possible, however, for a person's genetic inheritance to directly affect their health-related behaviour? It may be, for example, that alcoholism is partly hereditary; Sher (1991) describes evidence that the children of alcoholics are more likely to become alcoholic themselves. Although it is notoriously difficult to determine whether a correlation such as this is due to genetic factors or arises as a result of social learning, some psychologists argue that, although there probably is no such thing as an 'alcoholism gene', certain genetically inherited personality traits may pre-dispose an individual towards alcohol abuse.

Behaviourist learning theories

Classical conditioning could explain certain health-related behaviours such as 'comfort eating', for example. If a parent regularly offers a child sweets or chocolate at the same time as physical and emotional affection, then the child may learn to associate sweet foods with the reassuring feelings that arise out of parental love. In later life, the child may try to recreate these pleasant feelings by eating chocolate when he is stressed or depressed. Another example of how classical conditioning could effect health behaviour is based on the concept of one-trial learning; a single frightening or painful visit to a dentist, for example, could create an irrational fear of dentists, leading to avoidance.

A striking example of how **operant conditioning** can effect health behaviour is the study by Gil et al. (1988).

EVALUATION ISSUES

ETHICS

The 'behavioural change' approach to promoting health – based on the assumption that a key factor in maintaining good health is the individual's lifestyle – raises ethical issues as it can lead to 'victim-blaming'. There have been cases where doctors have refused to treat certain patients because they felt that they had brought their illnesses on themselves.

FOR CONSIDERATION

The link between genes and alcoholism may be subtle. Richard Burton, the famous actor, was quoted as saying that he would never have become an alcoholic if he had ever suffered a hangover. The ability to drink heavily without getting a headache the following morning may be linked to the way the body metabolises alcohol, and this may be partly affected by genetic inheritance.

- Why do you think some people drink more than others?

KEY STUDY

Direct observation of scratching behaviour in children with atopic dermatitis
Gil, Keefe, Sampson, McCaskill, Rodin and Crisson (1988)

Aim: To investigate the effect of distraction and of parental reactions on children's scratching behaviour.

Sample: 15 boys and 15 girls (mean age 5.6 years) who were being evaluated for severe atopic dermatitis at Duke University Medical Center, USA.

Method: Each child was video-taped for 10 minutes while interacting with their parent. For 5 minutes, they took part in a structured task (playing with Lego) and for the other 5 minutes, in an unstructured task (sitting in front of the camera with the toys out of reach). The researchers observed the child's scratching behaviour (scratching or rubbing themselves, or asking the parent to scratch them) and the parents' behaviour (scratching or rubbing the child, attempting to stop the child from scratching, paying attention to the child). Two observers practiced scoring until their agreement scores routinely exceeded 85 per cent.

Results: Children engaged in more scratching behaviour during the unstructured task than during the structured task. They also scratched themselves more when the parents responded to their behaviour by scratching or rubbing them, or by paying them attention. When parents paid attention to their children for not scratching themselves, the children's scratching behaviour was reduced.

Conclusions: When parents pay attention to their children's scratching behaviour, even if it is to tell them to stop, this seems to reinforce the scratching behaviour, and make it worse. When parents ignore the scratching, and pay attention to their children when they stop scratching themselves, then the scratching behaviour is not reinforced and is consequently reduced. Parents should (1) not reinforce the scratching behaviour by paying attention to it; (2) pay more attention to the child when he engages in non-scratching behaviour; (3) try to distract the child; (4) not try to stop the child from scratching.

KEY DEFINITIONS

Classical conditioning is a process in which the individual associates an automatic response with a neutral stimulus. Ivan Pavlov (1849–1936) described this process after he noticed that laboratory dogs would salivate when he turned a light on because they had learned to associate the light with the presence of food.

Operant conditioning is when people respond to reward or punishment by either repeating a particular behaviour, or else stopping it. If an individual carries out a behaviour that clearly seems to be bad for her health, such as smoking cigarettes, a deeper look may well reveal benefits for the individual, such as social approval, the nicotine buzz and so on.

Social learning occurs when an individual observes and imitates another person's behaviour, either because the individual looks up to that person as a role model or else through vicarious reinforcement, that is, the individual sees the person being rewarded for his or her actions. A study that illustrates this process was carried out by Albert Bandura (1965), see page 18.

Social learning can clearly be very influential in encouraging people to do things that are bad for their health. For example, a teenager may take up smoking because she has an admired elder brother who smokes, or may try illegal drugs because she sees other people taking them and having a good time. Another example of how vicarious reinforcement can lead to unhealthy behaviour concerns young people with eating disorders who see images of very thin models in magazines being rewarded with success, money, glamour and fame. On the other hand, many health promotion campaigns use positive role models to try to get people to lead healthier lifestyles.

Social and environmental factors

There are many different social and environmental factors contributing to people's health behaviour. For example, a common explanation for young people taking drugs or smoking cigarettes is '**peer pressure**'. It may be that people imitate their peers because of the explanation given above, that is, vicarious reinforcement; they see others getting a reward for a certain behaviour, so they copy it. A different psychological concept that can explain how peer pressure works is **conformity** in which people act the

EVALUATION ISSUES

REDUCTIONISM

Many psychologists criticise behaviourist learning theories as reductionist; they are based on the assumption that human beings respond automatically to specific situations. Not only does this imply a lack of free will, but it ignores the effect on behaviour of cognitive factors.

CD-ROM

See Health: Theoretical approaches: Classical conditioning and also Operant conditioning.

same as members of their own social group in order to fit in, to gain social acceptance or to reinforce their social identity.

Emotional factors

There are obvious ways in which an individual's emotional state could affect his or her health behaviour; people who are stressed or depressed are more likely to smoke, drink, eat an unbalanced diet and have accidents. Sigmund Freud suggested that people's behaviour can be affected by the desire to alleviate negative emotional states.

The main **ego defence mechanisms** described by Freud are briefly set out below, with examples showing how they can affect health behaviour:

- **Denial** is where people pretend to themselves that a certain event simply did not happen, or that a particular situation does not exist. A health-related example of denial is when someone has a symptom that may indicate the onset of a life-threatening disease, such as cancer, and is so scared of accepting that he might be ill that he stops perceiving the symptom at all.
- **Suppression** is where people deliberately and consciously try not to think about things that might upset them. They know that they have a worrying symptom, but they make efforts to distract themselves from even thinking about it.
- **Repression** also involves pushing thoughts out of the conscious mind, but in this case the process is unconscious. Examples of this are when someone has a doctor's appointment that he or she is dreading and forgets to go, or when people forget to take unpleasant medication.
- **Rationalisation** involves justifying or making excuses for an action in order to convince oneself that it is not so bad. For example, the teenager who watches a health promotion video about the dangers of tobacco and then says, 'I don't need to worry because I'm not as old as the people in the video, and I'll have given up smoking by the age of 25' is using rationalisation as a defence mechanism.

3.1.2 HEALTH BELIEF MODELS

People's cognitions – their beliefs, opinions, motivations and so on – clearly have an impact on their behaviour in general and their health behaviour in particular. It is often said, for example, that you cannot get someone to give up smoking or drugs unless that person wants to. Cognitive psychologists would argue that it is important to understand the cognitive determinants of behaviour because, by changing these, the behaviour itself can be modified. This section examines two different, but related, theories that attempt to explain how our beliefs and opinions can affect our health behaviour.

The Health Belief Model

The Health Belief Model was initially developed in the 1950s as a theory to explain the widespread failure of people to take part in preventive health campaigns, such as the free tuberculosis screening programme introduced by the Public Health Service in the USA (Hochbaum, 1958).

The Health Belief Model is made up of the following components:

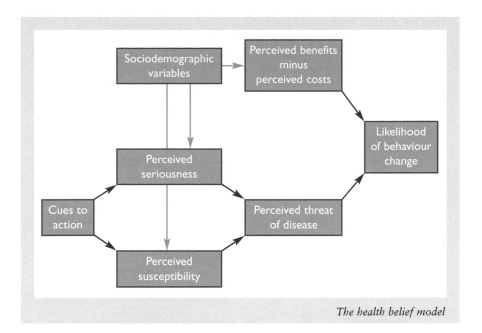

The health belief model

- **Perceived threat of disease:** many health promotion campaigns attempt to create the perception of risk by presenting information about how serious the threat is. An example of this would be to show someone who had died as a result of taking ecstasy. However, the chances of dying from a single ecstasy tablet are so low that this probably puts very few people off taking the drug. So, in order to convince individuals that there is a threat of disease (**perceived threat**), you have to convince them first that the outcome of the behaviour is potentially serious (**perceived seriousness**) and second that they themselves are at risk (**perceived susceptibility**).
- **Perceived benefits and barriers:** once an individual has accepted that there is a real threat, she will not change her behaviour unless she believes that this will actually reduce the threat.
- **Cues to action:** in his original research, Hochbaum (1958) suggested that perceived threat of disease in an individual is triggered by cues to action, for example a magazine article or a friend falling ill.
- **Sociodemographic variables:** the Health Belief Model recognises that its key elements – perception of threat, and of the costs and benefits of a certain action – are affected by certain modifying factors such as age, gender, ethnicity and socio-economic status, and our previous experience, education and knowledge.

Theory of Reasoned Action/Theory of Planned Behaviour

The Theory of Planned Behaviour (Ajzen, 1991) is an extension of an earlier model, the Theory of Reasoned Action (Ajzen and Fishbein, 1980). The **Theory of Reasoned Action** assumes that people's behaviour is determined by their intentions; in other words, first we decide to do something, and then we do it. Intention to behave is determined by the following two factors:

- **Attitude towards the behaviour:** this is the individual's personal beliefs about the possible consequences of the behaviour. For example, if an individual believes that taking more exercise will be good for him, then he is more likely to take exercise.
- **Subjective norm:** this represents social influence (this is not considered by the Health Belief Model) and consists of the individual's beliefs about other people's attitudes to the behaviour. For example, a person

EVALUATION ISSUES

VALIDITY OF THE HEALTH BELIEF MODEL

- The Health Belief Model is a decision-making model that describes how a person will arrive at the decision to change their behaviour; it does not guarantee that the behaviour will occur.
- Many health behaviours are done out of habit, and the Health Belief Model does not take this into account.
- Using these points it could be argued that the Health Belief Model is not a valid explanation for all behaviours.

EVALUATION ISSUES

VALIDITY

Sutton (1997) says that the Theory of Reasoned Action seems to explain about 50 per cent of variations in intention to behave between people, and about 25 per cent of variations in actual behaviour. Sutton states that although the theories are useful for prediction, they do not provide an accurate description of how people make health-related decisions, and are therefore not valid for all situations.

Both the Theory of Reasoned Action and the Theory of Planned Behaviour predict intention to behave and intention does not always lead to actual behaviour therefore they are not effective in explaining all behaviours.

may well take friends' or family members' opinions into account when deciding whether to give up smoking. If the individual perceives that his friends disapprove of smoking, and this matters to the individual, then he is more likely to decide to give up.

The **Theory of Planned Behaviour** adds a third, very important, factor to the Theory of Reasoned Action. **Perceived behavioural control** refers to how confident the individual is that he will succeed in changing his behaviour. If a person feels confident that he can give up smoking, for example, then he is more likely to decide to try. This belief, which is very similar to the notion of **self-efficacy**, is based on past experiences and also on the individual's perception of possible obstacles that might crop up in the future. Perceived behavioural control not only affects the intention to behave, but can also have a direct impact on whether the behaviour is actually carried out. Someone with high perceived behavioural control is likely to try harder to convert his intention to behave into actual behaviour.

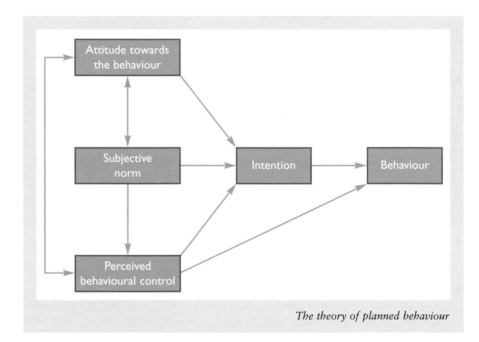

The theory of planned behaviour

KEY STUDY

Application of the Theory of Planned Behaviour to two dietary behaviours: roles of perceived control and self-efficacy
Povey, Connor, Sparks, James and Shepherd (2000)

Aim: To examine the application of the Theory of Planned Behaviour to specific dietary behaviours. The study looks at a specific component of the Theory of Planned Behaviour (perceived behavioural control), which Povey et al. argue is made up of self-efficacy and locus of control.

Sample: 390 people responded to an advert placed in a regional newspaper asking for volunteers for a 'research project on attitudes towards food'.

Method: Half of the participants were sent a 'low fat diet' questionnaire (144 responded) and the other half were sent a 'five portions of fruit and vegetables' questionnaire (143 responded). Overall, about 70 per cent of the sample were female, with ages ranging from 9 to 91 (mean age 41). Respondents were paid £5 on receipt of the completed questionnaires.

⚖ EVALUATION ISSUES

EFFECTIVENESS

Many studies have found that, in fact, the most effective way to change behaviour is to limit the barriers (that is, by making healthier choices easier choices) thus increasing self efficacy, and the least effective way is to try to convince people of the seriousness of the situation.

▶

Participants were sent two questionnaires, a month apart. The first questionnaire included demographic questions (age, gender and so on) designed to measure self-efficacy and locus of control, and questions about the extent to which the participants felt the need to eat less fat/eat five portions of fruit and vegetables per day. The second questionnaire was designed to measure the participants' actual diet and consisted of a 63-item food frequency survey.

Results: For each of the two dietary behaviours, locus of control and self-efficacy were good predictors of intentions. When it came to actual behaviour, high self-efficacy was significantly correlated with eating less fat and with eating more fruit and vegetables, but the correlation was weaker with behaviour than with intentions. Locus of control was not significantly correlated with actual behaviour.

Conclusions: Povey et al. concluded that the Theory of Planned Behaviour can be applied to the two specific dietary behaviours they examined, and especially the self-efficacy component. They suggest that health promotion programmes aimed at improving diet should target people's sense of self-efficacy.

Is diet a result of an internal or external locus of control?

In the Theory of Planned Behaviour, the notion of perceived behavioural control represents the individual's beliefs about his or her ability to carry out successfully a certain behaviour. Bandura (1986) refers to this concept as self-efficacy. Clearly, high levels of self-efficacy are likely to be linked to greater motivation to change behaviour; people who feel more confident that they can succeed are more likely to attempt health-related behaviour change and will show greater perseverance.

Wallston et al. (1978) developed a scale specifically designed to measure the extent to which people perceive their state of health as being under internal or external control. Their **Multidimensional Health Locus of Control Scale** (MHLC) identifies three distinct ways in which people attribute their health status:

- **Internal health locus of control** (IHLC): someone with a strong IHLC will feel responsible for her own health and will believe she can improve her health by taking action. There is quite a lot of research evidence to indicate that having an IHLC is good for your health.
- **Powerful others health locus of control** (PHLC): this refers to the belief that other people are responsible for your state of health, either for the bad (for example, 'I only smoke because my friends make me') or for the good (for example, 'If I do what my doctor tells me, then I will stay healthy'). People with a strong PHLC are less likely to take personal responsibility for changing their own lifestyles, but are more likely to seek help from health professionals.
- **Chance health locus of control** (CHLC): people with a strong CHLC tend to be fatalistic about their health (for example, 'There's nothing I can do about it; if I'm unlucky then I will get ill' or 'There's no point looking after my health; I might get run over by a bus tomorrow'). This group is the least likely to take responsibility for looking after their own health.

If it is true that people who tend to attribute health internally end up being healthier, then it may be productive to look at ways for modifying people's locus of control, either by carrying out research into why people develop specific attribution styles, or by developing forms of treatment that can help people feel more in control of what happens to them.

3.1.3 DEVELOPMENTAL, CULTURAL AND GENDER DIFFERENCES IN HEALTH BEHAVIOURS

The previous section focused on ways in which behaviours and lifestyles may affect health. Related to this are the cultural factors that might influence these ways of living. In particular this section will focus on **gender** and **social class**, and how these factors influence inequalities in health and health care.

Gender and health

Although sex is obviously a biological category, the illnesses that women suffer can sometimes be related to their gender role in society, which is a cultural construct. The health of women is quite different to the health of men in many ways, and this affects their use of the health services. Women and men differ in their illness and mortality rates, and many of these differences reflect social and cultural differences between women and men. Some examples include:

- women outlive men in our society by about five to six years
- men between the ages of 15 and 44 have a three to four times higher mortality rate than women from accidents, suicide and violence (Arber, 1999)
- women suffer from more reported mental health problems than men (Ussher, 1997)
- men report higher levels of alcohol and drug dependence.

Biological differences

There are, of course, biological differences that affect the illnesses, needs and the provision of health services for men and women. For example, health care for women has largely focused on their reproductive needs and all the associated services, such as contraception, abortion and infertility. 'Well women' clinics provide screening services that are focused on women's biological differences from men, i.e. cervical and breast screening. Many researchers would argue that this reproductive focus has meant that women's health in other areas has been neglected.

Cultural/psychosocial differences

More important perhaps are the social and environmental influences on health that have little to do with biological differences. Gender roles and relationships affect both women's and men's health. There are a number of ways in which women's roles affect their health, such as the fact that women are stereotyped by society as 'carers'. Because of this they often find themselves caring for sick or elderly relatives and they are, by and large, the unpaid carers of young children. Women are more often on the receiving end of domestic violence than men, and many women bring up young children alone. Perhaps for these reasons, women tend to be more susceptible to stress and depression than men, and this has consequences for their mental and physical health.

Some conditions that women suffer from have been examined from both a biological and a psychosocial perspective, and these make an interesting comparison, in particular conditions such as pre-menstrual syndrome (PMS), postnatal depression (PND) and the menopause. With all of these conditions medical interpretations focus on the biochemical changes associated with hormone levels. According to the medical model, these hormonal changes account for the psychological and physical problems reported by women. However, it can be argued from a psychosocial approach that there are more complex relationships between a range of factors that may affect physical and psychological symptoms.

One of the most important factors to consider is the fact that not all women suffer equally from these symptoms, and according to Ussher (1997) this shows very clearly the importance of psychosocial explanations. The study by Ruble (1977) illustrates this clearly.

KEY STUDY

Premenstrual symptoms: a reinterpretation
Ruble (1977)

Aim: To examine the physiological basis of pre-menstrual symptoms, and to question the validity of women's self-reports of these symptoms.

Sample: 44 women undergraduates at Princeton University aged 18 to 24 were told they were taking part in research looking at a technique for predicting the expected date of menstruation.

Method: The research was carried out in the university infirmary. The women were interviewed (unknown to them) on the sixth or seventh day before their next period (calculated on the basis of previous information given to the researchers). The participants were randomly assigned to different experimental groups; pre-menstrual (one to two days until next period), intermenstrual (seven to ten days until next period) or control (given no information). They were 'tested' using an EEG machine, and told to which group they belonged. The women were then given a questionnaire in which they had to rate the extent to which they had experienced the symptoms in the questionnaire.

Results: Symptom rating of women who thought they were pre-menstrual was significantly higher than those who had been told they were intermenstrual for the symptoms of water retention, pain and change in eating habits.

Conclusions: Although Ruble recognised that demand characteristics may have affected the results of her study, she argued that the results show that learned associations or beliefs can cause a woman to overstate what she is actually experiencing or affect a woman's actual perception of her own body when she believes she is pre-menstrual. Ruble argues that this demonstrates that the extent to which psychological or physiological factors influence the pre-menstrual phase is open to question.

EVALUATION ISSUES

METHODOLOGY

Ruble (1977) recognised that demand characteristics might have affected the results of the study. However, she also argued that there are also other physical and psychological factors at work (nature/nurture).

Health care provision for men and women

The provision of health care for women has traditionally focused on their reproductive role. A further point that is interesting in the context of gender differences is that men and women suffering from the same condition may receive quite different treatment. Arber (1999) notes that women in the USA are less likely to receive kidney transplants than men, and that in the UK women are less likely than men to be offered a coronary artery bypass if they have heart disease. She also reports that women have appeared in very little research on AIDS or coronary heart disease. Many areas of research appear gender blind.

Stereotyping of men and women in terms of the norms and expectations of society is particularly problematic, since it can lead to misdiagnosis and labelling of illnesses. For example, women are more likely to be given a psychological diagnosis for a non-specific problem, whereas a man is more likely to be given a medical one. Labels can mean that the real cause of the problem is ignored.

FOR CONSIDERATION

- Why do you think that women tend to live longer than men?

Social class and health

There is a great deal of contemporary evidence to suggest that health varies according to socio-economic status. It could be argued that it is the single most important factor that explains health and illness. To be homeless and to live 'rough' carries a higher risk of mortality than any other group in the population. Any index of socio-economic status (including home and car ownership, income or class classification) appears to show similar trends, that is, the better the material circumstances, the lower the rate of premature mortality.

The Department of Health's report *Variations in Health* (1995) shows that of 66 major causes of death among men, 62 were most common among men in social class IV and V. Of 70 major causes of death among women, 64 were most common among women married to men in class IV and V (cited in Senior and Vivash, 1998). Deaths caused by respiratory diseases and accidents are the most highly correlated with social class. The lower the social class the higher the risk. Although the number of people in class V is reducing, the health gap between social class I and social class V is widening (Trowler, 1996). The only exception to this general trend is that the class differences in the deaths of babies under one year of age has narrowed considerably in recent years.

The most obvious cause of class inequalities in health is the differential access to resources between the different social classes. People in classes IV and V often have too little household income, live in unsafe, cold and damp housing, work in jobs where they are more likely to have accidents than people in other social classes, smoke and drink more as a result of stress, and are more likely to suffer from a major 'life event' that will then affect their health.

A further explanation is that the areas in which poorer people live are often those that have inadequate health services. The health service has its own hierarchy, and the best research and training hospitals are not always located where they are most needed.

There is also research to suggest that people in different social classes are treated differently by health professionals. Middle class people tend to be more demanding of the health service in terms of information and doctors' surgery time, for example. Doctors have been shown to respond to the questions of middle class people by answering questions and discussing treatments more fully.

One of the most convincing, but also one of the most problematic, explanations is that people in different social classes behave in ways that lead to worse health than people in other social classes. People in classes IV and V, for example, are more likely to behave in ways that damage their health (as has already been described) by smoking and drinking to excess, and eating a poor diet.

It is not only material factors that explain the behaviours and health of people in classes IV and V. There are a number of other factors that are also important to consider. One of these is how people feel about their 'relative' position in society. Evidence from Japan and other similarly affluent countries suggests that longest life expectancy occurs in places with the most equitable income distribution. As Wilkinson states 'It looks as if what matters about our physical circumstances is not what they are in themselves, but where they stand in the scale of things in our society. The implication is that our environment and standard of living no longer impact on our health primarily through direct physical causes, regardless of

EVALUATION ISSUES

ETHICS

One of the ethical problems with any explanation that focuses on the behaviour of a group of people is that it is likely to place 'blame' on that group for their particular health behaviours. However, there are considerable behavioural differences within, as well as between, social classes. The behaviour of poorer members of society is limited by factors that are often beyond their control, such as the availability of transport and shops.

our attitudes and perceptions, but have come to do so mainly through social and cognitively mediated processes' (1990, p. 405, cited in Carroll et al., 1997).

SECTION A EXAM QUESTIONS

a Describe one study about determinants of health-enhancing behaviour. [6]
b Discuss the difficulties of researching determinants of health-enhancing behaviour. [10]

a Describe one health belief model. [6]
b Contrast one health belief model with one other health belief model. [10]

a Describe one study of gender differences in health behaviours. [6]
b Discuss the usefulness of research into gender differences in health behaviours. [10]

CD-ROM

For Section B sample exam questions see Health: Sample exam questions.

3.2 HEALTH PROMOTION

Health promotion campaigns against smoking

This section examines approaches to health promotion, including the way in which health messages can be communicated effectively to their target audience, using examples of workplace, community and school campaigns. There are different approaches to health promotion; those that use a model of social change in that they are based on the belief that ill health arises out of power inequalities in society and that health promotion should be concerned with changing society, and the behavioural change and educational approaches that focus on modifying individual behaviour and cognitions, and make use of psychological theory. This section is based on the social regulation approach, focusing on changing individual behaviour rather than inequalities in society, as this is what psychological models of health promotion tend to focus on.

3.2.1 METHODS FOR PROMOTING HEALTH

This section focuses on three approaches to health promotion:
- fear arousal
- the use of the Yale Model of Communication
- increasing self-efficacy.

Fear arousal

The Health Belief Model says that perceived threat (made up of perceived seriousness and perceived susceptibility) is a prerequisite for healthy behaviour. In other words, people will not change their lifestyles unless they believe that they will become unhealthy unless they do so. The Theory of Planned Behaviour also includes perceived threat as a key factor. One obvious function of **fear arousal** in a health promotion campaign is to increase people's perceived threat by making the outcome of a particular behaviour seem very frightening. However, the role of fear arousal is not just to trigger the individual to make a cognitive decision to change his or her behaviour, but to arouse emotional tension. The theory is based on the idea that the individual will change his or her behaviour in order to reduce this tension. It is commonly believed that the more you frighten people, the more likely they are to change their behaviour. Almost all health promotion campaigns contain an element of fear arousal, and some are very frightening indeed.

The classic study by Janis and Feshbach (1953) suggested that strong fear arousal can be counter-productive. If a fear arousing message is so frightening that it creates a degree of emotional tension that the individual cannot deal with through behaviour change, then the individual will use ego defence mechanisms to cope. This avoidance actually reduces the chance of behavioural change.

FOR CONSIDERATION

There are many contemporary TV and radio campaigns that rely on fear arousal. Consider health promotion advertisements that your are familiar with (e.g. drink-driving, anti-smoking, etc.).
- To what extent do they use shock tactics in order to arouse fear?
- Do you think these adverts are effective? What evidence do you have?

EVALUATION ISSUES

EFFECTIVENESS

There is a tendency to use very shocking images in health promotion campaigns in order to make the 'unhealthy' behaviour seem very dangerous. However, it may be by making them too shocking they are encouraging ego defence mechanisms and reducing the effectiveness of the message.

KEY STUDY

Effects of fear arousing communications
Janis and Feshbach (1953)

Aim: To study the motivational effect of fear arousal in health promotion communications.

Sample: The entire 'freshman' class of a large Connecticut high school (mean age approximately 15, roughly equal numbers of males and females).

Method: Participants were divided into four groups. Three of the groups were given a 15-minute illustrated lecture on tooth decay and the importance of oral hygiene. The fourth group acted as a control. The three experimental groups were given different forms of the lecture:
- Form 1: strong fear appeal, emphasising the painful consequences of tooth decay and gum disease.
- Form 2: moderate fear appeal, in which the dangers were described in a milder and more factual manner.
- Form 3: minimal fear appeal, which rarely alluded to the consequences of tooth neglect.

Participants were given a questionnaire one week before the lecture (asking them about dental hygiene) a second questionnaire immediately after the lecture (asking about the immediate effects of the communication), and a third questionnaire one week after the lecture (asking whether their oral hygiene behaviour had changed).

Results: Janis and Feshbach found that higher levels of fear arousal resulted in greater anxiety about tooth decay immediately after the lecture (an increase of 42 per cent of the 'strong fear' group who felt 'somewhat or very worried' compared to an increase of 24 per cent for the 'minimal fear' group). There were no differences in the amount of information each group acquired from the lecture, but the 'strong fear' group appraised the communication more favourably than the other groups on a number of questions (for example, 'interesting', 'did a good job' and so on), but also thought that the lecture was more 'horrible' and 'disgusting'. However, when it came to assessing behaviour change, the 'minimal fear' communication was most effective: change in conformity to oral hygiene behaviour was 36 per cent for the 'minimal fear', 22 per cent for the 'moderate fear', 8 per cent for the 'strong fear' and 0 per cent for the control group.

Conclusions: The overall effectiveness of a health promotion communication is likely to be reduced by the use of a strong fear appeal. Janis and Feshbach argue that this is because when fear is strongly aroused but is not fully relieved by reassurances contained in the communication, the audience will become motivated to ignore or to minimise the importance of the threat.

The Yale Model of Communication

The Yale Communication Research Program was set up in the 1950s as a response to the increasing role of mass communication in the USA.

Hovland et al. (1953) focus on three aspects of communication; the communicator (who says it); the communication (what is said) and the audience (to whom is it said):
- **The communicator:** the crucial factor here seems to be the **credibility** of the source of the information. Low credibility sources are seen as more biased and unfair, and have a much weaker effect on the audience's opinions than high credibility sources. In research studies audiences learned as much information from high and low credibility communicators, but were much more likely to accept the conclusions advocated if the credibility of the source was high (although, these differences tended to disappear after a few weeks).
- **The communication:** Hovland et al. (1953) mention the use of fear in the message and argue that it seems reasonable to include fear arousal if

CD-ROM

For a discussion of different models of health promotion see Health: Theoretical approaches: Models of health promotion and Health: Real life applications: Improving health.

EXAM HINTS

Zimbardo has developed a version of the Yale Model, as part of this research programme. Other texts might cite his version, but it is the same basic model as that advocated in Hovland's original research.

EVALUATION ISSUES

EFFECTIVENESS

There are several ways of convincing an audience that a source of communication is credible, for example, using a doctor to explain why it is important to eat a healthy diet, using people who have had relevant personal experience (for example, using ex-drug addicts to talk to young people about substance use), or using people who are generally perceived as trustworthy and honest (using celebrities in health promotion programmes who have a good public image). This will make the message more effective.

necessary. They also mention other important features of the content of communication. For example, they found that in communication that deals with a complicated issue, it is better for the communicator to spell out the conclusions rather than rely on the audience. This is particularly true when the audience is either less well-informed or less 'intelligent'. On the other hand, when the message is fairly simple, or when communicating with well-informed people, it is more effective to let the audience reach its own conclusions. Another factor is the extent to which the audience actively participates in the communication; the more participation there is, the more the messages are internalised. This means that it is better to involve the audience in some way, maybe through discussion, or even asking them to repeat the message to others.

- **The audience:** Hovland et al. (1953) found that certain individuals are more susceptible to persuasion than others. For example, people with low self-esteem, depressive tendencies and 'social inadequacies' are more likely to be influenced by persuasive communications. Also, people with a strong sense of group conformity will be more resistant to messages that are contrary to the standards and beliefs of the group. If people with low self-esteem are more likely to respond to health promotion messages, why is it that such people tend to lead less healthy lifestyles? In contemporary society people are constantly bombarded with messages from many media sources. We receive many more messages promoting unhealthy lifestyles than healthy ones, and so it makes sense that individuals who are more susceptible to persuasive communication lead less healthy lives. Rather than attempt to 'counter-persuade' such people, it may be better to help them regain their self-esteem, so that they become more resistant to negative health messages.

Increasing self-efficacy

Some health promotion campaigns, while based on communication, are so simple, that anyone can practice them. Many health promotion campaigns involve difficult decision making processes, and are hard to put into practice in spite of good intentions. Others however need no more than a very easy change in behaviour that can give the people carrying them out a sense of efficacy, as there is no sense of difficulty or failure. A good example of one such campaign is the Department of Health's campaign to reduce cot death. The campaign lists six straightforward steps to reduce cot death. The most simple of these is to put the baby to bed on its back. Other campaigns that might be compared to this include a campaign to reduce chip pan fires. Although many people do not feel confident in tackling fires, the simple message that everyone could put into practice was that chip pans should not be more than half full (this prevents the majority of fires from starting).

3.2.2 HEALTH PROMOTION IN SCHOOLS, WORKPLACES AND COMMUNITIES

There are many different settings in which health promotion can take place, for example, in schools, in workplaces, in local communities, in hospitals and other health care places or in the mass media. The characteristics of a successful health promotion programme will depend largely on its setting.

Health promotion in the workplace

There are two reasons why the workplace is a useful setting for health promotion: first, it is a good way to gain access to a large captive audience and second, many behaviours linked to ill health occur within the workplace. This is underlined by the following figures published by the Health Education Authority in 1997 (cited in Naidoo and Wills, 2000, p. 266):

- 18 per cent of deaths in the UK are work-related
- 6 per cent of adults suffer ill health associated with work
- 15 million working days are lost every year in the UK as a result of work-related illness or injury (including stress-related illness).

There are several ways in which health promotion can occur within the workplace, including:

- adequate health and safety policies
- occupational health, e.g. first aid and medical treatment, health screening
- health education, e.g. advice about healthy lifestyles
- provision of facilities and services such as gyms, stress counselling and so on
- creating a healthier environment, for example, by providing a healthy diet in the canteen or by banning smoking (see Parry et al., 2000).

KEY STUDY

Out of sight, out of mind: workplace smoking bans and the relocation of smoking at work
Parry, Platt and Thomson (2000)

Aim and background: To evaluate a smoking ban implemented at a Scottish university in 1997.

Method: The university implemented a policy of a complete smoking ban, a policy that is accepted by many workplaces and colleges around the country.

Results: At first sight, it seems reasonable to ban smoking from public places: it makes it harder for smokers to smoke, meaning that they may cut down on their daily cigarettes; it protects non-smokers from environmental tobacco smoke; and it keeps the place cleaner. Comments from non-smokers at the university before the smoking ban was implemented seemed to back this up. They said '... we should be much more concerned about air quality and not exposing non-smokers to carcinogenic fumes' '... the university should do nothing to make life easier for those who want to inflict toxins on people around them and who have no choice but to breathe in their effluent'.

An alternative to banning smoking completely is to create dedicated smoking areas, but this was also unpopular among non-smokers, who said things like '... I see no reason why the university should be forced to provide dedicated areas'.

Once the ban was implemented it seemed to be accepted by university staff, and led to some reduction in levels of smoking and a reduction of environmental tobacco smoke inside the buildings. However, the smoking ban also led to a number of unintended consequences:

- environmental tobacco smoke shifted from inside the buildings to just outside, as smokers congregated around the entrances
- smokers at the university became more visible and gained a higher profile
- there was an accumulation of smoking debris in certain areas outside the buildings
- sympathy for smokers actually increased as they were perceived to be discriminated against.

▶

Some people would argue that individuals have the right to choose to engage in behaviour that may be harmful to themselves, and that to prevent them from doing so is unethical. Others might argue that to allow people to harm themselves is unethical. However, most would agree that it is legitimate to prevent people from engaging in behaviour that harms others.

Conclusions: The authors conclude that, while smoking bans are successful in reducing smoke pollution in workplaces, they do not really solve the problem of smoking at all. Banning smoking from inside buildings simply shifts the problem elsewhere (in fact, many smokers reported that they had started smoking more outside working hours as a result of the ban). The authors do not support the idea of designated smoking areas on the grounds that it is difficult to ensure that smoke pollution does not leak out from such areas, and that this, while appearing to condone smoking, also serves to ghettoise smokers and render them invisible. They recognise that the main aim of smoking bans is to reduce environmental tobacco smoke, but argue that the only long-term solution to the problem is to provide help for smokers to cut down or quit smoking.

Health promotion in schools

Many health-related behaviours become habitual at a fairly young age, and teenagers in particular begin to behave in ways that can cause serious problems later on. For example, very few people take up cigarette smoking if they have not already done so by the age of 18, and young people are particularly vulnerable to the dangers of substance mis-use and unsafe sex. Therefore, it makes sense to start health education as early as possible, and schools seem to be an ideal setting for this; there is a captive audience, already studying in an educational environment, and teachers can be specifically trained to provide high quality health education. In fact, various government publications (ranging from national curriculum subject orders to the non-statutory framework for teaching personal, social and health education) suggest that the following topics could be taught in schools:

- substance use and mis-use
- sex education
- family life education
- safety
- health-related exercise
- food and nutrition
- personal hygiene
- environmental aspects
- psychological aspects.

Unfortunately, the practice of health promotion in schools does not always match up to its good intentions, and many young people are critical of the health education they receive. This may be due to a lack of time and resources, or maybe teachers are inadequately trained in providing health education.

- Consider the health education you have received at school; was it effective? If not, why not?

Health promotion in the community

Community-based health promotion is based on the assumption that social and environmental factors play an important role in people's health, and that it is possible to modify social structures in ways that encourage people to lead healthier lives. The key environmental and social change needed to improve health is to reduce poverty, as negative social conditions are the most important contributors to ill health. However, this involves political activity that is beyond the scope of most health promotion professionals, who consequently attempt to make whatever changes they can within the current sociopolitical climate. Specific examples of health promotion in the community include:

- local environmental campaigning (for example, against road pollution, for safer roads and more green spaces)
- 'social' campaigning (for example, for better quality housing and adequate policing against racist attacks)
- improving local services (for example, adequate provision of public transport, shops, post offices, health services and community centres)

- improving the social environment (for example, encouraging community or voluntary organisations and self-help groups)
- encouraging specific behaviour (for example, getting shops to ask for ID before selling cigarettes to young people and encouraging people to check up on elderly neighbours).

One such current initiative is called 'Walking the Way to Health'. This is an initiative sponsored by organisations such as the British Heart Foundation and the Countryside Agency which gives simple advice about the benefits of walking, and encourages people to take up walking by providing information about local walks.

3.2.3 PROMOTING HEALTH: A CASE STUDY

This section focuses on a study by Davis Kirsch and Pullen (2003) in which the authors describe and evaluate a school-based programme in the USA aimed at persuading children to wear bicycle helmets. Approximately 500 000 children visit the hospital or the doctor every year in the USA as a result of cycling injuries, and head traumas account for 140 000 of these visits. Every year 252 children die from cycling crashes, and 97 per cent of these were not wearing helmets. Since children suffer higher rates of death and injury from cycling accidents than other groups, and wearing a helmet is thought to reduce the risk of serious injury, it makes sense to design a health promotion programme aimed at persuading children to wear cycling helmets.

Davis Kirsch and Pullen (2003) describe a school educational programme named Safety Central, launched in 1997 and aimed at 4th-graders. The programme had two key approaches:
- to increase children's levels of **self-efficacy**: this was done by improving their skills (practising fitting and wearing a helmet), providing them with an experience of success (through an activity sheet) and persuasion (being encouraged by valued others, e.g. parents and teachers)
- to increase children's **fear arousal** by showing them a video that was designed to increase children's perceptions of their susceptibility to an injury and by sending a letter home to parents aimed at increasing parents' perception of the severity of a cycling accident. They also made the health behaviour easier by providing each child with a free helmet.

Davis Kirsch and Pullen (2003) evaluate the effectiveness of the Safety Central programme through the use of a questionnaire and by direct observation.

KEY STUDY

Evaluation of a school-based education programme to promote bicycle safety
Davis Kirsch and Pullen (2003)

Aim: To evaluate the effectiveness of the Safety Central programme, initiated by the Center for Childhood Safety in the Pacific North West of the USA in 1997.

Sample: Five schools chosen to represent the demographic make-up of the community (involving a total of 11 teachers and 284 children aged 10–12 years; 51 per cent were girls); all five schools had been using the Safety Central programme during the previous two years. Four

EVALUATION ISSUES

EFFECTIVENESS

Is it more effective to instigate health promotion campaigns in schools, in the workplace or in the community? The advantage of health promotion in schools is that the target group are young and it may be possible to prevent people getting into the habit of behaving in ways that are damaging to their health. In contrast, adults spend a great deal of their waking time at work, and so programmes within the workplace are a very good way of reaching many people. However, school-based and workplace programmes tend to focus on the role of the individual in changing his behaviour, and the advantage of community-based programmes is that they tend to modify the social and physical environment so that 'healthier choices become easier choices'.

EVALUATION ISSUES

THEORETICAL APPROACHES

Safety Central was based on two cognitive theories of health behaviour which can be used for comparison:
- the Theory of Planned Behaviour, which incorporates the notion of perceived behavioural control, or the individual's beliefs about her ability to succeed. Bandura (1986) refers to this as self-efficacy (see page 28)
- the Health Belief Model, which incorporates the notions of perceived threat (made up of perceived seriousness and perceived susceptibility) and perceived costs of the health behaviour (see page 82).

METHODOLOGY

One methodological criticism of this study is lack of a proper control group. It may have been better to use five schools that had taken part in Safety Central and compare them to five schools that had not, rather than rely on children who had come from other schools as the control group. Another problem is the fact that they did not collect enough observational data to draw any conclusions (although the two observers reached 100 per cent agreement on the data that they did collect); the researchers only allowed one day's observation for each site.

observation sites were chosen: two schools which had taken part in the Safety Central initiative, and two which had not, to serve as controls; observations were carried out in and around the schools and in nearby parks.

Method: Each child was given a 14-item questionnaire to complete. Children from two of the schools, and from another two control schools, were observed in and around the schools. The observers recorded the date, time and weather; the gender, ethnicity and approximate age of the children; whether they had a helmet and whether they were using it properly; and whether they were alone or with others.

Results:
- 84 per cent of the children had been in the participating schools during 4th grade, when the Safety Central programme was taught and 16 per cent came from schools that did not participate in the programme.
- 90 per cent of children reported owning a bicycle helmet.
- 74 per cent said they had worn a helmet on their last cycle ride; significantly more of these were female, and the older the children were, the less likely they were to have worn a helmet.
- Children who had been in the 4th grade of a school that used the Safety Central programme were significantly more likely to wear helmets.
- 55 per cent were able to identify correctly three checkpoints for proper helmet fit.
- In response to the statement 'I am a good bike rider so I don't have to wear a helmet', 82 per cent said this was 'not at all like me'.
- 50 per cent responded 'a lot like me' to the statement 'I know how to fall so I don't get hurt'.
- Unfortunately, the observation data were not useful, as very few cycle riders were seen in the observation sites.

Conclusions: The authors conclude that the Safety Central programme is effective in teaching safety messages to children, and that knowledge retention and safe behaviour was evident over a 1–2 year period. They suggest that a booster session should be introduced at grade 6 (two years after the original programme), to re-fit the helmets and to reinforce the message about susceptibility to injury. The authors also express concern that 50 per cent of their sample believed that they could avoid injury by 'knowing how to fall'. They suggest that initiatives aimed at encouraging children to attribute cycling injuries more externally by stressing the limited control held by individuals in an accident would be useful. Finally, they stress the importance of reducing the costs of the health behaviour they are trying to encourage, by making low-cost, 'cool' looking helmets readily available.

FOR CONSIDERATION

Can you spot where the following theories come into the Safety Central programme?
- the Theory of Planned Behaviour
- the Health Beliefs Model
- Attribution Theory.

CD-ROM

For Section B sample exam questions see Health: Sample exam questions.

SECTION A EXAM QUESTIONS

a Describe one study of health promotion. [6]
b Discuss the ethics of research into health promotion. [10]

a Describe one study of health promotion in schools. [10]
b Discuss the strengths of promoting health in schools. [10]

a Describe one study of health promotion in a worksite. [6]
b Evaluate the effectiveness of health promotion in worksites. [10]

SUBSTANCE USE AND ABUSE

The substances on which this section will focus are alcohol and tobacco, with some reference to the use of illegal drugs. There is obvious interest in the use and mis-use of these substances, and from a psychological perspective it is important to consider why people use (and in particular mis-use) these substances and how substance mis-use can be prevented or alleviated.

3.3.1 DEFINING SUBSTANCE USE AND ABUSE

When does 'use' become 'mis-use'?

Most people will have tried alcohol and tobacco at some stage in their lives, and many will have tried psychoactive drugs also. For the majority the use of these substances never becomes a problem. Many people drink regularly, and moderate consumption of alcohol (within government guidelines; currently 21 units per week for men and 14 units per week for women) may actually enhance health rather than detract from it. There is evidence to suggest that these drinkers have lower morbidity and mortality rates (i.e. they get less illness and live longer) than heavy drinkers and those who abstain altogether (Rimm et al., 1991).

Rosenhan and Seligman (1984) suggest that three factors indicate what they call **substance abuse**:
- pathological use and an inability to stop
- the use has problematic effects upon the person's life; with their work, family or friends
- the pathological use lasts for at least one month.

Addiction

People are often described as having 'addictive' personalities, and researchers now look at the ways in which people can become addicted to certain types of behaviours (gambling or sex, for example), as well as certain types of substances. Sarafino (1994) defines **addiction** as '… a condition, produced by repeated consumption of a natural or synthetic substance, in which the person becomes physically and psychologically dependent on the substance' (1994, p. 206).
- **Physical dependence** is the condition in which people have developed a **physical tolerance** of the substance, and will have negative side effects or **withdrawal symptoms** if they stop taking the substance.
- **Psychological dependence** is the condition in which people come to rely on a substance because they enjoy the effect it has on them, either directly or through association, without necessarily being physically dependent on it.

Ogden (1996) describes two distinct psychological approaches to the understanding of addiction. The first approach takes a medical perspective and argues that:
- addictions are discrete, a person is either addicted or not
- addictions are illnesses
- the individual is seen as the problem
- the addiction cannot be reversed
- treatment requires total abstinence.

KEY DEFINITIONS

The DSM-IV (the current diagnostic manual of the American Psychiatric Association) classifies **alcohol abuse** as a maladaptive drinking pattern described in much the same way as Rosenhan and Seligman describe substance abuse in general. Those who abuse alcohol are diagnosed on the basis of one of the following:
- recurrent drinking in spite of its affect on personal obligations
- continued drinking in spite of legal or personal problems associated with its use
- recurrent drinking in situations where this is dangerous.

EVALUATION ISSUES

REDUCTIONISM

It would be reductionist to assume that addiction is purely physical; if this were the case, then physical techniques for reducing substance mis-use (such as nicotine patches for people trying to cut down on cigarette smoking, or methadone for heroin addicts) would be very effective. These techniques help, but often do not work on their own; psychological and social interventions are also required.

The medical perspective thinks of addiction as an 'illness' and therefore not really the individual's fault (unless, perhaps, they wilfully refuse to seek treatment for the illness). In contrast the social approach tends to see addicts as victims of a social system that, for example, means that people of a lower socio-economic class are much more likely to mis-use substances. A third attitude is to attribute moral weakness to substance mis-users. The notion that addicts are morally reprehensible is fairly widespread. This view would be considered unethical by the other two approaches, who see addicts more as victims.

Nicotine is the addictive chemical in cigarettes

- Have you ever met anyone who you consider to be mis-using a particular substance?
- What was it about their behaviour that led you to think this?
- What do you think are the reasons they mis-used the substance?

It could be considered reductionist to explain substance mis-use simply in terms of physical addiction or arising mainly from genetic factors.

The second approach, related to social learning theory, argues that:
- addictive behaviours are learned
- addictive behaviours can be unlearned
- addictive behaviours are not discrete, but lie on a continuum
- addictive behaviours are no different from other behaviours, and treatment involves abstinence or unlearning the behaviour.

Physiological and psychological effects of substances

Nicotine is the addictive chemical in cigarettes, and it is this that produces very rapid and strong effects. When a person smokes, the nicotine is absorbed very quickly in to the blood stream through the membranes in the mouth, throat and lungs. It is carried to the brain where it triggers the release of a number of chemicals, including **acetylcholine** and **norepinephrine** which have the effect of enhancing concentration and alertness, and increasing pleasurable feelings. These chemicals also reduce feelings of tension and anxiety.

Alcohol affects the central nervous system and, depending on the amount of alcohol consumed, this effect can range from physical relaxation and a reduction in feelings of anxiety to serious impairment in judgement and co-ordination. Large amounts of alcohol consumed in a short space of time can paralyse vital reflexes and cause death. However, most people use alcohol because of its relaxing effect. Alcohol reduces the production of **catecholamine** (a chemical that produces a sense of arousal and is associated with stress). More recently alcohol has also been shown to increase the production of substances in the bloodstream that protect the blood vessels from cholesterol.

Psychoactive drugs have many and various physiological effects, for example the effect of heroin on chemicals in the brain can cause feelings of euphoria and intense well-being. Stimulants such as cocaine produce physiological and psychological arousal that give feelings of confidence and well-being, and hallucinogens such as marijuana produce distortions in perception and feelings of relaxation. Psychoactive drugs can cause physical harm to the body, and contribute to accidents. Babies can be born addicted to drugs such as heroin and cocaine if their mothers use them during pregnancy.

3.3.2 THEORIES OF SUBSTANCE ABUSE

There are many reasons why people start and continue to mis-use substances, and these reasons can be grouped into three categories; **physical**, **psychological** and **social and environmental**. Most clinicians now take a bio-psychosocial approach and recognise that it is a combination of these factors that has an overall effect on the likelihood of mis-use by an individual.

Physical factors affecting mis-use

There is evidence to suggest that genetic factors may have an influence on substance mis-use. The effects of both alcohol and nicotine are influenced by genetic factors to some degree. Family, adoption and twin studies have shown that there may be a link to alcoholism (Sayette and Hufford, 1997). Genetic variation in the function of dopamine receptors and liver enzymes that metabolise nicotine may influence whether a person is more or less vulnerable to nicotine addiction (Moolchan et al., 2000). However, most researchers in the field would argue that the reasons why one person becomes a smoker and another does not are primarily psychological and social. The key study by Moolchan et al. (2000) described below points to psychological and social causes, but also indicates that some of the reasons that people smoke may be physiological.

CD-ROM

For a study that provides evidence for a genetic cause of alcoholism, see Health: Additional key studies: Sayette and Hufford (1997).

KEY STUDY

A review of tobacco smoking in adolescents: treatment implications
Moolchan, Ernst and Heningfield (2000)

Aim: To review research on tobacco smoking in adolescents.

Method: Moolchan et al. did not collect primary data themselves, but reviewed data previously collected by other researchers. This included data on the risk factors for adolescent smoking, the characteristics of nicotine use in adolescents and treatment intervention for adolescent smoking.

Results:
- 42.7 per cent of US students in grade 9 have used tobacco.
- 75 per cent of teenage smokers will smoke as adults.
- Smoking can become a way for adolescents to instantly appear independent and mature while fitting in with peers.
- 75 per cent of adolescent smokers have one or both parents who smoke.
- Adolescents who smoke report more symptoms of depression than those who do not smoke.
- Adolescents who smoke are more likely to have ADHD than those who do not smoke.
- Female smokers are more confident, outgoing, rebellious and socially skilled than male smokers, who are more likely to be socially insecure.
- Adolescent girls pre-occupied with dieting and weight are more likely to become smokers.
- Smoking cessation treatment programmes for adolescents have been disappointing because of low participation, high attrition and low quit rates.

Conclusions: Adolescent smoking is influenced by a range of environmental and biological factors, and treatments aimed at helping adolescents to quit smoking have not been very effective up to now.

EVALUATION ISSUES

NATURE/NURTURE

Moolchan et al's study (2000) suggests that there are physical, psychological and social causes for smoking.

Psychological factors affecting mis-use

When looking at psychological factors that affect the mis-use of cigarettes, alcohol and drugs, it is useful to refer to the models of health behaviour discussed on pages 82–85. The Theory of Planned Behaviour for example, can be used to understand the cognitive factors that may contribute to a person starting, continuing or stopping smoking. If the Theory of Planned Behaviour is applied to an individual who smokes, then it might explain her behavioural intentions in the following ways:
- A negative attitude to the behaviour would be that smoking does not necessarily lead to health problems.
- A negative subjective norm would be that her friends did not particularly want her to give up smoking, or if they did, that the individual does not care what her friends think.
- A negative sense of behavioural control is that the individual feels that she cannot manage without cigarettes in the company of these friends.

If all these factors are in place then the individual is less likely to intend to behave in a positive way (i.e. not smoke), and, according to the model,

FOR CONSIDERATION

Behaviourist psychologists could argue that television programmes and films can encourage substance mis-use. Scenes in soap operas, for example, often make the association between alcohol and either celebrating a happy event, or coping with a crisis.

- Do programme makers have a moral duty to avoid such associations?
- Does the state have the moral right to impose restrictions on what should and should not be shown in the media?

FOR CONSIDERATION

- Why do you think that young people smoke cigarettes?
- Is it their fault that they started smoking in the first place?
- How easy is it to give up smoking?

behavioural intention leads to a change in the behaviour. Similarly, this model can be used to explain why people drink too much alcohol, or use harmful drugs.

The beneficial effects that adolescents, in particular, associate with smoking, drinking and taking drugs are important in explaining the initial use of these substances at this time. One area that has recently been the focus of research is risk-taking behaviour. Adolescence is the first time that young people have the opportunity to take risks as a mark of their growing independence. Involvement in the use of substances such as marijuana, tobacco and alcohol is seen to promote a person's sense of independence and maturity and enhance their own self-image (Moolchan et al., 2000). Peer pressure is also an important influence; a longitudinal study conducted in the USA showed that an important indicator of a high school student's moving from trial to use of cigarettes was their friend's smoking and approval and cigarettes being offered to them by friends (Robinson et al., 1997).

Some studies suggest that personality traits may indicate a likelihood that a person will smoke, mis-use alcohol or take drugs. Sensation seeking personality types and impulsiveness are traits thought to relate to alcoholism (Sayette and Hufford, 1997).

Many of the reasons why people become addicted to various substances can be related to the behaviourist theories of **classical** and **operant conditioning** and **social learning theory**. The idea that, at least in part, addictions are learned is one that has already been mentioned above.

- An example of alcohol use being reinforced by **classical conditioning** is the way in which people learn to associate drinking with having a good time, or celebrating something.
- In relation to **operant conditioning** people drink alcohol, for example, to increase pleasant feelings (**positive reinforcement**), and to decrease or avoid negative feelings (**negative reinforcement**).
- An example of **social learning** is the way in which people often drink because it is seen as acceptable behaviour by their friends and family. Children often **model** their behaviour on adults, and studies show that children of parents who smoke are twice as likely to do the same themselves than the children of parents who do not. Adolescents for whom alcohol becomes a problem are also likely to have parents who drink moderately to heavily themselves (Orford and Velleman, 1991).

Social and environmental factors affecting mis-use

Overall there has been a drop in the number of people who smoke in western countries. However, there has been a steady rise in the number of young women who smoke compared to young men. One interesting finding about the differences between adolescent male and female smokers is that young women who smoke tend to be self confident, socially skilled and rebellious, compared to young men who tend to be socially insecure (Moolchan et al., 2000).

Perhaps one of the most important cultural factors that has had an impact on female smoking over the last 30 years is the desire to be slim (Moolchan et al., 2000). There are many ways in which our society, like many others has promoted low body weight, and cigarette smoking is seen as a way to curb appetite. In the 1950s and 1960s women often advertised cigarettes, usually shown looking elegant and sophisticated. With changes in government legislation, and a reduction in advertising of cigarettes this reduced dramatically. However, in the last few years the number of models shown smoking cigarettes has increased. Although these are not identified with a particular brand, this still sends messages to young women who are conscious of the way they look.

Drug and alcohol use do not appear to be closely linked to gender differences, although fewer black and Asian women smoke and drink than white women. This has been related to cultural values and religion.

As has already been discussed, age is a crucial factor in developing addictions. Most people who go on to become addicted to nicotine start smoking in secondary school. Drug addiction also tends to develop in adolescence or young adulthood, although this does vary according to the type of drug, and is linked to availability.

Availability and social acceptability cannot be overlooked as factors that shape substance use and mis-use. Both cigarettes and alcohol are seen as perfectly acceptable in our society, and although there are age restrictions on when individuals can buy them (16 for cigarettes and 18 for alcohol) drinking and smoking often start much younger than this. Attitudes to drugs change over time, ecstasy was legal until its use became widespread in the 1980s, and the use of marijuana is now being examined in the light of research that suggests it may relieve certain medical conditions.

KEY STUDY

Predictors of risk for different stages of adolescent smoking in a bi-racial sample
Robinson, Klesges, Zbikowski and Glaser (1997)

Aim: To identify the risk factors associated with different stages of cigarette use in adolescents.

Sample: 6967 7th-graders from 39 schools in the middle southern USA.

Method: Each participant was given a wide-ranging questionnaire.

Results:
- 37.8 per cent of participants had tried smoking and 4.1 per cent said they were regular smokers.
- The best predictor of experimentation with cigarettes was the perception that they are easily available and affordable.
- Regular smoking was heavily influenced by cost.
- The children generally rated the social value of cigarettes as low, but were much more likely to smoke if their friends smoked.
- Girls were more likely to smoke if their parents did, but not boys.
- 39 per cent believed that smoking can reduce body weight and 4 per cent said they had actively used cigarettes as a dietary strategy.

Conclusions: A range of social influences contribute to both experimental and regular smoking, and this has implications for smoking prevention programmes.

EVALUATION ISSUES

SAMPLING/REPRESENTATIVENESS

Robinson et al's study (1997) has a very large sample which means that the results are likely to be representative and therefore generalisable to the southern USA.

3.3.3 PREVENTING AND TREATING SUBSTANCE ABUSE

One of the points made above was that it is in adolescence that many of these addictive behaviours start. There are two ways of dealing with addiction, either to prevent it happening in the first place, or to treat it once it has happened (i.e. help people quit using the substance). Most of the initiatives that are targeted at adolescents are directed at prevention rather than treatment.

Prevention

Most methods of prevention involve public health interventions. For children and adolescents these are often targeted through schools and colleges. For adults this occurs more commonly through the workplace, or in the doctor's surgery. Primary prevention programmes in schools often focus on the negative social aspects of smoking like bad breath and clothes that smell. Young people are more likely to be affected by this kind of message than one that is directed at the health risks, which seem remote to young people.

In the workplace, strategies are usually directed at smoking, and usually involve no smoking policies that ban smoking in all public areas. Smokers may be relegated to one smoking room that is open at particular times. However, studies on the effect of no smoking policies show conflicting evidence. Some show that there is a drop in overall smoking rates, but other studies suggest that people smoke more outside office hours to compensate.

Government legislative interventions take several forms. Recently in the UK, and in a number of other European countries, the Government has restricted tobacco advertising, or in some cases banned it altogether. These initiatives do seem to have reduced the number of smokers. The cost of smoking and drinking may also be prohibitive, especially for children. Ogden (1996) applies the Health Belief Model to this by pointing out that higher price might be a perceived cost and an incentive to change behaviour. There are now also many places where smoking is banned, such as aeroplanes and tube trains. Some restaurants and bars operate no smoking policies. It could be argued that in the long run this will cause the cues to smoke and drink to be removed, but it might simply mean that people just go elsewhere instead.

Doctor's surgeries are effective places to promote health education messages, and people in waiting rooms are a passive audience for posters and leaflets. More important perhaps is the view of the doctor as a credible source of information.

Quitting

There are a number of different ways to treat people who have a problem with a particular substance. There are various drug treatments for smokers and drug users that can help them to reduce and finally quit taking a substance, and there are various behavioural and cognitive therapies that can be used.

Relapse prevention

This approach to treatment recognises that there is a risk of relapse and tries to focus on the situations in which this might occur. Rather than focusing on the lapse as a failure, this approach tries to help patients identify the situation that caused a lapse or might cause a lapse in the future, and to develop strategies to cope, or to avoid the situation in the first place.

Skills training

The ability to cope involves skills training in which a person is encouraged to develop their assertiveness, so that they develop strategies to refuse a drink or a cigarette, for example. People are also encouraged to use behavioural strategies such as chewing gum, or doing something in particular when they have a craving for alcohol or cigarettes. Skills training also encourages people to use support groups.

Self-help groups

Many alcoholics, drug users and smokers gain a great deal of support from self-help groups such as Alcoholics Anonymous. These groups meet to discuss the experiences of those who are trying to abstain or control a

CD-ROM

For a study that investigates the benefits of GPs advising their patients not to smoke, see Health: Additional key studies: Russell et al. (1979).

EVALUATION ISSUES

EFFECTIVENESS/RELIABILITY

Prevention or treatment methods need to be judged on their level of effectiveness. This can be measured in terms of the number of people engaged in a specific behaviour (e.g. the percentage of young people who smoke) or the success rate of a treatment programme (e.g. the percentage of people who are still clean six months after the start of the treatment). However, self-report measures are unreliable in this area, as people tend to underestimate or lie about their use, and more objective measures can be expensive and intrusive.

dependence. Members can discuss their fears, and get social support from other members, who can reassure and encourage them.

Aversion therapies

Aversion therapies involve trying to extinguish the behaviour by introducing unpleasant stimuli, for example electric shocks or unpleasant pictures or films. Smokers are sometimes encouraged to smoke continuously as an aversive therapy. This behaviourist technique, based on the theory of classical conditioning, is relatively effective, but cannot be used for all smokers.

KEY STUDY

Successful treatment of smokers with a broad-spectrum behavioural approach
Lando (1977)

Aim: To compare a 'broad-spectrum' treatment programme for smokers (i.e. using a range of techniques) to a control group receiving aversive conditioning only.

Sample: 16 men and 18 women recruited by an announcement in the local newspaper in Iowa, USA. The mean age of participants was 31.2 years and they had been smoking an average of 12.4 years. The mean number of cigarettes smoked a day was 28.7.

Method: Before the experiment, participants kept a diary of their smoking for one week, to provide baseline data. They were then randomly assigned to two groups. The experimental group received six 45-minute treatment sessions over one week. They were told that smoking was a learned activity rather than an addiction and that the treatment was designed to disrupt their normal style of smoking. During the week they were urged to smoke as much as possible (at least twice their normal amount) and the researchers even set up daily 'laboratory smoking' sessions, in which participants were made to smoke continuously for 25 minutes. They were told that they would be expected to abstain from smoking after the week was over, and were asked to come to seven follow-up sessions over the next two months. During these one-hour sessions, participants discussed the difficulties they were facing in giving up smoking. They also had to sign contracts promising to pay a fine for every cigarette smoked and providing self rewards for successful abstinence. The control group were told that their treatment would consist of one week's aversive conditioning, and then they would have to maintain abstinence on their own.

Results: 76 per cent of experimental participants (as opposed to 35 per cent of controls) were still not smoking after six months.

Conclusions: Lando concludes that this broad-spectrum approach, combining aversion therapy, rewards and punishments, social support and attitude change is potentially a very effective way of helping people stop smoking.

SECTION A EXAM QUESTIONS

a Describe one theory of substance abuse. [6]
b Discuss the validity of theories of substance abuse. [10]

a Describe one method of preventing substance abuse. [6]
b Discuss the problems of researching methods of preventing substance abuse. [10]

a Describe one method of quitting substance abuse. [6]
b Contrast one method of quitting with other methods of quitting substance abuse. [10]

EVALUATION ISSUES

ETHICS

It could be argued that behaviourist treatments are not as ethical as other treatments, as they attempt to manipulate behaviour, sometimes using unpleasant methods. Self-help groups could be argued to be more ethical as they respect the individual's right to more autonomy.

? FOR CONSIDERATION

Most people would agree that it is better to prevent young people from mis-using substances in the first place, than to attempt to treat them once they are physically of psychologically addicted.

• Do you feel that prevention programmes have been effective with you and people you know?
• What do you think is the best approach to encouraging people to quit mis-using a particular substance?

CD-ROM

For Section B sample exam questions see Health: Sample exam questions.

3.4

HEALTH AND SAFETY

Accidents are a major cause of death and illness in the UK. Some groups are more vulnerable than others. Children, disabled people and old people are particularly vulnerable to accidents, and men are more likely to die from accidents than women. Accidents are the most common cause of death in people under 30 years of age. **Health and safety** initiatives are aimed at reducing the frequency and severity of accidents. This section examines different types and causes of accidents and then questions whether the concept of **accident-proneness** has any validity. It concludes by describing ways in which accidents can be reduced.

3.4.1 DEFINITIONS, CAUSES AND FACTORS AFFECTING ACCIDENTS

Accidents are usually caused by more than one factor. Pheasant (1991) argues that an accident may be caused by a combination of unlikely circumstances that cause an unexpected event. A recent example of this, which had tragic consequences, was the series of circumstances that came together to cause the crash of the French Concorde just outside Charles de Gaulle Airport (Paris) in July 2000. The crash was caused by a piece of metal that punctured one of the tyres of the plane. This sent shrapnel up into the wing, bursting the fuel tanks, which caused the fire. The small piece of metal had fallen off the fuselage of another plane that had taken off on the same runway minutes before Concorde. Runways at airports are inspected for debris several times a day. However, on this particular day another factor that may have precipitated the problem was that the morning inspection of the runway at Charles de Gaulle had been postponed because of a fire drill. Concorde had been flying for nearly 30 years with no fatalities, and in this one accident over 100 people were killed.

When an accident is as serious as this, or when it is on a large scale, it is sometimes referred to as a **disaster** or a **catastrophe**. Sometimes catastrophes are caused by what are known as 'acts of God'– natural disasters such as earthquakes or floods – but more often disasters are caused by human error or mechanical failure, as in the case of the Concorde crash. Even with mechanical failure, human error may be the cause because the equipment was not checked carefully enough or it was mis-used in some way. Pheasant argues that accidents are either caused by **'unsafe behaviours'** or they are caused by **'unsafe systems'** in the work place. With the former it becomes necessary to change the behaviour, and with the latter to change the system.

Causes of accidents

Roberts and Holly (1996) list what they call the 'basic causes' of accidents in hospital settings. These could also be applied to other workplaces:
* Inadequate equipment or maintenance of equipment: inadequate or inadequately tested equipment increases the risk of accidents occurring.
* Abuse or mis-use of equipment, or failure to check equipment: these can all cause harm. Roberts and Holly cite an example of a boy who

KEY DEFINITIONS

Pheasant defines an **accident** as '... an unplanned, unforeseen or uncontrolled event, generally one which has unhappy consequences' (1991, p. 176).

EVALUATION ISSUES

ETHICS

Researchers who believe that accidents are mainly caused by unsafe systems would argue that it is unethical to blame individual human error as this leads to misplaced guilt and a failure to tackle the root cause of the problem. In contrast, people who believe that the cause of an accident is unsafe behaviour, would criticise those who blame the system on the grounds that it lets the culpable individuals off the hook.

suffered irreversible brain damage caused by a foreign body passing from an anaesthetic tube into his trachea and remaining there unnoticed, obstructing his airway for long enough to cause brain damage.

- Inadequate work standards: risks can develop through a lack of training and supervision.
- Lack of knowledge: this could be how to use equipment safely and effectively, for example.
- Inadequate physical or mental capacity to do the job required: either because the person is physically unable, or because he or she may be drinking too much, or has some kind of mental illness.
- Mental or physical stress: this can make people vulnerable to accidents. It appears that most of these are to do with human error on some level.

Roberts and Holly go on to describe the types of error that health care professionals can make that can lead to accidents in a hospital setting. They describe situations in which what they call type I and type II errors can occur:

- **Type I** errors are due to 'omission' through a lack of knowledge about up-to-date or acceptable practice, for example, inadequate diagnosis or treatment being given in an Accident and Emergency department of a hospital.
- **Type II** errors occur through 'commission', that is, when something is done that should not have been done. For example, a surgeon might take out the wrong kidney, or sever an artery through lack of concentration.

KEY STUDY

What are the principal causes of accidents with bicyclists?
SWOV Institute for Road Safety Research (1997)

Aim: To investigate the specific factors that contribute to the incidence of cycle accidents.

Sample: Victims of cycling accidents in Amsterdam were selected by means of a stratified random sample. Participants were divided into three groups; cyclists who sustained an injury while riding, stationary cyclists and cycle passengers. All victims had been taken to hospital as a result of the accident, but only 19 per cent were admitted, the other 81 per cent returned home after first aid treatment.

Method: Participants were given a written questionnaire to complete.

Results:
- 53 per cent of the accident victims fell while riding, 29 per cent collided with another party and 24 per cent collided with an object.
- 7 per cent of respondents attributed their accident to a technical cycle defect; 28 per cent blamed their own behaviour; 27 per cent blamed the behaviour of other road users; 14 per cent blamed the condition of the road surface; and 24 per cent attributed their accident to 'other causes'.
- 8 per cent said that the accident would have been avoided if the cycle had been better maintained.
- 30 per cent of the cyclists whose accidents occurred at night and who were riding without lights said the accident would have been avoided if they had put their lights on.

▶

- 4 per cent of cyclists were wearing helmets and they suffered fewer head injuries despite the fact they tended to ride considerably faster.
- For bicycle passengers (i.e. children in cycle seats), 73 per cent caught their feet between the spokes; 70 per cent of cycles had no wheel spoke cover, or a broken one, and 20 per cent of cycle seats were regarded to be of poor quality.

Conclusions: This study appears to suggest that in the main it is unsafe behaviours that cause accidents rather than unsafe systems. The authors make four specific recommendations on the basis of their research:
- there should be legal quality requirements in the manufacturing of bicycles
- adults should be made more aware of safe child transport (wheel spoke covers and better cycle seats)
- the wearing of cycle helmets should be promoted
- road surfaces should be improved.

Some psychologists are interested in whether there are certain types of people who are more likely than others to have, or cause, accidents. One of the causes of accidents is sometimes related to what is often referred to as 'accident proneness'.

3.4.2 PERSONALITY AND ACCIDENT PRONENESS

The concept of accident proneness is one that has been studied by many different psychologists. Some studies suggest that there are those who are 'risk takers' and those who are 'risk avoiders', and the basis of their behaviour is their overall attitudes to risk and danger and their view of the world. There are some people who seek out the adrenaline rush they experience from racing a car or parachuting out of a plane, and there are other people who would never engage in what they would consider to be such high-risk activities.

Studies of accidents in childhood sometimes use the term **'injury-prone personality'** to describe what happens to some children. Aggression is a predictor of injury in childhood, as is over-activity, and boys are three times as likely to be injured as girls (Pitts, 1996). However, Jaquess and Finney (1994) argue that economic deprivation is a more important indicator of the likelihood that a child will have an accident. They studied a group of economically deprived children who were participating in a summer camp scheme and found that a disproportionately high number of the children who had accidents at the summer camp had also had accidents in the preceding year, and went on to have further accidents in the year after the summer camp.

The idea that some people are accident prone, or have accident-prone personalities, may be to do with psychological or physical characteristics, or the situation in which a person is working, for example, some people may be exposed to more risks than others. Pheasant (1991) describes accident proneness in terms of 'personal characteristics' such as cognitive abilities and personality traits (for example, how extrovert a person is) and 'transient states', which may be to do with illness or mood (something that affects the person, but is not lasting). He argues that extroverts, for example, have more accidents than introverts, perhaps because they are more impulsive. He also argues that accident-prone people may have problems with their cognitive abilities. For example, accident-prone drivers may have what is called 'field dependence', that is, they are not very good at extracting relevant information from a complicated perceptual field.

Psychoanalytic theory can be used to explain accident proneness as a form of withdrawal from a situation. Early studies, for example Hill and Trist (1953), have shown that accident-prone workers are also likely to have higher absenteeism than other workers, and these studies have drawn parallels between accident proneness and absenteeism, as both being examples of 'withdrawal behaviour'.

In terms of transient states, Pheasant (1991) cites the inevitable example of menstrual periods making women more accident prone. Illness is also likely to make people more accident prone, either because they are not physically capable of performing the tasks they are trying to do or because their illness makes them lose concentration. Similarly, mood can have an effect on concentration and a person's ability to think clearly and positively about what they are doing.

? FOR CONSIDERATION

- Do you know someone whom you consider to be 'accident prone'?
- What leads you to this belief?
- Why do you think this person has so many accidents?

KEY STUDY

Accident proneness: the history of an idea
Haight (2001)

This is a review article tracing the history of the concept of **accident proneness** in relation to traffic accidents.

The concept of 'accident proneness' was first used when Greenwood and Woods (1919) noticed that accidents to women working in munitions factories during the First World War were not occurring according to the probability distribution one would expect by chance. They discovered that, for each individual woman, accidents were distributed according to the expected distribution, but that some women had a higher average number of accidents than others. This average value was defined as 'accident proneness'.

The concept of accident proneness was attractive as it implied that it was not someone's fault if they were clumsy, but there was no way of determining an individual's level of accident proneness in advance. Over the next 30 years, hundreds of papers were published attempting to find some kind of psychological measure that would correlate with people's accident experience, with no success.

Shortly after the Second World War, researchers began criticising the concept of accident proneness and Johnson (1946) reviewed 200 studies and showed that the statistical conclusions of each one were logically unwarranted. Arbous and Kerrich (1951) described accident proneness as '... a figment of the imagination resulting from wishful thinking'. By the late 1950s, 'accident proneness' had fallen into disuse and disrepute and the concept was struck a fatal blow in the 1960s by Ralph Nader and William Haddon, who argued that vehicle design, rather than driver characteristics, was the key factor in road accidents. Attention was focused on making cars safer rather than the diagnosis and removal of 'accident prone' drivers.

Recently, however, interest in the driver as a factor in accidents has started to re-emerge with the discovery of a suitable villain that everyone could blame; the drunken driver. Traffic police are trained to spot drunk drivers and tend not to look for the cause of accidents in road design or vehicle ergonomics. Of course, the difference between being a 'drunk driver' and being 'accident prone' is that the former is morally reprehensible, whereas clumsiness is perfectly excusable.

▶

Haight concludes by pointing to three causes of road accidents:
- factors internal to the driver
- factors related to the road
- purely random factors.

He argues that the third set of factors have been greatly underestimated, probably because people feel that if no blame can be attached, then no countermeasure can be prescribed. However lightning is a random factor, and it is possible to deal with this by installing lightning rods. Seat belts are similar to lightning rods in that they ameliorate the effect of random factors in traffic accidents. Haight finally suggests that the search for the 'accident prone personality' was a search for a scapegoat and that advances in car and road technology have meant that more and more accidents are caused by random factors. The goal should be to reach a situation in which 100 per cent of accidents are caused by random factors.

3.4.3 REDUCING ACCIDENTS AND PROMOTING SAFETY BEHAVIOURS

Where young children are concerned, it is usually adults who have to take responsibility for promoting safe behaviours and preventing accidents. It is therefore adults who are targeted in health promotion and accident prevention campaigns rather than children. There are some messages that can be conveyed to children such as road safety, for example, the Green Cross Code in the 1970s, which is currently being conveyed by two cartoon hedgehogs. In contemporary society, however, there are fewer messages conveyed through the media, and more being taught in schools through Personal, Social and Health Education (PSE).

Wortel et al. (1994) describe four safety behaviours that parents can engage in that prevent accidents among pre-school children:
- educating the child about risks
- adequate supervision of the child
- making sure that the child's environment is safe
- giving first aid when an accident has happened.

Some studies suggest that parents must understand the importance of their own role in eliminating risk and preventing accidents. In their survey, Langley and Silva (1982) found that only 39 per cent of parents whose child had had an accident in the pre-school period changed their behaviour to prevent further accidents. Most of the parents who did not change their behaviour did not feel that it was possible to prevent the accident.

The workplace is one of the obvious targets for accident prevention campaigns and the promotion of safe behaviours. Some risk is unavoidable in certain jobs, for example, in occupations such as fire-fighting, deep-sea diving and fishing at sea, there is an inevitable risk that goes with the job. However, where possible these risks are minimised.

Oborne (1982) (cited in Pitts, 1996) uses a learning theory approach to understanding safety. He argues that often safety routines and practices take a lot of time, and that these behaviours are less likely to be reinforced than behaviours that are often quicker and easier, although more risky. It is useful therefore to focus on ways of making safe behaviours easier, and less time consuming to perform.

Pitts (1996) argues that there is now agreement in the literature on safety about how to try to prevent accidents in the workplace. She lists the following actions as the most important:

- to eliminate the hazards from the workplace
- to remove the individual from exposure
- to isolate the hazard
- workers can be issued with personal protection, such as protective clothing.

A paper which describes how managers should deal with what it calls 'accident repeaters' suggests that companies must strengthen 'safety culture' by using education and training, rather than blame and punishment to address the problem (SSA, 2003). Involving the workforce and seeking their views and participation in programmes of accident prevention will enable people to take greater personal control of their own safety. Defining clear targets for reducing accidents, and closely monitoring and reviewing the effectiveness of such programmes gives 'repeaters' a greater sense of self-efficacy in their ability to reduce the number of accidents in which they are involved, without apportioning blame.

The use of cycle helmets

A number of recent studies have looked at initiatives to encourage safe behaviour in children and adults alike, such as laws to make the use of seat belts compulsory for everyone. In her chapter on accidents and injuries, Pitts (1996) reviews recent studies on the promotion of the use of cycle helmets in various parts of the world. In a recent study in Maryland (USA), the use of cycle helmets was compared in three counties; one in which a law had been passed in 1990 making it mandatory for everyone under the age of 16 to wear an approved helmet, one in which publicity about proposed legislation was widespread, and one in which there were no laws or publicity.

Using self-report measures, the increase in helmet use rose from 11.4 per cent to 37.5 per cent, 8.4 per cent to 12.6 per cent and 6.7 per cent to 11.1 per cent respectively. Observations of the use of cycle helmets in the three counties found slightly different increases: from 4 per cent to 47 per cent, 8 per cent to 19 per cent, and in the county with no laws or publicity, there was a decrease during the period of survey. There is an obvious effect of legislation and campaigns.

A second study that shows the importance of what is known as passive intervention (legislation) was carried out in Australia. In one state in Australia, after ten years of health promotion about the importance of cycle helmets, their use was made compulsory by the state government. There was an immediate increase in helmet use from 31 per cent in March 1990 to 75 per cent a year later. The number of cyclists killed from head injuries decreased by 48 per cent in the first year, and by 70 per cent in the second year after the legislation had come into effect. This study explains the way in which the promotion of safe behaviours can be more effective if laws are passed to support these initiatives.

SECTION A EXAM QUESTIONS

a   Describe one study of causes of accidents. [6]
b   Discuss the problems of researching causes of accidents. [10]

a   Describe one study of personality and accident proneness. [6]
b   Discuss the validity of the concept of accident proneness. [10]

EVALUATION ISSUES

USEFULNESS

Pitts' suggestions for reducing accidents focus on actions taken by employers, rather than individual workers. These safety procedures are useful, but in the case of the first three actions they may not always be possible or practical.

EVALUATION ISSUES

THEORETICAL APPROACH/EFFECTIVENESS

Self-efficacy plays a key role in programmes aimed at reducing accidents. If people know what action they are supposed to take, and feel confident that they are able to take the appropriate action, then they are much more likely to do so. Thus making the initiative effective.

FOR CONSIDERATION

- 'There is no such thing as a genuine accident'. Do you agree with this statement?

CD-ROM

For Section B sample exam questions see Health: Sample exam questions.

3.5 PAIN

Everybody experiences pain at one time or another in their lives, and the most obvious association for most people is between pain and injury; the more severe the injury the worse the pain. However, it is not uncommon for people who have been severely injured not to feel pain (at least for a certain period of time) and for people who are not injured, or who have recovered from an injury, to experience lasting pain. These are examples of a number of phenomena that are difficult to explain and that have lead many of those who write about pain to describe what they call the 'puzzle' of pain (Melzack and Wall, 1996). It is very important to try to understand pain; according to Karoly it is '[the] most pervasive symptom in medical practice, the most frequently stated "cause" of disability, and the single most compelling force underlying an individual's choice to seek or avoid medical care' (1985, p. 461).

3.5.1 TYPES AND THEORIES OF PAIN

In attempting to define pain, Melzack and Wall say 'The word "pain" represents a category of experiences, signifying a multitude of different, unique experiences having different causes, and characterised by different qualities varying along a number of sensory, affective and evaluative dimensions' (1996, p. 46).

Some of the more simplistic definitions look at pain from a physiological perspective; others have tried to incorporate the emotional component of pain. For example, Merskey (1986) defines pain as 'an unpleasant sensory and emotional experience associated with actual or potential tissue damage, or described in terms of such damage'.

The purpose of pain

Pain performs several different functions:
- Prevention of further injury: pain caused by damage or injury can prevent a more severe injury from occurring, such as the warning pain from a blister on your foot telling you not to carry on walking.
- Learning: the pain caused by a burn would teach a child to avoid touching a hot stove.
- Aiding recovery: an ankle that has been sprained hurts to make the injured person rest the limb so that the injury can heal.
- Warning: pain can warn the individual of an underlying illness and encourage them to seek medical attention.

For most people pain can serve a number of useful functions. However, many people suffer from pain that appears to serve no useful purpose and this is more difficult to explain. Rather than providing any of the functions listed above, pain such as this can become an overwhelming problem in itself.

An example of pain that serves no useful purpose is phantom limb pain, where a limb may cause excruciating pain long after it has been amputated. A very high proportion of people who have had amputations suffer from phantom limb pain. Pain in phantom limbs can be severe and is described by sufferers as 'cramping, shooting, burning or crushing'.

KEY DEFINITIONS

Organic pain is that which is obviously related to tissue damage and when the pain is largely caused by that damage.

Psychogenic pain is where the underlying causes are seen to be largely psychological.

Acute pain is a more or less intense pain that lasts until healing has begun, for example, the pain of appendicitis or of a broken limb.

Chronic pain is much more persistent. It can be constant or intermittent and pain is said to be chronic if it has lasted for three months or more.

External pain is easy to locate at the point of injury, but **internal pain** is often 'referred' from the actual site of the problem. Referred pain can be acute or chronic. A well-known example of referred pain is caused by appendicitis. The first sign of appendicitis is often pain in the middle of the upper abdomen, while the appendix itself is on the lower right-hand side of the abdomen. With angina and heart attacks, severe pain is often felt in the left arm.

Types of pain

Pain is not just a simple sensation; it can vary in quality, intensity, duration, location and frequency. The type of pain a person experiences will differ according to the origin and duration of the pain. In describing different types of pain, people often refer to the distinction between organic and psychogenic pain, and between acute and chronic pain. Pain can be either organic or psychogenic and, at the same time, it is either acute or chronic.

Most contemporary researchers recognise that organic and psychogenic factors play an important role in the experience of most pain. The absence of an obvious cause does not imply that the pain is not real and this is important to recognise. A study by Gillmore and Hill (1981) showed that nursing students were seen to react less favourably to the pain of patients who did not have a specific diagnosis, in other words, they valued a medical diagnosis more than the patients' subjective experience. Chronic pain often increases or maintains high levels of anxiety. When medical treatment has not helped, the pain can take over the lives of those who suffer from it, and people with chronic pain can develop a desperate sense of helplessness and hopelessness. Acute pain describes temporary pain that is distressing, but the worry will reduce as the condition improves.

Injury without pain

This may take the form of either episodic analgesia or congenital analgesia.
- **Episodic analgesia** is a reasonably common condition and, in fact, most of us have experienced this at some time in our lives. It occurs when a person injures herself but does not feel the pain for some minutes or hours afterwards. Carlen et al. (1979) carried out a study of Israeli soldiers who lost limbs in the Yom Kippur War. They did not feel any pain from these injuries until many hours after they had been wounded. Carlen et al. describe how they were fully aware of the situation and were surprised that they felt no pain.
- **Congenital analgesia** is a very rare condition in which some people are born without the ability to feel pain at all. These cases are well documented and have generated a great deal of research.

Pain without injury

There are many people who feel pain for which there is no known cause. Back pain often has no apparent physiological basis, and certain types of headaches such as migraines have no proven pathology. Two types of pain that are often described as not being caused by injury are causalgia and neuralgia.

Early pain theories

Early pain theories describe pain within a biomedical framework. These theories work on the assumption that there is an automatic response to pain. Descartes was one of the earliest writers on pain. He believed that there was a direct pathway from the source of the pain to an area in the brain that detected painful sensations.
- **Specificity theory**: developed by Von Frey (1895), this theory argues that the body has separate sensory receptors for perceiving touch, heat and pain and that these receptors are sensitive to particular sensations.
- **Pattern theory**: this is based on similar assumptions of the relationship between the stimulus and the response. Pattern theory, however, argues that there is no separate system for perceiving pain and that the receptors for pain are shared with other senses such as touch. Pattern theory argues that too much stimulation can cause pain.

Some injured sports players may not feel pain until after the game

CD-ROM

For a case study of congenital analgesia see Health: Real life applications: Congenital analgesia.

KEY DEFINITIONS

Causalgia is described as severe, burning pain; it appears to occur at the location of some previous severe injury and is caused by nerve damage. Only a minority of patients with such wounds develop causalgia, but the pain lasts for a long time after the wound has completely healed.

Neuralgia occurs in various forms and like causalgia it is associated with peripheral nerve damage. However, neuralgia is a different type of pain to causalgia. Neuralgic pain is described as shooting or stabbing along the pathway of a nerve. Neuralgia can occur suddenly and often as the result of very gentle stimulation.

REDUCTIONISM

Neither specificity nor pattern theory includes a psychological approach to pain, and organic pain is seen as the only 'real' pain. Both these theories are reductionist, in that they assume that the sensation of pain has a single cause (i.e. tissue damage).

EVALUATION ISSUES

EFFECTIVENESS

Melzack and Wall's study (1965) gives a more effective explanation of pain mechanisms because it includes a psychological component, such as levels of anxiety if the injury is serious, or relief if it is minor.

- **Gate control theory:** Melzack and Wall developed the gate control theory in the 1960s to explain types of pain that were recognised but could not be understood in terms of the previous models of pain. Examples of this type of pain include phantom limb pain and tension headaches. The gate control theory also explains the lack of pain under certain circumstances, such as episodic analgesia after traumatic injury. Gate control theory adds a psychological component to an understanding of pain.

KEY STUDY

Pain mechanisms: a new theory
Melzack and Wall (1965)

This is not a clinical study but an article describing a new theory of pain (which almost 30 years later is still dominant in pain research). Melzack and Wall start off by describing specificity theory and pattern theory and by describing data that cannot be explained by these theories. For example, the fact that causalgia pain can be triggered by light touch contradicts the theory that there are separate nerves for pain and for touch and suggests that intense pain can be experienced by the central nervous system without much input from receptor fibres. Pattern theory, which suggests that pain is caused by overstimulation of touch receptors, is contradicted by physiological evidence that reveals that different types of receptor fibres do seem to perform different functions. Gate control theory allows for physiological specialisation of nerve fibres and for input from the central nervous system.

Melzack and Wall (1965) argue that there is a neural 'gate' in the dorsal horn section of the spinal cord. According to gate control theory there are three factors that affect our experience of pain and opening and closing the gate:
- the amount of activity in the small pain fibres
- the amount of activity in large peripheral fibres
- messages that descend from the brain.

The more intense the stimulus at the skin surface, the more activity there is in the pain fibres, which causes the gate to open; this results in a greater transmission of T cells which is experienced by the central

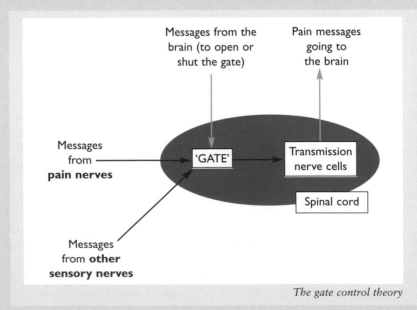

The gate control theory

nervous system as pain. The gate can be closed by increased activity in the peripheral fibres and by messages descending from the brain. However, the gate can also be opened by messages from the brain, such as anxiety about the pain. The notion that the brain can directly affect the transmission of T cells by closing the gate can explain episodic analgesia. Melzack and Wall describe how American soldiers injured at the Anzio beachhead during the Second World War denied that they felt any pain from their extensive wounds; they were so relieved at escaping alive from the battlefield that they perceived the injuries as very positive, and this attitude caused the gate to close.

Melzack and Wall conclude their article by describing two therapeutic implications of gate control theory. The first involves either decreasing the small pain fibre stimulation (by removing the source of the pain, or by the use of peripherally acting medication, i.e. by preventing 'pain messages' reaching the gate in the first place) or increasing the large peripheral fibre stimulation and thereby closing the gate. This last technique is called counter stimulation. Melzack and Wall describe a treatment for causalgia that involves bathing the limb in gently moving water followed by a massage. Crudely speaking, by blocking the gate with non-pain signals, fewer pain messages can get through. In this way, gate control theory explains why 'rubbing it better' really works. A second therapeutic implication suggested by Melzack and Wall is that gate control theory points the way to the development of new drugs that, instead of numbing the brain or the pain receptors, could actually serve to close the gate and lower the perception of pain.

? FOR CONSIDERATION

A third therapeutic implication of gate control theory, not mentioned by Melzack and Wall (1965), is to persuade the brain to send messages that will close the gate. Getting patients to think in a positive way about the pain, to stay calm and relaxed and to distract themselves from the pain can relieve the experience of pain.

- Do you believe that it is possible to use 'mind over matter' to reduce the perception of pain? If so, how?

3.5.2 MEASURING PAIN

Perception of pain is modified by a wide range of situational, behavioural and emotional factors making it an especially subjective experience. This means that other people's pain is very difficult to assess. However, the assessment of pain is important for research and as a diagnostic tool for medical treatment.

Physiological measures of pain

The most obvious way to measure pain physiologically is to assess the extent of the tissue damage or injury, that is, the more injured someone is, the more pain they must be in. However, as mentioned above, the relationship between tissue damage and the subjective experience of pain is very complex and this is not a valid way of assessing pain.

Muscle tension is associated with painful conditions such as headaches and lower backache, and it can be measured using an **electromyograph** (EMG), which measures electrical activity in the muscles. Some link has been established between headaches and EMG patterns, but EMG recordings do not generally correlate with pain perception (Chapman et al., 1985) and EMG measurements have not been shown to be a useful way of measuring pain.

Another approach has been to relate pain to **autonomic arousal** (i.e. the 'fight or flight' response). By taking measurements of pulse rate, skin conductance and skin temperature, it may be possible to measure the physiological arousal caused by experiencing pain.

Finally, since pain is perceived within the brain, it may be possible to measure brain activity, using an **electroencephalograph** (EEG), in order to determine the extent to which an individual is experiencing pain. It has

⚖ EVALUATION ISSUES

VALIDITY

The advantage of physiological measures of pain is that they are objective. On the other hand, they involve the use of expensive machinery and trained personnel. Their main disadvantage, however, is that they are not valid. For example, autonomic arousal can occur in the absence of pain; being wired up to a machine may be stressful and can cause a person's heart rate to increase. A person's perception of their pain may also affect their level of arousal; if someone is very anxious about the process of having his or her pain assessed, or else is worried about the meaning of the pain, this will cause physiological changes not necessarily related to the intensity of the pain being experienced.

been shown that subjective reports of pain do correlate with electrical changes that show up as peaks in EEG recordings; moreover, when analgesics are given, both pain report and waveform amplitude on the EEG are decreased (Chapman et al., 1985). However, the correlation between subjective experience of pain and EEG measures is relatively weak, and so this is not a completely reliable technique.

Observations of pain behaviours

People tend to behave in certain ways when they are in pain; observing such behaviour could provide a means of assessing pain. Turk, Wack and Kerns (1985) have provided a classification of observable pain behaviours.

- Facial/audible expression of distress: grimacing and teeth clenching; moaning and sighing.
- Distorted ambulation or posture: limping or walking with a stoop; moving slowly or carefully to protect an injury; supporting, rubbing or holding a painful spot; frequently shifting position.
- Negative effect: feeling irritable; asking for help in walking, or to be excused from activities; asking questions like 'Why did this happen to me?'
- Avoidance of activity: lying down frequently; avoiding physical activity; using a prosthetic device.

A commonly used example of an observation tool for assessing pain behaviour is the UAB Pain Behaviour Scale designed by Richards et al. (1982). This scale consists of ten target behaviours and observers have to rate how frequently each occurs. The UAB is easy to use and quick to score; it has scored well on inter-rater and test-retest reliability. However, correlation between scores on the UAB and on the McGill Pain Questionnaire is low, indicating that the relationship between observable pain behaviour and the self-reports of the subjective experience of pain is not a close one. This is perhaps not surprising given the number of social and psychological factors that can affect what people say about their pain (for example, anxiety, depression, the need to let others know how ill they are and so on).

Turk et al. (1983) describe techniques that someone living with the patient (the observer) can use to provide a record of their pain behaviour. These include asking the observer to keep a pain diary, which includes a record of when the patient is in pain and for how long, how the observer recognised the pain, what the observer thought and felt at the time, and how the observer attempted to help the patient alleviate the pain. Other techniques are to interview the observer, or to ask the observer to complete a questionnaire containing questions about how much the pain interferes with the patient's normal activities and social life, the effect of the pain on family relationships and on the moods of both patient and observer.

Self-report measures

Because pain is a subjective, internal experience, the assessment of pain is therefore best carried out by using patient self-reports, and this is by far the most frequently used technique.

The McGill Pain Questionnaire (MPQ), developed by Melzack (1975), was the first proper self-report pain measuring instrument and is still the most widely used today. Its design was largely based on research previously carried out by Melzack and Torgerson (1971).

CD-ROM

- One way to assess pain behaviours is to observe them in a clinical setting. Keefe and Williams (1992) identified five elements that need to be considered when preparing to assess any form of behaviour through this type of observation. See Health: Additional key studies: Keefe and Williams (1992).
- For a copy of the UAB Pain Behaviour Scale see Health: Measurement scales: UAB.
- Carroll (1993a) lists the different dimensions of pain that sufferers can be questioned about. See Health: Additional key studies: Carroll (1993a).

The first 20 questions on the McGill Pain Questionnaire (MPQ) consist of adjectives set out within their sub-classes, in order of intensity. Questions 1 to 10 are sensory, 11 to 15 affective, 16 is evaluative and 17 to 20 are miscellaneous. Patients are asked to tick the word in each sub-class that best describes their pain. Based on this, a pain rating index (PRI) is calculated; each sub-class is effectively a verbal rating scale and is scored accordingly (that is, 1 for the adjective describing least intensity, 2 for the next one and so on). Scores are given for the different classes (sensory, affective, evaluative and miscellaneous), and also a total score for all the sub-classes. In addition, patients are asked to indicate the location of the pain on a body chart (using the codes E for pain on the surface of the body, I for internal pain and EI for both external and internal), and to indicate present pain intensity (PPI) on a 6-point verbal rating scale. Finally, patients complete a set of three verbal rating scales describing the pattern of the pain.

KEY STUDY

On the language of pain
Melzack and Torgerson (1971)

Aim: To identify what words people use to describe pain for use in the design of a reliable and valid self-report pain measuring questionnaire.

Sample: Doctors, patients, university graduates and students.

Method: In the first part of the study, Melzack and Torgerson asked doctors and university graduates to classify 102 adjectives into groups describing different aspects of pain. They then asked a sample of doctors, patients and students to rate the words in each sub-class for intensity.

Results: As a result of the first part of the study, Melzack and Torgerson identified three major psychological dimensions of pain:
- sensory: what the pain feels like physically; where it is located, how intense it is, its duration and its quality (for example, 'burning', 'throbbing')
- affective: what the pain feels like emotionally; whether it is frightening, worrying and so on
- evaluative: what the subjective overall intensity of the pain experience is (for example, 'troublesome', 'unbearable').

Each of the three main classes was divided into a number of sub-classes (16 in total). For example, the affective class was sub-divided into tension (including the adjectives 'tiring', 'exhausting'), autonomic (including 'sickening', 'suffocating') and fear (including 'fearful', 'frightful', 'terrifying').

Conclusions: Pain is a multi-dimensional experience; as well as actual physical sensation, subjective experience of pain is affected by the individual's emotional response to the pain and by what the pain means to the individual. The experience of pain has physical, affective and cognitive components and any valid self-report instrument has to measure all three.

Measuring pain in children

An interesting problem with measuring pain is how to do this with children. It seems that even very young children experience pain in much

CD-ROM

For a copy of the McGill Pain Questionnaire (MPQ) see Health: Measurement scales: MPQ.

EVALUATION ISSUES

EFFECTIVENESS

The use of pain behaviour scales with children needs to be treated with caution; behavioural ratings do not always relate exactly to experienced pain intensity. Children can exhibit distress for emotional reasons, even when they are not in pain; some children can be very stoical and calm even though they are suffering. It is important to know the child well when interpreting her pain behaviours as signs of suffering.

FOR CONSIDERATION

Pain is a purely subjective experience and so is impossible to measure objectively, and subjective measures are open to bias.

- Why do you think that people may report, or act as if, they are in more or less pain than they really are?

the same way as adults, but the fact that they have limited or no language abilities creates difficulties in assessing their pain.

As children mature, they experience an increasingly wide range of physical sensations and learn to describe the various dimensions of the experience of pain in language that is used by those around them, i.e. family, friends, what appears on TV.

When questioning young children about their pain, it is important to use vocabulary they are familiar with and to take into account the developmental stage they are at. A 3-year-old would be unable to complete the McGill Pain Questionnaire not only because of the sophisticated vocabulary, but also because the child may not have learned, for example, to distinguish between internal and external pain.

Observing pain behaviours is a valuable way of measuring pain in children, particularly if they are too young to communicate through the use of language. Such pain behaviours include crying and moaning, flailing about and grimacing (although these behaviours are also carried out in the absence of pain).

Specific scales have been developed for recording pain behaviour in infants, both by parents and health care professionals in a clinical setting. Most ways of assessing pain in children consist of interviews or behavioural assessments, but researchers are now developing appropriate self-report methods. It is possible to ask children about the pain they are experiencing once they have reached a certain age, but certain specific skills are required. It is very important to establish a good rapport with the child and this may be especially difficult if he or she is suffering. Questions have to be asked in the right way, using terminology and concepts that the child is familiar with, and the interviewer has to ensure that the child does indeed understand the questions being asked. Difficult or upsetting questions should be interspersed with easier ones. Finally, the answers given by the children need to be interpreted correctly.

An increasing number of self-report scales for use with children are being developed. Children are able to report how much and what kinds of pain they are experiencing, but the scales used must be appropriate to their developmental level and their language abilities. For example, instead of asking young children to rate intensity of pain on a scale from 1 to 10, they can be presented with a set of line drawings of faces displaying increasingly severe expressions of pain.

The Varni/Thompson Pediatric Pain Questionnaire is an example of a self-report scale specifically designed for children (McGrath and Brigham, 1992). This includes visual analogue scales, colour-coded rating scales (in which the children have to pick colours that represent 'no hurt', 'a little hurt', 'more hurt' and 'a lot of hurt', then colour in a body chart) and verbal descriptors to provide information about the sensory, affective and evaluative dimensions of the pain. The questionnaire also asks parents and doctors for information about the child and the family's pain history (including pain relief interventions) and about socio-environmental factors that might affect the pain.

3.5.3 MANAGING AND CONTROLLING PAIN

Pain management is an area of research that has grown considerably in the last 20 years. Carroll (1993b) argues that this has lead to considerable change in the clinical practice of pain treatment. It is still very common for pain relieving drugs to be the main focus of treatment, especially with acute pain, although drugs are also often used for chronic pain without proper pain assessment. There are obvious reasons for this, when time and money are in short supply, and patients often have a long wait to be referred to a specialist who might use other methods to control and manage their pain. Attitudes to pain have changed and the idea that pain is to be 'expected' or is 'natural' is outdated. It is now considered that 'patients have a right to no pain' Carroll (1993a, p. 1). Pain relief in childbirth is a good example of this, where epidural blocks are widely used in contemporary maternity units. Some of the methods for controlling and managing both acute and chronic pain are considered below.

Medication

The most common form of treatment for both acute and chronic pain is medication:

- **peripherally active analgesics** (e.g. aspirin) act at the site of the pain
- **centrally active analgesics** (e.g. morphine) act within the central nervous system
- **local anaesthetics** (e.g. novocaine) act to block all messages from the site of the pain
- **indirect drugs** (e.g. anti-depressants) work by improving mood (and closing the 'gate').

The main ways of administering drugs for acute pain are either through injection or pills. One technique for giving intravenous painkillers is through patient-controlled analgesia. This involves the use of an infusion pump where the patient can press a button to administer a dose of the drug. The doses are regulated by amount and frequency to prevent overdose. Using patient-controlled analgesia avoids the delay in treatment of pain by busy ward staff, and can also give patients a greater sense of control over their pain. Citron et al. (1986) looked at the effects of patient-controlled analgesia on a group of male cancer patients with severe pain. Citron found that their rate of morphine use declined dramatically over a period of two days, when they were able to dose themselves.

Surgical methods

Surgery is used, for example, in the treatment of trigeminal neuralgia where the nerve transmitting the pain messages is actually destroyed by means of a heated needle inserted into the face. The problem with this type of treatment is that it can cause numbness in the face around the site of the nerve, and occasionally can cause paralysis. Another more successful treatment for pain is synorectomy, where the surgeon removes inflamed membranes in arthritic joints. However, these procedures are usually only used as a last resort if all other methods have failed.

Physical therapy for pain

There are two main ways of using physical methods to alleviate pain; counter-irritation such as TENS (transcutaneous electrical nerve stimulation), and physiotherapy or massage.

- Counter-irritation: TENS machines are used by placing electrodes on the skin where patients feel pain, then stimulating the area with a mild electric current.
- Physiotherapy and massage: physiotherapy involves the use of exercises to enhance stamina and relieve pain. Some pain responds well to

? FOR CONSIDERATION

Different people cope with pain in different ways.

- Why do you think that some people are more resilient to pain than others?
- How good are you at coping with pain?
- To what lengths would you go to avoid experiencing pain?

⚖ EVALUATION ISSUES

EFFECTIVENESS

There are particular problems with using drugs to treat chronic pain, e.g. addiction, tolerance and possible side effects. In spite of these problems, medication is still commonly used for acute and chronic pain, not least because if used correctly, it can bring real relief from pain.

TENS – a physical method used to alleviate pain

Operant conditioning used as a treatment for pain is not effective for everyone, for example, those whose relatives and friends are not very supportive cannot always use this method. People with progressive chronic pain cannot be helped using this technique. Another problem in the use of this method is that some people may not want to engage in well behaviours, for example, those who are receiving some kind of benefit (such as disability payments, time off work and so on) for displaying sick-role behaviours.

It is important that distraction is realistic and credible; asking someone to carry out a pointless task to distract his or her attention may not work. Something more meaningful, however, such as reading a book or watching a film might give more lasting relief. Similarly, a limitation of the use of imagery is how well a person is able to use his imagination, as some people are better than others at this technique. Cognitive approaches, such as pain redefinition, require patients to be articulate and willing to think and talk about their pain. This means that well-educated people are likely to find this type of therapy more useful than other people.

CD-ROM

For a detailed discussion of other pain management techniques see Health: Real life applications: Other treatments for pain.

physiotherapy, for example, the pain of arthritis is eased by keeping joints supple, and neck and back pain often responds well to physiotherapy and massage. Sometimes this kind of therapy does not relieve the pain directly, but because it can increase strength and stamina, patients can engage in more activity as a distraction from the pain, enhancing their self-efficacy and control.

Behavioural approaches to chronic pain

Pain behaviours are a sign that a person is in pain. Fordyce (1973) identifies operant pain behaviours that are conditioned to exist because of a number of different reinforcers such as attention from family and friends. People who suffer from chronic pain often learn to avoid activities that they have previously associated with an increase in their pain. Operant conditioning attempts to remove the gains of sick-role behaviour by identifying and rewarding well behaviour. The two main aims of operant conditioning that follow on from this are to increase a patient's level of activity and reduce dependence on drugs (Turner and Chapman, 1982).

Cognitive approaches to pain

Redefinition is a process that involves a person replacing fearful or distressing thoughts about pain with more positive or realistic thoughts (Fernandez, 1986). Explaining clearly what causes a chronic pain or giving accurate information about a procedure that has not yet taken place can help patients redefine how they feel about the experience when it happens. Reducing anxiety may reduce the expectation of pain and therefore the experience of it (Anderson and Masur, 1983).

Distraction is a method where those in pain focus on a non-painful stimulus in their immediate environment. Doctors' treatment rooms often have pictures on the walls (especially for children) to distract attention away from any uncomfortable or painful procedure. Magazines and books also help to focus attention away from the cause of the visit. Beales (1979) described the use of distraction in a study that looked at how nurses distract children with conversation while a doctor is stitching a wound. Often children noticed no pain until the doctor commented on some aspect of the procedure, at which point Beales points out the children start to notice the pain.

Patients can learn to use **imagery** by focusing on an image that is incompatible with or unrelated to the pain. This is sometimes referred to as non-pain imagery or guided imagery (Sarafino, 1994). An example of this might be a warm relaxing image, such as a beach or other place that the patient might enjoy. Imagery works well with mild to moderate pain, rather than strong pain (Ralphs, 1993).

Pain clinics

Pain clinics have been developed specifically to treat chronic pain. Pain clinics focus on a multidisciplinary approach to the management and control of pain. Clinics use assessment and treatment methods that involve a number of different components, for example, drug therapy, physical treatments, psychotherapy and cognitive and behavioural approaches. The aim of the pain clinics is to reduce a person's pain, improve his lifestyle, enhance social support, allow personal control and reduce drug intake and the use of medical services. Pain clinics will use the treatments described above in addition to a whole range of other treatments.

a   Describe one theory of pain. [6]
b   Contrast one theory of pain with another theory of pain. [10]

a   Describe one way of measuring pain. [6]
b   Discuss the validity of measures of pain. [10]

a   Describe one method of controlling pain. [6]
b   Discuss the effectiveness of methods of controlling pain. [10]

CD-ROM

For Section B sample exam questions
see Health: Sample exam questions.

3.6 STRESS

? FOR CONSIDERATION

In modern life, we are often presented with threatening situations that cannot be dealt with effectively by increased physical activity (this can happen when driving in traffic, for example). If the flight or fight response leads to increased physiological arousal, and this is not 'used up' by increased physical activity, it can leave one feeling 'edgy' (this process may partly account for road rage).

- Can you think of any other situations in which the fight or flight response can have a negative impact?

Stress is one of the areas in which the interaction between psychology and health is most obvious. It is generally accepted that stress provides a clear example of how a person's mental state can affect his or her physical condition, and vice versa. This section begins by looking at different theories about the causes and sources of stress, then goes on to describe the psychological and physiological effects of stress, different ways in which stress can be measured, and how stress can be controlled or managed.

3.6.1 CAUSES/SOURCES OF STRESS

The 'fight or flight' response and the General Adaptation Syndrome

One of the earliest theories of stress was developed by Walter Cannon in 1929. He noticed that animals and human beings undergo certain physical changes when they are threatened and that these changes consist of physiological arousal; they have the effect of providing the organism with the physical resources to escape from the threatening situation, either by fighting the threat or by running away.

In the 1930s, Hans Selye extended Cannon's theory to include the physical harm caused by over-arousal. He developed a theory called the General Adaptation Syndrome, which has three stages:

1 **The alarm reaction**: this is the same as Cannon's fight or flight response. Selye found that the increased physical arousal that occurs during this stage is linked to the release of hormones by the endocrine system. When these substances reach the bloodstream, the fight or flight responses are triggered. By undertaking experiments on rats, Selye concluded that organisms are incapable of maintaining a constant alarm reaction for lengthy periods of time; they die within hours. In order to survive, organisms enter a second stage, the stage of resistance.
2 **The stage of resistance**: here, the physiological arousal present during the alarm reaction is reversed to allow the body to recover, ready to face the next threat. However, even this process cannot be kept up for ever, leading to a third stage, the stage of exhaustion.
3 **The stage of exhaustion**: by now, the body is no longer able to recover from the alarm reaction. Selye describes it as 'at the end of a life under stress, this was a kind of premature ageing due to wear and tear' (Selye, 1977, p. 33).

Cognitive conflict

There are several theories that describe stress as a psychological response, rather than a purely physiological one. For example, Festinger (1957) developed the theory of **cognitive dissonance** in which inconsistencies in a person's cognitions lead to an unpleasant psychological feeling, which in turn can motivate attitude change. For example, if an individual thinks he or she should give up smoking but does not do so, this will lead to the feeling of dissonance. The individual is motivated to reduce this unpleasant feeling by either changing their behaviour (that is, giving up smoking) or changing their attitude (that is, by convincing themselves that they do not really want to give up smoking after all, or at least not yet). This theory

⚖ EVALUATION ISSUES

REDUCTIONISM

Cannon's fight or flight theory and Selye's General Adaptation Syndrome both define stress as an automatic physiological response to an external stressor. This is a reductionist approach as it ignores psychological and social factors.

describes stress as an unpleasant psychological feeling caused by inconsistencies or contradictions in a person's cognitions.

Cognitive appraisal theory

This theory, developed by Richard Lazarus and his colleagues in the 1970s (Monat and Lazarus, 1977) takes biological, psychological and social factors into account.

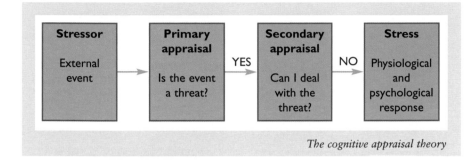

The cognitive appraisal theory

The experience of stress is triggered in the first place by an external event known as a stressor. Once the individual becomes aware of the stressor, she engages in **primary appraisal**; deciding whether the condition is a threat to her health. At this stage, the individual could deploy ego defence mechanisms to persuade themselves that they are not really ill; in this case, the stressor is not perceived as a threat, and the individual will feel no stress.

However, if the stressor is perceived as threatening, the individual moves to a stage known as secondary appraisal, in which she evaluates whether she feels able to cope with the demands of the situation. Someone with a high level of self-efficacy and a strong internal locus of control is more likely to feel confident about this, in which case little stress will be experienced. However, if the individual is not very confident about his or her ability to cope with the demands of the situation, then that individual will experience the physiological and psychological responses associated with stress.

KEY STUDY

Association of specific overt behaviour pattern with blood and cardiovascular findings
Friedman and Rosenman (1959)

Aim: To find a link between certain behaviour patterns and coronary heart disease.

Sample: Three groups of men were used:

Group A consisted of 83 men displaying a particular behaviour pattern, as follows:
- an intense, sustained drive to achieve self-selected goals
- a strong competitive attitude
- a persistent desire for recognition and promotion
- doing lots of things at once, constantly subject to deadlines
- rushing physical and mental tasks
- extraordinary mental and physical alertness.

These men were identified by colleagues at work and almost all of them agreed to take part in the study.

▶

Friedman and Rosenman's study (1959) seems to suggest that behaviour patterns relating to heart disease may be inherited although it could be argued that this is open to debate.

Group B also consisted of 83 men (businessmen or union officials) and were selected to match the group A sample in terms of age and physical characteristics, but to be exactly the opposite in terms of behaviour patterns.

Group C was made up of 46 unemployed blind men. These were chosen on the grounds that their visual impairments would lead to a lack of drive and ambition (like group B), but that they would exhibit a chronic state of insecurity and anxiety as a direct result of their disability.

Method: The researchers carried out the following assessments for each participant:
- A personal interview about parental incidence of coronary heart disease, past and present illnesses, hours of work and sleep, smoking habits, physical activity and dietary habits. The participants' behaviour during the interviews was observed for evidence of Type A behaviour (e.g. impatience).
- A survey of dietary and alcohol ingestion.
- A cardiovascular survey looking for medical indications of possible coronary heart disease.

Results:
- Group A men worked more hours per week (51 hours on average) than group B (45 hours). Group C men were all unemployed.
- Group A men were significantly more active than group B, but not than group C; all three groups showed similar sleep patterns.
- There was no difference in the calorie intake or the amount of fat eaten between groups A and B, although group C ate more than the other two groups.
- A greater proportion of group A men smoked cigarettes than the other two groups, and they also smoked more cigarettes a day on average.
- Group C men drank less alcohol than the other two groups.
- More group A men had a family history of coronary heart disease.
- On all the medical indicators of possible coronary heart disease, group A men seemed significantly more at risk than the other two groups (as much as five times more likely than group B).

Conclusions: Friedman and Rosenman concluded that men displaying certain behaviour patterns are more likely to contract coronary heart disease. Some possible confounding variables, such as sleep and diet can be eliminated at once, as there was no difference between the groups. Others (exercise, tobacco, hours of work and alcohol) were eliminated because there was no correlation within each group between these factors and the risk of coronary heart disease. The fact that group A men were more likely to have a family history of coronary heart disease led Friedman and Rosenman to speculate that the behaviour patterns associated with groups A and B may be partly inherited. This last conclusion has led to psychologists thinking of these behaviour patterns as personality traits.

CD-ROM

- For more information on how psychological and social factors can affect stress see Health: Real life applications: Psychosocial factors and stress.
- For a version of a Type A measurement scale see Health: Measurement scales: Type A measurement scale.
- For a description of the medical effects of stress see Health: Real life applications: Effects of stress.

Psychosocial factors and stress

The conclusions of Friedman and Rosenman (1959) suggest that being a Type A or a Type B personality may contribute to how stressed an individual gets, and that these personality traits may be partly hereditary. This represents a biological explanation of why some people get more stressed than others.

There are two reasons why it is useful to be able to measure people's levels of stress: first, it may help with clinical diagnosis, and second, it is necessary for carrying out research into the causes and effects of stress, and the effectiveness of specific coping techniques. Stress can be assessed either by measuring the stressors themselves or by measuring the effects of stress.

Measuring stress responses can be done by looking at the physiological effects of stress (either by measuring these directly, or asking people to report on their perception of how aroused they feel), the psychological effects (by using self-report techniques to assess mood and attitudes) or the behavioural effects (either by observing people's actual behaviour, or asking them, or others, to report on it).

The text that follows examines three of the techniques for measuring stress in more detail; physiological measures of stress responses, life events and daily hassles.

Physiological measures

The fight or flight response consists of increased physiological arousal triggered by hormonal changes. This leads to two different approaches to measuring stress physiologically:
- using blood or urine samples to measure hormone levels in the body
- using a polygraph to measure physiological arousal.

A polygraph is a machine that measures blood pressure, heart rate, respiration rate and galvanic skin response (that is, how much someone is sweating; this is done by passing a small electrical current across the surface of the skin and measuring the resistance).

The advantages of measuring stress in these ways are that they are reliable and objective and provide quantitative results. The disadvantages are that they are expensive, requiring specialist equipment and trained personnel. Also, physiological arousal is not simply affected by stress; pain can cause arousal, and an individual's level of arousal will be affected by other factors such as gender, weight, activity and consumption of substances. It is also feasible that having blood taken or being wired up to a polygraph machine actually causes stress in itself, detracting from the validity of these measurement techniques. Finally, physiological ways of measuring stress measure an alarm reaction; it is possible to feel psychologically stressed without experiencing immediate changes in physiological arousal.

Life events

One technique for assessing the stressors in an individual's life is to look at their social environment. Someone who is poor, the victim of harassment or discrimination, in a stressful job (for example, with long hours or that involves responsibility for other people's lives), or who has a difficult or disadvantaged home life is likely to be experiencing stress. However, this does not enable us to examine in detail the specific circumstances of a particular person. A more individualistic approach would be to ascertain how many actual stressful life events have taken place over a certain period of time, on the assumption that certain events in people's lives are going to cause them stress, and the more of these events that occur, then the more stress there will be.

The earliest attempt to create a life events scale for measuring stress was by Holmes and Rahe (1967). They established their Social Re-adjustment Rating Scale (SRRS) by asking a large (but not particularly representative)

CD-ROM

For a copy of the Social Re-adjustment Rating Scale (SRRS) see Health: Measurement scales: SRRS.

EVALUATION ISSUES

VALIDITY/ETHNOCENTRICITY OF THE SRRS

Apart from the fact that the SRRS seems very outdated (for example, 'wife beginning or stopping work' scores 26 points) and ethnocentric (for example, 'Christmas' scores 12 points), it has some other major problems. For instance, items such as 'death of a close family member' are ambiguous as people may interpret the word 'close' differently. Furthermore, the scale fails to take the meaning of the life event for the individual into account. 'Pregnancy', for instance, may be a very positive event for one individual and a personal disaster for another. All these points mean that it has problems of validity.

Although life events scales are cheaper than physiological measures (as they do not require specialised equipment), they are also less objective. Apart from the ambiguity mentioned on p. 123 in deciding whether a life event has actually happened, these scales are vulnerable to falsification.

![CD-ROM icon] CD-ROM

For a copy of a Daily Hassles scale see Health: Measurement scales: Daily hassles scale.

![scales icon] EVALUATION ISSUES

VALIDITY

Psychologists disagree about whether the life events approach or the daily hassles approach is the most valid way of measuring stress. Both techniques are currently used in practice. However, one advantage of life events scales is that they are slightly more objective; they simply ask the respondent to state whether specific events have occurred, whereas the daily hassles scale expects respondents to rate events according to severity.

sample to rate the degree of social re-adjustment required to adapt to 43 separate life events (such as 'death of a spouse', 'personal injury or illness', 'retirement' and so on). Items that were judged as requiring greater levels of re-adjustment were considered more stressful and had more points allocated to them (for example, 'divorce' was 73 points, 'son or daughter leaving home' was 29 points and so on). Individuals' levels of stress are measured by asking them to state how many life events have happened to them in the past 12 or 24 months, then the points for these items are added up.

An attempt to overcome the problem that the same event may cause different levels of stress in different people was built into a scale called the Life Events and Difficulties Schedule (see Harris, 1997). Without actually asking people about their subjective reactions to specific life events, this scale takes into account the likely meaning of each event for the person concerned on the basis of what most people with a similar background would feel. The interviewer uses a set of previously developed rules, based on extensive lists of precedents to translate the respondents' life events into a stress score (for example, 'pregnancy' would score much less for a married woman who already has a child than for a 16-year-old).

Daily hassles

Kanner et al. (1981) challenged the life events approach to measuring stress arguing, first, that the correlation between life events and stress-related disease is not as strong as people claim, and second, that the irritating, frustrating and distressing demands arising out of everyday life are more closely linked to stress. They called these demands 'daily hassles' and developed a scale that measures stress by asking people to rate how irritating or annoying these hassles are to them.

Kanner et al. also recognised that certain everyday events can have a positive effect on stress, and they called these daily uplifts. The Hassles Scale consists of a list of 117 hassles generated by the researchers (for example, 'misplacing and losing things', 'declining physical abilities', 'not enough time for the family', 'concerns about owing money', 'pollution'); similarly, the uplifts scale consists of 135 items (for example, 'being lucky', 'relating well with friends', 'getting a present', 'being complimented').

On both scales, respondents are asked to circle which items happened to them during the previous month, then rate each of these on a three-point scale relating to severity (for the hassles) and frequency (for the uplifts). Kanner et al. claim that their hassles and uplifts scales are a much better way of measuring stress and therefore predicting stress-related illness than life events scales.

KEY STUDY

Comparison of two modes of stress measurement: daily hassles and uplifts versus major life events
Kanner, Coyne, Schaeffer and Lazarus (1981)

Aim: To see whether the daily hassles and uplifts scales are more accurate in predicting stress than a life events scale.

Sample: 100 participants (52 women, 48 men; all white, well-educated and comfortably well off) were selected from a population of 7000 previously identified for another study in Alameda County, USA.

Method: Each participant was assessed once a month for ten consecutive months using:
- a daily hassles and a daily uplifts scale developed by the researchers
- a life events scale similar to the SRRS (Holmes and Rahe, 1967)
- the Hopkins Symptoms Checklist of psychological symptoms
- the Bradburn Morale Scale to measure psychological well-being.

Results: Kanner et al. found that the hassles scale was a better predictor of psychological symptoms than the life events scores. When the effects of the life events scores were removed, the hassles score and the symptoms were still significantly correlated. The uplifts score was positively related to symptoms for women but not for men.

Conclusions: From this study it seems that daily hassles are a more valid way of measuring stress than life events. Interestingly, daily uplifts may be useful in measuring stress in women, but not in men.

3.6.3 MANAGEMENT OF STRESS

This section describes several specific techniques for managing stress in the context of Lazarus' cognitive appraisal theory (see page 121). The diagram below shows how the stress management techniques relate to this theory.

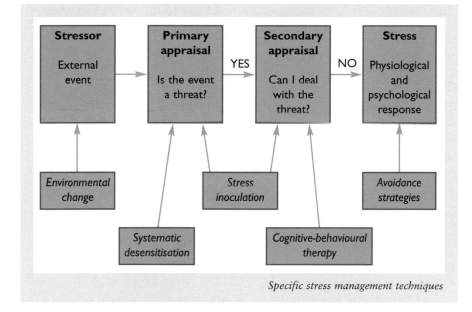

Specific stress management techniques

Environmental change

One way to prevent people from experiencing stress is to deal with the events and circumstances (that is, the stressors) that trigger the stress in the first place, for example, installing sound-proofing to eliminate noise pollution, breaking off a bad relationship, or deciding to stop taking part in dangerous activities.

Systematic desensitisation

There are circumstances in which an individual perceives a threat arising from a particular stressor, but this perception is somehow deluded or irrational. People with phobias or obsessive-compulsive disorders would fit into this category. For example, if a therapist has a client who is too anxious to leave his or her house, or has a phobia about a kind of everyday object such as balloons, it does not seem particularly helpful to

Systematic desensitisation is an effective behaviourist technique based on the principle of classical conditioning. In contrast a cognitive technique applied to treating phobias, in which the therapist explains to the patient that the anxiety-provoking stimulus is not actually threatening, is less effective as most people with phobias already recognise that their fears are irrational.

attempt an environmental change aimed at removing the stressor. Rather, it would be better to alter the individual's perception of threat.

Systematic desensitisation is a technique often used to help people with irrational fears (phobias). The patient is asked to relax and then presented with the anxiety-provoking stimuli at progressively more intense levels. Gradually, he or she stops associating the stimulus with anxiety or fear, and going out to the shops or balloons are no longer perceived as threatening.

Stress inoculation

Meichenbaum (1985) adapted the process of systematic desensitisation into a technique he called stress inoculation, in which people are exposed to stressful situations step-by-step, not only allowing them to get used to the situation and perceive it as less threatening, but also offering them an opportunity to develop specific coping skills and therefore to feel more confident about their ability to deal with the threat.

As participants are gradually introduced to the stressful situation, they are encouraged to express their thoughts and feelings through a series of self-statements. A child with a phobia about going to the dentist, for example, could be read stories about dentists and shown pictures before being taken for a first visit in which he or she would simply sit in the waiting room for a while. Eventually, the child could look into the treatment room, sit in the chair, become familiar with the instruments and so on, before treatment actually takes place. Specific coping skills relevant to this situation could include relaxation techniques in the waiting room or mental distraction during the treatment itself.

Cognitive-behavioural therapy

Cognitive-behavioural therapy (CBT) focuses on the secondary appraisal stage of the cognitive appraisal theory of stress in that it has the dual aim of encouraging participants to be realistic about their ability to cope with specific stressors (that is, challenging negative thoughts), and also to actually improve that ability by developing appropriate skills and strategies.

This form of therapy is commonly used to help people with anxiety and depression, and takes place in one-to-one therapy sessions, in group therapy, or even through self-help manuals. It incorporates a wide range of techniques. (See Gilbert, 2000 and Fennell, 1999).

Techniques used in cognitive behavioural therapy include:
- getting participants to examine the evidence to support their thoughts and feelings (for example, 'Why do you think that nobody at school likes you?', 'What makes you think that you cannot write this essay, have you successfully written an essay like this in the past?')
- considering alternative assumptions and conclusions (for example, 'Maybe your friend shouted at you because they are worried about something and not because they do not like you any more')
- writing down the advantages and disadvantages of a particular course of action in order to help clarify conflicts and dilemmas (this is particularly appropriate in cases where the source of stress is a difficult decision that has to be made)
- designing 'experiments' in order to test things out and rehearse new skills (this technique is similar to that of stress inoculation)
- questioning self-critical thoughts in order to develop a higher sense of self-efficacy.

CD-ROM

For a practical example of stress management see Health: Real life applications: Managing anxiety.

KEY STUDY

Brief cognitive therapy for panic disorder: a randomised controlled trial
Clark, Salkovskis, Hackmann, Wells, Ludgate and Gelder (1999)

Aim: To test the effectiveness of a briefer, more cost-effective cognitive treatment programme for panic disorder (Note: although the authors of this study refer throughout to their treatment as 'cognitive' it does have a behavioural component and consists of a form of CBT).

Sample: Patients with panic disorder were referred by GPs, psychiatrists and psychologists in Oxfordshire. They were then assessed to check that they satisfied the criteria for panic disorder (e.g. at least three panic attacks in the three weeks prior to interview), that they were free from other psychiatric disorders, that they had not received CBT for panic before, and that they were willing to accept random allocation to groups. 42 patients (aged 18–60) participated in the study.

Method: Patients were randomly divided into three groups:
- FCT: these patients received full cognitive therapy (12 one-hour sessions over three months)
- BCT: these patients received brief cognitive therapy (five one-hour sessions over three months)

Both these groups had two booster sessions in the following three months.
- Control: this group were put on a waiting list for three months and received no treatment during this time. At the end of the first three months, they were randomly assigned to one of the two treatment groups.

The treatment received by patients consisted of a mixture of cognitive techniques and behavioural experiments intended to modify misinterpretations of body sensations. For the BCT group, some of the treatment procedures were done using self-study modules.
- Module 1 described cases of panic attacks and helped patients recognise the symptoms of panic in themselves.
- Module 2 focused on patients' worst fears about the feelings they experienced in panic attacks and helped them find other, less frightening, explanations for their bodily sensations.
- Module 3 explained how the use of 'safety behaviours' can prevent cognitive change and helped patients identify their own safety behaviours (an example of a safety behaviour would be someone who feels that they need to hold on to the furniture in order not to fall over during a panic attack).
- Module 4 looked at behavioural experiments in which patients were encouraged to drop safety behaviours during panic attacks.

Patients were assessed on a range of measures (number of panic attacks, panic-related cognition, agoraphobic avoidance, etc.) by an independent assessor who was unaware of each patient's treatment condition (i.e. a double-blind design).

Results: Patients in the FCT and BCT groups did significantly better on all measures than the control group, but there were no significant differences in outcome between the two treatment groups.

Conclusions: CBT is a very effective way of treating panic disorder and a brief treatment programme involving less than half the amount of therapist time and self-study modules was as effective as the full treatment programme.

EVALUATION ISSUES

EFFECTIVENESS

Clark et al's (1999) study shows that CBT is very effective in treating panic disorders, even if the therapy is less than half the duration of a normal course.

Avoidance strategies

All the stress management techniques described above are problem focused in that they involve dealing with the external and internal causes of stress. An alternative approach is to use emotion-focused techniques in order to minimise the negative effects of stress. At first glance, it seems obvious that the first of these approaches is likely to be more effective. Simply making oneself feel less stressed without tackling the stressors themselves (for example, by taking stress-relieving medication) seems to be a short-term solution only. However, there are situations in which emotion-focused techniques are more appropriate, for example, where the individual is powerless to do anything about the stressor, or where the levels of anxiety are so high that tackling the root cause of the stress seems impossible.

Physiological techniques for dealing with the effects of stress include physical relaxation, biofeedback (in which patients are put in front of a machine that shows their heart-rate, breathing rate and blood pressure, and attempt to lower these by the use of their will), and the use of recreational drugs. If an individual complains to his or her doctor of feeling over-stressed, then there is a wide range of tranquillisers or anti-depressants that can be prescribed. Alternatively, people can use psychological avoidance techniques in order make themselves feel less stressed (see the section on ego defence mechanisms, page 292).

SECTION A EXAM QUESTIONS

a Describe one piece of research into sources of stress. [6]
b Evaluate research into sources of stress. [10]

a Describe one measure of stress. [6]
b Discuss the validity of measures of stress. [10]

a Describe one way of managing stress. [6]
b Discuss the problems of investigating stress management techniques. [10]

? FOR CONSIDERATION

- How good are you at managing your own stress?
- Which techniques do you use to lower your stress level?
- Which techniques are most effective, in the short term and in the long term?
- Are certain techniques more suitable for particular types of stress?

◉ CD-ROM

For Section B sample exam questions see Health: Sample exam questions.

ADHERENCE TO MEDICAL ADVICE

3.7

In the area of health care there is an increasing emphasis on self-care and personal responsibility for health. This is reflected in the need for patients to understand and adhere to complicated advice and information, and if necessary to treat themselves with a range of medicines.

Kent and Dalgleish (1996) describe a study in which many parents of children who were prescribed a ten-day course of penicillin for a throat infection did not ensure that their children completed the treatment. The majority of the parents understood the diagnosis, were familiar with the medicine and knew how to obtain it. Despite the fact that the medication was free, the doctors were aware of the study and the families knew they would be followed up, by day three of the treatment 41 per cent of the children were still being given the penicillin, and by day six only 29 per cent were being given it. This study very clearly illustrates the problem of non-adherence.

The costs associated with non-adherence can be high. The illness may be prolonged in the patient and he may need extra visits to the doctor. These are not the only costs, however, as the person may have a longer recovery period, might need more time off work or even require a stay in hospital. Non-adherence may lead to as much as 10–20 per cent of patients needing a second prescription, 5–10 per cent visiting their doctor for a second time, the same number needing extra days off work, and about 0.25–1 per cent needing hospitalisation (Ley, 1997).

3.7.1 WHY PATIENTS DO NOT ADHERE

The reasons why patients do not adhere are complex and may be multidimensional. For example, the more complex the regime the less likely the patient is to adhere fully, and the more likely he or she is to make mistakes. The length of the treatment also has an effect; the longer the treatment the lower the adherence becomes. Some adherence involves the person making a change in a behaviour that is long standing, and this type of adherence also appears harder to maintain than adherence to a regime for taking medication.

Perceived threat

Kent and Dalgleish note that mothers who felt their children were susceptible to illness and who perceived this threat as serious were more likely to adhere to the treatment regime prescribed by their doctors and to keep appointments for check-ups than mothers who did not hold these beliefs. It is also true that patients' decisions to stop following advice are affected by how serious they perceive their illness to be. In studies where patients have been asked why they have stopped taking medication, the findings suggest that it is because they no longer feel ill and no longer consider their illness to be serious enough to need the medication. Caldwell et al. (1970) also considered that this was connected with the patients' perceptions of their sick role; when they no longer felt ill the role no longer applied, and so they felt less inclined to follow the doctor's advice in the way that they did when they felt ill.

KEY DEFINITIONS

Adherence (sometimes referred to as **compliance**) is defined as people doing what they are told to do; in this case adhering to the advice or medication given to them by a health professional. This advice may involve adherence to medical regimes (such as taking pills), lifestyle changes (such as cutting down on foods high in fat or stopping smoking) or preventive measures (such as using condoms or wearing cycle helmets).

EVALUATION ISSUES

EFFECTIVENESS

The Health Belief Model and the Theory of Planned Behaviour (see pages 82–85) both stress the importance of perceived threat (made up of perceived seriousness and perceived susceptibility) in making health decisions. Kent and Dalgleish (1996) argue that it is not the ideas about seriousness on the part of the doctor that are important, it is the perceived seriousness of patients that make them adhere effectively. The way in which they see their perceived illness does have a significant effect on the likelihood that they will adhere.

Rational non-adherence

One reason why people might not adhere is that they are concerned about the possible side effects of their treatment. Adherence decreases if the treatment seems worse than the illness, and this is particularly true if it affects cognitive functioning. Patients are prepared to suffer some physical discomfort as a side effect – nausea, for example – but are less willing to suffer problems with concentration, visual disturbance or sense of balance (Kent and Dalgleish, 1996).

Related to this is the idea that the diagnosis or treatment may be wrong. While the majority of patients have to trust their doctors, whom they accept must be more knowledgeable than themselves, doctors still need to convince their patients that they know what they are talking about (they must be credible), and that the treatment they are suggesting is the best one for that particular patient. Non-adherence may become a problem if the patient does not believe in the effectiveness of the treatment offered.

Social support

Family circumstances may affect the likelihood that a person will adhere to medical advice. The level of social support a person receives from family and friends may be important in affecting how far they adhere to the medical regime given to them. Whether or not family members are living in the same house as the patient is also an indicator of how effective this will be (Kent and Dalgleish, 1996). When family members are present, they suggest that adherence is twice as good as when the patient is living alone.

KEY STUDY

Depression is a risk factor for non-compliance with medical treatment
DiMatteo, Lepper and Croghan (2000)

Aim: Depression and anxiety are common in medical patients and are normally associated with decreased health care utilisation. This is a review article of studies aimed at finding correlations between patients' non-adherence to medical treatment and their levels of anxiety and depression.

Sample: The authors looked at 25 studies carried out between 1968 and 1998, 12 of these were about depression and 13 about anxiety.

Method: In order to qualify for this review, previous studies had to measure adherence and patient depression or anxiety and involve patients who were not being treated for depression or anxiety, but had been asked to follow a medical regime by a doctor who was not a psychiatrist.

Results: The studies examined by the authors showed that there seems to be no correlation between anxiety and non-adherence, but a strong correlation between depression and non-adherence.

Conclusions: Compared with non-depressed patients, depressed patients are three times more likely to fail to adhere to the medical regime that has been prescribed for them. The authors point out that it remains to be determined whether treating depression will result in improved patient adherence but that the recognition of depression as a risk factor for non-adherence has the potential to improve health care outcomes for some patients.

EFFECTIVENESS

The finding of DiMatteo et al.'s study (2001) is effective because in showing that there is a correlation between depression and non-adherence the practical implications are that doctors can screen patients for depression, and hence predict non-adherence or, on the other hand, take the fact of non-adherence as a indicator of possible depression, and treat the patient accordingly.

Self-efficacy and conformity

Payne and Walker (1996) suggest that because people who have low self-esteem and low self-efficacy do not value their own ideas, they are more likely to adhere to medical advice because they value what the doctor tells them more than someone with high self-esteem. Similarly, a number of factors have been shown to be important in predicting the likelihood that a person will conform (or adhere), and one of these is if a person perceives that someone else has greater expertise than them (i.e. has a 'powerful others' locus of control); this is often true of how people regard doctors.

Another factor that affects conformity is that people are more likely to conform if they have relatively little information on which to base their judgement; the less information, the higher the rate of conformity. This may seem counter-intuitive, but combined with some of the other factors already mentioned, Payne and Walker (1996) argue that many situations relating to patient adherence in health care are like this. Doctors tend to explain things to their patients on a 'need to know' basis, which leaves patients with little real knowledge about their condition or treatment.

Patient–practitioner relationships

It has been found that when patients believe their doctors to be concerned and interested in them, they are more likely to adhere to the medical advice given by a doctor. While status can have some effect, and the advice of a consultant might carry more weight than the advice of a less experienced doctor, it is still the individual approach of a particular doctor that is of the most importance to patients. This approach is reflected in the style of the doctor. Should doctors be distant and professional, or should they be more personal and friendly? There is no concrete answer to this question, as individuals prefer different doctoring styles, but it illustrates the idea that there are recognisable differences in style, that have been labelled by health psychologists as doctor-centred, co-operative and patient-centred:

- **Doctor-centred** relationships between patient and doctor revolve around the doctor being active and the patient being passive in the interactions that they have. The doctor is in charge and does not consider the patient's opinions in the decision-making process about treatment.
- **Co-operative** (sometimes known as guidance co-operative) relationships between patient and doctor involve the doctor adapting the treatment to some degree to meet the wishes of the patient, but ultimately retaining the power and authority in the interaction.
- **Patient-centred** relationships between doctors and patients are more about a process of negotiation, where the patient can accept or reject the doctor's opinion, and is given the choice about how best to fit the available treatment options into her own lifestyle.

Different patients vary in which style they prefer their doctor to adopt, but problems arise most frequently when a doctor and patient have different styles and expectations. However, many studies show that a doctor-centred approach is the one that elicits the lowest level of adherence.

The complexity of the message

The complexity of the instructions that patients have to follow can have a marked effect on their ability to understand and remember what they must do. One of the most straightforward problems for patients is remembering what doctors have told them to do, and it is important not to underestimate the importance of this simple problem, as it can seriously undermine adherence in spite of the best intentions a patient may have. Kent and Dalgleish (1996) cite studies that have found that patients forget what doctors have told them within a very short period of time. Different studies have found that patients can forget up to 50 per cent of what they were told almost immediately after their consultation.

? FOR CONSIDERATION

- Have you ever failed to do what you were told by a doctor?
- Why didn't you adhere to the medical advice you were given?
- What were the consequences of your non-adherence?

One of the difficulties with measuring adherence is the different ways in which patients might not adhere. These might vary from missing the occasional dose of medicine, to taking it at the wrong time or in the wrong amount, to deciding not to take it at all, for example, patients who are feeling better or who want to discover how they feel if they do not take it. Another difficulty is that patients may well not be honest about the extent of their non-adherence.

• Why do you think this may be the case?

⚖ **EVALUATION ISSUES**

EFFECTIVENESS OF PHYSICAL MEASURES OF ADHERENCE

Physical measures, although reliable and objective, may not be very effective in giving the full picture. Although a blood or urine test might be able to determine whether a particular drug is present, and in what quantity (although it is not always possible to do this), it cannot always tell when the medication was taken or how regularly it is taken. It is also time consuming and expensive to use this process in order to check adherence.

⚖ **EVALUATION ISSUES**

EFFECTIVENESS OF SELF-REPORT MEASURES OF ADHERENCE

Self-report measures are particularly problematic, for some of the reasons outlined earlier. People tend to over-report their adherence. This may be deliberate for a particular reason such as rational non-adherence, but often patients report what they think the doctor wants to hear or what they wish they were able to achieve. Sometimes patients' perception of what they are doing is inaccurate because they may not fully understand the method of treatment or the implications of not sticking to the regime they have been given. This method of checking on patient adherence (although one of the most widely used) is therefore very subjective and open to bias, and cannot be fully effective.

There are various ways to measure patient adherence. These can be divided into those that use physical measures, those that use self-report measures, and those that use observational measures.

Physical measures

Physical measures of measuring patient adherence include:
• blood tests
• urine tests
• outcomes, that is, an improvement in patient health, such as a drop in blood pressure.

Biochemical tests can determine whether the medication has been used recently, and in some cases how much has been used. Adherence can be measured in terms of outcomes, although people may get better even if they do not adhere.

Self-report and behavioural measures

Self-report and behavioural measures of patient adherence are the most commonly used ways of measuring adherence and include:
• patient's reports
• devices that measure how many times the pill container is opened or measures out doses of medicine.

Doctors, especially those in general practice, are most likely to ask their patients whether they are sticking to their regime. Ley (1988) noted that while 78 per cent of patients reported themselves to be adhering to their regime, more objective measures estimated the level of adherence to be closer to 46 per cent.

KEY STUDY

A cohort study of possible risk factors for over-reporting of antihypertensive adherence
Choo, Rand, Inui, Ting Lee, Canning and Platt (2001)

Aim and background: The measurement of medicinal adherence is difficult because direct observation of medication use is usually impossible. The most practical way of measuring adherence is to ask patients, but this can be very inaccurate. Assuming that patients who do not get better must have been non-adherent can unfairly mislabel some adherent patients as non-adherent. Other, more 'objective', techniques such as pill counts, drug levels, pharmacy dispensing records and electronic medication monitors are difficult to implement due to cost or obtrusiveness. This study aims to compare self-reporting with electronic monitoring for patients with high blood pressure.

Sample: 286 individuals (mean age: 55 years; age range: 18–84 years; 50 per cent female; 33 per cent black; 67 per cent college graduates) on single-drug anti-hypertensive therapy in a large managed care organisation in New England.

Method: Participants who consented were given a baseline questionnaire that asked them about their socio-economic status, the medication they were on, their adherence, their health beliefs, their health status and the amount of social support they had access to. During the monitoring period of three months, they were asked the following adherence question 'While you were using the special medication bottle, on how many days in an average week did you forget to take a pill?' At the same time, their 'actual' adherence was measured by means of electronic monitoring vials containing the medication. Participants were informed of the purpose of the electronic medication monitor.

Results: 21 per cent of participants admitted to missing doses of medication on one or more days per week, but the electronic monitoring showed the true figure to be twice as high (42 per cent). Participants who over-reported their adherence tended to be of lower socio-economic status, to have a lower perceived health risk from non-adherence and to be on more than one daily dose of medication.

Conclusions: There is a clear tendency for patients to over-report their adherence; factors related to socio-economic status, perceived risk from non-adherence (i.e. a health belief) and the dosing regimen may influence how accurately patients recall and report their adherence.

Observational measures

Observational measures of patient adherence include:
- reports of friends and/or family
- the doctor's estimate
- attendance at the clinic or surgery.

Reports of family and friends can be helpful, as this participation usually means that the relatives or friends are offering social support alongside the observation. This should mean that the patient will receive encouragement to adhere to the advice they have been given.

3.7.3 IMPROVING ADHERENCE

At the beginning of this section it was suggested that whether or not a patient adheres to medical advice depends on a number of factors. It is difficult to differentiate between these factors in terms of their importance, as this will vary for each individual patient. However, there are some very simple and effective ways of improving patient adherence that seem to work for the majority of patients, whatever their circumstances.

KEY STUDY

Fluoxetine for depression in diabetes
Lustman, Griffith, Freedman and Clouse (2000)

Aim: Depression is prevalent in patients with diabetes and previous research suggests that it may be linked to non-adherence to the treatment regime. This study aims to see whether treating diabetic patients with the anti-depressant fluoxetine will improve their level of adherence.

Sample: The researchers advertised for participants within the Washington University Medical Center, and in the city of St Louis. Volunteers with a history of suicidal behaviour, bipolar mood disorder, any psychotic disorder, current alcohol or substance abuse disorder or who were currently on psychoactive medication were excluded. The remaining volunteers were screened for depression and the final sample consisted of 60 patients with diabetes and major depression.

Method: Participants were randomly assigned to two groups; one receiving fluoxetine, and a control group receiving identical looking

EVALUATION ISSUES

EFFECTIVENESS/VALIDITY AND RELIABILITY OF OBSERVATIONAL MEASURES OF ADHERENCE

- Observational measures are reasonably valid, especially if they are used in conjunction with another method such as a patient self-report or a blood or urine test. Often the person carrying out the observation helps to reinforce the treatment programme, and encourages the patient to adhere, so this is an effective method of measuring adherence and ensuring that adherence is maintained.
- According to research, one of the least valid ways of measuring adherence is to ask the doctor about their patient. While regular check-ups and attendance at clinic can be seen as reliable methods, doctors themselves often overestimate the adherence of their patients (Ley, 1997).

EVALUATION ISSUES

EFFECTIVENESS/USEFULNESS

Lustman et al.'s (2000) study shows how effective drug therapy can be for the treatment of depression, and is useful because the diabetics who took fluoxetine had greater control of their diabetes after only 8 weeks.

placebos. The design was double-blind, meaning that neither participants nor the researchers who were assessing them knew who had been given the fluoxetine. Over a period of eight weeks, the experimental group were given daily doses of fluoxetine, and the level of depression for all participants was measured using the Becks Depression Inventory (BDI) and the Hamilton Rating Scale for Depression (HAMD). Blood sugar levels were monitored to measure how much control the diabetic patients had over their illness, and this was assumed to be a valid measure of the patients' adherence to their medical regimen. Participants who remained seriously depressed after the eight-week study was over were referred for further psychiatric treatment or psychotherapy.

Results: As expected, the participants who were given fluoxetine were significantly less depressed than the control group. They also showed much healthier blood sugar levels.

Conclusions: After only eight weeks of being treated with fluoxetine, diabetic patients tended to develop better control over their blood sugar levels, which was very probably as a result of better adherence to the treatment regime. It is, of course, possible that the fluoxetine had a direct effect on their diabetes, but this study provides strong evidence to suggest that one way of improving patient adherence (at least in diabetic patients) is to reduce their level of depression.

Social support

As was suggested earlier, the involvement of friends and family can encourage adherence. This can happen in a general way, perhaps with the friend sitting in on the consultation so that he is aware of the treatment programme; or the supporter can reinforce the treatment by actually being involved in the administration of the medication or monitoring the patient's use. If this is not possible, then support groups can play a very important role. Support groups for particular illnesses often encourage coping strategies, and can offer help and guidance about treatment and medication.

Providing information

There is evidence to suggest that the more instructions a patient is given, the less he remembers. One way of dealing with this problem is to reduce the number of instructions and to make them as straightforward as possible. Another way of dealing with the problem of recall is to base instructions on the psychological theory of the primacy effect. The basis of this theory is that people remember best the information that they hear first. Ley (1988) suggests that in simplifying communication the doctor should take account of all these factors, as well as using repetition, stressing the importance of adherence and making follow-up appointments.

Behavioural methods

Behavioural methods of encouraging patients to adhere include providing prompts and feedback for the patient, for example, in the form of labelled pill dispensers or those that make a sound at the time the medicine should be taken. Telephoned reminders can also be used, as can rewards for adherence. Rewards might range from the approval of the doctor (social reinforcement) to a reward from the relative or support group, such as a trip or meal out (material reinforcement).

Ley (1997) lists a straightforward set of guidelines for improving adherence, which includes a number of the examples given earlier:

FOR CONSIDERATION

Some researchers argue that medical students tend not to be trained in improving adherence as effectively as they might be.
• What specific training should they receive in this area?

- to make the treatment as simple and quick as possible
- to find out what individual patients' health beliefs are in order to evaluate whether the patients have an accurate perception of the seriousness of their condition and are aware of their susceptibility to the condition or the consequences of that condition
- to tailor the treatment to fit in with the patient's lifestyle
- to make sure patients are satisfied with the amount of information given about the treatment
- to make sure patients understand exactly what they must do and understand why the treatment is as it is
- to provide written guidelines for the treatment
- if possible, to involve a friend or family member in the process of treatment and adherence
- to provide support and back-up, and sort out problems as they arise.

SECTION A EXAM QUESTIONS

a Describe one study of why people do not adhere to medical advice. [6]
b Evaluate research into non-adherence to medical advice. [10]

a Describe one way of measuring adherence/non-adherence. [6]
b Discuss the validity of measures of adherence/non-adherence. [10]

a Describe one way of improving adherence. [6]
b Discuss the problems of improving adherence. [10]

EVALUATION ISSUES

EFFECTIVENESS

While all of the techniques described above may be very effective in improving adherence, there are certain practical implications that have to be considered. For example, some of the suggestions may take up additional time and money that doctors feel they do not have. However, improving adherence may save time and money in the long term, as patients will not need to visit the doctor as frequently.

CD-ROM

For Section B sample exam questions see Health: Sample exam questions.

3.8 THE PATIENT–PRACTITIONER RELATIONSHIP

Underlying many of the factors affecting levels of adherence is the relationship between the doctor and the patient. The section that follows examines how this relationship can also affect other aspects of the treatment process, such as how satisfied patients feel with the way they are being treated and how effective the communication is between the patient and the doctor.

3.8.1 PRACTITIONER AND PATIENT INTERPERSONAL SKILLS

Interpersonal skills are very important in shaping doctor–patient interactions. The information that is gained during the consultation is of vital importance in the diagnosis and treatment of any condition, since in order to carry out diagnostic testing a doctor must first understand the nature of the problem. Studies that have looked at whether patients are happy with their treatment have focused on the process of the consultation. Some of these studies have discovered that whether or not patients are satisfied with their treatment relates to how the doctor communicates with them and whether, in the process of communicating, the patients feel they have been given enough information by the doctor, which has been explained sufficiently clearly. Effective communication between doctor and patient is fundamental in situations where patients are expected to make important decisions affecting their own or a relative's health. It can reduce patient anxiety about procedures and treatments and without effective communication patients can become unsure or unhappy about their treatments, which may lead to non-adherence or mistrust of the doctor.

The effectiveness of doctor–patient communication has a great deal to do with the interpersonal skills of the doctor concerned. According to Weinman (1997), many doctors have their own attitudes and beliefs about the patient's role in the consultation process. However, Weinman considers that one of the most important things the doctor must understand is the patient's own expectations. This is a difficult process and one that requires a great deal of sensitivity. The interviewing technique that doctors develop is important because it has a lot to do with how satisfied the patient is with the consultation.

KEY DEFINITIONS

Kent and Dalgleish (1996) argue that there are both **cognitive** and **emotional components** to a patient's satisfaction with their care.

- **Cognitive satisfaction** relates to how happy patients are with their understanding of the explanation of their diagnosis, treatment and prognosis.
- **Emotional satisfaction** is related to the doctor's non-verbal behaviour. The doctor's tone of voice is important in showing interest, and body posture can be equally important. Patients want their doctor to appear interested and concerned by their condition.

KEY STUDY

Communication in the hospital setting: a survey of medical and everyday language use among patients, nurse and doctors
Bourhis, Roth and MacQueen (1989)

Aim: To examine the use of language between health professionals and their patients.

Sample: The study was carried out using three groups of respondents: 40 doctors, 40 student nurses and 40 patients.

Method: All respondents were asked to complete a written questionnaire about the use of medical language (ML) and everyday language (EL) in the hospital setting. The first section asked about the amount of medical and everyday language the respondent used in the hospital with members of the other groups in the study. The second section asked the respondent to estimate how much ML and EL other members of their own group used with the other groups in the study. The third section asked the respondent to evaluate (on a 7-point scale) the appropriateness of the use of ML and EL among the study groups in the hospital setting. The fourth section asked the respondents for background information and about their attitudes to various communication issues in the hospital.

Results:
- Doctors' self-reports of their efforts to use EL with their patients was confirmed by other doctors but not by patients or nurses.
- Patients' self-reports stated that they themselves used EL, although those with limited knowledge of ML used this to try to communicate better with doctors.
- Doctors did not encourage the use of ML by their patients, and reported the strongest preference of all the groups for patients to use EL.
- Nurses were seen by all three groups as 'communication brokers' between the EL of the patient group and the ML of the group of doctors.
- All three groups agreed that EL was better for use with patients, and that use of ML often led to difficulties in communication.

Conclusions: One of the overall conclusions drawn from the results of the study was that doctors used ML as a way of maintaining their status in relation to their patient group and as a way of maintaining the power and prestige accorded to doctors within society as a whole. The fact that nurses were prepared to 'converge' with the doctors and patients is taken as an indication that they are less status conscious than doctors. Bourhis et al. suggest that the results show that experienced doctors and nurses, as well as students, might benefit from courses focused on helping people to understand the motivation behind the use of language and to improve effective communication between hospital staff and patients.

Increasingly doctors are trained in interpersonal skills in medical school and are taught skills such as active listening. Active listening can help the patient to communicate more easily. It includes using eye contact, open-ended questions and responding positively to patients, while listening to their descriptions of their problems. These kinds of skill are taught through role-play and observation with real patients. There is evidence that this kind of training does improve communication skills (Weinman, 1997).

Maguire and Rutter (1976) argue that a useful strategy for medical students is to use video to see themselves interacting with patients. In one study students were divided into two groups; one in which they used video during a consultation with a patient, and a control group in which they did not have access to this feedback. The video group were also given written notes of a model for interviewing recommended by Maguire. A week later the medical students in both groups interviewed a second patient. The experimental condition gained three times as much relevant information from the patients as the control condition.

In their model of an appropriate interviewing technique, Maguire and Rutter distinguish between the content of the interview (that is, what information is collected) and the process (how it is collected):

The content of the interview should contain the following:

- The details of the problem: the doctor should recognise that there may be more than one problem and that these could be emotional and social, as well as physical. Having established the main cause of concern, the doctor should ask if there are any other problems the patient might like to mention.
- The impact on the patient and his family: the doctor should find out about the effect of the illness on the patient's relationships with family members, work, and his emotional state.
- The patient's view of their problems: a patient's belief about his illnesses is very important as it can often explain the patient's behaviour in relation to his illness.
- Predisposition to develop similar problems: the patient's background and early health record may be important.
- Screening questions: these questions should provide the opportunity for the doctor to touch on areas that have not been covered. If, for example, the doctor has concentrated on the patient's physical well-being then she might ask about that patient's psychological state.

The process should include the following:
- Beginning the interview: the doctor should greet patients appropriately and show them where to sit if they have not met before, in order to put them at their ease.
- The procedure of the interview: to help patients understand what is happening, the doctor should explain how the interview will take place in order to put patients at their ease. For example, the doctor should explain if she is going to take notes.
- Obtaining relevant information: doctors frequently interrupt their patients, but it is better for doctors to ask open-ended questions, then encourage a response from the patient by using active listening techniques.
- Ending the interview: it is important to allow time at the end of a consultation to allow the patient to ask questions and for the doctor to review and sum up what has been discussed.

One of the most difficult areas of communication relates to breaking bad news. Trainee doctors are now taught how best to convey this kind of information and how to deal with distressed patients or relatives. What is appropriate for one person may be difficult for another to cope with. Non-verbal behaviour may give clues as to how the patient feels, whether he is embarrassed, for example. Hogbin and Fallowfield (1989) describe a simple procedure that can help to communicate difficult or sensitive information concerning certain types of diagnosis. They recommend using a tape-recording of the consultation, which the patient can then take away. This helps patients and relatives to go back to information that they may have found too overwhelming to grasp at the time of the consultation.

Non-verbal communication

As well as the obvious need for verbal communication, a great deal of the interaction between doctor and patient takes place at a non-verbal level. Non-verbal communication can influence verbal communication to a considerable degree. Whether patients perceive their doctor to be receptive and understanding may relate to the non-verbal signals he or she is giving, just as much, if not more, than the verbal ones. Similarly, the response of patients will tell the doctor a certain amount about how they are feeling, how receptive they are to what the doctor may be saying, and how likely they are to be able to adhere to the treatments and instructions that have been given.

Facial expressions, as well as other forms of body language, can be closely related to a person's emotional state and can indicate to the doctor how the patient is feeling. Eye contact tells the patient and the doctor whether the other person is listening. Eye contact can be used by a doctor to gauge whether patients understand what is being said, whereas patients might look at the eye contact a doctor is making in order to gauge his interest in and empathy with them. Videotaped research suggests that patients talk while the doctor makes eye contact, and hesitate or stop talking when the doctor looks away or starts making notes.

Posture and position in the consulting room can facilitate or hinder a consultation. Leaning towards the patient can be interpreted as the doctor showing interest in that patient. Restlessness on the part of the doctor or the patient can be interpreted in different way; as perhaps the desire to end the consultation if it is the doctor who is being restless, and as a need to change the subject or to say something else on the part of the patient. The doctor must be particularly aware of these cues, so that he understands how to help the patient say what they want to communicate to the doctor, without feeling intimidated or uncomfortable in the presence of the doctor.

The position of the doctor, and also of her desk, is important. Status can be related to the position of the desk in a consultation room, and to the position of the doctor behind the desk.

? FOR CONSIDERATION

Consider the doctors you have been treated by during your lifetime.
- How good were they at communicating with you?

3.8.2 PATIENT AND PRACTITIONER DIAGNOSIS AND STYLE

Payne and Walker (1996) are interested in how doctors engage in what Goffman (1971) calls impression management. They argue that learning to become a doctor involves more than just knowledge, claiming that being a doctor also includes looking and behaving like a doctor. It involves a hierarchical relationship with nursing staff and patients, in which it is clear who is in charge. They argue that doctors have their own particular 'props' that set them apart from other people in the hospital and define who they are; the stethoscope and the white coat, for example. This role management is used by some doctors more than others and researchers have identified two distinct 'practitioner styles' as described below.

Doctor-centred relationships

These are characterised by the doctor taking charge of the interaction. There have been a number of studies carried out into the interaction between doctors and their patients, and these appear to confirm that the majority of interactions are still based on a doctor-centred style. These studies categorise interaction into groups of behaviours. In a meta-analysis of some of these studies, Roter (1989) found that doctors:
- give information in approximately 35 per cent of their communications
- ask for information in about 22 per cent of their communications
- talk positively to the patient about 15 per cent of the time and negatively about 1 per cent of the time
- try to relate to their patients 10 per cent of the time (what Roter calls 'partnership building') and make social conversation 6 per cent of the time.

However, patients give information about 50 per cent of the time, and ask questions less than 10 per cent of the time.

EVALUATION ISSUES

EFFECTIVENESS

It may well be the case that patient-centred consultations take more time than doctor-centred ones, and this is an important issue for hard-pressed and busy GPs. However, some doctors would argue that this is effective because by spending more time on individual consultations, the patients adhere to their medical treatment more and are less likely to return for a follow-up consultation, so time is saved in the end.

EVALUATION ISSUES

EFFECTIVENESS/USEFULNESS

Savage and Armstrong's study (1990) is interesting because it shows that for many patients the most effective style was directive. This is useful because it can help doctors become more aware of patients' needs (although this may not be the same for all patients).

FOR CONSIDERATION

- Would you say that your own GP was more doctor-centred or patient-centred?
- What do you think of your GP's consultation style?

Patient-centred relationships

These are characterised by more open-ended questions and allow more time for patients to raise their own concerns. It is often possible to tell the style of the doctor by the length of the waiting time in her surgery. Patients often choose which of the doctors to visit at the local practice depending on the nature of their problem. If it is a straightforward medical problem that they already understand and for which they may simply need some penicillin, the patient may choose one doctor. If their problem is less specific or they need some support and advice from their doctor, the person may choose a different member of the practice.

Although these styles have been described as quite different, one is not necessarily better or worse than the other. Individual patients prefer different styles and if they have a choice, they will chose to consult with the doctor who suits their own style best.

KEY STUDY

Effects of general practitioner's consulting style on patients' satisfaction: a controlled study
Savage and Armstrong (1990)

Aim: To compare the effect of different types of communication styles of doctors on their patients' satisfaction with their consultation. These styles are described as 'directing' and 'sharing'.

Sample: The study was carried out in an inner London general practice, where patients were free to chose which doctor they consulted. Some 359 participants were selected randomly, and from this original sample the results from 200 participants were used.

Method: The 200 participants were either given a directed consultation that included statements such as 'You are suffering from …', and 'It is essential that you take this medication'; 'You should be better in … days' and 'Come and see me in … days', or they received a sharing consultation that included statements such as 'What do you think is wrong?' and 'Would you like a prescription?'; 'Are there any other problems?' and 'When would you like to come and see me again?'. The consultations were tape-recorded. The patients were given two questionnaires, one immediately after the consultation and one a week later, to assess their satisfaction with the consultation.

Results: Overall the patients reported a high level of satisfaction with their consultations. However, the group who had received the directed consultation reported a higher level of satisfaction than those in the sharing group. The directed group reported significantly higher levels of satisfaction with the explanation given by the doctor, and with their own understanding of the problem, and were more likely to report that they had been 'greatly helped' than the sharing group.

Conclusions: The results show that the style of consultation does affect patient satisfaction, and appears to contradict contemporary conventional ideas that sharing decisions about treatment is popular with patients and enhances the relationship between doctor and patient.

Patient communication style

Like doctors, patients have different ways of communicating that can either help or hinder the doctor. For example, patients with the same condition may well focus on very different symptoms, and describe these to the doctor. The doctor has to be aware of the possibility of this happening. Some patients who go to see a doctor about a specific medical problem might actually have other problems they want to discuss with the doctor. Although the doctor needs to allow for the possibility of a range of problems presenting themselves, it can make it more difficult for the doctor to find the root cause of the problem. On the other hand, patients might find it difficult to express their symptoms clearly, and this again might make it possible for the doctor to misinterpret or misdiagnose.

A further consideration is that patients might also find it difficult to speak to the doctor for social or cultural reasons. It may be inappropriate for an Asian woman to see a male doctor, or if she does she may not feel at ease explaining symptoms. While this is obviously not the fault of the patient it can make it difficult to communicate effectively. Language barriers and cultural differences can sometimes be a problem, too.

3.8.3 USING AND MIS-USING HEALTH SERVICES

The publication Living in Britain – 2001 (Office for National Statistics, 2002) contains information from the General Household Survey (GHS), which has documented major changes in British households, families and society since 1971, and which includes a series of questions about health and the use of health services. Overall, females were more likely than males to have made use of health services. This may be partly due to women visiting practice nurses for reasons associated with family planning and pregnancy. However, men were more likely than women to have attended an outpatient or casualty department. Use was highest among children aged less than 5 and adults aged 75 and over.

Overusing health services

There have always been political arguments about health service funding, but however much money goes into the NHS, there will always come a point where treatment cannot be provided because of lack of funds. It is important, therefore, for people not to mis-use health services by receiving treatment they do not need. Unnecessary treatment can also have other adverse effects. In 1999, the government published guidelines on the over-prescribing of antibiotics, not to save money but because of fears that over-prescription was leading to the rise of drug-resistant diseases.

Individuals who have a tendency to overuse health services are often referred to as 'hypochondriacs' and are assumed to be malingering or else to be imagining symptoms that do not really exist. However, most hypochondriacs are interpreting benign symptoms (such as a mild stress headache) as signs of serious illness (e.g. a brain tumour). There does seem to be a link between hypochondriasis and neuroticism as researchers have discovered correlations between levels of neuroticism and the number of medical complaints. It is possible, of course, that being ill causes individuals to become neurotic, but prospective studies do seem to indicate that neuroticism leads to complaints rather than the other way round.

Munchausen's syndrome is a very rare condition in which the individual repeatedly seeks out medical treatment by falsely claiming to have symptoms of serious illness. Munchausen's is known as a factitious disorder, which means that the patient is either consciously pretending to have symptoms that don't really exist, or else deliberately harming themselves in order to produce symptoms. Another form of the disorder is Munchausen's by proxy. This is when a person induces or fakes the

KEY DEFINITIONS

Hypochondriacs have a tendency to worry excessively about their own health, to monitor their bodily sensations more closely than other people, to complain about medical conditions which they do not have and to believe they are ill even if they have been told by doctors that this is not the case.

Neuroticism is a 'broad dimension of normal personality that encompasses a variety of specific traits, including self-consciousness, inability to inhibit cravings, and vulnerability to stress as well as the tendency to experience anxiety, hostility and depression' (Cost and McCrae, 1985; cited in Sarafino, 1994).

It could be that **Munchausen's syndrome** arises from an extreme need to seek attention. The treatment (based on the principle of operant conditioning) would be to ignore people with the condition and not offer them the reinforcement they crave; the danger with this approach is that the patient may escalate the self-harm in order to make treatment imperative. Another explanation is that as a result of past experience the patient has made a classical conditioning association between being cared for by medical staff and some kind of positive affect (e.g. feeling loved).

symptoms of an illness in another person in order for them to receive medical treatment. In almost all cases, the person with Munchausen's syndrome by proxy is a parent (usually the mother), and the 'victim' is their child. In many cases the parent actually inflicts physical injuries on the child in order to make medical treatment necessary, and so this condition is often thought of as a form of child abuse.

Underusing health services

A much larger problem for health services than people who seek out treatment that they do not really need, is people who delay seeking treatment when they are genuinely ill. Such delay can, of course, have serious consequences for the health of the individual and there are many studies that show that people have a tendency not to seek medical help immediately and that this often results in a poorer outcome of treatment. On the other hand, as explained above, most people would be reluctant to seek medical help prematurely, so the psychological processes involved in deciding to seek medical help and then actually doing so are very important. The classic study by Safer et al. (1979) investigates and describes these processes in detail.

EVALUATION ISSUES

USEFULNESS/GENERALISABILITY

Although Safer et al.'s study (1979) may be useful in helping to understand the complexity of the reasons why people delay seeking medical attention, it is not widely generalisable because the study was only carried out in four clinics in one inner city hospital in the USA.

KEY STUDY

Determinants of three stages of delay in seeking care at a medical clinic
Safer, Tharps, Jackson and Leventhal (1979)

Aim: Previous studies on delay in seeking medical help have focused on the total time from when a symptom is first noticed to the time that treatment starts. Safer et al. argue that different factors will affect delay at different times, and it is more useful to break down total delay into three sequential stages:
* appraisal delay: the time taken for the patient to recognise a symptom as a sign of illness
* illness delay: the time taken from deciding that one is ill to deciding to seek medical care
* utilisation delay: the time taken from deciding to seek medical care to actually getting it.

This study aims to discover which psychological factors affect delay at each of these three stages.

Sample: The study was carried out in the waiting rooms of four clinics in a large inner-city hospital in the USA. Interviewers approached patients who were there to report a new symptom or complaint and asked them a series of questions that took about 45 minutes. A total of 93 patients were interviewed, with an average age of 44 years. 60 per cent of the sample was black. They were interviewed by a black, female nurse and a white, male undergraduate.

Method: Participants were asked about when they first noticed the symptom ('What was your very first symptom or sign that you might be sick, and when did it first occur?'), when they decided that they were ill ('Was there some point when you began to feel you were really sick?') and when they decided to seek medical help ('At what time did you decide to see a doctor'). They were also asked a range of other questions, some open and some closed, aimed at discovering the factors that may have contributed to the decisions involved in getting medical help.

Results:
* There were no statistically significant correlations between appraisal delay, illness delay and utilisation delay, implying that the factors that

contribute to delay at each of these three stages operate independently from each other.

- The mean total delay was 14.2 days (statistically adjusted to reduce the impact of outlying values).
- Three variables correlated significantly with appraisal delay: the presence of severe pain, whether the patient had read about his symptoms, and the presence of bleeding. This implies that pain and bleeding are the two key symptoms that make people think they are ill, and that reading about symptoms actually has the opposite effect. Safer et al. explain this last finding by describing reading about symptoms as passive monitoring (as opposed to active monitoring which involves self-examining the symptom or looking for other symptoms) and that this activity is likely to be time-consuming and to lead to further information searching rather than decision-making, thus increasing appraisal delay.
- Three distinct variables correlated significantly with illness delay: whether the symptom was new or had been experienced before, whether the patient imagined negative consequences of being ill, and gender. Patients experiencing old symptoms spent longer deciding that they needed to seek medical help, as did patients who were reporting more negative imagery. Females had longer illness delays than males.
- Three variables correlated with utilisation delay: patients who were concerned about the cost of treatment delayed for longer, patients with a painful symptom delayed for less long, as did patients who believed that their illness could be cured.
- Finally, there was one other variable that was found to correlate with total delay but not with any one of the three stages: patients with personal problems in their lives (at work, within the family, etc.) had a longer total delay.

Conclusions: The authors conclude that different factors mediate delay at each of three different stages, and that there is little point carrying out research that simply looks at total delay.

FOR CONSIDERATION

- How could the findings of Safer et al. (1979) be used to plan interventions to reduce delay at each stage? For example, to reduce appraisal delay, people could be encouraged to think of themselves as potentially ill for reasons other than pain or bleeding (e.g. breast lumps, palpitations, etc.). To reduce illness delay, patients could be helped to cope with negative imagery, and to think of old and new symptoms as equally important. To reduce utilisation delay, patients' concern about the cost of treatment needs to be reduced, and patients need to be convinced that the treatment will cure them. How could this be achieved?

SECTION A EXAM QUESTIONS

a Describe one study of patient-practitioner interpersonal style. [6]
b Discuss the ethics of research into patient-practitioner interactions. [10]

a Describe one piece of research into using health services. [6]
b Discuss the usefulness of research into using health services. [10]

a Describe one piece of research into mis-using health services. [6]
b Discuss the problems of researching mis-use of health services. [10]

CD-ROM

For Section B sample exam questions see Health: Sample exam questions.

CHAPTER **4** ‖ PSYCHOLOGY AND ORGANISATIONS

CHAPTER 4: INTRODUCTION

In the twenty-first century the world of work is changing rapidly; the introduction of new technologies and the decline of traditional industrial occupations has put pressure on organisations to change and adapt. Psychology has many important roles to play in understanding the culture within organisations and in helping to explain the behaviour of individuals, groups and the organisation as a whole. As the nature of working life has changed from the industrial pre-war age, so has the role and emphasis of organisational psychology. This is reflected in the variety of terms used for this applied area of psychology.

At the beginning of the twentieth century, Organisational Psychology was primarily concerned with assessment and selection of personnel for industrial tasks. This was demonstrated by the introduction of intelligence tests for the selection of army recruits to different roles in the US army during the First World War (the work of Yerkes, cited in Gould, 1982). In the 1920s Elton Mayo carried out extensive investigations into work conditions in American factories (see page 196), and through his work, developed insights into group processes and also the effects of carrying out research in the workplace. At that time, the emphasis of Organisational Psychology was the application of scientific methods and principles to work practices in order to maximise productivity, with little attention being paid to the welfare or happiness of workers. A new era developed in the 1960s with a more humanitarian approach, that recognised the importance and value of the individual in organisations. It was during this time that many theories were developed with an emphasis on the needs of workers to feel valued and satisfied in their work (Hertzberg, 1966; McClelland, 1965).

Recent trends in Organisational Psychology are towards improving the quality of working life and the effectiveness of structures within the organisation. The services of organisational psychologists are in ever-increasing demand. According to BPS (2001), the main aims of occupational psychologists are:
* to increase the effectiveness of the organisation or group
* to improve the job satisfaction of the individual.

There are several aspects involved in the work of organisational psychologists, and examples of the areas in which they may be employed are outlined below:

Aspect	Example of practice
Working with individuals	Work stress, leadership style
Consultancy	Managing change, appraisal systems, reward systems, communication systems
Assessment and training	Selection, job satisfaction, motivation, psychometric testing
Vocational guidance	Job analysis, interview techniques
Ergonomics (the fit between the worker and the physical environment)	Work conditions, job satisfaction
Health and safety	Work conditions, temporal conditions, quality of working life

This chapter will examine the application of established psychology in organisations, in addition to the psychological theories and insights which have emerged from studying people at work.

KEY DEFINITIONS

There are a number of interchangeable terms used in the application of psychology to the workplace. In 1921, the National Institute of Industrial Psychology (NIIP) was formed in the UK, and the term **Industrial Psychology** was the term of preference. In the 1950s **Occupational Psychology** was the term most commonly used, and it remains the term currently used by the British Psychological Society (BPS). In Europe, the term **Work Psychology** is popular, while in the USA the field is known as **Industrial and Organisational Psychology (IO Psychology)**. In this chapter the term 'Organisational Psychology' is used, but it could be replaced by any of the above terms.

SELECTION OF PEOPLE FOR WORK

In order for organisations to perform effectively it is essential that the workforce can carry out the tasks that they are set; for this to happen, personnel are selected from potential employees, who meet the requirements of a particular position. It is important that the skills and aptitudes of an employee match the job specification to ensure that both employer and employee are satisfied. For example, a candidate with a degree may not be happy working in telephone sales as a full time occupation. They would be seen by the employer as a bad investment as they would soon tire of the work and leave. This would then be costly for the employer who would have to re-advertise and re-train a new employee. In this way qualifications could lead to an employer refusing to consider your application on the ground that you are over qualified.

Occupational psychologists may play a part in the process of finding the right person for a job, in a consultancy role, through selection techniques or devising and administering psychometric tests to differentiate between applicants. Companies would recruit the services of an occupational psychologist for such purposes, and also to monitor and report back on the success of the selection process over time.

The following section will consider the role of psychology and the use of psychometric tests and interviews in the selection of people for work. It will also focus on how selection decisions are made, and discuss the reliability and validity of such decisions.

4.1.1 PERSONNEL SCREENING AND PSYCHOMETRIC TESTING

Personnel selection is the means by which employers pick the employees most suited to vacant positions. It is usual to start with the job description and find a person to fit it (although the process can occur the other way around, assessing an individual's potential, and finding them a job to suit). To achieve a match between an applicant and a position, Makin (1996) argues that four underlying assumptions are made:

- Any particular job has relatively stable characteristics.
- Individuals have relatively stable characteristics.
- The characteristics of both job and individuals can be matched.
- Accurate matching will result in improved organisational outcomes (e.g. reduction in staff turnover, increased profit/efficiency/results).

Screening

When considering an applicant for a job, screening can take a variety of forms:

- biographical data (letter of application, CV, references)
- interview
- presentation/simulation by candidates
- performance on psychometric tests
- assessment of applicant's past performance
- a trial period, after which a permanent position may be offered.

The great majority of positions are filled using the first two of the above methods. However, when there are a large number of applicants for a few jobs, or when time is critical or the quality of the recruitment decision needs greater depth of information concerning the applicants, the other methods may be utilised.

Psychometric testing

Psychometric tests should be objective and use controlled, uniform procedures carried out by trained personnel (this being a centre-piece of the work of organisational psychologists). Scoring should be standardised, and scores referenced to norms (Toplis, Dulewicz and Fletcher, 1987).

There are a great variety of psychometric tests at the disposal of organisational psychologists. The main categories are listed below:

- **Personality tests**: used to determine whether the applicant has the right personal characteristics for the job. There are many established general tests of personality, such as Cattell's 16 Personality Factors (1965) or Eysenk's (1964) Introversion/Extraversion Scale. In addition there are tests specific to organisational use, such as the Organisational Personality Questionnaire (see below for examples of these types of test). These may be particularly important in certain jobs like management or selling. The Transformational Leadership Questionnaire (TLQ) is another example of a psychometric test used by organisations to identify leadership potential in managers. Its use is described on page 179.
- **Intelligence tests**: used to obtain an applicant's level of general intelligence.
- **Cognitive or construct tests**: used to establish how an individual perceives and interprets the world around them. For example Kelly's Personal Construct Theory (1955) or Rotter's Locus of Control test (1966).
- **Aptitude tests**: these are projective tests, devised to indicate an individual's potential to perform on certain tasks in the future. An example of one of these is the numerical task used in the Phillips and Dipboyle (1989) study (see page 153).

Personality and cognitive tests

Cattell (1965) devised a means of measuring personality by systematically reducing a very large number of personality traits to 16 Source Traits. These traits are thought to be enduring aspects of personality, and can be used to predict future behaviour. The 16 traits are bi-polar, that is, they are based along a continuum and the individual gets a rating on that trait. Factor A, for example, concerns social interaction; at one extreme lies 'Reserved, detached, critical' and at the other 'Outgoing, warm-hearted'. Factor C ranges from 'Affected by feelings, easily upset' to 'Emotionally stable, faces reality'.

The 16 Personality Factor (16PF) instrument is made up of 187 questions. Each question has three possible forced choices: 'agree', 'uncertain', 'disagree', although the instructions discourage over-use of the 'uncertain', option. After completion the scoring leads to a profile, indicating where on each of the 16 factors an individual is.

Hartson and Mottram (1976) used the 16PF to differentiate between the personalities of different occupational groups. The questionnaire was completed by 603 middle managers who were attending a management course at a UK college. They discovered that the managers from different backgrounds varied in the following ways:

- **sales managers**: extrovert, competitive, impulsive and unconventional
- **accountants**: critical, aloof, rigid in their attitudes
- **personnel managers**: tender-minded, introspective, tolerant and romantic

- When completing psychometric tests on personality, it is tempting to bend the truth. It is difficult to admit to traits or behaviours that are not socially desirable. Individuals may therefore respond by choosing the response which shows them in a more positive light, rather than being honest.
- The predictive validity of personality tests is low, and has been correlated to a value of –0.2 (Tett et al., 1972). This indicates that personality tests are poor predictors of future behaviour.

There is much debate around the use of intelligence tests. The WAIS tests a range of cognitive abilities and places the individual's score within a normal distribution, so that in comparison to others who have taken the test, one is either average, or above or below average. However, many psychologists argue that the IQ score it generates is not a valid indicator of intelligence, since there are many different types of intelligence, and such tests only measure a few of them. There are also many other problems with the use of such psychometric tests, such as practice effects, fatigue and the fact that they are only a 'snapshot' measure; on the day of the test an individual may not be performing as well as they usually would.

For an in depth discussion on the problems surrounding the attempts to measure intelligence, refer to the article by Gould, *A nation of morons*, a commentary on the work of Yerkes who devised intelligence tests for army recruits in the USA in 1915. This was covered in the OCR AS Psychology course. The work of Yerkes is also an example of the early use of psychometric testing in selection, and so could be included in this section for A2.

- **engineers:** cautious, conventional, self-reliant and introspective
- **production managers:** tough-minded, conventional, assertive.

Saville and Holdsworth (1984) devised the Occupational Personality Questionnaire (OPQ). The OPQ consists of 11 questionnaires, some of which are used for selecting personnel. The scoring of the questionnaires gives a personality profile of 30 traits, sub-divided into three main categories:

- relationships with people (9 traits, including affiliative, out-going, persuasive)
- thinking style (11 traits, including artistic, innovative, conscientious)
- feelings and emotions (10 traits, including worrying, optimistic, decisive).

The OPQ has been shown to have good criterion-related validity, in that its findings are supported by similar psychometric tests.

KEY STUDY

The Weschler Adult Intelligence Scale (WAIS)
Weschler (1981)

The WAIS is the most widely used intelligence test for adults (16–74 year-olds). The WAIS measures IQ (intelligence quotient) by deviation, that is, standardisation of the test produces a normal curve, with the mean score of 100, and scores above and below the mean being evenly distributed. The WAIS was developed in order to address the problem of the Stanford-Binet IQ test relying too heavily on language ability, and not being designed for use on adults (Wechsler, 1981). It is made up of two sections; a verbal scale and a performance scale (as shown below).

Verbal scale (tests are not timed):
- information: general knowledge.
- comprehension: ability to use knowledge in a practical setting.
- arithmetic.
- similarities: conceptual reasoning.
- digit span-testing: short term memory (repeating strings of numbers forward or backward).
- vocabulary: word meaning.

Performance scale (tests are timed):
- picture arrangement: visual efficiency (spotting missing items in pictures).
- picture arrangements: sequencing of information (storyboards).
- block design: multicoloured blocks arranged to match pictures.
- object assembly: jigsaws.
- digit symbol: memorising and ordering abstract patterns.

The WAIS has been shown to be a reliable and valid psychometric test (Atkinson et al., 1987). However, the test measures how good one is at completing a particular test and one's score is only relevant to the standardised scores of others who have done the same test. The WAIS, like other IQ tests tells us how well an individual does on that test, and may be an indicator of their intelligence, but it should not be considered as an absolute measure of intelligence.

4.1.2 TYPES AND PITFALLS OF SELECTION INTERVIEWS

Interviews are a familiar method used to obtain information about an individual in psychology, and the selection interview used by organisations works in the same way, and has similar advantages and disadvantages. An interview is an opportunity for the interviewer to find out more about the applicant and his suitability for the job, and also for the interviewee to find out more about a prospective employer. For many people the interview process is a stressful experience since the behaviour, both verbal and non-verbal, of the applicant is being closely scrutinised, and the outcome (getting a job) can be crucial.

The interview is often regarded as the most important factor in the selection process, when it is usually only the middle stage of three:
1   analysis of pre-interview data: application form, CV, test scores, references
2   the interview: a face-to-face exchange of information
3   decision-making: about whether to hire or not.

Traditional interviews may be quite haphazard affairs. There is a familiar pattern to follow; the applicant waits to be called into the interview room, she is greeted by the interview panel, interviewers ask questions and the interviewee responds, there may be a chance for the interviewee to ask questions, the interview concludes and the applicant goes home to wait tentatively by the telephone for a decision. However, the traditional interview process can vary from setting to setting and be a completely different experience for subsequent interviewees. Questions are often irrelevant to the position on offer, and the experience and competence of interviewers can vary. **Structured interviews** are an improvement on unstructured ones as interviewers get together before the interview to decide on what questions to ask, and sometimes agree on what would constitute 'good' answers.

The traditional interview is riddled with pitfalls. Some are summarised below:
- **Social desirability**: the interviewee discerns from the wording of the questions or the body language of the interviewer, the response the interviewer is looking for. This could mean that the success of the interviewee is a reflection of his perception of the situation rather than their suitability for the job.
- **Lack of interviewer reliability**: interviewers may disagree on the quality of the interviewee's responses due to a lack of pre-agreed consensus on what constitutes desirable responses (Latham and Saari, 1980).
- **Poor standardisation of questions**: different questions may be asked in interviews for the same job, or too much time may be spent on personal or irrelevant questions (Latham and Saari, 1980).
- **Bias**: interviewers may discriminate between applicants on the basis of race, gender or even accent (Awosunle and Doyle, 2001).
- **Self-fulfilling prophecy**: pre-selection information may influence the judgement of the interviewee's interview performance, so that their interview behaviour is interpreted in a more or less positive way (Phillips and Dipboyle, 1989).
- **Projective validity**: an applicant's ability to impress in the interview does not necessarily correlate with their ability to do the work for which they will be appointed.

In response to the failings of the traditional interview, Latham and Saari (1980) developed the **situational interview**. By providing interviewers with standardised questions, specific to the job applied for, and training interviewers to score interview responses, a higher relevance of questions and inter-rater reliability can be achieved.

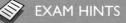

KEY DEFINITIONS

Traditional or **unstructured interviews** are those that have little structure or pre-planning. The interview experience can be very different for each applicant, and the information gathered about applicants is unlikely to be uniform.
Structured interviews attempt to standardise the questions asked, and the interpretation and relative weighting of the applicants' responses. One of the most structured forms of interviewing is the situational interview.

EXAM HINTS

The problems with traditional interviews described in the text may be used to evaluate selection interviews in the exam.

The validity of the situational interview in Latham and Saari's (1980) study was high compared to traditional interviewing techniques.

FOR CONSIDERATION

Reflect on job interviews you have experienced.
- Did they take the form of traditional or situational interviews?
- What kind of questions were you asked?

KEY DEFINITIONS

Clinical decision-making: decisions about who to appoint are made subjectively. Performance on all aspects of the selection process may be taken into account, but essentially, the judgement of an experienced selector will determine the best applicant.

Actuarial decision-making: sophisticated mathematical techniques are used to weigh the scores from the various selection methods. For these to be applied, quantifiable measures must be used throughout the selection process. The applicant with the highest overall score would be appointed.

KEY STUDY

The situational interview
Latham and Saari (1980)

In response to concerns that traditional interviews lack reliability and validity, Latham and Saari devised the situational interview. The theoretical assumption upon which the interview is based is that what people say correlates highly with what they do (Locke's Goal Setting Theory, 1968). Rather than being asked irrelevant questions in the interview, behavioural scenarios are given to interviewees, and they are asked what they would do in that situation. Questions were created by using critical incident technique, that is, posing a problem which could actually occur in that particular industry.

Example of a critical incident:

'Your spouse and two teenage children are sick in bed with a cold. There are no relatives or friends available to look in on them. Your shift starts in three hours. What would you do in this situation?'

Experienced personnel in the relevant industrial field rate the possible answers, and assign a rank order to each response. In the case of the above incident:
- 'I would stay at home; my spouse and family come first' (1)
- 'I would phone my supervisor and explain the situation' (3)
- 'Since they only have a cold, I'd come to work' (5).

This rating system is agreed by a number of raters to ensure consistency of measures. Interviewers are then trained on technique, so that they only ask the pre-agreed questions, and that they are able to quickly assign a score for each response using the above rating system as a benchmark. The number of critical incident-based questions is determined by time; no interview should exceed one hour. In the interview, one interviewer poses the questions and at least two other interviewers rate the interviewee's responses.

Latham and Saari conducted research to test the predictive validity of the situational interview. The situational interview was administered to 56 applicants for entry-level work at a pulp mill. The applicants were hired and assessed on their job performance by their supervisors one year later. The supervisors were unaware of the workers' original interview score. A correlation between the performance in the situational interview score and performance rating on the job was carried out, and was found to be significant.

Conclusions: The situational interview is a more reliable and valid tool than the traditional interview. Questions are only work-related, and responses are ranked in an objective way by using benchmarks for scoring, which have high inter-rater reliability. Interviewers are also trained, which decreases the effects of bias and experience. The predictive validity was quite good; indicating that people do act as they say they will, however, working out a desirable response in the interview may still play a part.

4.1.3 PERSONNEL SELECTION DECISIONS

Once the selection process has been completed, decisions are made about whom to appoint in two ways: clinically or actuarially.

The situational interview is geared to the actuarial method, since the interviewee's responses are rated by the interviewer with reference to a benchmarked scoring system. The interviews conducted by the American companies in the Phillips and Dipboyle (1989) study (see below) are more clinical, in that, although data are available from a number of sources, and much of it is quantifiable, the decisions on who to appoint were subjectively made, and based on initial impressions made of the applicants.

KEY STUDY

Personnel selection decisions: correlational tests of predictions from a process model of the interview
Phillips and Dipboyle (1989)

Aim: To investigate the influence of pre-interview impressions of an applicant on the subsequent conduct of the interview and decisions to hire an applicant. In other words, to see whether the self-fulfilling prophecy plays a role in the appointment of staff.

Sample: 34 male interviewers and 164 applicants whose ages ranged from 21 to 51 years, for employment in the selling of financial products (research carried out in the USA).

Method: Field study; applicants were assessed in three stages:
- Selection for interview was based on candidates' applications and scores on a standardised test (50 item numerical ability and economics knowledge test).
- Interview: an unstructured format, which led to selection to the next stage.
- Simulation: an intensive set of exercises designed to simulate the tasks of an account executive. Performance was rated on a 5-point scale.

Interviewers were given a questionnaire to complete before and after the interview to establish their impressions of applicants. Applicants were also given a questionnaire regarding their impressions of the interviewer, how they felt the interview had gone and their opinion of the job and the company.

Findings: Interviewers' pre-interview evaluations were positively related to post-interview judgements about suitability of applicants for employment. The performance by applicants who had made favourable pre-interview impressions was attributed to internal factors (i.e. the performance of the applicant was interpreted as being genuine, rather than a response to being in the interview setting). The information available from simulation scores was largely ignored in the decision-making process, although this is a more valid predictor of future performance.

Conclusion: Despite the emphasis on the role of the interview in selection, more importance may be placed on the quality of pre-interview data. Pre-interview impressions were found to be very important in colouring the subsequent evaluations made by interviewers as to the suitability of applicants, even when more rigorous data were available. This lends support to the role of self-fulfilling prophecy in recruitment (the applicant's performance in the interview will be interpreted to fit in with the pre-interview impression), as it sways the impression of the interviewer in the decision to hire.

KEY DEFINITIONS

Self-fulfilling prophecy: this is the psychological concept that individuals or groups will come to resemble the expectations that have been made of them.

EVALUATION ISSUES

VALIDITY

Phillips and Dipboyle's (1989) study suggests that the validity of the interviewer can be called into question, as pre-interview evaluations may be more important in influencing the decisions interviewers make than the interview itself.

In arriving at a selection decision using the actuarial method, interviewers will take into account ratings of the applicant's selection materials and performance. **Cut-off points** will be established for the different aspects of the selection procedure and the applicants' data is compared with these criteria. For example, when a cognitive ability test has been used to screen applicants, only those who exceed the agreed threshold score will be considered for the position. When looking at the written applications for the job, the number of matches between the **essential** and **desirable** qualifications will be scored, and the decisions made about who to move on to the next stage of the selection process. The process should be objective, that is, scoring should be uniform for all applicants, but this is easier for some parts of the selection procedure (e.g. test scores or qualifications) than others (e.g. interviews) where there is more likelihood of subjective interpretation of performance. Also, some parts of the selection process may be more influential than others, and colour the impressions formed about applicants' performance on other measures used for selection. The validity of selection decisions should also be considered, since the selection process becomes pointless if the data, which informs it, is not what it seems.

Reliability of selection procedures

The reliability of selection decisions can be questioned on a number of fronts:

- **Selection tests:** these may be scored differently by different scorers, particularly when responses are to open-ended questions, or responses are of a qualitative nature.
- **Biographical data:** the information gleaned from references and letters of application may be weighed differently by different judges.
- **Observations:** ratings of applicants' performance can be influenced by prior judgements made about an applicant based on other assessments, or by bias towards particular applicants held by assessors.
- **Evaluation of past performance:** this can be affected by expectations. A candidate who has worked well in the past will be more likely to make a positive impression, as their performance is judged as internal (due to personality characteristics) rather than external (due to positive situational factors).
- **Interview performance:** this is subject to inconsistency in questions asked by interviewers and the time given to asking irrelevant questions, as well as weighting given to different interviewee responses. Interviewers may also vary in terms of experience.

Validity of selection procedures

How good are different selection procedures at predicting future performance? Are people honest when they write letters of application? Are referees always telling the truth, or are they trying to off-load a poor employee? Are ability and personality tests good predictors of future potential, or do they demonstrate practice and socially desirable responses?

Hunter and Hunter (1984) carried out a meta-analysis of the literature on the validity of predictors for entry-level jobs for which training would occur after hiring. Their findings are summarised below:

Validity of predictors for entry-level jobs

Predictor	Mean validity	Sample size
Cognitive ability test	0.53	32 124
Job simulation activity	0.44	*
Biographical information	0.37	4 429
Reference	0.26	5 389
Experience	0.18	32 124

FOR CONSIDERATION

- Which do you think is the best strategy for appointing people to jobs: clinical (in which the selector makes a largely subjective decision) or actuarial (in which the decision is made as a result of objective numerical data)?

EXAM HINTS

The problems with selection procedures described in the text can be used to evaluate selection procedures in the exam.

Predictor	Mean validity	Sample size
Interview	0.14	2 694
Training rating	0.13	*
Academic achievement	0.11	1 089
Education	0.10	32 124
Age	0.01	32 124

*Sample size not available
Adapted from 'Validity and Utiility of predictors of job performance,' Hunter and Hunter 1984.

The mean validity is a correlation coefficient of the relationship between each predictor and subsequent performance. A validity coefficient of 1 would represent a perfect correlation. Hunter and Hunter (1984) concluded that cognitive ability tests were the best predictors of performance for entry level jobs, outstripping biographical data and performance at assessment centres, where job simulation exercises are carried out. The cost of using cognitive ability tests is offset by savings made by companies in recruiting suitable staff, but such tests should be recognised as standardised tests, and scored by trained personnel. Hunter and Hunter also propose that such tests be used in combination with other selection procedures, to further increase validity.

SECTION A EXAM QUESTIONS

a Describe one method of personnel screening. [6]
b Evaluate the validity of methods of personnel screening. [10]

a Describe one type of selection interview. [6]
b Discuss the weakness of selection interviews. [10]

a Describe one psychometric test used in the selection of people for work. [6]
b Evaluate psychometrics tests used in the selection of people for work. [10]

CD-ROM

For Section B sample exam questions see Organisations: Sample exam questions.

4.2 HUMAN RESOURCE PRACTICES

In the 1980s, human resource management became the accepted term for what used to be known as 'personnel' functions in organisations. It encompasses many of the roles of personnel management, and recognises the importance and value of people in an organisation. It promotes the importance of shared goals between the management and the work force, and the concept that success is often due to the commitment and skills of the workers. The people who work for an organisation are often its most expensive resource in terms of paying out salaries, and it is good business sense to maintain a flexible, co-operative and adaptive work force.

Human resource practices are the means by which organisations recruit, manage and motivate employees. The roles of the organisational psychologist are in training, performance appraisal, reward systems and personnel selection. Many psychology graduates are recruited into the field of human resources, as they are seen to possess the knowledge of 'how people work'.

4.2.1 JOB ANALYSIS AND JOB ANALYSIS TECHNIQUES

Job analysis

Job analysis is the systematic deconstruction of a job into its component parts. A list is made of the job's tasks and responsibilities, equipment used, the position of the job within the organisational hierarchy, together with the knowledge, skills, abilities and other characteristics (KSAOs) required to do the job. The job analysis is the starting point for many human resource practices, and its products include:

- job descriptions
- job specifications
- job evaluation performance criteria.

These may then be used for a number of organisational functions, including job design, recruitment (advertising jobs and job specifications) and selection, employee development, compensation, equal opportunity practices and performance appraisal.

Job analysis techniques

The information used for job analysis may come from a number of sources:

- written material: existing job descriptions, organisational training manuals
- job holder's reports: information from interviews, questionnaires, or diaries kept by workers
- colleagues' observations
- direct observation by trained personnel
- critical incident technique.

The **critical incident technique** mentioned above involves employees writing down incidents of good and bad practice that have actually occurred in their jobs. These incidents are then sorted into categories that can be used to describe the main components of the job. Finally the incidents are reappraised into examples of good and bad practice. Critical incident

CD-ROM

For examples of job descriptions using a job analysis technique, see Organisation: Real life applications: Job descriptions.

CD-ROM

A comprehensive example of collected job descriptions is the DOT, which can be accessed on-line: see Organisation: Real life applications: DOT.

technique can be used to write job descriptions, as a tool to discriminate between interviewees (see p. 152 *The situational interview*) or to select individuals for promotion. An advantage of critical incident technique is that the descriptors of job elements are stated by the people who are actually doing the job.

There are problems associated with the methods used to analyse jobs. A jobholder may be suspicious about the use that will be made of the information they provide. If they feel the analysis will lead to their supervisors requiring more effort from them, they may not include everything that they normally do. As an exercise that feeds into performance related pay, the worker may include items that they do not usually do as routine. Colleagues may not have sufficient insight into what their fellow workers do, or may be influenced by factors such as **halo effects** towards their preferred colleagues or negative bias due to poor inter-personal relationships or prejudice.

Combinations of the above techniques are used in varying degrees in specialised job analysis techniques. Functional job analysis and the Position Analysis Questionnaire are described in more detail below.

Fine and Wiley (1974) describe how **Functional Job Analysis (FJA)** is widely used in the USA in conjunction with the **Dictionary of Occupational Titles (DOT)**, which classifies and gives general descriptions of over 40 000 jobs. The analyst begins with the general description of the job from the DOT, and then interviews and observes a worker in a more detailed study of a particular job. The analyst focuses on the tasks carried out over a period of time and assesses them in terms of how they contribute towards an expressed objective.

A sample DOT entry is shown below:

Job: 166.267-018 Job Analyst

Collects, analyses, and prepares occupational information to facilitate personnel, administration and management functions of an organisation. Consults with management to determine type, scope and purpose of study. Studies current organisational, occupational data and compiles distribution reports, organisation and flow charts, and other background information. Observes jobs and interviews workers and supervisory personnel to determine job and worker requirements. Analyses occupational data, such as physical, mental and training requirements of jobs and workers and develops written summaries, such as job descriptions, job specifications and lines of career movement. Utilises and develops occupational data to evaluate or improve methods and techniques for recruiting, selecting, promoting, evaluating and training workers and administration of related personnel programs. May specialise in classifying positions according to regulated guidelines to meet job classification requirements of civil service system and be known as Position Classifier (government ser.).

Source: US Department of Labour, Dictionary of Occupational Titles (1991)

The middle three numbers on the DOT are indicators of three areas: data, people and things, and are used to give further information on the key elements of the job:

⚖ **EVALUATION ISSUES**

SUBJECTIVITY

There are problems when using the critical incident technique; first because the process is time consuming, and second, the categorisation of the job elements into separate categories is subjective, as is the decision as to whether a certain behaviour is 'good' or 'poor'. For example, when considering the performance of a waiter who is extremely attentive, some people may see his behaviour as desirable, where others could perceive his constant attentions as irritating.

⚖ **EVALUATION ISSUES**

METHODOLOGY

Direct observation requires skilled personnel, who are trained in rating procedures, and even when trained observers are available they may not be physically present when some aspects of the job are performed. The behaviour of workers under observation may also change due to their awareness of being watched. Written records of job descriptions are likely to become out-of-date, particularly with the advances in and adoption of new technology.

🔑 **KEY DEFINITIONS**

Halo effect, or halo error is the result of an evaluator being influenced positively by an individual performing well in one aspect of behaviour. This impression is then generalised to other aspects of behaviour. For example, a receptionist who is very efficient in screening phone calls may be judged to be efficient in other aspects of the job, when this may not be the case.

Consider the following jobs:
- air traffic controller
- waitress
- plumber.

Which of the key data, people and things would be the most appropriate for each job?

Key indicators used in the *Dictionary of Occupational Titles* descriptors

Data	People	Things
0. Synthesising	0. Mentoring	0. Setting up
1. Co-ordinating	1. Negotiating	1. Precision working
2. Analysing	2. Instructing	2. Operating–controlling
3. Compiling	3. Supervising	3. Driving operating
4. Computing	4. Diverting	4. Manipulating
5. Copying	5. Persuading	5. Tending
6. Comparing	6. Speaking–signalling	6. Feeding–offbearing
	7. Serving	7. Handling
	8. Taking instructions-helping	

For the above position of job analyst, the numbers 267 denote, analysing, speaking-signalling and handling.

The FJA is a popular and cost-effective tool. It has been useful in research designed to investigate how well people are performing their jobs. In a study of over 200 nursing assistants in nursing homes (Brannon, Streit and Smyer, 1992) it showed that nursing assistants were spending too much time on report writing and changing bedding, and not enough time giving care and attention to their patients.

KEY STUDY

The Position Analysis Questionnaire
McCormick et al. (1972)

The PAQ is a standardised instrument, and is the most widely used and researched method of job analysis in the USA. The questionnaire is completed by the worker or by an observer (either a colleague or an analyst). It contains 187 job elements that are arranged into six categories:
- Information input: where the worker gets information needed to perform a job, e.g. a photographer would need to keep up-to-date with new developments in specialist publications.
- Mental processes: the kinds of reasoning and analysis needed to perform a job.
- Work output: the tasks and equipment needed.
- Relationships with others: these would vary depending on the type of job; a counsellor would be geared towards listening, and an air traffic controller would need to be assertive.
- Job context: the conditions in which the individual works.
- Miscellaneous aspects.

Each of these categories are rated on a five point scale, from 1 (not very important) to 5 (very substantial), with an 'N' option, for 'does not apply'. The (convergent) validity, of the PAQ has been researched by comparing the responses of jobholders with their supervisors' ratings, and findings have shown good agreement.

⚖ EVALUATION ISSUES

EFFECTIVENESS

FJA and PAQ are both effective methods of job analysis and widely used in the USA. Comparison studies of the PAQ and the FJA have shown that the FJA provides a more detailed and comprehensive analysis than the PAQ, whereas the PAQ is more cost effective and easier to use (Anderson and Wilson, 1997). A combination of methods would yield the best job analysis, but that in turn would make the process more costly and time consuming.

4.2.2 PERFORMANCE APPRAISAL TECHNIQUES: ADMINISTRATION AND PROBLEMS

It is common practice in many working environments for workers' performance to be assessed by supervisors, to ascertain whether individuals are doing their jobs properly. In most cases performance appraisal is an annual event and the outcome of the appraisal is used to identify training needs, staff development and progression, and to determine rewards such as pay increases. Before the face-to-face performance appraisal meeting takes place, information is gathered from a number of sources. Reference will be made to written data such as records from the previous appraisal meeting and targets that were set at that meeting, job descriptions or written reports about a worker by a line manager. Observations may be made using behavioural objectives of a worker on task. In some cases a worker may attend an assessment centre, where multiple raters will assess the individual's performance on specific work criteria. The outcome of the performance appraisal is fed back to the employee, and concerns or commendations are passed on to management.

Administration of the appraisal system

Although appraisal meetings usually take place annually, they may also take place when a probationary period comes to an end, or when a unit of work has been completed. Who administers performance appraisals and the difficulties associated with the occupation of the appraiser's role are considered below.

Possible appraisors and problems associated with them

Appraiser	Possible problems
Supervisor: often considered the most appropriate choice due to their position to observe and evaluate a subordinate.	• May not have adequate experience • Personal bias may be held towards worker • May be distant from subordinate and unfamiliar with what they do.
Self: the person with the greatest insight into what they do.	• Tendency to elaborate on successes and ignore failings • Distrust of process.
Peers: co-workers are able to evaluate their colleagues closely over a long period of time.	• Tendency to rate friends more positively • Negative bias towards less popular colleagues.
Subordinates: this bottom-up viewpoint gives a worker's perspective of the performance of a superior.	• Well-liked superiors may be given better ratings than less popular bosses who may be more competent • Subordinates may fear the consequences of honesty.
Others: clients or external consultants may be employed, particularly to appraise the performance of more senior managers, or as part of an organisational review.	• Too distant from the organisation • Costly.

A possible way to improve conventional appraiser failings is to carry out 360 degree feedback. This technique was used in staff development programmes in the early 1990s, but it is becoming more widely used in the UK as a performance appraisal tool. Assessment ratings are gathered from a number of sources, e.g. subordinates, peers, superiors, clients and self. These assessments are collated and integrated by the human resource manager or by an external consultant, then fed back to the 'target' manager in the form of a profile on the individual.

EVALUATION ISSUES

RELIABILITY

Research on the effectiveness of the 360 degree feedback method is in its early stages but some studies suggest that care should be taken to avoid the same rater errors of traditional methods (Fletcher et al. 1997).

Problems with performance appraisal techniques

De Nisi and Mitchell (1978) analysed peer ratings in performance appraisal with the aim of evaluating their use. They carried out a review of existing literature relating to peer ratings as predictors and criterion measures. Their findings included the following:

- Peer ratings have low construct validity; they do not agree with ratings from other sources (e.g. supervisors', or self-ratings).
- Members from sub-groups (e.g. gender, race or graduate/non-graduate status) rate fellow group members more positively.
- Friendship positively influences ratings.
- The stability of peer ratings over time may be due to the inability to avoid stereotypes.
- Persons who receive negative ratings from peers are prone to retaliate in subsequent rounds of appraisal.

De Nisi and Mitchell (1978) recommend caution in the use of peer appraisal unless raters are asked to comment only on areas where they are able to make objective observations on peer behaviour. Also peer appraisal can be used for feedback, where it would aid individual self-improvement rather than for use in performance management. They stress that any peer rating findings should always be from anonymous sources.

FOR CONSIDERATION

Look at the McBriarty (1998) study.
- Who carries out the appraisal?
- Why did a 'forced distribution' have such negative effects on the officers?

EVALUATION ISSUES

EFFECTIVENESS

McBriarty's study (1988) shows that appraisals can be ineffective at best and demotivating and harmful in many cases.

KEY STUDY

Performance appraisal: some unintended consequences
McBriarty (1998)

Aim: To evaluate the organisational impacts of the US Air Force Officers' performance appraisal system after the introduction of forced distributions in 1974.

Background: In the late 1960s and early 1970s it became clear that the appraisal instrument used by the US Air Force for its officers was subjective and imprecise. By 1973, 90 per cent of officers were achieving the highest ratings and were deemed to be of high quality performance potential. This was attributed to reliance on anecdotal evidence and a tendency to avoid conflict. As a solution to the extremely high preponderance of top ratings, a forced distribution was incorporated into the appraisal system, as it was assumed that performance potential should follow a normal distribution. The Air Force Personnel Centre stipulated that appraisers must allocate 22 per cent of officers to the highest rank, 28 per cent in the next highest block and that the remaining officers be distributed in the remaining 50 per cent, in other words, 'the bottom half'. Appraisals made by initial raters were then reviewed by an additional rater and finally by an endorser. Endorsers seldom had first hand knowledge of those being appraised, and had varying degrees of experience in appraisal techniques. It soon became clear that the single most important factor in the appraisal system was the officer's 'performance potential' rating.

Sample: 200 Air Force officers.

Method: Interviews with Air Force staff, participation in conferences about the appraisal system and a review of internal documentation relating to the system.

Findings:
- Motivation plummeted. Officers who were used to being highly regarded after years of positive appraisals found themselves with lower than average ratings. This led to uncertainty about their future and organisational disinvestments culminating in many leaving the Air Force.

- Supervisor/subordinate relationships fell apart. Officers in the lower 50 per cent could either accept that the system was wrong or that their supervisor was in error. This led to suspicion towards supervisors and a weakening of relationships.
- Teamwork suffered as 'looking out for number one' became critical in the promotional ladder. Pressure on those in the top bands increased as they became more self-reliant.
- Future promotion prospects for the lower 50 per cent dwindled, since the better tasks were allocated to the top 50 per cent and the 'below averages' had little opportunity to show their worth.

Conclusions: McBriarty concluded that systems which try to impose a neat mathematical agenda, such as forced distributions, ignore the importance of the interpersonal factors and support systems that an organisation needs in order to function. The appraisal system was seen by the officers as an unpleasant intrusion into their working lives. Instead of enhancing the Air Force officers' development, the system led to weaker management and dysfunctional behaviour in individuals.

? FOR CONSIDERATION

- If you were asked to advise a manager on how to carry out staff appraisal, what would you tell her to do, and what should she avoid?

One other difficulty in the administration of performance appraisal occurs when an individual receives feedback on their limitations. Most appraisers are uncomfortable about making critical comments and fear defensive reactions from the worker. Critical feedback and awareness that performance is regarded as less than satisfactory can result in loss of motivation and reduced performance, particularly when the outcome of performance appraisal is linked to promotion and rewards.

Contemporary trends in UK organisations are to use performance appraisal for staff development outside the rewards system, with potential being assessed using psychometric tests or assessment centres.

4.2.3 REWARD SYSTEMS

Two theoretical perspectives that can be applied to reward systems are **exchange theory** and **operant conditioning**.

Exchange theory operates along the lines of 'You work for me and in return I give you something that you need'. Operant conditioning explains incentive systems in terms of the individual learning desired work behaviour. If past behaviour by a worker has been reinforced, the individual will anticipate that the same behaviour will be rewarded in the future. The rewards available in organisational settings may be **intrinsic** or **extrinsic**. Intrinsic rewards are described in more detail in section 4.6: 'Motivation to work', on page 185. Extrinsic rewards are considered below.

In order for rewards to be effective, they must be desired by the individual. There would be little incentive for a vegetarian to work harder in December to earn a Christmas turkey. Financial rewards for work seem on the surface to be highly desirable for the majority of people; since money can be exchanged for things they specifically want (Lawler, 1981). Managers and Union leaders often view pay as the single most important reward. However, research has found that pay is not always the most valued reward for many employees. Nealey (1964) found that employees' did not rate pay as their top priority and that preferred rewards differed with age.

🔑 KEY DEFINITIONS

Extrinsic rewards are rewards external to an individual. They are physical, tangible things like money, food, clothing or accommodation.
Intrinsic rewards are internally experienced by the individual. They are less observable than extrinsic rewards and include feelings of pride in your accomplishments, or a sense of worth gained through being part of a well-integrated team.

KEY STUDY

Preference for alternative rewards
Nealey (1964)

Aim: To discover whether pay or alternative incentives are seen as desirable by workers.

Sample: 1133 male trade union workers (International Brotherhood of Electrical Workers), who returned questionnaires (8300 were sent initially).

Method: Union members were surveyed using questionnaires with six options of rewards:
- reduction in working hours per week
- pension benefits
- union shop (all members would have their union fees paid)
- hospital insurance
- 6 per cent raise in pay
- three additional weeks of vacation.

Each of the above incentives would cost the company the same outlay.

Results: The results are shown in the graph below:

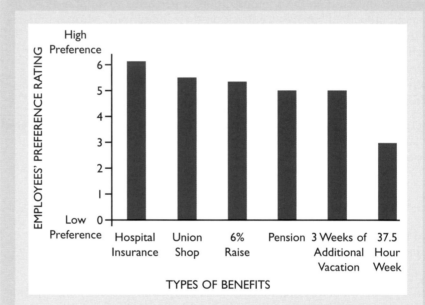

In addition to the findings above, Nealey also discovered that age played a role in preferences. For workers over 40, pension benefits were most highly valued, and hospital insurance was the top choice of men aged 30–40.

Conclusions: Nealey concluded that there are individual differences in what people find rewarding, and that increasing pay may not be the most desired option. Although the sample is large in the study, it is all male and from only one occupational field, which means there may be problems with generalising the findings to a wider population. Also, the participants in this American study would have to pay towards health care, which may not be the case for British workers who have free care provided by a state system.

Despite psychological evidence pointing to the inadequacy of financial incentives as desirable rewards, an increasing number of employers have implemented **performance related pay** (PRP) into organisations. Performance appraisal systems and job analysis systems may be used to assess which point on a salary scale a worker will be paid, or whether or not he is eligible to receive a pay increase. The reasoning behind performance related pay is that it is more cost effective for companies to reward individual workers or teams who meet targets for their efforts. This in turn gives recognition to workers who get results. In practice, performance related pay has not been the incentive it was meant to be, and instead it has been divisive, increasing competition, undervaluing team effort, and de-motivating for those who are not judged to have met their targets (Hutton, 1995).

Another way of rewarding good work behaviour is the behaviourist approach of implementing **token economies**. A study of the use of a token economy in open cast-mining is described on page 203.

SECTION A EXAM QUESTIONS

a Describe one job analysis technique. [6]
b Discuss the weaknesses of job analysis techniques. [10]

a Describe one technique of performance appraisal. [6]
b Contrast this technique with other techniques of performance appraisal. [10]

a Describe one reward system used in organisations. [6]
b Evaluate the effectiveness of reward systems used in organisations. [10]

? FOR CONSIDERATION

Intrinsic and extrinsic rewards can work against each other. Extrinsic rewards such as a pay increase or a company car can alter the carefully balanced social systems within the workforce. The worker who is rewarded may feel ostracised by colleagues who feel they also worked hard for the same reward. The intrinsic rewards experienced by the successful worker, for example camaraderie and group acceptance, may then decline.

• Consider how intrinsic and extrinsic rewards could work against each other in organisations that have introduced performance related pay.

CD-ROM

For a critique of the use of reward systems by Kohn (1993), see Organisations: Additional key studies: Kohn (1993).

CD-ROM

For Section B sample exam questions see Organisations: Sample exam questions.

4.3 GROUP BEHAVIOUR IN ORGANISATIONS

Selection systems focus on recruiting individuals, but although some very accomplished individuals exist, organisations need teams to enable growth and creativity. Groups or teams can be comprised of a number of individuals who have conflicting qualities that could not co-exist within one person. Teams can regroup and accommodate new members when existing members leave, where a talented individual may be very difficult to replace. In general, teams can achieve an aim or goal that could not be easily accomplished by an individual working alone. Organisations can move forward by benefiting from the wealth of collective knowledge and ideas that are generated by groups working together. According to Unsworth and West (2000), four conditions must be met for a collection of individuals to be considered as a team:

- members have shared goals
- members interact with each other
- members have well defined and interdependent roles
- members have an organisational identity as a team.

Team working allows people to work effectively and productively but there are also difficulties associated with teams, including co-ordination (the bigger the team, the more barriers there will be to arranging meetings, integrating and passing on information), motivation and communication. The following section will look at some aspects of group behaviour and consider the benefits as well problems that can occur in group situations.

4.3.1 GROUP DECISION-MAKING STRATEGIES AND PITFALLS

Team decision-making has four steps (Unsworth and West, 2000):
- describing the problem
- identifying possible solutions
- evaluating and choosing the best solution
- implementing the solution.

To describe a problem, one must first be aware that there is a problem. Some members of groups may interpret problems as threats to existing practices and relationships, and discourage fellow group members from raising them in order to maintain the security of prevailing systems (Miceli and Near, 1985). Research has indicated that teams that are aware and responsive to problems are more effective (Maier, 1970).

Generating solutions often involves brainstorming ideas from group members. This can be effective when people feel their contributions will be considered seriously, and when everybody gets their chance to contribute.

Evaluation of alternative solutions and the arrival at a decision for action is perhaps the most critical stage in the decision-making process. One psychological contribution is known as the **risky shift** phenomenon (Stoner, 1961). The risky shift phenomenon was put forward by Stoner to explain why members of a group made riskier choices when they made decisions together than they did as individuals prior to the group activity. He presented business studies students with problems based on case studies involving choices that the central character had to make. The problems were presented to individuals who had to evaluate an acceptable level of risk in each scenario. The same individuals then considered the same problems in groups, and Stoner found that the group decisions following discussion were riskier than those made by individuals. Wallach and Kogan (1965) believed that the explanation for why risky shift happens is due to an effect known as **diffusion of responsibility**.

KEY STUDY

The role of information, discussion and consensus on group risk-taking
Wallach and Kogan (1965)

Aim: To investigate which of the three components of group decision-making produces a risky shift:
- provision of information about other peoples' judgements
- group discussion
- achievement of information.

Sample: 360 college students (180 of each sex). Participants received payment or credit for experimental participation.

Procedure: An 'opinion questionnaire' was issued to individuals in each group of five participants. The questionnaire asked respondents to put themselves in the shoes of the central character in a number of scenarios which could occur in everyday life. Participants had to indicate the degree of risk they felt was acceptable in each scenario. The risk scores for each participant were used as a baseline measure.

The individuals were then allocated to single-sex groups of five and put in one of the following conditions:

1 **Group discussion leading to consensus:** individual participants were given a booklet of scenarios, on which they marked their risk evaluation for each situation. They were then allocated to a group and told to arrive at a consensus decision after five minutes of discussion.
2 **Group consensus without discussion:** after their individual decisions the group had to arrive at a consensus decision by balloting. A number of rounds took place where each individual's choice was displayed on a board along with the rest of the group's, until all choices were consistent.
3 **Group discussion without consensus:** after making their individual choices, participants were issued with the same questionnaire and asked to discuss each item with their group of five. They were then asked to make their subsequent choices individually in their booklets.

Results: A significant shift towards enhanced risk-taking was found for condition 1, replicating Stoner's work. In condition 2, there was no systematic shift in risk taking, but rather an averaging out effect was observed. In condition 3 the difference in pre- and post- discussion choices showed the same degree of riskier shift that was observed in condition 1.

Conclusions: Wallach and Kogan assert that 'group discussion provides the necessary and sufficient condition for generating the risky shift effect'. They also speculate that the process of verbal interaction causes the individuals to assume a group identity, which in turn allows the individuals to share the responsibility for any decision. They suggest that it is the 'diffusion of responsibility' effect, which explains the risky shift phenomenon, since all the members of the group will share the 'blame' of making a bad decision.

⚖ EVALUATION ISSUES

GENERALISABILITY

The samples used in Stoner's (1961) original research and in Wallach and Kogan's (1965) study are both drawn from student populations. Student populations differ from 'normal' populations in a number of ways; they are slightly more intelligent than the 'average' population, they are predominantly of a narrow age range, they have little life experience and they are likely to try and work out the aim of the research, and alter their behaviour accordingly. These characteristics make them an unsuitable sample group to generalise from.

⚖ EVALUATION ISSUES

ECOLOGICAL VALIDITY

Risky shift research has largely been carried out using hypothetical scenarios evaluated in laboratory conditions. The behaviour of real groups in real settings, where decisions must be made to address genuine problems, may not mirror that of these research findings. However, it would be intrusive and alter the working dynamics of groups if researchers attempted to investigate behaviour by observing real life situations.

FOR CONSIDERATION

Stoner (1961) also reported the occurrence of 'cautious shift', when groups made less risky choices than individuals. Look at the hypothetical scenario below:

An old friend has offered Mr B, an optician, a partnership. His current job in Vision Express is not very well paid, but he has been paying into the works pension scheme for ten years, and his job is secure. He has a wife and three young children. He will need to invest his entire savings in the partnership offer, but if it is a success, he will end up being considerably better off.

• Would a group decision about Mr B's choice be riskier or more cautious than an individual's decision?

CD-ROM

For a discussion of the characteristics of groupthink, and its application to the Challenger space shuttle disaster in 1986, see Organisations: Additional key studies: Moorhead et al. (1991).

EVALUATION ISSUES

PRACTICAL IMPLICATIONS

While in most group decision-making situations, cohesiveness may be desirable as it brings with it greater motivation, there are times when cohesion can lead to errors in decision-making, due to the effects of polarisation as seen in 'risky shift' and 'groupthink'. In both cases, the input from individuals may have been useful in preventing poor decisions being made, but the effect of polarisation towards a group decision overrides the individual's input.

Risky shift is an example of group polarisation because individual members of a group move away from an individual position to a shared, group stance. Polarisation has an influence on group decision-making and in some instances this influence can have very negative effects. Janis (1972), introduced the concept of **groupthink** to explain a number of real life decisions with disastrous consequences. One of these cases was the Bay of Pigs crisis, when President Kennedy authorised the CIA to help Cuban exiles mount an 'invasion' of Communist Cuba. The invasion was an abject failure, and the event served to exacerbate an already antagonistic relationship between the USA and the Soviet Union, increasing the frictions between the two nations in what was known as the 'Cold War'. In analysing such political decisions, Janis suggested that under certain conditions, commitment to the group overrides the member's ability to assess situations realistically. The following conditions combine to create groupthink:

• an extremely vital decision must be made, usually within severe time constraints
• the group is already cohesive
• the group is isolated from outsiders
• the leader has a preferred solution which he or she actively seeks to implement with the group's backing.

Fortunately, President Kennedy learned from the mistakes of the Bay of Pigs and avoided the pressures of groupthink in the subsequent Cuban missile crisis.

The final stage of decision-making is to implement the solution. Landy and Trumbo (1976) suggest that where the members of groups are active members of the decision-making process, they are less likely to allow the implementation to fail. Having arrived at a final decision high levels of commitment are needed from the team to ensure that the result is put into practice and that the time and energy spent in decision-making is not wasted; members of a cohesive group are more likely to support each other in maintaining post-decision change.

4.3.2 TEAM ROLES AND TEAM BUILDING

Team roles

Members of groups assume roles within the group, and these roles define the behaviour of the individuals within the group, and the expectations of others in the group in relation to the role occupants. The most comprehensive research into team roles was carried out by Belbin (1981) in collaboration with Henley College over a number of years. Belbin's sample were managers in their late 30s attending management training courses at Henley. These managers were given group exercises to reflect the complexity of decision-making faced by executives.

Initially, Belbin tried various combinations of team composition, with the team members being matched after screening on intelligence and personality. Teams that comprised of the most intelligent managers (Apollo teams) instead of doing brilliantly, fared disastrously. Teams made up of members with similar personality profiles showed interesting differences. Generally, extrovert teams did better than introvert teams, and 'stable extroverts' got on extremely well, but before long their social activities (playing pool, for example) began to interfere with their team-planning tasks, leading to errors.

Belbin went on to experiment with team roles and found that the most successful teams consisted of a mixture of individuals each occupying a specific role, as shown in the table below:

Belbin's Team Roles

Title	Characteristics	Qualities
Company worker (CW)	Conservative, dutiful, predictable.	Organising, practical common sense, hard working, self-disciplined
Chairman (CH)	Calm, self-confident, controlled	Welcoming, encouraging contributions from others, focused
Shaper (SH)	Highly-strung, dynamic, outgoing	Drive and readiness to challenge inertia or complacency
Plant (PL)	Unorthodox, individualistic.	Imagination, inspiration, intellect
Resource investigator (RI)	Enthusiastic, curious, extrovert	Good at contacting people and exploring options
Monitor-evaluator (ME)	Sober, prudent, unemotional	Judgement, level-headed, detached
Team worker (TW)	Sensitive, sociable, team player	Responsive to people and situations
Completer-finisher (CF)	Conscientious, perfectionist, orderly	Ability to follow through

(adapted from Belbin, 1981)

In his early experiments with team composition, Belbin discovered that some teams that should have been doing well were failing. The problem seemed to be that the teams lacked a person in the group who generated ideas. This observation gave rise to the role of 'plant', that is, an individual with the specific role of coming up with ideas, who was planted in the failing teams. Belbin concluded that teams made up of members filling all eight roles would prove adequate for any challenge. In teams where there are less than eight members, some talented individuals may have the skills to occupy two roles, having a primary and a back-up role to offer. To Belbin, 'Teams are a question of balance. What is needed is not well-balanced individuals but individuals who balance well with one another.'

In 1993, Belbin added a ninth role, **technical specialist**, an expert who provides the team with knowledge and experience. He also re-named two team roles, so that company worker is now referred to as **implementer**, and chairman has become **co-ordinator**.

Team building

In today's organisations, teams are growing in importance and it is necessary to support teams so that they can become effective. The work of Belbin (1981) has been used to develop team functioning of management groups by team members learning which role they occupy and then being allocated to form well-balanced teams. Belbin's approach would be to select and bring together individuals to arrive at an optimal solution for team effectiveness. This approach may be difficult to follow in organisations where there are teams already in existence, or in small

⚖ EVALUATION ISSUES

USEFULNESS

While it is possible to manipulate the attributes of team members in experimental exercises, it may be more difficult in organisational settings to find a team that is made up of all eight roles. Also, in the selection of people for management positions, it may be difficult to find a candidate with the role requirements to occupy a vacant position. These factors make it difficult to apply Belbin's recommendations in organisational settings in a useful way.

 CD-ROM

For a copy of Belbin's Self Perception Inventory see Organisations: Measurement scales: Belbin.

EFFECTIVENESS

- The success of team building exercises such as Dyer's hinges on the dedication of the manager to follow-through the team's decisions and keep the momentum going. Individual differences in managers in terms of their commitment to supporting change will affect the success of team building exercises. Also, consultants, who play a key role in team building, will possess different levels of experience and knowledge of the organisation which are important factors in the effectiveness of the intervention.
- The success of team building initiatives is only likely where the prevailing organisational culture supports development. Some organisations place value on people achieving their own personal goals, and these organisations are not so concerned about the needs of the group. In such organisations team building may prove to be ineffective.

EVALUATION ISSUES

EFFECTIVENESS

Interventions that allow participation from team members are more likely to succeed than those that are imposed by managers or outsiders. Team building exercises are only effective in the long term when the impetus for change is sustained and supported by the organisation over a period of time. While team members may enjoy a day away from work to develop team goals and working practices, they will become sceptical of the benefits if there is insufficient follow-up when they return to work.

FOR CONSIDERATION

- List the possible reasons why team-building exercises could fail.
- What conditions are needed for success?

companies where there are insufficient members of the management team to fill all of the discrete roles. An alternative way to develop teams was put forward by Dyer (1984).

Dyer's approach is to analyse and develop existing teams with the assistance of an external consultant. The purposes of the team building exercise are to:
- remove barriers to communication
- clarify the roles of members of the group
- resolve misunderstandings of members
- share information.

In order to achieve these objectives, a day is set aside away from work and its interruptions. Prior to the meeting, individual members of the team provide their own answers to the following questions:
- What prevents you from being as successful as you would like to be in your position?
- What prevents staff in your team from functioning effectively?
- What works well in your team and is worth keeping?
- What suggestions do you have for improving the quality of working relationships?

At the meeting, the consultant asks the team to share their answers to the above questions, and from there the group prioritises issues to work on. The consultant also plays a critical role in supporting the manager in implementing agreed changes after the meeting.

Finally, clarification of both team and individual goals is widely regarded as important in team building. West and Unsworth (1997) outline ten steps to developing a clear and motivating team vision, as shown below.

KEY STUDY

Developing a team vision
Unsworth and West (1997)

Unsworth and West suggest the following key factors in helping to develop a team vision:
- Organise a team meeting that everyone can attend. An 'away day' can often facilitate the process.
- Ask each team member to write down his views on the various elements of team vision.
- Pair team members and ask them to discuss areas of agreement and differences relating to the team vision.
- Bring the discussion back to the whole team, with each pair feeding into the discussion. Bring about consensus through debate and full participation of all team members.
- Articulate a new team vision that all parties agree to.
- From the mission statement, develop a list of team goals.
- For each goal, develop objectives that are **shared, attainable, clear and measurable.**
- For each objective, devise an action plan.
- Prepare a document that sets out the mission statement, goals, objectives and action plans for team members. This should be given to team members for comments and revision (if necessary).
- Repeat the process regularly to incorporate changes to team membership and environment that may influence the team's vision.

Conflict is not necessarily a bad thing. In instances where groups are too polarised (too committed to group agreement), someone who challenges the way things are can prevent the group from making errors. In fact, minority dissent can bring about enduring change in attitudes through sustained task-related conflict due to the cognitive and social dissonance it causes. In such cases, conflict can improve the effectiveness of decision-making (Nemeth and Owens, 1996). However, conflict can also have damaging effects on groups and be counter-productive to the organisation and the individuals within it. Robins (1974) identifies three major sources of negative conflict:

1 **Communication**: misunderstandings may be due to poor communication.
2 **Structure**:
   - size: the larger the group and the greater its specialisation, the greater the likelihood of conflict
   - ambiguity: the lack of a clear definition of where responsibility lies can lead to inter-group fighting over resources
   - leadership: an over-emphasis on participative-leadership, where group members are involved with decision-making, can lead to conflict with the expression of too many different points of view
   - rewards: when group members see others benefiting from rewards that they themselves feel entitled to, it can lead to dissatisfaction and jealousy
   - interdependency: where groups have very distinct roles and concerns from each other, for example, line-managers and staff specialists, there is enormous potential for disagreement and conflict (Dalton 1950).
3 **Personal factors**: the value systems to which individuals adhere are a significant variable in social conflict. They determine people's outlook and behaviour and their view of their work, and the work of their colleagues. Differences in value systems can give rise to prejudice and discrimination.

Social identity theory and racial conflict

Social identity theory implies that team members perceive themselves as belonging to in-groups and other workers as out-group members. This perception in turn may lead to prejudice and discrimination. With the rise of multinational corporations, and increasing ethnic and cultural diversity, indigenous workers may feel threatened by people with different cultural identities, particularly when resources are scarce. This awareness of differences and categorisation of individuals into in- and out-groups can lead to racial conflict, despite legislation on equal opportunities.

Research suggests that being aware of cultural differences is the key to managing diversity. Girndt (1997) has outlined how to make team members aware of, and recognise, misunderstandings in interactions. Girndt identifies four important signals of misunderstanding:
- time delays in responding to information
- non-verbal signs of offence
- withdrawal from an interaction
- verbal signs of anger.

After identifying that a misunderstanding has occurred, the reasons for the misunderstanding must be made explicit. Girndt proposes that to expose the reason for the misunderstanding an individual can explain her own

EVALUATION ISSUES

ETHNOCENTRISM

The meaning of a 'team' may change across cultures. Cultures such as the UK, USA and Australia are strongly individualistic, and teams are seen as a collection of distinctive persons, each making a specific contribution. In more collectivist cultures, like India and Japan, teams are viewed as sharing responsibility for all aspects of the work. There may be more interpersonal conflict in groups where there is a greater sense of individuality rather than collectivism.

beliefs and behaviour, and then ask the other party to give their perspective on the event. Alternatively, the individual's behaviours and beliefs are compared with others of their cultural group. When the differences between the cultural groups have been aired, the team can negotiate ways of addressing the same issue in the future. This may take the form of a compromise between the cultures, or the adoption of the beliefs/behaviours of one of the cultures, or new rules, that all parties can agree to, being generated. In this way the value systems and methods of working are brought into the open, and misunderstandings are less likely to escalate.

Thomas (1976) identified five main styles of conflict management:
- **Competition**: using an assertive and directive style, the manager resolves conflict by using authority and threats of disciplinary action.
- **Collaboration**: using discussion, all parties involved in the conflict come face to face to discuss issues and arrive at a mutually beneficial outcome.
- **Avoidance**: one party in the conflict withdraws to avoid open confrontation. Where withdrawal is not possible, the issues at the centre of the conflict are suppressed, and not referred to. In the latter case, the underlying source of conflict is not addressed, but parties can continue to work with each other.
- **Accommodation**: one party retracts, and puts the other party's interests first. This is regarded as altruistic behaviour, where appeasement allows resolution.
- **Compromise**: both parties agree to give way, with any allowance in one direction being balanced by a gain in the other. Both sides win, but there is an acknowledgement of give and take.

Thomas (1977) went on to suggest how the different approaches could be used in different situations, since sometimes a particular style would be more appropriate. However, others challenge this assumption, believing that individuals are predisposed to dealing with issues in a preferred style, and they will use this whatever the situation (Sternberg and Soriano, 1984).

When conflict is between groups, another strategy that could be used is to set **superordinate goals**, or common goals, for all of the involved groups to attain. A classic study which highlights this approach was carried out by Sherif (1967), with American boys on summer camp, known as the 'Robber's Cave' experiments. After causing the boys to become members of two cohesive groups, Sherif and his colleagues set them up in direct competition with each other, to win desirable trophies that only the winning group would receive. Very quickly, hostility between the two groups escalated, resulting in name-calling and sabotaging behaviour. To resolve the conflict, Sherif gave the two groups communal time together, to eat and watch movies. Instead of reducing the conflict, these meetings just served as venues for the opposing groups to continue baiting each other. The research team then manipulated situations and cut off the water supply to the camp. To get the water supply back, both groups had to work co-operatively together. Over a number of subsequent tasks with superordinate goals, Sherif noted the two groups began to integrate and relationships were formed between boys who had been their former enemies.

In an organisational context, such resolution of conflict by striving for a superordinate goal may come about when the continuing survival of the organisation depends on the workers all working together, although this would be a real situation, rather than one engineered by the management.

GENERALISABILITY/ EFFECTIVENESS

- The sample in the Robber's Cave research were all boys, who did not know each other before the summer camp, unlike workers in organisations who have built up prejudices against out-group members over substantial periods of time, so this study may not be generalisable to organisational settings.
- The superordinate approach was effective for the boys at summer camp, but this may be because the two groups of boys were of equal status. In organisational settings, there may be power differentials, where one group is more powerful than another and this may reduce the chances of collective co-operation between different factions.

SECTION A EXAM QUESTIONS

a Describe one group decision-making strategy. [6]
b Discuss the pitfalls of group decision-making. [10]

a Describe one classification of team roles. [6]
b Discuss the usefulness of researching team roles. [10]

a Describe one way of managing group conflict. [6]
b Discuss the effectiveness of managing group conflict. [10]

 FOR CONSIDERATION

- Using the information in this section, suggest how conflict between two departments in a large superstore could be reduced.

 CD-ROM

For Section B sample exam questions see Organisations: Sample exam questions.

4.4 INTERPERSONAL COMMUNICATION SYSTEMS

Communication is the process by which an individual (or group), the 'sender', transmits some type of information, the 'message' to another person (or group), the 'receiver'. The message is encoded into a medium for transmission. The means of transmission varies; it can be verbal, non-verbal or electronic in nature, and when the message arrives the receiver must decode it, usually returning a reply to the sender.

Communication in organisations has a number of functions:
- **direct action**: getting people to behave in a desired fashion
- **co-ordination of action**: sharing of information and working together
- **socialisation**: developing friendships and support systems within the workplace.

Poor communication is frequently cited as a reason for poor job satisfaction and industrial discord. The British Airways check-in workers dispute which disrupted many peoples' summer holidays in 2003, was attributed to a lack of communication about new procedures for clocking in for the check-in staff. The new procedures were implemented without consultation, resulting in check-in staff taking industrial action. Psychology has an important role in the understanding and improvement of organisational communication to help ensure that people are clear about what their roles are, and that their communication systems are effective.

4.4.1 TYPES OF COMMUNICATION CHANNEL AND INFLUENCES ON THEM

Verbal communication: the written and spoken word

Verbal communication can take a number of forms or channels, and vary in its capacity to convey information. Face-to-face discussions are very rich in terms of the large amounts of information they can transmit and the immediate feedback that is available to all parties. At the other end of the scale, flyers and bulletins are essentially one-way communications, which often get filed directly into the bin by the recipient. The former, richer channels of communication are **interactive**, and include telephone conversations and video conferencing. The latter, leaner communication channels are **static**, in that they are passively received, and include media such as memos, letters, faxes and voice mail (Lengel and Daft, 1988).

Different communication channels are used depending on the nature of the message being transmitted. Daft, Lengel and Trevino (1987) propose that oral media are preferable to written media when the message is ambiguous, and written media is preferable when the message is clear. They surveyed managers to discover their preferences for different communication channels. The findings showed that managers preferred the use of oral media (such as telephones or face-to-face channels) when the message was ambiguous (for example, 'getting an explanation for a complicated technical matter'). When the message was clear (for example, 'giving a subordinate a set of cost figures'), the managers preferred the more expedient use of written channels. Daft et al. then went on to investigate whether the managers' sensitivity to communication channel usage was

🔑 **KEY DEFINITIONS**

Encoding: the sender transforms an idea into a form that can be understood by the receiver. This could be in written form or orally transmitted.

Decoding: the process by which the receiver interprets the message from the sender.

Noise: factors which distort the message at any point in the communication process. For example, distraction, poor encoding or decoding of the message or overload experienced by the receiver.

related to the managers' effectiveness. They found that media-sensitive managers, who were skilled at choosing the best communication channel for the delivery of the message, were rated most highly by their company in terms of their performance. The ability to choose the most suitable communication channel could be a factor in leadership effectiveness, or used as an evaluative point on 'individual differences' in leaders (see section 4.5.2, pp. 180–181).

Non-verbal communication

Non-verbal communication has in the past been considered to be the channel for communicating emotion and interpersonal relationships, and as such a channel contrasted with speech. More recently, this separation of non-verbal behaviour and speech has been reviewed, in the acknowledgement that the two systems are inter-related (Bull, 2001). Non-verbal communication has a number of forms:

- facial expressions
- gaze and pupil size
- proximity
- body language
- style of dress
- time: being kept waiting
- vocal features: intonation, stress, speech rate.

In communication, these cues are used to support the spoken word, or to partake in group interactions (even with the nod of the head or a hand gesture) more expediently than waiting for a gap in the conversation. Often, the sincerity of the speaker is judged by the non-verbal indicators they give, and the meaning of what is actually said is inferred from non-verbal signals.

Influences on communication channels

There are a number of influences on communication channels which can enhance or interfere with communication. Barriers to communication are often referred to as **noise** in the communication cycle. Noise can be due to human or environmental factors, these are summarised below:

Human barriers

- **Encoding/decoding difficulties**: a good idea may be poorly converted due to problems with linguistic expression, and the understanding of the message may be impaired due the use of poor expression and jargon.
- **Selectivity**: receivers of messages may ignore information in which they are not interested.
- **Cultural differences**: the conventions of exchanges differ from one culture to another. Interactions may be misinterpreted due to misunderstandings of the cultural norms. In Japan, it is considered rude to ask a superior a question directly, whereas in the West, being direct is considered an attribute.
- **Overload**: individuals are bombarded with too much information, and are unable to read the circulars or staff guidance information.
- **Feedback difficulties**: the sender presumes that the message has been received and understood, but there may be difficulties in the feedback system. Overload may prevent the recipient from replying, or where the feedback is negative, refrain from replying due to anticipated repercussions.

Environmental barriers

- **Technological problems**: electronic communication systems can be brought down by computer viruses or system crashes.

EVALUATION ISSUES

CAUSALITY

In the work of Daft et al. (1987), the suggestion that being skilled at choosing appropriate communication channels is directly responsible for the manager's success may be questioned. The successful manager may possess a range of managerial skills of which media sensitivity is only one.

Tannen's (1995) study is useful because it raises awareness of gender differences in communication style, so that workplaces can address these problems.

• **Poor work conditions:** very noisy and crowded environments can prevent the message from being heard in the first place.

KEY STUDY

Gender differences in communication
Deborah Tannen (1995)

Deborah Tannen is an American socio-linguist who has researched the communication between men and women in the workplace. She observed and interviewed male and female employees and found that men and women frequently miscommunicate due to differences in the ways they have learned to use language.

According to Tannen, men use language to communicate status, and, for them, conversations are to transmit information. For women, conversation is a vehicle to build and reinforce social bonds, and they encourage participation and inclusion by asking tag questions (with expressions like, 'don't you agree?', 'isn't it?' being added to the end of sentences to elicit involvement). Perceptions of content of conversations of the opposite sex are also different; women see male topics as dry, boring cataloguing of facts on financial matters, cars and sports; while men regard female conversation as gossipy and trivial. In the work environment, men deal with problems by giving advice, and women offer support. Men see women as 'too emotional' and women complain that men 'do not listen'.

Tannen also found that people in powerful positions tend to reward those whose linguistic style matches their own. As a result in the majority of organisations where men are in charge, contributions of women tend to be downplayed, due to their contributions being misinterpreted. A woman who tries to match the male style of communication can be perceived by men as being pushy and aggressive.

Tannen suggests that the way forward is to make men and women aware of the differences in communication style, and use their knowledge to make the most of the talents of members of the opposite sex.

FOR CONSIDERATION

Think about when you have overheard single-sex groups in conversation.
• Are Tannen's (1995) observations about male and female communication accurate?

4.4.2 COMMUNICATION NETWORKS AND CYCLES

Early research on formal communication networks was carried out by Leavitt (1951). He experimented with different arrangements of people in five-person networks, and found that the arrangement of connections in the networks affected both the efficiency of the network and the levels of satisfaction experienced by the individual members (see below).

KEY STUDY

Some effects of certain communication patterns on group performance
Leavitt (1951)

Aim: To investigate communication networks and their effects on behaviour.

Sample: 100 male undergraduates, divided into groups of five members.

Procedure: Each participant in the group was allocated an identifying colour (red, white, brown, yellow, blue) and seated at a circular table with partitions. The participants could communicate by passing written slips to other people around the table, but the experimenter could manipulate the connections between individuals. There were four communication patterns as indicated below:

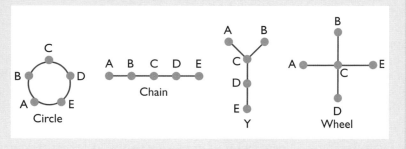

Different communication networks

Each participant was given a card on which appeared five symbols. The cards had different symbols (from a set of six) for each participant. The task for the group was to find out which symbol they had in common. There followed 15 trials which were randomised. When a member of the network had solved the common symbol, he lit up a light in his partition. When all partition members lit their lights, the trial was ended and a new one initiated. Observers then recorded the behaviour of each network and noted the time taken to solve each trial, and the correctness of the solution. The participants were then asked to fill in a questionnaire about the organisation of their group and their own experience of the task.

Results: In the wheel, chain and Y networks, a pattern of action was established after four or five trials, and this was adhered to for the rest of the trials. Occupants of central positions in the above networks, acted as leaders in the activity. The circle, having no centralised position, showed no consistent operational organisation. The circle network also generated more messages to its members than the other arrangements. Of all of the networks, the wheel was considerably faster. The greatest satisfaction for all members was in the circle, and central positions on the other networks. The peripheral members of the wheel experienced the least satisfaction, due to being less involved in the problem analysis.

Conclusion: Occupants of central positions in communication networks are more likely to emerge as leaders and experience greater satisfaction than the occupants of peripheral positions. The circle network, while being the least efficient, allowed all members to be equally involved, which increased their satisfaction with the task.

CD-ROM

For more information on Leavitt's trials see: Organisations: Additional key studies: Leavitt (1951).

EVALUATION ISSUES

ECOLOGICAL VALIDITY

In research on communication networks the tasks are problem-solving ones, usually involving symbol differences. The members of the networks are unknown to each other, and are only allowed to communicate in written form unlike a normal workplace. The networks in studies operate in laboratory conditions. These factors contribute to low ecological validity in the studies.

EVALUATION ISSUES

EFFECTIVENESS

The efficiency of centralised networks depends on the characteristics of the individual who occupies the central position. Individuals who are able to process information quickly, and who function well under pressure will contribute to the efficiency of the network.

KEY DEFINITIONS

Saturation: the maximum amount of information a single group member can process in the network. When saturation levels become too great the individual becomes overloaded, and can no longer function effectively.

Later research found that there was a relationship between network composition and the nature of the task. Leavitt's network investigations had used only very simple tasks, and in those cases centralised networks had solved the problems more efficiently. This is due to the central members having an important organisational role in filtering and sorting information, deciding which information to reject and which to pass back to the other network members. However, the greater the complexity of the task, the more saturated the central member becomes and this detracts from their effectiveness. Shaw (1964) suggested that centralised networks are more efficient on simple tasks, and de-centralised networks work better for complex tasks.

Socialising and interacting informally with colleagues is a very important aspect of work. During these interactions information is passed informally from one person to another, and this gives rise to the informal network known as the **grapevine**.

The grapevine usually communicates using oral channels, but the increased efficiency of e-mail communication has opened up a great opportunity for people to transmit news inside and outside the organisation. Davis (1976) suggested that the following factors give rise to the formation of grapevines:
- formal communication channels do not provide enough information
- feelings of insecurity promote a greater reliance on informal channels
- conflicts between individuals are offloaded on to supportive colleagues
- there is a need to disseminate new information quickly throughout the organisation.

Although the common perception of grapevine networks is that the quality of information is questionable and that most of the content is fuelled by rumour, there has been research that shows that the transmission of information can be very accurate (Walton, 1961). In their grapevine research, Sutton and Porter (1968) studied 79 employees in a US tax office and found that employees could be placed into three categories:
- **Isolates**: these were individuals who received less than 50 per cent of information but seldom passed it on.
- **Liaisons**: these received over 90 per cent of information. Managers often tended to be liaisons and only 10 per cent of non-managers were liaisons. Liaisons receive and pass on information.
- **Dead-enders**: these individuals were party to most of the information but rarely passed it on.

4.4.3 IMPROVING COMMUNICATION FLOW

Given the central role played by communication in organisations, increasing the efficiency of the communication flow will benefit both the organisation and the individuals who work within it. In order to improve communication it is necessary to remove the barriers to communication. This section will look at reducing overload of individual members, improving errors in encoding and de-coding messages and the use of information communication technology (ICT).

Reducing overload

One way of combating overload is to introduce filters into the system. The amount of information that is sent to a key individual, such as a manager can be streamlined by introducing **queuing** and the information can be prioritised by employing **gatekeepers.** These systems are often run by company PAs (personal assistants), many of whom are invaluable to their bosses. In medical settings, reception staff allocate appointment times and a queuing system, so that heath practitioners are not overloaded.

Improving encoding and decoding

Often, as organisations develop, the linguistic shorthand (or jargon) that is used proliferates. Jargon is a barrier to communication when the receiver is unclear of the meaning of frequently used terms. In his study of a large American organisation, Kanter (1977) found that jargon was developed within departments; and other departments who were not familiar with the terms felt left out. He also discovered that wives and relatives were also baffled by the use of over 100 work related terms which they could not understand. In order to improve communication flow across the organisation, Kanter argues that the use of jargon should be kept to a minimum. An additional strategy is to adopt the **KISS** principle, that is 'keep it short and simple' when communicating.

To further improve communication at an interpersonal level, good listening skills are essential. An attentive and interested listener will encourage the speaker to develop points and enhance the clarity of the message. This also reinforces feedback, so that the sender is aware of how well their message has been received. Hamilton and Kleiner (1987) state the following rules for becoming an effective and reflective listener:

- stop talking; you cannot speak and listen at the same time
- be friendly; smile, make eye contact
- show you want to listen; keep your hands still, look at the speaker not your watch
- remove distractions; close the door and turn off your phone
- empathise with the speaker; try to consider the speaker's feelings, try to think about how they are feeling (angry, upset, fed-up)
- be patient; allow the speaker to finish what they are saying, without jumping in and putting words in their mouths
- keep calm; do not let your temper get the better of you
- keep criticism to a minimum; even positive criticism can stifle openness
- ask questions; clarify the speaker's points using paraphrases ('so what you're saying is ...').

ICT and enhanced communication flow

The electronic office links managers, clerical employees, professional workers and sales personnel in a communication network that uses computerised data storage, transmission and retrieval systems. These systems have the potential to improve effective communication by:

- making information more easily available
- facilitating the free flow of information
- increasing the accuracy of information
- making information flow faster.

The most common form of ICT in the workplace is e-mail. Corbett (1997) reported that e-mail has increased the use of the grapevine as a means of communication. The benefit for management of workers using e-mail is that the content of transmissions can be monitored. However, workers may resent this intrusion into their personal correspondence.

SECTION A EXAM QUESTIONS

a Describe one type of communication channel. [6]
b Discuss the weaknesses of different types of communication channel. [10]

a Describe one communication network. [6]
b Discuss the effectiveness of different types of communication network. [10]

a Describe one way of improving communication flow. [6]
b Discuss the problems of improving communication flow. [10]

EVALUATION ISSUES

ASSUMPTIONS

Managers may assume that ICT will benefit their employees and improve communication. Although e-mail is a fast means of communicating, many employees miss the richness of face-to-face interactions. Also, to further increase speed of communication, users invent short hand and jargon, which in turn act as barriers to communication. Finally, in most organisations there are 'technosceptics' who distrust ICT, and prefer the traditional reliance on paper and hard copy. These individuals can refuse to co-operate with the introduction of technological advances, and are resistant to adapting to ICT.

? FOR CONSIDERATION

A small insurance company decides to try to improve its internal communication by giving all of its office workers lap top computers.
- Consider the benefits and possible barriers to enhancing communication flow that this would lead to.

CD-ROM

For Section B sample exam questions see Organisations: Sample exam questions.

LEADERSHIP AND MANAGEMENT

Leading and managing the behaviour of others is considered a cornerstone of **social influence**, and psychology can be applied to help us understand how and why certain individuals exert this influence over others. In the world of work, the role of the leader or manager is central to the successful functioning of an organisation, and individuals are evaluated on their ability to lead in addition to their ability to contribute effectively in a team.

The differences between **leaders** and **managers** is outlined by McKenna (1991), who claimed that leadership is a force that creates a capacity among a group of people to do something that is different or better. This could be reflected in a more creative outcome, or a higher level of performance. In essence, leadership is an agency of change, and could entail inspiring others to do more than they would otherwise have done, or were doing. By contrast, management is a force more preoccupied with planning, co-ordinating, and supervising routine activity, which of course can be done in an inspired way. Managerial leadership could be viewed as an integral part of the managerial role, and its significance grows in importance as we move up the organisational hierarchy.

The following section will look at some of the theories psychologists have proposed to explain why and how certain individuals become leaders, and the different styles leaders and managers employ in order to influence others, as well as investigating the relationship between leaders and followers.

4.5.1 THEORIES OF LEADERSHIP

Dispositional or trait theories

In this section, a good starting point might well be the old adage that, 'a leader is born, not made'. This is the main thrust of the **trait** theories, which hold the belief that it is one's innate personality that predicts the likelihood of becoming a leader. The lay belief in what is known as 'great man' theory is that a leader will possess characteristics such as intelligence, extroversion and dominance, which predispose their attaining a leadership position. This has been largely refuted.

More recently, research in business settings has shown that certain traits are more visible in those in leadership positions, in particular 'flexibility'. Kirkpatrick and Locke (1991) found that clusters of traits, which they call the 'right stuff' were more apparent in leaders. Possession of the right stuff or qualities like drive, self-confidence and cognitive ability, are seen by Kirkpatrick and Locke as being characteristics of successful leaders.

Examples of the world's most influential leaders might include people like Martin Luther King, Gandhi, Margaret Thatcher, Tony Blair and even Adolph Hitler. These famous individuals are good examples of charismatic or transformational leaders. According to Conger (1991) such leaders have the ability to make 'ordinary people do extraordinary things'. Such is the extent of their influence that they use their exceptional persuasive charm to direct nations, for better or for worse. However, although these leaders may go down in history, they are usually operating in the political arena,

EVALUATION ISSUES

VALIDITY

The validity of trait theories has been challenged due to the lack of empirical support. Mann (1959) found that, in his review of over 100 studies that had attempted to correlate personality characteristics with leadership, only very weak relationships were found for the traits of intelligence, extroversion, dominance and sensitivity. He concluded that leaders vary only marginally from non-leaders.

Martin Luther King

Adolf Hitler

Richard Branson

not in an organisational setting. It may well be that they have the power to change the direction of companies, or turn around failing businesses, but what would they do after they accomplish what they set out to? Perhaps a good example of a charismatic leader in an organisational setting would be Richard Branson, whose company began as an independent record label, and now incorporates air, train, radio and holiday companies.

Until recently, insights on transformational leadership have been generated largely in the USA, and have focused on **distant** leaders, for example, leaders at the head of large companies, rather than **close** leaders. In their *Development of a New Transformational Leadership Questionnaire*, Alimo-Metcalfe and Alban-Metcalfe (2001) have focused on managers working for local government in the UK. Their questionnaire has been developed to identify the core characteristics and qualities of transformational leaders, and could be used to assess transformational skills in managers at all levels in an organisation.

KEY STUDY

Development of a new transformational leadership questionnaire
Alimo-Metcalfe and Alban-Metcalfe (2001)

Aim: To develop a questionnaire identifying transformational leadership, which identifies constructs, and factors associated with 'nearby/close' leaders.

Sample (i) Identification of constructs: local government managerial staff from 11 local authorities were identified as having transformational qualities, 21 male and 22 females were interviewed. Also, 56 National Health Service managers at different management levels were interviewed.

Sample (ii) Piloting of the new TLQ: a random sample of 1464 managers from four managerial tiers (Chief Executive, Director, Assistant Director, Middle manager) returned the questionnaires.

Method: The researchers focused on the leadership qualities of 'nearby/close' managers, i.e. supervisors and middle managers. In the first phase of the research they interviewed managers and identified 48 constructs, or 'leadership dimensions'.

In Phase 2, pilot questionnaires were constructed, using questions generated from the identified constructs. The questionnaire comprised of 176 items with likert-type scales for responses. Analysis of responses led to the emergence of nine first-order factors.

? FOR CONSIDERATION

Using the nine aspects of transformational leadership identified by Alimo-Metcalfe and Alban-Metcalfe:
- Consider a leader/teacher/manager you know well. How would they score as a transformational leader under each of the criteria?
- How would the above leaders (see photographs) score under each of the criteria?

- The pilot testing of the Transformational Leader Questionnaire (TLQ) was carried out on a large sample, consisting of four managerial tiers, which means the findings from the pilot should be generalisable. However the sample was drawn from local government workers, reducing its generalisability to similar occupations. This is recognised by Alimo-Metcalfe and Alban-Metcalfe as they suggest the questionnaire, the TLQ local government version, is only for use with local government workers.

- The development of the TLQ was carried out using local government workers, who were asked to give information about their managers. This gives the research high ecological validity, although filling in the questionnaires may not be a typical feature of their normal working experiences.

KEY DEFINITIONS

Participative style: leaders invite workers to be part of the decision-making process, actively encourage them to take part in discussions and take on board suggestion from the workforce.

Directive style: leaders have entire control over the decision-making process, they tell workers what to do and expect their directives to be carried out.

Results: Nine factors were found to be aspects of transformational leadership:
- genuine concern for others
- political sensitivity and skills
- decisiveness, determination, self confidence
- integrity, trustworthiness, honest and open
- empowers, develops potential
- inspirational networker and promoter
- accessible, approachable
- clarifies boundaries, involves others in decisions
- encourages critical and strategic thinking.

Genuine concern for others was the most important factor in determining transformational leadership. The pilot questionnaire led to the TLQ-LGV (Transformational Leader Questionnaire-Local Government Version) being developed.

Conclusion: The factors emphasise what transformational leaders do for their followers, and show a connectedness between leader and subordinate.

Situational theories

An alternative to the trait approach is to look at **situational factors.** Could it be the case that anyone is a potential leader, given the right circumstances? Leavitt (1951) found in his experiments with different communication networks (see page 174), that individuals who occupy central positions in networks would assume a leadership role. Participants in wheel, chain and Y networks (see page 175) can communicate only with the central person, who has to manage the input and output and organise the flow of information. Due to the role they have in the network, occupants of the central positions emerge as leaders; thus situational factors are important in determining who becomes a leader.

4.5.2 LEADERSHIP/MANAGEMENT STYLES

This section looks at leadership and management styles, including the classification of different styles, such as **participative** and **directive**.

KEY STUDY

Effect of leadership style on boys in activity clubs
Lewin, Lippitt and White (1939)

Aim: To observe the effect on the behaviour in boys clubs, when the style of adult leadership is varied.

Sample: 20 boys aged 10, in four groups of five members. Prior to the research the members of each group were matched, to ensure the same pattern in each group as a whole.

Method: Clubs for 10-year-old boys were organised on a voluntary basis. Each club had an adult leader who ran the group in one of three styles:
- **Authoritarian/autocratic:** leader told the boys what they had to make, whom they could work with, and was aloof and impersonal.
- **Democratic:** leader discussed projects with the boys and allowed them to choose what to make and who to work with. The leader participated in the activities and made constructive comments.

- *Laissez-faire*: the boys were left to do as they wanted. The leader only took a role when a boy directly requested help.

The behaviour of the boys was observed at 1-minute intervals during the club sessions. The activities in the club included mask making, soap carving and model aeroplane construction. Every six weeks each group rotated the leader, and was exposed to a different style of leadership. Each adult leader used all three styles to ensure that any effect was due to style rather than the adult's personality. The boys were interviewed throughout the 5-month experimental period, and asked about their perception of the different leaders, and the other boys.

Measures: Lewin et al. were interested in which style of leadership would result in the boys in the groups:
- doing the most work
- behaving co-operatively or aggressively
- experiencing satisfaction with the leader.

Results: 19/20 boys liked their democratic leader better than their autocratic leader. Quotes: Democratic leader, 'he never did try to be the boss, but we always had plenty to do'. Authoritarian leader, 'we just had to do things; he wanted us to get it done in a hurry'. Boys felt the *laissez faire* leader was, 'too easy going', although seven of the boys preferred this. Observations confirmed that boys in the autocratic group were more aggressive towards each other, and did little when the leader left the room. In the democratic group, the boys got along better, and continued to work in the absence of a leader. In the *laissez-faire* condition there was more aggression (but not as much as in the authoritarian group) and very little work was done whether the leader was present or not. Similar amounts of work were completed in the democratic and autocratic groups, but the *laissez-faire* group produced very little.

Conclusions: The authors concluded that the boys preferred the democratic style of leadership, and better co-operation between group members occurred in the democratically led clubs. This difference was due to the style adopted by the leader.

? FOR CONSIDERATION

Think of three teachers you have been taught by, one of each leadership style (autocratic, democratic, *laissez-faire*).
- Which style led you to do more work?
- Which style did you prefer?

⚖ EVALUATION ISSUES

GENERALISABILITY/ ECOLOGICAL VALIDITY

In Lewin, Lippitt and White's (1939) study the generalisability is low because the sample used was small (n=20) and the participants were all 10-year-old boys. The tasks undertaken are not typical of everyday working situations, and so the ecological validity is also low.

Contingency models

These are models where an outcome is dependent on a number of factors; for example, in Fiedler's Contingency Theory (1967), the effectiveness of a leader depends on the style employed, relationships between the leader and the workers, the esteem in which the leader is held and the nature of the task to be accomplished.

There are a number of **contingency theories**, the best known being Fiedler's Contingency Theory (1967). Fiedler developed a scale with which to measure the 'Least Preferred Co-worker' score of an individual leader, or LPC score. A leader who scores highly on the LPC scale values relationships with others; their least preferred colleague is seen in a favourable light. They would seek to excuse the behaviour of their least favourite colleague in terms of 'they aren't as bad as all that'. A low score on the LPC scale would indicate a leader who seeks to do a job well but at the expense of her relationship with her co-workers.

The success of the leader is not only dependent on their leadership style (relationship or task centred), but also on situational variables, which allow the leader to exert their influence. These are:
- leader-member relations (How well do they get on with each other?)
- task structure (How difficult is a solution? How many possible solutions are there?)

Fiedler believed that the LPC score is a stable characteristic, and that it may be a better solution to change the leader to fit the situation rather than the other way around. His theory has been challenged due to this assumption, as the least preferred co-worker may not be a permanent member of staff, or may be generally agreed to be everyone's 'worst nightmare'. The theory does not allow for this, or for the mellowing of relationships with the LPC over time. Also the LPC score is somewhat ambiguous as a measurement, and the behaviour towards the LPC may not reflect the leader's feelings about them.

CD-ROM

For a copy of the decision tree, see Organisations: Theoretical approaches: Decision tree.

EVALUATION ISSUES

EFFECTIVENESS

Normative theory suggests that managers need to consider the answers to the decision tree questions in order to discover which style of leadership is the most effective. The application of the appropriate style to a given situation may not be straightforward, however, as some managers may have difficulty in adopting a style which is alien to them. Even though training courses can provide managers with information and practice of the varying styles, there are still those who will resort to their preferred style when they return to the workplace.

- position-power (the capacity of the leader to dispense rewards or sanctions).

According to the theory, task oriented leaders will be more successful in either very easy or very difficult situations. They will be the best leaders in a crisis, when decisions are needed quickly, and relationships can be sacrificed. Relationship-oriented leaders are better in the in-between situations, when a leader needs the subordinates on-board to make a solution effective.

Vroom and Yetton (1973) developed the concept of leadership styles. They believed that the reduction of styles to relationship-orientation and task orientation was over-simplified. In their **normative model**, they propose four styles:

- Autocratic (A): the manager makes the decision using the information at their disposal. Subordinates may supply information, but they are not involved in the decision-making process.
- Consultative (C): subordinates give suggestions to the problem either individually or in groups. The manager makes the final decision, which may not reflect the input from subordinates.
- Group-dominated (G): the problem is tackled by the subordinates and the manager working together until a mutually agreeable solution is reached.
- Delegative (D): the manager provides the delegated subordinate with information. The delegate has responsibility for solving the problem.

The above styles are adapted to work either in making decisions with groups or with individuals. Vroom and Yetton suggest that decision rules can then be used to inform the manager of the best approach to use in a given situation. The manager needs to ask herself a series of questions in order to determine, by a process of elimination, which style of leadership will be the most effective. These questions are guided by a **decision tree**. Some of the factors that need consideration include:

- the quality of the final decision; is the outcome very important ?
- the amount of information needed; does the leader have enough expertise to make the decision alone?
- the commitment of the workers to the decision; are the workers behind the decision?
- the levels of support needed from workers to make the decision work; will the decision fail if the workers are half-hearted?

Vroom and Jago (1988) have revised the original model to include more sensitive situational variables and the original options on the decision tree have been modified from yes/no answers to options on a scale from 1–5. The revised model is more complex; however software is available for managers to use in order to arrive at the appropriate management style quickly.

4.5.3 LEADER–WORKER INTERACTION AND SATISFACTION

In their review of participation and satisfaction, Miller and Monge (1982) found that people-centred, or participative, leadership was a determinant of job satisfaction. When workers have been surveyed on their preference of decision styles, a preference for participative procedures was discovered (Field and House, 1990), even when the model indicated that an autocratic style would be most effective. It would seem that workers like to be part of the decision-making process, or at least to feel as if they are part of it.

Being more involved in decision-making allows the individual a greater sense of personal control, which in turn reduces the stress levels of workers and increases their job-satisfaction. According to Jane Henry (2003), the trends in organisational structure over the past 20 years have led to the individual worker being more valued, and initiatives such as IIP (Investors in People) require that managers now give more attention to individual development needs.

Transformational leadership also has a role to play in leader–worker interaction and satisfaction. In their analysis of the TLQ-LGV, Alimo-Metcalfe and Alban-Metcalfe, comment that genuine concern for others, which was considered to be the most important leader attribute, incorporates an interest in and a sensitivity to the needs of others, actively supporting their development, giving personal job-related support, communicating positive expectations and taking time to develop a team. It could be concluded that, the more closely a leader exhibits transformational qualities, the greater the satisfaction experienced by workers will be.

SECTION A EXAM QUESTIONS

a   Describe one study of management style. [6]
b   Discuss the difficulties of researching management style. [10]

a   Describe one study of leader-worker interaction and satisfaction. [6]
b   Discuss the problems of investigating leader-worker interaction and satisfaction. [10]

EVALUATION ISSUES

VALIDITY

Organisations may report that initiatives such as IIP are taking place, when in fact they are only paying lip service to them because they are aware that outsiders expect to see them in place.

EVALUATION ISSUES

ETHNOCENTRISM

Care should be taken when applying these maxims to non-western organisations, since the values and beliefs of the industrialised world may not be the same everywhere else.

FOR CONSIDERATION

According to McGregor (1960), managers hold two different perceptions of workers. The first, referred to as 'Theory X' managers, believe that workers are essentially lazy, and need careful supervision to ensure they stay on-the-job. The second type, or 'Theory Y' managers believe that workers can enjoy their jobs and will work well if they feel appreciated.
*   How would each type of manager keep the workers on-task?
*   Which type of manager would workers prefer?
*   Which workers would experience greater satisfaction?

CD-ROM

For Section B sample exam questions see Organisations: Sample exam questions.

4.6

MOTIVATION TO WORK

As organisations must work in increasingly competitive and global conditions, with pressure to downsize and devolve responsibility, the pressures on the workforce increase. In order for the organisation to function effectively, the workers must be motivated to work to the best of their capacity so that the organisation as a whole can meet its targets. In 1996 the Institute of Personnel and Development (IPD) issued a research-based summary of factors that are essential for organisations to remain flexible in the face of change:

- people are better motivated when work satisfies economic, social and psychological needs
- motivation improves if attention is paid to job design and work organisation
- people work more effectively within a participative management style.

4.6.1 THEORIES OF MOTIVATION

Motivation is a very complex area of psychology, since motivational factors can be different from one individual to another, and these may change with the prevailing economic climate. Reflecting this, there are more theories of work motivation than can be covered within the scope of this section, but essentially theoretical perspectives fall into three categories:

- motivation through extrinsic rewards at work
- motivation through intrinsic rewards at work
- motivation through social relationships at work.

The above categories are not always discrete, as there can also be inter-relationships between these three elements of motivation.

Needs theories

In his seminal work on motivation, Maslow conceptualised motivational needs in an ascending order, with physiological needs being the essential needs common to all human beings. Only when a lower order need has been achieved will the higher needs become desirable to the individual, and the lower, achieved needs will cease to be motivators. In 1954, Maslow explained the hierarchical system in terms of its application to the

Example of needs being met in an organisational setting

Needs	Relation to organisational settings
Self-actualisation	Taking up a challenge, e.g. modernising the organisation
Esteem needs	Job title; responsibilities
Social (love) needs	Social belonging at work
Safety and security needs	Permanent job, pension scheme
Physiological needs	Basic wage to buy food, clothing and accommodation

workplace. In 1971, Maslow explained that his model was not intended as a rigid description of the development of human needs, but that the hierarchy was to illustrate the complexity and inter-relationship of needs within an individual. He also recognised the role of individual differences, in that individuals might place different emphasis on the importance of higher needs, and some people may pursue more than one need at a given time, for example, social needs and esteem needs may both be satisfied by an individual organising a successful social function for colleagues.

Maslow's contributions to the understanding of motivational factors have generated a number of other theories, among them, McGregor's (1960) theory X and theory Y; McClelland's (1965) avoidance, achievement, power and affiliation theory, Herzberg's (1966) hygiene and growth factors; and Alderfer's (1972) ERG theory.

Cognitive theories

In addition to needs theories, there are a number of theories that focus on the **perception of rewards** as motivators to work. Adams (1965) gave the name **equity theory** to the simple assertion that people within organisations like to be treated fairly. That is, they feel they should experience the same benefits as others for the same work. This is an aspect of **social comparison**, which is applied to an individual's perception of how others are treated in relation to themselves within an organisation. The comparisons are expressed in terms of **inputs** and **outcomes**.

The assessment of input/outcome relationships is based on objective information, such as salary, holiday entitlement and benefits, company car, as well as subjective information, such as the perception of how much effort has been made or the perceived dedication to the organisation. The equity theory formula can be expressed as follows:

$$\frac{\text{Outcome (self)}}{\text{Input (self)}} \quad \text{vs.} \quad \frac{\text{Outcome (other)}}{\text{Input (other)}}$$

When there is a balance between the input and outcome of the self in comparison with the input and outcome of another person, then the individual experiences a sense of equity. When there is an imbalance in the comparison, they will experience inequity.

In order for equity to be experienced, the ratios of the outcomes to incomes must be equal. If an individual perceives a colleague to work harder than themselves, they will still experience equity, even when the colleague's outcomes are higher, because the difference is seen to be fair. However, when an individual perceives their colleague to be getting more, or the same as them for doing less, they will experience feelings of inequality, which will in turn lead to motivation to act to restore equality. This will bring about any of the following changes:

- **Alter input:** if it is felt that rewards are insufficient, efforts may be reduced.
- **Alter outcomes:** the individual may ask for a salary rise.
- **Alter self-perceptions:** the individual may re-evaluate their original perceptions of inputs.
- **Alter perceptions of others:** the original evaluation of the outcomes of the other may be reconsidered. Perhaps they work longer hours, or have fewer breaks.
- **Change the focus of comparison:** the original comparison figure may be reassessed and found to be an unfair person for comparison with. A different member of the workforce may be a more valid other.
- **Exit the situation:** the individual may feel their best option is to move to another area within the organisation, or leave the organisation.

EVALUATION ISSUES

VALIDITY/EFFECTIVENESS

Maslow's critics have argued that there are problems in the ways individuals perceive and rank needs and the use of the hierarchical model to predict a person's motivation. While Maslow's hierarchy of needs theory is an interesting way to consider human functioning, it fails to offer employers guidance on how to motivate staff.

CD-ROM

For a full description of social comparison theory, see Organisations: Theoretical approaches: Social comparison theory.

KEY DEFINITIONS

Inputs are the things that the individual brings to the job, such as education, past experience, loyalty, knowledge and effort.
Outcomes are the returns the individual gets for their working experience. These include wages, social interactions and intrinsic rewards.

EVALUATION ISSUES

INDIVIDUAL DIFFERENCES

People have differences in their perceptions of reality. What a manager sees as an incentive may be regarded differently by some workers, even as an insult. For example, a manager with poor communication skills may intend to verbally reward her workers but her actions may be misinterpreted or regarded as insincere. Another criticism that has been made of equity theory is that many people may not engage in the social comparisons that the theory assumes. Workers who are engaged with their work focus on their own situation. Also people who work alone within the organisation may not have others available for comparison.

A study on Equity theory and movivation in American baseball players is detailed in section 4.6.3 (see p. 189).

Self-efficacy and goal setting

Bandura's (1977) theory of self-efficacy is a useful mechanism to help understand the role of goal setting in organisations. The theory explains why attaining a goal or objective in one's working life can result in feelings of increased self-worth and competence. In a work setting this leads to a sense of pride in one's achievements and increased motivation towards future targets.

One of the most useful theories of motivation is Locke's (1968) **goal setting theory**. Locke hypothesised that individuals are motivated by conscious goals, which they work towards. By harnessing the workers' objectives to the desire to achieve goals, managers can enhance and direct the performance of the workforce. There are two key factors to goal setting:

* **Goal difficulty:** this is the extent of the challenge a goal has for an individual. If the task set is too difficult, the individuals cannot see themselves actually achieving it. However, if a very challenging goal has a large incentive attached to it, the worker will strive harder to meet it.
* **Goal specificity:** this applies to the clarity and precision of the stated goal. A goal which is clearly defined is more easily understood and thus more likely to be achieved. Some areas within an organisation are more difficult to set specific goals in, such as raising staff moral, or increasing positive working relationships.

Locke and Latham (1979) expanded the theory to include two further key characteristics:

* **Goal acceptance:** this is the extent to which an individual accepts a goal.
* **Goal commitment:** this is the degree to which the individual internalises the goal.

Moorhead and Griffin (1992) see goal setting as a useful, short-term strategy for harnessing motivation, although they argue that 'goal-setting theory is not really a theory but simply an effective motivational technique'. Goal setting in an applied organisational setting is described in the next section (management by objectives), and in a study by Ivancevich (1977) in section 4.6.3 (see page 188).

4.6.2 IMPROVING MOTIVATION

If theories of motivation are applied in an organisational context, there should be an improvement in the motivation of the workforce. Below are some suggestions for how the theories described in the above section could be applied.

Possible applications of motivation theories to organisations

Theory	Application
Equity theory	Avoid underpayment, and overpayment of staff. Give thorough explanations to staff regarding pay freezes or redundancy, in order for them to understand the fairness of such undesired outcomes.

CD-ROM

For detailed description of self-efficacy see Health: Theoretical approaches: Self-efficacy.

EVALUATION ISSUES

ETHNOCENTRISM

The vast majority of theories of motivation have been proposed by western psychologists, predominantly from North America. These theories assume that motivation applies to the individual's experience within an organisation. In other cultures, more value may be placed on the importance of the family or the wider community, and belonging and conforming to organisational groups, rather than on the individual. The emphasis on motivation from an individual's perspective may therefore be ethnocentric.

Theory	Application
Needs theories	Organisations should meet the physiological needs of their employees by promoting a healthy workforce and meet esteem needs by giving workers recognition for their achievements.
Goal setting theory	Set goals that are specific and attainable while challenging to the worker. Monitor goals, give feedback and reward progression. Allow the individual to participate in setting their goals.

FOR CONSIDERATION

- Choose one theory of motivation and outline in detail how you would apply it in an organisational setting to improve motivation.

Management by objectives

Management by objectives (MBO) is an organisation-wide application of goal setting theory, to improve the motivation and satisfaction of individual workers and to develop the productivity and cohesiveness of the organisation as a whole. MBO works in a cyclical fashion that is usually implemented in the following ways:

- **diagnosis**: this allows an understanding of employees needs
- **planning**: the MBO approach is explained and endorsed by management and workers
- **definition of the employee's job**: this is a prerequisite to goal setting
- **goal setting**: time-specific goals are set by the worker
- **superior's review**: the worker's goals are assessed and, if necessary, modified. Goals are agreed by the worker and line-manager
- **interim review**: progress towards targets is evaluated. Targets may be adapted to meet changing situational factors
- **final review**: subordinates meet with managers to see if the success criteria for goals have been met. The outcome of the review feeds into the next MBO cycle.

EVALUATION ISSUES

EFFECTIVENESS

In his 1981 meta analysis of 185 studies on the effects of MBO on employee satisfaction and productivity, Kondrasuk (1981) found that there was mixed support for the effectiveness of MBO. He concluded that MBO could be effective in its initial stages, when impetus and enthusiasm are high, but that after two years, the positive effects of MBO wore off.

Job design

An alternative way of improving motivation is to make the work that needs to be done more interesting, and thus intrinsically more motivating to the individual. Two approaches used to increase the motivational properties of jobs are **job rotation** and **job enrichment**, and a model designed to increase the motivational potential of jobs is Hackman and Oldham's **Job Characteristics Model** (1975). The model focuses on five core characteristics of a job, which are:

- **skill variety**: the number of skills and talents a job requires
- **task identity**: the extent to which a worker sees a job through to its conclusion. In car production, the involvement of a worker in seeing a car coming from its component parts to a completed vehicle
- **job significance**: the perceived importance an occupation has to others inside and outside an organisation. A doctor is perceived to have a more important job than a shop assistant
- **autonomy**: the amount of independence a job occupant has in planning and carrying out work
- **feedback**: the extent to which direct and clear information is available with regard to current performance. A salesperson can evaluate how many items are sold each day, but an advice worker may not have clear data concerning how much of their advice has been acted upon.

Each core characteristic is given a numerical loading that is combined to give a Motivational Potential Score, or MPS. Hackman and Oldham

KEY DEFINITIONS

Job rotation: this aims to give the worker a greater variety of different tasks and to increase the worker's experience within the different areas of an organisation. This leads to the worker having a broader set of skills at their disposal.

Job enrichment: the practice of giving employees a high degree of control over their work. This encompasses having more tasks to perform at a higher level of skill and responsibility. Setting tasks that require higher order skills increases the vertical job loading.

(1975) designed the Job Diagnostic Survey, which is completed by the jobholder to measure scores on the five core characteristics. According to the model:

- the more meaningful a job is perceived to be, the greater the personal and work benefits
- the more an employee seeks personal growth, the more positive will be the reaction to a demanding task
- when jobs incorporate high levels of the five core job characteristics, workers will experience high levels of motivation, report high satisfaction with work and have less absences from work.

4.6.3 MOTIVATION AND PERFORMANCE

This section will consider whether theories of motivation do have an impact on performance in organisations. Two studies are outlined that examine field research on goal setting theory and equity theory.

FOR CONSIDERATION

Evaluate the studies by Ivancevich (1977) and Lord and Hohenfeld (1979), in terms of:
- Generalisability
- Ecological validity
- Measures
- Implications

EVALUATION ISSUES

GENERALISABILITY

The generalisability of Ivancevich's study (1977) is low because the manufacturing areas in the study were different. The sample is also small making it difficult to generalise.

KEY STUDY

Goal setting and its effects on performance and satisfaction
Ivancevich (1977)

Aim: To investigate the effects of different goal-setting treatments.

Sample: 195 skilled technicians and supervisors.

Design: Longitudinal field experiment, lasting 1 year.

Method: Three manufacturing plants with no previous experience in goal setting were allocated randomly to one of three conditions:
- Plant 1: participation in goal setting of workers (n=58)
- Plant 2: assignment to goals by superiors (n=59)
- Plant 3: comparison ('Do your best') (n=62).

Training in goal setting was given to Plants 1 and 2, consisting of role-plays, case analyses, group discussions and lectures. Specific goals relating to unexcused absenteeism, service complaints and cost of performance were set, either with the participation of the workers (Plant 1) or by supervisors (Plant 2), or workers were encouraged to try their best on the above items, but without any use of goal setting (Plant 3).

Measures: Performance measures on absenteeism, service complaints and cost of performance were taken at baseline, and after 6, 9 and 12 months.

Satisfaction was measured using the 'work' and 'supervision' scales on the Job Descriptive Index (JDI), this is described in detail on page 194.

Results: Ivancevich found that the plants with assigned and participative goal setting were superior to the 'do your best' plant. Plant 2 fared better than the participative plant. However, the improvements in the experimental groups in terms of satisfaction and performance declined substantially after 9 months.

Conclusion: Ivancevich recognises the limitations of generalising the findings from one manufacturing area and a relatively small sample. However there does appear to be an improvement in performance and satisfaction of the workers who experienced goal setting. These gains do not endure after the first year, but Ivancevich suggests that refresher training or the use if reinforcements may help in sustaining improvements.

KEY STUDY

Equity effects on the performance of major league baseball players
Lord and Hohenfeld (1979)

Aim: To test the role of the equity theory of motivation in a real life setting.

Background: Taking advantage of a change in the contractual agreement legislation for baseball players, whereby contractual bonds between owners and players were limited to one year, rather than for perpetuity, the researchers predicted that major league players would experience inequity. While playing out their existing contracts, the players would be aware of inequalities in their earnings, compared with other players with new contracts, which would be widely publicised in the media. They would thus perceive that their fellow players were benefiting from substantially higher compensation for the same job. In addition, most players in the study had experienced cuts in their pay since the introduction of the new legislation, enabling them to make a self-comparison with their former earnings.

Hypothesis: The experience of inequality would produce motivation to restore equality. This would result in altered inputs by the non-signed players.

Sample: 23 major league players, who were playing out their options during 1976, ten of whom signed a new contract part way through the season.

Procedure: Performance data for each player were gathered for the 1976 season from the *New York Times, Sporting News* and *The Baseball Encyclopaedia*. The data were collated for two periods, the first part of the season (1976A) before any of the players signed new contracts and the second part (1976B), after which ten of the players had new contracts.

Results: A significant reduction in performance was found (batting average, home runs and runs batted in) for all players in the data collected during 1976A. However, there was a recovery to normal levels of performance in the players who had signed up for new contracts during 1976B.

Conclusion: Lord and Hohenfeld concluded that perceptions of inequality were motivational factors that led to the decrease in performance of the players. This lends empirical evidence to support the equity theory, particularly since the players who established new contracts recovered performance levels after a perceived improvement in outcome/input perceptions.

Implications: The researchers draw attention to the indirect effects of multi-million dollar contracts for individual players, as these could give rise to perceptions of inequality among other players on the same team, who do not receive the same remuneration for their efforts.

Although it is assumed that improved motivation will lead to higher levels of performance, this may not always be the case. Riggio (1999) asserts that there are other variables in the workplace that influence performance:

- **Systems and technology variables:** throughout the world, workers who are well motivated are unable to perform to their potential due to poor equipment and resources. In such cases low levels of performance are often attributed to poor motivation, when in fact it is the lack of finance to buy modern equipment or to access new technologies.

- **Individual differences:** some individuals may be highly motivated, but lack the skills and abilities required to do their job effectively. An example is a new recruit, who is keen but inexperienced with work systems and practices.
- **Group dynamic variables:** most performance is measured by team output, and it is common for workers to be members of groups. As was discussed in section 4.3 (see p. 164), group membership can influence the individual. An individual may be well motivated, but may not perform optimally due to conformity to group norms.
- **Organisational variables:** within the organisation there may be a team or unit that is under performing. This will affect the overall performance of the organisation as a whole, even though many of the workforce are motivated and working hard.

SECTION A EXAM QUESTIONS

a Describe one theory of motivation to work. [6]
b Evaluate one theory of motivation to work. [10]

a Describe one way of improving motivation at work. [6]
b Contrast one way of improving motivation to work with another way of improving motivation to work. [10]

a Describe one study of the relationship between motivation and performance. [6]
b Evaluate the relationship between motivation and performance. [10]

For Section B sample exam questions see Organisations: Sample exam questions.

THE QUALITY OF WORKING LIFE

Most British people will spend approximately 45 years of their lives working five days a week, with 30 days off a year. With so much of our lives being spent in a working environment, it is important to address the quality of working life. According to Seyle (1974, 1985), all organisms require stimulation in order to function. He proposed that there is an optimal level of arousal, when individuals are stimulated into action. Too little stimulation leads to boredom and frustration, and over-stimulation will lead to reduced effectiveness, overload and eventually, to exhaustion. He also differentiated between stressors that affect the organism positively and coined the term **eustress** for the positive state experienced, and those which are negative and harmful and lead to a negative state, **distress.**

Organisational psychology plays an important role in addressing the balance between work stress (distress) and job satisfaction (eustress). In practice this involves an organisational psychologist assessing the levels of stress and work satisfaction that are experienced by individuals, reducing the impact of distress and increasing the experience of eustress.

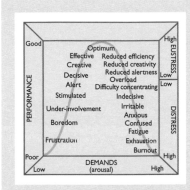

Arousal graph

4.7.1 WORK STRESS: CAUSES AND EFFECTS

Causes of stress

Stressors in organisational settings can be either discrete, one-off events, or long lasting and continuous. Wheaton (1996) described these as **event** stressors and **chronic** stressors.

In considering work stress as negative stimuli or noxious events that may occur in the working environment, Le Blanc et al. (2000) categorised stressors into four categories: job content, working conditions, employment conditions and social relations at work. These are summarised below:

Aspects of working life and related stressors

Category	Stressor
Job content	Work over-/under-load, complex work, monotonous work, too much responsibility, dangerous work, conflicting/ambiguous demands.
Working conditions	Toxic substances, noise, vibrations, lighting, radiation, temperature, work posture, physically demanding work, dangerous situations, lack of hygiene, lack of protective devices.
Employment conditions	Shift work, low pay, poor career prospects, flexible labour contract, job insecurity.
Social relations at work	Poor leadership, low social support, low participation in decision making, liberties, discrimination.

(adapted from Le Blanc et al, 2000)

> ### 🔑 KEY DEFINITIONS
>
> **Event stressors** are one-off problems that put the worker under pressure. They are time-limited, and although they are stressful, they are manageable.
>
> **Chronic stressors** are problems and issues that are 'so regular in the enactment of daily roles and activities or defined by the nature of daily role enactments or activities that they behave as if they are continuous for the individual' (Wheaton, 1996).

In addition to the impact of organisational stressors, certain individuals may, by their behaviour, increase their exposure to stress. These individuals were identified by Friedmann and Rosenman (1959) as exhibiting Type A behaviour (see section 3.6.1). According to Friedmann and Rosenman (1959) Type A behaviour is characterised in the following ways:
- an intense, sustained drive to achieve often poorly defined personal goals
- an eagerness to compete in the majority of situations
- a persistent desire for recognition and achievement
- continuous involvement in several activities at the same time, constantly subject to deadlines
- always rushing to finish activities
- extraordinary mental and physical alertness
- impatience and restlessness

Individuals who exhibit Type A behaviour are often perceived as 'workaholics', who prioritise work above family or life outside of work. They are thus more likely to be found in professional and managerial positions.

Effects of stress

In 1956 Hans Seyle suggested that the body reacts in a similar way to a wide variety of stressors and he called this process the **general adaptation syndrome**, or GAS. The GAS has three phases, which are outlined below:
- **Phase 1 Alarm:** the brain perceives the stressor and the autonomic nervous system (ANS) and the hypothalamic-pituitary link are activated.
- **Phase 2 Resistance:** the ANS and hypothalamic-pituitary link work together to maintain a high state of arousal, channelling resources to the muscles, increasing heart rate and blood pressure. The body produces adrenaline and cortisol. If the individual can take action during phase 2 to alleviate the stressor the parasympathetic nervous system (PNS) returns the body to its normal state. However, if the individual cannot avoid or cope with the stressor the body reinitiates the alarm stage, which in turn activates the resistance stage and the final phase will eventually follow.
- **Phase 3 Exhaustion:** the repeated demands made on the body begin to take their toll. This impacts on the heart, blood vessels and adrenal glands, and depletes the efficiency of the immune system. The continued state of exhaustion leads to progressively worse illnesses, such as headaches, stomach ulcers, hypertension (high blood pressure) and heart attacks.

Seyle's GAS explains why the men in Friedmann and Rosenman's (1959) study on Type A behaviour were more likely than Type B (individuals who display the opposite behaviours to Type A) to suffer from heart attacks. It is an example of the direct effects of stress on physical health. Health can also suffer due to the indirect effects of stress, such as increasing behaviours known to be harmful to physical well-being, like smoking, drinking alcohol and missing meals and sleep.

In addition to physiological reactions to stress, the individual may also suffer psychologically. Reactions may be affective (relating to mood), cognitive-behavioural (the individual interpreting and responding to the work environment) and motivational. When an individual is subjected to prolonged stress that they are unable to resolve, they are vulnerable to chronic stress complaints, such as **burnout**. Burnout can occur as a result of unrelenting exposure to stress at work. It is characterised by feelings of exhaustion, both physical and psychological. Individuals then begin to experience feelings of negative attitudes towards themselves and others, culminating in their diminished belief in their own abilities and accomplishments. (Greenberg and Baron, 1995).

Le Blanc et al. (2000) sum up the research that has been carried out on the effects of job stressors. They conclude that job stressors affect all workers, but to a greater or lesser degree depending on the influence of three categories of individual difference variables:
- genetic characteristics (such as, gender, constitution, physique)
- acquired characteristics (such as age, social class, skills, education)
- dispositional characteristics (such as Type A/B behaviour, coping styles, locus of control, hardiness).

4.7.2 MEASURING JOB SATISFACTION

Measuring job satisfaction is a complex task as it cannot be directly observed, it is not a stable experience and individuals will try to best guess the purpose for which the information will be used, and answer accordingly. The perception of job satisfaction may also vary according to the worker's emotional state, and other factors that are not related to work, for example characteristics of their home life. Job satisfaction measurement is informed by psychological attempts to measure attitudes, and the best method available to do this is to use self reports.

? FOR CONSIDERATION

- List the reasons why you work, or why members of your family work.
- How high on the list does job satisfaction come?
- Which occupations have high job satisfaction?

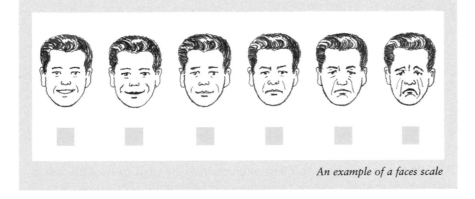

An example of a faces scale

In early attempts to measure job satisfaction, Kunin (1955) devised the **faces scale**. The faces scale is simple to use as it requires individuals to tick the box of the face that best represents the way they currently feel. Kunin carried out cross-cultural studies to ensure that people from different backgrounds and cultures interpreted the faces in the same way. The faces scale is no longer used on its own as it is regarded as lacking sufficient detail, and because some workers have reported it to be demeaning. However, the faces scale was used by Smith et al. (1969) in the development of the most widely used job satisfaction scale in the USA, the Job Descriptive Inventory (JDI), which is outlined below.

CD-ROM

For a full copy of the JDI see Organisations: Measurement scales: JDI.

EVALUATION ISSUES

VALIDITY AND RELIABILITY/
INDIVIDUAL DIFFERENCES

- The JDI was validated using the scale to measure satisfaction in a range of different samples; students, a farmers' co-operative, employees in a large electronics manufacturing company and bank employees. The JDI data was found to have good concurrent validity and good reliability across the various samples. Split half estimates of the JDI have shown an average reliability correlation co-efficient of 0.79.

- One of the most problematic aspects of measuring attitudes, such as job satisfaction, is the arbitrariness of descriptions. A factor that leads to satisfaction for one individual may not do so for another. Low pay is a good example; when a worker depends on their salary as the sole source of finance for the family, low pay will be experienced as unsatisfying. If another worker does the same job, but their partner also contributes to their overall income, low pay may not be a factor in their experience of satisfaction, since the money earned is not the most important reason for working. One way of overcoming the problem of individual differences is to ask two questions for each item, the first to establish how important the item is to the employee and a further question to rate their experience of satisfaction with that item.

KEY STUDY

The Job Description Inventory (JDI)
Smith, Kendall and Hulin (1969)

The JDI measures satisfactions within five areas of a job:
- the experience of the **work**
- **pay**
- opportunities for **promotion**
- the experience of **supervision**
- the experience of **co-workers**.

Under each heading is a list of phrases, which the worker marks with a 'Y' (for yes) if it applies, 'N' (for no) if it does not apply, and a '?' if the respondent is in doubt. For example:

Pay
- Income adequate for normal expenses   ——
- Satisfactory profit sharing   ——
- Barely live on income   ——
- Bad   ——
- Income provides luxuries   ——
- Insecure   ——
- Less than I deserve   ——
- Highly paid   ——
- Underpaid   ——

In order to interpret the scores on the JDI, scores are compared to standardised norms, based on data from a sample of 2000 men and 600 women. An individual's score can be compared with normative scores with respect to age, gender, job level, education and community prosperity. Thus an individual's score on the JDI can be compared with norms to establish whether the worker is satisfied more or less than other workers with the same demographic characteristics.

Smith et al. (1969) state that the advantages of using the JDI are:
- it measures specific areas of job satisfaction, rather than global satisfaction
- the language used is at a low verbal ability level, making the scale accessible to a broad range of users of English
- the responses are job-referent, rather than self-referent
- some of the phrases describe objective features of the job which have a direct influence on satisfaction.

Two alternative methods to questionnaires may be used to measure job satisfaction; critical incident technique and interviews. Critical incident technique asks the worker to give examples of things they like or dislike about their jobs. The examples of incidents are then analysed to give themes to the incidents. As an example, a worker may like being left to work independently, but dislike being checked up on too regularly. These incidents would be allocated to descriptors concerning supervision issues. The process allows a more individualistic analysis of job satisfaction than the use of a standard questionnaire, but is far more time consuming to carry out.

Interviews may also be used to gain an understanding of job satisfaction. Interviewers can probe more deeply into the areas of dissatisfaction, and the skilful interviewer can gain greater depth and clarity of understanding than can be gained from questionnaire responses. However, the process would be time consuming and open to the possibilities of bias, socially desirable answers and demand characteristics.

4.7.3 INCREASING JOB SATISFACTION AND QUALITY OF WORKING LIFE

Increasing job satisfaction has been reported in a number of different areas in this chapter. These are summarised below:
- Improving communication (see page 176): satisfaction is improved when communication systems are effective and when individuals can participate in decentralised networks.
- Leader–worker interaction (see pages 182–183): workers are more satisfied when a participative style of leadership is adopted.
- Motivation (see page 188): the job characteristics model, job enrichment and job rotation add to satisfaction.
- Work conditions (see pages 196–204): allowing individuals to have personal space and work in safer environments increases their experience of satisfaction.

Greenberg and Baron (1995) make the following recommendations in promoting job satisfaction:
- Pay people fairly: workers are happier when they perceive they are getting a fair day's pay for a fair day's work. This suggestion is based on equity theory (see page 185).
- Improve the quality of supervision: this means having good lines of communication, being treated with respect and having competent supervisors and managers.
- Decentralise the control of organisational power: include workers in decision-making, this increases their sense of ownership.
- Match people to the jobs they have an interest in: allow workers to do the work they enjoy, and give them greater autonomy.

Quality of work life (QWL) has its origins in organisational development (OD). QWL programmes are intended to 'humanise' the workplace, creating environments that enhance employee motivation, satisfaction and commitment. An offshoot of QWL is the quality circle. Quality circles are made up of a small number of workers who work at the same level and report to the same supervisor. The circle members meet regularly on a voluntary basis and are given support and training in interpersonal skills, problem solving and technical aspects of the job. The quality circle makes suggestions to the management on ways of improving the quality of working life and increasing efficiency in their organisation. The main obstacle to quality circles is a lack of support for their recommendations by the management (Van Fleet and Griffin, 1989).

SECTION A EXAM QUESTIONS

a Describe one way of measuring job satisfaction. [6]
b Discuss the validity of ways of measuring job satisfaction. [10]

a Describe one method of increasing job satisfaction. [6]
b Discuss the effectiveness of methods of increasing job satisfaction. [10]

? FOR CONSIDERATION

- Using the information above, make two recommendations on how to improve the job satisfaction and quality of working life for shop-floor workers in a car assembly plant.

◎ CD-ROM

For Section B sample exam questions see Organisations: Sample exam questions.

4.8 ORGANISATIONAL WORK CONDITIONS

Working conditions in western societies have changed considerably over the past 100 years, with the introduction of Health and Safety Legislation and developments in **ergonomics**. There still remain occupations where working conditions put a strain upon the workforce, such as the emergency services and heavy industry. In jobs like these, the worker may be endangered due to the nature of their job, which may involve working in physically dangerous environments. There are also other factors to consider; some working environments, such as working in very high or very low temperatures, in poorly lit conditions, in overcrowded settings and working long hours or shift work have been shown to affect individuals in the following ways:

- worker performance (productivity)
- worker satisfaction
- worker health
- worker stress.

The following sections consider research from a range of working conditions and give insights into negative environmental experiences for workers and the effects these working conditions can have on individuals. It is also important to consider the role of organisational psychology in improving working environments.

4.8.1 PHYSICAL AND PSYCHOLOGICAL CONDITIONS OF WORK ENVIRONMENTS

Physical conditions of the work environment

Lighting

In the 1920s, Elton Mayo carried out a series of studies on the effect of the physical environment on worker productivity at the Hawthorne plant of the Western Electric Company. The most famous of these were on lighting, carried out over a five year period, investigating how altering the intensity of illumination affected productivity. Mayo used a group of five women (two of whom were replaced during the study as they were too slow), who were assembling electrical relay switching. He varied the lighting intensities from very bright to very dull. Interestingly, he discovered that output increased both when it was brighter and duller, even when the workers were operating in moonlight equivalent conditions. Mayo concluded that the worker's performance changed due to the fact that the women believed that their involvement in the experiments would lead to an improvement in their working conditions, and so they had increased their work-rate. This phenomenon became known as the **Hawthorne effect**.

Subsequent research on lighting indicates that increasing illumination leads to improved performance up to a point, but too much lighting can have a negative effect. The optimal level of lighting will depend on the nature of the work being done, and there are handbooks to indicate desirable levels of illumination for different tasks. In general, high levels of glare, lack of natural light and illumination levels too low for a given task can have negative effects on performance, productivity and satisfaction, and increase worker stress (Sutton and Rafaeli, 1987).

Temperature

The human body is homeostatically controlled to maintain a core temperature of 37°C. Workers who labour in extremes of hot or cold are vulnerable to heat stroke and hypothermia, both of which can kill. In richer countries, employers may install cooling and heating systems, however in some jobs, for example, in refrigeration plants or blast furnaces, or jobs that require outdoor work in severe conditions, employees may be subjected to temperature extremes.

Effects of temperature on employees

Fahrenheit	Effect
25	Manual performance declines by 15%
45	Accidents at munition plant increase by 30%
50	Accidents increase by 35%
55	Manual performance declines
70	'Ideal' temperature
80	Tracking errors double
85	Coal mine accidents triple
90	20 gold mine workers die in 16 months
92.5	Aggression increases
95	Cognitive errors double after 7 hours of exposure
98	Telegraph errors increase by 500%

The effect of heat stress on the performance of tasks that require high levels of concentration was investigated by Beshir et al. (1981) (see below). Their findings have important implications for jobs that require high levels of vigilance from workers, such as radar tracking or equipment monitoring in nuclear plants.

KEY STUDY

Time on task effect on tracking performance under heat stress
Beshir, El-Sabagh and El-Nawawi (1981)

Aim: To investigate the effect of environmental heat on tracking performance.

Sample: Six fit, male undergraduates.

Procedure: The participants were required to track a beam of light on a visual display by keeping alignment with the display using a hand control. They undertook the tracking task for 120 minutes, with measures being recorded at 30-minute intervals.

Conditions: The task was carried out at 20°C (control), 26°C and 30°C.

Measurements: Deviations of the tracking beam from the display were recorded.

EVALUATION ISSUES

INDIVIDUAL DIFFERENCES

The effects of high temperatures can be exacerbated by other factors such as humidity and the wearing of protective clothing, which prevents the worker from sweating as the material becomes saturated. Individual differences, such as heat tolerance (see Beshir et al., 1981) and acclimatisation also need to be taken into consideration.

Results: Deterioration in tracking performance was observed in all conditions after 90 minutes, however this effect was more evident in the higher temperature conditions, with twice as many errors being recorded at 26°C after 30 minutes. There was little difference between the 26°C and 30°C levels of performance. Noticeable differences between participants were recorded.

Conclusions: Increasing temperature to 26°C led to impairment in tracking ability after 30 minutes, indicating that heat stress impairs performance on tasks which require high levels of cognitive attention. There are also variations between individuals in the extent to which they are affected by heat stress.

Noise

Many people work in noisy environments. Noise may be caused by heavy machinery on construction sites or in factories, by the heating and cooling systems that are in place to alleviate the negative effects of temperature in the work environment, or due to design features, such as open plan offices.

The average noise in factories is about 100 decibels. Noise levels over 90 decibels can cause hearing loss if exposure is regularly for more than eight hours a day. Examples of noise levels and research on its effects are shown in the table below.

The perception of noise was investigated by Glass and Singer (1972) who concluded that there are three factors which influence the individual's response to noise:
- Volume: noise above 90 decibels is psychologically disturbing and causes hearing loss.
- Predictability: if noise is regular, for example from machinery in factories individuals can habituate to it.
- Perceived control: if an individual feels they have some control over noise, the effects of noise are reduced, even when no real difference has been made.

Effects of noise at different levels

Cause of noise	Loudness of noise (in decibels)	Effect of noise
Rocket launch	180	
Gunshot blast	140	
Jet takeoff	130	Brief exposure can result in permanent deafness
Disco	120	
Riveting machine	115	Maximum legal exposure to noise
Power lawn mower	110	A person cannot speak over a sound at this level
Textile-weaving plant	100	Blood pressure increases

Cause of noise	Loudness of noise (in decibels)	Effect of noise
Food blender	95	Cognitive performance is reduced Employees report more illness and somatic complaints
	93	Angry people become more aggressive Driving performance decreases
City traffic	90	Legal acceptable noise limit for 8 hour day
Computer card verifier	85	Helping behaviour decreases
Train (100 feet away)	80	Reaction time decreases by 3%
Car	75	
Noisy restaurant	70	Telephone use is difficult
	68	Reduced detection of grammatical errors during proofreading
	65	Hearing loss can occur in sensitive individuals
Normal speech	60	
Normal noise at home	40	
Soft whisper	30	
Breathing	10	

Thus, loud unpredictable noise over which the individual perceives they have no control is the most damaging.

Psychological work conditions

The environmental design of work areas can create psychological effects which impact upon worker satisfaction and worker stress. In attempts to increase worker contact and enable better supervision of workers, **open plan offices** have increased in popularity. While open plan designs may enhance communication, there are psychological costs in terms of working conditions. Oldham and Fried (1987) suggest that open plan environments, in which there is a total absence of offices or partitions for workers, and where managerial and supervisory staff work alongside other workers, can lead to **overstimulation**. The crowding and increase in interactions combined with a lack of privacy and personal space caused by too many people occupying insufficient space leads to a state of psychological discomfort which is stressful and impairs the quality of working life.

Oldham and Fried (1987) used a sample of 109 full-time office employees (101 women, 8 men) from 19 open plan offices in a large Midwestern University (USA). They investigated the following variables:
- **social density**: total number of individuals in a given area
- **room darkness**: on the premise that the office will seem more crowded in darker conditions
- **number of enclosures**: walls/partitions around workers
- **interpersonal distance**: the distance between each worker and the nearest other worker.

The researchers recorded the characteristics of each office according to the above variables. Workers completed the 'general' and 'growth' sections of the Job Diagnostic Survey (see pages 187–188) and answered the question 'Where do you spend your coffee breaks?' Office turnover was measured 24 months after the initial survey of work conditions. Employees in the study were more likely to exhibit discretionary withdrawal (leave the office during breaks), experience dissatisfaction and quit their jobs when:
• the office was rated as dark
• few enclosures were present
• employees were seated closely together
• many employees occupied the office.

These effects were increased when more of the above factors were reported as occurring together. Oldham and Fried (1987) concluded that the conditions of open plan offices lead to the employees experiencing overstimulation, and this, in turn, leads to dissatisfaction, and workers behaving in ways to reduce the overstimulation, i.e. leaving the office during breaks or quitting their job.

In open plan environments, workers may experience lack of privacy and control over their **personal space.** Another consequence of these environments is increased environmental noise, which can contribute to stress levels and prevent the worker from doing their job efficiently.

Sutton and Rafaeli (1987) have proposed two concepts that may be helpful in understanding individual differences in the experience of work conditions:
• **The Detachment Hypothesis:** overloaded employees will concentrate more on their jobs than their less loaded colleagues. High levels of concentration on the job will mean that they are less bothered by the negative intrusions of their physical surroundings, such as temperature or noise.
• **The Aggravation Hypothesis:** intrusions and distractions may be more stressful to employees who have heavy workloads. Characteristics of the work environment (e.g. excessive heat or cold), that get in the way of them completing their work, may be perceived as more stressful when compared to their colleagues who have lesser workloads.

4.8.2 TEMPORAL CONDITIONS OF WORK ENVIRONMENTS

In the twenty-first century, we live in an era where we expect around the clock service and the demands on organisations to work 24 hours a day are increasing. In some organisations workers have traditionally worked shifts to meet productivity demands and increase efficiency, or because of the nature of the services they provide. It is now common for people to work shifts, in the USA and Canada, 25 per cent of the workforce do (Jamal, 1981), but there are physical and psychological costs to the individual.

Daus, Saunders and Campbell (1998) have identified the main detrimental effects to be as follows:

Psychological effects
• **Stress** due to disruption of Circadian Rhythms (see below) and disruption of family and social life.
• **Affect** (mood) irritability, apathy and depression.
• **Drug dependence** on stimulants like caffeine in order to stay awake and sleeping pills to sleep.

Physiological effects

- **Sleep debt:** many individuals experience poorer quality of sleep, and have less sleep.
- **Decreased alertness and concentration.**
- **Gastrointestinal problems:** difficulties with digestion.

The human body is adapted to follow a 24-hour cycle or a **Circadian Rhythm,** sleeping during the night and being awake during daylight. For most people, body temperature, metabolism and hormone production follow the 24-hour cycle and are synchronised to external cues, and at night the body should be inactive. Working night shifts reverses the body's natural Circadian Rhythms, leading to a state of **internal desynchronisation.** This disruption of the body's natural rhythms results in people being stressed, experiencing difficulties in digestion and concentration, and experiencing sleep problems. These effects are similar to the experiences of jet lag, which are experienced by airline staff. Jet-lag effects have been shown to be decreased when travelling in an east–west direction and increased when travelling from west to east. This can be explained by looking at the body's natural cycle, as the human biological clock has a 25-hour cycle, and so it is easier for the body to adapt if the day is made longer, in the case of pilots, 'following the sun' in the east–west direction.

This idea was put into practice to improve the quality of working life for mineral miners working on the Great Salt Lakes in Utah.

KEY STUDY

Great Salt Lake Minerals and Chemicals Corporation, Utah Blakemore (1988)

In 1980, two sleep specialists from Stanford University, Czeisler and Coleman, were invited by the president of GSL, to advise the management how to help 150 employees who were having trouble sleeping. The GSL workers followed a shift pattern that seemed designed to be the most disruptive schedule for normal bodily rhythms, that is, a week on day shift, followed by a week on night shift, then a week on evening shift. These work schedules had the effect of rotating the workers' body clocks backwards by eight hours each week.

The sleep specialists recommended that:
- the shift patterns should move forwards to better reflect the body's natural cycle
- each shift should last for three weeks, as it takes most people longer than one week to adjust to a change to a new time zone.

After a three-month trial period the researchers asked the management to provide measures of productivity. GSL workers were also asked to fill in questionnaires.

Results: Productivity (as measured by the number of tons of potash loaded and hauled per hour) had improved by 20 per cent. The workers reported better health, feeling more alert, and an improvement in morale and job satisfaction. They also said there was less bickering and back-biting. These effects were more apparent in the workers who had their shifts extended to three weeks.

Conclusion: The change of shift work rotations and durations to allow physiological adaptation to natural Circadian Rhythms is beneficial to workers. Initially the workers were resistant to the changes in their work patterns, but after one year 90 per cent of the workforce accepted the changes.

KEY DEFINITIONS

Circadian Rhythms: this term originates from the Latin: *Circa* (around) *Dies* (a day). Circadian Rhythms are the cycles of waking and sleeping and other physiological functions (heart rate, breathing, metabolism, hormonal levels) which are natural for animals. Human beings have adapted to be at their most alert during the hours of daylight, and to sleep when it is dark. Our body's resources are at their lowest during the early hours of the morning, and at their highest in the mid-afternoon.

Internal desynchronisation: (Aschoff, 1964) is a physiological cause of stress that is experienced due to the internal bodily controls (endogenous cues) and external environmental cues (exogenous cues) being out of normal alignment.

EVALUATION ISSUES

INDIVIDUAL DIFFERENCES

While most people's bodily rhythms will adjust after 14 days on a new schedule, some people take less time, and can adjust in one or two days. These can be compared to those whose body clocks never adjust.

EVALUATION ISSUES

ECOLOGICAL VALIDITY

Many sleep studies are carried out under laboratory conditions and Blakemore's (1988) study is a good example of a study with high ecological validity as it was carried out in the field.

Jamal (1981) proposed that the effects of shift work would be more pronounced when employees worked on variable shifts rather than on fixed shifts, as the latter would be able to adjust both internally and socially. He carried out a comparison of shift work schedules and their effects on workers. Jamal predicted that workers on variable shifts will experience less job satisfaction, less emotional and physiological well-being, less organisational commitment and poorer mental health than workers on fixed shifts. 580 nurses (97 per cent of the sample were females) in two Canadian hospitals were asked to complete a structured questionnaire. 440 useable questionnaires were returned. Absence and lateness were collected for each respondent from hospital records. Routine oriented schedules were those which had fixed hours (day, evening or night). Low-routine oriented schedules were those with rotational shifts. The questionnaire had questions relating to mental health, job satisfaction, social involvement (attendance of church or ethnic group, civic or social clubs), organisational commitment and anticipated turnover (the worker was asked how likely it was that they would leave their current job within two years).

Significant differences were found between fixed shift and rotating shift employees. Nurses on fixed shifts scored higher on mental health, job satisfaction, social involvement and organisational commitment. When demographic variables were compared (age, sex, marital status, place of socialisation, cultural background and seniority) the only factor that emerged as significant was marital status and organisational commitment (higher in married nurses). Jamal (1981) concluded that workers on shifts can adapt to changes in their routines when the shifts they work are fixed. Rotational and variable shift workers experience more disruption both in their biological clocks and in their life outside of work, which has negative physical, social and emotional consequences for the individual.

4.8.3 REDUCING NEGATIVE EFFECTS OF WORK ENVIRONMENTS FOR INDIVIDUALS

As mentioned on page 196, an important approach to enhancing the quality of working life is a perspective known as **ergonomics**, which focuses on minimising the physical demands and biological risks in the workplace. It has a number of positive outcomes (Maund, 1999) including:
- less physical effort
- less physical fatigue
- fewer health problems
- lower absenteeism
- higher job satisfaction.

When looking at reducing the negative effects of temporal conditions due to shift work (see Jamal, 1981 and Blakemore, 1988), the following recommendations can be made:
- **Incorporate fixed shifts**: by having shifts organised in a fixed pattern, workers are more able to adjust physically and socially. Indeed some workers prefer to work night shifts as it allows them more flexibility for childcare.
- **Make each shift rotation at least two weeks in duration**: this allows more time for the individual to adjust to new working conditions.
- **Rotate shifts forward**: this produces less physiological strain on the body.

In terms of the physical design of working spaces, negative effects of the working environment can be reduced by paying attention to worker preferences for personal space and the socialisation needs of the workforce.

Sutton and Rafaeli (1987) investigated the effects of different office designs on office workers.

KEY STUDY

Characteristics of workstations as potential occupational stressors
Sutton and Rafaeli (1987)

Aim: To investigate overstimulation in open plan environments and to suggest ways to reduce it.

Sample: 127 office workers from three separate insurance offices.

Conditions:
- Office C (control) was completely open plan
- Office D (density) was open plan, but had fewer occupants per square metre
- Office P (partitions): work stations had partitions on three sides

Procedure: Office D and Office P workers moved to new offices from open plan offices. The researchers took measures of density and partitions and the participants completed questionnaires three months before and three months after the change of office environment. Office C data were collected for comparison.

Measures: Respondents rated the following items on a seven point Likert Scale:
- crowding
- task privacy
- communication privacy
- office satisfaction
- work satisfaction
- performance
- stimulus/stress screening (how able are you to screen interruptions to your work?)
- need for privacy.

Results: Workers in Office P and Office D reported a significant improvement in task privacy, crowding and office satisfaction. Employees who had low stimulus screening (they felt unable to prevent interruption to their work) and high need for privacy reported the greatest improvements.

Conclusion: Sutton and Rafaeli suggest that for the majority of office workers the change from crowded, open plan offices into ones that afforded greater personal space or greater privacy increased job satisfaction and reduced stress. They also commented on the demands of the work on the employee, stating that where work was demanding these effects would be more likely to occur, but where work was less stimulating and demanding, workers may prefer more open plan arrangements.

⚖ **EVALUATION ISSUES**

GENERALISABILITY

The samples in both of the studies used in this section are from a narrow range of occupations; mines and offices. The samples are large enough to generalise from but such generalisations are limited to similar occupational fields.

For employees who work in dangerous environments with heavy equipment, the best way to reduce the negative effects of their environment is to make the workers engage in safer behaviour. One approach that has been shown to be effective is to introduce a **token economy** system, to encourage safer behaviour. One such study was conducted by Fox et al. (1987), who carried out a longitudinal study from 1972–1983 to investigate the long-term effects of a token economy on safety performance in open-pit mining. The sample consisted of workers from two open-pit mines, one in Wyoming (uranium ore) and one in Arizona (coal). Workers were office staff, foremen

The token economy system outlined in the Fox et al. study was extremely effective in reducing the negative effects of the work environments. Critics of token economy systems often raise the point that token economies are only effective in the short-term, yet this system was working for a period of over ten years.

FOR CONSIDERATION

In some situations it may be difficult to reduce work stress by changing the working environment.
• Can you suggest any psychological interventions to help workers manage their stress?

CD-ROM

For Section B sample exam questions see Organisations: Sample exam questions.

and supervisors, labourers, electricians, scraper operators and lube workers. Prior to the introduction of the token economy the number of days lost due to on-the-job injuries was eight times the national average.

Six weeks before the introduction of the stamp system, workers were told about the reward scheme where they would be awarded a number of trading stamps in their pay checks which could be exchanged for thousands of items in local stores (in 1972, 3000 stamps could be exchanged for a spice rack. Other items included microwave ovens, cuckoo clocks and even shot guns). Stamps were awarded for:
• remaining free from injury that month
• belonging to a group where no one had time off due to injury
• not being involved in damaging equipment
• making safety suggestion
• unusual behaviour that prevented accidents.

Workers lost stamps if:
• they or any of their group were injured
• they caused damage to equipment
• they failed to report an accident.

In both mines there was a substantial decrease in days lost due to injury which reduced to 25 per cent of the national average. There was a reduction in work-related deaths or permanent injuries. The reduction in costs from reduced damage to the companies far exceeded the costs of running the token economy. Fox et al. (1987) concluded that the introduction of the token economy system reduced the number of injuries to workers by increasing their safety behaviours. The system had long-term beneficial effects on safety behaviour. The authors noted that workers may fail to report accidents in order not to lose stamps, but there was still a great improvement in accident rates, and substantial reductions in cost to the companies.

SECTION A EXAM QUESTIONS

a Describe one study of physical conditions of work environments. [6]
b Evaluate the usefulness of research into physical conditions of work. [10]

a Describe one study of the psychological conditions of work environments. [6]
b Evaluate research into the psychological conditions of work environments. [10]

CHAPTER 5 | PSYCHOLOGY AND ENVIRONMENT

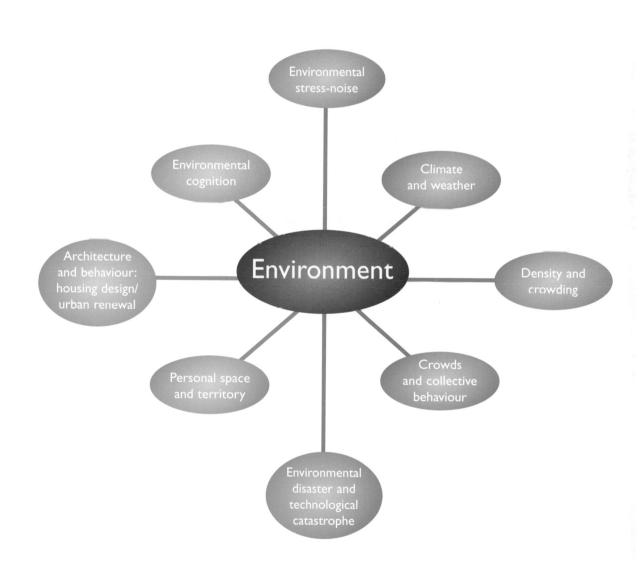

CHAPTER 5: INTRODUCTION

Environmental psychology developed at the end of the 1950s and early 1960s in the USA. Initially it began with a campaign linked to the building of psychiatric hospitals. Architects responsible for building these hospitals were more concerned with the structure of the building than the needs of those who would be using the buildings. For example, the layout of the building linked to the care required and possible interactions with other patients was not the focus of the design process, rather greater priority was given to the actual physical structure of the building. Architects began to turn to psychologists for information on cognition and social and human behaviour in an attempt to make the buildings that they were designing more satisfactory to those who were going to be using them. This created architectural psychology, focusing on the designs of buildings, which was particularly important after the Second World War as so much rebuilding was required due to the devastation that occurred during the war. This linked with topics such as behavioural geography, which was looking at human-environment relations, and the new interest in environmental problems. These areas and others were brought together and the term environmental psychology evolved.

Initially the main concern was simply the physical environment. However, over time, it developed into the larger issue of the relationship between human behaviour and the socio-physical environment. Research began to investigate topics such as wayfinding, how individuals navigate their way around their own and new environments, the effects of environmental stressors, such as noise and air pollution on human behaviour, the promotion of environmentally friendly behaviour and the impact of climate and weather. Environmental psychology aims to be problem focused, attempting to improve human beings' interaction with their environment.

Environmental psychologists now focus directly on the interaction between behaviour and the environment and it is important to look at both the physical and social environments. In order to understand the physical environment it is necessary to look at relevant social factors; for example, in the physical environment a law court is just a building, but through the process of socialisation we behave in a certain way if we are in a courtroom. Thus environmental psychology is concerned with both the social and physical environment and people's interaction with these.

🔑 **KEY DEFINITIONS**

Environmental psychology has been defined as 'the study of the interrelationships between the physical environment and human behaviour' (Burroughs, 1989).

5.1 ENVIRONMENTAL STRESS – NOISE

Environmental stressors are occurrences in the environment around us that lead to individuals experiencing an increase in arousal levels, generally leading to more negative feelings or behaviours. Stressors can include such things as pollution, traffic and travel. However one of the greatest environmental stressors, and the one that will be considered in this section, is noise.

5.1.1 DEFINITIONS AND SOURCES OF NOISE

The most straightforward definition of noise is that it is 'unwanted sound that creates a negative affective response' (Baron, 1984). The most important part of this definition is the 'unwanted' element. This therefore means that what is considered to be noise will vary between individuals, as what is 'unwanted' by one individual may be considered acceptable by another. This is the psychological component of noise; the perception of whether it is a sound that is wanted or unwanted. *Social Trends* 1995 reported that a third of people said that noise spoiled their home life to some extent. People said that noise made them feel angry, resentful and anxious.

Glass and Singer (1972) found that there are three major dimensions that influence how annoying people find noise to be outlined below:
- **Volume**: although generally the louder the noise the more annoying it is, this is not always the case. For example, people talking quietly in the silent area of a library can be classified as noise according to Baron's definition. However, more usually noise levels of above 90 dB (decibels) are considered to be both physically and psychologically damaging.
- **Predictability**: unpredictable noise is likely to be more annoying than predictable noise. Individuals can tune out constant stimuli (such as predictable noise) while non-constant stimuli (such as unpredictable noise) requires more attention. Therefore unpredictable noise leads to greater increases in arousal and thus is more stressful.
- **Perceived control**: noise is more annoying if individuals have no control over it, therefore loud music from a neighbour's party would be more annoying than loud music from your own party. If people perceive that they have no control over the noise that they are exposed to, it can ultimately lead to learned helplessness.

Research by Borsky (1969) suggested that other factors that can influence how annoying noise is include:
- if one perceives the noise to be unnecessary
- if the person making the noise doesn't seem to care about others
- if the person hearing the noise believes that it is hazardous to their health
- if the person hearing it associates it with fear
- if the person hearing it is dissatisfied with other aspects of their environment.

Sources of noise

Noise can be generated in many different ways (as shown in the table below) and two of the major sources of noise are transportation noise and occupational noise.

The approximate intensity of different sources of noise

Source of noise	Approximate intensity (dB)
Threshold of hearing	0
Pin dropping at 10 m	10
Whispering	20
Quiet office noise	30
Quiet conversation	40
Average office noise	50
Normal conversation	60
Busy street traffic	70
Lawnmower	90
Walkman at maximum level	100
Power tools	110
Threshold of pain	130
Military jet take-off	140
Perforation of eardrum	160

Transportation noise

Cars, buses, trains, planes and other forms of transport are an integral part of everyday life, yet all of these individually and collectively generate a great deal of noise. Noise levels near to motorways and roads have been measured and found to frequently reach levels of 90 dB; this level of noise is psychologically disturbing and repeated exposure to this level of noise could lead to hearing damage.

Research conducted into the effects of noise generated by transport has generally found it to have a negative effect. Fidell, Barber and Schultz (1991) found that the more exposure to transport noise community members had, the greater their reported levels of annoyance. Ising et al. (1990) used a more objective measure to examine the effects of aircraft noise. They found that exposure to aircraft noise was associated with high blood pressure and hearing problems as well as general annoyance.

Occupational noise

Noise can occur in the workplace across a wide range of different vocations. For example Raloff (1982) found that construction workers may be subjected to noise levels of up to 100 dB, aircraft mechanics to levels of between 88 dB and 120 dB and coalminers are exposed to noise levels of between 95 dB and 105 dB. All of these go above the level which is regarded as safe, and therefore all possibly risk damage to their hearing. Some of the problems that can arise from occupational noise include:
- possible deafness
- interference with speech, which can in turn lead to feelings of isolation and a reduction in job satisfaction
- interference with warning systems; for example, fire alarms, which raises health and safety issues
- annoyance at constant noise leads to increased stress levels.

Other negative effects have also been identified. Meecham and Smith (1977) found that the higher the levels of occupational noise employees had been exposed to the higher the rate of admissions to psychiatric

CD-ROM

For further detail on how the decibel scale works see Environment: Real life applications: The Decibel scale.

EVALUATION ISSUES

REDUCTIONISM

It would be reductionist to say that transport noise alone has negative effects as it is likely that there will be other environmental factors that may also be associated with transport, such as increased pollution that may be contributing to the stress that people suffer.

FOR CONSIDERATION

Research suggests that noise in the workplace creates a range of physical and psychological problems.
- How could employers aim to reduce occupational noise and what would the benefits of this be?

Working with aircraft can mean being subjected to extremely high noise levels

EFFECTIVENESS

It is important to remember that while correlational research can effectively demonstrate that two variables have altered at the same time, cause and effect cannot be inferred. It is not possible to say that the change in one variable has caused the change in the other variable.

CD-ROM

For other studies on noise, see Environment: Additional key study: Belojevic, Slepvic and Jolkovljevic (2001) and Maxwell and Evans (2000).

EVALUATION ISSUES

ECOLOGICAL VALIDITY/ETHICS

The studies by Cohen et al., Hambrick-Dixon, and Bronzaft and McCarthy are all field studies and therefore have high levels of ecological validity. They also avoid the ethical problems associated with deliberately exposing participants to noise. The drawback however is the lack of control and even when participants are matched it is possible that external factors are influencing the results.

hospitals. Ising and Melchert (1980) found that workers who wore ear defenders to protect themselves from occupational noise had lower blood pressure and lower levels of adrenalin in their urine than those workers who did not wear ear defenders. Although research does demonstrate clear benefits of wearing ear defenders, often workers are reluctant to do so, as many believe that it does not fit with their image and it also reduces communication with colleagues even further.

5.1.2 NEGATIVE EFFECTS OF NOISE ON PERFORMANCE, SOCIAL BEHAVIOUR AND HEALTH

Noise and performance

A great deal of research has been carried out into the effects of noise on performance. The studies have covered performance on a wide range of tasks and the findings have been mixed, demonstrating that the features of noise can affect the extent to which it alters performance. Attempts have also been made to link the effects of noise to other characteristics such as personality. However, general findings have been that more errors are made in noisy than in quiet conditions.

Cohen, Glass and Singer (1973) conducted a field experiment comparing two groups of children living in a New York apartment block. One group lived on the lowest floor, the others on the highest floor. The noise was greater on the lower floor. The children were matched for factors such as age and social class, but the researchers found that the children who lived on the lower floor performed less well on auditory discrimination tasks, leading to the conclusion that noise was responsible for this difference.

Bronzaft and McCarthy (1975) investigated the reading ability of children whose school was near to a train track in New York. They found that the reading ages of the children whose classrooms were nearest the tracks were lower than their counterparts. Hambrick-Dixon (1986) studied children in day care centres, and compared children who attended day care near to busy roads, with a noisy environment, and those who attended day care in a quieter setting. The children had to perform tasks in laboratory conditions and the children who attended noisy day care performed better under noisy conditions. This suggests that it is possible to adapt to noise levels.

KEY STUDY

Psychic cost of adaptation to an environmental stressor
Glass, Singer and Friedman (1969)

Aim: To test, via two laboratory experiments, whether loud unpredictable noise rather than loud predictable noise would lead to greater frustration and poorer performance on tasks requiring care and attention.

Participants: In experiment 1, 48 female undergraduates aged between 17 and 24 who were paid $3.40 for taking part. In experiment 2, 18 female undergraduates aged between 17 and 22, also paid $3.40.

Method: Experiment 1: participants were tested individually. There were two different types of noise stimuli used; fixed intermittent (predictable), where 9 second noise bursts were presented every minute for 23 minutes, and random intermittent (unpredictable), where both the length of the noise bursts and the interval between them was random (the overall amount of noise exposure equalled the fixed intermittent group).

Participants were further subdivided, and half of both groups were subjected to 110 dB of noise and the other half of each group was subjected to 56 dB; a third group acted as a control group who completed the tasks without noise. During the 23 minutes, the participants were asked to complete three separate tasks requiring both verbal and numerical skills. They were asked to work quickly on the tasks but to try not to make any mistakes. Their performance was measured in two ways, first, skin conductance was measured as this has been shown to demonstrate the individual's adaptation to the noise, and second, the number of errors made on the tasks.

Following this stage of the experiment the participants' tolerance to frustration was tested as they were then asked to complete some puzzles, without noise and on their own, some of which were unsolvable. The number of attempts they made at the unsolvable puzzles was taken as the tolerance to frustration. Second, they were asked to complete a proof reading task and the number of errors not spotted was recorded. Finally, participants completed a questionnaire to ascertain how unpleasant they had found the noise.

Experiment 2: two groups were exposed to random 110 dB noise. One group were told that they could stop the noise by pressing a button if they wished, therefore having perceived control. The other group had no control. The rest of the procedure followed the same format as experiment 1.

Results: In experiment 1 the unpredictable noise group had lower tolerance to frustration and made more errors on the proof reading task. In experiment 2, although none of the participants used the control button, those who had perceived control showed greater tolerance to frustration and made fewer proof reading errors.

Conclusions: The first experiment demonstrates the impact of noise, particularly unpredictable noise and illustrates that there can be after-effects following exposure to noise. The second experiment looks at the variable of control and its effect on the experience of noise. This experiment found that perceived control is an important factor in reducing the impact that noise has.

Noise and social behaviour

Attraction

Noise can affect individuals personal liking for each other, and how physically attractive they find one another. Bull et al. (1972) found that when participants were exposed to 84 dB of background noise, in most cases it led to less liking of other participants; however, it did not affect females' liking of others who were similar to themselves, who had been in the situation with them. Kenrick and Johnson (1979) also found that females' attraction towards others who were exposed to noise remained unchanged, but their liking of others who had not been in the same situation was reduced. Both of these studies demonstrate that females in particular seem to form an emotional bond with others that they have shared an experience with. Noise has been found to distort individuals' perceptions of others, as the concentration required to attend to the noise means that less attention is paid to others' characteristics.

Aggression

A variety of studies have been conducted to examine the effect that noise has on aggressive behaviour. Several researchers have suggested that if

Although no real electric shocks were given in Donnerstein and Wilson's (1976) study, asking participants to deliver electric shocks to 'victims' in this type of study can be considered unethical. Despite the fact that no shocks are given, participants do not know during the experiment that the shocks are not real and therefore leave the study with the knowledge that they were willing to potentially harm another participant.

The use of laboratory studies to investigate noise and aggression means that there is a lack of ecological validity, particularly in the way aggression is measured. Angering participants in an artificial setting and measuring aggression via electric shocks is not generalisable to the real world.

individuals have a tendency to be aggressive and they are exposed to noise, they are likely to become more aggressive. Research has not generally found that noise alone can make a non-aggressive person aggressive.

The majority of the research investigating the link between noise and aggression has been conducted in a laboratory setting, for example, Donnerstein and Wilson (1976) investigated the effect of unpredictable noise in a laboratory study. Participants had to give 'victims' electric shocks. Half of the 'victims' angered the participants and half did not. Participants were either exposed to 1 second bursts of 55 dB noise or 1 second bursts of 95 dB noise. When the number of electric shocks was measured, it was found that angered participants delivered more electric shocks, and the 95 dB of noise only increased the aggression levels for angered participants. Donnerstein and Wilson carried out a second study to investigate the effects of having control of noise and whether it reduced the level of aggressive behaviour. Participants were asked to work on maths problems and were exposed to either no noise, 95 dB of noise that was unpredictable and uncontrollable, or 95 dB of noise that was unpredictable but that they could stop at any time. Again they were asked to administer electric shocks, however this was after the noise had stopped, measuring the after-effects of noise. The participants were either provoked to anger or not directly after the maths problem. Findings illustrated that more shocks were given by angered participants and the unpredictable, uncontrollable noise only increased aggression for angered participants.

Helping

Research has also been conducted to investigate whether exposure to noise increases or decreases helping behaviour towards others. Mathews and Canon (1975) devised several innovative studies to try and test this and the key study described below is an example.

KEY STUDY

Environmental noise level as a determinant of helping behaviour
Mathews and Canon (1975)

Aim: To investigate the effects on helping behaviour of exposure to noise in both a laboratory and field setting. Experiment 2 also aimed to test the effect of noise level on cue-utilisation, how much attention was paid to cues that indicated whether an individual was in greater need of help.

Participants: In experiment 1 there were 52 male participants; in experiment 2 there were 80 male participants.

Procedure: Experiment 1 was a laboratory experiment in which participants were split into three noise exposure groups; 48 dB (normal noise), 65 dB (low noise) and 85 dB (high noise). Participants reported for a study that they believed was on interpersonal perception, and were asked to wait in a 'waiting room' with another person (a confederate of the experimenter) who was holding a large pile of papers. The experimenter returned and asked the confederate to come and take his turn in the study, when he got up to go he dropped all the papers. The independent variable was the level of noise in the room during the period of study and the dependent variable was the presence or absence of helping behaviour, measured by whether participants helped to pick the papers up.

Experiment 2 was a field experiment to investigate whether the effects of noise on helping were the same in the real world. The experiment took place in a curving tree-lined low density street in a student residential area. A confederate, who was either a 'high need' individual (wearing a cast on his arm), or a 'low need' individual (not wearing a cast) sat in a parked car. When a suitable participant approached, the confederate received a signal from another confederate, who was positioned across the street; he got out of a car and dropped a pile of books. Noise was added for half of the participants by a third confederate using a lawnmower, generating 87 dB of noise nearby. Again helping behaviour was measured by the amount of help the participant gave to pick up the books.

Results: In the first experiment, they found that 72 per cent of the participants in the normal noise condition helped pick up the papers, compared to 67 per cent in the 65 dB condition and 37 per cent in the 85 dB condition. In the second experiment, the results demonstrated that noise had little effect for the low need individual but for the high need individual helping dropped from 80 per cent to 15 per cent with the occurrence of noise.

Conclusions: This study illustrates that the greater the level of noise the less helping behaviour was demonstrated. These studies seem to suggest that noise is taking some attention from the current situation as people have to attend to the noise; environmental cues are therefore missed and behaviour changes as a result.

EVALUATION ISSUES

METHODOLOGY – LABORATORY VS. FIELD EXPERIMENTS

Mathews and Canon initially carried out a laboratory experiment that while highly controlled, lacked ecological validity. Their second study, a field experiment, overcame the issue of ecological validity yet was obviously less controlled. This therefore means that there are other possible reasons for the passers-by not helping besides the noise.

Other studies support the suggestion that noise leads to environmental cues being missed, for example Page (1977) approached people directly with a request for change and found that people were less likely to respond if it was noisy.

Noise and health

The most obvious effect of noise on health is the temporary or permanent loss of hearing. Constant noise levels above 90 dB can lead to hearing loss. On a daily basis everyone is subjected to noise from a variety of sources and it is possible to adapt to this. Often people who are used to city life do not really notice how noisy it is, but do notice the silence if they go to the countryside. Although it is possible to adapt to noise it does seem to have a detrimental effect on hearing; for example, Rosen et al. (1962) found that 70-year-old Sudanese nomads had the same hearing ability as 20-year-old Americans, and daily noise levels in the USA have increased in the years since this finding.

Other effects on health are less conclusive. Most research has found a link between high levels of noise and increases in blood pressure. Cohen et al. (1977) found that high intensity noise was linked with a range of physical symptoms including headaches, nausea, anxiety and sexual impotence; while Cameron et al. (1972) found a correlation between reported exposure to noise and reported acute and chronic illness.

As it is difficult to conduct controlled research to investigate the effects of noise on health some researchers have studied the effects on animals instead. Millar and Steels (1990) found that exposing animals to noise led to a constriction in their blood vessels. Raloff (1982) also conducted animal research to investigate the proposal that taking certain drugs affected the extent to which noise impacts on health. He found that animals who were given antibiotics and then exposed to noise showed greater hearing loss than those not given antibiotics.

An alternative way to attempt to examine the link between noise and health is by conducting a laboratory experiment. Egerton et al. (1987)

EVALUATION ISSUES

METHODOLOGY/ETHICS

Many studies looking at the link between noise and health use correlational techniques, which lead to problems identifying cause and effect. It is only possible to say that as noise levels increase so do health problems. It is not possible to say that noise causes health problems. In order to demonstrate causality, it is necessary to expose people to noise and then see if it causes any harm, but this is clearly unethical. Studies of this kind have been done on animals, but this raises the question of whether it is possible to generalise to human beings.

Using participants with mildly high blood pressure allowed potential health effects to be monitored. However this raises the ethical issue of protection of participants. Is it right to expose people with existing health problems to high levels of noise to see if it affects them further?

FOR CONSIDERATION

• List situations where music is played where it would be considered to have a positive effect on people.

EVALUATION ISSUES

ECOLOGICAL VALIDITY/ GENERALISABILITY

The fact that the Konecni study was conducted in an artificial environment with what could be considered an unrealistic task means that the study lacks ecological validity. Therefore it is difficult to conclude from such studies whether the results can be generalised to real life settings.

carried out an experiment using participants with mildly high blood pressure. The participants were exposed to noise of 105 dB for 10 minutes and their blood pressure was monitored. There was a significant rise in blood pressure during the exposure to noise, suggesting that exposure to noise may have a direct effect on health.

Overall, noise does seem to have an impact on a range of different aspects of our lives. However, it is not possible to conclude that noise always affects individuals, rather there seem to be mediating factors, such as individual differences and level and source of noise, that affect the impact that noise has upon us.

5.1.3 POSITIVE USES OF SOUND (MUSIC)

The previous sections have focused on noise which is considered to be unwanted sound. However, there are many different sounds that occur that are wanted, the main one being music. Although music preferences are down to individual taste, listening to music is generally seen as being a positive experience.

Listening to music often leads to an increase in our performance and a generally positive view of the situation that we are in. However, it is important that the style of music is selected carefully. Music that is highly arousing can lead to an increase in arousal and thus a more negative response than would be expected otherwise. For example, in a study by Konecni (1975) participants were either insulted or treated neutrally by an experimental accomplice before being exposed to music of varying arousal levels. The participants were given the opportunity to give fake electric shocks to the accomplice and those who had been insulted and exposed to arousing music gave most shocks. This clearly demonstrates that the type of music is important when trying to create a positive mood.

Music played in supermarkets can have an effect on how people shop. For example, Milliman (1982) found that fast tempo music led to shoppers moving around the store more quickly, but spending less money than when slow tempo music was played. In a separate study, Milliman found that fast tempo music played in a restaurant led to people eating their food more quickly, whilst slow tempo music led to more money being spent on drinks at the bar. These studies demonstrate that music can affect how we perceive the environment that we are in. This was also shown in the key study by North and Hargreaves (1996) described below.

KEY STUDY

The effects of music on responses to a dining area
North and Hargreaves (1996)

Aim: To determine whether liking for music is positively related to responses towards the environment in which that music is experienced. A secondary aim was linked to the complexity of music, in that moderately complex music is predicted to be the most well liked.

Participants: 285 university students at an East Midlands university.

Method: Participants were approached at dining tables, between 11.00 am and 2.30 pm, and asked to complete a short questionnaire about the cafeteria. While completing the questionnaire different types of music were played via a loud speaker situated next to a welfare advice stall set up by the experimenters. Each participant completed the questionnaire while listening to one particular type of music. Participants in each music type are as follows; 64 in the low-complexity new age, 74 in the high-complexity new age, 43 in the moderate-complexity new age, 55 in the moderate-complexity organ and 49 had no music.

The questionnaire aimed to measure the participants liking for the cafeteria, how happy they would be return there, how likely they would be to visit the advice stall and how much they liked the music that was playing. The experimenter staffing the advice stall also noted down the number of people that visited and any complaints that were made about the music.

Results: A positive correlation was found between the liking for the music and the liking for the atmosphere of the cafeteria, the desire to return to the cafeteria, and the likelihood of visiting the advice stall. Responses to the environment tended to be more positive in the moderate-complexity new age style music than in the other three music conditions.

Conclusions: The results indicate that positive responses to musical stimuli are associated with positive responses to the listening situation.

In conclusion, it appears that sound can be used in a positive way. Music can be used to stimulate or reduce arousal dependent upon the music used and what the situation requires, thus altering the way in which people perceive situations. Music can also be used to positive effect by stimulating and recreating memories which remind people of happier times, or it can be used as a way of distracting people from focusing on their current situation. The crucial factor in using music to positive effect seems to be selecting the right type of music for the particular situation.

SECTION A EXAM QUESTIONS

a Describe one study of the negative effects of noise on social behaviour. [6]
b Evaluate research into the negative effects of noise on social behaviour.. [10]

a Describe one study which looks at the negative effects of environmental noise. [6]
b Evaluate the ecological validity of studying environmental noise in a laboratory. [10]

a Describe one positive use of sound. [6]
b Evaluate research into the positive use of sound. [10]

💿 CD-ROM

For Section B sample exam questions see Environment: Sample exam questions.

Most individuals are aware that they feel different during the different seasons of the year, and when experiencing different types of climate and weather while on holiday. However, are these differences measurable, and does there seem to be any specific link between types of climate and weather and effects on performance and other behaviours? This section will examine how climate and weather can be classified and the effects that it has on us.

5.2.1 DEFINITIONS AND TYPES OF CLIMATE AND WEATHER

An important distinction to make is between the terms 'climate' and 'weather'. Climate refers to the average weather conditions over a period of time, while weather refers to a particular condition at a particular point in time.

There are generally considered to be three main types of climate: hot, cold and temperate. The type of climate that a country experiences is determined by its global position, more specifically, its proximity to the equator. Thus the UK's climate would be considered to be temperate, the poles would be classed as cold and most of Africa would be considered to be hot.

Weather, however, is not stable and covers the range of different conditions that a country may experience over a period of time. For example, temperature changes, rainfall and winds may all occur in a given country, but the extent and severity can vary greatly. Rainfall occurs in most countries but in some it will be infrequent and light while in others it will be relentless, often leading to flooding. Therefore, there are wide variations in weather conditions.

When examining the research that has been conducted to investigate the effects of climate and weather, it is useful to consider three perspectives that have been used to determine these effects:

- Climatological determinism suggests that climate causes a range of behaviours, such as heat causing riots. This perspective has had some support for centuries, with the belief that climate had an impact in determining how advanced different civilisations became. However, few today would support such a direct cause and effect relationship between climate and weather and behaviour, as there is recognition of the many other variables that may also influence behaviour.
- Climatological possibilism suggests that climate sets limits within which behaviour may vary, such as light winds allow people to engage in certain types of behaviour such as sailing, yet gale force winds prevent such behaviour as it would make sailing dangerous.
- Climatological probabilism falls between the above two perspectives, and suggests that climate does not determine behaviour but does influence the likelihood that some behaviours will occur, for example, due to temperature changes, people swim outdoors in some countries but rarely in others.

These three perspectives are not mutually exclusive and may overlap. The other influence that is inextricably linked to climate and weather, as

EVALUATION ISSUES

METHODOLOGY

It is difficult to clearly identify patterns of weather in some countries due to the size of the country or the variability of the weather. Thus research that is conducted to examine the effects of the weather on individuals must be clear in its defined area of study and the comparisons that are attempting to be made.

FOR CONSIDERATION

- Make a list of all the different weather conditions that you have experienced in the place that you live.
- Explain how these have affected your behaviour.

EVALUATION ISSUES

CAUSALITY/REDUCTIONISM

Research cannot conclude that it is the climate and weather alone that are affecting behaviour as this would be reductionist, it may be the geographical location or some other factor affecting behaviour. It would be impossible to separate these variables. Therefore conclusions about the impact of climate and weather should be made cautiously.

mentioned earlier, is geographical location. People's behaviour may be affected by the location they live in and the facilities that are available rather than simply being affected by the climate and weather that they experience.

5.2.2 EFFECTS OF CLIMATE AND WEATHER ON PERFORMANCE AND SOCIAL BEHAVIOUR

Although any change in weather can affect an individual's behaviour the most well researched weather conditions are temperature and light. Therefore these are the conditions that this section will focus upon.

Temperature and performance

In general, research has shown that temperatures above 32°C will impair mental performance (for example, reaction time, memory and the ability to complete mathematical calculations) of unacclimatised participants after as little as 2 hours exposure. Physical performance suffers after 1 hour.

Studies have been conducted in a range of different settings in an attempt to identify if there is any support for the above claim. Although it is possible to conduct laboratory studies to investigate this, the results from the ones that have been done have not been conclusive, possibly due to the lack of ecological validity.

Classroom studies have tested children's performance in schools of varying temperatures. Pepler (1972) conducted a study in schools with and without air conditioning in Portland, Oregon. The schools were matched geographically as was the socio-economic status of the students. In schools without air conditioning, test scores showed more variance as temperatures rose, while in air conditioned schools there was no such variability, even on the warmest days. Wyon (1970) conducted a study that examined children's reading performance in controlled temperatures between 68°F and 86°F. Findings showed that performance declined as temperature rose, yet at the highest temperature performance did rise again slightly. This study suggests that the relationship between temperature and performance may not be a straightforward linear relationship.

Other studies have been conducted in the workplace and findings show that exposure to industrial heat can cause dehydration, loss of salt and muscle fatigue, which together can reduce endurance and hence impair performance. Therefore, it is important to ensure that workers have protective clothing, are not exposed to intolerable heat for prolonged periods, and have sufficient fluid intake. When new, workers will need time to adapt to the hot environment. This was demonstrated by a review study carried out by Adam (1967). He reviewed a number of British military studies and found that 20–25 per cent of troops become heat casualties with serious deterioration in combat effectiveness when moved to tropical temperatures without acclimatisation; thus supporting the idea that time is needed to adjust.

Again research evidence is not wholly conclusive, with studies finding the full range of outcomes; heat improves performance, heat impairs performance and heat both improves and impairs performance. This lack of agreement in the findings may be due to the following factors:
- Heat initially causes a startle reaction and this may lead to an increase in performance.
- Provins (1966) suggested that heat may lead to over-arousal which, beyond an optimal point, would lead to a decrease in performance, eventually leading to physical exhaustion.

? FOR CONSIDERATION

Consider when you have been sitting exams.
- How might temperature have affected your performance?

💿 CD-ROM

For a conversion chart for temperature from Celsius to Fahrenheit see Environment: Real life applications: Temperature scales.

⚖ EVALUATION ISSUES

ECOLOGICAL VALIDITY/ REPRESENTATIVENESS

While classroom studies have high ecological validity, the sample (schoolchildren) is not representative of the whole population and therefore results are not fully generalisable.

- As heat stress increases it leads people to perceive a lower level of personal control, which in turn leads to a drop in performance.
- Individuals have different thresholds for heat; those with the lowest body temperatures are most tolerant of higher ambient temperatures.

Light and performance

It is difficult to study the effects of light and temperature separately as changes often go hand in hand. As temperature increases in the summer months so does the number of daylight hours, and as the number of daylight hours reduces in the winter the temperature starts to drop. When researching the effect that light has on behaviour it is important to remember that it has three dimensions:
- brightness
- timing of exposure
- type of light (short wavelength or long wavelength).

Munson and Ferguson (1985) conducted a study that examined the performance of elementary schoolchildren under either cool white or daylight bulbs. Performance was tested after two weeks and again seven to eight weeks later. They found that when performance on a hand steadiness task was measured, the children who had worked under daylight bulbs made fewer errors. This suggests that cool white light may have led to higher levels of arousal, thus leading to children making more errors. This could therefore have important implications for lighting in schools.

Campbell and Dawson (1990) support the suggestion that increased light leads to increased arousal having examined the alertness of shift workers. Employees worked one night under quite dim light and the following night worked under one of three conditions, dim, moderate or bright lighting. Those who worked in the bright light group performed best and were most alert. This study therefore suggests that people perform best in bright light, which could be associated with summer. Therefore, extra lighting may need to be provided during the winter months to compensate for the greater darkness that may lead to reductions in performance.

Temperature and social behaviour

Attraction

Individuals exposed to high ambient temperatures report feeling uncomfortable and irritable. Griffitt (1970) demonstrated that there was a decrease in interpersonal attraction when individuals are experiencing the effects of heat or cold (see below).

KEY STUDY

Environmental effects of interpersonal affective behaviour
Griffitt (1970)

Aim: To investigate the impact of effective temperature manipulation on interpersonal evaluative responses as shown by attitude similarity-dissimilarity.

Participants: 40 male and female students from an American university.

Method: To prevent them being fully aware of the experimental aim participants were told that the experiment was investigating 'judgemental processes under altered environmental conditions'. They were asked to wear cotton Bermuda shorts and a cotton blouse or shirt, to reduce the

▶

impact that clothing could have on the level of comfort they felt. Before the experiment actually began, all participants were pre-tested on a 44 item attitude scale. Participants were allocated to identical rooms, the only difference being the temperature. Two different temperatures were used, 90.6°F (hot) and 67.5°F (comfortable). For the first 45 minutes the participants completed a range of paper and pencil tasks finishing with a short form of the Mood Adjective Check List (MACL) to attempt to assess the feelings that they were experiencing.

The next phase of the experiment involved making judgements about an anonymous stranger based on inspection of the stranger's responses to the 44 item attitude scale (as completed before the experiment). These were fictitious, but half the participants in each temperature condition were given the responses of a stranger who agreed with them 25 per cent of the time, and the other half were given responses that agreed 75 per cent of the time (these were matched to the ones that the participants had completed before the experiment). The strangers were rated on the Interpersonal Judgement Scale (IJS) which generates an attraction score ranging from 2 to 14.

Results: The mean attraction scores were lower in both levels of agreement in the hot condition. The greatest difference between the comfortable and hot condition was for the stranger's responses that only agreed 25 per cent of the time with the participant who was rating them.

Conclusions: Increases in temperature were associated with more negative feelings and led to lower perceived attraction towards a stranger suggesting that weather, specifically temperature, can have an important impact on social behaviour.

Rotton (1983) suggested that when the stress is not actually shared with someone who is present attraction decreases, but if someone is there to share the distress the decrease in attraction may not occur. This is similar to the findings for the impact of noise on attraction, particularly for females (see page 211).

Aggression

There is a general belief that temperature has an effect on aggressive behaviour and people talk about the 'long hot summer effect'. Some data support this view, for example, the riots in the USA in 1967 were found to start on days when the temperature was 27°C or above.

There are three main ways of studying temperature and aggression that have been used:
- Geographic region studies: these compare crime rates (seen to be a measure of aggression) across different regions of a country or a continent.
- Time period studies: violence is measured at different time intervals and results are correlated with temperature in an attempt to investigate the link between heat and aggression.
- Concomitant temperature study: the temperature is known at the actual time of the study, and thus at the time of the aggression, which can therefore more accurately identify any relationship.

Concomitant studies have found that aggression often increases with heat, for example, Baron (1976) found that car drivers honked their horns more when temperatures were above 29°C than when they were below. For drivers in air conditioned cars heat did not increase horn honking.

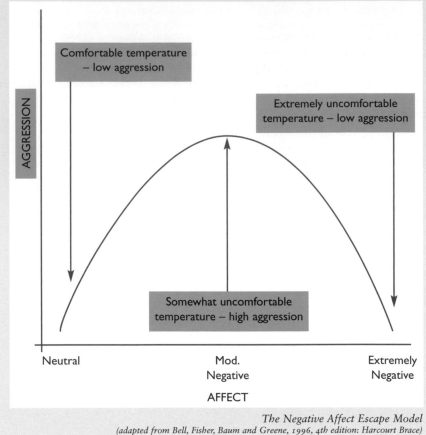

The Negative Affect Escape Model
(adapted from Bell, Fisher, Baum and Greene, 1996, 4th edition: Harcourt Brace)

Baron and Bell (1975) conducted a concomitant laboratory study where participants were either insulted or complimented before being given the opportunity to be aggressive by administering electric shocks. This was conducted in two different temperature conditions; comfortable (23°C) or hot (35°C). They found that in the comfortable condition the insulted participants were more aggressive but in the hot condition found the reverse; reduced aggression was shown to the insulting confederate while more aggression was shown to those who had been friendly. Several other studies have also found that provoked subjects in a hot laboratory showed relatively low levels of violence.

Baron and Bell (1976) have put forward an explanation for this: The Negative Affect Escape Model, which links to the inverted U hypothesis.

This model suggests that up to a critical point the negative affect caused by heat increases aggressive behaviour, but beyond this point stronger negative feelings actually reduce aggressive behaviour.

Geographic and time studies have failed to find this relationship and therefore there is the suggestion that finding this inverted U relationship is due to laboratory methodology or other factors affecting the geographic and time studies.

Helping

Again it is difficult to draw any definite conclusions from the studies that have been conducted to investigate the relationship between temperature and helping behaviour. Page (1978) found that when participants were leaving an uncomfortably hot experimental room they were less likely to volunteer their assistance than those who had been in a more comfortable environment.

Light and social behaviour

Attraction

Gergen et al. (1973) carried out an experiment to investigate the effects of light and dark on people's social behaviour. Participants volunteered to take part in an environmental psychology experiment. They were taken individually to a darkened room, where they had to remove their shoes and empty their pockets before being left with the other participants in the dark for up to an hour. There were four males and four females in each session and each had been told that at the end of the session they would be escorted from the room alone and they would never see the other participants again. Control groups had the same experiences in the room but the lights were left on.

A number of differences between the two groups were found. First, in the control group conversation was continuous for the whole session with individuals not really moving from their original seats, while in the darkened room people talked much less and moved around much more. Second, in the control group there was virtually no touching, while in the darkened room all of the participants touched each other accidentally and nearly all of them reported touching someone else deliberately. Hugging and kissing both occurred in the dark room and almost 80 per cent reported feeling sexual excitement. All of these behaviours did decline in the dark room if the participants thought that they would see each other again.

Helping

Cunningham (1979) found that sunlight seems to increase helping behaviour. People were stopped on the street and asked to help with an interview by answering a number of questions. People were told that there were 80 questions in total, but that they were not expected to answer them all, and asked how many they would answer. People were willing to answer more questions the more sunshine was present regardless of other weather conditions, such as low temperatures. This therefore suggests that social behaviour can be influenced by the amount of light that we are exposed to; the greater the natural light levels the greater the helping behaviour.

5.2.3 EFFECTS OF CLIMATE AND WEATHER ON HEALTH

Temperature and health

Body temperature should be close to 37°C (98.6°F) and death occurs at temperatures below −25°C and above 45°C. Therefore, it is important to consider what the potential health effects of heat are within this range.

The human body does have effective mechanisms to help it cope with heat and cold. These mechanisms are controlled by the hypothalamus in the brain; for example, if we get too hot the body tries to lose heat by sweating, panting and peripheral vasodilation (blood vessels near the surface of the skin dilate which in turn allows more blood to flow from the core of the body taking excess heat with it). However, if adaptive mechanisms fail a number of physiological disorders can result. Temperatures of above 39°C can have major effects on health; heat exhaustion will occur along with a decline in bodily function. As heart rate increases so does perspiration, leading to a reduction in blood volume and thus blood pressure falls. As the brain is starved of oxygen fainting may occur and in the most severe cases this can lead to coma and ultimately death.

CD-ROM

For a discussion of the effects of weather on health, see Environment: Real life applications: Why sunshine is good for you.

As 14 million work days are lost annually in the USA due to colds, it would be useful if a definite link with temperature could be found. Colds have been related to indoor temperature and atmosphere. However, humidity has an effect and therefore temperature does not tell us the whole story. It thus becomes more difficult to separate the factors. High temperatures and moist heat are also known to create problems for those with heart disease, but again finding a definite link is difficult.

Light and health

One other way that climate and weather has been linked to health is by looking at the effects of light. Psychological well-being and mental health can be affected by the amount of light individuals are exposed to. Generally research has suggested that psychological well-being, as measured by moods, is more positive in the summer, when sunlight is greatest (for example, the key study by Cunningham (1979) described below) while a lack of light in the winter months is often associated with negative moods.

KEY STUDY

Weather, mood and helping behaviour: quasi experiments with the sunshine Samaritan
Cunningham (1979)

Aim: In the second of two experiments that were carried out within this piece of research, Cunningham was aiming to test whether mood was affected by sunlight and thus whether there would be a positive correlation between helping behaviour and sunlight.

Participants: 130 parties dining during the afternoon at a moderately expensive climate-controlled restaurant in a shopping centre in Chicago.

Procedure: The experiment was conducted on 13 randomly selected days in April, May and June in 1978, with ten parties being observed on each day. The temperature outside varied from 4°C to 27°C but was constant at 21°C inside. On each test day one of six waitresses was asked to record information about the first ten parties of people she served after 1.00 pm. She had to record the number of people in the group, the total amount of the bill, the amount of the tip, the sex and approximate age of the person leaving the tip and whether alcohol had been served. Prior to recording the customer's details the waitress had to record her own mood, rated on a five point scale. Weather information was obtained from the Chicago Forecast Office.

The naturally occurring independent variable was the weather conditions and the dependent variable was the relation of the amount of money left as a tip to the total bill for the meal, thus linking to the mood of the customer, with the belief that those who were in a better mood would leave a greater tip.

Results: Sunshine and temperature were both significantly positively correlated with tipping behaviour, suggesting that weather affects our mood and behaviour. The study also found that both sunshine and temperature were significantly related to the positive mood of the waitress. However, the waitress's mood was not a predictor of tipping behaviour, suggesting that the effect of weather on tipping may have been mediated by the mood of the customers.

Conclusions: Although it is difficult to identify a cause and effect relationship between customer mood and the weather, this piece of research and similar previous research seems to suggest that the reason that tipping behaviour altered with the weather is due to the alterations in mood of the customers linked to the weather. This gives support to the general belief that we are happier when the sun is shining.

? FOR CONSIDERATION

- How could employers minimise the effects of changes in the weather on working conditions in an attempt to prevent it affecting workers' health?

Seasonal affective disorder

The lack of light during the winter months and its possible connection to the condition known as Seasonal Affective Disorder (SAD) is also of great interest. The symptoms of SAD include severe depression, fatigue, lethargy and a craving for high carbohydrate food. The prevalence of SAD among people living in countries where daylight hours are drastically shortened in the winter months suggests that there is a link between the symptoms and light levels. Rosenthal et al. (1984) initially identified the potential link as, working at the National Institute of Mental Health in the USA, they noted how mood appeared to decline in the winter months and increased again as the days became longer in the spring. In an attempt to investigate this link they tested those individuals with negative mood by exposing them to one of two different light levels. First, a dim yellow light and second a much brighter light that was similar to natural daylight. They found that the first had no effect, while the latter produced an improvement in mood in most of those who were exposed to it. This therefore supports the suggestion that SAD is linked to light levels.

The main type of treatment for SAD is light therapy. This involves the patients being exposed to several hours of very bright artificial light on a daily basis. This has to be at least ten times the intensity of normal artificial lighting. The patients have to sit close to a light box, allowing the light to shine directly into the eyes. This has been found to be effective in up to 85 per cent of diagnosed cases.

Other more recent research has questioned the link between light and SAD as it has found occurrences of SAD during the summer months in some countries. Srisurapanont and Intaprasert (1999) found a high occurrence of SAD in the summer months in people from the northern tropics, thus also suggesting a possible link between SAD and temperature. This therefore reinforces the difficulties associated with attempting to investigate the effects of temperature and light separately as they are so closely linked.

CD-ROM

For further information on SAD, see Environment: Theoretical approaches: Psychobiology of SAD.

SECTION A EXAM QUESTIONS

a Describe one study of the effects of climate and/or weather on performance. [6]
b Evaluate the strengths of research into the effects of climate and/or weather on performance. [10]

a Describe one study of the effects of climate and/or weather on health. [6]
b Discuss the validity of research into the effects of climate and/or weather on health. [10]

CD-ROM

For Section B sample exam questions see Environment: Sample exam questions.

5.3 DENSITY AND CROWDING

The world's population is increasing, and has more than doubled in the last 40 years. It is therefore an undeniable fact that the presence of other people affects various aspects of our lives. We encounter other people in a range of different circumstances in our daily lives, from public transport on the journey to work, to the crowded supermarket when we go shopping. This section will examine the impact that high density situations can have on both humans and animals.

5.3.1 DEFINITIONS OF DENSITY AND CROWDING

Density is the number of people in a prescribed space, for example, in a square kilometre. It is therefore a physical condition and can be separated into two types:
- spatial density occurs when there is the same number of people but the size of the space alters
- social density occurs when the number of people alters but the space stays the same.

As spatial density occurs when the actual size of the space varies yet the number of people remains the same it may lead to physical disruption, invasion of space and physical constraints. For example, during a busy Saturday afternoon in a city centre one floor of a department store has to be closed due to an emergency; all the shoppers will initially have to move to other floors thus increasing the spatial density.

An increase in social density has different effects as the number of people increases which can lead to a greater need for social structure, increased interactions and a greater threat to feelings of control. For example, if a bus full of passengers all go straight into the same shop to do their Christmas shopping on arrival at town the social density would increase.

Crowding is the experience of the people in a given setting and is a subjective psychological concept. This means that feelings of crowding will vary from individual to individual as it involves a personal interpretation of the level of density. Therefore some people will feel 'crowded' more quickly than others.

It might be expected that situations of similar density would lead to the same reactions. However, there are a number of different factors that can affect how crowded an individual perceives a situation to be. These include:
- the relationship with the people involved
- the duration of the experience
- the physical context of the experience
- the meaning of the experience.

Measures of density and crowding
Although it is relatively easy to gain a measure of density in a real life setting by counting the number of people in a given space, it is more difficult to measure crowding. The effects of density tend to be measured most frequently in laboratory experiments because levels of spatial or

social density can easily be manipulated and participants can be asked about the way that the different situations make them feel. However, there are obvious disadvantages with this method of measurement. Firstly, it does not create situations that are generalisable to the real world, thus limiting the usefulness of the results. It also only allows measurement of the short-term effects of density as practically and ethically it would not be possible to keep participants in the artificial situation for an extended period of time. Therefore, the experience participants have in a laboratory study cannot be likened to living in a high density environment on a 24-hour basis.

In an attempt to overcome such problems psychologists have attempted to measure density and crowding in the real world. However, while this makes any findings more generalisable, it does not allow causality to be inferred as it is not possible to control for all external factors. Thus the measured effects may not be due to crowding but due to other factors, for example, pollution or noise level. In order to attempt to control for other factors, psychologists have examined real life situations that involve a high level of external control, such as hospitals or prisons. This in turn creates other problems with generalisability as the sample is not representative.

Correlational research has also been used to assess the impact of density and crowding, correlating levels of density with various aspects of behaviour. As ever, the drawback with correlational research is the fact that it is not possible to infer causality. An alternative way of studying density and crowding which allows for greater control and manipulation of variables is to conduct animal studies; these are discussed in the section that follows.

Animal studies of density and crowding

Research that examines the effect of density and crowding on animals can be classified in to two main groups: natural studies, investigating how increased density affects animals in their natural habitat and laboratory studies, where the density is artificially manipulated and the effect it has on the animals is examined.

Natural animal studies

A range of different animals have been investigated in their natural environment, perhaps most famous is the study of lemmings.

Dubos (1965) studied lemmings (small rodents that have short tails and fur covered feet) living in the Scandinavian mountain regions. It is well documented that every 3–4 years the lemmings go down to the edge of the sea and many of them fall over the edge and drown. This was believed to have been a biologically pre-programmed event to prevent overcrowding and limit their numbers. However, on closer examination, this research found that the event was frenzied with many of the lemmings dying accidentally. The researchers proposed that the reason for this was that their rapid reproduction led to a great increase in density which in turn influenced brain and adrenal functioning.

Another natural study carried out earlier by Christian, Flyger and Davis (1960) investigated Sika Deer on James Island, and came to a similar conclusion. They examined the records that were kept about the deer and found that initially in 1916 there had been four deer on the island. By 1955, this had increased to between 280 and 300 deer. However, three years later half of the deer had died, and by 1960 only 80 deer were left. The researchers were concerned by this sudden decline in the deer

EVALUATION ISSUES

METHODOLOGY/ECOLOGICAL VALIDITY

The strength of these two studies is that they have examined the effects of natural increases in density in the animal's natural environment. However, this means that the researchers did not have control of all of the possible outside influences and thus it is possible that there could be a different reason for this type of behaviour that the researchers were not aware of.

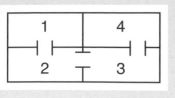

Housing unit

population, and post-mortems were conducted on the deer. They found that they appeared to have been in good shape with shiny coats and well developed muscles. However, their adrenal glands were ten times larger than normal, and after further testing to eliminate possible causes the researchers concluded that the adrenal glands were enlarged as a result of stress. This stress was believed to have been as a reaction to the crowding.

Experimental animal studies

Studies of animal density that have been carried out in a controlled environment have aimed to control other variables and thus try to gain a more direct insight into the effects of high density. One of the most important studies in this area was carried out by Calhoun (1962).

KEY STUDY

Population density and social pathology
Calhoun (1962)

Aim: To investigate the impact of overpopulation on the social behaviour of rats.

Sample: A number of laboratory-bred rats.

Procedure: A small number of rats were put into a housing unit that was capable of holding up to 48 rats. The unit was divided into four pens and an important feature was how the pens connected together. Pens 1 and 4 were not connected together and were therefore termed 'end pens'. Each of the four areas had the same facilities such as food and sleeping platforms; only the access was different. Initially the rats behaved in a normal manner with male rats building a harem, mating and defending their territory whilst female rats occupied themselves nest-building, rearing their young and resisting the advances of males outside of their harem. Gradually with continued reproduction the density in the housing unit began to increase.

Results: The overcrowding had negative effects on the social behaviour of the rats, with the worst behaviour being found in pens 2 and 3, termed the 'behavioural sink' areas. In these two pens neither males nor females carried out their roles effectively. Between 80 and 90 per cent of all new-born pups died before being weaned as the mothers showed no maternal behaviours. Male behaviour deteriorated and they pursued the females relentlessly. Without the protection of a dominant male the females were unable to resist the advances which resulted in over half of them dying due to disease by the sixteenth month of the study.

In pens 1 and 4 the rats did attempt to engage in normal social activities even when it became more populated. Infant mortality was around 50 per cent and females survived longer than their counterparts in pens 2 and 3. Overall in pens 1 and 4 behaviour resembled that of normal rats.

Conclusions: This study clearly shows the detrimental effects to both social and reproductive behaviour of higher levels of density. As density increased the social order disintegrated and a new one emerged. Calhoun suggested that each species has an optimal group size and if this is exceeded the cost to the species is great.

The overall conclusion from the animal studies is that high density has a negative effect on both health and social behaviour. However, as these studies are only on a limited number of species it is not possible to fully generalise the results to all animals.

5.3.2 EFFECTS OF DENSITY AND CROWDING ON HUMAN HEALTH, SOCIAL BEHAVIOUR AND PERFORMANCE

Following on from the findings of the animal studies on density, research has been undertaken to investigate the impact that high density can have on humans, including the effects on health, social behaviour and performance.

Crowding and health

Researchers have examined the effect of increased social density on prisoners, as obviously they are unable to escape their environment and effects can be monitored over a period of time. McCain, Cox and Paulus (1976) researched the impact of different levels of density among prisoners and found that those inmates living in conditions of low social and spatial density were ill less frequently than those living in higher densities. They conducted further research and found that inmates who lived in higher density settings were more likely to suffer from high blood pressure and that high density was linked to higher death rates among prisoners.

Lundberg (1976) studied male passengers on a commuter train and compared high and low density conditions. There were enough seats for everyone even in the most crowded conditions. Urine samples were collected to measure for levels of adrenaline and higher levels were found after the high density journeys, suggesting increases in arousal and thus increases in stress. Further results found that regardless of how crowded the train was, those who boarded at the first stop had lower adrenaline levels than those who boarded the train half way through the journey. Although their journey was longer, 72 minutes rather than 38 minutes, the control they experienced, by being able to choose their seats in an initially low density situation, led to them being able to cope with the higher density situation. Heshka and Pylypuk (1975) also conducted a study that took physiological measures following exposure to high density in the participants' natural environment. Levels of cortisol, a steroid compound produced by the adrenal cortex, were measured (as high levels of cortisol indicate high levels of stress). Students who spent the day in a high density shopping centre were compared with students who stayed on a relatively low density college campus. They found that males who had been in the high density situation had higher levels of cortisol than the control group, but females showed no difference.

Baron et al. conducted a study, also in a natural environment (student accommodation) to assess the effects of high density living on factors such as health (see below).

? FOR CONSIDERATION

- Before examining the psychological research that has been conducted, consider what you think the effects of high density environments will be on human health, social behaviour and performance and try and explain your suggestions.

⚖ EVALUATION ISSUES

REPRESENTATIVENESS

While McCain et al's study was carried out in a natural environment, the sample used (prisoners) cannot be said to be representative of the general population and therefore the results cannot be generalised.

⚖ EVALUATION ISSUES

EFFECTIVENESS

The results of Heshka and Pylypuk's study could suggest that females cope better with high density situations than males. However, it is possible that using a shopping centre as the high density situation may simply reflect greater enjoyment from shopping for females; this therefore questions the effectiveness of this study.

KEY STUDY

Effects of social density in university residential environments
Baron, Mandel, Adams and Griffin (1976)

Aim: To examine the potential long term consequences of high density living on academic performance and health.

Participants: 144 male students from five high-rise university dormitories where unexpected tripling had occurred in rooms normally used as doubles. 102 were three to a room and 42 were two to a room.

Method: Participants were given seven different measures to complete in an hour. Five of these were in the hall study lounges. These were: a

▶

present living situation questionnaire, a comfortable interpersonal distance measure, a privacy scale, a past spatial history focusing on past living experiences and an internal-external locus of control scale. The other two measures: a room evaluation scale and a series of territorial maps, were given in the individual dorm rooms.

Results: The major triple-double differences were as follows:
- Evaluation of living space: triples rated their living space as more cramped and saw their rooms in more negative ways than doubles.
- Self-perception of privacy and control: triples were less satisfied with their privacy and with the co-operation they received from their roommates in achieving privacy.
- Interpersonal adjustment: triples perceived that they received less co-operation from roommates and were less satisfied with their roommates.
- It was also found that triples visited the health centre more frequently but the difference was not significant. There were no overall significant differences in academic performance.

Conclusions: This study demonstrates that living in a high-density environment in the real world can have a negative effect on an individual's liking for others and also have a negative impact on their health.

Research has also been conducted in a more controlled environment to examine the effects of density. Evans (1979) carried out a laboratory experiment conducted with mixed sex groups of five males and five females in a three and a half hour study, in either a small room or a large room. Participants' heart rate and blood pressure were measured before the experiment began and again after three hours; it was found that in high density conditions participants had higher blood pressure and pulse rates than those in more spacious conditions.

Crowding and social behaviour

Aggression

Research into aggression and crowding has found that in some cases high density leads to aggressive behaviour while other studies have found the reverse. This has led to the suggestion that both high and low density do not necessarily lead to aggression while moderate density does, suggesting an inverted U relationship. It is possible that the reason for the increase in aggression is linked to the frustration aggression hypothesis and people become frustrated at being in a high density situation. Research also suggests that gender may affect aggression levels linked to density, with males being more aggressive. For example, Freedman et al. (1972) found that increased spatial density was associated with increased aggression in males but not in females.

Ehrlich and Freedman (1971) gave people various games to play, in varying sized rooms and found that the smaller rooms led to increased competitiveness and aggression, thus demonstrating the impact of spatial density. Palmstierna, Huitfield and Wistedt (1991) reported the effects of social density by looking at the behaviour of 163 acute care psychiatric patients over a 25 week period and found that the major predisposing factor to aggressive attacks was the number of patients around.

Many of the studies have found inconclusive results as they are not 'real world' studies. The short term nature of them makes the methodology very weak. However, it is difficult to study crowding in the real world other than using correlations between, for example, spatial density and crime statistics which suggest that there is a relationship between high density and some types of crime.

Attraction

The general finding is that high density leads to decreased attraction, both physical attraction and liking towards others. Research has also found that merely expecting higher density levels can lead to a reduction in attraction; Baum and Greenberg (1975) found that expecting to experience high social density was enough to elicit dislike. In their study, students who were told that they were waiting for ten people initially liked the people less than those who were told that they were waiting for four people. The key study described on page 227 by Baron et al. (1976) found similar results.

There also appear to be gender differences in the impact that density has on attraction levels, with males experiencing a more extreme reaction. Epstein and Karlin (1975) conducted an experiment where males and females participated in same sex groups of six, solving puzzles. The participants were asked afterwards to say how similar they perceived the others to be. They found that males rated others more negatively in the high spatial density groups whereas females rated the others more positively in high density situations.

The differences in the levels of attraction shown by males and females could be due to different personal space zones or to more co-operative socialisation of females and more competitive socialisation of males. This links to social norms, with it generally being seen as acceptable for females to discuss problems and support each other and as less acceptable for males to do this.

Research has suggested that one way in which individuals deal with high density is to withdraw from the situation. Withdrawal may occur in anticipation of the high density or as a reaction to it. The consequences of withdrawal due to density may be a disruption to social support networks. This in turn can have a negative effect as these are the networks we often rely upon during times of stress which are therefore not available. For example, Evans and Lepore (1993) found that individuals from crowded homes were less likely to seek social support when they needed it and rated others as less supportive than those from less crowded homes. Individuals from crowded homes were also less likely to offer support to others.

Helping

Much of the work that has looked at density and helping has been carried out in field studies which have obvious benefits over the laboratory research that has been carried out into other effects of density. It has been found that the greater the density the less the helping behaviour.

One field experiment that has been carried out with students was conducted by Bickman et al. (1973). They compared acts of helping behaviour in high, medium and low density dormitories. Envelopes which were stamped and addressed were dropped in the dorms and helpfulness was measured by the number that were picked up and placed in the mail. They found that 58 per cent mailed the letters in the high density dorms, 79 per cent in medium density dorms, and 88 per cent in low density dorms. This therefore demonstrates that more helping behaviour occurred in the lower density situations. Jorgenson and Dukes (1976) investigated social density and compliance in cafeterias. A notice was placed in the

It is questionable how effective the measurement of helping is in both of these studies as neither is a very true to life measure. Mailing a letter or removing rubbish does not truly assess whether an individual would give help in a real situation such as assisting a person who has fallen. Therefore the results cannot be fully generalised to real life situations.

One explanation for why density affects performance to varying degrees is via the Yerkes-Dodson law. Increased density leads to increased arousal and therefore may initially lead to an increase in performance. In contrast, more complex tasks require more attention and as the high density situation also requires attention it may lead to poorer performance on tasks.

cafeteria asking people to return their trays, and they found that more people did this in low density conditions.

One reason why the level of helping behaviour may be reduced in crowded situations links to the concept of diffusion of responsibility. The more people that are present in a situation that requires help, the less often help is given. This may be due to the fact that people diffuse responsibility among themselves with no-one feeling that they ought to be the one to help.

Crowding and Task performance

Once again there have been a variety of studies carried out to test the impact that density has on task performance, including both laboratory and field experiments. It would seem likely that if density has a negative physiological effect and a negative effect on our social behaviour it will also have a negative effect on task performance. In a laboratory experiment, Paulus et al. (1976) found that both high spatial and social density led to decreases in complex maze task performance, with high social density having a greater effect than high spatial density.

Aiello, Epstein and Karlin (1975) conducted a field study looking at student dorms. They had two conditions: three people in a two person dorm (high density) or two people in a two person dorm (low density). They found that there was a decrease in complex task performance for the higher density condition.

This suggests that university students living in low density settings may get better marks than those living in high density settings. The increased density may overload an individual's information processing ability which in turn will lead to a poorer performance of tasks which require higher level cognitive skills.

A field study was also carried out by Saegert, MacIntosh and West (1975). They tested participants in a socially dense department store and at a busy railway terminal. One of the tasks was to produce a cognitive map of their environment, enabling them to give directions to others. The results showed that their ability to do this was impeded by the high density. Similarly a field study was conducted by Bruins and Barber (2000) outside a supermarket. Eighty people were asked to take part at either crowded or uncrowded times. Findings demonstrated that the performance was worse, particularly for mental tasks, under crowded conditions.

Research has also found that there is the possibility that being in high density situations will have lasting after-effects. Evans (1979) found that participants who had been exposed to high density situations later showed less persistence at solving unsolvable puzzles than those who had been exposed to low density situations.

5.3.3 PREVENTING AND COPING WITH THE EFFECTS OF CROWDING

When looking at crowding it is also important to consider how people cope with crowded situations; as soon as crowding is anticipated we start to use coping strategies, such as withdrawing from the situation. There are however certain factors that affect the impact of crowding, and thus affect how we deal with it. These include factors such as the reason for being in the crowded situation, the people with whom the experience is being shared and the opportunities for escape from the crowd. It is also important to remember that crowding is a subjective experience and thus the experience of crowding will differ for different individuals; therefore there cannot be a 'best way' to cope, as different strategies will work for different people.

Preventing crowding

A number of factors linked to building design could affect the extent to which people feel crowded in a high density setting. First, it seems that having some space that an individual can claim to be her own, regardless of actual size, prevents the effects of density and leaves people feeling positive. For example, as described in the key study below, Cox et al. (1984) found that prisoners who had small single cells were more satisfied with their environment than those who had larger cells but had to share with another prisoner. Therefore when designing new buildings it may be beneficial to create more spaces for individuals rather than large communal areas to minimise the effects of high density living. Similarly Baum and Valins (1977) found that high-density accommodation that had been subdivided led to a reduced feeling of crowding. One reason for this is that the separation of the building into smaller units reduced the number of unnecessary social interactions and thus reduced some of the feelings of high density.

When planning new buildings, the size and shape of the rooms should be taken into account. Rectangular rooms tend to feel less crowded than square rooms, as do rooms where there are sufficient windows and doors. Curved rooms tend to feel more crowded as do high rise buildings. Therefore when designing new buildings it would be beneficial to take such factors into account to attempt to satisfy the eventual inhabitants and hopefully reduce the potential feelings of crowding.

KEY STUDY

Prison crowding research
Cox, Paulus and McCain (1984)

Aim: To investigate the effects of crowding on inmates' physical and psychological health in state prisons.

Participants: Archival data from four prison systems, Illinois, Mississippi, Oklahoma and Texas on over 175 000 inmates was used alongside information collected directly from more than 2500 inmates.

Method: The prison environment was chosen as crowding, defined as aversive levels of density, was long-term, intense and inescapable. The prisons where the data were collected from ranged in population from 500 to 3000 and the housing units varied from spacious single rooms to densely populated dormitories for 70 or more inmates.

Results: Increases in prison population without a proportionate increase in facilities are associated with an increase in rates of death, suicide and psychiatric problems while decreases in population are accompanied by a reduction of these factors and inmate on inmate attacks and self-mutilations. Double cells led to negative effects on disciplinary infraction rates and illness complaint rates compared to single cells and open dormitory housing led to increased negative psychological reactions and increased illness-complaint rates compared to single or double cells.

Conclusions: Overall in a prison environment the greater the density the greater the negative effect. Therefore these findings have important implications for the design of prisons, in that providing inmates with some individual space will lead to positive effects both physically and psychologically.

EVALUATION ISSUES

REPRESENTATIVENESS/ GENERALISABILITY

The sample that has been used in this study is not fully generalisable as prison inmates are not representative of the population as a whole. Also, as archival data from different prison systems was used, it was difficult to compare the data exactly as different recording systems were in operation thus making it more difficult to establish reliability.

FOR CONSIDERATION

- Plan a building, such as a student hall of residence or prison, taking into account factors that may lead to a reduction in feeling of crowding in those using it.

Coping with the effects of crowding

Individual differences

Individual differences can have an effect on our ability to cope with crowding. For example, males are more likely to experience the effects of crowding than females, particularly in the short term, but may cope better in the long term. This could also be linked to an individual's preference for personal space. People with a need for a large interpersonal space are more badly affected in high density settings (Aiello, 1977). Men tend to like larger amounts of personal space, particularly when interacting with other men. The level of personal space required could also help to explain cultural differences in the ability to cope with crowding, as Mediterranean people experience the most negative effects when in a crowded situation.

Perceived control

The more control a person has over the crowded environment the less negatively they experience it, thus the perceived crowding is less. Schmidt and Keating (1979) identified three types of control:
- Cognitive control: having accurate information, for example, knowing the reasons for the crowding and the likely duration of the crowding.
- Behavioural control: having the ability to work towards a particular goal, for example, trying to limit the time spent in the high density situation.
- Decisional control: having choices available, for example, deciding to move to a lower density location.

They suggested that if one or more types of control are present there will be a reduction in crowding stress. Rodin, Soloman and Metcalf (1978) investigated perceived control and attempted to manipulate the amount of control people had in a lift. By observing people in the lift they found that there was a tendency to gravitate towards the control panel (i.e. trying to have some control). Therefore they manipulated whether or not people were able to stand near the control panel and found that those given control felt better and thought that the lift was larger when questioned afterwards. This suggests that if people feel that they have a choice, and have a feeling of control over the situation, the perception of the high density is not as negative.

Social conditions

The ability to cope with crowding is also influenced by the relationship the individual has with the other people in the situation. The high density will be interpreted less negatively if the individual experiences it with people he likes. This also raises the issue of the reason for the density. If people are sharing a pleasant experience, for example a concert, it is less likely to be perceived as crowded in a negative manner. Whereas, if people are experiencing density in an unpleasant situation, for example, trapped in a broken down tube train in rush hour, it is likely to be perceived negatively.

Coping strategies

One of the main coping strategies employed to limit the impact of high density is social withdrawal. This includes behaviours such as averting the gaze and using negative body language to attempt to block any potential intrusions. Evans et al. (2000) found that living in high density environments seems to predispose individuals to utilise social withdrawal as a coping strategy. Those people who have learned to use social withdrawal in their high density living are then able to use it as an effective coping strategy in other high density situations.

EVALUATION ISSUES

EFFECTIVENESS

It is difficult to determine whether individuals are using a coping strategy to help them to deal with the high density environment and thus difficult to assess how effective different coping strategies may be in reducing the stress created.

SECTION A EXAM QUESTIONS

a Describe one animal study of crowding and density. [6]
b Discuss the extent to which animal research on crowding can be generalised to humans. [10]

a Describe one study of the effects of crowding on social behaviour. [6]
b Evaluate the usefulness of research on crowding and social behaviour. [10]

a Describe one study of the effects of crowding on performance. [6]
b Evaluate the ecological validity of research into crowding and performance. [10]

CD-ROM

For Section B sample exam questions see Environment: Sample exam questions.

5.4 CROWDS AND COLLECTIVE BEHAVIOUR

There is little doubt that in certain circumstances people behave differently in crowds from the way they do when they are alone. There are many famous examples of this, ranging from the murderous lynch mobs in South America to the public outpouring of grief by the crowds at Princess Diana's funeral. Crowds may also become frantically fearful, particularly in emergency situations. One such case occurred when a fire broke out in a Chicago theatre in 1903; there were 602 victims many of who had been smothered or trampled to death as exits were blocked by masses of people.

According to one view put forward by LeBon in the late nineteenth century, when people are in crowds their individual conscience and autonomy are suppressed and they revert to what he termed a primeval, animalistic state. Thus people in crowds become alike and infect each other with whatever emotion they are experiencing; the more people the greater the emotion. This section examines the different types of crowd and how people respond to crowded situations.

5.4.1 DEFINITIONS AND TYPES OF CROWD

? FOR CONSIDERATION

- Make a list of as many famous or personal examples of crowd behaviour that you have read about or experienced.
- Try and link these to the different types of crowd discussed later in this section.

It is difficult to give a precise definition of a crowd. It is different to crowding (which relates to the psychological experience of high density situations) as it involves people coming together. However, a crowd is more than a collection of individuals; there may be a large numbers of shoppers in a department store at Christmas time, but this would not be classified as a crowd as the individuals are acting autonomously and not gathering together with any shared sense of purpose. For a crowd to be so defined there needs to be a reason for the individuals coming together, for example, a sports match or concert, even if it is only for a limited duration.

The crowd adopts a shared identity for the duration of their gathering and the resultant behaviour can be either positive or negative. Positive crowd behaviour can include peaceful protests, while negative crowd behaviour often involves violent and aggressive behaviour. Crowd behaviour also tends to follow 'rules'. These are unwritten ground rules that members of the crowd follow. Often even apparently uncontrolled, unpredictable behaviour is following an unwritten set of rules.

Types of crowd

There are a variety of types of crowd, three of which are briefly described below.

The panicky crowd

In certain situations crowd behaviour turns to panic. Panic occurs within a crowd when all individuals are competing with each other. This occurs due to the lack of trust and co-operation of the crowd members. The optimum solution for all members in a fire, for example, is to escape. However, this will only happen if everyone trusts each other. If this trust is lacking, each individual will do the next best thing given his motives and expectations of what the others will do. He will run to the exit and hope to get there first. The problem is that everyone makes the same assumption, and thus they all arrive at the exit at the same time and jam the exit. Such panic depends on the crowd's beliefs about the escape routes; if the people in the crowd recognise that all the exits are open and readily accessible they will not stampede. Similarly, if all exits are firmly blocked, for example, if a mine collapses, then people in a crowd tend to stay where they are.

The hostile crowd

With a hostile crowd the individuals within the crowd are united against others outside their group. This links to Social Identity Theory (see page 237). However intense an individual crowd member's hatred of the other group, it would probably not be enough to make him go to the extremes a crowd will if he were alone, due to both social and moral restraints. Therefore, there are factors within crowds that appear to weaken these restraints:

- Anonymity: this produces a state of deindividuation (see below).
- Diffusion of responsibility: a diminished fear of retribution. It is hard to prove who did what and guilt becomes diluted.
- Pluralistic ignorance: the crowd often is not as cohesive as everyone thinks, yet all the waiverers assume everyone else is settled and therefore do not voice their opposition.

The apathetic crowd

One reason for an apathetic crowd is that individuals within it often fail to identify the situation appropriately. Within the apathetic crowd nobody takes responsibility for any action, as everyone assumes someone else already has and thus apathy prevails.

5.4.2 CROWD BEHAVIOUR AND CROWDS IN EMERGENCY SITUATIONS

Research into crowd behaviour has demonstrated that the high density can influence behaviour in a number of ways. For example, arousal levels increase as an overload of stimuli leads to an inability to process all of the information. This in turn can lead to a loss of control. These findings suggest that crowd behaviour is irrational and uncontrolled; however, this is not always the case. Often crowds appear to be following unwritten rules, and several theories that attempt to explain the reasons for the differences between individual and crowd behaviour are examined below.

Deindividuation

Deiner (1979) suggests that once an individual is in a crowd, she loses a sense of separateness because self-awareness is blocked leading to an inability to monitor behaviour and thus leading to deindividuation.

Without appropriate self-regulation restraints, we are less concerned about the opinions of others and are therefore less rational and more impulsive. Prentice-Dunn and Rogers (1982) suggest that there are two routes via which socially appropriate behaviour in crowds could increase:

- private self-awareness: conscious attention to our feelings, beliefs and behaviours
- public self-awareness: the extent to which we care what other people think about our behaviour.

When in a crowd, private self-awareness decreases as the attention shifts from ourselves to others. Noise, increased arousal and other events cause us to focus outwardly on the situation, lowering the attention that we pay

EVALUATION ISSUES

VALIDITY

Identifying the type of crowd in a valid way can be difficult, particularly on occasions when the gathering of a crowd is unexpected. It may be that crowds can demonstrate a combination of different behaviours or that the type of crowd may change as time or the event progresses.

KEY DEFINITIONS

Festinger defined **deindividuation** as a state of affairs in a group where individual members do not pay attention to other individuals as individuals and, correspondingly, members do not feel that they are being singled out by others.

to ourselves leading to a reduced awareness of our beliefs. There is a subsequent loss of personal identity and an increased likelihood of behaving in a way in which we would usually consider to be unacceptable. Public self-awareness is affected when the number of others increases, thus leading to increased anonymity of individuals. Diffusion of responsibility may also occur, as in a large crowd individuals feel less responsible and this, coupled with the inability to identify individuals, compounds the disregard for social norms.

Research that supports the notion of deindividuation includes Zimbardo (1969). He investigated whether deindividuation affected demonstrations of aggression. Female undergraduates saw a woman being interviewed who was either pleasant or obnoxious. The participants were then asked to administer electric shocks to the woman (a confederate of the researcher) as an evaluation of the interview. Half of the women gave the fake 'shocks' wearing their own clothes and name badges and the other half were dressed in lab coats and hoods and had no name badges (thus deindividuating them). Results showed that the deindividuated women were indiscriminate in the shocks they gave, showing no difference to the pleasant or obnoxious woman. They also held the shock button for twice as long as the identifiable women.

The concept of deindividuation can help to explain the apparently impulsive and irrational behaviour that is seen in crowds. However, it cannot explain why some crowds are violent and others are not, and it does not take the intent of the crowd into account.

Emergent norm theory

An alternative explanation of crowd behaviour is emergent norm theory which suggests that rather than becoming deindividuated, members of crowds are still self-aware and are following norms. Turner and Killian (1972) proposed that two key factors are needed for crowd behaviour to change:

- The crowd must develop a new (emergent) norm for behaviour, such as aggression.
- Individuals in crowds need to be identifiable thus increasing the social pressure on them to conform to the new norms.

The new norms of behaviour tend to develop from the actions of a small number of distinctive individuals whose behaviour stands out from the others. When individuals are in new situations they tend to look to others for guidance about how to behave, and so these few individuals become role models. Reicher and Potter (1985) conducted research into the St Paul's riots in Bristol in 1980 and demonstrated that although the behaviour of the 3000 strong crowd appeared to be chaotic they were not acting in an irrational uncontrolled manner. The damage to property was restricted to police buildings, banks and other buildings that represented the establishment. The effects of the riot did not spread to other areas of Bristol but remained within the St Paul's district. The rioters claimed not to have lost their sense of personal identity but expressed a pride in their community. This suggests that the rioters were following unwritten rules or norms of behaviour.

Emergent norm theory can help to explain why some crowds are aggressive while remaining calm, as it depends upon the norms that are developing. It also suggests that crowds are groups of individuals who come together with a shared purpose. However, critics argue that crowds rarely come together for no reason and thus some norms must already exist.

EVALUATION ISSUES

ECOLOGICAL VALIDITY/ GENERALISABILITY

As Zimbardo's study was a laboratory study it lacked ecological validity due to the unrealistic nature of the task. It is also questionable whether the results can be applied to real life crowds based on a small sample of female students.

EVALUATION ISSUES

THEORETICAL APPROACH

As emergent norm theory suggests that individuals follow norms, this means that they must have some degree of self-awareness which directly contradicts the deindividuation explanation of crowd behaviour which suggests that when individuals become part of a crowd they lose their self-awareness.

Social identity theory

An alternative explanation of crowd behaviour links to Social Identity Theory. This also helps to explain the predictable behaviour of crowds, as it suggests that groups develop an identity and are hostile towards others who do not share this identity, thus separating people into in-groups and out-groups. As our social identity is linked to our self-esteem, it is important to believe that the group that we belong to is superior to the other group. This theory is based around Tajfel's work that suggests that simply belonging to a group is sufficient to create in-group feelings and thus once in a crowd, belonging to that crowd could be enough to create these types of feelings.

Crowds and emergency situations

When individuals are in a crowd that is facing an emergency situation it appears to reduce their ability to make appropriate decisions about what to do and thus their response seems to be one of two extremes. First, individuals within the crowd may fail to appropriately assess the situation as a real emergency and thus remain too calm and not take any extra steps to remove themselves from the situation. This has been suggested as one possible explanation of the death toll at the Kings Cross underground fire. Donald and Canter (1992) researched what had happened in the 1987 fire and found that three quarters of those who died had carried on with their normal behaviour, apparently not responding to the seriousness of the situation, thus suggesting that they remained calm and did not panic enough (see below).

CD-ROM

For a description of the 1987 King's Cross fire see Environment: Additional key studies: Donald and Canter (1992).

KEY STUDY

Intentionality and fatality during the King's Cross underground fire
Donald and Canter (1992)

Aim: To examine data relating to the King's Cross fire to discover whether those who perish in fires behave in any way significantly differently than those who survive. Thus examining how crowds respond to an emergency setting.

Method: Data were collected consisting of statements from family and friends of the victims concerning their believed destinations and intentions. Also used was a map of named body positions supplied by the Fire Brigade and statements from witnesses who were in locations close to those who perished.

The body positions showed four main locations where people perished and, of the 31 victims, sufficient information was gathered to piece together the likely intentions and actions of 24 of them.

Results: The statements that were pieced together, along with information from the scene suggested that the behaviour of those who died was essentially rational and following their usual behaviour. There was no evidence to suggest that the victims had panicked and it appeared that people behaved as individuals among a large number of other people.

Conclusions: From the behaviour of the victims and the survivors, the evidence is that people do continue a sequence of actions even if they are not the most appropriate or the most likely to ensure survival. This could have important practical implications as people need to understand, or be told that their usual behaviour is not appropriate in an emergency situation.

EVALUATION ISSUES

ECOLOGICAL VALIDITY

Although Donald and Canter's (1992) study was carried out after the event it has high ecological validity as it looks at a real life situation.

Second, others may panic too much, and this overwhelming panic in an emergency can lead to loss of life as some individuals act in what is a rational way for their own survival but will have a negative effect on the overall crowd's behaviour. As a few individuals panic due to the emergency and try to escape others begin to follow, resulting in chaos as the sense of panic escalates and the others also try to escape. Panic behaviour is not considered to be within the control of the individual as it is seen as neither logical nor rational. Panic behaviour also tends to be associated with behaviour within a crowd rather than on an individual level and thus as crowds are also seen as more likely to be irrational, crowds in an emergency situation suggest a high level of panic behaviour is likely. The Chicago theatre fire in 1903 referred to on page 234 is an example of the extraordinary amount of fear and panic that can be generated within a crowd in an emergency situation.

It is possible that less panic is shown if an emergency occurs in a familiar crowded environment, for example, in the workplace or commuting. This may be because these are situations that people are familiar with and therefore have existing schema about how to behave and if everyone follows the written or unwritten rules there is a reduced likelihood of widespread panic. It has therefore been suggested that in order to understand behaviour, it is first necessary to understand the cognitive processes involved. Research has shown that people tend to act in a way that is consistent with the role that they are in and the type of behaviour that they were engaging in prior to the emergency. Therefore people seem to follow both social roles and place rules. However, in novel situations where the other individuals in the crowd are likely to be strangers, no schema exist and this leads to individuals looking to others for cues as to how to behave. As the majority of the crowd are strangers to each other in these type of situations there is no existing trust between them which may mean some individuals are more likely to try to and ensure their own survival at the expense of others (see 'For Consideration' box).

The fire dilemma helps us to understand that all decisions made by individuals in crowds have an impact on others and what seems to be a rational choice for an individual may not be the best choice for the good of the rest of the crowd. The problem, however, is that without trust in the others there is also likely to be panic and chaos in emergency situations.

5.4.3 CONTROLLING CROWDS AND PREVENTING PROBLEMS

It is not possible to prevent crowds from gathering, and therefore it is important to attempt to understand how they can be best controlled to prevent problems from arising. It is difficult to determine a singular best way of controlling crowds because there is no overall agreement as to the underlying cause of crowd behaviour.

If deindividuation can explain crowd behaviour, the installation of CCTV surveillance systems may prevent anti-social acts occurring. According to deindividuation these acts occur due to the loss of self-awareness and personal identity, thus the presence of CCTV will mean that individuals can be identified and therefore, hopefully, will be deterred from behaving anti-socially. However, in cases where behaviour of the crowd can be explained as following unwritten rules, intervention can lead to greater problems as it upsets the balance and understanding within the crowd; and thus police presence may be beneficial to control the crowd but exuberant intervention can create further problems.

Police presence is essential in order to control rioting crowds

Waddington et al. (1987) proposed a model to analyse past social events and disorder. This aims to provide an explanation of the behaviour and possible intervention strategies to reduce anti-social behaviour in similar future situations. They proposed six different levels of analysis that can be used to understand the behaviour:

- Structural levels: the structure of society will directly influence the way that some individuals will respond, for example, the effects of pit closures on miners.
- Political/ideological levels: if government decisions are having an impact on individuals, for example large increases in council tax, problems may develop.
- Cultural levels: shared norms and values which influence behaviour, such as belief in racial equality.
- Contextual levels: the sequence of events that lead up to the crowded situation, including initial triggers and the reactions that follow.
- Spatial levels: the location of the crowd, where the crowd has gathered or where the demonstration was taking place.
- Interactional levels: how the interactions between individuals are conducted, for example, between opposing fans or between the police and fans.

These levels are not meant to be hierarchical and interaction of two or more levels is needed to determine the behaviour, as any level alone is not sufficient. Therefore if behaviour can be interpreted in terms of these factors it may be possible to understand what is creating problems and how the problems can be controlled.

As a result of their analysis of events, Waddington et al. (1987) also made five recommendations for controlling crowds:

- Those responsible for controlling the crowd should have communication skills training.
- Crowds should be allowed to be self-policing whenever possible.
- If the police are involved effective communication with crowd members should be encouraged.
- Minimum force should be used by the police to prevent potential negative reactions from the crowd.
- The police and any other enforcement agencies should be accountable to the community rather than autonomous.

SECTION A EXAM QUESTIONS

a Describe one type of crowd (collective behaviour). [6]
b Discuss the strengths of weaknesses of the research conducted into crowds (collective behaviour). [10]

a Describe one study of theory of crowd behaviour in emergency situations. [6]
b Discuss the difficulties of studying crowd behaviour in emergency situations. [10]

a Describe one study of controlling crowds. [6]
b Evaluate research into controlling crowds. [10]

CD-ROM

For an example of controlling crowds, see Environment: Real life applications: World Cup crowd control, Asian style.

EVALUATION ISSUES

USEFULNESS

Although the suggestions in Waddington et al. (1987) provide a clear framework for interpreting crowd behaviour and thus analysing behaviour to prevent problems from occurring, the main problem is that, as many crowds develop spontaneously, there may be little opportunity to conduct such an analysis. This may make it difficult to apply the suggestions that they make.

FOR CONSIDERATION

- Based on evidence from the research, what suggestions would you make to somebody organising an open-air music festival seeking advice on controlling crowds so that no problems occur.

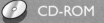

CD-ROM

For Section B sample exam questions see Environment: Sample exam questions.

5.5 ENVIRONMENTAL DISASTER AND TECHNOLOGICAL CATASTROPHE

EVALUATION ISSUES

USEFULNESS

It is difficult to precisely define at what point an event is considered to be a disaster or catastrophe, and some may only be categorised after the event once the effects are able to be assessed.

Environmental disaster has a tremendous impact on people. However, the effect is not simply the physical impact upon those directly involved. There can also be complex psychological effects that can lead to a range of problems for those involved directly or indirectly and their families and friends. Psychologists are interested in examining these effects; however, this often proves difficult for a number of reasons such as ethical issues and assessing how best those suffering psychological effects can be helped. As research develops, psychologists are also beginning to investigate the benefits of being prepared and the impact this has on longer term effects.

5.5.1 DEFINITIONS, CHARACTERISTICS AND CAUSES OF DISASTERS AND CATASTROPHES

Definitions and causes of disasters and catastrophes

Natural disasters are difficult to define precisely but generally they:

The damage caused to buildings after a natural disaster such as an earthquake

- are from natural forces that are not under human control, such as earthquakes, floods and volcanic eruptions, however, it is possible that human behaviour has an impact on the severity of the disaster, for example, poor construction standards in earthquake areas
- must cause damage or death before they are seen as a disaster; a hurricane occurring in an uninhabited area which leads to little damage or loss of life is unlikely to be considered a disaster.

Therefore disasters are also identified by the amount of damage and disruption that they cause to individual, group and organisational functioning. In the USA, one way of defining disasters is when the Government believes that there has been damage of sufficient severity to warrant major disaster assistance.

Technological catastrophes are human made rather than naturally occurring, usually due to error or miscalculation. These include such things as air and train crashes, nuclear accidents and toxic contamination. Again the scope of the impact is one of the factors that determines at which point the event is labelled as a catastrophe. Technological catastrophes may threaten our feelings of control more than natural disasters as they shake our confidence to a greater extent as generally they could have been prevented and thus are not supposed to happen.

Technological catastrophe – the Potter's Bar train crash (May 2002)

Characteristics of disasters and catastrophes

Although there is some overlap in the identifying characteristics of disasters and catastrophes there are also some major differences. The following table summarises the main characteristics of each:

Characteristics of disasters and catastrophes

Natural disasters	Technological catastrophes
Due to natural forces	Due to human error
Unpredictable (although some countries and specific geographical areas are known to be more likely to experience particular types of natural disaster, for example, earthquakes) and uncontrollable	Unpredictable and uncontrollable
Often sudden but may sometimes have warning, for example, via weather reports	Sudden, generally occur without any warning
Generally have a limited duration. Many natural disasters, such as hurricanes, are over relatively quickly allowing those involved to assess the impact and begin coming to terms with it. Others many be longer lasting, for example, droughts	Duration is variable. More likely to be longer lasting, for example, the effects from a nuclear accident. However, occasionally the duration would be brief, e.g. a power cut
Generally have an identifiable low point; a point that can be said to be the worst the event is going to get, after this passes the situation may start to improve	Many do not have a clear low point making it difficult to know whether the worst has happened or is yet to come. Those with a clear low point are easier to cope with
Visible destruction, for example, buildings are destroyed, transport networks damaged and trees uprooted	Often have no visible destruction, for example radiation or toxic contamination

? FOR CONSIDERATION

- Carry out an Internet search to generate two lists of events. First, events that could be considered to be natural disasters and second, those that could be seen as technological catastrophes.
- Outline the defining features of them.

5.5.2 BEHAVIOUR DURING DISASTERS AND CATASTROPHES AND THE EFFECT ON INDIVIDUALS

During the disaster or catastrophe a wide range of behaviours may be demonstrated with a variety of factors influencing individual behaviour. During the event generally people do not panic. People may:

- run and hide; this is perhaps most likely if there is prior warning of the disaster or catastrophe allowing individuals or communities to put contingency plans into action and evacuate the area. However, even with warning not all individuals flee the impending event as some are in denial and do not quite believe that it is really going to happen
- stay and watch; this frequently occurs when events are sudden and those involved are in a state of denial as they are unable to fully accept the scene that is unfolding. There are many amateur videos of disasters, such as hurricanes, tornadoes and even events like the collapse of the World Trade Centre on 11 September 2001, as people stay and watch without considering their own safety
- display positive and negative behaviour; during and immediately after a disaster people tend to need greater social support and this can be provided by others who have been directly or indirectly involved. However the severity of the situation can affect how successfully others are able to provide this support. Negative behaviour that is displayed at the time of disasters includes looting often starting even while the rescue efforts are still underway.

Behaviour during a technological catastrophe is often similar to that occurring during natural disasters. Fritz and Marks (1954) reviewed a number of human made catastrophes and found that panic did not usually

? FOR CONSIDERATION

The behaviour of individuals during disasters and catastrophes is very difficult to measure accurately.
- Why do you think research into this area would be problematic?

⚖ EVALUATION ISSUES

EFFECTIVENESS/METHODOLOGY

There are a number of problems in trying to study disasters as it is impossible to know where they are going to occur and therefore it is difficult to measure behaviour as it happens, particularly if the event is relatively short lived. It is also impossible to be able to measure the mood of those involved before the event to enable firm conclusions about the effects of the disaster to be drawn.

occur and when it did it was usually to escape immediate threat. Less than 10 per cent of victims interviewed reported feeling out of control.

An article by Wraith and Gordon has attempted to dispel some myths about the way that people behave during disasters. These are outlined below.

KEY STUDY

Human responses to natural disasters
Wraith and Gordon (cited in *The Australian Emergency Manual Disaster Recovery* (1996) Emergency Management Australia)

The myths outlined below have been dispelled by knowledge as increasing research on disasters is being done. However, understanding the short and long term effects of disasters is at an early stage and the knowledge of how to reduce the effects is even less well developed. Unfortunately, it is only by accumulating more experiences of human suffering in disasters that this knowledge can be gained.

Myth	Reality
People in danger will panic	Panic during disasters is very rare. Panic is only likely to occur if there is an immediate perceived threat of death or people feel trapped, but even then panic is rare
In the face of danger people only think of themselves	The majority of people in disasters behave with concern for others and thus this should be taken into account when disaster planning
Too much information is likely to scare people into behaving erratically	Often people are reluctant to believe that threats are real if they are unexpected. However, if information is accurate, people do tend to act responsibly and may seek guidance from others
Unless there is an obvious emotional disturbance people are unaffected by the disaster	The majority of people who are disaster survivors do not experience severe mental health problems. Most draw on their coping strategies to deal with the situation. However, the stress of the situation can affect all those who have been involved
Children are not affected by disasters	Following initial reactions to the disaster, such as nightmares, children often appear to cope very well, forgetting about what has happened. However, they often express their fears and problems connected to the disaster in other ways after the event
Communities affected by disasters will never recover	Although the community may never return to its pre-disaster state it does not mean that it cannot recover. Gradually reconstruction will take

▶

Myth	Reality
	place as the individuals within the community attempt to rebuild social and physical aspects of the community
Workers in the disaster situation are not affected by the disaster	Anybody entering the disaster situation becomes in some way involved. Heavy emotional demands are placed on rescue workers. This must be acknowledged and provision for helping them come to terms with the events should be provided

There have been different models proposed to attempt to explain behaviour during a disaster. These include the following:
- Physical science and complementary panic model: this predicts that when people realise that they are in danger they will head for emergency exits, assuming that they are nearby and visible. This suggests that an individual's primary concern will be to save themselves and escape the situation.
- Affiliative model: this predicts that people will move towards their companions first, thus suggesting that the primary concern will be the well being of loved ones, before individual escape.

Sime (1985) examined how shoppers and staff behaved as they became aware of a fire that ultimately killed 50 people in a department store. Using interviews they found that shoppers used the affiliative model, trying to ensure the safety of friends or loved ones first, while staff used the physical science model, perhaps due to the fact they were at work and thus less likely to be with loved ones.

Factors affecting behaviour during disasters

Behaviour can be influenced by situational factors and individual differences. Situational factors include the following:
- Event duration: the longer the duration of the disaster the greater the probability that those involved will be exposed to threat or actual harm. Thus the longer the duration the greater the potential for panic, or alternatively as events continue, learned helplessness may begin to develop.
- Low point: if the event has a clear low point, when things are as bad as they are going to get, and those involved are aware that things will get better after that point it can have an impact on behaviour. Once people realise that they have survived and the worst is over they can start to think that they may be able to help others. Disasters that do not have a low point often lead to greater unsettled behaviour as people are fearful for longer and concerned that the worst is yet to come.
- Warning: less warning can lead to greater problems, but giving warnings may cause problems too; if warnings are given without sufficient time to act upon them greater panic will arise. Alternatively, it is possible that if warnings have been given in the past that turned out to be false alarms, new warnings will not be taken seriously.

Individual differences that affect behaviour during disasters include the following:

ETHICS

Alongside the problems with measuring the behaviour of disaster victims, there are also important ethical issues to consider. Is it possible to gain informed consent from those being studied? If not, should the study be taking place? It is also possible that asking victims about their experiences may recreate distress which could also be considered to be unethical.

CD-ROM

For a study on the effects of disasters, see Environment: Additional key studies: Solomon and Thompson (1995).

- Personality variables: Sims and Baumann (1972) noted that the heaviest concentration of tornadoes in the USA was in the Midwest but most tornado related deaths occur in the South. After eliminating natural differences for this they suggested that it might be due to differences in personality linked to perceptions of danger. Further investigation found there were differences in people's locus of control. Illinois (Midwest) residents felt that luck had less to do with their fate and therefore took more precautions as the storm approached. Alabama (South) residents paid less attention to warnings and took fewer precautions as the storm approached.
- Age: Thompson, Norris and Hanacek (1993) looked at the evidence connected to age and response to disaster and they suggested that:
  - older victims are more likely to be injured
  - older victims have fewer resources and therefore may show more distress
  - older victims may be able to cope more efficiently than younger victims
  - the middle age group have the greatest burden for caring in the event of a disaster as they often have responsibility for their children and for elderly relatives.

Thompson et al. examined these four suggestions in a study of 831 adults from four areas affected by Hurricane Hugo with varying degrees of severity. Results showed that variables such as injury, life threat, personal loss and financial loss affected the level of distress shown at varying time intervals after the event. As age interacted with these factors, the conclusion was that the middle age group were most greatly affected.

Other factors that affect how people behave during disasters include:
- life threat
- injury
- witnessing death or injury
- death/injury of friend or relative
- preparedness of the community
- social cohesion of the community
- financial loss
- property/possession loss
- separation from family.

Effect of disasters and catastrophes on individuals

Having considered the different types of behaviour that may be displayed by individuals during a disaster, it is also important to examine what effect the disasters have on those involved. Psychologists are interested in investigating the likely duration of the effects. Do people return to normal immediately after the disaster has passed, or are the effects likely to be longer lasting?

The impact and severity of the effects will be dependent upon individual involvement in the disaster. Factors such as whether the individual's life was threatened and how much bereavement was suffered, whether he lost his home and belongings and the extent to which the community was disrupted will all have an influence on the effects of the disaster. Whether the event was a natural disaster or a technological catastrophe also affects how people are influenced by the situation.

Initial effects of the disaster include physiological arousal responses, which in turn lead to anxiety and stress. If the disaster has an obvious low point and is over quite quickly it is possible that the stress response will be limited simply to the duration of the event. This stress is linked to primary stressors, i.e. the events of the disaster. However, if the disaster lasts for a more prolonged period of time and the individual is threatened by the events, the stress response may continue and possibly last for years after the event. This stress is linked to secondary stressors such as loss of housing, jobs and other life changes as a result of the disaster. As time passes the initial feelings of being glad to be alive may start to be replaced by psychological and/or physical symptoms.

Those suffering from stress for a prolonged period after the disaster may be experiencing Post Traumatic Stress Disorder (PTSD). This can develop after any type of disaster, but is more likely after technological catastrophes due to the fact that they are human made and thus shake our confidence to a greater extent.

Psychiatrists have classified PTSD symptoms into three categories; intrusive symptoms, avoidant symptoms and symptoms of hyperarousal.

Intrusive symptoms	Flashbacks. Onslaught of emotions that have no cause. Emotions that bring tears, fear or anger
Avoidant symptoms	Avoids close emotional contact with family. Diminished emotions and only capable of carrying routine tasks. Person seems bored, cold or preoccupied. Avoids situations that are reminders of the traumatic events
Symptoms of hyperarousal	Easily irritable. Have trouble concentrating. May develop insomnia. Suffer from panic attacks. Has trouble breathing and may have increased heart rate

Those suffering from PTSD following a disaster tend to experience most intrusive symptoms as they continually experience flashbacks. Treatment for PTSD is considered in the following section.

5.5.3 PSYCHOLOGICAL INTERVENTION BEFORE AND AFTER EVENTS

Intervention before events

Intervention before an event would be in the form of warnings of the impending situation. Obviously this is not always possible due to the naturally unpredictable nature of disasters and catastrophes. However, particularly for weather-related disasters it is often possible to give some form of warning.

Warnings allow people to have a greater sense of control of the situation as they are better able to prepare for events. If an area is identified as a likely area for floods, precautions can be taken within the community, for example ensuring access to sand bags and wherever possible permanently reinforcing weak-spots to reduce the severity of the flooding. Those likely to be involved in the disaster can make decisions about whether to stay and risk danger or flee from the danger situation. This heightened sense of control makes people feel better psychologically even if in the long run it makes little difference to the outcome of the situation.

Lack of warnings lead to an intense feeling of shock and disbelief as people try to interpret the events that they see unfolding. Thus, no warning would lead to a greater sense of denial.

Intervention after events

Instructions

Immediately after an event has occurred intervention can take the form of attempting to help people escape to safety. Providing clear instruction can help people to understand what is happening and thus help to save lives.

EVALUATION ISSUES

GENERALISABILITY

The study by Sugiman and Misumi (1988) cannot be generalised to all countries or nationalities as the sample is only representative of one country. Thus it may be factors that are unique to that group of people that led to the results rather than the different methods that were used.

CD-ROM

For a larger discussion of coping styles, see Environment: Real life applications: Coping with disasters.

This is because it prevents people panicking and all rushing to escape, which may endanger others; Sugiman and Misumi (1988) conducted a Japanese study that compared two methods of assisting escape:
- follow directions method: leaders tell people where to go in loud voices with vigorous gestures
- follow me method: leaders actually take a few people to where they should go.

They found that the 'follow me' method worked best when there were only a few (approximately four) people otherwise the 'follow directions' method was better. This could have important implications for those responsible for giving instructions at the time of a disaster. The problem, however, is often related to who is responsible and the extent to which people are prepared to listen in an emergency situation.

Coping styles

Once the disaster has passed, survivors have to find ways of coping. There are three main strategies that they can use:
- Emotion focused coping; using an emotional strategy to alleviate the stress, such as attending counselling sessions.
- Problem focused coping; do something practical to improve the situation
- Denial of the situation to reduce the feelings of stress.

Different disasters may benefit from certain types of coping style. For example, if the problem is very difficult to solve, a problem focused approach would increase the distress. Studying the effects of the Three Mile Island nuclear accident, where information released about the incident was incomplete and contradictory and people were fearful of the effects after the event, Baum et al. (1983) found that people using emotion focused coping dealt with the incident better.

Treating PTSD

There are a range of different ways of treating PTSD in an attempt to help those suffering from it to regain a sense of control and re-establish a sense of safety in their life. The different forms of therapy available include:
- Cognitive-behavioural therapy: the aim of this therapy is to focus on correcting the sufferer's painful and intrusive thoughts and patterns of behaviour. This is done by teaching relaxation techniques and examining and attempting to alter the person's mental processes. A research article by McNally, Bryant and Ehlers explored, amongst other factors, the benefits of early intervention using cognitive-behavioural therapy. A summary of this is described below.

KEY STUDY

Does early psychological intervention promote recovery from post traumatic stress?
McNally, Bryant and Ehlers (2003)

Aim: This article is a review of the risk factors for PTSD, recommendations for crisis intervention and the identification of individuals at risk of chronic PTSD, and research on early interventions based on cognitive-behaviour therapy. The article also examines the controversy regarding early aid for trauma survivors linked to its social, political and economic context.

This summary focuses only on the research linked to the early intervention based on cognitive-behaviour therapy (CBT).

Summary: Many of the psychological treatments for PTSD symptoms, in the initial weeks and months after traumatic events, have been adapted from CBT programs. Initial research was unable to identify the extent to which these relieved symptoms more than would be expected with natural recovery. Therefore the aim of more recent research has been to assess the usefulness of CBT. Foa, Hearst-Ikeda and Perry (1995) used a CBT approach, in four weekly two-hour sessions, with ten victims of rape or aggravated assault within several weeks of the trauma. Ten other victims received only repeated assessments. Follow-up assessments two months and five and a half months after the assault revealed that the treated patients at two months had fewer symptoms of PTSD. However, by the second assessment there was very little difference. This suggests that intervention accelerates natural recovery.

Other programs have examined the effectiveness of CBT beginning one to three months after the trauma occurred. Ehlers et al. (2003) worked with road traffic accident victims and in follow-up assessments one year after the trauma those who had received CBT were significantly less likely to be demonstrating PTSD symptoms than those receiving repeated assessments or those in a self-help condition. Similar results were found in a study by Öst, Paunovic and Gillow (2002). Working with victims of crime who had PTSD, they randomly assigned them to either a CBT group or a waiting list for treatment. At the end of the CBT sessions measures were taken to examine the level of PTSD symptoms and it was found that only 5 per cent of the CBT group still had PTSD compared to 65 per cent of the waiting list group.

Conclusions: Overall, CBT treatments delivered up to three months after the trauma showed promising results for survivors with PTSD. Compared to those who received no treatment CBT appears to promote recovery from trauma.

- Behaviour therapy: working on behaviourist principles, the aim is to reduce the panic feelings that are provoked by various stimuli. This is done by desensitisation as the therapist gradually exposes the sufferer to the panic-inducing stimuli until the panic reduces.
- Psychodynamic psychotherapy: as PTSD results in part from the difference between the individual's personal values and the reality that they witnessed during the disaster, psychodynamic psychotherapy aims to help the individual examine these values and the behaviour that violated them during the disaster. The aim is therefore to resolve the conscious and unconscious conflicts that were created.

SECTION A EXAM QUESTIONS

a Describe one study of the effects of a technological catastophe on individuals. [6]
b Evaluate the use of self-report as a method or researching the effects of disasters and catastrophes on individuals. [10]

a Describe one study of behaviour during a natural disaster. [6]
b Discuss the ethics of researching how people behave during disasters and/or catastrophes. [10]

a Describe one psychological intervention after a disaster or catastrophe. [6]
b Discuss the difficulties of researching psychological interventions after a disaster or catastrophe. [10]

EVALUATION ISSUES

INDIVIDUAL DIFFERENCES/ GENERALISABILITY/USEFULNESS

There are several issues that are raised by the review of research conducted by McNally et al.

- There needs to be an awareness of individual differences when delivering CBT treatments as some people demonstrate benefits after relatively few sessions while others require up to four or five weekly sessions. This needs to be taken into account before conclusions about effectiveness can be made.
- The samples that were used in the majority of the research studies were victims of accidents or crime. Therefore the results gained may not be generalisable to disaster survivors as the experiences of trauma are different. However, it must be remembered that it is very difficult to swiftly conduct research into disasters due to their unpredictable nature.
- It is also important to remember that trauma does create other issues besides PTSD such as an increase in substance abuse or depression. This research has only examined the usefulness of CBT in reducing PTSD symptoms and thus it is possible that other problems still exist but have not been measured.

FOR CONSIDERATION

- What advice could you give to a local authority who are looking to provide some support to residents who are living in an area prone to flooding?
- How could they help residents before and after events?

CD-ROM

For Section B sample exam questions see Environment: Sample exam questions.

5.6 PERSONAL SPACE AND TERRITORY

An important influence on behaviour is the impact of other people, and in particular our interactions with other people. When interacting with each other individuals like to keep a certain amount of distance between themselves and those that they are interacting with. This is known as personal space and the amount required varies, based upon a number of different factors. A further way that humans protect their interactions with others is by defending space or territory that they believe to be their own. Again the amount of territory that we believe that we have, and the extent to which we are willing to defend it, varies according to the situation. Both of these concepts will be discussed in this section.

5.6.1 DEFINITIONS, TYPES AND MEASUREMENT OF PERSONAL SPACE AND TERRITORY

KEY DEFINITIONS

Two types of personal space have been identified:
- **alpha personal space** is the objective, externally measurable distance and angle between interacting individuals
- **beta personal space** is the subjective experience, i.e. the individuals' sense of the above.

FOR CONSIDERATION

- Think of ways that personal space could be measured in the real world.
- What would be the drawback with such methods of measurement?

What is personal space?

Personal space is a portable invisible boundary surrounding us, into which others may or may not be allowed. It regulates how closely we interact with others. Personal space always relates to interaction with other individuals.

For some species personal space is necessary to regulate behaviours such as feeding. Personal space can also be used as a communication channel to let others know the type of relationship that exists between others and us.

Types of personal space

Hall (1966) identified four categories of personal space:
- intimate: 0–45 cm; very close relationships, but also situations where social rules allow contact, e.g. sport (near = body contact; far = whispering)
- personal: 45–120 cm; good friends (near = intimate; far = friends)
- social: 1.2–3.5m; business type relationships (near = informal; far = formal)
- public: 3.5m+ (near = speaker and audience; far = public and important figure).

It is important to remember that we tend to perceive people as nearer than they really are.

Measuring personal space

The main methods of measuring personal space are described below, each having its advantages and disadvantages. It is commonly accepted that due to the sensitive nature of measuring personal space there is no ideal method.
- Simulation methods involve using inanimate objects such as small felt figures or dolls and manipulating their positioning to demonstrate personal space. This was used primarily in early research. This method is able to measure beta personal space but not alpha personal space.
- Stop-Distance Method is better for measuring alpha personal space. It is studied in a laboratory setting, but in a live encounter. Participants are asked to stand some distance away from the experimenter and walk

slowly towards the experimenter. Alternatively, the experimenter may walk towards the participants, who tell the experimenter when to stop. Wherever they stop, this distance is taken as the measure of alpha personal space.

- Naturalistic observation involves observing the effects passers-by or confederates have on others by looking at varying degrees of the invasion of personal space.
- Questionnaires can be used to present participants with an imaginary scenario in which they have to rate how comfortable they would feel. Duke and Nowicki's (1972) self-report measure, the Comfortable Interpersonal Distance Scale, is an example of such a measure.
- Virtual environment measures: with advances in technology it is now possible to measure personal space in a virtual reality environment, gaining accurate measurements as individuals navigate around a virtual environment without an awareness of the measurements being taken, thus removing the conscious decision-making process involved with some of the other measures. An outline of how this method is used is described in the key study below.

KEY STUDY

Interpersonal distance in immersive virtual environments
Bailenson, Blascovich, Beall and Loomis (2003)

Aim: In the first of two experiments the researchers aimed to investigate personal space in a virtual environment containing a virtual human. They hypothesised that participants would leave a larger personal space bubble around virtual humans who maintained eye gaze with the participants than those who did not.

Participants: 80 students from an introductory psychology course, both male and female with a mean age of 19.6 years.

Method: Participants completed two blocks of trials, one block with female virtual humans and one block with male virtual humans and there were five trials in each block. Gaze behaviour was also varied as either high gaze or low gaze. The order of the blocks was counterbalanced across the participants. Participants wore a head-mounted display (HMD) that included a display monitor over each eye. While wearing the HMD, the outside world could not be seen. The system that was used redraws the virtual environment 30 times a second, separately for each eye. To prevent the aim of the study influencing the results all participants were led to believe that it was a study about memory. Participants were told that they had to walk towards the stationary person and read the name and number that was located on a patch on his or her shirt; this was large enough to be read from a distance of 0.75 metres. They were told that they would be asked questions about this as well as about the person's clothing, hair colour and eye colour.

After the two blocks of trials were completed the HMDs were removed and the participants were given a recall task where they had to recall all the names and numbers on the patches. A matching task and a social presence questionnaire were also completed.

Results: The minimum distance of personal space that participants assumed between themselves and the virtual human was taken. The mean front minimum distance was 0.51 m and the mean back minimum distance was 0.45 m with the difference between these being significant. A significant difference was also found between the high and low gaze conditions with a greater distance being maintained in the high gaze

⚖ EVALUATION ISSUES

VALIDITY/ETHICS/METHODOLOGY

- The Stop-Distance Method is a more valid measure of personal space than simulation methods, but the individuals are still aware of the distancing process therefore the decisions are still conscious unlike personal space in real life.
- Although naturalistic observation is the most ecologically valid method of measuring personal space it is also the most problematic. The main issue is that it is highly unethical as it involves observing people's reactions without their consent. It is also influenced by external variables as the experimenters do not have control over the situation.
- One of the main problems that can arise when using a questionnaire is that people may not tell the truth. This may be deliberate or because they are unable to accurately imagine the situation or because they are trying to give socially desirable responses. Therefore although it is quick and easy to administer it may not generate accurate results.

⚖ EVALUATION ISSUES

GENERALISABILITY/ ECOLOGICAL VALIDITY

The use of a virtual environment to measure personal space as used in the study by Bailenson et al. (2003) overcomes many of the problems outlined earlier as it allows a measure of personal space to be taken accurately and without the participants being aware that it is being measured, thus generating more accurate results. However, there may also be disadvantages with this use of a virtual environment to measure personal space. First, as the technology is new and it is only measuring virtual interactions it may not be possible to generalise to the population as a whole. Second, due to the nature of the environment, it does not capture real physical interactions and thus may not take into account factors that could influence the personal space distance maintained in real world interactions.

CD-ROM

For further information see
Environment: Additional key studies:
Wells (2000)

KEY DEFINITIONS

Sommer (1969) defined **territory** as
' visible, relatively stationary, visibly
bounded, and tends to be home
centred, regulating who will interact'.
Territoriality can be said to be a
pattern of behaviours held by an
individual or group based on
perceived, attempted or actual control
of a definable physical space, object or
ideas that may involve habitual
occupation, defence, marking and
personalisation.
Marking: placing an object or
substance in a space to indicate one's
intentions.
Personalisation: marking in a
manner that indicates one's identity.

EVALUATION ISSUES

METHODOLOGY

- The use of field experiments has
  provided the richest source of
  data linked to territory research.
  However, they can be problematic
  as they can be difficult to set up
  and conduct. There may also be
  ethical problems if those involved
  have not given consent.
- There are a number of potential
  problems with using surveys and
  interviews as a way of measuring
  territory. As with personal space it
  is difficult to imagine territory and
  how we react to people invading
  it out of context. It is also possible,
  as with any self-report scale that
  questions are misinterpreted or
  socially desirable answers are
  given.
- When observing territorial
  behaviour it is possible to
  misinterpret behaviours and it
  may be difficult to conduct
  ethically.

condition. Participants also maintained a significantly greater distance
from the female virtual humans than the male virtual humans.

Conclusions: The study allowed a realistic measure of personal space to
be taken while the participants were unaware as to the purpose of the
study. The results supported previous suggestions regarding the size and
shape of the personal space 'bubble'.

What is territory?

Territory is usually considered to be a physical space that we believe we
have some ownership of on either a temporary or permanent basis.
Territory can be seen as belonging to one individual or a group of
individuals, and it is a relatively stationary area often with visible
boundaries.

Types of territory

Altman (1975) identified three types of territory that are used by
humans:

Primary
- Primary territories are most important.
- The individual feels that it is their own, therefore there is a high sense
  of ownership.
- It is relatively permanent and individuals are very defensive of it.
- Examples include bedroom or family home.
- Primary territories are extensively personalised.

Secondary
- The individual is seen as one of a number of temporary owners.
- It may be personalised for the period of legitimate occupancy.
- Examples include classrooms or lockers at the gym.

Public
- The territory does not belong to anyone and therefore control is
  difficult to assert.
- The occupant is seen as one of many possible users.
- Some temporary personalisation may occur.
- Examples include areas of a beach or a local park.

Measurement of territory

It can be very difficult to measure territory and it is particularly difficult to
carry out laboratory studies. This is due to the fact that the very nature of
territory is something that individuals feel they have some degree of
ownership of, and thus it is not possible to recreate easily in an artificial
setting, therefore other methods have to be employed.
- Field experiments involve a certain degree of experimental
  manipulation and control by the researcher, for example invading
  territory in a real world setting such as student dorms and measuring
  reactions to this.
- Surveys and interviews: an alternative way to study territory is simply
  to ask people about their territory and their defence of it using either
  questionnaires or interviews. These can be a quick and relatively easy
  way to gather an insight into territory.
- Naturalistic observations involve watching a real life location, such as a
  workplace, and noting down the behaviour observed using unobtrusive
  measures such as the level of personalisation and marking.

What happens if personal space is invaded?

Personal space is invaded when another individual interacts at a distance that feels uncomfortable. This distance will vary depending upon who the person is and what the interaction is about. Other factors may also influence the point at which personal space is considered to be invaded and these will be considered later in this section.

There are a number of possible effects of an invasion of personal space and these include an increase in physiological arousal and an attempt to leave the situation.

Physiological arousal

It is difficult to gain an accurate measure of the level of physiological arousal linked to the invasion of personal space as if the participants know that their arousal levels are being monitored it can affect results. The key study below conducted by Middlemist et al. (1976) demonstrates an innovative, although not entirely ethical, way of measuring the impact of the invasion of personal space on arousal.

> **KEY STUDY**
>
> *Personal space invasion in the lavatory: suggestive evidence for arousal*
> Middlemist, Knowles and Matter (1976)
>
> **Aim:** To examine the proposal that invaded personal space leads to an increased level of arousal.
>
> **Participants:** 60 males who visited a men's public lavatory at an American university.
>
> **Method:** The men's lavatory contained three urinals and the men were unknowingly randomly assigned to one of three conditions:
> * the experimenter stood directly next to the participant
> * the experimenter stood at the opposite end of the urinals
> * the experimenter was not present.
>
> These conditions were manipulated by the experimenters placing a cleaning bucket by either the centre or right urinal to indicate that it was not to be used. Condition 1 represented a high level of personal space invasion, while in condition 3 there was no personal space invasion. The men were observed by another experimenter using a periscope from inside a cubicle. Two key measures were taken, first how quickly the participant began to urinate and second how long he urinated for.
>
> **Results:** On average, the men in condition 1 took twice as long to begin urinating (9 seconds) and persisted for significantly less time (18 seconds) compared to the men in condition 3 who took only 5 seconds to begin urinating and urinated for 25 seconds.
>
> **Conclusions:** The results suggest that invaded personal space in a lavatory leads to an increase in autonomic arousal, thus affecting urination.

Flight behaviour

Another possible consequence of invading an individual's personal space is that they leave the situation more quickly than would have happened without the invasion.

A study conducted by Felipe and Sommer (1966) provided evidence for the hypothesis that avoidance behaviour, in this case leaving the situation, was

? FOR CONSIDERATION

People tend to feel uncomfortable when their personal space is invaded.
* Think of factors that may affect how people respond to their personal space being invaded, and consider the different ways that they may respond to an invasion of personal space.

◎ CD-ROM

See Environment: Real life applications: Keep your distance and Environment: Theoretical approaches: Physiological signs of arousal.

EVALUATION ISSUES

ETHICS

Although the study by Middlemist et al. (1976) generated some interesting results, it cannot be said to be an ethical study. Participants were not asked for consent and were observed while urinating without their knowledge. However, it could be argued that if participants were asked for consent they either would have refused to take part in the study or it would have affected their arousal levels.

GENERALISABILITY

Due to the location of Felipe and Sommer's (1966) study it is not possible to generalise the results to the whole population as the patients may have certain characteristics that influenced the way that they responded that may not be typical of all people.

the result of negative emotions due to the invasion of personal space. The study was conducted at a 1500-bed psychiatric hospital. Patients spent a great deal of time sitting alone outside and this is where the invasion was staged; a stranger, an experimental confederate, went and sat down approximately 15 cm away. If the patient moved along the confederate also did, to maintain close proximity. It was found that after one minute 20 per cent of the invaded patients had left the situation compared with none of a control group (personal space was not invaded as they were watched from a distance). After 20 minutes two thirds of the invaded group had left the situation compared with only a third of the control group. These results do seem to demonstrate that invaded personal space leads to a flight response.

Felipe and Sommer (1966) conducted a further study and obtained similar findings in an almost empty university library. A female experimenter sat very close to female students even though there was plenty of other available space. After 30 minutes 70 per cent of the students had left the library.

Konecni et al. (1975) also found similar results when pedestrians' space was invaded as they waited to cross the road. The closer the confederate stood the quicker the pedestrian crossed the road. Thus suggesting that the greater the invasion of personal space the more anxious a person is to escape.

Factors influencing the reaction to the invasion of personal space

There are a number of factors that affect the amount of personal space required and thus affect at what point an individual believes personal space to be invaded.

Gender is one factor that affects the amount of personal space required, with research finding that males and females prefer different amounts of personal space which is also affected by who they are interacting with. Gifford (1987) found that males like to have most personal space when interacting with other males, followed by females interacting with other females. Males interacting with females and vice versa wanted least personal space. Fisher and Byrne (1975) investigated gender differences in response to the invasion of personal space by studying both male and female students in a university library. Confederates either sat next to, one seat away from, or opposite the participants. Each participant was asked to complete a questionnaire about the experience. The results demonstrated gender differences as males were less comfortable having the space invaded opposite them, but did not mind invasion from the sides. Females showed the reverse, disliking invasion from the sides more than from opposite them.

Age can also influence the required amount of personal space and Hayduk (1983) suggested that personal space increases with age. Children do not show the same awareness of personal space, but need for personal space appears to increase as we get older. By the age of 12, children use personal space like adults.

Different cultures have preferences for different amounts of personal space, for example, Arabs only like a small amount of personal space. Collett (1971) trained English men to act in the same way as Arabs with regard to eye contact and the use of space. Following interaction with Arabs it was found that those who had been 'trained' were liked better by the Arabs.

The situation can affect the closeness of interactions. King (1966) found that in friendly situations the amount of personal space required is smaller than in unfriendly situations. Tedesco and Fromme (1974) studied participants interacting with a confederate in either a competitive or co-operative situation. The participants were then taken into another room and their interpersonal space was measured. They found that the co-operative group chose smaller amounts of personal space than those from the competitive group.

The status of an individual can affect interactions. The greater the difference in status the larger the amount of interpersonal space that is chosen. Burns (1964) showed participants a film of an office setting with someone giving a message to another person. It was found that when there was a large difference in space people judged the other person to be a subordinate, while when there was a small personal space the individuals were judged to be equal.

Effects and consequences of the invasion of territory

It is more difficult to conduct research to investigate the impact of the invasion of territory as it is a challenge to find ways that are ecologically valid and thus meaningful. There is also the issue that it is sometimes difficult to make the distinction between personal space and territory in that if personal space has been invaded, in some cases territory will have also been invaded.

Research has shown, both with animals and humans, that invasion of territory often leads to an aggressive response. The more well established the territory the stronger the reaction to invasion.

There are considered to be three main types of territorial infringement (Gifford, 1997):

- Invasion: an outsider physically enters territory usually with the intention of taking control of it, this could occur during war time.
- Violation: a more temporary infringement, usually the goal is not ownership but annoyance or harm, for example burglary. This type of infringement can occur by accident, for example, a boy goes into the female toilets.
- Contamination: this involves the deliberate leaving of something that messes up your territory, for example, waste left in your garden.

According to Knapp (1978) the way in which we react to infringement of our territory will depend upon a variety of factors, as shown below:

Who is the infringer?	Is it a friend or a stranger?
Why did the infringement occur?	Was it deliberate or accidental?
What type of territory was infringed?	Was it primary, secondary or public?
How was the infringement accomplished?	Personal contact is worse than physical infringement.
How long was the duration of the infringement?	Was it temporary or permanent?
Where did the infringement occur?	Was there other usable territory nearby?

Aggression resulting from invasion of territory is quite rare in humans. Humans tend, wherever possible, to resolve territorial invasions via negotiation. Linking in to Knapp's suggestions, evidence demonstrates that aggression is most likely to result from invasion of territories that are not fully established. Ley and Cybriwsky (1974) found that if territorial boundaries were not properly established it led to greater inter-gang violence than when boundaries were clearly established. The reason for this difference could be due to the fact that if boundaries are clearly established in the first place there is less likelihood of the territories being invaded.

Factors influencing the reaction to the invasion of territory

The factors that influence the response to the invasion of territory are similar to those linked to the invasion of personal space.

Gender is an important influence and Mercer and Benjamin (1980) investigated territoriality in student dormitories. Students were asked to draw a map of their double occupancy room and mark which areas they thought were theirs, which were their roommates and which they shared. Results showed that males drew larger areas as belonging to themselves. Similarly Haber (1980) found that markers that appeared to belong to men were more effective at preventing an invasion of territory and men's desks were less likely to get invaded.

Social factors may also have an effect. Taylor, Gottfredson and Brower (1981) found that friendly neighbourhoods in Baltimore had fewer problems of territorial control and felt more responsible for neighbourhood space than those where people were unfriendly or did not know their neighbours.

Culture may influence how territory is seen in the first place, and thus affect how individuals respond to it being invaded. Smith (1981) compared Germans, French and Americans marking out beach space. It was found that generally males claimed more than females regardless of nationality, and groups claimed less per person than couples or people alone. The main cultural difference was that Germans engaged in much more marking of territories and erecting boundaries, and claimed larger spaces than the other two nationalities. This suggests that territory and territoriality are at least in part shaped by upbringing and society. The number of other people in a given situation can also have an impact. Sommer (1969) investigated territory and invasion of territory and found that in low density situations any marker in a library was effective while in high density situations personal possessions were more effective at preventing invasion.

Research has also been conducted to examine the impact of control and whether the possession of territory helps humans to dominate activities and win. Harris and McAndrew (1986) found that if people were asked to sign a petition (for something that was against their wishes) they were most likely to say no if they were on primary territory, suggesting that they felt more in control. This also links to home field advantage whereby teams are more likely to win when they are on their home territory.

5.6.3 DEFENDING PERSONAL SPACE AND TERRITORY

Defending personal space

There is no simple way of defending personal space, as the amount required varies depending upon so many different factors and it is often not known when an invasion is going to occur. One possible way of defending personal space is to have some sort of barrier, such as a bag or a newspaper, to limit the proximity others can attain, however this is not a very practical solution; therefore defending personal space may be better thought of as optimising personal space in different situations. One example of how this can be done is via seating arrangements. There are two main types of seating arrangements that can affect how much interaction individuals have. First, sociofugal design is when chairs are arranged to keep a greater amount of personal space between people, generally with people facing away from each other, for example, back to back seating at an airport lounge. Second, sociopetal design encourages interaction and therefore tends to reduce the amount of personal space available. The chairs tend to be arranged in a more informal way often facing each other, for example, people sitting facing each other at a round table.

Other research examining interactions could give further clues about how we defend personal space. When we feel uncomfortable we are less likely to disclose personal information. For example, in a study by Stone and Morden (1976) students were asked to discuss personal topics with a therapist at a distance of either 2 feet, 5 feet or 9 feet. It was found that most personal information was disclosed at the 5-foot distance. This could suggest that at closer distances students felt the need to defend their personal space and thus were less willing to disclose personal information.

Defending territory

One of the best ways of defending territory links to proposals made by Jacobs (1961) and Newman (1972) about defensible space. This theory proposes that certain design features, for example real or symbolic barriers, separating public territory from private territory and the ability to be able to observe suspicious activity (surveillance) will increase the resident's sense of security and reduce invasion of the territory, thus reducing crime.

A number of studies have found support for this theory although it is not clear to what extent criminals take into account defensible space features.

Newman (1972) studied crime rates in two housing projects in New York. Both housed the same number of people:
- Brownsville had small blocks for five or six families built around courtyards which meant that areas were defensible and people tended to know their neighbours.
- Van Dyke had high rise blocks separated by large parks with people keeping themselves to themselves.

Crime rate was 50 per cent greater in Van Dyke. Therefore Newman suggested that four factors were important:
- Maintained territory suggests to outsiders that the area is private.
- Smaller groups means that it is easier to defend territory, spotting intruders, etc.
- High rise blocks mean that there is no individuality that would suggest privacy or territory.
- Buildings in public spaces are more likely to be vandalised.

The theory of defensible space was tested in the key study by MacDonald and Gifford (1989), described below.

KEY STUDY

Territorial cues and defensible space theory: the burglar's point of view MacDonald and Gifford (1989)

Aim: To investigate how burglars interpret territorial and surveillability cues and whether it links to defensible space theory.

? FOR CONSIDERATION

Different situations require a different amount of interaction.
- Consider when it might be most appropriate to have a sociofugal design and when it would be more appropriate to have a sociopetal design.

CD-ROM

For another study on defending territory, see Environment: Additional key studies: Perkins, Wanderman, Rich and Taylor (1993).

EVALUATION ISSUES

REDUCTIONISM

While Newman's ideas go some way to explain the different levels of crime and satisfaction with different housing projects there have been criticisms. One of the main criticisms is that the proposals do not take other factors into account which may also influence crime and satisfaction. For example, social factors, such as employment levels or size of family and number of children may also have an impact which is not considered within the defensible space proposals.

Participants: 44 male burglars (24 adult and 20 young offenders) detained in prison, all of whom had been convicted of breaking and entering at least once.

Method: 50 photographs of residential single family houses were used, each providing as much information as was possible about the site. The photographs had been rated by five students prior to the study from an original sample of 121 photographs. Five photographs were rated as highly representative and five not very representative of the five categories that the researchers were examining:

- actual barriers
- symbolic barriers, such as low fences or flower borders
- traces of occupancy
- road surveillability
- occupants' surveillability.

Each offender was tested individually in a small interview room. Seven cardboard numbers (1–7) were spread out across the table and the offender was told that they would be shown 50 photographs that they had to rate whether the houses were likely to be broken into. The houses that were most likely to be broken into had to be put under number 1 and those least likely to be broken into had to be put under number 7. They were asked to put at least three houses under each number. Following sorting the photographs the offenders were asked to provide reasons for the photographs sorted into the most extreme piles.

Results: Vulnerability was judged to be lower if at least three-quarters of the house or yard could be seen from the road and if the house had a solid front door with no glass. Greater road surveillability was associated with less vulnerability as was occupants' surveillability but to a lesser extent. Symbolic barriers actually seemed to increase vulnerability and there was no link to vulnerability between actual barriers and traces of occupancy.

Conclusions: The results strongly support the defensible space proposal that surveillable property will be less vulnerable. However, symbolic and actual barriers do not seem to be a deterrent to burglars as this suggests that there will be goods worth stealing in the house. Therefore this study does not fully support Jacobs and Newman's proposals.

EVALUATION ISSUES

GENERALISABILITY

Although MacDonald and Gifford's study does not fully support the proposals of the defensible space theory there are issues with the generalisability of the study. First the sample used were all male and all convicted burglars which is not representative of the population but could be considered an appropriate group to test. Second, the results only relate to the crime of burglary. They do not give any insight into whether certain defensible space features are linked to other types of crime such as vandalism.

Other research has also found similar results linked to defensible space and the extent to which it reduces the likelihood of territory invasion. Wise and Wise (1985) found certain features, which meant less surveillance was possible, increased the chances of a hold up in a bank. Edney (1972) found that homeowners who used clear markers were expecting to live there longer and also showed more vigilant behaviour. Also people who displayed 'no trespassing' signs were quicker to respond to a knock at the door, again suggesting that they were protecting their territory. Newman (1980) also suggested streets that have defensible space features such as speed bumps, communal spaces and clearly marked out gardens have less incidences of crime.

a   Describe one way of measuring territory. [6]
b   Discuss the problems of measuring territory. [10]

a   Describe one study of the consequences of invading personal space. [6]
b   Discuss the ethics of research into personal space invasions. [6]

a   Describe one study of defence of territory. [6]
b   Discuss applications of research on defence of territory. [10]

CD-ROM

For Section B sample exam questions
see Environment: Sample exam
questions.

ARCHITECTURE AND BEHAVIOUR: HOUSING DESIGN AND URBAN RENEWAL

The environment around us can have a significant impact on our behaviour. An important aspect of this links to the type of buildings that we spend our time in and how satisfactory these are in terms of design. It is now generally recognised that the way in which individual buildings, complexes of buildings and even communities are designed can alter how we interact within them and thus impact on our health and behaviour. Therefore it is essential that when planning and designing new buildings there is a consultation process with those who the buildings are intended for.

? FOR CONSIDERATION

- What effects do you think living and working in a busy city may have on individuals?
- Consider the possible effects, both positive and negative, on health and social behaviour.

5.7.1 THEORIES AND EFFECTS OF URBAN LIVING ON HEALTH AND SOCIAL BEHAVIOUR

Theories of urban living

It is possible to examine the impact of city living using a number of theoretical explanations. Four of the main explanations of how urban living affects individuals will be considered here.

Overload theory

Overload theorists suggest that living in a busy city will expose individuals to an abundance of stimulating experiences. These can include high noise levels, high density situations and the necessity to successfully navigate around the city. Due to the fact that many stimulating experiences are present at any one time it means that not all can be adequately processed and thus individuals become overloaded. In order to deal with this overload, coping strategies need to be employed; these can range from the ways in which an individual prioritises dealing with the stimuli, to shifting the burden onto others. Constantly employing coping strategies can be costly to the individual as it can lead to fatigue, while unsuccessful coping can have a more detrimental effect on both health and behaviour.

Adaptation level theory

This theory does not suggest that urban living will necessarily lead to an overload causing negative effects, but rather the effects will vary dependent upon the individuals involved. The intense level of stimulation can lead to either positive or negative effects dependent upon the past experiences of the individual. Therefore, for some people the vast array of activities within the city may be around their optimal level of stimulation while for others it would be too intense. Therefore due to the huge range of stimulation within the city it is important that individuals find a level that is appropriate for them. Exposure to the increased levels of stimulation over a period of time does however seem to lead to adaptation by the majority of people.

Environmental stress theory

This approach links certain types of stimulation more specifically to the negative effects of urban living rather than simply suggesting any stimuli can lead to a negative effect (as with overload theory). The specific stimuli that lead to negative effects include noise and crowding (see pages 213 and 227). The experience of such directly negative stimuli may lead to a stress response which can include emotional, behavioural and physiological components. As a result of the stress response coping strategies are needed which, if successful, may lead to adaptation to the negative stimuli, while unsuccessful coping will lead to long-term negative effects.

Behaviour constraint theory

This theory suggests that urban living actually constrains behaviour in a way that does not happen to those living in rural areas. Behaviour is constrained by aspects of the environment, such as not going out at night alone because of fear. Our initial response to our behaviour being constrained is an attempt to reassert our freewill. However, if our behaviour remains constrained by the environment around us it is likely that learned helplessness will develop, where people feel unable to do anything about their situation and thus stop trying. Although certain constraints will occur due to city life it is likely that different constraints arise for those living in more rural areas, for example, outings having to be planned more precisely due to the less frequent public transport services.

Having considered the different explanations for how urban living can affect people it is important to consider the actual impact on both health and behaviour.

Effects of urban living on health and social behaviour

Health

The effects of urban living on health are not universal as they depend on individual differences as well as the health issue in question. It may be that certain groups of people are more likely to experience city life as negative and thus it could have a greater impact on health. These groups would include those who are unemployed, or those who are living alone away from families without any social support.

Levine et al. (1988) found that cities that experienced a fast pace of life had a greater number of deaths from coronary heart disease. Ford (1976) found that in busy cities where pollution levels are higher there were increased levels of emphysema, bronchitis and lung cancer. However, Hay and Wantman (1969) found only slight differences in the rates of high blood pressure when comparing New York city figures to national figures, and Srole (1972) found arthritis and rheumatism rates to be lower in New York city than they were nationally. Evidence appears far from conclusive and health issues must be considered on an individual basis.

Another health related issue that has been examined is mental health. Again results are mixed, Kovess et al. (1987) examined the differences in depressive disorders between urban and rural dwellers in French Canada. They found lower rates of depression in rural areas. Srole (1976) however, reported that urban dwellers are less likely to display signs of imminent nervous breakdown than those living in small towns. Researchers have also been interested in establishing a link between suicide and urban and rural living, but no conclusive results have been established.

Social behaviour

It is difficult to clearly identify urban living as leading to differences in social behaviour as there are many other variables that could influence results which are impossible to control. However studies suggest that those

EVALUATION ISSUES

REDUCTIONISM

The theories that are outlined above are possible explanations of the impact that urban living has on behaviour. However, it is possible that a combination of these may be better able to explain the effects. Therefore each theory can be said to be reductionist as it only considers one explanation.

EVALUATION ISSUES

GENERALISABILITY

It is difficult to isolate one variable as responsible for differences in individuals' health. Thus it is possible that factors other than living in the city are responsible for any differences such as access to specialist medical facilities.

living in smaller more rural towns are often friendlier towards strangers than those living in urban areas. This is demonstrated by fewer interactions and less eye contact among urban dwellers. This was highlighted by a study conducted by Milgram (1977) where undergraduates approached strangers in the street and extended their hands in a friendly manner. Only 38.5 per cent of city dwellers reciprocated compared to 66 per cent of more rural dwellers.

It has been suggested that population density, rather than population size, is linked to whether or not prosocial behaviour is shown. This was demonstrated in the key study by Levine et al. (1994) described below. These findings support overload theory which suggests that the external demands placed upon city dwellers lead to a state of overload which then distracts attention away from cues that influence social behaviour.

KEY STUDY

Helping in 36 US cities
Levine, Martinez, Brase and Sorenson (1994)

Aim: First, to investigate differences in helping behaviours in cities and regions across the USA. Second, to investigate whether population density is a stronger predictor of helping behaviour than population size, and third, to examine what other factors influence helping behaviour.

Participants: A range of people from 36 US cities. These were: three large (population greater than 2 000 000), three medium (population between 950 000 and 1 450 000) and three small (population between 350 000 and 600 000) cities from each of the four census-defined regions of the United States.

Method: Six different measures of helping were used:
- Dropped pen: a pen was deliberately dropped and the experimenter who dropped it carried on walking.
- Hurt leg: the experimenter, walking with a heavy limp and leg brace, dropped a pile of magazines.
- Change for a quarter: the experimenters asked oncoming pedestrians for change.
- Helping a blind person cross the street: the experimenter, wearing dark glasses and carrying a cane waited for assistance to cross the road.
- Lost letter: the percentage of dropped stamped addressed envelopes returned was measured.
- United Way contributions: per capita contributions to United Way campaigns for each area for 1990 were calculated from records.

Three experimenters, all male, collected almost all of the data across the different cities. All were college age and casually dressed. Standardised procedures were followed and inter-experimenter reliability was checked.

Results: The strongest finding was the highly significant negative correlation between population density and helping behaviour. Population size was also significantly negatively correlated with helping.

Conclusions: This study demonstrates that rather than simply city living affecting helping, the density (the number of people in a particular area of space) is a greater predictor of whether an individual will receive help or not.

One factor that may influence people's willingness to help in urban areas is a fear of crime. People feel a greater need to protect themselves which detracts from helping others. It is also possible (linking to overload theory) that so much time is taken up attending to environmental cues that other important cues (such as somebody requiring help) are missed.

5.7.2 URBAN RENEWAL AND BUILDING DESIGN

Urban renewal

Urban renewal is an attempt to rejuvenate areas of towns as they become run-down. Porteus (1977) defined urban renewal as an integrated set of steps taken to maintain and upgrade the environmental, economic and social health of an urban area. The belief was that renewal would lead to improved housing, safer neighbourhoods and a greater level of business activity.

However, urban renewal over the last 50 years has involved changing housing in many areas to tower blocks which has not always been successful (see defensible space page 255). Often as part of the renewal, those who had been living in the areas affected had to relocate, which has had a negative psychological impact. Therefore it appears that in order for urban renewal to be successful, building design needs to be carefully considered.

Building design

To what extent does architecture influence behaviour? There is no overall agreement as to the degree that building design affects behaviour. It is generally accepted that a building has to fulfil more functions than simply being a roof overhead.

Several different viewpoints have been proposed to suggest the extent to which buildings affect behaviour. Architectural determinism is the view that the built environment directly shapes the behaviour of the people within it, thus suggesting that our behaviour will be altered by the building that we are in. However, some believe that this is too deterministic and propose at the other extreme that the major determinant of our behaviour is the individual, thus a building is what we make of it. This viewpoint is known as architectural possibilism (Porteus, 1977). As these are the two extreme viewpoints a third option is architectural probabilism (Porteus, 1977) which is half way between the other two. This suggests that architecture determines behaviour to an extent, but is modifiable by people; for example, one can move chairs and desks around in a classroom to make the building more appropriate for a particular situation.

Whichever viewpoint an individual subscribes to, Lang (1987) suggested that designed environments must fulfil three basic purposes:
- commodity; functional purpose, i.e. what is the building for?
- firmness; structural integrity, i.e. for how long will it last?
- delight; aesthetics, i.e. is it pleasing to the eye?

The extent to which architects listen to the information given by psychologists links to what is known as the applicability gap (Russell and Ward, 1982). The applicability gap suggests that gaps occur due to needs not being met, for example between designers and those using the buildings.

Architects attend to design criteria while psychologists focus on the effects the design of the building will have on behaviour, such as the impact on privacy, territoriality and personal space. Research carried out by psychologists could assist those designing buildings and make the finished building more satisfactory for those using it.

The contribution to design by psychologists

Privacy

Altman (1975) defined privacy as 'the selective control of access to the self or one's group'. This identifies the fact that we have a need to separate ourselves from other people; we need to be able to personalise our space (see page 255).

Vinsel et al (1980) found that college students who dropped out of college for non-academic reasons were less likely to have been able to achieve adequate privacy in their dorms; thus highlighting the importance of appropriate building design if personal satisfaction is to be achieved. Privacy has also been found to be important in the workplace, as Sundstrom et al (1994) acknowledged. Following a survey of more than 2000 workers it was found that auditory privacy is also an important consideration as more than 54 per cent of respondents said that they were bothered by noise at work.

Windows and illumination

Many recent building designs have included rooms that have no windows or very small windows, with the view that appropriate lighting can be created artificially. However, research has suggested that in many cases there is no substitute for natural lighting, and that windows allow us to see some aspect of the outside world. Karmel (1965) looked at the effect of windowless schools which had initially been designed to reduce distraction, lower heating costs and prevent vandalism. Findings demonstrated that the lack of windows did not seem to have any consistent effect on learning, but did produce negative moods, suggesting user dissatisfaction. Similarly Ulrich (1984) examined the impact that windows could have within hospitals (see key study below). In other working environments windows have also been found to affect both health and personal well-being. For example, Hollister (1968) found that in an underground factory in Sweden workers suffered more than usual from fatigue headaches, and Heerwagan and Orians (1986) report that windowless offices in a university had posters of landscapes on the walls, potentially suggesting that a view of the outside world helps people cope with work stress.

KEY STUDY

View through a window may influence recovery from surgery
Ulrich (1984)

Aim: To examine the restorative effects of natural views on surgical patients in a suburban Pennsylvanian hospital to investigate whether a hospital window view could influence a patient's emotional state and also affect recovery.

Participants: 46 patients, 30 female and 16 male, who were selected from their records and had undergone cholecystectomy, a common type of gall bladder operation, between 1972 and 1981. Patients were aged between 20 and 69 and matched on certain criteria to create the two groups, one with a view of trees, the others with a view of a brick wall.

Method: Data were taken from patient records for all 46 participants. Five different types of information was taken to assess any effects of different window views:

- number of days in hospital
- number and strength of analgesics each day
- number and strength of doses for anxiety, including tranquillisers and barbiturates
- minor complications such as persistent headaches and nausea
- nurses' notes relating to a patient's condition.

Results: The patients' records showed that overall patients with window views of trees spent less time in hospital compared to those with views of brick walls. A significant difference was also found between the two groups linked to the amount of analgesics taken in the critical period of days two to five following surgery, with the tree view group needing less. No significant difference was found between the number of anxiety drugs needed. More negative comments were found on the notes of the brick wall view group.

Conclusion: Overall, in comparison to the brick wall view group the tree view group had shorter post-operative stays, had fewer negative evaluative comments and took lower doses of analgesics. Thus this study suggests that the design of buildings can be important, having a potential effect on behaviour and well-being of those using them.

Closely linked to the issue of windows is that of illumination, as rooms have to be lit to an appropriate level either naturally or artificially. It is generally believed that lower levels of light are more appropriate if greater intimacy and quiet conversation are required, whereas high levels of light are more suitable in kitchens, the workplace or to increase surveillability in primary territories. This general belief has been supported by Gergen et al. (1973) who found when students were placed in a dark room for several hours considerable verbal and physical intimacy took place (see page 221).

Colour

There is a general belief that room colour affects perception of room size and room temperature. Rooms painted in oranges and reds are considered to be warm, while blues and greens are thought to be cooler.

Berry (1961) conducted research to investigate the effects of colour on participants in a heated room. Participants performed a driving simulator task and were told that the lights generated a lot of heat; they were then told to tell the experimenter if they got too hot. No differences in tolerance to heat were found, regardless of whether the colour was green, blue, yellow or amber. However, when participants were asked later to rank the colours according to the heat they transmitted, they said red was hot and blue was cold. This suggests that it is simply our expectations of certain colours rather than any real effect. However, Baum and Davis (1976) found rooms that were painted light green appeared larger and less crowded than identical rooms that had been painted dark green, suggesting that colour does have an impact on our perception of space.

Stone (2001) conducted a study investigating study environments and looked at the impact of three different colours; red, white and blue and the effect on satisfaction. Findings showed that the most positive moods were experienced in the blue rooms and the least positive were experienced in the red rooms. Therefore, maybe colour should be a consideration when designing classrooms and study areas.

Furnishings

The type and arrangement of furniture has been found to have an effect on behaviour, for example, the seating arrangement in a classroom. Sommer (1969) found that horseshoe patterns of seating led to more interest and participation than rows of desks facing the front. Sociopetal seating is open and welcomes interaction while sociofugal seating is closed and discourages contact (see page 255). Sommer and Ross (1958) found that in a geriatric hospital when chairs where arranged along the walls little interaction took place, yet when the seating was arranged into small groups an increase in interaction was noted.

Ornstein (1992) gave executives and students pictures of a variety of companies' reception areas, and found that both judged those with upholstered chairs at right angles and prominent floral displays as the most likeable and considerate. Those with four chairs around a table, contemporary artwork and plants were seen as moderately considerate, while least considerate were those who had chairs directly opposite each other across a coffee table.

FOR CONSIDERATION

• Taking the above factors into account design a new classroom, office or reception area, explaining the reasons for your choice of the various design features.

5.7.3 COMMUNITY ENVIRONMENTAL DESIGN

Community environmental design is more than simply urban renewal, as it offers the residents of a neighbourhood the opportunity to have some input into the redesign of an area of their community or the new development of an area. The aim of this is that it will provide an understanding of the needs and wants of the people already living there, and therefore the people who will be using the new area.

One of the main things that residents in a neighbourhood want to try to prevent is crime, and designers need to attempt to create environments that will minimise the likelihood of crime occurring. In the past it was believed that by making buildings vandal-proof and less appealing the levels of crime would be reduced. This was the belief behind the Pruitt-Igoe project in St Louis which was built in 1974. High rise blocks of flats were built containing more than 2700 separate flats. It was designed to maximise the use of space and minimise crime. Hallways in the buildings were tiled to enable any graffiti to be easily removed, the light fittings were indestructible and there were vandal-resistant radiators and lifts.

EVALUATION ISSUES

EFFECTIVENESS

Building design is only one factor that will influence the level of crime and therefore other factors must also be taken into account such as the types of people who will be living together and the amount of space that families have to live in.

However, residential satisfaction with the project was low as the design failed to create any sense of community, and there was no defensible space (see page 255). As a result the supposedly crime-resistant buildings were in a state of disrepair, with over half of the buildings empty by 1970; the whole project was eventually demolished. This would suggest that other factors should be taken into account when designers attempt to minimise crime. New areas should be built to create defensible space where possible, allowing easy surveillability to occur (see McDonald and Gifford key study page 255). This should in turn allow for a greater sense of community to develop which also reduces the likelihood of crime occurring.

Residents are often keen to develop a sense of a social community and thus design opportunities for interaction should be provided, e.g. more social facilities such as leisure centres and more public areas such as parks, but these would need to be well maintained. Research has demonstrated that those who live in areas where there is a strong sense of community and therefore a greater amount of social support available have better psychological and physical health (for example, Holahan and Moos, 1981).

Designers also need to consider post-occupancy evaluation (POE). Sommer (1969) looked at a psychiatric hospital that had spent some pension fund money on new furniture, air conditioners and TVs. They failed to consult the patients beforehand and found that these changes actually led to less social interaction. This highlights how the physical design can be created for the needs of the staff or the environment rather than the needs of those using it, therefore demonstrating the importance of communication between all those involved in any type of community redesign.

SECTION A EXAM QUESTIONS

a Describe one theory of urban living. [6]
b Evaluate theories of urban living. [10]

a Describe one study of community environmental design. [6]
b Evaluate the usefulness of research into community environmental design. [10]

FOR CONSIDERATION

Think of an area in your community that could be redesigned. Imagine that you are a psychologist working with designers to create the new environment.

- What features would the residents want to see? Explain your suggestions.

CD-ROM

For Section B sample exam questions see Environment: Sample exam questions.

ENVIRONMENTAL COGNITION

This section will focus on how we understand and remember the environment around us. Each time that we visit the same place we are able to imagine the route that we need to take, and use the mental representation that we have stored to help us to get there rather than have to ask for directions each time. Environmental cognition therefore brings together different disciplines; for example, the link between psychology, geography and town planning. Consideration will be given to how information is stored as well as how we can test the ability to use the knowledge that we have stored. Some people appear to be better at this type of spatial understanding than others, so individual differences will also be considered. Linked to this is whether it is possible to improve the ways that cognitive maps are stored and used, and how this can be helped to assist wayfinding. Finally the impact of our scenic environment will be assessed.

5.8.1 DEFINITIONS, MEASUREMENT, ERRORS AND INDIVIDUAL DIFFERENCES IN COGNITIVE MAPS

Definitions

The initial discovery that mental representations of the spatial world were stored and could be used to help find a particular place came from animal research. Tolman (1948) studied the way that rats learned in experimental mazes. Using conditioning techniques, rats learned to follow a particular path to reach food. This learned path was then blocked and it was found that instead of taking an alternative, previously reinforced path, the rats would take a novel one which led more directly to the end goal. This suggested that some kind of learning had occurred linking the whole maze, as they were aware of where the end was in relation to the start. Tolman termed this representation that they had acquired a 'cognitive map'.

Interest in the use of cognitive maps in humans developed in the 1960s when Lynch, who was interested in town planning, asked people from three cities – Boston, Jersey City and Los Angeles – to draw sketch maps of their city and give detailed descriptions of the route they took home from work. From these he was able to identify certain elements that seemed to be common across maps from all three cities.

Elements of cognitive maps (Lynch):
- Paths: routes along which people travel, for example, roads and footpaths.
- Edges: boundaries or non-travelled lines, for example, shores of lakes, edges of cliffs, building walls.
- Districts: moderately sized areas that city residents perceive as having a particular character, for example, the West End.
- Nodes: well-known points that people travel to and from, often at the juncture of pathways, for example, major road junctions, bus stations.
- Landmarks: easily-viewed elements which can be used as reference features, for example on a grand scale, a tall building such as a church spire, or on a smaller scale a statue.

KEY DEFINITIONS

Cognitive maps have been defined by Downs and Stea (1973) as 'a process composed of a series of psychological transformations by which an individual acquires, stores, recalls and decodes information about the relative locations and attributes of the phenomena in his everyday spatial environment'.

FOR CONSIDERATION

- Draw a map of the town or city where you live and describe the route that you take home from school or college each day.

CD-ROM

For more information on cognitive maps, see Environment: Theoretical approach: What are cognitive maps and why are they useful? and Environment: Real life applications: Cognitive maps at the supermarket.

Subsequent research has supported the existence of these five distinct elements when examining cognitive maps.

Measurement of cognitive maps

Psychologists are interested in measuring our ability to mentally represent our spatial environment as it provides an invaluable insight into how we successfully navigate around our world and are able to travel extensively without too many problems arising. There are a variety of ways that researchers can attempt to measure an individual's spatial cognition and each has its strengths and weaknesses. One problem, however, arises when trying to make comparisons between studies, as different methods have often been used which makes direct comparisons difficult.

Sketch maps

Perhaps the most obvious method to use is that designed by Lynch, asking individuals to draw a sketch map. They are required to draw the map of a particular area, for example, their home town or local neighbourhood, to gain an understanding of the internal representation that they have of that area. Using this technique, Appleyard (1970) found that one of two main types of map was drawn, spatial or sequential.

Recognition tasks

Initially recognition tasks were used as a way of checking the reliability of sketch maps. Individuals are asked whether they recognise certain features, such as landmarks. Photographs of local landmarks would be shown interspersed with photographs of non-familiar landmarks, as a way of testing how well people store details of their spatial environment. This became a technique in its own right as it overcame the problems of varying levels of drawing skills. The impact that the use of features such as landmarks had on learning a particular route was examined in a study by Tlauka and Wilson (1994) which is described below.

KEY DEFINITIONS

Spatial sketch maps: maps that consist mostly of landmarks and districts thus representing what is usually considered to be a birds eye view.

Sequential sketch maps: maps that are predominantly constructed of elements that may be encountered while travelling from one place to another, for example, paths and nodes.

EVALUATION ISSUES

USEFULNESS/RELIABILITY/VALIDITY

There are a number of potential problems with sketch maps. First, an overview of an area is required to enable an individual to draw a map of the area and it is unlikely that people will have this. The maps that are produced will be subject to individual differences with those people who are better at drawing producing better quality maps, therefore some maps may be difficult to interpret due to poor drawing skills. However, despite these problems sketch maps are probably the most reliable and valid way of measuring spatial knowledge.

EVALUATION ISSUES

USEFULNESS

The main problem that occurs with the use of recognition tasks in Tlauka and Wilson's study (1994) is that it is always much easier to recognise something than it is to accurately recall something. Therefore individuals will be able to recognise landmarks but that does not mean that they would have included them on a sketch map if they were asked to draw one. This method would also not test our perception of distances.

KEY STUDY

Route-learning in a computer-simulated environment
Tlauka and Wilson (1994)

Aim: To test whether participants would perform a route-learning task more efficiently in an environment with landmarks compared to one without.

Participants: Experiment 1: 32 students from Leicester University, approximately equal numbers of males and females with a mean age of 21.

Experiment 2: a different group of 32 students from Leicester University, with a mean age of 23.

Method: Experiment 1: participants were asked to find their way through a simulated environment, moving through a series of rooms on a computer screen using the keyboard to select the appropriate door to move to the next room. Each participant was tested individually and received six trials. A trial was complete when the participant reached room 15. At this point the environment was re-set back to the starting position in room 1 and the next trial commenced. The difference between the two groups was whether there were landmarks between the two doors, to act as reference points and thus

ECOLOGICAL VALIDITY

Although Tlauka and Wilson's (1994) study was a laboratory experiment conducted via a computer simulation and thus lacking ecological validity the findings do have real life application. The interference task is true to life because whenever individuals are trying to give or follow directions there tend to be other distracters such as noise that prevent the task being given full attention. Therefore the fact that in this study landmarks were recognised and assisted route-learning, even when participants were distracted, highlights their potential importance in the real world.

assist recognition of which of the two doors was the correct one to open, or not.

Experiment 2: the same procedure was followed but in this experiment the participants in both groups were asked to count backwards in threes starting at 911, to act as a distraction task.

Results: Experiment 1: no significant difference was found between the two groups in the number of correct door choices that were made.

Experiment 2: the landmark group chose significantly more correct door choices than the non-landmark group.

Conclusions: The fact that there was no difference between the two groups in experiment 1 suggests that either the landmarks did not make the scene more distinctive or the non-landmark group were using some strategy to remember the correct order of door choices. Experiment 2 was conducted in an attempt to assess the likelihood of it being due to the latter and with the distraction tasks landmarks did aid learning, while without the landmarks the learning strategies used in the landmark condition were not able to be used.

USEFULNESS

This technique is difficult to compare to the others as it does not assess an individual's full knowledge of an area as only distance knowledge is considered. It is also generally accepted that distance tends to be hard to estimate thus leading to inaccuracies in judgement.

Multidimensional scaling

This technique involves the use of distance estimates to assess an individual's mental representation of the spatial environment. Individuals are asked to estimate distances between different features, such as distance between buildings, landmarks or towns, which then leads to a computer-generated map being created to position the buildings according to the estimates given.

An example of how this technique has been used is in a study by Moar (1978). Housewives from Glasgow and Cambridge were asked to give distance estimates between different cities in the UK. From these estimates, maps were created to demonstrate where they perceived the different places to be in relation to each other. It was found that Glasgow housewives exaggerated the size of Scotland while Cambridge housewives exaggerated the size of England. See an example of the maps below.

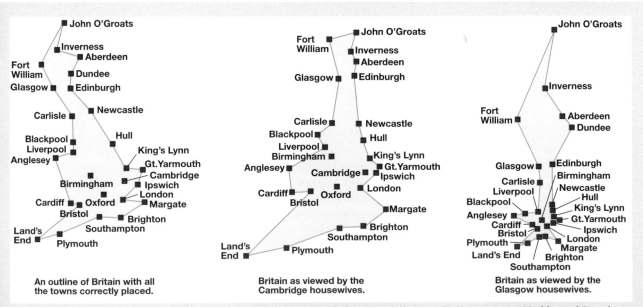

An outline of Britain with all the towns correctly placed.

Britain as viewed by the Cambridge housewives.

Britain as viewed by the Glasgow housewives.

Adapted from Susan Cave (1998) Applying Psychology to the Environment, *Hodder and Stoughton.*

Errors made in cognitive maps

There are a number of different types of error that can be made when our cognitive maps are being tested. Three of the main ones are described below.

Incomplete detail

When maps are drawn some details may be omitted; for example, minor roads or buildings that could affect the overall usefulness of the map.

Distortion

Detail that is included may not be represented accurately. For example, roads tend to be drawn as straight rather than curved, and most commonly junctions are drawn inaccurately at right angles, as mis-estimation of intersection angles occurs (with acute angles being overestimated and obtuse angles being underestimated). Often sizes of buildings or landmarks are distorted, as are the distances between certain features.

Augmentation

On some maps detail is omitted and it is also common for non-existent detail to be added, as we inaccurately represent the area in our mind. This is often linked to our expectations of particular occurrences built out of experience. For example, an engineer working in Guyana included a railway line that did not exist in a sketch map of the area, because his experience led him to predict that there would be a rail connection between a steel mill and a mining port.

Individual differences in cognitive maps

Research has found that there are individual differences in the ability to draw cognitive maps, and further investigation has identified a number of different factors that appear to affect accuracy.

Familiarity

The more familiar a person is with an environment the more detailed and accurate the sketch maps that they produce are. Appleyard (1970) argued that maps were more spatial than sequential for long term residents, rather than newcomers to an area. When we move to a new area Gärling et al. (1981) reported that the basic path and node structure was learned first, and as an individual spends more time in the environment other details such as landmarks are filled in. This can also explain why sketch maps produced by children tend to include fewer landmarks than adults' maps. Siegal and White (1975) suggested that the development of children's spatial representations follows a similar course to adults' in a new environment.

Gender differences

Research by Maccoby and Jacklin (1974) demonstrated that males tend to have better visual and spatial skills on pencil and paper tasks than females, and this would suggest that males would be better at producing cognitive maps than females. Appleyard (1976) found that maps drawn by males tended to be more accurate than females' maps. However, one explanation for this at the time was that males had greater exposure to the cities than females, because their careers took them into cities more often. This would probably not be such a valid explanation nowadays.

Many studies have found that males and females are similarly accurate, but stylistically different. For example, females seem to focus on landmarks and districts, while males focus more on paths (McGuiness and Sparks, 1979). They also found that females were less accurate in placing buildings with respect to spatial terrain, but more accurate with respect to their distance from each other. Further research demonstrated that females did know the locations of many of the roads but just did not include them on their maps unless specifically asked to do so. Ward, Newcombe and Overton (1986) found that males are more likely than females to use compass directions and mileage estimates when they are asked directions. However, when females were asked to phrase their directions in these terms, females were just as successful as males. Again this suggests that the genders may just be stylistically different.

Research suggests that part of the difference between males and females can be attributed to motivation, as it is generally considered that a good sense of direction is important for males, thus they are more motivated to produce accurate directions or maps. Certainly they are often more willing and less anxious about providing these than females.

5.8.2 DESIGNING BETTER MAPS AND WAYFINDING

Wayfinding

It is very rare to be truly lost, but navigating our way around a new or unfamiliar environment can be stressful. It may be necessary to ask for directions or to consult a map, as without experience of an area any mental representation is limited. Gärling et al (1986) proposed that when people are trying to find their way in a new environment, they go through a four stage process which is basically a decision-making exercise:

- Stage 1: determine the location, i.e. identify the building or street that you need to visit.
- Stage 2: localise the destination, i.e. find out where it is, for example, the address.
- Stage 3: select a route, i.e. choose the route that will get you to the location, this may involve looking at a map or asking for directions.
- Stage 4: decide the method of transportation, i.e. consider factors such as distance and ease of travel before deciding how to get to the location.

However, if wayfinding is a problem-solving task, then certain features in the environment can have an impact on how easy it is to navigate around a particular location.

Gärling et al. (1984) proposed that three main features of the physical environment affect how successfully people are able to find their way around. First, differentiation, which is the extent to which the different aspects of the environment are similar to or distinguishable from each other. Buildings that are free-standing are better remembered, as they are more distinctive and this assists wayfinding, while buildings that are clustered together and look very similar make it hard to remember them and thus may hinder accurate wayfinding. Evans et al. (1982) demonstrated that buildings that were distinctive were better remembered, and features such as colour coding improved people's ability to navigate around a particular building.

Second, the degree of visual access, the extent to which different parts of buildings are visible from different perspectives, can also have an impact upon wayfinding. The more visible a building or feature is, the more useful when wayfinding. Thus buildings that can be seen from different locations within a town, such as a tall church spire, can be used as a reference point for navigation, while areas where visual access is limited, such as single-storey buildings or car parks, will not be useful for wayfinding.

The final feature that was identified is the complexity of spatial layout; the more complicated the layout the harder wayfinding is. Complexity links to the number of floors a building has and how many ways there are of reaching these, as well as how complex the layout of each floor is. Thus simple floor plans have been found to assist wayfinding in campus buildings (Weisman, 1981).

Wayfinding was tested in a study by Devlin and Bernstein (1995) (see below) in an attempt to assess the importance of cues such as landmarks and the usefulness of different forms of wayfinding information.

? FOR CONSIDERATION

- Try to think of examples of how colour coding has been used in public buildings or areas to assist wayfinding.
- How could the concept of differentiation linked to wayfinding be incorporated into the design of a new public building, such as a supermarket or hospital?

KEY STUDY

Interactive wayfinding: use of cues by men and women
Devlin and Bernstein (1995)

Aim: The study was designed to examine the use of wayfinding information, specifically testing the use of landmarks within the context of maps, written directions, and written directions supplemented by photographs. Gender differences were also examined.

Participants: 277 first-time visitors to a college admissions building, 126 males and 151 females, ranging in age from 10 to 60 with the majority being high school students.

Method: All aspects of the experiment were conducted using a touch screen monitor with participants experiencing a computer simulation of a tour of the college from point A, the admissions building, to point B, the computer annex. Seven different tour conditions were used in total which participants were randomly assigned to. These were:
- 14 photographs of the college tour
- 14 photographs supplemented with directional text on 9 of the photographs
- 14 photographs supplemented with directional text on the same 9 screens but additionally making reference to landmarks
- 9 screens with the directional text
- 9 screens with the directional text and the reference to landmarks
- a campus map with the specific tour route highlighted with a heavy line
- a campus map with important landmarks graphically presented as well as the route line.

Before beginning the tour the instructions on screen told the participants to 'pay close attention' as they would be asked to 'find their way through the computer simulation afterwards'. The test required the participants to indicate from a choice of direction arrows on different screens which would be the right way to go as suggested by the original simulated tour. The number of errors made and time taken was recorded. Participants were also asked how confident they were about their ability to find their way on the test condition.

Results: The error data indicated that the photographs with the landmark text condition, the photographs with the general text condition and the map with landmarks condition each produced significantly fewer errors than the general text condition, the landmark and route line and the route line only conditions. Overall, males made significantly fewer errors than females and were more confident about their ability.

Conclusions: This study therefore highlights the importance of the use of reference points, particularly landmarks, when designing maps to assist wayfinding.

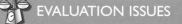

⚖ EVALUATION ISSUES

GENERALISABILITY

The results from this study cannot be fully generalised as the majority of the participants were high school students and thus may be more familiar than the general population with the use of computers and the type of computer simulations that were used in the Devlin and Bernstein study.

Designing better maps

One of the main factors which assists wayfinding when consulting a map is an indication as to your current position or location. These are known as 'you are here' maps, as they clearly identify where an individual is in reference to the rest of the map, which in turn assists wayfinding as the unfamiliar surroundings are put into context.

Certain factors make this type of map more useful. First, if structure matching is used it enables map users to more accurately orientate themselves. The map needs to make it possible to pair buildings or features that can be seen in the environment with the corresponding points on the maps. Therefore three-dimensional maps are most useful for structure matching with the clearest maps containing labels that resemble the labels in the actual setting. If the map is placed in a location where the buildings or features that are depicted on the map are clearly visible in the environment, this allows for the most accurate matching.

Orientation of the map is also important, and where possible the map should be orientated in the same direction as the setting it refers to. People tend to find wayfinding easier if the direction that they are walking, and the direction that they are following on the map correspond. Research by Levine et al. (1984) supported this belief that maps are most useful if they are what is known as 'forward-up'. This is so-called as the tendency is to make the map and the direction of travel match (even to the extent that people will turn maps upside down when travelling north to south to enable a greater sense of correct orientation).

5.8.3 THE SCENIC ENVIRONMENT

The scenic environment relates to how pleasant or beautiful different environments are thought to be. If asked to describe a scenic environment, different people may describe the same thing, or perceptions may vary as they may be influenced by individual differences.

In general, expert opinion and research using descriptive assessments have found that people tend to prefer environments that are naturally occurring and unspoilt (such as mountains, deserts and countryside) to man-made environments (such as housing estates or city centres). Psychologists have attempted to investigate what features linked to the natural environments are preferred to the man-made environment. Findings have suggested that the existence of water and vegetation enhance people's liking of the scene as does apparent tranquillity. These preferences link in to Kaplan and Kaplan's (1989) suggestion that preferences that are demonstrated could be linked to evolutionary factors, such as the extent to which the environment could afford people vital resources such as food or shelter.

How people make decisions about what is and is not aesthetically pleasing has been investigated, and Berlyne (1960, 1974) proposed a general model of aesthetics which contained two main concepts that linked to the choices that are made. First, collative stimulus properties (that is, features in the environment that elicit some type of comparative response) and second, specific versus diversive exploration. Specific exploration occurs when arousal is due to a particular stimulus that is investigated to satisfy curiosity, while diversive exploration occurs due to understimulation and thus involves searching the environment for arousing stimuli. As a result of this model four factors were identified as contributing to the judgements that we make. These are:
- complexity; how varied are the features of the environment?

CD-ROM

For a description of the upside-down map, designed to make travelling easier see CD-ROM: Environment: Real life applications: Upside-down map.

FOR CONSIDERATION

- Collect a selection of pictures depicting different types of environment, both natural and man-made.
- Ask others to rate which they perceive to be the most beautiful.
- Is there any consistency?

- novelty; how unusual are the features within the scene to us?
- incongruity; is there an apparent mismatch between features in the scene and their context?
- surprisingness; the extent to which the features that we can see in the scene are expected.

Berlyne's later work suggested that the judgements made in connection with the two concepts outlined above varied along two dimensions: uncertainty-arousal and hedonic tone. The uncertainty-arousal dimension suggests that as uncertainty about the environment increases so does arousal, while hedonic tone (degree of pleasantness) is related to uncertainty in an inverted U. As uncertainty increases, arousal first increases then decreases. This is linked to diversive exploration and as the inverted U hypothesis suggests people are happiest with a moderate amount of arousal and stimulation. This would suggest that people select preferred environments that create a moderate level of arousal.

An alternative model that has been proposed in an attempt to explain environmental perception is the preference model (Kaplan and Kaplan, 1989). In creating their model they asked people to classify a large range of photographs of different environments on a variety of dimensions, including similar-dissimilar and like-dislike. Following statistical analysis they identified two main dimensions that influenced aesthetic preference:
- Environmental content: natural scenes without human activity depicted were preferred to man-made scenes.
- Spatial configuration: scenes that appeared to be open, but not lacking definition, rather than closed in scenes were preferred.

They suggested that these preferences were perhaps linked to desire for survival, yet people also like scenes that are interesting and not dull. Kaplan and Kaplan went on to suggest four main components that influence our environmental preference:
- Coherence: the more 'together' a scene appears to be (rather than disjointed) the greater the preference for it.
- Legibility: is it possible to understand and categorise the contents of a particular scene? The more legible an environment the greater the preference.
- Complexity: scenes with a greater number of different features are preferred.
- Mystery: if there is the suggestion of further detail but this is hidden from immediate view then the scene will gain greater preference.

While these factors are not totally dissimilar to those proposed by Berlyne, the Kaplans suggest that if an element of cognitive processing is required to interpret the scene depicted it will receive a higher degree of interest and liking thus taking more factors into account.

Research has been conducted to examine whether people's preferences for various environments link in with the proposals made. One example of such research is described in the Purcell et al. (1994) study below.

KEY STUDY

Preference or preferences for landscape?
Purcell, Lamb, Peron and Falchero (1994)

Aim: To investigate whether expressed preferences for landscapes are affected by contextual factors such as the purpose of the

▶

EVALUATION ISSUES

THEORETICAL APPROACH

The main problem with the model that was proposed by Berlyne is that both natural and man-made environments could create similar feelings linked to the above factors, yet findings demonstrate that people tend to choose natural environments when asked. Often natural environments do not have the high level of complexity that was suggested to be important by Berlyne yet they are still preferred. Also, the model does not take into account the individual differences that will occur linked to other factors such as familiarity.

environment, for example, as a place to live, work or visit on holiday.

Participants: 192 university students, equal numbers of males and females ranging in age from 18 to 30 years old. 96 students from each of two different locations – Sydney, Australia and the Padua region in northern Italy. Both areas are located close to large bodies of water on predominantly river plains with mountain ranges in close proximity.

Method: Stimulus material was created by taking colour slides of 12 different scene types identified as existing in both locations, for example, industrial area, street by water, hills, etc. Two examples of each scene type were taken in both locations providing a total of 48 slides.

The two groups of participants were tested in their own country and in each case the slides from both countries were shown, however, the analysis focused of the slides from the participants' country of origin. Slides were projected in a dark room for 5 seconds each. Participants were to record in an answer booklet their responses to the following questions on a 7-point scale, 1 denoting not at all and 7 denoting as much as possible:
- How much they liked the scene.
- Whether they thought that the environment was built or natural.
- How much would they like to live and work in the environment.
- How familiar they were with the place.
- How much they would like to visit the place on holiday.

Results: Overall preferences were shown by both groups for natural scenes of forests and lakes with low preference shown for industrial areas. However, when the results were analysed further to examine preferences of the different environments for different purposes, differences began to emerge. Australians showed a lower preference for the landscape and hill scenes as places to live and work, possibly reflecting the fact that these are a considerable distance from the city centre and thus offer relatively limited career opportunities for graduates. Preferences for places to visit on holiday were also linked to how familiar the participants perceived the scenes to be, with the greater the familiarity the lower the preference for visiting it on holiday. This suggests that the participants would rather visit somewhere unfamiliar and dissimilar to home on holiday.

Conclusions: The study provides evidence for the fact that preferences for the scenic environment are complex and a singular judgement about liking of different scenes is probably not sufficient to accurately assess preference, as when examined in more detail other factors have an effect on the judgements made.

EVALUATION ISSUES

REPRESENTATIVENESS

While the sample used in the Purcell et al. (1994) study can be considered to be a reasonable size and also drawn from different locations it cannot be said to be fully representative, as only university students were used and their preferences, particularly linked to where they would like to live and work may not accurately reflect the views of the general population.

SECTION A EXAM QUESTIONS

a Describe one way of measuring cognitive maps. [6]
b Discuss the validity of ways of measuring cognitive maps. [10]

a Describe one study of individual differences in cognitive maps. [6]
b Discuss whether individual differences in cognitive maps are due to nature or nurture. [10]

a Describe one study of the effects of scenic environment on individuals. [6]
b Discuss the problems of researching the effects of scenic environment on individuals. [10]

CD-ROM

For Section B sample exam questions see Environment: Sample exam questions.

CHAPTER **6** | PSYCHOLOGY AND CRIME

CHAPTER 6: INTRODUCTION

This chapter focuses on the contribution that psychology can make to our understanding of criminal behaviour and its consequences. It is important to establish early on what is meant by 'crime', and this is not as straightforward as it might seem. In law a crime is an act that violates the law, and for which a person can be prosecuted and punished. However, many individuals have their own sense of what constitutes criminal behaviour, and this varies between social groups as well as between cultures and over time. It is important to consider the difference between morality and criminality, as sometimes these can contradict each other. For example there are acts which are considered to be morally wrong and are also illegal, such as murdering someone. However, there are acts that may be considered to be morally acceptable by some people in society, but they are still illegal, such as using some soft drugs, and acts which some people find morally offensive but are not illegal, such as blood sports. There is a section in this chapter on morality and crime, but for the most part the legal definition of a crime in American and most European states is what is being referred to here.

Psychological theory cannot explain everything about criminal behaviour, and other disciplines such as sociology, criminology and economics have developed their own theories that explain some elements of criminality. However, psychological theory can be applied to certain behaviours and situations, and psychological research and methods can be used to understand some criminal conduct, and the responses of those who work with criminals, such as the police, the courts and the prison service. This chapter also looks at the effect of witnessing a crime, and victims of crime and their responses to victimisation; and here too psychological evidence can be applied to the reaction of victims and witnesses. Cognitive, behavioural, developmental, psychoanalytical and psychobiological theories can all be applied to the study of the causes and effects of crime.

EXPLANATIONS OF CRIMINAL BEHAVIOUR

There are many theories that try to explain the reasons why people commit crime. Many of the more sociological theories look at the environment of the criminal and political issues such as poverty. While these obviously play an important role, this section deals with some of the different kinds of areas that psychologists have focused on over the years. The first area looks at theories of criminal behaviour and focuses on biological theories, personality theories and theories that relate to behaviourism. The second area looks at studies that try to explain the many individual and cultural differences that exist between crime rates and types of crime, such as gender and ethnicity. Finally, the third area in this section looks at theories and studies that deal with the social psychology of the criminal, in other words the types of social processes that might affect criminal behaviour.

6.1.1 THEORIES OF CRIMINAL BEHAVIOUR

Biological theories

Historically the medical profession and early psychologists concentrated on physical characteristics to explain criminality. Lombroso (1836–1909), an Italian army doctor, argued that criminals were born with a genetic predisposition towards crime. In 1876 Lombroso published a book entitled *L'Uomo Delinquente*, in which he spelt out his theories about the physical differences between criminals (who he called *homo delinquens*) and non-criminals. Lombroso argued that criminals were more primitive than other people, and that this was evident in their physical features such as a heavy jutting jaw, low brow, a flattened nose, protruding ears and extra toes, fingers and nipples. His evidence was gathered in prisons, and amongst army recruits.

In the eighteenth and nineteenth centuries there were many pseudo-scientific methods of determining criminality. Phrenology was one such 'science', popular in the USA and UK. It was developed by a Viennese doctor called Franz Joseph Gall, who felt the lumps and bumps on the skull, measured the skull using callipers, and related these measurements to character defects. In nineteenth-century Edinburgh, a lawyer called George Combe took interested middle class men into prisons to show them the physical traits of the prisoners. During these trips he would guess the crimes of the inmates from the shape of their heads. By 1900, Combe had sold 350 000 copies of his book *The Constitution of Man*. Phrenology was taken seriously well into the twentieth century, and the British Phrenological Society was not disbanded until 1967.

In recent years, technological advances in the field of brain imaging have renewed interest in linking criminality to physiological factors. Raine, Buchsbaum and LaCasse (1997) used Positron Emission Tomography (PET) scans to compare the brains of violent criminals with control groups. These scans are able to measure the activity of specific parts of the brain, and they did find that, in certain respects, the brains of violent murderers do work in different ways. Raine et al. (1997) suggest that brain abnormalities may be responsible for the violent acts of some murderers. However, the fact that murderers tend to have brain dysfunction does not

Lombroso's criminal types

necessarily mean that this is directly responsible for the violence; many violent killers were themselves physically abused as children, and it may be the experience of abuse that leads to violence, and perhaps also to brain damage. Despite this limitation, there is likely to be an increasing quantity of research into the possible brain abnormalities of criminals, with all sorts of implications for the criminal justice system. For example, whether or not an individual can be held responsible for an act of violence arising directly out of a brain injury.

Personality theories

Theories that appear much more psychological in their approach to understanding criminality often use personality as a basis for explaining antisocial behaviour. These theories argue that personality is in part determined by genetic factors, but also recognise the important effect that social and environmental influences have.

Hans Eysenck's theory of crime argues that personality affects a person's ability to behave appropriately in different situations. Originally Eysenck described two personality dimensions, extroversion (E) and neuroticism (N). In his later work he also describes a third dimension, psychoticism (P). These dimensions are described along continuums, most people falling in the middle, with a few who have extreme characteristics at either end. According to Eysenck (1977), personality is affected by the **cortical and autonomic nervous systems** that affect people's ability to be conditioned by environmental stimuli.

Eysenck argues, for example, that extrovert people are cortically under-aroused, and therefore will need to seek out excitement and stimulation to optimise cortical arousal. An introvert, however, is cortically over-aroused and therefore avoids stimulation to keep arousal at a manageable level. Eysenck relates emotionality (measured by the neuroticism scale) to the autonomic nervous system (ANS). Individuals at the high extreme of the neuroticism scale have an ANS more prone to chemical change, and are likely to react more strongly to external stimuli, and be moody and restless. Individuals with a low N score have a more stable ANS and are more calm and controlled. Measured on these two dimensions it is possible to plot a person's E and N scores, and to relate this score to personality characteristics, which can in turn be related to criminal tendencies.

Eysenck argues that successful social conditioning depends on personality type. A person who is a stable introvert (Low N; Low E) will condition best, and a person who is a neurotic extrovert (High N; High E) will be the hardest to condition. It follows on from this that neurotic extroverts will be over-represented in criminal statistics as they are the least likely to have appropriate socially-controlled responses to external stimuli. Stable introverts are least likely to offend with the other two personality types, stable extrovert (High E; Low N) and neurotic introverts (Low E; High N) somewhere in the middle.

The psychoticism scale (P) assesses personality traits such as aggression, sensation seeking and a lack of feeling for others. The scale has not been as widely applied as the other two, although Eysenck (1977) argues that psychoticism is very closely related to criminality, especially in terms of crimes that involve aggression.

Hare (2001) is particularly interested in the personality characteristics of psychopaths. People with psychopathic personality traits tend to be over represented in the prison population of violent offenders. Until recently explanations of criminality linked to personality theories were out of

🔑 KEY DEFINITIONS

The **cortical (somatic) nervous system** is responsible for voluntary, conscious sensory and motor functions.
The **autonomic nervous system** is responsible for non-voluntary activity, such as breathing.

💿 CD-ROM

For a copy of Eysenck's personality questionnaire (EPI), see Crime: Measurement scales: EPI.

⚖ EVALUATION ISSUES

THEORETICAL APPROACH

Eysenck's theory has a lot of support and many studies confirm his ideas. However the theory cannot be related to all types of crime, and it may be the case that other aspects of personality, that Eysenck does not measure, are more closely related to crime.

favour, but there has been a resurgence of these ideas with the work of theorists such as Hare. Hare's ideas about the nature of psychopathy, and the scale that he designed to measure this, help to explain the link between personality and criminal behaviour.

EVALUATION ISSUES

NATURE/NURTURE

Early biological theories focus on physical features alone, in contrast to personality studies that recognise the link between genetic and environmental factors that can cause criminal behaviour, and social learning theory (p. 281) which focuses on environmental and cognitive processes.

KEY STUDY

Psychopaths and their nature
Hare (2001)

In referring to the 'nature' of psychopaths, Hare is expressing the belief that their behaviour (i.e. human predatory violence) owes more to individual personality than to the social and environmental factors that underlie most other types of violence. He describes psychopaths as grandiose, arrogant, callous, dominant, superficial and manipulative. They are short-tempered, unable to form strong emotional relationships and are lacking in empathy, guilt or remorse. They lead socially deviant lifestyles that include irresponsible and impulsive behaviour and a tendency to violate social conventions. Psychopaths make up about 1 per cent of the general population, but around 25 per cent of the prison population; it is easy to see how psychopathic personality traits lead directly to using intimidation and violence as tools to achieve power and control over others.

Hare argues that the personality traits that define adult psychopathy start to show in early childhood, sometimes as a combination of conduct disorder and ADHD. These traits are influenced by social and environmental forces, and it is likely that genetic factors contribute significantly, although the biological and environmental mechanisms responsible for psychopathy are not well understood. One piece of evidence for a genetic cause is that psychopathy is a disorder that seems to occur in every culture, and is always associated with violent behaviour. Another is that, unlike other non-psychopathic criminals, psychopaths engage in criminal behaviour from an early age and for much of their lives, and their tendency towards violence decreases very little with age. There is little evidence that suggests that psychopaths respond to treatment, which again suggests that psychopathy is an enduring, if not immutable, personality trait, but it may also mean that no one has yet come up with an effective treatment. Hare goes on to consider why certain people show psychopathic personality traits and describes in detail recent research using neuro-imaging and other technology. It seems that the brains of psychopaths work differently from those of 'normal' people, and are physiologically different in some respects. This would certainly explain why psychopaths are so resistant to treatment, although Hare suggests that they might be responsive to biological interventions, particularly if introduced at an early age.

Psychopathy in an individual can be identified by means of a psychometric test, and the most commonly used one was designed by Robert Hare: the Hare Psychopathy Checklist-Revised (PCL-R). This checklist assesses the interpersonal and affective components of the disorder, as well as the socially deviant lifestyle aspects. It uses a semi-structured interview, a review of case history materials and behavioural observations. A score of 30 is typically used as a diagnostic cut-off for psychopathy. Hare has also designed a scale for use with children (the PCL:YV).

Until recently, a common view was that personality traits are not particularly helpful in predicting violent behaviour, but Hare argues against this, saying that an egocentric, cold-blooded and remorseless psychopath is much more likely to be violent. He quotes several prospective studies that show a link between high scores on the PCL-R and future acts of violence. For example, Gran et al. (1999) looked at the relationship between the PCL-R and violent re-offending in a sample of 352 personality disordered offenders. 68 per cent of participants with a high PCL-R score re-offended within four years, whereas only 24 per cent with a low PCL-R score did so. In fact, Hare argues that the PCL-R is often the best predictor of violence available.

In summary, Hare is making a strong argument in favour of a personality theory of criminal behaviour, at least as far as psychopaths are concerned. He describes the psychopathic personality and the neurological abnormalities with which it is associated. However, he does not really shed much light on the question of where personality comes from in the first place, i.e. how much of it is a result of genetic or acquired physiological abnormalities and how much arises out of social and environmental influences.

Behaviourism: classical/operant conditioning and social learning theory

The behaviourist theories of classical and operant conditioning have been widely used to explain criminal behaviour. Classical conditioning is about learning through association; for example, as a result of abusive childhood experiences a person might learn to associate sexual arousal with pain and dominance. In later years, this association may lead them to sexually abuse others. With operant conditioning a person learns through reward and punishment, and this can be applied to criminal behaviour as a person can be rewarded for their crime either materially in terms of what they steal, or through the rewards of status or self esteem that crime confers within a group of friends or peers. According to operant conditioning if the person is punished for their behaviour they are less likely to repeat it; if caught and punished a burglar may stop breaking into people's houses.

Classical and operant conditioning are based on empirical research using animals, that was then applied to human behaviour; social learning differs from other behaviourist approaches in that it takes account of cognitive processes in its approach to human behaviour. Bandura (1965) argues that social learning occurs through imitation, where the person watching the modelled behaviour uses cognitive processes to learn the behaviours they might use themselves. Bandura states that this learning occurs in three ways: through **external reinforcement** (operant conditioning; a person might steal for the financial gain), **vicarious reinforcement** (seeing someone else rewarded for a behaviour and imitating it; seeing the social status another person gets from stealing a car, and copying the behaviour) and **self reinforcement** (feeling clever and raising self esteem as a result of the behaviour; avoiding detection having committed a crime for example).

6.1.2 INDIVIDUAL AND CULTURAL DIFFERENCES IN CRIMINAL BEHAVIOUR

Psychologists have looked at a whole range of individual and cultural factors that might cause criminal behaviour. Factors such as age, gender, ethnicity and social class have been examined, alongside influences such as family background, parenting styles and parental relationships, the school, the peer group and poverty. This section will focus on age and gender.

EVALUATION ISSUES

EFFECTIVENESS

Operant conditioning is currently widely applied within the criminal justice system. However, re-offending rates are very high which suggests that punishment is not a particularly effective deterrent.

EVALUATION ISSUES

THEORETICAL APPROACH

Social learning is considered to be a very useful theory in the area of criminology and is widely used by psychologists, sociologists and criminologists.

FOR CONSIDERATION

• Do you think that people are 'born criminal' or is this something that is learned?

 CD-ROM

For a fuller discussion of social learning theory, see Crime: Theoretical approaches: Social learning.

Age

Juvenile crime accounts for about 30 per cent of serious offences in the UK and the USA (Farrington, 1987). Hollin (2001) discusses the nature of juvenile crime, and distinguishes between what are called **status** offences and **index** (**notifiable**) offences. Status offences are those that relate to young people and not adults; offences such as driving under age, truancy and drinking under age. Index offences are those that are more serious such as burglary or arson. Delinquency increases from the age of 8 until 16 or 17 years of age, when it starts to decrease into the early 20s. A study by Wolfgang et al. (1987, cited by Hollin, 2001) suggests that in the USA it is not individual juveniles that commit more crime as they get older, but a general increase in the number of offenders during teenage years.

There are many different factors that might account for the high rates of juvenile crime. The few longitudinal studies that have been carried out have identified a number of key problems that appear to be important in explaining the **incidence** of both status and index crimes among young people, although these are only indicators and the research is far from conclusive. The Cambridge Study in Delinquent Development is a longitudinal study that was started in 1961 with a group of 8- and 9-year-old boys. The results of this study have been published in numerous articles and books over the years, and the key findings are described below (Farrington, 2002). This study suggests that it is problems associated with poverty, large families, harsh parenting, low IQ and difficulties at school that are some of the key factors in the development of juvenile delinquency.

Gender

There are marked statistical differences in the recorded crime levels between men and women, and men are found guilty of 80 per cent of all crime, with women only committing a reported 20 per cent. The types of offences are also very different with 80 per cent of female offences being for theft and fraud, compared to men who commit a much wider range of crimes.

There is little agreement over what causes these differences and various explanations have been put forward. Some argue that the sex differences in offences may be caused by bias in reporting crime, and in the processing of female suspects. Eaton (1986) argues that women (and men) who conform to gender stereotypes are more likely to be treated fairly by the courts than those that are seen as 'deviant', such as lone parents or gay people, as courts tend to reflect the conservative nature of society.

Other theorists focus on other psychological and social reasons for the differences. The fact that women are more likely to conform to social norms and values than men has been used as an explanation for low levels of female crime compared to male crime (Heidensohn, 1985). From an early age girls are encouraged to conform more than boys, and are more subject to parental control. The key study described below suggests that, for women, there is a link between being victimised and becoming involved in criminal activity.

KEY STUDY

Commission on women and the criminal justice system
The Fawcett Society (2003)

The Fawcett Society (named after a prominent suffragette) is a charitable organisation whose aim is to campaign for the equality of women in society. In November 2003, the Fawcett Society published a controversial report arguing that women tend to turn to crime for different reasons to men, and that the criminal justice system is failing to take this into account in its treatment of female offenders. Recent Home Office figures show that the majority of female prisoners re-offend within two years of being released, suggesting that they are becoming more hardened criminals. Despite overall decreases in crime the number of women jailed for burglary rose by 49 per cent in 2003; there were also sharp increases in convictions for robbery and violence. Over the last ten years, six times as many women as before are serving prison sentences of ten years or more, but less than life imprisonment.

The Fawcett Society report suggests that the reason women are increasingly committing serious and violent crimes is because they have been brutalised by violence against them. Half of women prisoners say they have been hit by a partner; this is more than twice the rate for the general population. One third say they have suffered sexual abuse. More than a third of sentenced female prisoners have attempted suicide at some point in their lives and two thirds were either on drugs or drinking heavily in the year before going to prison. The report argues that there is a closer link between women who are victims and women who offend than there is with men. It calls for better treatment and routes of escape for victims of domestic violence and suggests that the number of women offenders could be lowered by reducing the number of women victims.

6.1.3 SOCIAL PSYCHOLOGY OF THE CRIMINAL

The social psychology of the criminal explains behaviour in terms of the social process that can affect the likelihood of criminal activity. One of the social processes widely thought to affect behaviour, particularly in a group, is deindividuation. Zimbardo (1970) argued that certain conditions such as anonymity, or involvement with a group, and the related state of arousal could cause deindividuation. In this state people are less self aware, and have the feeling that they no longer stand out. This feeling of anonymity combined with a decrease in concern for the consequences of the behaviour can lead people to do things they might not otherwise do, or allow them to do things that they might not were they not deindividuated.

In a recent article Zimbardo (2004) describes some of his original research into deindividuation. The procedure involved young women giving electric shocks to two other women; one of whom had been rated as pleasant and the other of whom had been rated as unpleasant prior to the start of the experiment. The participants could see the two victims through a one-way mirror. The participants were tested in groups of four. Some groups of women had their appearances concealed, and were given numbers to identify them instead of using their names. This made them deindividuated. The women in the other groups were called by their names and made to feel special. These women were individuated. The results showed clearly that the deindividuated women gave twice as many shocks to both victims than the individuated women did, and that the individuated women gave fewer shocks over time to the woman that they had rated as pleasant before the start of the experiment.

Zimbardo and various colleagues tested his theory of deindividuation in many different situations, and with different types of people, and came to the same conclusions each time; that if something makes people feel

CD-ROM

For additional material on gender and ethnicity, see Crime: Real life applications: Crime and ethnicity, Crime and gender.

EVALUATION ISSUES

GENERALISABILITY

It could be argued that these studies are not necessarily generalisable to all women, as there are many factors that will influence individual women's behaviour in relation to crime.

FOR CONSIDERATION

- What other social and cultural factors could be responsible for the differences in crime rates between men and women?

FOR CONSIDERATION

- Give examples of crimes that might be committed when a person is deindividuated.

anonymous they have the potential to do harm to others if the situation allows.

An extremely well-known study that looks at the social psychology of the criminal is the Cambridge Study described in the key study below. It deals with so many of the possible influences that can affect delinquent development, particularly in terms of family background, that it is widely quoted.

KEY STUDY

Key results from the first 40 years of the Cambridge Study in delinquent development
Farrington (2002)

Aim: The Cambridge Study in delinquent development began in 1961 and is a prospective longitudinal survey of the development of offending and antisocial behaviour in 411 South London males, born in 1953. The aim of the study was to see whether delinquent and criminal behaviour could be predicted, to explain why it began and why adult crime often ended as men reached their twenties.

Sample: Participants were taken from six state primary schools in South London; it was overwhelmingly a white, urban, working class sample of UK origin.

Method: The boys were interviewed and tested at school at ages 8, 10 and 14. They were interviewed in the research office at ages 16, 18 and 21, and in their own homes at ages 25, 32 and 46. There was some attrition; for example, at age 32, the researcher only managed to interview 378 out of the 403 original participants who were still alive. The tests in schools measured intelligence, attainment, personality and psychomotor impulsivity. In the interviews, participants were asked about living circumstances, employment, personal relationships, children, illnesses and injuries, drinking and drug use, fighting and offending behaviour. The mothers of the boys were also interviewed every year (when the boys were 8 to 15) and asked about the boy's personality, family income and size, employment, history of psychiatric disorders, child-rearing practices and closeness of supervision of the boy. At 8, 10, 12 and 14, teachers answered a questionnaire about the boys' behaviour at school. The researchers also asked for reports from the boys' peers and searched criminal records for evidence of offending.

Results:
- 40 per cent of the sample were convicted of a criminal offence before they were 40 (compared with a national average of 31 per cent).
- Offending increased up to age 17 and then decreased.
- The average duration of criminal careers was about 7 years.
- The criminal careers of siblings and partners was similar to the participants', although female relatives had a lower rate of conviction.
- The conviction careers of parents were very different; they started much later and lasted much longer.
- Offenders were very persistent, but there was little specialisation in actual crimes committed.
- 6 per cent of the sample seemed to be 'chronic' offenders.
- Boys whose first conviction was early tended to become the most persistent offenders.
- Participants tended to move from co-offending in their teens to lone offending in their twenties.
- Recruiting of less experienced offenders was common, especially for burglary.

- Reasons given for offending were utilitarian (i.e. for material gain) or hedonistic (i.e. for enjoyment or excitement).

Farrington identifies the following risk factors for offending:
- Poor families, low standard housing, physical neglect by parents (but not low economic status as defined by occupational prestige or by having working mothers).
- Parents with convictions and delinquent older siblings.
- Poor parental child-rearing behaviour (i.e. harsh or erratic), parental conflict.
- Poor parental supervision (i.e. lax in enforcing rules or undervigilant).
- Broken homes or separations from parents.
- Nervous or ill mothers, fathers with erratic job histories.
- Low intelligence and low school achievement.
- Rated as 'daring' by parents and peers.
- Hyperactive, poor concentration, impulsive.
- Unpopular with peers.
- Below average height and weight.

Conclusions: In attempting to explain offending and antisocial behaviour by working class males, Farrington lists biological and social risk factors (see above) but also suggests that there exist 'energising' factors (e.g. desire for material goods, status and excitement) and 'inhibiting' factors (e.g. conscience, empathy). His model also includes cognitive processes (e.g. cost-benefit analysis) and other factors such as life events and opportunity for crime. He argues that all of these various factors interact with each other. Farrington concludes that there do exist individual differences between people in what he calls 'anti-social tendency', which is relatively stable from childhood to adulthood. The most important predictors of antisocial tendency are impulsivity, low intelligence or attainment, family criminality, poverty and poor parental child-rearing behaviour. Farrington takes a 'social psychological' approach in recognising the important impact of social factors, but he also recognises that other factors, such as biological or cognitive, are influential and his model tries to explain criminal behaviour in terms of an interaction between all of these various influences.

EVALUATION ISSUES

USEFULNESS/ REPRESENTATIVENESS/ GENERALISABILITY

- The Cambridge Study is particularly useful because it looks at so many factors to explain criminality and is therefore not reductionist.
- The sample is large, the study is longitudinal, and in spite of this has not suffered high levels of attrition (92 per cent of the original sample were still involved at the age of 30).
- It could be argued that the results of the study are generalisable because the sample is large and representative.

SECTION A EXAM QUESTIONS

a Describe one theory of criminal behaviour. [6]
b Contrast one theory of criminal behaviour with one other theory of criminal behaviour. [10]

a Describe one study of cultural differences in criminal behaviour. [6]
b Discuss the problems of investigating cultural differences in criminal behaviour. [10]

a Describe one study of the social psychology of the criminal. [6]
b Evaluate the methods used to investigate the social psychology of the criminal. [10]

CD-ROM

For Section B sample exam questions see Crime: Sample exam questions.

6.2 CRIME-VICTIM INTERACTION

This section examines some of the ways in which crimes are recorded, and consequently how victims of crime are identified. It also looks at fear of crime and how victims respond to crime. The response of victims partly determines the likelihood of their reporting the crime, and the type of reaction they have to the criminal at the time, whether they will intervene or remain passive in the process.

6.2.1 WHO ARE THE VICTIMS?

Official figures from the Home Office based on reported and recorded crime have long been used by the government and the police to indicate whether levels of crime are increasing or decreasing, and to examine which types of crime are increasing and decreasing. While these official figures are useful to explain levels of **recorded** crime, it is widely recognised that they only show a partial picture of the true levels of crime in society.

This is because a great deal of crime goes unreported and therefore unrecorded. There are some crimes also that may be reported but do not make their way into official statistics, as in the case of domestic violence for example, where a police warning may be all that occurs, or the person who reports the incident withdraws their complaint soon after. The level of unreported and unrecorded crime is sometimes referred to as the '**dark figure**' (an analogy is often made to the tip of an iceberg) what is visible is only a tiny fraction of the total number of crimes committed within society. The graph opposite shows the percentage of reported crimes that the police record – for example, of all reported vandalism, the police record 70% of incidents.

An alternative way of finding out about the level of crime in society is to carry out **offender** and **victim surveys**. These are self-report measures in which people are either asked about crimes they have committed in the last year, or in the case of victim surveys, crimes that have been committed against them in the last year. Offender surveys reveal information about the offenders who are not caught and processed by the police, and they can help in giving an accurate picture of victimless crimes, such as using illegal drugs.

Victim surveys have the advantage of giving details of the extent and type of crime, and also the effects of crime in terms of fear of crime and the impact of crime on victims. The best known victim survey is the British Crime Survey. This survey is conducted every year, and is widely quoted. Its sample is usually in the region of 10 000–12 000, and it builds up a detailed picture through the use of a number of questionnaires for each participant.

One of the problems with the British Crime Survey is that it does not use people under the age of 16 in its samples. However, other surveys have been conducted in order to find out about levels of crime among younger people, for example the British Youth Lifestyle Survey (2000) was designed to obtain information about crimes against young people.

In a report entitled *Crime in England and Wales*, Simmons and Dodd (2003) bring together statistics from the British Crime Survey (BCS) and the number

EVALUATION ISSUES

VALIDITY

Because a great deal of crime goes unreported and unrecorded, the Home Office statistics cannot be a valid picture of crime.

EVALUATION ISSUES

REPRESENTATIVENESS

It is not clear that the samples of people who fill out offender surveys are really representative of the population; they often tend to be opportunity samples of students and young people who are readily available.

EVALUATION ISSUES

VALIDITY

It is possible that people filling out this kind of survey might lie or misrepresent the true level of their crimes, either by over or under-representation. Even though they are anonymous, victim surveys seem to suggest that offender surveys under-represent some crimes, especially those of a sexual nature and domestic violence.

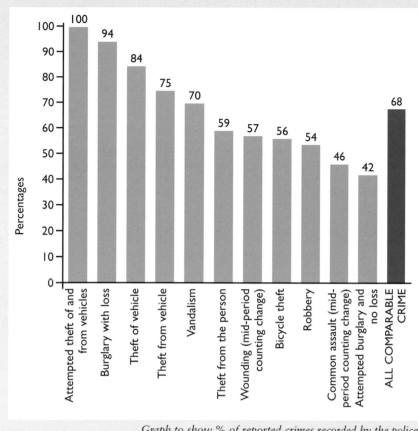

Graph to show % of reported crimes recorded by the police
(Source: British Crime Survey 2002/3: Home Office)

of crimes recorded by the police using Home Office statistics. The key finding of the 2002/2003 report was that crime had fallen by 2 per cent compared to the previous year, and by 25 per cent since 1997. The risk of becoming a victim of crime in 2003 is at an all time low of 27 per cent (compared to 40 per cent in 1995). Furthermore, the number of detections recorded by the police rose by 8 per cent from the previous year. The British Crime Survey also looks at who is most likely to become the victim of crime:

- Well-off professionals living in town and city areas have a high risk of burglary and of vehicle theft.
- Vehicle-owning households in multi-ethnic low-income areas are most at risk of vehicle theft.
- Household crime is highest in Yorkshire and the Humber region, and lowest in Wales.
- The South-East had the lowest rate of overall crime, and London the highest.
- People living in rural areas have a significantly lower risk of being the victims of burglary, violent crime or vehicle theft than people living in towns and cities.

Simmons and Dodd (2003) found that almost 75 per cent of the public believe that the national crime rate is rising:

- 38 per cent of respondents believed that the crime rate had risen 'a lot', and 35 per cent believed it had risen 'a little' despite the fact that the total number of reported crimes has fallen by 17 per cent since 1999.
- 43 per cent of tabloid newspaper readers believed that crime had risen 'a lot' compared to 26 per cent of broadsheet readers.
- 13 per cent of people said they felt 'very unsafe' walking alone in their area after dark, and another 21 per cent felt 'a bit unsafe'.

EVALUATION ISSUES

METHODOLOGY

One of the problems with victim surveys is relying on the memory of the victim, as this may be flawed or biased in some way.

FOR CONSIDERATION

Young men have a very high chance of being victims of crime. Victim surveys suggest that some people are more likely to be at risk than others, and some people are more likely to experience repeat victimisation.

- Why might young men and especially young Afro-Caribbean men have a high chance of being victims of crime?

For more details of Simmons' and Dodd's study, 'Crime in England and Wales', see Crime: Additional key studies: Simmons and Dodd (2003).

- There was a small increase in the numbers of people worried about teenagers hanging around, and a small decrease in the numbers worried about car and violent crime.
- 59 per cent of victims were satisfied with the way the police dealt with their incident.

The key study by Nayak (2003) described below investigates fear of crime in children.

EVALUATION ISSUES

GENERALISABILITY

Nayak's (2003) study has a large sample, but it could be argued that it is not generalisable to all children, as only one school in a predominantly white working-class area was used in the study.

KEY STUDY

Through children's eyes: childhood, place and the fear of crime
Nayak (2003)

Aim: To understand fear of crime from children's perspectives.

Sample: 449 12–15 year old pupils, balanced in terms of gender, from a mainly white secondary school located within a predominantly working class area in the North of England.

Method: After piloting the study on a small sample of children, a survey was given to the participants during their PSE (personal and social education) lessons. Respondents were asked not to speak to their peers while filling out the survey, and they were assured that their responses would remain confidential. The survey contained both quantitative and qualitative questions.

Results:
- Around half (51 per cent) of respondents had either been stopped, stopped and searched, or taken to the police station, but this figure was higher for children living on the council estate, compared to those from other suburban districts. Despite this, nearly all respondents saw the police as necessary and many agreed that a greater police presence would be welcome, although they were also critical of the way that the police treated them.
- While children did recognise a range of social problems in their communities (e.g. theft, drug abuse, street violence), the overwhelming majority (82 per cent) felt 'safe' in their localities. Children felt much safer hanging around in the streets than in local parks (53 per cent perceived these as 'unsafe' at night); the streets seemed to offer children their own space outside the parental home, and the opportunity to 'have a laugh' and relieve boredom. At the same time as being treated as youth 'gangs' by the police, groups of children gathering together outside felt themselves to be the subjects of intimidation from older teenagers. Respondents seemed to distinguish between other children, who were perceived as safe, and youths, who were potentially threatening. They perceived their own 'gang' as something that would protect them from other youths and from 'stranger danger'.
- One of the most prevalent hazards perceived by children was being injured by dangerous car drivers; their accounts showed a sharp awareness of 'hot spots' and 'problem' areas in the neighbourhood.

Most children perceived drugs to be a significant problem in their localities, but they had a good knowledge of drugs and the areas associated with drug use.

Conclusions:
- Children were appreciative of the role and function of the police, but critical of policing tactics.

- Groups of children congregating outdoors were critical of adults' inability to distinguish between children 'hanging out' and criminal 'gangs'; unlike adults, children do not necessarily perceive the presence of other children in public places as a threat. However, they did fear 'gangs' of older youths and perceived their own gangs as protective.
- Children perceived danger from those committing car crime and those using hard drugs, but they also had a clear idea of which 'danger' areas to avoid.
- From this research, Nayak concludes that children should be seen as knowledgeable, active agents in the community, rather than the 'innocent' subjects of parental protection, or dangerous, 'ostracised' outsiders. Closer consultation between youth services, residents, children and the police would be helpful in developing better community relationships.

6.2.2 VICTIM RESPONSES

There are many different reactions to victimisation, and this section will examine some of these. Most people have experienced some kind of threat, even if it is not directly linked to criminal activity, and it is obvious to most of us that our responses are either the same or different to those of others in a similar situation. Understanding how people cope with victimisation is an important area of psychological research, particularly because many people need help to overcome such experiences.

How people cope does not always bear any relation to the type of crime that was committed against them. While there is some evidence to show that victims of the same types of crimes do experience similar symptoms in their response to these crimes, this may not always be the case. Stephenson (1992) reviews studies that suggest that robbery and rape victims may experience similar responses of anxiety and low self esteem, although robbery victims recover quicker. However, other factors are likely to affect individual responses, such as age, sex, the severity of the trauma and where the event took place. It is also important to remember that although some crimes, for example rape or abuse, will have a greater effect on their victims than burglary of an empty house might, the after effects of the 'lesser' crime cannot be ignored. A study by Brown and Harris (1989) (cited by Stephenson, 1992) used interviews with women who had been victims of burglary in Utah, USA to examine the effects of the 'depth of territorial intrusion'; in other words they were looking at the effect of more or less invasion of privacy in the person's home. They found that the more the intruders had gone through personal effects, and the greater the number of rooms they had entered the worse the psychological trauma. The damage caused, and the value of the property stolen was less important than these other factors. Brown and Harris also found that coping strategies such as checking locks and talking to neighbours had little effect on stress in the short term, or on fear of future victimisation.

Locus of control and attribution

One important psychological theory that can be applied to the experience of victimisation is **locus of control** (Rotter, 1966). This can be applied to victims of crime, as it is probable that people who have an internal locus of control are likely to experience more distress than a person with an external locus of control because they blame themselves in some way for their victimisation. However, a person with an internal locus of control is

> ### KEY DEFINITIONS
>
> **Locus of control** refers to how individuals attribute responsibility. A person who has an **internal** locus of control is likely to blame themselves when something happens to them and attribute responsibility to their own intentions, personality or behaviour. Someone with an **external** locus of control is less likely to do this, as they are more likely to see the event as beyond their control, they are likely to blame other people, the situation they found themselves in, or else attribute the event to 'luck'.

Attributional error is when individuals make mistakes in placing responsibility for events; this can have very serious implications in crime-related situations. For example, if a victim of a crime blames themselves for what happened (i.e. internal attribution), this can lead to feelings of guilt and worthlessness, and victim support often focuses on trying to persuade people that it was not their fault they were victimised. On the other hand, it can be helpful for victims to make internal attributions because it may make them feel more able to avoid being a victim in the future. An example of **self-serving attributional bias** is when perpetrators of crimes blame the victims or the situation instead of themselves (external attribution); this can alleviate feelings of guilt but is a barrier to genuine remorse.

more likely to avoid the situation that caused the offence in the future, whereas a person with an external locus of control is more likely to see a possible re-occurrence as unavoidable.

Ainsworth (2000) notes that in making judgements about victims others will often make an **attributional error** of judgement in relation to the victim's behaviour; commonly making an internal (dispositional) attribution for behaviour. It is often the case, at least in part, that the victim is blamed for their own misfortune, e.g. in the case of 'mugging' in certain neighbourhoods, or late night attacks, the person is held partly responsible for being there in the first place. In contrast, people are likely to make external (situational) attributions for their own victimisation, e.g. it was bad luck or their lift didn't turn up on time.

Post-traumatic stress

Post traumatic stress disorder is now a widely recognised reaction to victimisation, and although PTSD does not affect everyone, it is particularly common if the victimisation involves violence. PTSD was first diagnosed in soldiers returning from the Vietnam war, but it probably explains many reactions to severe trauma that were interpreted differently at the time. For example, many soldiers were executed for cowardice during the First World War, when in reality they were probably suffering severe reactions to the experience of war. In the USA it has been estimated that the prevalence of crime-related PTSD in the general population is around 1 per cent and that there is a great deal of evidence to suggest that the experience of criminal victimisation leads to problems with mental health. In a study of the victims of burglary, robbery and assault, it was found that 75 per cent were experiencing distress or sleeping disorders 1–3 weeks after the incident. The key study below sets out the official definition of PTSD.

KEY STUDY

DSM-IV Criteria for PTSD, diagnostic and statistical manual of mental disorders

The DSM-IV defines a 'traumatic event' as one that involves the threat of death or serious injury to self or others, and in which the person's response involves fear, helplessness or horror.

PTSD is present if all of the following apply:
- The traumatic event is 're-experienced' by the individual in the form of recurrent and intrusive recollections, recurrent distressing dreams, reliving the experience (i.e. hallucinations or flashback episodes), and psychological and physiological distress at exposure to cues that symbolise the traumatic event.
- The individual engages in persistent avoidance of stimuli associated with the trauma, by avoiding thoughts, conversations or activities associated with the event; by being unable to recall important aspects of the traumatic event; by withdrawing from other people or from normal activities; by having a restricted ability to feel love and by feeling that the future is short and bleak.
- The individual shows persistent symptoms of increased arousal such as insomnia, irritability, difficulty concentrating, hypervigilance and an exaggerated startle response.

Furthermore, the disturbance has to last for more than one month and must cause clinically significant distress or impairment in social or occupational functioning.

CD-ROM

For a full description of the DSM-IV criteria for PTSD see Crime: Theoretical approaches: DSM-IV/PTSD.

Joseph et al. (1997) argue that crime involving random violence can be particularly distressing. They cite an example of a shooting in a restaurant in the USA in which 21 people died, after which nearly a third of the community in which it happened said they were seriously affected by the incident. In another multiple shooting incident that took place in a small town, 80 per cent of those having family or friends involved in the incident exhibited symptoms of PTSD.

Rape is one of the most traumatic events and has the highest rate of PTSD (around 76 per cent of rape victims meet the criteria for PTSD within a year of the assault). In addition to PTSD, rape victims are likely to suffer from other psychological problems such as anxiety and fear, sexual dysfunction and problems in social adjustment. The psychological effects of rape are now known as 'Rape Trauma Syndrome'.

Rape trauma syndrome

Physical	Psychological	Behavioural
Insomnia/nightmares	Depression/tearfulness	Inability to go out
Poor appetite/weight loss/swallowing and eating problems	Anxiety, flashbacks guilt and self-blame	Avoidance of rape-related stimuli; social withdrawal
Menstrual irregularities	Decline in sexual enjoyment	Increasing dependence on others
Difficulty in micturation (urinating)	Poor concentration	Alcohol/drug abuse
General non-specific complaints: weakness/dizziness/ general malaise/ faintness/nausea/ increased muscle tension	Irritability and apathy, phobias	Moving house/cutting off phone NB: Pregnancy/sexually transmitted disease/ AIDS risks

Post Traumatic Stress Disorder can also affect people who regularly deal with violence and crime as part of their job. From of a sample of 37 Dutch police officers who were involved in serious shooting incidents, only three were found to be symptom free. It was also found that not one of these officers had tried to get help from doctors or psychologists; perhaps because of a culture in the police force that discouraged officers from discussing emotional reactions.

All of the examples given above involve a single traumatic incident, but one example of victimisation that can be prolonged and repeated is childhood sexual abuse. This seems to lead to a more complex form of PTSD which includes enduring personality changes and high risk of repeated harm, either self-inflicted or at the hands of others. Victims of this type of abuse are often misdiagnosed as having personality disorders as many of the symptoms overlap. In a recent national survey of over 2500 Americans, 27 per cent of women and 16 per cent of men reported being the victims of child sexual abuse, and most of these victims exhibited a range of dissociative and autodestructive behaviours, such as substance misuse or self-harm.

In spite of the suffering that leads to the onset of PTSD, it is a condition that can be overcome, or at the very least the effects can be reduced with effective therapy, such as cognitive behavioural therapy, or group therapy.

CD-ROM

For a further study that explores the multiple causes of PTSD, see Crime: Additional key studies: Joseph et al (1997).

Ego defence mechanisms

Freud describes how people use a range of techniques to make themselves feel better in certain situations, especially at times of anxiety or stress. He calls these **ego defence mechanisms,** and these can help to explain how some people respond to and cope with victimisation. These mechanisms work by distorting or denying reality. Freud describes a number of ego defence mechanisms:

- **denial:** where people simply pretend to themselves that something did not happen
- **suppression:** where people deliberately try not to think about things that might upset them
- **repression:** an unconscious process of pushing thoughts out of the mind
- **rationalisation:** justifying or making excuses for something
- **displacement:** where a person has negative feelings about something but redirects them towards a safer target
- **projection:** where thoughts or feelings a person might be ashamed of are unconsciously attributed to someone else.

Suppression may be used a great deal to cope with victimisation; a person might try not to think about what has happened, and might try to distract themselves with activities that help them avoid confronting their thoughts and fears. **Denial, repression** and **suppression** for example, might be used where the person cannot cope with the feelings that their experience of being a victim generates, such as sexual abuse of some kind. All of the ego defence mechanisms Freud describes can be used to explain victim responses to crime.

6.2.3 CRIME REPORTING AND INTERVENTION

Intervening at the time of the incident, or reporting a crime that has been committed against a person, would appear to be a straightforward response to victimisation. However, whether or not a person responds in this way is based on a complex set of factors that can illicit very different reactions.

The key study below shows how many factors are associated with reporting and intervention. In their survey of over 44 000 reports of victimisation reported in American National Crime Surveys between 1973 and 1982, Webb and Marshall (1989) found that factors associated with the incident itself were most likely to cause a victim to report the crime; with gun crime and crimes that involved multiple offenders the most likely to be reported.

EVALUATION ISSUES

EFFECTIVENESS/REDUCTIONISM

- Although ego defence mechanisms can protect the individual in the short term, or perhaps from less serious incidents, longer term coping strategies such as psychotherapy may be necessary for some individuals.
- It may be reductionist to try to label a victim's response to crime. They may experience all or none of the reactions described. While PTSD includes a recognised range of symptoms and accounts for many behavioural and psychological reactions, some diagnoses may be inaccurate, or partial.

CD-ROM

For more information about ego defence mechanisms, see Crime: Theoretical approaches: Ego defence mechanisms.

FOR CONSIDERATION

- Do you think it is useful for people who have experienced traumatic events to relive their experiences by talking about them?

FOR CONSIDERATION

- Write a list of factors that may influence whether or not a crime is reported.

KEY STUDY

Response to criminal victimisation by older Americans
Webb and Marshall (1989)

Aim: To investigate whether age and other variables have an impact on victims' self-protective action or police reporting. Webb and Marshall looked at three different categories of variables that may have an impact on how people react while being victimised, and whether they report the crime to the police afterwards. **Victim characteristics** include age, ethnicity, gender and socio-economic status; **incident characteristics** include the presence or absence of a weapon, single versus multiple offenders and the seriousness of the crime; **contextual characteristics** refer to the neighbourhood and community. There had been very little previous research on the victim's decision to resist attack, but the victim's decision to report the crime had been much studied. The key factor is the degree of harm suffered by the victim, but there are other factors: females are more likely to report than males, black people more than white

---

people, older more than younger, married more than single, better educated more than less well educated.

Sample: Evidence was collated from the National Crime Survey (NCS) data on criminal incidents over the period from 1973 to 1982.

Method: The NCS questionnaire asks victims what, if anything, did they do to protect themselves during the incident, and whether they, or someone else, informed the police afterwards.

Results: None of the characteristics examined were strongly related to self-protective action or police reporting. Age was the most important factor, with older people doing least to defend themselves, and being more likely to report the incident to the police. Males were more likely to physically defend themselves when attacked, whereas females were more likely to use non-physical strategies and were more likely to report the crime. Similarly, black people were less likely to have defended themselves and more likely to have reported the incident. Poorer and less well-educated people were all slightly less likely to defend themselves, and slightly more likely to report the crimes (this last finding is in contradiction to previous research). Regarding the type of crime, victims of rape were more likely to have defended themselves than victims of armed robbery. Victims of more serious crimes, or crimes in which a weapon was used, were more likely to report them to the police. Interestingly, the presence of a weapon did not influence the victims' decision to defend themselves. Incidents with multiple offenders were less likely to be resisted and more likely to be reported. None of the contextual characteristics had an effect.

Conclusions: Age of victim and severity of crime were the two most influential factors, but none were particularly strongly related to self-protection or police reporting. It is interesting to note that in all situations where the victims are more likely to defend themselves, they are less likely to report the crime to the police.

EVALUATION ISSUES

GENERALISABILITY

Webb and Marshall's study has a large sample and it is representative as a result of this (although it may not be generalisable outside the USA).

EVALUATION ISSUES

VALIDITY

Studies such as that by Webb and Marshall (1989) show that the validity of crime statistics may be questionable

Piliavin's (1969) model of **bystander intervention** suggests that witnessing a crime creates psychological arousal in a bystander. This will be higher the more empathy the bystander has with the victim, the closer they are to the incident and the longer the incident continues without help. Psychological arousal is an unpleasant feeling, and one way of reducing it is by helping or going to get help. The decision whether to help or not is made by considering a **cost reward matrix** (i.e. by weighing up the pros and cons). The bystander considers the costs and rewards of helping, and the costs and rewards of not helping.

Kidd (1985) looked at bystander intervention in crime reporting, and argued that when people see a crime committed they become emotionally aroused (especially if they are involved), and this arousal can cause them to behave in an impulsive way. People who intervene are often found to be more reckless than other people in the population, and to have higher levels of aggression than average.

EXAM HINTS

You can use the core study you looked at in the AS modules as an example of bystander intervention – although the stooges were not criminal, Piliavin's study shows how people weigh up the costs and rewards of helping.

SECTION A EXAM QUESTIONS

a Describe one study of fear of crime. [6]
b Discuss the methods used to investigate fear of crime. [10]

a Describe one study of victim responses to crime. [6]
b Discuss the usefulness of research into victim responses to crime. [10]

a Describe one study of crime reporting. [6]
b Discuss the difficulties of investigating crime reporting. [10]

CD-ROM

For Section B sample exam questions see Crime: Sample exam questions.

OFFENDER PROFILING

Offender profiling has become a very popular tool in films such as *Silence of the Lambs* and in TV series such as *Cracker*, and many people feel that they understand the work of a profiler. The reality however, is not as straightforward as such examples would have us believe. Profiling is a very well known, but little understood, method used by the police to help them in the apprehension of suspects, and its success is debatable; some would argue that it is an invaluable tool, while others would suggest that much of it is common sense.

6.3.1 DEFINITIONS, APPROACHES AND DEVELOPING A PROFILE

There is no clear single definition of an offender profile, and profiling varies to some degree between individual profilers, and the approach to profiling that they adopt. One of the first recognised profiling techniques came from the FBI in the USA but it is possible to recognise the expertise of profiling in cases as early as those such as that of Jack the Ripper in London (1888). Early attempts at understanding the perpetrator of a crime were not labelled profiles, and were carried out by the police, rather than 'experts' in the field of forensic psychology; however they bear the hallmarks of early versions of what later became known as offender profiling.

Copson (1995) argues that the police need four types of information from profilers:
- the type of person who committed the crime
- how great a threat they pose in the future; are they likely to strike again?
- the possibility that the case is linked to others
- how the police should interview suspects; what sort of strategies should they use?

Most of those who produce profiles, and those who use them, argue that there are only certain types of crime for which a profile is useful. These crimes are usually serious offences such as rape, murder (especially sexual murder), arson and kidnapping. It is also important to remember that profiling does not solve the crime, it can only offer an indication of the type of person who might have committed the crime.

Profiling is based either on a **scientific approach** which uses, for example, statistical analyses of types of offence, relationships between characteristics of the offence (such as what was done to the victim), and the geographical distribution of offences, or a **clinical approach** which uses personality theories to explain characteristics of the offender and looks at underlying psychological processes drawing on the experience and expertise of the profiler. These approaches are not mutually exclusive, as profilers often use a range of techniques; and furthermore profiling can be subdivided according to the emphasis of the profiler (for example some profilers that use scientific methods are known for their geographical approach, which focuses primarily on the location of the offences).

KEY DEFINITIONS

Blau (1994) defines **offender profiling** as 'a method of helping to identify the perpetrator of a crime based on the nature of the offence and the manner in which it was committed. The process attempts to determine aspects of a criminal's personality makeup from the criminal's choice of action before, during and after the criminal act'. The basic premise of offender profiling is that information left by the offender at the crime scene, both in terms of their behaviour and forensic evidence, can lead to conclusions being drawn about the person who committed the crime.

EVALUATION ISSUES

GENERALISABILITY

Profiling can only be used for a small number of specific types of offence, so it is not widely generalisable.

The FBI approach

As discussed above, the FBI were the first to develop a systematic profiling technique in the USA, devised in their 'Behavioural Science Unit'. This method was developed alongside their ability to analyse forensic evidence, since they needed to know the kind of person who might be responsible for producing the evidence. This profiling method was devised on the basis of a study carried out on 36 convicted serial murderers, whose crimes had a sexual orientation. These people (including Charles Manson and Ted Bundy) were interviewed at length, and then categorised according to whether they were classified as 'organised' or disorganised'. It appeared from the crime scenes that crimes were either premeditated and planned carefully, the victim being a targeted stranger, or that they were more sudden and unrehearsed with little attempt being made to hide clues.

The table below illustrates some of the main features of 'organised' and 'disorganised' killers identified by the FBI.

Features of organised and disorganised killers

Organised	Disorganised
High intelligence; socially and sexually competent; may be a skilled worker; very controlled during crime; living with a partner; mobile, usually owns a car; follows the crime reporting in the newspaper	Average intelligence; socially and sexually incompetent; unskilled, may be irregular worker; anxious during crime; living alone; lives or eats near crime scene; little interest in the media coverage of crime

Ressler (1998) describes the four main stages that are used in profiling by the FBI:

- **Profiling inputs:** police reports, evidence from the crime scene, forensic evidence, background of the victim.
- **Homicide type and style:** number of victims, types of victims (whether a certain type of person has been victimised), location of victims.
- **Crime assessment:** how did the offender and the victim behave? During this stage a reconstruction of the event may be useful.
- **The actual criminal profile:** this is the last stage, and is based on the previous three stages. This is the profile from which the police can then target likely suspects.

The investigative psychological approach

This is the approach adopted by David Canter from the University of Liverpool. He has become one of the UK's most well known profilers, and has been famously responsible for profiling cases such as that of the so-called 'Railway Rapist', John Duffy, in which his profile was remarkably accurate. Canter uses some similar techniques to the FBI, and initially started by building up a database on convicted offenders. For example, Canter and Heritage (1990) studied 66 sexual assault cases which had been committed by 27 offenders. From these cases they identified 33 offence characteristics that they argued were common in these types of cases. The common characteristics included things such as blindfolding, gagging, use of a weapon, use of a disguise, verbal violence and aggression, demeaning towards the victim, complimenting the victim and stealing items belonging to the victim. These are in no particular order, and the contradictory nature of some of the items reflects the fact that offenders obviously behave in different ways. On the basis of this evidence, and by using multivariate analysis, Canter and Heritage could build up a picture of the types of factors that might be associated with each other and which were less likely to be connected.

EVALUATION ISSUES

METHODOLOGY

The FBI approach is based on interviews with a very small number of convicted murderers, and the same could be said of Canter and Heritage's study (see below) based on 66 offences committed by 27 offenders.

CD-ROM

For a further study that looks at the different approaches to profiling, see Crime: Additional key studies: Bekerian and Jackson (1997).

KEY DEFINITIONS

Multivariate analysis: this is a technique of statistical analysis based on correlating data, and finding patterns of behaviour in this data. Multivariate analysis has to be carried out with great care, and used with caution, because although it may produce accurate results, it can also produce very misleading data. For example, if several statistical tests are carried out on a set of data using a 5 per cent level of significance, then one would expect 1 in 20 to provide a positive result by chance, even if there is no relationship between the variables.

For a description of a profiling technique that looks at the area in which a crime was committed, see Crime: Real life applications: Geographic profiling.

EVALUATION ISSUES

THEORETICAL APPROACHES

The scientific approach adopted by Canter can be contrasted with the more clinical approach adopted by Boon and Britton. These two approaches have quite different starting points, although there is inevitably some overlap in their techniques.

FOR CONSIDERATION

Some people see criminal profiling as a useful tool that helps the police catch criminals who might otherwise not be found. Others argue that at best it is a waste of time and at worst it might encourage the police to harass innocent people simply because they fit the profile.
• What do you think?

EVALUATION ISSUES

GENERALISABILITY

Profiling can only be used in a limited number of cases, and is therefore not generalisable to all crimes or criminals.

EXAM HINTS

Section 6.3.2 can be used for evaluation purposes in a section A or B question in the exam.

Canter argues that these associated activities shed light on the way in which the criminal behaves in their everyday life. Using statistical analysis in this way Canter argues that it is possible to build up a picture of a wide range of factors that can be associated with each other to give a profile of the offender.

Canter has identified five characteristics of a profile that are particularly important in helping with police investigations:
• criminal history
• domestic and social characteristics
• residential location
• personal characteristics
• a history of occupation and education.

The clinical approach

Boon (1997) describes how he and other psychologists who are involved in helping the police with profiling certain cases use theoretical models, such as those that relate to personality, to try to understand the types of people who will have committed certain types of crime. He argues that he uses different psychological approaches and theories depending on the case, and that much of this is based on his own experience. Britton (1997) uses a clinical approach in his profiling strategies, and looks at each case in isolation, rather than looking at the statistical analysis of previous cases. Copson et al. (1997) argue that profiling is about inferring a motive from the evidence at the crime scene, combined with a theoretical understanding that can explain why a person might behave in this way. Some theorists argue that it is of little use to be able to predict behaviour if there is no understanding of what motivated the behaviour; the more that is understood within a clinical framework the better the overall understanding of criminal behaviour.

6.3.2 BIASES AND PITFALLS IN PROFILING

This section highlights some of the problems with profiling, and as such will be useful for evaluation purposes. As has already been discussed, one of the problems with offender profiling is that it can only be used for a number of very specific types of crimes; these are usually violent crimes, often sexual in nature that may be quite sadistic. Offender profiling is not perceived to be useful for crimes which, although serious, are motivated by material gain, such as robbery. Another related problem, is that because the types of crime for which offender profiling is used are quite rare it is difficult to fully evaluate the effectiveness of profiling, as there are relatively few profiles to use, and by no means all of these are successful.

KEY STUDY

Coals to Newcastle? A study of offender profiling
Copson (1995)

Aim: This paper was commissioned by the Metropolitan Police in order to evaluate the potential for offender profiling to assist with the investigation of serious crime.

Sample: Detectives from 48 of the 56 police forces in the UK took part in this study. Their responses covered 184 individual cases, 105 solved and 79 unsolved. Most of the cases (113) involved murder and 50 cases

▶

involved rape or serious sexual assault. The remainder of the cases involved arson, extortion, abduction and threatening telephone calls. In each case, offender profiling advice had been sought; the 184 cases included the work of 29 different 'profilers' (although two people were responsible for almost half the cases).

Method: A questionnaire survey was used to determine the attitudes to offender profiling of the officers dealing with the cases. Profiling advice had been sought by the police for four reasons:

- to help predict characteristics of unknown offenders
- to help the police understand the offender's behaviour and enable them to assess the future level of threat
- to provide strategies for interviewing suspects and witnesses
- to link a series of offences by behavioural traits.

Results:

- Only 14 per cent of respondents claimed that profiling had helped solve the case.
- Only 16 per cent said that they had directly acted on advice received from the profiler.
- Only 3 per cent said that the advice had led to the identification of an offender.
- However, 83 per cent said they had found the advice useful because it helped understand the case or the offender, or else because it confirmed their own opinion.
- 69 per cent said they would use profiling again.

The majority of detectives in the survey did not perceive any particular benefit from the prediction of offender characteristics. This may be because the predictions were inaccurate, or maybe the officers failed to act upon the predictions, or did not recognise their usefulness.

Conclusions: Most detectives perceive the benefits of offender profiling as an intelligent second opinion leading to the introduction of new ideas about the crime. They seem to feel that offender profiling helps in an indirect way, rather than directly solving the case.

EVALUATION ISSUES

USEFULNESS

Overall, studies suggest that offender profiling is thought to be useful, although not necessarily in terms of actually apprehending the offender.

Similar studies have also been carried out in other European countries such as the Netherlands, and in the USA. In the Netherlands a study carried out by Jackson et al. (1993), in which they interviewed 20 police officers for whom profiles had been prepared, showed that overall there was a high level of satisfaction with the profiles, but more in terms of the information about how the enquiry should be conducted (interview techniques, for example) than with the profile leading to the apprehension of the suspect. Similarly, in the USA Douglas (1981) conducted a review of the costs and benefits of profiling within the FBI, and found that although profiling did not actually lead to the apprehension of many criminals, the benefits in terms of focusing the investigation, saving time, and the level of detail the profiles produced, outweighed the costs.

Finkel et al. (1990) carried out an interesting piece of research in which they compared five groups on their ability to develop a profile of a suspect in a homicide and in a sex offence. The groups they 'tested' were expert profilers, detectives with profiling experience, detectives without profiling experience, clinical psychologists and undergraduates. The results showed that profilers were more accurate than non-profilers in the sex offence case, but that the detectives without profiling experience were more accurate than profilers on the homicide case. These results might suggest that police experience is more important than psychological training on certain types of cases.

EVALUATION ISSUES

ETHNOCENTRIC BIAS

There has been little work done on whether profiling techniques can be applied in different societies. Most profiling work has been carried out in western societies, and therefore it could be argued that the methods employed, and the theoretical basis of profiling might not be applicable in other cultures.

FOR CONSIDERATION

- Is profiling worth the effort?
- Write down a list of the advantages and disadvantages of profiling?

The following case study is an interesting example of an attempt to profile a murderer who left little forensic evidence at the crime scene. Although the profile was ultimately unsuccessful, it provides a detailed case to examine and raises some serious issues about the way in which profiles and profilers should be used by the police.

Rachel Nickell

The Rachel Nickell murder

On a sunny morning in July 1992, 23-year-old Rachel Nickell was sexually assaulted and battered to death while walking with her dog and 2-year-old son on Wimbledon Common in South London. Rachel Nickell's murder was followed by an intense public response, perhaps because the victim was young and attractive; perhaps because she was killed in front of her little boy in broad daylight in an area that was not generally considered dangerous.

Rachel parked her car at around 10 am and was seen 20 minutes later walking towards Windmill Wood. The attack occurred about 500 yards from the car park, where the path runs through a lightly wooded area; Rachel's body was found about 4 metres from the path. Rachel's little boy must have witnessed the entire incident but was not physically hurt; police were very careful about interviewing him in any depth because they did not wish to fix horrific memories in his mind. Most of Rachel's clothes had been removed and she had been sexually assaulted and stabbed 49 times; in cutting her throat the murderer had practically decapitated his victim.

There was very little forensic evidence at the scene of the crime; no blood, semen, saliva or hair samples. All that the police found was a shoe print. Eye-witnesses were not much more helpful either; out of the 100 people in the area at the time of the murder, two described a man washing his hands in a stream about 150 metres from the scene of the crime. The public interest in this case made it very important to the investigating police officers to solve the crime as quickly as possible and, in the absence of physical clues, they called in an offender profiler, Paul Britton.

Britton's first task was to establish a clear picture of the kind of person Rachel was by interviewing family and friends; in his book *The Jigsaw Man* (1997) he says, 'Different women present different levels of vulnerability. Was Rachel a high-level risk victim or a low-level risk victim? If I know that then I can begin to know how particular the killer was in choosing her.' His first thoughts were that the fact that Rachel's little boy was left unharmed meant that she had not known her attacker and that this was unlikely to be a domestic murder or an argument gone wrong. The nature of the attack pointed towards a violent sexual psychopath.

Based on his past contacts with sexual killers, Britton then started to draw up a profile of the murderer. He decided that:

- the offender would be aged between 20 and 30 (most sexual attacks are committed by young men, and Britton felt that this incident was the first murder committed by this particular person)
- he would have an inability to relate to women in ordinary conversation
- he would have a history of failed or unsatisfactory relationships, if any
- he would suffer from some form of sexual dysfunction, like difficulty with erection or ejaculatory control

- he would be attracted to pornography which would play a role in his sexual fantasy life, some of which would be violent
- he would only have average intelligence and education (on the grounds that the attack was brutal, frenzied and chaotic)
- if employed, he would work in an unskilled or labouring occupation
- he would be single and have a relatively isolated lifestyle, living at home with a parent or alone in a flat or bedsit
- he would have solitary hobbies and interests, perhaps including martial arts or photography
- he would live within easy walking distance of Wimbledon Common and would be thoroughly familiar with it; he would not be a car user
- he would be very likely to kill another young woman at some point in the future.

The police received more than 2500 calls in the first month after Rachel's murder, but they were no nearer an arrest. The breakthrough came when Britton's profile of the killer was broadcast on *Crimewatch*. Within four hours, 300 calls were received and the name of Colin Stagg came up four times. Stagg fitted Britton's profile exactly and a witness who saw him a few hours after the murder said that he looked 'strangely excited' and had just washed his hair. He told her that he had been on the Common just 10 minutes before Rachel had died. He was arrested immediately and police now had three days to interview him before they had to charge him or release him. Stagg consistently denied any involvement in the crime, but his responses to questions strengthened the match with Britton's profile; for example, he admitted that intercourse with several girlfriends had failed as a result of his sexual inadequacy. The police could find no physical evidence connecting Stagg to the murder but he remained an important suspect, and this was reinforced a month later when they were handed a letter written by Stagg to a woman he contacted after she had placed a lonely hearts advert in a London magazine; the letter described a fantasy about having sex with a stranger in a public park.

At this point in the investigation, the police and Britton decided upon a very unusual strategy; they would design a covert operation, based on Britton's assumption of the killer's characteristics, designed to lead to the 'implication or elimination' of Stagg as the prime suspect. An undercover policewoman, who adopted the name Lizzie James, claimed she was a friend of the woman who had passed Stagg's letter to the police and found his fantasies interesting. However, Stagg did not confess to the murder and he appeared as a timid and insecure person, anxious to impress Lizzie James. Stagg replied, 'I'm terribly sorry but I haven't.' Despite his constant denials, the police felt that Stagg had said some things to James about Rachel Nickell's murder that he could only have known if he was the killer. Meanwhile, the pressure of keeping up the pretence was driving Lizzie James towards a nervous breakdown. Stagg was arrested and charged with the murder of Rachel Nickell.

The evidence of Britton's profile and the information obtained from Lizzie James was thrown out of court. The judge argued that 'the police had shown excessive zeal and had tried to incriminate a suspect by deceptive conduct of the grossest kind'. He commented that the prosecution case was almost entirely based upon a profile formulated from Britton's speculation and intuition. Stagg was acquitted, Rachel's killer has never been found, and Paul Britton was pilloried in the press and brought before a British Psychological Society disciplinary hearing.

⚖ **EVALUATION ISSUES**

METHODOLOGY

Britton states that his conclusions about Rachel's murderer were not 'pulled out of the air' and refers to 120 years of psychological experimentation and a vast database of knowledge from around the world. He says, 'All of these conclusions were drawn from what we know about men who kill women in this way.' However, his critics accuse him of using intuitive rather than scientific methods. Intuition has its strengths as it can lead to true conclusions that more scientific approaches would not reach; however, intuition is subjective and therefore easily affected by personal prejudice.

💿 **CD-ROM**

Another well-documented profile can be found in Crime: Real life applications: Famous cases in profiling: the Railway Rapist. See also Crime: Real life applications: Geographic profiling. This describes how profilers look at the area where the crimes were committed, as in the railway killer case.

⚖ **EVALUATION ISSUES**

ETHICS/ VALIDITY/ EFFECTIVENESS

- There are ethical problems with the way in which Britton encouraged the police to use leading questions, and entrap the suspect using deception.
- In this example the judge called into question the validity of Britton's profile, as it was based almost entirely on intuition.
- This case study highlights the fact that although the profile may be accurate it does not always lead to the apprehension of a suspect. The profile cannot solve the crime, it can only lead to possible suspects.

FOR CONSIDERATION

• What is your opinion of the part played by criminal profiling in the Nickell case?

CD-ROM

For Section B sample exam questions see Crime: Sample exam questions.

a Describe one type of offender profiling. [6]
b Consider the weaknesses of offender profiling. [10]

a Describe one bias of offender profiling. [6]
b Discuss the validity of offender profiles. [10]

a Outline one case study of offender profiling. [6]
b Evaluate the usefulness of one case study of offender profiling. [10]

CRIMINAL THINKING PATTERNS

This is an area that looks at how cognitive psychology can be applied to criminal thinking patterns. Many psychologists interested in this area have argued that criminals think in different ways to non-criminals, and that it is these thinking patterns that are partly responsible for criminal behaviour.

CD-ROM

To find out how moral you are, go to Crime: Measurement scales: Morality, to test yourself.

6.4.1 MORALITY AND CRIME

If a person behaves in a moral way then they can be said to be adhering to conventionally accepted standards of behaviour, in other words they follow the norms and values of society and follow the laws that are made to support these norms and values. Morals distinguish good and bad behaviour, or right from wrong. How societies develop moral codes of behaviour has interested philosophers for centuries, and many psychologists have looked at the way in which individuals develop their own sense of morality.

Kohlberg is well known for his theory of moral development, and although others have also looked at the development of morality, it is Kohlberg who has specifically applied his theories to crime. Like Piaget, Kohlberg argues that moral reasoning develops over time as children pass through maturational stages into adolescence. Kohlberg describes three levels of moral development: **preconventional morality**, **conventional morality** and **post conventional** or **principled morality**. At each level there are two stages (as shown in the table below). Level one morality is a stage of moral reasoning associated with pre-adolescence, level two is a stage of moral reasoning associated with most adolescents and adults, and level three is a level of morality that only some adults will attain.

The three levels of moral development

Level 1 Preconventional morality	
Stage 1 Obedience and punishment	Obedience to those who have power (parents and teachers) is important. The need to avoid punishment directs actions.
Stage 2 Instrumental purpose	This stage is characterised by the desire to meet ones own needs first and foremost, while recognising the needs of others.
Level 2 Conventional morality	
Stage 3 Conformity	Roles and responsibilities are important. Behaviour is judged in terms of good intentions, and a concern for others.
Stage 4 Law and order	A commitment to social order and the upholding of laws, and contributing to the group or institution is seen as important in this stage.

Level 3 Post conventional morality	
Stage 5 Social contract, individual rights	In this stage self is distinguished from others, whilst recognising the importance of values and rules relative to the group.
Stage 6 Universal ethical principles	The reason for doing right is governed by justice and human rights, a sense of dignity, and the validity of universal moral principles.

CD-ROM

For examples of Kohlberg's moral dilemmas see Crime: Theoretical approaches: Piaget and Kohlberg's 'Theories of Moral Dilemmas'.

EVALUATION ISSUES

EFFECTIVENESS

One of the problems with Kohlberg's theory is that moral reasoning may not be directly related to actions. A person might understand the moral issues related to what they are doing, but there may be other factors that influence the likelihood that they will proceed.

EVALUATION ISSUES

METHODOLOGY

There are few longitudinal studies on moral development. Lower stages of moral development may be a consequence of criminality rather than a cause; criminals justify their behaviour to themselves by using preconventional levels of moral reasoning; it is only wrong if I get caught.

Progression from one stage to the next is dependent upon appropriate cognitive development and the ability to understand the perspective of others (social perspective or role taking). Social experiences, and involvement with groups of people in different situations is critical to this process. Kohlberg applies this theory to offenders, and argues that they may function at a lower stage of moral development than non-criminals (many functioning at level 2). Kohlberg designed a number of moral dilemmas in which people in the dilemmas faced difficult decisions; participants were asked to say what they would do faced with the same dilemma but Kohlberg was not interested in what decision they made but rather how they justified their decision, and at what stage of moral development their justification lay.

There is a lot of evidence to support Kohlberg's view; for example Hudgens and Prentice (1973) argue that mothers of delinquents show lower moral reasoning than the mothers of non-deliquents, and the study by Palmer and Hollin (see below) illustrates the relationship between lower levels of moral reasoning and delinquency.

There is also evidence that shows that criminals are not a homogenous group in terms of their moral reasoning. For example, a study by Thornton and Reid (1982) (cited in Hollin, 2001) argues that offenders who commit crimes such as assault, murder and sex offences show more mature moral judgement than those who offend for financial gain, committing crimes such as robbery, burglary and fraud. The offenders who commit crime for personal gain tend to be operating at a preconventional level. Jennings et al. (1983) argue that lower level moral development may be associated with recidivists (criminals who re-offend) rather than all criminals per se, and age may also be a factor in relating crime to levels of moral development. Blackburn (1997) argues that preconventional thinking tends to be more common in younger offenders and in psychopathic criminals.

KEY STUDY

A comparison of patterns of moral development in young offenders and non-offenders
Palmer and Hollin (1998)

Aim: To see whether the development of moral reasoning on questions relating to offending behaviour among male delinquents is delayed compared to non-delinquents.

Sample: 332 non-offenders aged between 13 and 22 years (210 female and 122 male), obtained through schools in the West Midlands and a university; 126 convicted male offenders aged between 13 and 21, obtained through a Young Offender Institution and at Magistrates' Courts (the offences committed by the offender sample were mainly burglary and car theft).

Method: All participants were given a questionnaire that asked about socio-economic status and also incorporated two specific measures:
- The Sociomoral Reflection Measure-Short Form (SRM-SF) measures moral reasoning. It consist of 11 questions which assess respondents' moral reasoning in relation to contract and truth, affiliation, life, property and law, and legal justice.
- The Self-reported Delinquency Checklist (SRD) was used to see whether the officially delinquent and non-delinquent samples were really exhibiting different levels of offending behaviour.

Respondents were assured that the questionnaires were entirely confidential.

Results: The SRD Checklist confirmed that the offender sample had offended significantly more than the control group. The SRM-SF showed that the male offenders had the least mature moral reasoning and were predominantly reasoning at Kohlberg's preconventional level. The majority of non-offenders were using conventional reasoning. Furthermore, female non-offenders showed a more mature level of moral reasoning than male non-offenders.

Conclusions: Delinquents seem to have deficits in their moral reasoning, with less mature reasoning exhibited in the value areas relating specifically to delinquent behaviour. It may be that interventions aimed at raising levels of moral reasoning in those areas could lead to a decrease in offending behaviour.

Behaviourist theories such as classical conditioning can also be applied to a study of morality and crime. Eysenck argues that conscience is no more than a conditioned emotional response. For example, when a child is smacked for stealing this produces pain and anxiety. If the child is told 'You must not steal' as they are smacked, eventually the words 'You must not steal' produce anxiety as a conditioned response; so when the child thinks about stealing they feel anxious. According to Eysenck these feelings enable the child to develop their conscience, and make a moral judgement not to steal. This theory suggests that what we believe to be universal moral principles are merely conditioned responses, determined by the way we were treated in the past.

6.4.2 SOCIAL COGNITION AND CRIME

This area of research relates to the way in which offenders interpret other people's behaviour; how they process information in a social context. As with the previous section, there is some evidence that criminals think about their own behaviour and the behaviour of other people in different ways to non-criminals.

Yochelson and Samenow (1976) attempted to identify a criminal personality by looking at the role of errors and biases in the thinking patterns of criminals. Their sample was made up of 240 male offenders in community clinics and a psychiatric hospital in Washington DC, with whom they carried out interviews. They suggest, along with other cognitive psychologists such as Hudgens and Prentice (1973), that parental influence is very important in shaping thinking patterns. Due to the errors and biases

EVALUATION ISSUES

SAMPLING/GENERALISABILITY

Kohlberg's early work was only carried out on men, and most studies on moral development have been carried out on juveniles, including Palmer and Hollin (1998). These studies lack generalisability.

KEY DEFINITIONS

In the process of **classical conditioning**, people learn to associate specific responses such as fear, guilt and so on with neutral stimuli, simply because those stimuli were presented coincidentally with stimuli that elicited those responses for real. Watson and Rayner (1920) successfully conditioned a small boy into developing a phobia of a white rat, by frightening him with a loud noise every time he stroked the rat.

CD-ROM

For a full description of Watson and Rayner's (1920) study see Education: Additional key studies: Watson and Rayner (1920).

FOR CONSIDERATION

Consider people you know personally who have committed crimes.
- Would you consider them to have a different morality than non-criminals?

that have developed in their thinking patterns these offenders make a series of 'incorrect' choices, and therefore behave in ways that are unacceptable to other people in society. Yochelson and Samenow describe non-offenders as being responsible in their thoughts and actions, whereas offenders make more than 40 'thinking errors' that cause them to behave in this way. These thinking errors include:

- closed thinking: not receptive to criticism, good at pointing out and giving feedback on the faults of others
- external attribution: views self as a victim; blames others (family, childhood, social conditions, the past, etc.)
- perception of self: focuses only on own positive attributes and fails to acknowledge own destructive behaviour
- lack of interest in 'responsible' behaviour: finds responsible living to be unexciting and unsatisfying
- lack of time perspective: does not use the past as a learning tool; expects others to act immediately on demand
- fear of fear: has irrational fears but refuses to admit them; has a fundamental fear of injury or death; has a profound fear of put-downs
- perceives a need for personal control: has a compelling need to be in control of every situation; uses manipulation and deceit; refuses to be dependent unless it is possible to take advantage of someone
- perception of uniqueness: thinks of self as different and better than others; expects of others that which he fails to do; combines fear of failure with super-optimism; gives up at the first sign of failure
- ownership attitude: perceives all people, places, and things as objects to possess; has no concept of the ownership rights of others; uses sex for power and control, not intimacy.

Another interesting area of social cognitive development is that which concerns violence and aggression. This is clearly related to criminality, since so much crime is based on violence or the threat of violence. Based on human and animal behavioural studies, Robert Blair has argued that a cognitive **violence inhibiting mechanism** (VIM) exists. This violence inhibiting mechanism is activated by non-verbal distress signals from a victim and it initiates a withdrawal response in a conflict situation. The VIM is thought to have evolved as an innate physiological mechanism in animals, but to be linked to early socialisation experiences in humans.

According to Blair, distress cues from a victim in a conflict situation (for example a fight) will automatically trigger the VIM, which then interrupts the violent behaviour in the aggressor. This generates an emotional reaction in the aggressor, which is perceived as aversive (e.g. guilt or remorse) because it is initiated by a withdrawal response and is therefore consistent with a change in behaviour.

Blair's VIM theory is linked to Schachter and Singer's (1962) two stage theory of emotion; they suggest that the individual first experiences a physiological response, which indicates that an emotion is being felt, but that the precise nature of the emotion (fear, excitement, etc.) is determined by a cognitive interpretation of the situation.

Blair describes a process of classical conditioning in which the repeated pairing of the VIM activation with aversive emotional reactions will lead to a situation in which thinking about aggression becomes aversive. A classically conditioned association can also be made between activation of the VIM and the aggressor's perception of the victim's internal state, so that the VIM can be activated without distress cues. In other words, the aggressor recognises that someone in the victim's situation would be

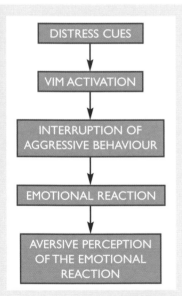

Diagram of the violence inhibiting mechanism

distressed without the need for them to actually display distress cues. Blair argues that the cognitive process of VIM activation that results from role-taking of the victim's internal state generates an emotional reaction such as **empathy**. In the key study described below, Blair et al. (1997) suggest that in violent offenders the VIM is not working properly, either as a result of physiological dysfunction or arising from specific childhood experiences.

KEY STUDY

The psychopathic individual: a lack of responsiveness to distress cues?
Blair, Jones, Clark and Smith (1997)

Aim: To investigate the psycho-physiological responsiveness of psychopathic individuals to distress cues and to threatening and neutral stimuli.

Sample: Participants were residents at Broadmoor Special Hospital or Wormwood Scrubs prison. The PCL-R (Hare's Psychopathy Checklist-Revised, see page 280) was used to identify 18 psychopathic and 18 non-psychopathic men, matched for IQ and ethnicity. All of the men were serving life sentences for murder or manslaughter. Seven of the psychopathic and four of the non-psychopathic prisoners refused to participate.

Method: Each participant viewed a series of 28 colour slides: ten practice slides, five showing distress cues (e.g. a crying face), five showing threatening images (e.g. a shark, a pointed gun) and eight showing neutral objects (e.g. a hairdryer, a book). Skin conductance activity (SCR) was measured while the participants viewed the slides.

Results: Compared to the control group, the psychopaths showed reduced electrodermal responses to the distress cues. In contrast, there was no difference in responses to the threatening stimuli and the neutral stimuli.

Conclusions: Blair et al. conclude that the lack of responsiveness to distress cues in psychopaths interferes with the normal functioning of the Violence Inhibiting Mechanism (VIM). According to the VIM model, the normally developing child possesses a VIM that initiates a withdrawal response when activated by distress cues. The operation of this physiological mechanism is explained and facilitated by parents explaining to children that it is wrong to hurt others. If this moral socialisation does not occur at an early age, then this can result in the failure to develop the moral emotions and reduced suppression of aggression. Furthermore, if this is coupled with a maladaptive social environment or other cognitive impairments, it may lead to the development of psychopathy.

An influential study that has looked at the ways in which children process information and then adjust their behaviour accordingly as a response to that situation, was carried out by Crick and Dodge (1994). This model argues that children come to a social situation with a 'database' made up of memories of past experiences, rules that have already been learned, social schemas and social knowledge. The social situation itself provides the child with an array of cues that then have to be processed. The child's behavioural response in any situation is a result of the processing of those cues, and this processing is influenced by the content of each individual's database.

KEY DEFINITIONS

Attribution refers to where people place the blame for events. One dimension of attribution is internal/external. An **internal attribution** is to blame one's own personality or motivation, whereas an **external attribution** is to blame other people, or bad luck.
Attributional bias occurs when an individual systematically makes faulty attributions. For example, an individual who, for some reason, has developed a tendency to believe that when bad things happen to them, it is as a result of someone else deliberately trying to hurt them (rather than their own incompetence, or simple bad luck), will feel paranoid and may react in an over-aggressive manner towards others.

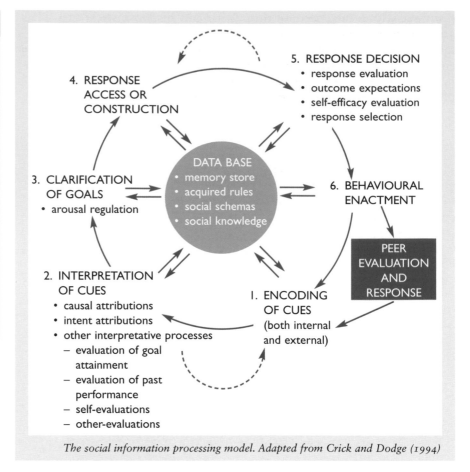

The social information processing model. Adapted from Crick and Dodge (1994)

EVALUATION ISSUES

REDUCTIONISM

While Crick and Dodge's study is a very thorough review of the cognitive processes in social adjustment, they recognise that this approach does not take account of non-cognitive factors fully enough, such as gender, age and the social context in which the children are operating.

EVALUATION ISSUES

ECOLOGICAL VALIDITY

Another problem that Crick and Dodge recognise with their approach is the lack of ecological validity in their research, as they used hypothetical situations to assess the children in their study. It is possible that studying the actual social interactions of children may illicit different results.

The figure above is reproduced from Crick and Dodge (1994) and it represents the authors' social information-processing model of children's social adjustment. This model recognises that

- during step 1, the child **selectively attends** to particular **situational** and **internal cues**, and encodes them (i.e. mentally notes their existence). For example, if a child is hit by a ball in the back in a school playground, he will notice a variety of pieces of situational and internal information, for example, who threw the ball, who they were with, what they were doing, the look on their face, whether the ball hurt, etc.

- during step 2, these **cues are interpreted**, for example, was the ball thrown at his back on purpose, was it intended to hurt him, did he deserve to be hurt, was the person who threw the ball pleased he was hurt, had they tried to hurt him in the past, etc. It is easy to see how both the selection of which cues to notice, and the interpretation of those cues, depends on the child's social 'database'.

- during step 3, the child **selects a desired outcome** for the situation. For example, not getting hurt any more, getting even with the person who threw the ball, making friends with the person who threw the ball, etc. The goal selected will be the result of previous social tendencies and of the specific situation the child finds himself in.

- during step 4, the child **accesses from his memory different possible responses to the situation or, if the situation is a new one, constructs possible new behaviours**. In this example, possible responses could be falling over and crying, running to tell a teacher, throwing the ball back, asking the person who threw the ball why they did it, etc.

- during step 5, the child **has to select the best response**. He does this by evaluating the likely outcomes of different responses (outcome expectation), the degree of confidence he has in his ability to enact each response (self-efficacy), and the appropriateness of each response (response evaluation). In step 5, **the child acts upon the chosen behavioural response** and the outcomes of this behaviour, as well as other people's reaction to it. This **information is then fed back into the child's social 'database'** for use next time he is faced with a similar situation.

This is a kind of social problem-solving model that explains cognitive processes that are common to everyone, but the study also focuses on maladjustment and the behaviours of aggressive children. There is a great deal of research that looks at social maladjustment in childhood leading to criminal behaviour in adulthood, and how children develop their responses to others is closely related to the steps of this model. Using this model Crick and Dodge look at **attributions** and the hostile **attributional biases** that some maladjusted children will make in social contexts. A maladjusted child is much more likely than other children to think that the person who threw the ball (in the example given above) intended to hurt them, and they will then respond aggressively. This kind of reaction has obvious implications for aggressive responses later in life.

6.4.3 RATIONALITY AND CHOICE

The rational choice perspective argues that actions are motivated by self-interest, what is known as **expected utility,** the possible gain from committing crime. An offender might look for an opportunity to commit the crime, think that the benefits outweigh the costs, and make a rational decision to commit the crime; steal the car, or break into the house. Hollin (2001) argues that crime rates do appear to be linked to opportunity, at least to some degree; burglary has increased dramatically over the last 20 years as more houses are left empty during the working day.

The rational choice model relates the decision to commit crime to free will. A criminal is a person who decides rationally, of their own free will, to gain from the opportunity to commit a crime. Roshier (1989) argues that 'The goal of our rationality is personal satisfaction; rational self interest is the key motivational characteristic that governs our relationship with crime and conformity'.

In a car park with poor street lighting or a house with an open window, a criminal is simply a person who decides to take advantage of the opportunity that is presented to them. If criminal behaviour is seen as rational and a 'normal' choice in this context, this has implications for ideas about the law and punishment. Crime no longer becomes a moral problem but a practical one, and the purpose of punishment is to modify the likely outcome of an action in order to tip the scales in favour of not committing the crime. However, Hollin (2001) argues that the issue is not as straightforward as this, because although it can be argued that the offender's decision-making is rational, the content of the cognition about the offence may be problematic.

A model that can be applied to criminal intentions is the Theory of Planned Behaviour (Ajzen and Madden, 1986). This model has been applied to health behaviours and Stephenson (2001) argues that it can be

? FOR CONSIDERATION

Paranoia is the tendency to assume that people are acting in a hostile way.
- Why do you think that some people are more paranoid than others?
- Do you agree that paranoia can lead to violence?

EVALUATION ISSUES

THEORETICAL APPROACH

Some theorists would not agree with the idea of free will and rational choice, arguing that crime is determined by a number of factors that are beyond the individual's control.

applied to criminal behaviour in a similar way, as offenders are making a choice and planning their behaviour.

The model works in the following way:
- Intentions to perform a behaviour are determined by attitudes and motivations towards the behaviour (and beliefs about the consequences of the action). This is influenced by our need to comply with the expectations of significant others in our lives (subjective norm)
- Perceived control is also a factor, because circumstances or abilities might enhance or prevent the performance of the behaviour.

The Theory of Planned Behaviour can be applied to crime because the different parts of the model can be related to beliefs, but also to the circumstances that make it possible to commit a crime (perceived control); in this way the model explains the behaviour as a rational choice based on benefits that outweigh costs. Bennett and Wright (1984) argue that the majority of burglars plan their crimes very carefully and commit crime in a very rational way. In their study 59 per cent of burglars targeted a particular house and then broke in when the circumstances were appropriate. It is also important to recognise that criminals (like the rest of the population) will vary in their willingness to take risks, and in their commitment to norms; and that some offenders (emotionally disturbed offenders or young people, for example) may worry less about the threat of punishment than others.

There are many studies that look at the rational decision-making approach, and among these there are a number of studies that look at the rational decision not to commit crime. Using interviews these studies focus on career criminals, and give reasons for their decision to give up crime, and in so doing also explain why some criminals might continue (see key study below). Stephenson (1992) argues that it is a 'shock' that appears to be important in the decision to give up crime. 'It was often during the commission of their last crime that our subjects suffered this shock. One of them was wounded by the police during a shoot-out as he was leaving a bank. Another saw his partner killed by police bullets. A third told us that his accomplice had tried to kill him to get his share of the loot' (Stephenson, 1992).

As a result of events like this, these criminals re-assess the value of crime.

⚖ **EVALUATION ISSUES**

EFFECTIVENESS/REDUCTIONISM

The Theory of Planned Behaviour is an effective model to explain certain types of crime, because it looks at both beliefs and opportunity; this makes it less reductionist.

KEY STUDY

Understanding employment: a prospective exploration of factors linked to community-based employment among federal offenders
Gillis (2002)

Aim: Offender employment is generally considered to be a key factor in preventing recidivism; if prisoners are trained in skills that will enable them to get remunerative and satisfying jobs, then criminal behaviour becomes a less attractive option for them. The Theory of Planned Behaviour suggests that criminal behaviour is less likely if the individual intends not to commit a crime, and that this behavioural intention is affected by subjective norms and perceived behavioural control. This study investigates the Theory of Planned Behaviour in relation to offenders' employment after release from prison.

▶

Sample: 302 newly released offenders from five different sites in the USA volunteered to take part in the study; only 106 of these participated in the six-month assessment.

Method: Participants completed a questionnaire on release, six weeks after release and six months after release from prison that explored their employment history and asked them about their attitudes to employment.

Results:
- Offenders who stated a clear intention to gain employment were more likely to have jobs; this undermines one of the criticisms of the theory of planned behaviour, that it merely predicts intention to behave in a certain way and not actual behaviour.
- Offenders who felt that they had good chances of gaining employment were more likely to actually do so, again providing support for the theory of planned behaviour, which suggests that perceived behavioural control is a key factor in predicting behaviour.
- Offenders with higher levels of social support, or for whom it was important to gain employment were more likely to do so, whereas offenders who associated more with individuals involved in crime had lower levels of quality of employment; this supports the notion that subjective norms are an important factor in predicting behaviour.

Conclusions: Although this study does not focus on actual criminal behaviour, it examines employment of offenders, and this is closely linked to re-offending. Gillis concludes that an offender's intention to find and keep a job is a key factor in whether they gain employment and thus avoid re-offending, and that this intention is affected by their sense of self-efficacy and by their view of what other people expect of them. According to Gillis, these attitudes are amenable to change and she finishes by pointing the way to strategies that may increase offender employability, and hence reduce re-offending.

⚖ EVALUATION ISSUES

USEFULNESS

This study is useful as Gillis highlights issues that relate to the reduction of re-offending, rather than simply pausing on a criminal activity.

ⓘ FOR CONSIDERATION

- How convincing is the rational choice model for explaining criminal behaviour?
- Are there any crimes to which this model could not be applied? Why?

SECTION A EXAM QUESTIONS

a   Describe how one theory of morality links to criminal behaviour. [6]
b   Evaluate research into morality and crime. [10]

a   Describe one study of social cognition and crime. [6]
b   Discuss the problems of investigating social cognition and crime. [10]

a   Describe one study of rationality and criminal thinking patterns. [6]
b   Evaluate the validity of research into rationality and criminal thinking patterns. [10]

💿 CD-ROM

For Section B sample exam questions see Crime: Sample exam questions.

6.5 THE POLICE AND CRIME

Some of the sections in this chapter on the psychology of crime focus on the criminal, but in section 6.3 the work of the police, and in particular the work of profilers, was taken into account. This section considers the role of the police in a number of areas that relate to the psychology of crime. This is important because their role is obviously central to the understanding of who commits crime, and how criminals are processed in the system. There are two main themes in most of the psychological research that relates to the police; psychological studies of the police, and psychological studies and theories that relate to the work they do. This section starts by focusing on the police themselves, and examines the police personality, it then goes on to look at the work they do in apprehending and processing suspects, and the use of interview techniques.

6.5.1 POLICING AND THE POLICE PERSONALITY

Police officers are commonly thought to have a particular type of personality. US and UK police dramas on television are very popular indeed, and they present many of the stereotypes that have come to be associated with police. It is not surprising that common sense assumptions tend to be the ones that people remember. In both the UK and USA, the police are often thought to be authoritarian and conservative in their behaviour. Siegal argues that in the USA 'the typical police personality is thought to include authoritarianism, suspicion, racism, hostility, insecurity, conservatism, and cynicism' (Siegal, 1986; cited in Hollin, 2001).

Psychological studies do not portray such a clear picture of the police personality, and the results of such studies are mixed. Many studies have focused on the use of psychometric tests to determine the personality of the police. For example, Coleman and Goreman (1982) used four psychometric tests and open response questions on two groups of UK police officers in the Midlands, to analyse their attitudes towards questions about the death penalty, immigration and 'mixed marriage'. The two groups of officers were new recruits and officers with an average of 20 months service. Coleman and Goreman also used a non-police control. Analysis of the psychometric data revealed that both groups of police officers were more conservative (with a preference for conventional behaviour) than the control group. However, the control group did have higher levels of education than the police officers, and were significantly different in age, although Coleman and Goreman argued that this did not affect the results.

The key study by Gudjonsson and Adlam (1983) described below also uses psychometric tests to measure the police personality among UK police officers. The measures used in Gudjonsson and Adlam's study are different from those in Coleman and Goreman's study, and measure different personality traits.

Police officers – do they all have a particular type of personality?

EVALUATION ISSUES

GENERALISABILITY

Coleman and Goreman recognise that their sample is limited. They used police officers from only one area of the country, and question the generalisability from their sample. Coleman and Goreman also comment on the fact that attitudes are not always translated into actions.

KEY STUDY

Personality patterns of British police officers
Gudjonsson and Adlam (1983)

Aim: To investigate the personality profiles of serving police officers.

Sample: The researchers investigated four different groups of police officers (new recruits; probationary officers with 18 months service; constables with around 20 years service; senior officers with around 20 years service) and compared them to normative data from the general population.

Method: Two different psychometric tests were administered to the participants:

* The Eysenck Personality Questionnaire (EPQ), which contains three scales: Psychoticism (P) which measures 'tough-mindedness'; Neuroticism (N), which measures 'emotionality'; and Extraversion (E), which measures 'sociability'.
* The I5 test, which also contains three subscales: Impulsiveness (Imp), which measures the tendency to act without thinking; Venturesomeness (Vent), which measures a liking for adventure; and Empathy (Emp), which measures the degree of sympathy and understanding a person has towards the feelings of others.

Results:

* Recruits scored high on E, Imp and Vent, but low on P.
* Probationary constables scored low on E and Emp.
* The experienced constables and senior officers scored very low on Imp, Vent, Emp and P.

Conclusions: The fact that the recruits were extrovert, impulsive and venturesome reflects the image of the police as an exciting and stimulating job. However, the fact that police personality seemed to change as they spent more time in the job may reflect that the work has a sobering effect, or it may be that only certain types of new recruits end up staying in the job. The fact that experienced officers tended to score low on empathy may mean that the police as individuals do not care about others, or that the culture of the police encourages lack of empathy, but it could also be explained as a coping mechanism, and as reflecting the type of work the police do. Reassuringly, police officers score below average on psychoticism.

EVALUATION ISSUES

GENERALISABILITY/ ETHNOCENTRICITY

Most of the studies that have been carried out on police personality have used UK or US samples, with a few being carried out on other European police forces. It could be argued that this is ethnocentric, and that it cannot be assumed that studies carried out on these samples are representative of the personalities of police officers in other parts of the world, and cannot be generalised.

One of the issues raised by studies on police personality is whether the police have these personality traits before they join the force, or whether they learn them through being a part of the police force. There are psychological studies that look specifically at this issue, and these studies fall into two groups; those that subscribe to the 'predispositional model' (that which argues that these personality traits already exist), and those that favour a 'socialisation model' (arguing that it is membership of the police force that encourages these personality traits). Coleman and Goreman (1982) are in favour of a predispositional model, arguing that these personality traits exist before the recruits join the police, and in fact it is these traits that make police work appear attractive to these particular people. In contrast to this, Brown and Willis (1985) argue for the socialisation model, as they believe there is a police culture with specific values that encourages certain attitudes to develop in new recruits, and that these are reinforced over time.

EVALUATION ISSUES

THEORETICAL APPROACHES

The contrast between the predispositional and the socialisation model of police personality is similar to that between the dispositional and situational hypotheses that Haney, Banks and Zimbardo (1973) investigated in their prison simulation experiment.

It could be argued that to take one of these approaches without considering the effect of the other is reductionist. It is likely that personality trends among serving police officers arise out of the interaction between police culture and pre-existing traits.

CD-ROM

For a discussion of the public's perception of policing, see Crime: Real life applications: Public expectations and perceptions of policing.

Studies in the USA also look at these models, and are equally divided. For example, Austin et al. (1987; cited in Hollin, 2001) tested these two models by looking at the personality traits of police officers who had been made redundant. In particular they focused on how authoritarian they were. They argued that if there were a police culture that socialised officers into being authoritarian, then when they left the force this personality trait would reduce. On the other hand, if authoritarianism were dispositional, then it would remain constant. Austin et al. found no change in levels of authoritarianism, even after two years away from the force (although they did find that older ex-officers and black ex-officers were more authoritarian than younger ex-officers and white ex-officers).

6.5.2 DETERMINING AND PROCESSING SUSPECTS

How do the police decide whom to arrest? What happens when these people are taken into custody? The answers to these questions should be straightforward, but research suggests that the police are more likely to arrest certain types of people than others, and that whether these people are processed through the system also depends on a number of factors.

Research suggests that decisions to arrest are not based on legal criteria alone (Stephenson, 2001). Smith (1987) argues that the probability that the police will arrest a suspect (if they are present when the police arrive on the scene) can be ranked in the following order:

- when police action is requested by the victim
- when white people rather than people from ethnic minorities are the victim
- when threats are made towards the police
- in areas with high poverty levels
- when the people involved are both male, rather than a female victim
- if the people involved are known to the police
- if a weapon is used.

This study shows clear bias towards certain types of victims, and against certain types of suspects. Stephenson (2001) argues that the police are also likely to increase the level of conflict in these situations by calling for assistance on their radios, and threatening and sometimes intimidating suspects.

The key study by McConville, Sanders and Leng (1991) described below confirms some of the points made by Smith (1987), and raises a number of other issues about the arrest and processing of suspects.

KEY STUDY

Grading and sorting the suspect population
McConville, Sanders and Leng (1991)

The authors of this study observed and interviewed police officers at all the different stages of the prosecution decision-making process, and set out below is a summary of their study on what happens to suspects after they have been arrested, and why.

When a suspect is arrested, the police can decide to proceed with a prosecution, can caution the suspect, or can take no further action (NFA). There are several reasons why the police might arrest someone whom they do not wish to prosecute. It may be that the arrest arose out of a victim complaint that is later withdrawn (although, if the police wish to prosecute, they tend to ignore the victim's wishes), or it may be that the police are not convinced of the suspect's innocence, but take NFA because they cannot be sure of guilt. Perhaps the police do not believe that the offence deserves prosecution, and are therefore happier to caution the suspect; or maybe the police do not take the case to court in order to protect an informant, or simply because they are overworked and are trying to avoid additional paperwork. Sometimes the police may wish to prosecute a suspect, but choose not to do so, perhaps because they feel the case would not stand up in court due to lack of evidence.

In the large majority of cases, the decision about whether to caution, prosecute or take NFA, is made by the Custody Officer while the suspect is still in custody. In principle, the Custody Officer should make an unbiased and independent decision on the most appropriate course of action, based on the facts of the case. The authors describe evidence that suggests that Custody Officers do not make independent decisions. They found that Custody Officers are unable to isolate themselves from general policing concerns, so that they are likely to be harsher with suspects who threaten police officers, for example, and they are usually unwilling to contradict arresting officers. When one respondent was questioned about whether he had asked the arresting officer any questions, he said, 'Not at all. I accept that [the officer's] got no cause to be telling lies and the other chap has.'

McConville, Sanders and Leng also found that Custody Officers, like arresting officers, are affected by the demeanour, manner and dress of the suspect. For example, after deciding to give a woman arrested for shoplifting a caution, the Custody Officer said, 'She was … not – I hesitate to say this – the type of client we are normally used to dealing with … She was basically a lady of good character … it really was a one-off and she was a very clean, tidy lady.' Another officer, referring to a woman who was charged with stealing a purse, commented, '… I think she probably done it … I have to admit because of her background. She's come from a family who are in and out of here.' The authors discovered a very clear tendency to caution and take NFA against middle class suspects, and to prosecute working class suspects. The ambiguity and informality of the guidelines under which Custody Officers make such decisions allowed these biases to take place in a virtually uncontrolled manner.

Finally, McConville, Sanders and Leng found that Custody Officers do not always have the necessary information to make a truly independent decision; they do not know whether suspects have emotional or physical problems, whether they have fully confessed or not, and whether they have previous convictions. Also, they are entirely dependent on the information provided by the arresting officers, and this is often incomplete.

The authors conclude that the informal rules that apply to making arrests continue to influence decision-making in the police station. This allows officers to adopt a 'cop culture' that values 'experience' over 'going by the book'. This means that the official guidelines are ineffective in preventing officers introducing their own prejudices and stereotypes into the decision-making process.

EVALUATION ISSUES

ETHNOCENTRICITY/BIAS

Studies show that the police process suspects in very stereotypical ways – according to factors such as gender, ethnicity and age, for example.

The McConville et al. (1991) study focuses on a number of influences on police treatment of suspects. One of the areas that has been the subject of a considerable amount of research is whether or not the police are influenced by the ethnicity of the suspect. Early studies of police activity in US cities showed that the police appeared to be influenced by ethnicity in terms of how often they made arrests. Black and Reiss (1970) accompanied the police on patrol, and in 281 encounters, the police arrested 21 per cent of black suspects compared to 8 per cent of white suspects (although they argued that some of the offences committed by the black suspects were more serious). Smith and Visher (1982) studied 24 cities in the USA and argued that black suspects were more likely to be arrested than white, if other variables were controlled. They argued that the police had a stereotype of a 'type' of suspect.

The case of Jeffrey Dahmer (known as the Milwaukee Cannibal) illustrates these points very forcefully. Jeffrey Dahmer killed 17 young men between 1978 and 1991. His thirteenth victim, who he killed in May 1991, should have sparked police interest much earlier than it did, but unfortunately the racist attitudes of the police prevented them from acting sooner. In the early hours of the morning on 27 May 1991, two black girls saw an Asian boy running around incoherent and naked on a street in Milwaukee. A white man had followed him and was talking to him, but the situation and the boy's apparent fear of the white man made the girls call the police. When the police arrived however, they listened to the story of Jeffrey Dahmer, rather than that of the two black girls who had telephoned them. He appeared well spoken and convinced the police he and the boy were lovers, and that they had had a row. The police escorted them back to Dahmer's flat, but left them outside. After the police had left, Dahmer strangled the boy and dismembered him. If the police had run an identity check on Dahmer they would have found out that he was on probation for molesting children, and may have saved the life of 14-year-old Konerak Sinthasomphone, and four other victims.

Jeffrey Dahmer – the Milwaukee cannibal

Concerns over racism in the police have come to the fore in the UK with some high profile cases in which the police have been charged with 'institutional racism', which is thought to be widespread in the police force (in particular within the Metropolitan Police). The Stephen Lawrence case and the subsequent inquiry is a good example of the type of problems that the police force faces.

Stephen Lawrence, a young black man, was murdered on the night of 22 April 1993 in Eltham, South London. Over the next four years, police investigations, and even a private prosecution taken by Stephen's parents, failed to come up with convictions for the murder, despite eye-witnesses prepared to identify suspects. In 1997, Doreen and Neville Lawrence formally complained about the police investigation and the Home Secretary announced a judicial public inquiry into the matter led by **Sir William Macpherson**. What emerged from the Stephen Lawrence inquiry was a catalogue of police incompetence, corruption and racism. The police has always acknowledged that there exist a few corrupt or racist officers, but the inquiry went much further in its criticisms. It accused the Metropolitan Police Force of being **institutionally racist**. This means that it is not just a few 'bad apples' giving the force a bad name, but that the whole structure was riddled with racist practices. Institutional racism consists of organisational structures, policies, processes and practices that result in ethnic minorities being treated unfairly and less equally, often without intention or knowledge.

Institutional racism in the police is demonstrated by the following figures: at the time of Stephen's murder, the proportion of the population stopped and searched by the police was 14 out of 1000 for white people, and 108 out of 1000 for black people. Since the inquiry took place, Duwayne Brooks, Stephen's friend and a witness to his murder, has been arrested six times, once for stealing a car (it was his own car) and twice for carrying an offensive weapon (which turned out to be the tools he used in his job as a photocopier repair engineer). In all six cases, charges were eventually dropped because the police admitted that there was no crime actually committed.

The Macpherson Report (1999) made 70 recommendations, many aimed specifically at improving police attitudes to racism, and stressed the importance of a rapid increase in the numbers of black and Asian police officers. The government pledged to increase the number of officers from minority ethnic groups from around 2500 to 8000 by 2009. But a survey carried out on the second anniversary of the Macpherson Report in February 2001 revealed only 155 new officers from ethnic minorities had been recruited in the past year compared to an increase of 261 in the year following the report. Despite this, a survey of more than 1200 people showed that three quarters believed the police had learned from the Stephen Lawrence case and only 3 per cent believed the police were 'very racist'.

Critics of the Macpherson Report linked a rise in violent street crime in some areas to a drop in 'stop and searches' of black people because police officers feared being called racist. However, many black and Asian people, including Stephen Lawrence's father, Neville, who filed a complaint after being stopped in 2000, said they were still being unfairly targeted. In January 2001, figures from the Home Office showed that the fall in searches was greatest for white suspects with black people still five times more likely to be stopped in London than white people.

Stephen Lawrence

Explanations of police racism have been discussed in terms of the 'canteen culture' that some psychologists argue is responsible for socialising the police. Ainsworth (1995) argues that the police tend to have a view of the world influenced by the subculture of the organisation (not necessarily unique to the police). These attitudes can also be related to the need to conform to group norms, and Festinger's idea of social comparison theory can also be used to explain this behaviour. Festinger (1954) argued that people look to the group when they are unsure how to feel or act.

Although racism in the police force has caused much concern in recent years, there are other ways in which the police may bias their treatment of suspects. The police have been shown to treat women differently from men; age and sex are strongly correlated to the decision to caution rather than arrest; women and juvenile offenders are likely to be cautioned rather than arrested more often than adult men (Blackburn, 1997).

Attitudes of those who come into contact with the police also vary. Cox and White (1988) questioned 460 students who had received a 'ticket' for a traffic offence, compared to 373 students who had not. They found that interaction with the police appears to increase the experience of fear of the police. Although interaction did not affect perceptions of police competence, it did affect perceptions of police demeanour. The students who had been given a ticket for a minor traffic offence were more likely than the comparison group to believe that the police might hit and harass people, and that they might not provide for the safety of suspects once arrested.

 **EVALUATION ISSUES**

GENERALISABILITY

Although these studies suggest that the police are biased towards certain types of people, the majority have been carried out in a limited number of cities in the US and the UK, so it is difficult to generalise to all police forces from these studies.

FOR CONSIDERATION

- What are your feelings about the police force?
- Do these studies reflect your experience or perception of the police?

Interviewing

Interviewing is one of the main ways in which the police gather evidence about a crime. The police spend about 70–80 per cent of their time interviewing people who can help them with criminal investigations. The people who the police interview fall into four categories:

- victims
- witnesses
- complainants (those who report the crime)
- suspects.

These are not always mutually exclusive, but the ways in which the police approach an interview, and the techniques they use, may vary from individual to individual and case to case. Conducting an interview is very demanding, and the police have to adapt their interviewing style, while adhering to very strict rules and guidelines about the process itself. Kohnken (1999) illustrates the complexity of the process in the model shown below.

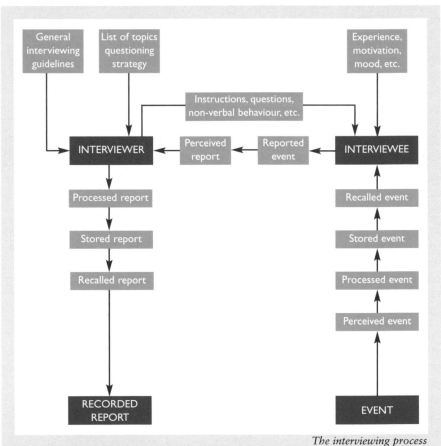

The interviewing process
(Reproduced with permission from John Wiley and Sons Ltd, Psychology in Legal Contexts, 1999, Bull, R. and Carson, D.)

EXAM HINTS

In an exam you could discuss the problems with interviewing in relation to eye-witness recall/testimony in section 6.6.

The ultimate goal of the interview is to get a true picture of what happened; but Kohnken (1999) argues that this is almost impossible, and that even highly trained police interviewers will never illicit a complete and accurate report (reasons for this are examined on pages 317–318 and 320–329). The key study by Milne and Bull (2003) described below summarises some of the current psychological research that is being applied to police interviewing tactics, and differentiates between the techniques used with witnesses and victims on the one hand, and suspects on the other.

KEY STUDY

Interviewing by the police
Milne and Bull (2003)

In this article, the authors describe recent initiatives and psychological research concerning investigative interviewing.

Interviewing witnesses/victims: professionals are increasingly acknowledging that interviewing of witnesses and victims can be just as important as the interviewing of suspects. If the first interview with an eye-witness to the crime is not carried out appropriately, then the whole investigation can fail. The fact that the term 'interrogation' has been replaced by 'investigative interviewing' reflects a change in ethos from an oppressive, suggestive and closed questioning manner, to a more open-minded, open-questioning search for the truth. In 1999, Milne and Bull developed a week-long course aimed at training the police in this new approach to interviewing. The programme was entitled PEACE, which stands for the different elements of an effective interview: planning and preparation, engage and explain, account, closure, evaluate. The PEACE course incorporates elements of two interviewing models: the **cognitive interview** (which is aimed at enhancing the memory of co-operative interviewees) and **conversation management** (which helps interviewers overcome resistance in interviews). Milne and Bull present evidence that the PEACE course and the cognitive interview are effective in experimental settings, but these approaches are only just beginning to be taken up by police officers in the field.

Interviewing suspects: there have been many criticisms of the way the police interview suspects, especially vulnerable suspects, because the focus tends to be on gaining a confession rather than interviewing to gain the facts. One study quoted by the authors suggests that police officers tend to judge the effectiveness of an interview simply on whether the suspect confessed or not. Another study, which examined 400 interviews of suspects in 1992, concluded that 'interviewing was a hit and miss' affair. Clarke and Milne (2001) evaluated 177 interviews, two-thirds of which had been carried out by PEACE trained officers, and found little difference between the two groups of officers, but argued that the 'untrained' sample were not completely naïve to the nature of PEACE. Comparisons of pre-PEACE and post-PEACE interviews do seem to suggest a clear improvement in ethos and ethical approach to interviewing. Clarke and Milne (2001) found that a high proportion of suspects were unco-operative in interviews and there is a need for research to develop 'tactics' that officers can use in such cases. However, the danger is that psychological tactics can lead to false confessions. A recent postal questionnaire (Holmberg and Christianson, 2004) suggests that the large majority of suspects perceive their police interviewers as displaying impatience, condemning attitudes and a lack of empathy. Many suspects feel insulted as human beings, and feel their interviews were characterised by '… aggression, a brusque and obstinate condemning approach, presumably aiming to extort a confession'. Interestingly, 'participants who perceive humanitarian attitudes from their interviewers were more likely to admit crime'.

Milne and Bull conclude that one way to improve standards in interviewing is to have appropriate training, and they make suggestions about how this could be achieved. Officers need specific courses on investigative interviewing as part of their basic training, and supervisors and managers also need training in the PEACE framework. There is also a need for specialist training to help officers deal with vulnerable groups, and such officers should undertake a skills assessment. Finally, interview advisers should be trained and appointed to advise and plan interview strategies at local level. Milne and Bull close by pointing out that, even with good training, not everyone will become a good interviewer.

EVALUATION ISSUES

ETHICS

Obvious concerns can be raised about some police interview techniques. Although the police are trained to interview in certain ways, research suggests that they do not always follow this practice.

EXAM HINTS

The cognitive interview technique is also described on page 326, details from which could be used in this section.

The Milne and Bull (2003) study suggests that the police have often been criticised for the way in which they interview suspects, and other studies support this view. Moston et al. (1992) carried out a study in the UK that suggested that in 70 per cent of cases police interviewers were already convinced of the guilt of the suspect before the interview began. They argue that the purpose of the interview is therefore to obtain a confession. Moston's research also highlighted the fact that suspects who exercised their right to silence were more likely to be charged than those who denied the offence but answered police questions.

Ainsworth (1995) suggests that the police have preconceived ideas about certain types of interviewees, especially suspects, and that this influences their techniques accordingly. When interviewing suspects Ainsworth (1995) argues that the police enter these interviews with five presumptions:

- Most suspects will lie to avoid conviction.
- There is usually an assumption of guilt, therefore the interview will provide weight to existing evidence.
- Most suspects can be persuaded to admit guilt, even if this takes time. Those that don't are 'skilled' rather than innocent.
- Experienced officers are particularly good at this persuasion.
- Innocent suspects will never make a guilty confession.

One of the main things that the police have to ascertain is whether the person they are interviewing is lying. Looking for non-verbal cues, such as averting the eyes, or appearing nervous, laughing or sighing is often used as an indicator of a person who is using deception (Oxford, 1991). However, research evidence does not always support these beliefs, and in fact it is often contradictory, and most evidence shows that people are not very good at spotting liars. Vrij (2001) suggests that looking at **indirect measures of deception** is more effective than looking for lies. Vrij suggests that police officers should attend not to whether they thought the suspect was lying, but whether the suspect was having to 'think hard'.

CD-ROM

To test how well you read non-verbal cues, go to Crime: Measurement scales: Spot the fake smile.

Negotiation

Negotiation differs from interviewing because the aim is not to extract information from the suspect, but to persuade them to stop committing a crime, and it is most widely used in hostage situations.

Ainsworth (2002) lists the different reasons why a hostage might be taken. He argues that the main types of incidents are:

- crimes where the hostage-taker has been forced to take a hostage because something has gone wrong
- for financial gain or for political reasons
- domestic incidents in which members of a family are held hostage by another member of the family
- situations where someone who is mentally ill takes people hostage who they believe might hurt them, or who they want to harm
- prison riots.

Hostage negotiation is very skilled, and members of police teams are usually trained to deal with such circumstances. Some of this training involves how to protect the hostages and the police officers involved. It is likely that there will be a primary and a secondary negotiator. The secondary negotiator usually advises the primary negotiator, and acts as a kind of coach, who can make suggestions as to how to direct the situation (Ainsworth, 2002). There are a number of roles that the psychologist can adopt in relation to negotiation techniques. They may be asked for their professional advice as a consultant, observer or negotiator in a situation (Hatcher et al., 1998), or they may be asked to help the police find people who would make good negotiators, with the use of psychometric tests. Getty and Elam (1988) found that good negotiators had excellent verbal skills, were empathetic and had a positive self image.

Negotiators will use 'active listening' skills, such as getting the person to talk about their feelings. This is thought to allow the hostage-taker to let out the anger, so that more rational and considered discussion and behaviour might progress from there (Ainsworth, 2002). This may stop the hostage-taker from acting quickly, or without thinking. It is important to check that the situation is progressing, and to understand whether this progression is positive or negative. Obviously the aim of the negotiation is to resolve the situation with the most peaceful outcome, but sometimes this is not possible, and the primary and secondary negotiators have to decide if and when action has to be taken. Hatcher (1998) suggests that negotiation is successful, and that 75 per cent of hostage situations are ended with the surrender of the hostage-taker. Butler et al. showed that in only 3 per cent of cases a hostage was killed (cited by Ainsworth, 2001).

Overall Hatcher et al. (1998) suggest that psychologists can play an important role in negotiation teams, through:
- looking at the decision-making processes of the hostage-taker
- examining the behaviour of hostages (especially if there is more than one)
- examining the training, and the skills needed to be a successful negotiator
- understanding and explaining the strategies of good negotiators
- helping hostage negotiation teams evaluate their own programmes.

SECTION A EXAM QUESTIONS

a Describe one study of the police personality. [6]
b Discuss the extent to which the police personality is a valid concept. [10]

a Describe one interviewing technique used by police. [6]
b Discuss the effectiveness of interviewing techniques used by police. [10]

a Describe one negotiation technique used by police. [6]
b Discuss the problems of investigating negotiation techniques used by police. [10]

PSYCHOLOGY OF TESTIMONY

The testimony that is given to the police, or in court, is often assumed to be accurate. However, it is likely that many factors may influence how precise this information is, and these things can inadvertently have an effect on the accuracy of the testimony that is given. There are a number of stages that are used in studies of memory that can be applied to eye-witness testimony: witnessing the incident (**acquisition**), the period of time while waiting to give evidence (**retention**) and giving evidence (**retrieval**). These can affect how well the person remembers the incident. Was the witness' acquisition of information good at the time, or was it partial or affected by fear or a focus on one specific thing? Was the witness interviewed soon after they saw the incident, or did they have to wait, with the possibility of their memory fading? Is the witness able to retrieve information for the police or in court, or are there factors such as stress or bias influencing their ability to remember?

Some researchers estimate that eye-witness misidentification is the most common cause of wrongful conviction (Yarmey, 2003), and psychological processes can help to explain some of the inaccuracies in testimony. An early study carried out in England and Wales in 1973 showed that there were 347 cases that year in which eye-witness testimony was the only evidence against the defendant, and in most of these cases the defendant was convicted, even though in over 50 per cent of cases the prosecution relied on the eye-witness testimony of only one person (Ainsworth, 2000).

6.6.1 COGNITIVE PROCESSES AND TESTIMONY

Acquisition

One of the most important factors in shaping testimony is how accurate the perception and memory of the event is (**acquisition**). If 20 adults were shown a videotape of a crime being committed, and then asked to write down what they had seen, it is likely that they would all recall slightly different details of the event. Perception is not objective, but is affected by an individual's subjective and selective interpretation of an event. When people give their account of a crime they have witnessed they swear to tell the 'whole' truth in court; this truth can only reflect their account of what it was they initially paid attention to when the crime was committed (Ainsworth, 2000).

Witnesses can leave out important details that they have forgotten, or did not pay attention to, but it is also possible that their **attitudes** affect the judgements they make. Duncan (1976) carried out a study in which he examined the effect that ethnicity had on people's perception of an event. Participants in his study watched one of two versions of a video in which two men had an argument that gradually became more angry, until one pushed the other. In one version the person pushing the other was white, and in the other version the person doing the pushing was black. All the participants were white American college students. Having watched one or other version of the video, the participants were asked to describe what they had seen in terms of whether the behaviour of the person doing the pushing was 'playing around' or could be considered to be 'violent behaviour'. The results of the study suggested that the perception (and memory) of the witnesses could be affected by the ethnicity of the aggressor. When the aggressor was white 67 per cent of the participants classified the behaviour as 'playing around'; however, when the aggressor was black 70 per cent of participants classified the behaviour as 'violent'.

Retention

Malpass and Devine (1981) show how **retention** of information can be affected quite considerably by the length of time between the event and the giving of evidence. Malpass and Devine compared the accuracy of identification of a suspect in witnesses who were asked for evidence immediately after an event (three days) and those who were asked after a period of five months. The results of the study show that after three days 83 per cent of witnesses made an accurate identification, compared to only 36 per cent after five months.

Retrieval

The work of Loftus is very important in this area of cognitive psychology. Having carried out a great deal of research into the accuracy of eye-witness testimony, she has been used as an expert witness on the efficacy of eye-witness testimony; and she has received many letters over the years from people claiming their friends or family were wrongly convicted on the basis of eye-witness testimony. Some of her most famous research relates to the unreliability of eye-witness testimony (**retrieval**). In 1974 Loftus and Palmer carried out a study to see if memory could be affected by the wording of questions asked after the event. They set up the study using two experiments in which participants watched video clips of car accidents, and were then asked questions about these clips. In each of five conditions in the first experiment and three conditions in the second, the verb in the question the participants were asked was changed. They found that the verbs in the questions elicited different responses from the participants in each of the conditions, and concluded from this that leading questions caused a distortion in the memory of the participants.

Loftus and Palmer (1974) argue that memory is **reconstructive** in that the single recall of an event is made up of two components: what the person perceives at the time of the event, and what they pick up afterwards (in this experiment the wording of the questions they were asked about the event). This has obvious implications for eye-witness testimony in court.

The key study by Malpass and Devine (1981) described below is similar to Loftus and Palmer (1974). Loftus and Palmer's study looked at the wording of **questions** asked to eye-witnesses and the effect it had on their answers; Malpass and Devine's study looks at the wording of **instructions** given to the eye witness and the effect these had on their responses.

KEY STUDY

Eye-witness identification: line-up instructions and the absence of the offender
Malpass and Devine (1981)

Aim: To investigate whether the instructions given to an eye-witness prior to an identification test can make a difference to the outcome.

Method: The researchers staged an act of vandalism during a lecture. The students present were asked to identify the vandal from one of two live line-ups within the following three days. Half the participants were presented with a line-up in which the vandal appeared and the other half in which he was absent (the second condition simulates a situation in which an innocent suspect is placed in a line-up). Half of the participants in each condition were given biased instructions: 'We believe that the person ... is present in the line-up. Look carefully at each of the five individuals in the line-up. Which of these is the person you saw ... ?' The participants were asked to circle a number from 1 to 5 indicating which person they thought was the vandal. The other half were given unbiased instructions: 'The person ... may be one of the five individuals in the line-up. It is also possible that he is not in the line-up. Look carefully at each of the five individuals in the line-up. If the person you saw ... is not in the line-up, circle ... If the person is present in the line-up, circle the number of his position.'

Results: 100 per cent of the subjects who saw the vandal-present line-up and who were given biased instructions made a positive identification, 75 per cent of which were correct. However, only 83 per cent of the participants in this condition who were given unbiased instructions made a positive identification (they were all correct). For the participants who viewed the vandal-absent line-up, 78 per cent who received biased instructions made a false positive identification, compared to 33 per cent who received unbiased instructions.

Conclusions: Biased instructions lead to significantly more false identifications than neutral instructions.

EVALUATION ISSUES

ETHICS

It could be argued that the Malpass and Devine study is unethical as it used deception, and could have caused distress to unwitting participants.

EVALUATION ISSUES

ECOLOGICAL VALIDITY

- Both Loftus and Palmer (1974) and Loftus (1974) lack ecological validity, the former because participants were shown a film of a car crash rather than a real one, and the latter because participants knew that they were not really convicting an offender.
- The Malpass and Devine (1981) study is ecologically valid, as it was carried out in a natural setting.

CD-ROM

For an interactive task on eye-witness testimony, go to Crime: Real life applications: Cognitive/eye-witness testimony experiment.

Loftus (1974) also carried out a study in which she looked at the influence of eye-witness testimony in court. She asked participants, acting as if they were jurors, to read an account of an armed robbery and a murder in which there was circumstantial evidence that the suspect was guilty. In one condition there was no eye-witness, in the second condition there was a credible eye-witness, and in the third the eyesight of the witness was called into question. The results showed that in the condition with no eye-witness only 18 per cent of the participants thought the defendant was guilty, compared to 72 per cent in the condition with a credible witness, and 68 per cent in the condition with the questionable eye-witness. Loftus argues that there are two conclusions to this study. First, that eye-witness testimony is very influential in jury decision-making, and second, that even a questionable eye-witness appears to influence the jury almost as much as a credible one.

Studies have shown just how influential eye-witnesses are, and there are no more credible eye-witnesses than the police. It is commonly assumed that if one of the witnesses is a police officer the suspect stands little chance of acquittal. There have been a number of psychological studies that look at whether the police are better at their perception (**acquisition**) and recall (**retrieval**) of events than the general public. However, these studies have shown that the police are just as prone to errors in their memories as the general population. Vernis and Walker (1970) (cited in Hollin, 1999) carried out an experiment in which a sample of police officers and a matched control group were shown some photographs, some of which contained various 'suspicious' elements (such as a car with an open door and a bag of tools inside). When they were asked questions about the photographs there was no difference in the recall of the police and the control group in terms of their memories of the suspicious situations, but the police officers were more likely to propose criminal intent in the scene.

Clifford and Bull (1978) describe another study carried out by Marshall and Hanssen in which participants watched a short film in which a man appeared to tamper with a pram net until a woman approached, at which point he walked off. The participants had to report back on what they had seen twice, once immediately after watching the film, and again after a week. The results showed that the police remembered more details than the control group immediately after the event, but a week later had no better recall than the control group, and were more likely to make what are called **errors of commission,** in which they remembered things that did not actually happen, for example 20 per cent said they saw the man take the baby out of the pram. This study (as in the previous study) shows that the police are more likely to interpret behaviour as criminal than the general public.

6.6.2 VARIABLES INFLUENCING ACCURATE IDENTIFICATION

The studies cited in the previous section can also be used in this one, since memory is a variable that is bound to influence accurate identification of a suspect or event. However, there are other variables (some of which have already been covered) that might also be influential; Wells (1978) describes these as **estimator variables** and **system variables.**

Estimator variables

The **weapon focus effect** has been widely reported, and is one variable that can influence accurate identification of a suspect or event. Weapon focus is the idea that a witness will focus more closely on the weapon than they will on the person holding the weapon. There is some debate as to the reason for this, as it is not clear whether it is (as some studies have suggested) the danger posed by the weapon, or (as other studies have shown) the unusualness of the situation that causes weapon focus. Loftus et al. (1987) showed two groups of participants two different films; in one the scene depicted a customer holding a gun in a restaurant, and in the other the customer was holding a cheque. In an identity parade, and in answer to specific questions afterwards, the participants who had been exposed to the 'cheque' condition were more accurate in their identification and answers than those in the 'gun' condition. Loftus concluded that this was caused by the weapon focus displayed in the gun condition.

In a study by Maass and Kohnken (1989) (cited in Stephenson, 2001), students were asked to take part in a study about sport and psychological well-being. In one condition students were exposed to a white-coated female experimenter with a syringe in her hand, who talked to the participants for 20 seconds before leaving. In the other condition the same experimenter did exactly the same thing except that she had a pen in her hand instead of a syringe. Of the two groups of participants the ones exposed to the 'pen' condition were much more likely to identify the experimenter accurately in an identification parade than in the condition with the syringe. Maass and Kohnken argue that the effect of the syringe is the same as the weapon effect at a crime scene. In the key study described below, Pickel (1998) looks at four possible explanations for weapon focus and concludes that it is unusualness that has the most important effect.

? FOR CONSIDERATION

It is debatable whether the finding that police officers are more likely to interpret behaviour as criminal is reassuring or worrying; on the one hand, it means that offenders are more likely to be arrested, but it also increases the chances of making false arrests.

• Why do you think the police make these errors of commission?

🔑 KEY DEFINITIONS

Estimator variables are variables over which the judicial system has no control such as the stress the witness is experiencing or the focus of the witness at the time of the incident (the effect of these variables can only be estimated).

System variables are factors that influence testimony over which the judicial system has some control, such as the questioning techniques of the police and the way in which a line up is constructed.

KEY STUDY

Unusualness and threat as possible causes of 'weapon focus'
Pickel (1998)

Aim: There are four possible explanations for the weapon focus effect:

1 Witnesses are simply attending to the weapon and ignoring the other details of the scene.

2 Witnesses are attending to all details equally, but demonstrate better memory for the weapon when tested later.

3 The weapon indicates a threat, which increases arousal, making the witness focus on the weapon.

4 The witness attends to the weapon because it is unusual.

The aim of this study is to test explanations 3 and 4: threat and unusualness.

Method: Participants watched a 2-minute video consisting of a scene from a hair salon, in which a man walks to the receptionist and she hands him money. Participants were split into five groups and each saw a version of the video in which the man held something different in his hand:
- nothing (control)
- scissors (high threat, low unusualness)
- handgun (high threat, high unusualness)
- wallet (low threat, low unusualness)
- raw chicken (low threat, high unusualness).

After 10 minutes, participants filled out a questionnaire. The first part focused on the receptionist who was seen as a control since she was viewed before the man walked in; the second section covered the man (target). They were asked to describe the target, what he was actually doing, and to identify him from a line-up.

Results: There was no difference in accuracy of descriptions of the target in the low-threat conditions, compared to the high-threat conditions. However, eye-witness accuracy was significantly poorer in the high unusualness conditions (although no weapon focus effect was observed in the line-up identifications).

Conclusions: Pickel suggests that the results of this study support the contention that it is not the threat of the object that creates the weapon focus effect, but rather the unusualness of the object that attracts the attention.

Another variable that can affect the accurate identification of the suspect or the event is the amount of stress felt by the witness at the time of the event itself, or in the courtroom afterwards. It is generally believed that the more stressful the event the poorer the eye-witness testimony (Stephenson, 2001). The Yerkes-Dodson Law supports this view, because it argues that a degree of arousal is beneficial for performance, but above this optimal level performance begins to deteriorate. If a witness or victim is particularly distressed they may find it difficult to take in information at the time of the event, and perhaps even more difficult to recall testimony in court. For most witnesses giving evidence in court is a stressful experience, not only because they have to recall unpleasant events, but also because the courtroom itself is an alien environment, and courts cannot offer much help to stressed witnesses; as a result of this their testimony may suffer (Ainsworth, 2002).

Ainsworth also notes that there is some evidence to suggest that stress can interfere with accurate recall in identification parades.

The type of event that the witness experiences is also an estimator variable that can affect identification. As has been discussed above, the event can cause arousal that may influence recall, but other factors about the event itself may also affect the memory of it. For example, Sporer (1997) found that the number of people involved in a crime had an influence on accuracy of recall; the more people involved the less accurate the recall of participants. However, this was also affected by how violent the crime was, and Sporer found that violence stops people being able to recall more complex events (such as those with multiple offenders).

The confidence of a witness in their ability to identify a suspect has been the focus of many psychological studies. Most of these have looked at the correlation between what witnesses saw (under experimental conditions) what they remembered when asked questions, and a confidence rating that they were asked to give themselves. This research has shown that there is little correlation between the confidence of the witness and the accuracy of their testimony. The problem that this research highlights is that jurors are influenced by the confidence of a witness and may well believe a confident witness although that witness may be wrong.

Systems variables

Much of the research on systems variables focuses on courtroom practices, and the questioning techniques that both the police and the judiciary use with witnesses. These questioning techniques can lead to a change in the perception or recall of the event. The wording of questions can sometimes be used to influence the witness; for example, a person can be asked 'How far away?' or 'How close?' an event or suspect was. The use of 'a' or 'the' has also been documented (Loftus and Zani, 1975); for example a witness could be asked 'Did you see a gun?' or 'Did you see the gun?' In the first question the witness is being asked whether there was a gun, in the latter question the presence of a gun is already implied. The witness may agree that they did see a gun, so that they appear observant, or the question may make the witness add to their existing memory with additional details that have been implied after the event.

This kind of distortion in the memory of the actual event has already been discussed on page 321, and Loftus and Palmer's work in 1974 remains seminal. In their work on the effect of leading questions they came to the conclusion that there are two parts to the experience of memory. The first is what the person perceived at the time of the event, and the second is information gathered after the event. These two things fuse together into one memory that becomes the 'truth' about the suspect or event.

There are a number of different types of questions that are used in asking witnesses about what they saw:
- Closed questions: specific questions that require a simple answer such as 'yes' or 'no'.
- Open questions: general questions in which the witness is allowed to describe events in their own words (these type of questions illicit the most accurate responses).
- Negative questions: questions that have a negative clause in them. For example 'Were you not wearing your glasses?'
- Double negatives: questions (sometimes statements) that contain two negatives (these can often be very confusing). For example 'It is not true to say that you were not wearing your glasses.'

METHODOLOGY—LABORATORY EXPERIMENTS VERSUS FIELD EXPERIMENTS

The problem with studies such as these is that they tend to focus on one or two variables, whereas in real life a witness may be influenced by many different things.

- Multi-part questions: where two questions are asked at once, these questions often require a detailed and descriptive reply. For example 'Is it true that it was dark, and that the alleyway was unlit?'
- Leading questions: these are questions where the question itself suggests the answer. For example 'The assailant was black?' This type of question is described in Loftus and Palmer's study.

One of the most significant problems witnesses face is a lack of understanding of the question that has been asked, and therefore an inability to answer. Kebbell et al. (2003) argue that not only are witnesses subjected to difficult and confusing questioning techniques, but they are often interrupted, giving the witness little time to give a full answer.

Hollin sums up the variables that can influence eye-witness testimony in the following table:

Variables influencing eye-witness testimony

Social	Situational	Individual	Interrogational
Attitudes; Conformity; Prejudice; Status of interrogator; Stereotyping	Complexity of event; Duration of event; Illumination; Time delay; Type of crime	Age; Cognitive style; Personality; Ethnicity; Sex; Background	Artists sketches; Computer systems; ID parades; Photofits; Mugshots; Training

6.6.3 AIDS TO RECALL/RECOGNITION: IDENTIKIT AND IDENTITY PARADES

There are a number of different ways in which witnesses can be helped to recall details that might assist with the recognition of a suspect. Some are more widely used than others, and this section will look at a number of these including identikit pictures and identity parades.

One of the most widely used aids to recall is the **cognitive interview technique** (CIT). Cognitive interviews can be useful with witnesses whether or not they were the victim. George (1991) argues that there is considerable variation between police forces in terms of how they interview witnesses, and Fisher and Geiselman, who devised the technique in 1984, argue that the police often inadvertently discourage the witness from remembering all they can by asking closed questions (which do not encourage elaboration) or by interrupting the witness. There is a sense of powerlessness on the part of the witness, with the police officer in a dominant role, and it is this kind of relationship that the cognitive interview attempts to break down. If the witness is put at their ease and allowed to take the dominant role, Fisher and Geiselman suggest that the witness is more likely to give as much information as they can. In a cognitive interview the witness is encouraged to relate their whole story without interruption, while the police officer takes an active listening role. Asking open ended questions, and avoiding a judgemental role on the part of the police is also encouraged. There are four stages in the cognitive interview:

- **Recreating the context:** this involves encouraging the witness to think about their involvement in the scene.
- **Focused concentration:** after allowing free recall of the situation the witness is asked to focus on one aspect of the event and focus on that.
- **Multiple retrieval attempts:** this is based on the idea that the witness may remember different details at different times, and may need more than one attempt to recall as much as they saw.

EVALUATION ISSUES

EFFECTIVENESS

Most studies of the CIT support its effectiveness and argue that witnesses remember more using this technique.

EVALUATION ISSUES

ETHICS

One of the problems with the implementation of the CIT is that although the police recognise its value, many police officers are reluctant to use it, especially with witnesses who may be upset or anxious, as they believe it may traumatise the witnesses further.

EVALUATION ISSUES

METHODOLOGY

Some police officers feel that CIT is too time consuming, and that the effort is not worthwhile. Kohnken et al. (1999) argue that about 85 per cent of the information retrieved using CIT was accurate, as opposed to 82 per cent from non-CIT.

- **Varied retrieval**: witnesses are sometimes asked to recount the event in a different order from the one in which it happened, in order to produce additional information.

Hypnosis has also been used to improve recall and recognition, and although its use is less widespread than it once was, it is an interesting technique that has been used with some success. At the height of its popularity it was widely used, especially after a few high profile cases in which it had been a great success. One of these cases involved a group of children in California on a school bus who were kidnapped. The children escaped unharmed, and the bus driver was able to recall the registration of the kidnappers' car while under hypnosis. The kidnappers were later caught and convicted (Ainsworth, 2002). The technique became particularly popular in the USA, where many police officers were trained in its use.

Identity parades, or **line-ups**, are commonly used to try to enable the witness to pick out the person they thought was involved in an offence. Although they are very useful, they have been subject to rigorous scrutiny as there are various ways in which the witness can be led during an identity parade. One of these is the simple wording of the information that accompanies the parade, such as explaining to the witness that 'likeness' is not enough, and that the person they saw may not be there (Stephenson, 2001).

This is important as the witness can easily be led to believe that the suspect is present and that they have to make an identification. Stephenson also suggests that police officers who know who the suspect is may unconsciously suggest who it is. He argues that the best way to avoid this is to have an officer conducting the identity parade who does not know who the suspect is.

Wells et al. (1998) carried out research that was used to write a guide to help with the administration of line-ups and photo spreads. The Technical Working Group for eye-witness Evidence within the US Department of Justice produced recommendations on the basis of this research for all stages of a criminal investigation involving eye-witness evidence. The recommendations were written in the form of a guide that contains the following advice for line-ups and photo-spreads:

Live line-ups

In composing a live line-up, the investigator should:
- include only one suspect in each line-up
- select foils who fit the witness's description of the perpetrator
- place the suspect in different positions in the line-up for different witnesses
- include at least four foils
- avoid using the same foils for two different line-ups with the same witness
- hide distinguishing marks, such as scars or tattoos, that have already been identified by the witness.

Prior to the line-up, the investigator should:
- instruct the witness that it is just as important to clear innocent people from suspicion as it is to identify guilty people
- instruct the witness that individuals present in the line-up may not appear exactly as they did on the date of the incident
- instruct the witness that the perpetrator may or may not be present in the line-up
- assure the witness that whether or not an identification is made, the police will continue to investigate the incident

? FOR CONSIDERATION

One of the problems with the testimony generated under hypnosis is how it is used. If it is used to help the police with their inquiries as in the kidnapping case then it appears justified, but Orne (1984) has raised concerns about people being given false memories under hypnosis and the police using this information as evidence.
- Do you think this kind of evidence is useful?

✎ EXAM HINTS

The study by Malpass and Devine (1981) outlined on pages 321–322 looks at the instructions given to witnesses prior to identity parades, and could be used in an essay on the topic described in this section.

• instruct the witness that they will be asked to state in their own words how certain they are of any identification.

The key study by Lindsay and Wells (1985) described below looks at the issue of how a line-up should be presented, as there is some debate about whether the foils should be presented together or separately.

CD-ROM

For an additional key study that explains guidelines for organising line-ups, see Crime: Additional key studies: Wells et al (1998).

EVALUATION ISSUES

EFFECTIVENESS

Sequential presentation of foils in a line-up is more effective than simultaneous presentation.

KEY STUDY

Improving eye-witness identifications from line-ups: simultaneous versus sequential line-up presentation
Lindsay and Wells (1985)

Aim: To investigate whether the typical procedure of presenting suspects and foils simultaneously in a line-up is more suggestive than asking witnesses to determine whether each alternative is or is not the perpetrator. The researchers suggest that this may be the case because in simultaneous presentation, witnesses are encouraged to choose the 'best' alternative, rather than make a positive identification.

Method: The researchers conducted staged thefts in view of undergraduate participants. Five minutes later, the participants were asked to identify the thief from a set of six photographs. Half of the participants were shown all six photos at the same time, and the other half were shown the photos sequentially. In the second condition, participants were asked to say whether each photo was the perpetrator, and the researchers held a stack of 12 photos even though they only showed 6; this was to prevent the participants from making an identification because they thought there were only one or two photos left. In each condition, half the participants were shown a thief-present array and half were shown a thief-absent array of photos.

Results: For participants who were shown the thief-present arrays, presentation style did not affect outcome: 58 per cent shown simultaneous photos and 50 per cent shown sequential photos correctly identified the thief. However, for participants who were shown the thief-absent arrays, 43 per cent of those presented with the photos simultaneously made false identifications, whereas this figure was only 17 per cent for those shown the photos sequentially.

Conclusions: Sequential presentation in a line-up reduces the false identification rate, thus making identification tests less suggestive.

The witness is sometimes asked to help develop either an **identikit** or a **photofit** picture of the suspect, as it is often difficult to describe a face using words. Identikit pictures are made up of drawn features, whereas photofit pictures are made up of photographs of facial features. Modern photofit tools allow witnesses to pick specific features (ears, eyes, spectacles, etc.) from an enormous database. The constructed image can then be digitally altered to make it look more accurate, and automatically aged in cases in which the witness is identifying someone they saw a while ago. These tools can even combine together images from different witnesses to produce a composite image. However, there is a fair amount of evidence that suggests that photofit images are not particularly accurate and Bruce (1988) suggests that this may be because of the limited number of features that the witness has to choose from, or because human beings do not naturally recognise faces by breaking them down into individual features. The first explanation is unlikely to apply to modern photofit technology, which provides witnesses with thousands of alternatives. However, human beings process facial features holistically, taking into account the relationship between features as well as the shape and size of individual features, and it is therefore very difficult to re-create a particular face by picking out individual features.

A paper by Gibson et al. presented to the British Machine Vision Conference in 2003 suggests that one way around the problem of asking witnesses to pick out individual features one at a time is to use 'evolutionary algorithms', which allow the witness to make choices between faces in order to get closer and closer to the actual face witnessed. One technique they propose, the Select-Multiply-Mutate algorithm, consists of presenting the witness with five faces and asking her to select the one that is most like the person she saw. This one is then multiplied five times and each copy is randomly mutated to produce a new generation. The witness then selects the most accurate fit from these images and the process is repeated until an accurate image is arrived at. Another technique, which is easier to operate but takes longer, is to present the witness at each step of the process with a new face displayed alongside the current best likeness. The witness simply has to choose the most accurate image of the two. The new face presented at each stage is not randomly generated, but takes into account previous decisions. Gibson et al. (2003) claim that the evolutionary approach is much more accurate than traditional composite generation.

SECTION A EXAM QUESTIONS

a Describe one study of cognitive processes and testimony. [6]
b Discuss the methods used to investigate cognitive processes and testimony. [10]

a Describe one study of witnesses' identification of suspects or events. [6]
b Discuss the validity of witnesses' identification of suspects or events. [10]

a Describe how one variable influences accurate identification of a suspect or event. [6]
b Evaluate the effectiveness of identikit and/or identity parades. [10]

CD-ROM

For Section B sample exam questions see Crime: Sample exam questions.

PSYCHOLOGY OF THE COURTROOM

In this section the focus is on the Anglo-American courtroom, in which lawyers present evidence within an adversarial framework, and then magistrates in a magistrates court or lay jurors in a crown court weigh up the evidence according to the rules given to them by the trial judge. The courtroom is a place that few jurors, witnesses or defendants will have much experience of, and they can be intimidating and alien environments, with set procedures and rules of behaviour. How lawyers use evidence, and how the jury makes decisions on the basis of that evidence is the subject of two of the areas in this section, and the use of children as witnesses, and the problems this can raise is the focus of the third.

6.7.1 TRIAL PROCEDURES AND PERSUASION TECHNIQUES

Trial procedures

There are two main types of trial systems, the **adversarial** and the **inquisitorial**. The **adversarial** system refers to the system in which the proceedings are structured like a dispute between two sides, with the role of the judge kept to a minimum. This system developed in the UK as a reaction to the historical mistrust of judges in inquisitorial roles in some European states, and it spread to the USA and the Commonwealth (McEwan, 1999). Other features of the adversarial system are the use of a jury, and the central role of the litigant and his or her advocates, as they are the ones who decide on the evidence, witnesses and the majority of the questions asked of the defendant and his or her witnesses. The **inquisitorial** system (more commonly used in Europe) gives judges a much more central role, and they may supervise the preparation of pre-trial evidence (this is sometimes because the police have much more power in court proceedings in Europe, and there was a concern that bias and corruption might influence proceedings). Judges in the inquisitorial system may also carry out a lot of the questioning of witnesses during the trial, with the advocate's role reduced to objecting to questions, and asking additional questions.

Griffiths (1970, cited in McEwan, 1999) refers to the inquisitorial system as the 'family model', with a basic trust of public officials, as opposed to the adversarial system that he refers to as the 'battle model' for obvious reasons. Faigman (2003) argues that neither system is entirely one thing or the other, and that they each use elements of the other in their proceedings. In the adversarial system elements of the inquisitorial system are used; such as those relating to rules about evidence, privileges conferred on the judge and the legal teams that tend to take control out of the victim and the defendants hands. Similarly in the inquisitorial system there are elements of the adversarial model; for example in the way that witnesses are presented, and the way in which representations are made by the counsel. McEwan (1999) argues that the modern adversarial system is moving closer to the inquisitorial system and one of the reasons for this is that most prosecutions are state funded and organised. This means that the prosecution lawyers tend to have much larger resources than the defence lawyers and the balance between the adversaries is unequal, making the adversarial process seem less fair.

Persuasion techniques

Persuasion plays a very important role in every trial. Judges and juries must evaluate the persuasive arguments of many different sources, for example, witnesses, the victim, the defendant and any expert witnesses that are called upon, such as pathologists, clinical psychologists and psychiatrists. The judge and jury must work out what the facts of the case are, whether all the evidence is admissible (allowed to be used), and which way the verdict should fall. In most trials this is a difficult and onerous responsibility, but in more complex trials with a lot of expert evidence and technical facts and details, some would argue that a lay jury is not capable of distinguishing fact from fiction. One of the reasons for this difficulty is the way in which arguments of guilt or innocence are presented to the court by both legal teams; barristers are experts in their field and extremely skilled at presenting persuasive arguments, not only in terms of the way in which they present the evidence and the order in which they present it, but also in the way they ask questions.

Yale model of persuasion

A psychological model that can be applied to these persuasive techniques is the Yale model of persuasion, put forward by Hovland and Janis as early as 1959. Hovland and Janis argue that there are a number of factors to consider in delivering a message to an audience so that it has the desired effect (of persuading the audience to behave or think in a certain way). These factors relate to the **source** of the information, the actual **message** itself, the **recipient** of the information and the **situation** in which the information is delivered.

The Yale model of persuasion suggests that, in order to be as persuasive as possible, the following should be taken into account:

- The **source** needs to be **credible, knowledgeable** and **attractive**: a barrister may spend some time in court trying to undermine the credibility of an eye-witness or an expert witness by questioning their general competence, rather than by examining their actual testimony. If the jury are led to believe that a particular witness is not reliable, or has a vested interest, then they are less likely to believe their evidence. An important aspect of being credible is to appear knowledgeable. In examining a friendly witness, barristers will try to establish first of all that they do actually know what they are talking about, and the opposing barristers will attempt to question this during cross-examination. Finally, lawyers, witnesses and suspects always make an effort to dress up for court cases, and the Yale model suggest that this would help them get their message across.
- The **message** should have some **emotional appeal** although too much will be off-putting. Barristers need to judge this very carefully in order to get the balance just right. The most important information should be presented first as this makes it easier for the jury to recall (the **primacy effect**). Finally, a two-sided message is more persuasive if the recipient is better educated, whereas a one-sided message is more effective if the recipient is less well educated. A barrister needs to build up an impression of the jury in order to decide whether to present a very black and white argument, or else a more ambiguous one which leads the jury in a certain direction but gives them the impression that they are making their own minds up.
- As mentioned above, the level of education of the **recipients** of the information (i.e. the judge and jury in a court case) is important, but so is their resistance to persuasion. Resistance to persuasion is increased by

EVALUATION ISSUES

EFFECTIVENESS

The Yale model of persuasion has been shown to be very effective with the right message and source.

The Yale model of persuasion has been applied to other areas in which people seek to affect the behaviour of others.

• Can you think of examples of other areas of psychological interest where this model may have been applied?

providing counter-arguments (which is what happens in a court case) or when the recipients become aware that someone is trying to persuade them (calling for subtlety on the part of barristers).

• The Yale model suggests that a message is more persuasive when presented in a more informal **situation**. A law-court is very formal, but barristers can increase the informality by joking with the jury and making direct eye-contact with individual members.

Story telling

One of the ways in which the message is used is to tell a story in court. **Story telling** is a widely researched method of persuading the jury to accept evidence; however, there is some debate over which method of telling stories is most effective. Barristers commonly manipulate the order in which they 'tell the story' of the events that are under scrutiny, and also bring out their witnesses in a certain order to persuade the court. The article by McArdle (2003) summarised below describes some of the techniques used by lawyers to persuade juries. However, there is evidence that juries are more easily persuaded when witnesses and evidence are presented in the sequence in which the events actually occurred, than in an order judged by the barrister as more likely to persuade them. Pennington and Hastie (1988) set up different juries in a mock trial and asked the prosecution and defence lawyers to present evidence either in the order of the events, or in an order judged to be most effective in persuading juries. The results indicate that 'story order' is significantly more effective in persuading juries than 'witness order'. In a later paper (Pennington and Hastie, 1990) they argue that the reason so many criminal court cases in the US result in guilty verdicts is that prosecution lawyers tend to use story order, and defence lawyers tend to use witness order.

⚖ EVALUATION ISSUES

EFFECTIVENESS

McArdle (2003) and other studies in this section show how cleverly professionals within the legal system use their knowledge to influence juries.

KEY STUDY

The order of witnesses is crucial
McArdle (2003)

This article from *Lawyers Weekly USA* (November, 2003) describes how a very successful lawyer, Christian Searcy Sr., manipulates the order in which he presents witnesses to win cases. Searcy suggests that, 'The first witness in the morning is generally better than the middle of the afternoon. The beginning and end of the week tend to be more memorable than the middle of the week. So there are prime times for witnesses.' One of Searcy's favourite strategies is to order evidence so that he presents a particularly revelatory or provocative piece of evidence on Friday afternoon, leaving the weekend for the jury to reflect on what was presented. Another strategy is to lead the case with an adverse witness. This runs counter to the primacy theory, that the first version of the story the jury hears becomes the prism through which they will assess all other information. However, Searcy argues that it is better for him to call the adverse witness first, and then call a helpful witness to rebut the adverse witness, rather than just call the helpful witness and leave it to the opposition to contradict the testimony with an adverse witness. Searcy prefers to tell the jury that they are about to hear from two conflicting witnesses, and that the second one is telling the truth.

Use of questions

One of the most influential ways in which the legal representatives of the victim or defendant can persuade the jury is through the use of questions.

Questioning in court is a very practiced and delicate skill. Certain questions are not allowed (such as leading questions), and other questions are encouraged (such as open questions). Carson and Pakes (2003) address the question of whether lawyers are able to put words into a witness' mouth. This is a particularly relevant question in England where courtroom procedure is based on an adversarial principle, and it is in the professional interests of both prosecution and defence lawyers to 'win' the case. Carson and Pakes describe a number of ways in which lawyers can get the answers they want from witnesses:

- **Leading questions**: A key rule in adversarial trial systems is that lawyers who call a witness are not allowed to ask leading questions, although this is permitted in cross-examination. Loftus and Palmer (1974) showed that merely changing one adjective in the wording of a question could alter eye-witness testimony. This suggests that leading questions can produce inaccurate evidence. Increasingly, the use of leading questions in a trial is being restricted, but the fact that this is still permitted in cross-examination means that there may be scope for manipulating witness' evidence in court. For example a lawyer would not be allowed to ask 'Was the car you saw blue?' but they could ask 'What colour was the car you saw?'

- **Directed questions**: Asking a witness 'Was the car you saw red?' is clearly a leading question, whereas 'What colour was the car?' is a directed question because it asks the witness to provide a specific piece of information determined by the lawyer. The lawyer is asking for a part of the total picture to be described, and important evidence could be excluded from the court proceedings. Directed questions can appear helpful to the witness, but they allow the lawyer to select what information is presented to the court.

- **Directed choices**: An example of this is 'Was the car red or brown?' In this case, it is possible for the witness to respond 'neither' but in practice witnesses are more likely to choose one of the options offered so as not to appear awkward or unco-operative in court. Lawyers can manipulate witnesses by making one of the choices inappropriate, for example, asking a witness whether an injury was 'life-threatening' or 'serious' could prevent the witness from saying that the injury was 'very serious'.

- **Short questions**: Lawyers tend to ask short questions to witnesses because it gives them more control over the testimony. If they ask long questions, with several parts, it invites the witness to give a long and convoluted answer. One of the most common forms of questions asked by lawyers in trials is a directed short choice, for example, 'Did you see the defendant hit the victim, yes or no?'

- **Casting doubt**: In a criminal case, the defence lawyers do not have to prove that the defendant is innocent but simply convince the jury that there is a reasonable doubt as to the defendant's guilt. Almost all criminal trials are based on persuasion rather than proof. Defence lawyers do not need to get prosecution witnesses to admit that they are liars, they just need to persuade them to accept that they may have been mistaken; this can lead to a reasonable doubt.

One technique that lawyers can use to attempt to cast doubt on a witness' evidence is by use of the word 'possible'. If a defence lawyer asks a witness 'Did you make a mistake' then the answer is likely to be 'no', but if they ask 'Is it at all possible that you made a mistake' then by saying 'no' the witness is saying that it is not even possible they were mistaken and this can sound very arrogant and the witness can lose credibility. On the other hand, if the witness admits that it is possible they were mistaken, then reasonable doubt is introduced; the witness is in a no-win situation.

EXAM HINTS

The Loftus and Palmer (1974) study can be used in an essay relating to this section. This study is one of the core studies that make up the AS syllabus.

EVALUATION ISSUES

ETHICS

There are a number of ethical concerns about using persuasion, leading questions and manipulation to convince a jury (see below).

In the following section the decisions that juries make will be examined in relation to the information above and other factors that can influence the verdict of the jury.

6.7.2 JURY SELECTION AND DECISION-MAKING

Juries are selected in slightly different ways depending on the particular judicial system, and the decisions they make are influenced by many different factors. Psychologists argue that some of these factors are to do with the evidence that is presented, while others are to do with what are called extra-evidential factors, such as group processes like conformity.

Jury selection

Green and Wrightsman (2003) cover several different aspects of the ways in which juries are selected in a number of different countries around the world. In the USA, court cases are preceded by *voir dire* procedures, which allow attorneys to question prospective jurors and even to give them lengthy written questionnaires asking about personal experiences and beliefs. Attorneys for each side are then able to eliminate as many prospective jurors 'with cause' (if they give a reason) and a certain number without cause. The ability to dismiss jurors in this way is referred to as a **peremptory challenge**, and this has been criticised on the grounds that it leads to discrimination against prospective jurors, wastes time and money, and makes the public more cynical about the jury system.

One study that looked at the potential effect of peremptory challenges, to see if jurors who would be biased against the defendant would be eliminated, was carried out by Olczak et al. (1991). They asked defence attorneys to examine 36 prospective jurors in a criminal case, and select the 'best' 12 and the 12 whom they would exclude. Interestingly, they found that attorneys were more likely to select jurors who convicted the defendant and reject ones who acquitted the defendant rather than the other way round (i.e. they tended to make the 'wrong' decisions). Other studies have shown that attorneys will try to eliminate jurors they think will be prejudiced against their client, but that having survived *voir dire* these jurors, when measured against a randomly chosen group of jurors, showed no significant differences in their attitudes.

In Scotland, peremptory challenges were abolished in 1995 on the grounds that they allowed defendants to 'stack the deck' with jurors unlikely to convict and because the practice angered and confused members of the public, and inconvenienced potential jurors. In some countries (e.g. Ireland, New Zealand) peremptory challenges are allowed, but lawyers are not allowed to question prospective jurors during *voir dire*; this could well invite decisions based on awareness of prospective jurors' superficial characteristics such as ethnicity, age, gender, class, etc. In England, prosecutors are allowed unlimited opportunity to 'stand a juror by', but this simply means the prospective juror returns to the pool and could be called on again. Defendants have no right to make peremptory challenges. Canadian juries are selected in a very different manner: two people ('lay triers') are selected at random from a pool of prospective jurors and when *voir dire* begins they listen to questions posed to the first two prospective jurors and decide whether they are impartial. Once the first two jurors have been selected, they then judge whether the next candidate is impartial and so on until all 12 have been selected.

Decision-making

The decisions juries make are influenced by many different factors, and some of the earlier sections of this chapter have looked at ways in which juries may be influenced, in particular by eye-witness testimony (see page 333).

Most psychological studies focus on the influence on the decisions that juries make in one of two areas: **evidential factors**, including eye-witness testimony (as has previously been described in section 6.6.2 on pages 323–6) and **extra-evidential factors**, including pre-trial publicity, and things about the witness such as their confidence, attractiveness, ethnicity and gender.

Extra-evidential factors

Pre-trial publicity can sometimes influence jurors, and a number of complaints have been made over the years that pre-trial publicity has had an adverse effect on jurors. in high profile trials jurors are often deliberately kept away from media coverage of the event.

A now dated, but none the less effective, study of the effect of pre-trial publicity was carried out by Padawer-Singer and Barton (1974) in which they gave a group of participants (mock jurors) newspaper cuttings about a defendant's criminal record and a confession that was later retracted. A second group of mock jurors were allowed to read newspaper articles about the case, but these left out the details about the criminal record and confession of the defendant. The two groups then listened to tape recordings of the trial. The results showed that 78 per cent of the jurors in the first condition (exposed to bias in the publicity) gave a guilty verdict, compared to 55 per cent in the second condition (those exposed to no bias). More recent research still confirms the results of this study; Steblay et al. (1999) carried out a review of 44 studies in which mock jurors were either exposed to adverse pre-trial publicity or less or no adverse publicity, and in each study the jurors in the adverse publicity condition were more likely to judge the defendant guilty. Some of the features that most affected the mock jurors decisions are commonplace in actual cases, such as the release of lots of information about the defendant and the case (prior to and during the trial), real as opposed to fictional or exaggerated information about the case, and at least a weeks' delay between exposure to the pre-trial publicity and the court case.

In the USA it is assumed that the *voir dire* process will screen out jurors who have been exposed to too much pre-trial publicity, and in England as well as the USA there is the assumption that judges will rely on 'common sense' to assess the effects of prejudicial pre-trial material (Greene and Wrightsman, 2003). In Australia the media can be fined for publishing material that might later be found to prejudice a case. Results from a survey in New Zealand, carried out by Lane (1999) (cited in Green and Wrightsman, 2003), suggests that pre-trial material may not influence the jury too much, and that the jurors are much more likely to focus on the evidence presented in the actual court itself.

One of the other factors that is thought to influence the jury is the confidence of the witness. This might be related to the fact that they are an expert witness, and therefore they have the credentials and experience that gives authority to their testimony; or it may be the certainty with which an eye-witness recounts their view of events, even if they were only a bystander at the time of the incident. Penrod and Cutler (1987) argue that witness confidence is the most important thing that jurors attend to when listening to evidence; however, this is problematic as confidence is not always related to accuracy.

EVALUATION ISSUES

RELIABILITY

Evidence suggests that eye-witnesses are not very accurate, and certainly not as accurate as they think they are. It is of serious concern that jurors can be biased by eye-witness testimony, and by other factors that have little to do with the case such as pre-trial publicity.

There are problems of reliability with both evidential and extra-evidential factors affecting the jury. Eye-witness testimony may be unreliable, but pre-trial publicity may also be biased.

There are also a number of research studies that have looked at extra-evidential factors that relate to the prejudices and biases of the jurors in their judgement of witnesses. For example, the attractiveness, gender and even the socio-economic status of a witness can have an impact. According to Bartol and Bartol (1994) there are three types of attractiveness: **physical**, **social** and **attitudinal**. In terms of physical attractiveness legal teams often coach their clients and witnesses to appear as attractive as possible in court, in terms of the way they dress, speak, and even in their posture in the witness box or dock. There are very good reasons for this as studies show that there is a greater tolerance of physically attractive people, and crimes that are committed by these people receive more lenient sentences than crimes committed by less attractive people. However, other studies suggest that the relationship between attractiveness and punishment may be a little more complex (see the key study below). In terms of **social attractiveness**, studies have found that if the defendant is socially attractive (with high social status) the jury will be more lenient towards the defendant, whereas if the victim has high social status (equal or higher than the defendant), the jury will favour the victim. Finally, in relation to **attitudinal attractiveness** people usually like people who conform to the same attitudes and beliefs as themselves, and jurors have been found to favour defendants whose attitudes match their own (Mitchell and Byrne, 1973). Mitchell and Byrne found that authoritarian jurors were less likely to find authoritarian defendants guilty, whereas this effect was not apparent in non-authoritarian jurors.

EVALUATION ISSUES

ECOLOGICAL VALIDITY

Studies with mock jurors lack ecological validity, as it is difficult to recreate the real context of the courtroom in an experimental setting.

KEY STUDY

Beautiful but dangerous: effects of offender attractiveness and nature of the crime on juridic judgment
Sigall and Ostrove (1975)

Aim: To test the hypothesis that physically attractive defendants will receive lighter punishments only when their attractiveness is unrelated to the crime. If the crime (e.g. swindling) involves persuasion and the accused may have used their attractiveness to con innocent victims, jurors may judge attractive people more harshly.

Sample: 120 mock jurors (60 male, 60 female) made up of college students who had agreed to take part in the study.

Method: Participants were randomly assigned into three groups. One third of the subjects were told that a female defendant was attractive, one third were told the defendant was unattractive and the remaining third were told nothing about the attractiveness. Each group was then split into two, with half the participants hearing about a burglary case, and the other half about a case involving fraud. The case accounts strongly implied guilt and the researchers asked subjects to recommend an appropriate sentence length, from 1 to 15 years in jail.

Results: Sigall and Ostrove found that attractiveness interacted with the type of crime. No difference was found between the gender of the jurors in terms of sentencing.

Mean sentence assigned (years):

Offence	Defendant		
	Attractive	Unattractive	Control
Swindle	5.45	4.35	4.35
Burglary	2.8	5.2	5.1

Conclusions: Sigall and Ostrove explained their results cognitively: in general, attractive people tend to be treated more generously as they are perceived as less dangerous and more virtuous. However, attractive people who 'mis-use' or take advantage of their beauty (e.g. in swindles or confidence tricks) are seen as more 'dangerous' and this incurs the animosity of the jurors, resulting in stiffer sentences.

The ethnicity of the defendant has long been thought to affect the decisions of juries. Looking at the prison population in the UK would suggest that there is bias in the sentencing of defendants from ethnic minority backgrounds; there are a disproportionate number of black male offenders in prison compared to the numbers of black men in the general population. It is possible that more black men commit the types of crimes that carry heavier sentences, but if the type of offence is controlled, significant differences still emerge (Ainsworth, 2000). Home Office figures also suggest that higher percentages of black offenders receive immediate custodial sentences than do white offenders committing the same crimes. A seminal piece of research by Hood (1992) (cited in Ainsworth, 2000) looked at a total of 2884 defendants appearing in Crown Court. Hood found that 48.4 per cent of white defendants were given custodial sentences compared to 56.6 per cent of black defendants. What is particularly interesting about his research is that he found that there were differences in the sentencing procedures of black and white defendants between different courts and between different judges. This was particularly apparent for moderately serious cases where the judge had some influence over the length of sentence, in contrast to trivial and very serious offences where the differences were minimal.

A key feature of jury decision-making is the fact that the 12 members of the jury have to make the decision collectively, and this introduces social psychological factors such as conformity and group dynamics into the process. In the classic film, *Twelve Angry Men* starring Henry Fonda, the jury start off with a clear majority believing in the defendant's guilt. In such cases, it is usual for the majority to persuade the minority to change their minds by discussing and eliminating the points of disagreement that are leading the minority to dissent. In this film, however, one individual consistently argues that guilt has not been established 'beyond all reasonable doubt' and manages to persuade the other members of the jury one by one. This raises the question of whether jury deliberations result in the verdict that best fits the evidence, or whether the faction that is best able to convince the others is the one that 'wins' the argument. In an ideal world, the jury members whose opinions are most respected ought to be those who have listened to and understood the evidence, who are not prejudiced in favour or against the defendant, and who understand the court process. In fact, juries tend to pay particular attention to individual members for a range of other reasons. For example, Saks and Hastie (1978, cited in Stephenson, 2001) noted that 'the person most likely to be chosen foreman is a high socio-economic status male who sits at the end of the table and initiates the discussion'. Lupfer et al. (1987, cited in Stephenson, 2001) found that jury members who emphasise the importance of universal principles and individual conscience are more likely to have their views respected. Such people are also more likely to vote for acquittal, and it is this scenario that is reflected in *Twelve Angry Men*.

EVALUATION ISSUES

ECOLOGICAL VALIDITY

Hood's research has high ecological validity as it was carried out using real data from real court cases.

EVALUATION ISSUES

EFFECTIVENESS

Many people would argue that trial by jury is likely to result in a fairer and less biased outcome than if the decision is made by a single judge or a small group of judges. However, if it is true that group decisions reflect the persuasiveness of their members, rather than the objective merits of the case, maybe jury decisions are less fair.

FOR CONSIDERATION

- Who do you think is best placed to determine whether someone is guilty of a crime: a jury of 12 citizens or judges specially trained for the job?

Research into the use of children as witnesses has increased in recent years, and legislation has changed to try to protect children from the effects of giving testimony in court either as a victim, or as a witness. Research has shown that children can suffer lasting trauma as a result of giving evidence, and this can cause cognitive and emotional difficulties that slow the rate of development in these children in relation to their peers (Bagley and Ramsey, 1986). This section will focus on the trauma children feel and the effect this has on their testimony, and what the judicial system has done to try to protect children.

Witness stress and effect on testimony

Spencer and Flin (1993) have developed a model of the stress experienced by child witnesses, and this includes the factors shown below.

Causes of stress:
• The crime (as a victim or eye-witness).
• The period before the trial (interviews and waiting for the trial).
• The trial (waiting in court, questions under examination and cross examination, seeing the accused person and the layout of the courtroom).
• The period after the trial (lack of understanding of the outcome, especially if the prosecution is unsuccessful).

Mediating factors:
• Pre-trial preparation.
• Social support (including family reaction).
• Personality.
• Age.

Effects of stress:
• The crime (post traumatic stress disorder).
• The period before the trial (anxiety, disruption of sleep, appetite, mood).
• The trial (anxiety, fear, lack of emotional control, interruption of cognitive and communication skills, which can lead to poor quality evidence).
• The period after the trial (positive effects: relief, and a sense of achievement; negative effects: lasting emotional and behavioural disturbance).

As the model suggests children suffer before, during and after the trial. Some psychologists have compared the trauma experienced by child witnesses in court to the experiences of women rape victims. These studies suggest that children can become so traumatised that their evidence is at worst of little or no use, and at best only a partial account. In cases of alleged sexual abuse where corroborating witnesses may be lacking, the testimony of the child is often central to the case, and difficulties of this kind can be very problematic.

As is suggested in the model proposed by Spencer and Flin (1993) Post Traumatic Stress Disorder (PTSD) can also be a serious reaction to the stress of the incident (as victim or witness). The symptoms of PTSD can include reliving the event over and over again, through the experience of flashbacks; but it can also cause persistent avoidance of the memory or situation, and in some people this avoidance is strong enough to cause amnesia (psychogenic amnesia) (Brooks, 1999). This has obvious implications for the testimony of a child in court.

CD-ROM

For more information on the testimony of children, go to Crime: Real life applications: Children's testimony.

Freud's theory of **ego defence mechanisms** can also be applied to child witnesses. Their experiences might cause suppression (where they deliberately try not to think about things that are upsetting) or repression (when thoughts are pushed out of the conscious mind); this in turn might make it harder to remember the events that took place, and lead to problems with testimony.

There are other studies however, that suggest that giving evidence can sometimes be beneficial for the child, as it allows the child to discuss the trauma they have suffered openly (especially in cases of sexual abuse) and can be a kind of coping strategy, increasing the child's sense of self-efficacy.

Protection for child witnesses

Recent legislation in England and Wales has sought to protect children who have to give evidence in court, and a number of initiatives are particularly relevant here:

- The 1988 Criminal Justice Act in England and Wales changed the law to allow children to give evidence via a video link from another room in the court building.
- The 1991 Criminal Justice Act in England and Wales now allows the use of video footage of interview evidence that was collected prior to the trial by the police or a social worker. However, these interviews can only be used if the judge agrees they were carried out appropriately.
- The emphasis on appropriate interviewing techniques in the 1991 legislation has led to an emphasis on good practice and training in the interviewing of children.

The research that psychologists have carried out in recent years suggests that children are usually able to give a useful account of what happened if they are interviewed properly; however, if interviewing is pressurised or uses leading questions that suggest answers this can severely bias the child's account (Bull, 1999). Research that has been carried out into cases where children witness complex events shows that children can reliably recall what happened. However, while their testimony is accurate, they very rarely give a full account (Bull, 1999).

One of the factors that has to be considered when using the testimony of children is the age of the child, as research suggests that younger children recall less than older children. For this reason young children often need more prompting, and questions have to be used more often than for older children. The key study by Saywitz et al. (1996) described below shows how young children may be able to be trained to help them remember events better.

⚖ EVALUATION ISSUES

ETHICS

This section deals with many of the ethical dilemmas that must be considered when using children as witnesses. The distress that giving evidence will cause is obviously of primary concern.

KEY STUDY

Preparing child witnesses: the efficiency of memory training strategy
Saywitz, Snyder and Lamphear (1996)

Aim: The study by Saywitz et al. comes out of a well-replicated finding that young children tend to recall less information about an event they have witnessed than older children (although what they recall is just as accurate). Young children are also more likely to acquiesce to suggestive leading questions than older children. The study evaluates a technique designed by Saywitz et al. to help increase the recall of young children; this would clearly be very useful where children are witnesses to criminal events, and also when they themselves are the victims.

▶

Method: Saywitz et al. used three groups of young children:
- Group 1 were trained in a range of techniques aimed at improving recall. These included the use of visual cues (e.g. schematic drawings of the scene of the incident) and other specific strategies previously shown to be effective with children.
- Group 2 received instructions to remember as much as possible, but received no special training.
- Group 3 received no instructions and no training.

All three groups were exposed to a staged live event and then their recall was tested.

Results: Group 1 (the trained group) correctly recalled significantly more information than the other two groups (between whom there was no difference). However, they also recalled significantly more incorrect information, and this was directly as a result of the use of visual cues.

Conclusions: The authors conclude that there is a great deal of scope for special training to improve the recall of child witnesses, but further research needs to be done to establish the most effective strategies.

There are a number of ways in which children can be interviewed to help them recall events, and to minimise the level of stress involved. The use of video links or footage has been mentioned and this involves the use of closed-circuit television. Many countries now use CCTV including the USA, UK, Canada, Australia and New Zealand. Using CCTV shields the child from confronting the defendant, and the child can be accompanied by a person approved by the judge.

A study by Flin et al. (1993) compared children interviewed in court using CCTV with children interviewed in open court, and found that there was less evidence of stress in those children interviewed using CCTV. The children interviewed using a video link cried less, spoke more loudly and more fluently, and gave more evidence than those in open court.

There are other ways in which children can be interviewed. One example is the use of props or toys to help children express things they cannot or do not want to say out loud. Another initiative that has been used increasingly with young children is the use of visual stimuli. Based on the work of Poole (1992) (cited in Bull, 1999) a green felt board is used on which there is an outline of the adult interviewer's head and the child's head. Young children tend to assume that adults know what the child knows, so in this technique the thoughts of the child are represented by using white triangles which are placed above the head of the child; as the interview progresses the triangles are moved over to above the adult's head, showing the child that the adult now knows what they do. Research using this technique suggests that it improves the amount that a young child recalls.

One of the most difficult questions about the evidence of children is how reliable and valid it is. Children are more suggestible and not very resistant to the influence of adults under normal circumstances, but in a court these effects may be much more serious. Children may lie to protect adults they know, or because they are scared, or they may say what they think the adult questioning them wants to hear. Research into whether it is possible to detect lies shows that there is no such thing as 'lie behaviour' (Bull, 1999). Research is being carried out into ways of checking the authenticity of the evidence children give. A relatively new technique known as Statement Validity Analysis (SVA) has been used with child victims of sexual abuse. It involves checking what children say against a number of 'reality criteria' which describe the way in which the child answers questions. The theory underpinning SVA is that the child will not be able to make up statements with reality criteria; so if their statements have these criteria they are likely to be true. Research suggests that SVA has good reliability and validity, although more research needs to be carried out in this area (Bull, 1999).

Understanding and acting upon the needs of children in court is fraught with difficulties; and although research is ongoing and has led to some good practice, as many of these studies suggest, more still needs to be done by the courts, the police and social services in order to protect children as much as possible from the stress of giving testimony in court.

SECTION A EXAM QUESTIONS

a Describe one study of persuasion techniques in the courtroom. [6]
b Discuss the usefulness of researching persuasion techniques in the courtroom. [10]

a Describe one study of decision-making in a jury. [6]
b Discuss the problems of researching decision-making in juries. [10]

a Describe one study of children as witnesses. [6]
b Evaluate the ethics of studying children as witnesses. [10]

? FOR CONSIDERATION

- Do you think it is fair to convict someone on the basis of evidence from a child?

CD-ROM

For Section B sample exam questions see Crime: Sample exam questions.

6.8 OFFENDER PUNISHMENTS AND TREATMENTS, AND PREVENTING CRIME

This section looks at the types of punishments that are commonly used to deal with offenders, and possible treatment once the courts have processed them. There is also a section on preventing crime; this looks at some of the community initiatives that have been put into practice to avoid crime being committed in the first place.

6.8.1 TYPES AND EFFECTIVENESS OF PUNISHMENTS

Types of punishments

There are two main types of punishments in western society; **custodial and non-custodial**.

Custodial:
- **Prison**: the current prison population in England and Wales is around 74 000 (2004). There are a large number of people employed in the prison service, and relatively few psychologists. Most prisons recognise that their main purpose is to remove offenders from mainstream society.
- **Special hospitals**: these institutions are not prisons, but are secure units in which treatment can take place (the wards are locked); they usually treat offenders whose criminal activities relate to some form of mental illness or instability.
- **Residential centres**: these are usually for young offenders, and use a mixture of therapeutic methods and a social learning approach to treat delinquents. Some follow a harsher regime of training and control.

Non-custodial:
- **Fines** vary widely in the amount a person has to pay, and the length of time they have pay it. A fine is sometimes used in conjunction with another punishment, such as removal of a driving licence.
- **Probation** is a period of time during which the offender has to report to a probation officer. The probation officer will supervise the offender, and sometimes the probation officer will also work with the offender on social skills training and other treatment programmes (see pages 346–348).
- **Community service** is a programme in which the offender has to work, for a given number of hours, on a project in the community. This may involve building, gardening or cleaning work.

The two most commonly cited reasons for punishment given by courts are that the offender deserved to be punished, and that punishment will reduce the rate of crime. The first reason is linked to **retribution** (and the future of the criminal is irrelevant with this reasoning). The idea of retribution is linked to the **just world hypothesis** in which the victim can feel that there is some justice if the offender is punished for what they did (Ainsworth, 2000). The second reason, that punishment will reduce the rate of crime, works in three ways: by **deterrence** (making the person think before committing the crime), **reform** (the offender might change while being

---

KEY DEFINITIONS

Custodial punishments involve the offender being put in some kind of prison or hospital for the duration of their sentence.

Non-custodial punishments include fines, probation and community service.

KEY DEFINITIONS

The **just world hypothesis** is a phrase originally coined by Lerner who argues that 'individuals have a need to believe that they live in a world where people generally get what they deserve and deserve what they get' (Lerner, 1978). This helps people maintain the belief that their world is stable and orderly and that they will not get punished unless they have done something to deserve it. In order to maintain the notion of a just world, it becomes necessary to punish criminals, not in order to teach them a lesson or to put other people off from committing crimes, but simply because they deserve to be punished.

punished) or by simply **removing the offender** from mainstream society (the offender cannot commit more crimes while in prison) (Hebenton and Pease, 1999). Other reasons for punishment include the criminal compensating for what they have done, or to communicate the seriousness of their wrongdoing to the offender and to society. Many psychologists and prison reformers argue that rehabilitation is not central to the ideas of the criminal justice system, and that punishment is much more about the criminal paying the price of their actions.

The concept of deterrence is based on the psychological theories of operant conditioning (which suggest that individuals will avoid behaviour for which they have been punished in the past) and social learning (which suggests that people consider the possible outcomes of a behaviour before acting). These outcomes can be deduced by observing what happens to other people performing the behaviour. In this way, punishing criminals makes other people less likely to commit crime.

According to Hollin (2001) the reasoning behind the idea that an offender deserves to be punished is the notion of free will. If it is assumed that the offender committed the crime knowingly, calculating the costs and benefits, then the offender must take the consequences of their actions. There is a widely known aphorism 'If you can't do the time, don't do the crime', and this appears to be borne out by the way in which the courts deal with most offenders. However, what constitutes an appropriate sentence for an individual crime is more difficult to establish. Historically, punishments were very severe regardless of the crime, with people being flogged, hung, branded and burned for theft as well as murder. In contemporary western society there is a consensus that the punishment should match the crime, and so the more serious the offence the more severe the punishment (Hollin, 2001). The decision therefore to give a custodial or non-custodial sentence, and the type of institution, length of sentence, amount of fine or community service that an offender is going to be subject to is left up to individual judges and magistrates to decide, within the guidance of existing laws.

The Theory of Planned Behaviour suggests that a key factor in the decision-making process is the perceived consequence of a particular behaviour. So if an individual recognises that the outcome of committing a crime will be punishment, they will be less likely to commit the crime. The logical consequence of this is to make punishment more severe, thereby increasing the deterrent effect (although it is generally accepted by psychologists that the perceived likelihood of getting caught is at least as important a factor as the perceived seriousness of the punishment). The most severe punishment is the death penalty, and it would be reasonable to assume that this would be a more effective deterrent than life imprisonment. However, there is a great deal of evidence from the USA that seems to contradict this, and even to suggest that the death penalty has a brutalising effect and actually results in an increase in the crime rate:

- During the last 20 years, the homicide rate in states (in the USA) with the death penalty has been significantly higher than in states without the death penalty.
- Of the 12 states without capital punishment 10 have homicide rates below the national average.

In the eight months after the execution of Robert Harris in California in 1992 (the state's first execution after a 25-year moratorium) crime statistics revealed slight increases in homicides.

KEY DEFINITIONS

Specific deterrence is concerned with punishing an individual offender in order to discourage her from offending again.
General deterrence is where people in general are discouraged from committing a crime by the threat of punishment if they are caught.

FOR CONSIDERATION

- What kind of punishments should we use in the UK?
- Do you agree with the way in which we punish criminals? Is it fair?

- In 1990, Oklahoma resumed executions after a 25-year moratorium. A comparison of murder rates between 1989 and 1991 uncovered no evidence of a deterrent effect and, in fact, researchers did find a significant increase in stranger killings.
- Researchers studied differences in homicides in 293 counties that were paired based on factors such as geographic location and demographic and economic variables. The pairs shared a geographical border, but differed on use of capital punishment. The authors found no support for a deterrent effect and, in fact, found higher violent crime rates in death penalty counties.

So why does the most severe possible punishment not seem to act as a deterrent? It may be that the threat of execution at some future date does not enter the minds of potential murderers. Most murders are carried out under the influence of drugs and/or alcohol, or while the killer is in the grip of fear or rage, or is panicking while committing another crime (such as a robbery). Perhaps a rational decision-making process simply does not take place at such times. It may even be the case that the severity of the punishment actually makes the potential murderer avoid thinking about the consequences of the crime, and thereby reduces the deterrent effect.

Effectiveness of punishment

Custodial

The most common type of custodial sentence is to be put in a prison. From a psychological viewpoint this is fraught with problems and it is the type of punishment that has been the subject of the most research. Ainsworth argues that societies' ideas about imprisonment are based on the behaviourist principles of operant conditioning, that punishment will reduce the likelihood that behaviour will re-occur. However the fact that re-offending rates are high shows that this is not true. Walker and Farrington (1981) compared first time offenders given probation or a suspended sentence with those imprisoned or fined, and found that those on probation were less likely to re-offend. Walker and Farrington also argue that the length of sentence has little relationship to re-offending rates, and found that among habitual criminals 85 per cent go on to re-offend.

Some people argue that prison is only effective if it is unpleasant, however this is not necessarily borne out by the evidence. Studies on crowding in animals, for example the work of Calhoun in the 1960s with mice and rats, showed that these animals develop pathological symptoms including aggression when left in crowded conditions. Calhoun's research can be applied to human populations in similar sorts of environments such as prisons, where inmates cannot physically remove themselves from the situation. Ainsworth (2000) looks at prison overcrowding and argues that studies suggest that in spite of the obvious difficulties this causes, recidivism rates are higher in offenders who are released from overcrowded prisons than those released from less crowded ones. Farrington and Nuttall (1980) suggest three reasons for this: in overcrowded prisons, inmates spend a lot of time locked up and therefore learn from each other, many offenders get very aggressive in these circumstances and are therefore more likely to offend upon release, and there is less opportunity for treatment programmes in crowded prisons.

There is no doubt that prison causes depression and stress, and it is widely known that suicide rates in prison are rising (suicide rates in

UK prisons are four times as high as in the rest of the population).

A public survey carried out by the Scottish Parliament (2002) found that people do not feel that prison is effective in rehabilitating offenders. The three main arguments are:

- that prison regimes are 'too soft' to bring about individual change
- that prisons are 'schools for crime' and, particularly for young offenders, simply expose people to damaging ideas and influences
- that the experience of prison has the effect of brutalising people or otherwise affecting their ability to function in 'normal' society.

Respondents did not perceive prison as being significantly more effective than a community penalty in terms of recidivism rates. In each case, on average, respondents thought that roughly 55 per cent of offenders would appear before the courts on a different charge within two years. Interestingly, this perception is a very accurate one and roughly 50 per cent of those who are given a prison sentence or community penalty will appear before the courts on a different charge within two years.

The effectiveness of special hospitals has been evaluated by various psychologists, notably Black (1982), who has carried out a number of follow-up studies of patients released from special hospitals such as Broadmoor. In one such study, Black (1982) noted that in a five-year follow-up study of 125 men discharged from Broadmoor, 101 had not been readmitted to a psychiatric hospital, and 70 had had no more court appearances. Of those that do re-offend after being in special hospitals (around 50 per cent), their crimes are often relatively minor (Bowden, 1981).

Non-custodial

The Prison Reform Trust (PRT) is a campaigning group that believes that prisons are the most shaming of all our public institutions. In a report from 2001 the PRT claims that the UK imprisons more of its people than virtually any other country in western Europe and believes that the vast majority of prisoners could be more humanely, economically and effectively dealt with in the community. The PRT advocates the use of more non-custodial punishments, such as a wider use of the probation service and community programmes.

The PRT website quotes the following figures in support of their arguments:

- Every prisoner costs about £25 000 a year to keep in custody. A night in a police cell costs more than a night in London's Dorchester Hotel.
- One fifth of all prisoners have not been convicted of any offence. Yet 40 per cent of these are not judged to need a prison sentence when they come to court.
- Only one in three prisoners is in prison because of an offence involving violence, sex or drugs. Many of the remainder have committed only minor, property offences.
- Up to a third of prisoners have some identifiable psychiatric disorder.
- Remand prisoners, who have not been found guilty of any crime, suffer the worst conditions and regimes.
- People who should be cared for by the mental health system wrongly end up in prison.
- On average, one prisoner commits suicide every four to five days.
- Community penalties cost less than prison and can work better.

Fines (although widely used for certain types of offences) are not always considered to be a deterrent. Although they can be paid in a number of ways, and over a period of time, a fine can be paid by someone other than the offender (such as a parent) which may reduce its effectiveness as a punishment. Some people also feel that they have 'got off lightly' if they are fined, and this may reduce the feeling of wrong-doing. Probation and community service are less expensive than prison, and by keeping people in the community, carry less stigma than a custodial punishment. However, it is difficult to assess the effectiveness of these programmes, and although some studies have shown re-offending rates to be lower, other studies argue that this is marginal.

A community justice programme that is advocated by The Restorative Justice Consortium focuses on both the offender and the victim. The Consortium defines restorative justice as seeking to ' ... balance the concerns of the victim and the community with the need to reintegrate the offender into society. It seeks to assist the recovery of the victim and enable all parties with a stake in the justice process to participate fruitfully in it' (1998).

This general definition leads to the following key objectives:
- To attend to the needs of victims (material, financial, emotional and social).
- To prevent re-offending by integrating offenders into the community.
- To enable offenders to assume responsibility for their crimes.
- To foster a community that supports the rehabilitation of offenders and victims and is active in preventing crime.

These aims are based on the assumption that crime has its origins in social conditions and in community relationships, and that communities should take responsibility for crime prevention. It represents an approach that stands in contrast to the traditional 'retributive' justice perspective.

6.8.2 OFFENDER TREATMENT PROGRAMMES

Offender treatment programmes are initiatives that actually try to change the behaviour of offenders with the aim that they do not re-offend. In this way they are closely related to psychological interventions, and many offender treatment programmes are designed and implemented by psychologists working closely with the prison service. England and Wales have had a prison psychological service since 1946; offenders on probation may be able to receive psychological services in the community, and juvenile offenders are often referred to educational psychologists or clinical psychologists or psychiatrists who work with children. Offender treatment programmes are varied, but often involve psychotherapy (individually or in groups), behavioural therapies and cognitive therapies. These therapeutic approaches overlap, and more than one approach is often applied to individual offenders. Treatment programmes may include the use of anger management, counselling and social skills training.

Anger management

Most people find it hard to contain their anger from time to time, but there are a group of offenders who have great difficulty managing their feelings of anger. Novaco (1975) stressed the role of cognition in emotional arousal, and argued that anger in some individuals comes to the surface more quickly because they are already upset about other things. Novaco suggests that people who are aroused in this way find that anger helps

KEY DEFINITIONS

A **retributive based approach** to criminal justice sees the state as the violated party and imposes punishment as a deterrent.
Restorative justice, on the other hand, sees the victim as the violated party and stresses dialogue, negotiation and restitution.

KEY DEFINITIONS

Behavioural therapy tries to modify maladaptive behaviour without examining its underlying causes, whereas cognitive therapy focuses on the individual's attitudes and attempts to challenge inappropriate beliefs.
Psychotherapy tends to explore the client's unconscious fears and needs, with a view to bringing these out into the open.

them to feel in control of a situation. In this case no attempt should be made to stop these individuals from feeling angry, but they should be taught how to control and manage their anger. People in this situation also need to be able to learn how to deal with situations of conflict without resorting to aggression. Ainsworth (2000) suggests that anger management programmes with offenders are run as group sessions and usually contain three stages:

- Cognitive preparation: in this stage the individual is asked to think about their own patterns of anger, and to reflect upon the effects of their anger. Although there may have been some benefits for the offender, they would be asked to look at the negative consequences for themselves and others.
- Skill acquisition: in this stage the individual is encouraged to learn more effective ways of dealing with anger, and the situations that cause it. The skills are both cognitive and behavioural; for example rehearsing thoughts about controlling anger, or using techniques such as relaxation and assertiveness training. Ainsworth argues that this is not to be confused with aggressiveness, as the individual can be taught how to make a point in a calm and effective way without resorting to aggression as they may have done in the past.
- Application practice: in this stage individuals are encouraged to practice their skills through role-play.

Social skills training

One of the problems that some offenders suffer from is their inability to communicate effectively, which may lead to frustration (and aggression). They might find social interaction difficult, and as a result might have found difficulty in finding or holding on to a partner, friends or a job. Simple things like appropriate levels of eye contact, conversational skills and body language can all be addressed in social skills training. This might enable the offender to have more satisfactory relationships outside prison or in the workplace. Vennard and Hedderman (1998) suggest that good offender treatment programmes include skills based training that helps to improve problem solving, and social interaction, as well as challenging the attitudes and beliefs that underpin the offending behaviour.

Andrews et al. (1990, cited in Ainsworth, 2000) identified a number of characteristics that they argue are effective in offender rehabilitation:

- The programmes are very structured, and address particular problems in distinct ways.
- The staff are committed and have anti-criminal values.
- The programme targets criminal attitudes and values.
- Problem solving using cognitive and behaviour methods is taught.
- Programmes can be applied beyond the context of the punishment.

However, as Hollin (2001) points out, although social skills training does appear to modify behaviour, there is no conclusive research to suggest that it prevents re-offending after punishment. There are also problems with the motivation of the offender to change, as individuals may not see the long-term benefits of doing so.

Token economies

The behaviourist approach to rewards for certain types of compliance has been shown to be effective in the short term in relation to controlling the behaviour of offenders, especially in institutions. In both young offender institutions and in adult prisons token economies have been used successfully to encourage offenders to follow rules and maintain the

? FOR CONSIDERATION

Anger management can be very effective in a general context, but can also be applied to specific situations in which the offender might be prone to particular types of outburst.
- Think of examples of where this may happen.

⚖ EVALUATION ISSUES

EFFECTIVENESS

Anger management courses can be very effective if there is enough on-going support given to the person trying to change their behaviour. Teaching new strategies is only part of the process, being able to implement them is another. This is also true of the other treatment programmes described in this section, for example token economies tend only to last for the duration of the programme.

KEY DEFINITIONS

In a **token economy** specific desired behaviours are clearly defined. When an individual performs these behaviours, they receive a token as **reinforcement**; these tokens can be collected and cashed in for some kind of material reward. Token rewards are based upon the theory of **operant conditioning**.

EVALUATION ISSUES

GENERALISABILITY

Treatment programmes are not always generalisable; what works for some people may not work for others, and there are many other factors to consider, such as the severity of the crime and the length of sentence.

EVALUATION ISSUES

EFFECTIVENESS

The Sex Offender Treatment Programme is very effective but has been devised for a very specific type of offender, and cannot be generalised.

institution. Privileges can include working in the kitchen or prison library, watching television or being able to use facilities such as pool tables or use gym equipment. Studies (mostly in the USA, where the use of token economies is popular) have shown that token economies do increase the behaviours that are encouraged. Hobbs and Holt (1976) used token economies in three of four hostels in a young offender institution (the fourth hostel acted as a control). In the three hostels with a token economy in place, where rewards included sweets, soft drinks, the use of recreation facilities and passes home, there was an increase in desired behaviour. However, it is hard to evaluate the success of these programmes after release, and there are few studies that indicate long term success.

A multidisciplinary approach is adopted in the offender treatment programme illustrated in the key study by Beech et al. (1998) described below.

KEY STUDY

An evaluation of the prison Sex Offender Treatment Programme
Beech, Fisher and Beckett (1998)

Aim: This report was commissioned by the Home Office to evaluate the effectiveness of treatment for sex offenders in Category C prisons. The Sex Offender Treatment Programme (SOTP) began in 1991 and is currently run in 25 prisons. The programme consists of about 80 two-hour sessions aimed at increasing the offender's motivation to avoid re-offending and developing the self-management skills necessary to achieve this. The treatment approach is 'cognitive-behavioural' and involves offenders working in groups. The advantage of group-work is that the offender has to publicly acknowledge his need to change, and groups provide a context in which socially acceptable values are conveyed and reinforced. The cognitive aspect of the treatment involves recognising the distorted thinking that allows the contemplation of illegal sexual acts and understanding the impact of sexual abuse on victims. The behavioural component involves reducing sexual arousal to inappropriate fantasies.

Sample: Six prisons were selected, and two treatment groups from each prison were studied in detail; a total of 82 child abusers were involved.

Method: Comprehensive psychometric data were gathered from each of the men prior to treatment. At the end of treatment 5 men had dropped out, leaving 77 who were re-tested and interviewed. Nine months later, participants were contacted again for testing and interviewing (56 men remained at this stage, roughly 40 per cent of whom had left prison by then). The psychometric tests were designed to measure change in four main areas:
- Denial/admittance of deviant sexual interests and level of offending behaviours: how ready the offender was to admit to fantasising, or to deny the offending behaviours and the harm done to victims.
- Pro-offending attitudes: distorted thinking about sexual contacts with children.
- Predisposing personality factors: e.g. low self-esteem, under-assertiveness, inability to be intimate with other people, poor coping with negative emotions and failure to accept responsibility for own behaviour.
- Relapse prevention skills: e.g. ability to recognise and avoid situations where there is a risk of re-offending, accept that he is still a potential offender, even after treatment.

Results: Significant improvements were found in all four areas investigated following the SOTP. One-third of the offenders ended up with profiles that were indistinguishable from those of non-sexual offenders. Offenders were divided into three groups, depending on special inadequacy measures ('deviance') and the degree to which they admitted to their offences ('denial'). The treatment was most effective for low deviancy/low denial men and least effective for high deviancy men (irrespective of level of denial). Of the 56 men who agreed to be seen after nine months, 32 were still in prison. Overall, the changes brought about by the treatment had been maintained. A key finding was that men who found it harder to recognise personal culpability also failed to perceive themselves as a risk in the future. The positive effects of the programme were more marked in men who had attended more sessions. Of the men who had been released, practically all said they found the programme helpful, and interviews with these men's probation officers indicated a high level of satisfaction with the treatment programme.

Conclusions: The SOTP is an effective treatment for sex offenders in prison, and men who fail to show improvement should be made to repeat the programme. Beech et al. end by pointing out that the only true way of measuring the effectiveness of this programme is to carry out recidivism studies at two, five and ten year intervals.

6.8.3 ENVIRONMENTAL CRIME PREVENTION

One of the problems with explaining criminality in terms of the disposition of the person who commits the crime, is that it draws attention away from the physical deterrents that can be implemented to stop crime from being carried out. However, if the rational choice approach to crime is adopted, then eliminating the opportunity for the criminal to make the choice (by locking windows and doors more securely, for example) will have a positive effect on levels of crime. This approach has two purposes: to reduce levels of crime in the first place, and to increase the likelihood of catching offenders.

Crime prevention takes many forms, and these range from the things people do at home to community-wide and government initiatives. Hollin (2001) refers to what he calls reducing opportunity in terms of 'hardening the target' and 'removing the target'. Hardening the target simply refers to the ways in which objects and buildings are strengthened to reduce the possibility of theft. Removing the target refers to the possibility of taking away the things that might be stolen or damaged.

Surveillance

Another way in which crime can be prevented is through increasing the risk of detection. Many of the ways in which this can be implemented are related to types of surveillance. There are two types of surveillance; formal and informal. Informal surveillance is through community schemes such as Neighbourhood Watch, where individuals within communities are responsible for watching over each other's properties, especially when individual householders are away. Signs are often used as a deterrent (on lamp posts and in windows) and in order to make residents feel safer. Research suggests that Neighbourhood Watch schemes are useful in encouraging community spirit and increasing awareness of safety measures and behaviours that individuals can engage with.

> **KEY DEFINITIONS**
>
> **Hardening the target** can include installing sophisticated locking systems and alarms in motor vehicles and protecting houses and offices with secure locks, alarms, gates and timer switches on lights.
>
> **Removing the target** includes the use of credit cards instead of cash (although credit cards can be stolen, they are much harder to use than cash). Using safe transport systems for late shift workers, especially if they are women, also increases safety and removes a possible target.

There are ethical concerns about the use of surveillance techniques. People do not give their consent, and although these methods have reduced crime in some areas, and have helped with detection rates, there are genuine concerns about the rights of individuals.

FOR CONSIDERATION

- Is it ethical to use surveillance in public areas in the UK?
- What are your views on the use of CCTV?

EVALUATION ISSUES

REDUCTIONISM

Newman's model is reductionist as there are other variables that influence crime rates, such as deprivation, for example.

Formal surveillance can be carried out by the police or some kind of security service; the police are often seen as a deterrent, although there are obviously not enough police officers on the street at any one time to have a significant impact. However, the police are often used in situations where there may be an increased likelihood of crime, such as football matches or other large gatherings of people (Hollin, 2001). Security guards are often used to watch commercial premises, and sometimes in private residential areas. There are a number of studies that show the way in which a uniform can affect the behaviour of bystanders, and this principle is applied to a number of jobs in the public sector where the person wearing the uniform may face hostility, or need authority to prevent criminal behaviour from occurring.

People such as traffic wardens, car park attendants, ticket inspectors and door personnel all reduce the likelihood of vandalism, theft and other forms of criminal activity. Surveillance does not always involve people, and increasingly CCTV is being used to watch people who might be engaging in criminal activity. CCTV is often used in city centres, public buildings, supermarkets and football matches for example. A study that looked at the effect of CCTV (Burrows, 1980; cited in Hollin, 2001) showed that crime levels dropped dramatically with the installation of CCTV in four underground stations. In those stations there were 252 offences in the year prior to the introduction of CCTV, and 75 offences in the year after installation. This is a drop of 70 per cent, compared to a fall of 38 per cent in underground stations without CCTV for the same period.

Another way in which formal surveillance can take place is in the use of electronic tagging. This has become much more popular in recent years, and has many advantages, including the reduced cost of keeping the offender out of prison. Tagging usually involves the offender wearing an electronic tag around their ankle, which can be monitored by telephone and computer. With the use of a tag, the police or probation service can impose restrictions on movement and implement curfews if necessary.

Defensible space theory

The other way to reduce crime is to design environments that discourage crime. In the 1960s Jane Jacobs and Oscar Newman developed a concept known as defensible space theory. Defensible space is created by certain features, such as boundary markers separating public from private territory, or places from which territory owners can observe activity within their territory. They argued that the problem with the high rise flats built in the 1960s and 1970s was that they had no defensible space; where territory is shared no one claims ownership or shows respect for public areas such as communal walkways, balconies, lifts and play areas. If people have boundary markers, such as fences or private balconies they are more likely to report the invasion of that space, and will look after it more carefully.

The key study below looks at a recent initiative implemented by a number of police forces around the UK in which they work with planners, architects and builders to reduce the opportunity for crime.

> **KEY STUDY**
>
> *Secured by Design*
> **Association of Chief Police Officers for England, Wales and Northern Ireland (ACPO) (2003)**
>
> Secured by Design is the UK Police flagship initiative supporting the principles of designing out crime. It has a number of key features:

▶

- Secured by Design (SBD) is the corporate title for a family of national police projects involving the design for new homes, refurbished homes, commercial premises, car parks and other police crime prevention projects.
- It is primarily an initiative to encourage the building industry to adopt crime prevention measures to assist in reducing the opportunity for crime and the fear of crime and creating a safer, more secure environment. Secured by Design supports one of the Government's key planning objectives; the creation of secure, quality places where people wish to live and work.
- Research by Huddersfield University shows that residents living on Secured by Design developments are half as likely to be burgled, two and a half times less likely to suffer vehicle crime and suffer 25 per cent less criminal damage.

Secured by Design functions on two levels:
- The Developers Award is a certificate given to building developments which, following consultation with local police Architectural Liaison Officers (sometimes called Crime Prevention Design Advisors), are built to conform to the ACPO guidelines and so reduce the opportunity for crime.
- Licensed products: Secured by Design licensed company status is awarded to those companies producing security products, including doors and windows, which pass standards and tests nominated by the police service as 'Police Preferred Specification'.

Extract from SBD guidelines on multi-storey dwellings:
- The security of the development is enhanced by discouraging casual intrusion by non-residents. Public access should, therefore, be restricted. An access control system should be provided. This may be a managed concierge system, a Proximity Access Control (PAC) system and door entry phone system, or a combination of both.
- Optimum natural surveillance should be incorporated, whereby residents can see and be seen. Measures should include an unobstructed view from dwellings of the site, its external spaces and neighbouring homes, to include external paths, galleries, roadways, communal areas, drying areas, landscaping, garages and parking areas.
- A monitored Closed-circuit Television (CCTV) system covering the site area, with particular focus on key access points may be required.
- Appropriate lighting should be carefully designed to cover potential high risk areas. Good lighting will deter intruders and reduce the fear of crime.
- Landscaping is an important feature of this initiative. Landscaping should not impede natural surveillance and must not create potential hiding places for intruders, especially adjacent to footpaths or close to buildings where it may obscure doors and windows. Frontages should be in open view. Ornamental walls and hedges should not exceed 1 metre in height. Grass or low ground cover planting only should be used within 2 metres either side of a footpath. The location and species of trees should not allow them to obscure lighting or CCTV, or become climbing aids. The specification should take account of maintenance needs to ensure continued compliance as plants grow. The correct use of certain species of plants can help prevent graffiti and loitering, and in addition to fencing may be used to define/reinforce boundaries. Defensive planting, i.e. Berberis or similar may be utilised to achieve this purpose.
- Enclosures to balconies at all levels should be designed to exclude handholds and to eliminate the opportunity for climbing up, down or across between balconies.

CD-ROM

For a further key study about environmental crime prevention, see Crime: Additional key studies: MacDonald and Gifford (1989).

- Secure bicycle storage for residents and visitors should be considered.
- Ground floor windows and those that are easily accessible to entry must have key operated locks. Where necessary, opening restrictors or similar built-in mechanisms will be required.

SECTION A EXAM QUESTIONS

a Describe one type of punishment. [6]
b Discuss the effectiveness of types of punishment. [10]

a Describe one study of an offender treatment programme. [6]
b Discuss the methods used to research offender treatment programmes. [10]

a Describe one environmental crime prevention programme. [6]
b Discuss the problems with environmental crime prevention programmes. [10]

CD-ROM

For Section B sample exam questions see Crime: Sample exam questions.

BIBLIOGRAPHY

PSYCHOLOGY AND EDUCATION

Arnot, M. David, M. and Weiner, G. (1999) *Closing the Gender Gap: Post-War Education and Social Change.* London: Polity Press.

Ausubel, D.P. (1960) The use of advance organisers in the learning and retention of meaningful verbal material. *Journal of Educational Psychology,* 51, 267–72.

Ausubel, D.P. (1977) The facilitation of meaningful verbal learning in the classroom. *Journal of Educational Psychology,* 12, 162–78.

Bandura, A. (1965) Influence of models' reinforcement contingencies on the acquisition of imitative responses. *Journal of Personality and Social Psychology,* 1 (6), 589–95.

Bandura, A. (1977) *Social Learning Theory.* Morristown, NJ: General Learning Press.

Bandura, A. (1986) *Social foundations of thought and action: a social cognitive theory.* Englewood Cliffs, NJ: Prentice-Hall.

Best, L. (1993) Dragons, dinner ladies and ferrets: sex roles in children's books. *Sociology Review,* 2 (3), 6–8.

Black, P. and Wiliam, D. (1998) Assessment and classroom learning. *Assessment in Education,* 5 (1), 7–70.

Boaler, J. (1997) Reclaiming scholl mathematics: The girls fight back. *Gender and Education,* 9 (3), 285–306.

Boring, E.G. (1923) Intelligence as the tests test it. *New Republic,* 35, 35–37.

Bradshaw, J. Clegg, S. and Trayhum, D. (1995) An investigation into gender bias in educational software used in English primary schools. *Gender and Education,* 7 (2), 167–74.

Bronzaft, A.L. (1981) The effect of a noise abatement program on reading ability. *Journal of Environmental Psychology,* 1, 215–22.

Brooks L. (1997) Dyslexia: 100 years on. *Dyslexia Review Magazine,* Spring 1997.

Bruner, J.S. (1961) *The process of Education.* Cambridge, Mass: Harvard University Press.

Claxton, C.S. and Murrell, P.H. (1987) *Learning styles: Implications for improving educational practices.* Washington, D. C., Clearing House on Higher Education.

Cohen, S. Evans, G.W. Krantz, D.S. Stokols, D. and Kelly, S. (1981) Aircraft noise and children: longitudinal and cross-sectional evidence on adaptation to noise and the effectiveness of noise abatement. *Journal of Personality and Social Psychology,* 40, 331–45.

Coles, G. (2000) *Misreading reading: the bad science that hurts children.* Portsmouth, NH: Heinemann.

DeFries, J. and Alarcon, M. (1996) Genetics of specific reading disability. *Mental Retardation and Developmental Dusabilities Research Reviews,* 2, 39–47.

Demie, F. (2001) Ethnic and gender differences in educational achievement and implications for school improvement strategies. *Educational Research,* 43 (1), 91–106.

Feuerstein, R. (1979) *The dynamic assessment of retarded performers: The Learning Potential Assessment Device: theory, instruments, and techniques.* Baltimore: University Park Press.

Fontana, D. (1995) *Psychology for Teachers.* London: Macmillan Press.

Freeman, J. (1979) *Gifted Children: Their identification and development in a social context.* Lancaster: MTP Press.

Gagné, R.M. (1985) *Conditions of Learning.* (4th edition) New York: Holt.

Gifford, R. (1997) *Environmental Psychology.* Needham Heights: Allyn and Bacon.

Gilroy, P. (1990) The end of anti-racism. *New Community,* vol 17, no. 1.

Gray, J.A. and Buffery, A.W.H. (1971) Sex differences in emotional and cognitive behaviour in mammals including man: adaptive and neural bases. *Acta Psychologia,* 35, 89–111.

Green, S. (2002) Criterion referenced assessment as a guide to learning – the importance of progression and reliability. *Paper presented at the Association for the Study of Evaluation in Education in Southern Africa International Conference,* Johannesburg, July 2002.

Griggs, S. and Dunn, R. (1996) Hispanic-American students and learning style. *Emergency Librarian,* 23 (2), 11–16.

Hall, J. (1989) Chronic psychiatric handicaps. In Hawton, K. Salkovskis, P.M. Kirk, J. and Clark, D.M. (eds) *Cognitive Behaviour Therapy for Psychiatric Problems.* Oxford: Oxford Medical Publications.

Haney, C. Banks, C. and Zimbardo, P. (1973) A study of prisoners and guards in a simulated prison. *Naval Research Reviews,* 30 (9), 4–17.

Hastings, N. and Chantrey Wood, K. (2002) *Reorganising Primary Classroom Learning.* Buckingham: Open University Press.

Hirohito, D.S. and Seligman, M.E.P. (1975) Generality of learned helplessness in man. *Journal of Personality and Social Psychology,* 31 (2), 311–327.

Honey, P. and Mumford, A. (1986) *Using your Learning Styles.* Maidenhead: Honey.

Honey P. and Mumford A. (1992) *The Manual of Learning Styles.* Maidenhead: Honey.

Hornby, G. (1999) Inclusion or delusion: can one size fit all? *Support for Learning,* vol. 14, no. 4.

Hyde J.S. Fennema, E. and Lamon S. J. (1990) Gender differences in mathematical performance: a meta-analysis. *Psychological Bulletin,* 107, 135–55.

Ireson, J. Hallam, S. Hack, S. Clark, H. and Plewis, I. (2002) Ability grouping in English secondary schools: effects on attainment in English, mathematics and science. *Educational Research and Evaluation,* 8 (3), 299–318.

Kegan, R. (1994) *In Over Our Heads: The Mental Demands of Modern Life.* Cambridge, Harvard University Press.

Kidd, R. and Hornby, G. (1993) Transfer from special to mainstream. *British Journal of Special Education,* 20, 17–19.

Kidscape (1999) *Long-Term Effects of Bullying.* Kidscape Survey, November 1999.

Kirby, M. et al. (1997) *Sociology in Perspective.* Oxford: Heinemann.

LeFrançois, G.R. (1997) *Psychology for Teaching* (9th Edition) Belmont: Wandsworth Publishing Company.

Lepper, M.R. and Greene, D. (1975) Turning play into work: effects of adult surveillance and extrinsic rewards on children's intrinsic motivation. *Journal of Personality and Social Psychology,* 31 (3), 479–86.

Meichenbaum, D. and Goodman, J. (1971) Training impulsive children to talk to themselves: a means of developing self-control. *Journal of Abnormal Psychology*, 77, 115–126.

Mirza, H. (1992) *Young, Female and Black*. London: Routledge.

Mirza, H. (1997) Black women in education: a collective movement for social change, *Black Feminisn: A Reader*. London: Routledge, 270–6.

Moreno, J.M. and Torrego, J.C. (1999) Fostering pro-social behaviour in the Spanish school system: a whole school approach. *Emotional and Behavioural Difficulties*, 4 (2), 23–31.

Myttas, N. (2001) Understanding and recognising ADHD. *Practice Nursing*, 12 (7), 278–280.

Neill, A.S. (1960) *Summerhill*. New York: Hart.

Piaget, J. (1969) *The Mechanisms of Perception*. New York: Basic Books.

Pilcher, J. (1999) *Women in Contemporary Britain: an Introduction*. London: Routledge.

Rogers, C.R. (1951) *Client-centred Therapy*. Boston: Houghton Mifflin.

Rogers, C.R. (1961) *On Becoming a Person*. London: Constable.

Rosenfield, P. Lambert, N.M. and Black, A. (1985) Desk arrangements effects on student classroom behaviour. *Journal of Educational Psychology*, 77 (1), 101–108.

Rosenthal, R. and Jacobson, L.F. (1968) Teacher expectations for the disadvantaged. *Scientific American*, 218 (4), pp.19–23.

Seligman, M.E.P. and Maier, S.F. (1967) Failure to escape traumatic shock. *Journal of Experimental Psychology*. 7 (74), 1–9.

Shield, B. and Dockrell, J. (2003) The effects of noise on the attainments and cognitive performance of primary school children. *Executive Summary Report*, South Bank University, London.

Smith, D.J. and Tomlinson, S. (1989) *The School Effect: A Study of Multi-Racial Comprehensives*. London: Policy Studies Institute.

Sommer, R. and Olsen, H. (1980) The soft classroom. *Environment and Behaviour*, 12 (1), 3–16.

Stone, M. (1981) *The Education of the Black Child in Britain: the Myth of Multiracial Education*. London: Fontana.

Trowler, P. (1996) *Investigating Education and Training*. London: Collins.

Vygotsky, L.S. (1983) School instruction and mental development. In Donaldson M, Grieve R and Pratt C, *Early Childhood Development and Education*. Oxford: Blackwell.

Vygotsky, L.S. (1962) *Thought and Language*. Cambridge, Mass: MIT Press.

Watson, J.B. and Rayner, R. (1920) Conditioned emotional reactions. *Journal of Experimental Psychology*, 3 (1), 1–14.

Wright, C. (1992) Early education: multi-racial primary school classrooms. In Gill, D, Mayor, B and Blair, M (eds) *Racism and Education: Structures and Strategies*. London: Sage.

Yee, D.K. and Eccles, J.K. (1988) Parent perceptions and attributions for children's math achievement. *Sex Roles*, 19, 317–33.

Zentall, S.S. (1983) Learning environments: a review of physical and temporal factors. *EEQ: Exceptional Educational Quarterly*, 4, 90–115.

PSYCHOLOGY AND HEALTH

Ajzen, I. (1991) The theory of planned behaviour. *Organisation Behaviour and Human Decision Processes*, 50, 179–211.

Ajzen, I. and Fishbein, M. (1980) *Understanding attitudes and predicting social behaviour*. Englewood Cliffs, NJ: Prentice-Hall.

Anderson K.O. and Masur F.T. (1983) Psychological preparation for invasive medical and dental procedures. *Journal of Behavioural Medicine*, 6, 1–40.

Arber, S. (1999) Gender. In Gordon D. Shaw M. Dorling D. and Davey Smith G. (eds) *Inequalities in Health*. University of Bristol: The Policy Press.

Bandura, A. (1965) Influence of models' reinforcement contingencies on the acquisition of imitative responses. *Journal of Personality and Social Psychology*, 1 (6), 589–95.

Bandura, A. (1986) *Social foundations of Thought and Action: A Social Cognitive Theory*. Englewood Cliffs, NJ: Prentice-Hall.

Beales, J.C. (1979) The effect of attention and distraction on pain among children attending a hospital casualty department. In Oborne DJ, Gruneberg, MM and Eiser, JR (eds) *Research in Psychology and Medicine*, vol 1. London: Academic Press.

Bourhis, R.Y., Roth, S. and MacQueen, G. (1989) Communication in the hospital setting: A survey of medical and everyday language use among patients, nurses and doctors. *Social Science Medicine*, 28 (4), 339–46.

Carlen, P. Wall, P.D. Nadvorna, H. and Steinbach, T. (1979) Phantom limbs and related phenomena in recent traumatic amputations. *Neurology*, 28, 211–17.

Carroll, D. and Bowsher, D. (1993) *Pain Management and Nursing Care*. Oxford: Butterworth-Heinemann.

Carroll, D., Davey Smith, G. and Bennet P. (1997) Socio economic status and health. In Baum, A. Newman, S. Weinman, J. West, R. and McManus, C. (eds) *Cambridge Handbook of Psychology, Health and Medicine*, Cambridge: Cambridge University Press.

Chapman, C.R. Casey, K.L. Dubner, R. Foley, K.M. Gracely, R.H. and Reading, A.E. (1985) Pain measurement: an overview. *Pain*, 22, 1–31.

Choo, P.W. Rand, C.S. Inui, T.S. Ting Lee, M. Canning, C. and Platt, R. (2001) A cohort study of possible risk factors for over-reporting of antihypertensive adherence. *BMC Cardiovascular Disorders*, 1 (6).

Clark, D.M. Salkovskis, P.M. Hackmann, A. Wells, A. Ludgate, J. and Gelder, M. (1999) Brief cognitive therapy for panic disorder: A randomised controlled trial. *Journal of Consulting and Clinical Psychology*, 67 (4), 583–589.

Davis Kirsch, S. and Pullen, N. (2003) Evaluation of a school-based education program to promote bicycle safety. *Health Promotion Practice*, 4 (2), 138–145.

DiMatteo, M.R. Lepper, H.S. and Croghan, T.W. (2000) Depression is a risk factor for noncompliance with medical treatment. *Archives of International Medicine*, 160, 2101–2107.

Freidman, M. and Rosenman, R.H. (1959) Association of specific overt behaviour pattern with blood and cardiovascular findings. *Journal of the American Medical Association*. 169 (12), 1286–95.

Gil, K.M. Keefe, F.J. Sampson, H.A. McCaskill, C.C. Rodin, J. and Crisson, J.E. (1988) Direct observation of scratching behaviour in children with atopic dermatitis. *Behaviour Therapy*, 19, 213–27.

Gilbert, P. (2000) *Overcoming depression*. London: Robinson Publishing.

Gillmore, M.R. and Hill, C.T. (1981) Reactions to patients who complain of pain: effects of ambiguous diagnosis. *Journal of Applied Social Psychology*, 11 (1), 13–22.

Goffman, E. (1971) *Asylums*. Harmondsworth: Penguin.

Haight, F.A. (2001) Accident proneness: The history of an idea. *Institute of Transportation Studies*, University of California.

Harris, T. (1997) Life events and health. In Baum, A, Newman, S, Weinman J, West, R and McManus, C (eds) *Cambridge Handbook of Psychology, Health and Medicine*. Cambridge: Cambridge University Press.

Hill, J.M. and Trist, E.L. (1953) A consideration of industrial accidents as a means of withdrawal from the work situation. *Human Relations*, 6, 357–80.

Hochbaum, G.M. (1958) *Public participation in medical screening programmes: a sociopsychological study* (Public Health Service Publication 572) US Government Washington DC: Printing Office.

Jacquess, D.L. and Finney, J.W. (1994) Previous injuries and behaviour problems predict children's injuries. *Journal of Pediatric Psychology*, 19 (1), 79–89.

Janis, I.L. and Feshbach, S. (1953) Effects of fear-arousing communications. *The Journal of Abnormal and Social Psychology*, 48 (1), 78–92.

Kent, G. and Dalgleish, M. (1993) *Psychology and Medical Care*. London: Saunders.

Lando, H.A. (1977) Successful treatment of smokers with a broad-spectrum behavioural approach. *Journal of Consulting and Clinical Psychology*, 45, 361–6.

Langley, J. and Silva, P.A. (1982) Childhood accidents: parents' attitudes to prevention. *Australian Pediatric Journal*, 18, 247–9.

Ley, P. (1988) *Communicating with Patients*. London: Chapman.

Ley, P. (1997) Compliance among patients. In Baum, A, Newman, S, Weinman J, West, R and McManus, C (eds) *Cambridge Handbook of Psychology, Health and Medicine*. Cambridge: Cambridge University Press.

Lustman, P.J. Griffith, L.S. Freedman, K.E. and Clouse, R.E. (2000) Fluoxetine for depression in diabetes. *Diabetes Care*, 23 (5), 618–623.

Maguire, P. and Rutter, D. (1976) Training medical students to communicate. In Bennett, A.E. (ed.) *Communication Between Doctors and Patients*. Oxford: Oxford University Press.

Meichenbaum, D. (1985) *Stress Inoculation Training*. New York: Pergamon Press.

Melzack, R. (1975) The McGill Pain Questionnaire: major properties and scoring methods. *Pain*, 1, 277–99.

Melzack, R. and Torgerson, W.S. (1971) On the language of pain. *Anesthesiology*, 34, 50–59.

Melzack, R. and Wall, P.D. (1965) Pain mechanisms: a new theory. *Science*, 150, 971–9.

Melzack, R. and Wall, P.D. (1996) *The Challenge of Pain*. London: Penguin.

Melzack, R, Wall, P.D. and Ty, T.C. (1982) Acute pain in an emergency clinic: latency in the onset and descriptor patterns. *Pain*, 14, 33–43.

Mersky H. (1986) Classification of chronic pain: descriptions of chronic pain syndromes and definitions of pain terms. *Pain*, Supplement 3, S1–S225.

Monat, A. and Lazarus, R.S. (eds) (1977) *Stress and Coping: an Anthology*. New York: Columbia University Press.

Moolchan, E.T., Ernst, M. and Henningfield, J.E. (2000) A review of tobacco smoking in adolescents: Treatment Implications. *Journal of the American Academy of Child and Adolescent Psychiatry*, 39 (6), June, pp 82–693.

Ogden, J. (1986) *Health Psychology: a Textbook*. Buckingham: Open University Press.

Orford, J. and Velleman, R. (1991) The environmental intergenerational transmission of alcohol problems: a comparison of two hypotheses. *British Journal of Medical Psychology*, 64, 189–200.

Parry, O. Platt, S. and Thomson, C. (2000) Out of sight, out of mind: workplace smoking bans and the relocation of smoking at work. *Health Promotion International*, 15 (2), 125–33.

Pitts, M. (1996) *The Psychology of Preventive Health*. London: Routledge.

Povey, R. Conner, M. Sparks, P. James, R. and Shepherd, R. (2000) Application of the Theory of Planned Behaviour to two dietary behaviours: roles of perceived control and self-efficacy. *British Journal of Health Psychology*, 5, 121–39.

Ralphs, J. (1993) The cognitive behavioural treatment of chronic pain. In Carroll D and Bowsher D (eds) *Pain Management and Nursing Care*. Oxford: Butterworth-Heinemann.

Richards, et al (1982) Assessing pain behaviour: the UAB Pain Behaviour Scale. *Pain*, 14, 393–8.

Rimm, E.B. Giovannucci, E.L. Willett, W.C. Colditz, G.A. Ascherio, A. Rosner, B. and Stampfer, M.J. (1991) Prospective study of alcohol consumption and risk of coronary heart disease. *Lancet*, 338, 464–8.

Robinson, L.A. Klesges, R.C. Zbikowski, S. and Galser, R. (1997) Predictors of risk for different stages of adolescent smoking in a biracial sample. *Journal of Consultative Clinical Psychology*, 65, 653–62.

Rosenhan, D.L. and Seligman, M.E.P. (1984) *Abnormal Psychology*. New York: Norton.

Ruble, D.N. (1977) Premenstrual symptoms: a reinterpretation. *Science*, 197, 291–2.

Russell, M.A.H. Wilson, C. Taylor, C. and Baker, C.D. (1979) Effect of general practitioners' advice against smoking. *British Medical Journal*, 2, 231–5.

Safer, M.A. Tharps, Q.J. Jackson, T.C. and Leventhal, H. (1979) Determinants of three stages of delay in seeking care at a medical clinic. *Medical Care*, 17 (1), 11–29.

Savage, R. and Armstrong, D. (1990) Effect of general practitioner's consulting style on patients' satisfaction: a controlled study. *British Medical Journal*, 30, 968–70.

Sayette, M.A. and Hufford, M.R. (1997) Alcohol abuse/acoholism. In Baum, A, Newman, S, Weinman J, West, R and McManus, C (eds) *Cambridge Handbook of Psychology, Health and Medicine*. Cambridge: Cambridge University Press.

Selye, H. (1977) Selections from the stress of life. In Monat, A and Lazarus, RS (eds) *Stress and Coping: an Anthology*. New York: Columbia University Press.

Strategic Safety Associates (2003) *Accident Repeaters*. SSA, Inc.

Sutton, S. (1997) The theory of planned behaviour. In Baum, A, Newman, S, Weinman J, West, R and McManus, C (eds) *Cambridge Handbook of Psychology, Health and Medicine*. Cambridge: Cambridge University Press.

SWOV Institute for Road Safety Research (1997) What are the principle causes of accidents with bicyclists? *SWOV Research Activities* No. 7. Leidersham, The Netherlands: SWOV.

Trowler, P. (1996) *Investigating Health, Welfare and Poverty*. London: HarperCollins.

Turk, D.C. and Meichenbaum, D. (1991) Adherence to self-care regimes: the patient's perspective. In Sweet J.J., Rosenskynad R.H. and Tovian S.M. (eds) *Handbook of Clinical Psychology in Medical Settings*. New York: Plenum.

Turk, D.C. Wack, J.T. and Kerns, R.D. (1985) An empirical examination of the 'pain-behaviour' construct. *Journal of Behavioural Medicine*, 8 (2), 119–30.

Turner, J.A. and Chapman, C.R. (1982) Psychological interventions for chronic pain. A critical review. 2. Operant conditioning, hypnosis, and cognitive behavioural therapy. *Pain*, 12, 24–46.

Ussher, J. (1997) Gender issues and women's health. In Baum, A., Newman, S., Weinmann, J., West, R. and McManus, C. (eds.) Cambridge Handbook of Psychology, Health and Medicine, Cambridge University Press.

Von Frey, M. (1895) Untersuchungen Über die Sinnesfunctionen der Menschlichen Haut Erste Abhandlung: Druckempfindung und Schmerz. Leipzig: Hirzel.

Wallston, K.A. Wallston, B.S. and DeVellis, R. (1978) Development of the Multidimensional Health Locus of Control (MHLC) Scales. *Health Education Monographs*, 6 (2), 160–70.

Weinman, J. (1997) Doctor–patient communication. In Baum, A, Newman, S, Weinman J, West, R and McManus, C (eds) *Cambridge Handbook of Psychology, Health and Medicine*. Cambridge: Cambridge University Press.

PSYCHOLOGY AND ORGANISATIONS

Adams, J.S. (1965) Inequity in social exchange. In *Advances in Experimental Social Psychology. Vol 2.* New York: Academic Press.

Alderfer, C.P. (1972) *Human Needs in Organizational Settings.* New York: Free Press.

Alimo-Metcalfe, B. and Alban-Metcalfe, R.J. (2001) The construction of a new transformational leadership. *Journal of Occupational and Organisational Psychology,* 74, 1–27.

Anderson, L. and Wilson, S. (1997) Critical incident technique. In D.L. Whetzel and G.L. Wheaton (eds), *Applied Measurement Methods in Industrial Psychology,* (89–112) Palo Alto, CA: Davies-Black.

Atkinson, R.L. Atkinson, R.C., Smith, E.E. and Hildgard, E.R. (1987) *Introduction to Psychology.* (9th edition). Orlando, FL: Harcourt Brace Jovanovich.

Bandura, A. (1977) Self-efficacy. *Psychological Review,* 84, 191–215.

BPS: The British Psychological Society (2001) *Careers in Psychology.* Student Information Leaflet.

Belbin, R.M. (1981) *Management Teams.* London: Heinemann Educational Books.

Belbin, R.M. (1993) *Team Roles at Work.* Oxford: Butterworth Heinemann.

Beshir, M.Y., El-Sabagh, A.S., El-Nawawi, M.A. (1981) Time on task effect on tracking performance under heat stress. *Ergonomics,* 24, 95–102.

Blakemore, C. (1988) *The Mind Machine.* London. BBC publications.

Brownell, J. (1985) A model for listening instructions: *Management Applications ABCA Bulletins,* 48(3). 39–44.

Bull, P. (2001) Nonverbal communication. *The Psychologist,* 14, 644–647.

Cattell, R.B. (1965) *The Scientific Analysis of Personality.* Hammondsworth: Penguin.

Cartwright, S. and Cooper, C.L. (1996) Public policy and occupational and health psychology in Europe. *Journal of Occupational Health Psychology.* 1, 349–61.

Chmiel, N. (ed) *Introduction to Work and Organizational Psychology: A European Perspective.* Blackwell Publishing Limited.

Cohen, S. and Weinstein, N. (1981) Non-auditory effects of noise on behaviour and health. *Journal of Personality and Social Psychology.* 37, 36–70.

Cooper, C.L., Sloan, S. and Williams, S. (1987) *Occupational Stress Indicator.* Windsor: NFER/Nelson.

Corbett, M. (1997) *Wired and Emotional.* People Management, June, p.26.

Daft, R.L. Lengel and Trevino. (1987) Message equivocality, media selection. *MIS Quarterly II,* 355–366.

Dalton, M. (1950) Conflict between staff and line managerial officers. *American Sociological Review,* 15, 107–120.

De Nisi, A.S. and Mitchell, J.L. (1978) An analysis of peer ratings as predictors and criterion measures and a proposed new application. *Academy of Management Review,* 3, 369–374.

Dyer, W.G. (1977) *Team Building: Issues and alternatives.* Reading MA: Addison-Wesley.

Eysenck, H.J. (1953) *The Structure of Human Personality.* London: Methuen.

Fiedler, F.E. (1967) *A Theory of Leadership Effectiveness.* New York: McGraw Hill.

Field, R.H.G. and House, R.J. (1990) A Test of the Vroom and Yetton model using manager and subordinate reports. *Journal of Applied Psychology* 75, pp362–6.

Fine, B.J. and Kobrick, J.L. (1978) Effects of altitude and heat on complex cognitive tasks. *Human Factors, 20,* 115–122.

Fombrun, C.J. and Laud, R.L. (1983) Strategic issues in performance appraisal: Theory and practice. *Personnel,* November – December, 23–31.

Fox, D.K., Hopkins, B.L. and Anger, W.K. (1987) Long Term effects of token economy on safety performance in open pit mining. *Journal of Applied Behaviour Anaylsis.* 20, 215–224.

Friedman, M. and Rosenman, R.H. (1959) Association of specific overt behaviour pattern with blood and cardiovascular findings. *Journal of American Medical Association.* 169, 1286–96.

Girndt, T. (1997) An intervention strategy to managing diversity: discerning conventions. *European Journal of Work and Organizational Psychology,* 6(2), 227–40.

Glass, D.E. and Singer, J.E. (1972) *Urban Stress.* New York: Academic Press.

Goldthorpe, J et al. (1968) *The Affluent Worker.* Cambridge University Press.

Gould, S.J. (1982) *The Mismeasure of Man.* New York: Norton.

Greenberg, J. and Baron, R.A. (1995) *Behaviour in Organizations.* (6th edn.) Prentice-Hall International Incorporated.

Grimshaw, J. (1999) *Employment and Health-Psychological Stress in the Workplace.* The British Library.

Hackman, J.R. and Oldham, G.R. (1975) Development of the job diagnostic survey. *Journal of Applied Psychology,* 60, 2, 159–170.

Hartston, W.R. and Mottram, R.D. (1976) *Personality Profiles of Managers: a study of occupational differences.* Cambridge, UK: Industrial Training Research Unit.

Hawkins, L.H. and Armstrong-Esther, C.A. (1978) Circadian rhythms and night shift working in nurses. *Nursing Times.* May 4th. 49–52.

Henry, J. (2003) Positive Organisations, *The Psychologist,* 16, No3, 138–139.

Herzberg, F. (1966) *Work and the Nature of Man.* Cleveland: World.

Hutton, W. (1985) *The State We're In.* London: Cape.

Institute of Personnel and Development, (1996) Occupational health and organisational effectiveness. *Key Facts,* December, p 1.

Ivancevich, J.M. (1977) Different goal setting treatments and their effects on performance and job satisfaction. *Academy of Management Journal,* 20, 406–419.

Ivancevich, J.M. and Matteson, M.T. (1980) *Stress at Work.* Glenview IL: Scott Foresman and Co.

Ivonson, G.H., Smith, P.C., Branwick, M.T., Gibson, W.M. and Paul, K.B. (1989) Construction of a Job In General Scale: A comparison of Global, Composite and Specific Measures. *Journal of Applied Psychology* 74, 193–200.

Jamal, M. (1981) Shiftwork related to job attitudes, social participation and withdrawal behaviour: a study of nurses and industrial workers. *Personnel Psychology,* 34, 535–547.

Janis, I.L., (1972) *Victims of Groupthink: A psychological study of foreign policy decisions and fiascos.* Boston: Houghton Mifflin.

Kanter, R.M. (1977) *Men and Women of the Corporation.* New York: Basic Books.

Kohn, A. (1993) Why incentive plans cannot work. *Harvard Business Review,* September/October, 54–63.

Kondrasuk, J.N. (1981) Studies in MBO effectiveness. *Academy of Management Review,* 6, 419–430.

Kunin, T. (1955) The construction of a new type of attitude measure. *Personnel Psychology,* 8, 65–78.

Latham, G.P. and Wexley, K.N. (1981) *Increasing Productivity Through Performance Appraisal.* Reading, M.A. Addison – Wesley.

Latham, G.P. and Saari, L.M. (1980) The situational interview. *Journal of Applied Psychology,* 65, 422–427.

Lawler, E.E., (1981) *Pay and Organisational Development.* Reading: Mass: Addison-Wesley

Leavitt, H.J. (1951) Some effects of certain communication patterns on group performance. *Journal of Abnormal and Social Psychology,* 46, 38–50.

Lazarus, R. and Folkman, S. (1984) *Stress Appraisal and Coping.* New York: Springer.

Lewin, K., Lippitt, R. and White, R. (1959) Patterns of aggressive behaviour in experimentally created "social climates". *Journal of Social Psychology.* 10, 271–99.

Locke, E.A. (1968) Toward a theory of task motivation and incentives. *Organizational Behaviour and Human Performance,* 3, 157–89.

Locke, E.A. and Latham L. (1979) *Organised dynamics.* New York: American Management Association.

Lord, R.G. and Hohenfeld, J.A. (1979) Longitudinal field assessment of Equity effects on the performance of major league baseball players. *Journal of Applied Psychology* 64, February, 19–26.

Makin, P.J., Eveleigh, C.W.J. and Dale, B.G. (1991) The influence of member role preferences and leader characteristics on the effectiveness of quality circles. *International Journal of Human resource Management,* 2, (2), 193–204.

Makin, P. Cooper, C. and Cox, C. (1996) *Organisations and the Psychological Contract.* The British Psychological Society.

Maslow, A. (1943) A Theory of Human Motivation. *Psychological Review,* Vol. 50, No 4, 370–396.

Maslow, A. (1954) *Motivation and Personality.* New York: Harper and Row.

Maslow, A. (1971) *The Farther Reaches of Human Nature.* Harmondsworth: Penguin Books.

Maund, L. (1999) *Understanding People and Organisations: An introduction to organisational behaviour.* Stanley Thornes.

Mayo, E. (1933) The Human Problems of an Industrial Civilisation. Cambridge. Harvard University Press.

McBriarty, M.A. (1988) Performance appraisal: some unintended consequences. *Public Personnel Management,* Winter, 423.

McClelland, D.C. (1965) Achievement motivation can be learned. *Harvard business Review,* 43, 6–24.

McCormick, E.J. Jeanneret, P. and Meacham, R.C. (1972) A study of job characteristics and job dimensions as based on the position analysis questionnaires. *Journal of Applied Psychology,* vol. 36, 347–68.

McGregor, D.M. (1960) *The Human Side of Enterprise.* New York: McGraw-Hill

Mckenna, E. F. (1998) *Business Psychology and Organisational Behaviour: A Student's Handbook.* (second edition) Psychology Press.

Moorhead, G. and Griffin, R.W. (1995) *Organisational Behaviour: Managing People and organisations.* (fourth edition), Boston: Houghton Mifflin.

Moorhead, G. Ferrence, R.K. and Neck, C.P. (1991) Group decision fiascos continue; Space Shuttle "Challenger" and a revised groupthink framework. *Human Relations,* 44, 539–550.

Nealey, S.M. (1964) Determining worker preferences among employee benefit programmes. *Journal of Applied Psychology,* 48,7–12.

Nemeth, C. and Owens, J. (1996) The Value of Minority Dissent. In: West, M.A. (ed.) *Handbook of Work Psychology.* Chichester: Wiley.

Oldham, G.R. and Fried, Y. (1987) Employee reactions to workspace characteristics. *Journal of Applied Psychology* 72,75–80.

Pennington, D.C. (1986) *Essential Psychology.* Sevenoaks, UK: Edward Arnold.

Phillips, A.P. and Dipboyle, R.L. (1989) Correlational tests of predictions from a process model of the interview. *Journal of Applied Psychology.* 74, 41–52.

Piliavin, M. Rodin, J.A. and Piliavin, J. (1969) Good Samaritanism: An underground phenomenon? *Journal of Personality and Social Psychology,* 13, 289–299.

Porter, L.W. (1961) A study of perceived need satisfaction in bottom and middle management jobs. *Journal of Applied Psychology,* 45, 1–10.

Reason, J. (1987) The Chernobyl Errors. *Bulletin of the British Psychological Society,* 40, 201–206.

Riggio, R.E. (1999) *Introduction to Industrial/Organizational Psychology.* (3rd edn.) Prentice Hall.

Robbins, S.P. (1989) *Training in Inter-Personal Skills: Tips for managing people at work.* New York: Prentice Hall.

Rotter, J.B. (1966) Generalised expectancies for internal versus external control of reinforcement. *Psychological Monographs,* 8 (1, whole number 609).

Saville & Holdsworth Ltd. (1984) *The Occupational Personality Questionnaires.* Thames Ditton, Surrey: Saville & Holdsworth Ltd.

Schufeli, W.B. and Enzmann, D.U. (1998) *The Burnout Companion to Study and Practice: a Critical Analysis.* London: Taylor and Francis.

Seyle, H. (1974) *Stress without distress.* Philadelphia: Lippincott.

Seyle, H. (1985) History and present status of the stress concept. In A. Monat and R.S. Lazarus (eds) *Stress and Coping* (2nd edn). New York: Columbia University Press.

Shaw, M.E. (1964) Communication networks. In Berkowitz, L. (ed) *Advances in Experimental Social Psychology,* vol 1. New York Academic Press.

Smith, P.C., Kendall, L.M. and Hulin, L.L. (1969) *The Measurement of Satisfaction in Work and Retirement.* Chicago: Rand McNally.

Sternberg, R.J.and Soriano, E.J (1984) Styles of conflict resolution. *Journal of Personality and Social Psychology,* July, 115–126.

Sutton, R.I. and Rafaeli, A. (1987) Characteristics of work stations as potential occupational stressors. *Academy of Management Journal.* 30, 260–276.

Tannen, D. (1995) *Talking 9 to 5.* New York: Avon.

Tanaka, M., Tochihara, Y., Yamazaki, S., Ohnaka, T. and Yoshida, K. (1983) Thermal reaction and manual performance during cold exposure while wearing cold-protective clothing. *Ergonomics* 26, 141–149.

Thomas, K. W. (1976) Conflict and Conflict Management. In M. Dunnet (ed), *Handbook of Industrial and Organisational Psychology.* Skokie, IL: Rand McNally.

Thomas, K.W. (1977) Toward multidimensional values in teaching: the example of conflict behaviours. *Academy of Management Review,* 2, July, 484–490.

Umstot, D. D. Bell, C.H. and Mitchell, T.R. (1976) Effects of job enrichment on satisfaction and productivity: implications for job design. *Journal of Applied Psychology*, 61, 4, 379–394.

Unsworth, K.L. and West, M.A. (2000) Teams: the challenges of co-operative work. In: Chmiel, N. (ED.) *Introduction to Work and Organizational Psychology: A European Perspective*. Blackwell Publishing Limited.

Van Fleet, D.D. and Griffin, R.W. (1989) Quality Circles: A review and suggested future directions. In C. L. Cooper and I.T. Robertson (eds.) *International Review of Industrial and Organizational Psychology*. Chichester: Wiley.

Vecchio, R. P. (1991), *Organisational Behaviour*. (second edition), Orlando, FL: The Dryden Press.

Vernon, H.M. (1936) *Accidents and their Prevention*. London: Cambridge University Press.

Vroom, V.H. and Jago, A.G. (1988) *The New Leadership: Managing participation in organisations*. New York: Prentice Hall.

Vroom, V.H. and Yetton, P.W. (1973) *Leadership and Decision Making*. Pittsburgh: University of Pittsburgh Press.

Walton, E. (1961) How efficient is the grapevine? *Personnel*, 28, 45–49.

Wallach, M.A. and Kogan, N. (1965) The Roles of Information, Discussion and Consensus in Group Risk-Taking. *Journal of Experimental Social Psychology*, 1, 1–19.

Wechsler, D. (1981) *Manual for Wechsler Adult Intelligence Scale*. (Revised). San Antonio, TX: The Psychological Corporation.

Weinstein, N.D. (1977) Noise and intellectual performance: A confirmation and extension. *Journal of Applied Psychology*, 62, 104–107.

PSYCHOLOGY AND ENVIRONMENT

Altman, I (1975) *The Environment and Social Behaviour*. Monterey, CA: Brooks/Cole

Appleyard, D. (1970) Styles and methods of structuring a city. *Environment and Behaviour*, 2, 101–117.

Appleyard, D. (1976) *Planning a Pluralistic City*. Cambridge, MA: M.I.T. Press.

Bailenson, J.N. Blascovich, J. Beall, A.C. and Loomis, J.M. (2003) Interpersonal distance in immersive virtual environments. *Personality and Social Psychology Bulletin*, 29, 819–833.

Baron, R.A. and Bell, P.A (1975) Aggression and heat: Mediating effects of prior provocation and exposure to an aggressive model. *Journal of Personality and Social Psychology*, 31, 825–832.

Baron, R.A. (1976) The reduction of aggression: A field study of the influence of incompatible reactions. *Journal of Applied Social Psychology*, 6, 260–274.

Baron, R.M. Mandel, D.R. Adams, C.A and Griffen, L.M (1976) Effects of social density in university residential environments. *Journal of Personality and Social Psychology*, 34, 434–446.

Baum, A. and Davis, G.E. (1976) Spatial and social aspects of crowding perception. *Environment and Behaviour*, 8, 527–545.

Baum, A. and Greenberg, C.I. (1975) Waiting for a crowd: The behavioural and perceptual effects of anticipated crowding. *Journal of Personality and Social Psychology*, 34, 667–671.

Baum, A. and Valins, S. (1977) Cited in Bell, P.A. Greene, T.C. Fisher, J.D. and Baum, A. *Environmental Psychology*. Harcourt Brace College Publishers.

Baum, A. Fleming, R. and Davidson, L.M. (1983) Natural disaster and technological catastrophe. *Environment and Behaviour*, 15, 333–354.

Berry, P.C. (1961) Effects of coloured illumination upon perceived temperature. *Journal of Applied Psychology*, 45, 248–250.

Bickman, L. Teger, A. Gabiele, T. McLaughlin, C. Berger, M. and Sunaday, E. (1973) Dormitory density and helping behaviour. *Environment and Behaviour*, 5, 465–490.

Borsky, P.N. (1969) Effects of noise on community behaviour. Cited in Bell, P.A. Greene, T.C. Fisher, J.D. and Baum, A. *Environmental Psychology*. Harcourt Brace College Publishers.

Bronzaft, A.L. and McCarthy, D.P. (1975) The effects of elevated train noise on reading ability. *Environment and Behaviour*, 7, 517–527.

Bruins, J. and Barber, A. (2000) Crowding, performance and effect: a field experiment investigating mediating processes. *Journal of Applied Social Psychology*, 30, 1268–80.

Bull, A.J. Burbage, S.E. Crandall, J.E. Fletcher, C.I. Lloyd, J.T. Ravenberg, R.L. and Rockett, S.L. (1972) Effects of noise and intolerance of ambiguity upon attraction for similar and dissimilar others. *Journal of Social Psychology*, 88, 151–152.

Calhoun, J.B. (1962) Population density and social pathology. *Scientific American*, 206, 139-148.

Cameron, P. Robertson, D. and Zaks, J. (1972) Sound pollutants, noise pollution, and health: Community parameters. *Journal of Applied Psychology*, 56, 67–74.

Cohen, S. Glass, D.C. and Singer, J.E. (1977) Apartment noise, auditory discrimination and reading ability in children. *Journal of experimental Social Psychology*, 9, 407–422.

Cox, V.C. Paulus, P.B. and McCain, G. (1984) Prison crowding research: The relevance for prison housing standards and a general approach regarding crowding phenomena. *American Psychologist*, 39, 1148–1160.

Cunningham, M.R. (1979) Weather, mood, and helping behaviour: Quasi experiments with the sunshine Samaritan. *Journal of Personality and Social Psychology*, 37, 1947–1956.

Deiner, E. (1979) Deindividuation, self-awareness and disinhibition. *Journal of Personality and Social Psychology*, 37, 1160–1171.

Devlin, A.S. and Bernstein, J. (1995) Interactive Wayfinding: Use of cues by men and women. *Journal of Environmental Psychology*, 15, 23–38.

Donald, I. and Canter, D. (1992) Intentionality and fatality during the Kings Cross underground fire. *European Journal of Social Psychology*, 22, 203–219.

Donnerstein, E. and Wilson, D.W. (1976) Effects of noise and perceived control on ongoing and subsequent aggressive behaviour. *Journal of Personality and Social Psychology*, 34, 774–781.

Edney, J.J. (1972) Property, possession and permanence: A field study in human territoriality. *Journal of Applied Social Psychology*, 31, 1108–1115.

Epstein, Y.M. and Karlin, R.A. (1975) Effects of acute experimental crowding. *Journal of Applied Social Psychology*, 5, 34–53.

Felipe, N.J. and Sommer, R. (1966) Invasions of Personal Space. *Social Problems*, 14, 206–214.

Fidell, S. Barber, D. and Schultz, T. (1991) Revision of a dosage-effect relationship for the prevalence of annoyance due to general transportation noise. *Journal of the Acoustical Society of America*, 89, 244–247.

Fisher, J.D. and Byrne, D. (1975) Too close for comfort: Sex differences in response to invasions of personal space. *Journal of Personality and Social Psychology*, 32, 15–21.

Ford, A.B. (1976) *Urban Health in America*. New York: Oxford University Press.

Freedman, J.L. Levy, A.S. Buchnan, R.W. and Price, J. (1972) Crowding and human aggressiveness. *Journal of Experimental Social Psychology*, 15, 295–303.

Fritz, C.E. and Marks, E.S. (1954) The NORC studies of human behaviour in disaster. *Journal of Social Issues* 10, 26–41.

Gärling T. Böök, A. and Linberg, E. (1984) Cognitive mapping of large-scale environments: the interrelationships of action plans, acquisition and orientation. *Environment and Behaviour*, 16, 3–34.

Geen, R.G. and O'Neal, E.C (1969) Activation of cue-elicited aggression by general arousal. *Journal of Personality and Social Psychology*, 11, 289–292.

Gergen, K.J. Gergen, M.K. and Barton, W.H. (1973) Deviance in the dark. *Psychology Today*, 7, 129–130.

Gifford, R. (1987) *Environmental Psychology, Principles and Practice*. (second edition) Boston: Allyn and Bacon.

Glass, D.C. and Singer, J.E (1972) *Urban stress*. New York: Academic Press.

Glass, D.C. Singer, J.E. and Friedman, L.W. (1969) Psychic cost of adaptation to an environmental stressor. *Journal of Personality and Social Psychology*, 12, 200–210.

Haber, G.M. (1980) Territorial invasion in the classroom: Invadee response. *Environment and Behaviour*, 12, 17–31.

Hayduk, L.A. (1983) Personal Space: Where we now stand. *Psychological Bulletin*, 94, 293–335.

Heerwagen, J.H. and Orians, G.H (1986) Adaptations to windowlessness: A study of the use of visual décor in windowed and windowless offices. *Environment and Behaviour*, 18, 623–639.

Heshka and Pylypuk (1975) Cited in Bell, P.A. Greene, T.C. Fisher, J.D. and Baum, A. *Environmental Psychology*. Harcourt Brace College Publishers.

Holahan, C.J. and Moos, R.H. (1981) Social support and psychological distress: A longitudinal analysis. *Journal of Abnormal Psychology*, 49, pp 365–370.

Hollister, F.D. (1968) Greater London Council: *A Report on the Problems of Windowless Environments*. London: Hobbs.

Ising et al. (1990) Cited in Bell, P.A. Greene, T.C. Fisher, J.D. and Baum, A. *Environmental Psychology*. Harcourt Brace College Publishers.

Jacobs, (1961) *The Death and Life of Great American Cities*. New York: Oxford University Press.

Jorgenson, D. O. and Dukes, F.O. (1976) Deindividuation as a function of density and group membership. *Journal of Personality and Social Psychology*, 34, 24–39.

Kaplan, S. and Kaplan, R. (1989) The visual environment: Public participation in design and planning. *Journal of Social Issues*, 45, 59–86.

Karmel, L.J. (1965) Effects of windowless classroom environment on high school students. *Perceptual and Motor Skills*, 20, 277–278.

Konecni , V.J. Libuser, L. Morton, H. and Ebbesen, E.B. (1975) Effects of a violation of personal space on escape and helping responses. *Journal of Experimental Social Psychology*, 11, 288–299.

Konenci, V.J. (1975) The mediation of aggressive behaviour: arousal level vs anger and cognitive labelling. *Journal of Personality and Social Psychology*, 32, 706–712.

Kovess, V. Murphy, H.B. and Tousignant, M (1987) Urban-rural comparisons of depressive disorders in French Canada. *Journal of Nervous Mental Disorders*, 175 (8), 457–66.

Lang, J. (1987) *Creating architectural theory: The role of the behavioural sciences in environmental design*. New York: Van Nostrand Reinhold.

Levine, M. Marchon, I. and Hanley, G. (1984) The placement and misplacement of you-are-here maps. *Environment and Behaviour*, 16, 139–157.

Levine, R.V. Martinez, T.S. Brase, G. and Sorenson, K. (1994) Helping in 36 U.S. Cities. *Journal of Personality and Social Psychology*, 67 (1), 69–82.

Ley, D. and Cybriwsky, R. (1974) Urban graffiti as territorial markers. *Annals of the Association of American Geographers*, 64, 491–505.

Lundberg, U. (1976) Urban commuting: Crowdedness and catecholamine excretion. *Journal of Human Stress*, 2, 26–32.

Lynch, K. (1960) *The Image of the City*. Cambridge, MA: The MIT Press.

Maccoby, E. and Jacklin, C. (1974) *The Psychology of Sex*. Stanford, CA: Stanford University Press.

MacDonald, J.E. and Gifford, R. (1989) Territorial cues and defensible space theory: the burglar's point of view. *Journal of Environmental Psychology*, 9, 193–205.

Mathews, K.E. and Canon, L.K. (1975) Environmental noise as a determinant of helping behaviour. *Journal of Personality and Social Psychology*, 32, 571–577.

McNally, R.J. Bryant, R.A. and Ehlers, A. (2003) Does early psychological intervention promote recovery from posttraumatic stress? *Psychological Science in the Public Interest* 4, 45–74.

Mercer, G.W. and Benjamin, M.L. (1980) Spatial behaviour of university undergraduates in double-occupancy residence rooms: An inventory of effects. *Journal of Applied Social Psychology*, 10, 32–44.

Middlemist, R.D. Knowles, E.S. and Matter, C.F. (1976) Personal space invasions in the lavatory: Suggestive evidence for arousal. *Journal of Personality and Social Psychology*, 33, 541–546.

Milgram, S. (1977) *The Individual in a Social World*. Reading, MA: Addison-Wesley

Millar, K. and Steels, M.J. (1990) Sustained peripheral vasoconstriction while working in continuous intense noise. *Aviation, Space and Environmental Medicine*, 61, 695–698.

Milliman, R.E. (1982) Using background music to affect the behaviour of supermarket shoppers. *Journal of Marketing*, 46, 86–91.

Moar, I. (1978) *Mental Triangulation and the Nature of Internal Representations of Space*. Unpublished PhD thesis, University of Cambridge.

Newman, O. (1972) *Defensible Space*. New York: Macmillan.

North, A.C. and Hargreaves, D.J. (1996) The effects of music on responses to a dining area. *Journal of Environmental Psychology*, 16, 55–64.

Ornstein, S. (1992) First impressions of the symbolic meanings connoted by reception area design. *Environment and Behaviour*, 24, 85–110.

Page, R.A. (1978) Environmental influences on prosocial behaviour: The effect of temperature. Cited in Bell, P.A. Greene, T.C. Fisher, J.D. and Baum, A. *Environmental Psychology*. Harcourt Brace College Publishers.

Pepler, R.D (1972) Cited in Bell, P.A. Greene, T.C. Fisher, J.D. and Baum, A. *Environmental Psychology*. Harcourt Brace College Publishers.

Porteus, J. (1977) *Environment and Behaviour*. Reading, MA: Addison-Wesley

Provins (1966) Environmental heat, body temperature and behaviour: An hypothesis. *Australian Journal of Psychology*, 85, pp 40–44.

Prentice-Dunn, S, and Rogers, R.W. (1982) Effects of public and private self-awareness on deindividuation and aggression. *Journal of Personality and Social Psychology*, 43, 503–513.

Purcell, A.T., Lamb, R.J., Peron, E.M. and Falchero, S. (1994) Preference or preferences for landscape? *Journal of Environmental Psychology*. 14, pp 195–209.

Raloff, J. (1982) Occupational noise – The subtle pollutant. *Science News*, 121, 347–350.

Rosen, S. Bergman, M. Plestor, M. Plestor, D. El-Mofty, A. and Satti, M. (1969) Presbycosis study of a relatively noise-free population in the Sudan. *Annals of Otology, Rhinology and Laryngology*, 71,727–743.

Rosenthal, N.E. Sack, D.A., Gillen, J.C. Lewy, A.J. Goodwin, F.K. Davenport, Y. Mueller, P.S. Newssome, D.A. and Wehr, T.A. (1984) Seasonal Affective Disorder: A description of the syndrome and preliminary findings with light therapy. *Archives of General Psychiatry*, 41, 72–80.

Rotton, J. (1983) Affective and cognitive consequences of malodourous pollution. *Basic and Applied Social Psychology*, 4, 171–191.

Russell, J.A. and Ward, L.M. (1982) Environmental Psychology. *Annual Review of Psychology*, 33, 651–688.

Saegert, S. MacIntosh, E. and West, S. (1975) Two studies of crowding urban public spaces. *Environment and Behaviour*, 1, 159–184.

Schmidt, D.E. and Keating, J.P. (1979) Human crowding and personality control: An integration of research. *Psychological Bulletin*, 86, 680–700.

Siegal, A.W. and White, S. (1975) The development of spatial representations of large scale environments. In Reese, H.W. (ed) *Advances in Child Development and Behaviou*r, NY. Academic Press.

Smith, H.W. (1981) Territorial spacing on a beach revisited: A cross-national exploration. *Social Psychology Quarterly*, 44, 132–137.

Sommer, R. (1969) *Personal Space*. Englewood Cliffs, NJ: Prentice-Hall.

Sommer, R. and Ross, H. (1958) Social interaction on a geriatrics ward. *International Journal of Social Psychiatry*, 4, 128–133.

Srisurapanont, M. and Intaprasert, S. (1999) Seasonal variations in mood and behaviour: epidemiological findings in the northern tropics. *Journal of Affective Disorders*, 54, 97–99.

Srole, L. (1976) The city vs the country: New evidence on an ancient bias. In Srole, L. and Fischer, A. (eds), *Mental Health in the metropolis* (second edition) New York: Harper and Row.

Stone, N. (2001) Designing effective study environments. *Journal of Experimental Psychology*, 21, 179–90.

Sugiman, T. and Misumi, J. (1988) Development of a new evacuation method for emergencies: Control of collective behaviour by emergent small groups. *Journal of Applied Psychology*, 73, 3–10.

Sunstrom, E. Town, J.P. Rice, R.W. Osborn, D.P. and Brill, M. (1994) Office noise, satisfaction and performance. *Environment and Behaviour*, 26, 560–579.

Taylor, R.B. Gottfredson, S.D. and Brower, S. (1981) Understanding block crime and fear. *Journal of Research in Crime and Delinquency*, 21, 303–331.

Thompson, M.P. Norris, F.H. and Hanacek, B. (1993) Age differences in the psychological consequences of Hurricane Hugo. *Psychology and Ageing*, 8, 606–616.

Tlauka, M. and Wilson, P.N. (1994) The effect of landmarks on route-learning in a computer-simulated environment. *Journal of Environmental Psychology*, 14, 305-313.

Tolman, E.C. (1948) Cognitive maps in rats and men. *Psychological Review*, 55, 189–208.

Turner, R.H. and Killian, L.M. (1972) *Collective Behaviour*. Englewood Cliffs, NJ: Prentice-Hall.

Ulrich, R. S. (1984) View through a window may influence recovery from surgery. *Science*, 224, 420–421.

Vinsel, A. Brown, B. Altman, I. and Foss, C. (1980) Privacy regulation, territorial displays, and effectiveness of individual functioning. *Journal of Personality and Social Psychology*, 39, 1104–1115.

Weisman, J. (1981) Wayfinding and the built environment. *Environment and Behaviour*, 13, 189–204.

Wyon, D.P. (1970) Studies of children under imposed noise and heat stress. *Ergonomics*, 13, 598–612.

Zimbardo, P.G. (1969) The human choices: Individuation, reason, and order versus deindividuation, impulse and chaos. Cited in Bell, P.A. Greene, T.C. Fisher, J.D. and Baum, *A. Environmental Psychology*. Harcourt Brace College Publishers.

PSYCHOLOGY AND CRIME

Ainsworth, P.B. (2000) *Psychology and Crime: Myths and Reality*. Harlow: Longman.

Ainsworth, P.B. (2002) *Psychology and Policing*. Padstow: Willan Publishing.

Austin, T.L., Hale, D.C. and Ramsey, L.J. (1987) The effect of layoff on police authoritarianism. *Criminal Justice and Behaviour*, 14, 194–210.

Bagley, C. and Ramsey, R. (1986) Sexual abuse in childhood: psychological outcomes and implications for social work practice. *Journal of Social Work and Human Sexuality*, 4, 33–47.

Bandura, A. (1965) Influence of models' reinforcement contingencies on the acquisition of imitative responses. *Journal of Personality and Social Psychology*, 1 (6), 589–95.

Beech, A., Fisher, D. and Beckett, R. (1998) *Step 3: An Evaluation of the Prisoner Sex Offender Treatment Programme*. London: Home Office.

Bennett, T. and Wright, R. (1984) *Burglars on Burglary: Prevention and the Offender*. Aldershot: Gower.

Black, D.A. (1982) A 5-year follow-up study of male patients discharged from Broadmoor Hospital. In Gunn, J. and Farrington, D.P. (eds) *Abnormal Offenders, Deliquency, and the Criminal Justice System*. Chichester: Wiley.

Black, D.A. and Reiss, A. (1970) Police control of juveniles. *American Sociological Review*, 35, 63–77.

Blackburn, R. (1997) *The Psychology of Criminal Conduct*. Chichester: Wiley.

Blair, R.J.R., Jones, L., Clark, F. and Smith, M. (1997) The psychopathic individual: A lack of responsiveness to distress cues? *Psychophysiology*, 34, 192–98.

Brown, L. and Willis, A. (1985) Authoritarianism in British police recruits: importation, socialisation or myth? *Journal of Occupational Psychology*, 58, 97–108.

Bruce, V. (1998) Identifying people caught on video. *The Psychologist*, 11 (7), 331–37.

Bull, R. (1999) Interviewing children in legal contexts. In Bull, R. and Carson, D. (eds) *Handbook of Psychology in Legal Contexts*. Chichester: Wiley.

Bull, R. and Carson, D. (1999) *Handbook of Psychology in Legal Contexts*. Chichester: Wiley.

Butler, W.M., Leitenberg, H. and Fuselier, D.G. (1993) The use of mental health professional consultants to police hostage negotiation teams. *Behavioural Sciences and Law*, 11, 213–21.

Canter, D. and Heritage, R. (1990) A multi-variate model of sexual offence behaviour. *Journal of Forensic Psychiatry*, 1 (2), 185–212.

Carson, D. and Bull, R. (2003) *Handbook of Psychology in Legal Contexts* (2nd edn.) Chichester: Wiley.

Carson, D. and Pakes, F. (2003) Advocacy: getting the answers you want. In Carson, D. and Bull, R. *Handbook of Psychology in Legal Contexts* (2nd edn.) Chichester: Wiley.

Clarke, C. and Milne, R. (2001) *National Evaluation of the PEACE Investigative Interviewing Course*. London: Police Research Award Scheme, report no. PRAS/149.

Clifford, B.R. and Bull, R. (1978) *The Psychology of Person Identification*. London: Routledge, Kegan Paul.

Coleman, A.M. and Gorman, L.P. (1982) Conservatism, dogmatism and authoritarianism in British police officers. *Sociology*, 16, 1–11.

Copson, G. (1995) Coals to Newcastle. Part 1: a study of offender profiling. *Police Research Group Special Interest Series: Paper 7*. London: Home Office.

Cox, T.C. and White, M.F. (1988) Traffic citations and student attitudes towards the police: an examination of selected interaction dynamics. *Journal of Police Science and Administration*, 16, 105–21.

Crick, N.R. and Dodge, K.A. (1994) A review and reformulation of social information-processing mechanisms in children's social adjustment. *Psychological Bulletin*, 115, 74–101.

Cusson, M. and Pinsonneault, P. (1986) The decision to give up crime. In Cornish, D.B. and Clarke, R.V.G. (eds) *The Reasoning Criminal*. New York: Springer-Verlag.

Douglas, J.E. (1981) Evaluation of the (FBI) psychological profiling. Unpublished. Cited in Copson, G. (1996) At last some facts about offender profiling in Britain. *Forensic Update*, 46, 4–10.

DSM-IV Criteria for PTSD (1994) Diagnostic and statistical manual of mental disorders, (4th edn.) American Psychiatric Association: Washington DC.

Duncan, B.L. (1976) Different social perceptions and attributions of inter-group violence: testing the lower limits of stereotyping of blacks. *Journal of Personality and Social Psychology*, 34, 590–98.

Eaton, M. (1986) *Justice for Women*. Milton Keynes: Open University Press.

Eysenck, H.J. (1977) *Crime and Personality*. London: Routledge, Kegan Paul.

Farrington, D.P. (2002) Key results from the first 40 years of the Cambridge study in delinquent development. In Thornberry, T.P. and Krohn, M.D. (eds), *Taking Stock of Delinquency: An Overview of Findings from Contemporary Longitudinal Studies*. New York: Kluwer Academic/Plenum Publishing.

The Fawcett Society (2003) Commission on Women and the Criminal Justice System: Interim report on women and offending. London.

Fisher, R.P. and Geiselman, R.E. (1984) *Memory-Enhancing Techniques for Investigative Interviewing: The Cognitive Interview*. Springfield IL: Charkes C. Thomas.

Flin, R., Boon, J., Knox, A. and Bull, R. (1993) The effects of a five-month delay on children's eye-witness memory. *British Journal of Psychology*, 83, 323–36.

George, R.C. (1991) *A field evaluation of the cognitive interview*. Unpublished M.A. thesis, Polytechnic of East London.

Gillis, C.A. (2002) Understanding employment: a prospective exploration of factors linked to community-based employment among federal offenders. *Forum on Correctional Research*, 14 (1), 3–6.

Greene, E. and Wrightsman, L. (2003) Decision making by juries and judges: international perspectives. In Carson, D. and Bull, R. *Handbook of Psychology in Legal Contexts* (2nd edn.) Chichester: Wiley.

Gudjonsson, G.H. and Adlam, K.R.C. (1983) Personality patterns of British police officers. *Personality and Individual Differences*, 4, 507–512.

Hare, R.D. (2001) Psychopaths and their nature. In Raine, A. and Sanmartin, J. (eds), *Violence and Psychopathy*. Dordrecht, The Netherlands: Kluwer Academic/Plenum Publishing.

Hatcher, C., Mohandie, K., Turner, J. and Gelles, M.G. (1998) The role of the psychologist in crisis/hostage negotiations. *Behavioural Sciences and the Law*, 16, 455–72.

Hollin, C. (2001) *Criminal Behaviour: A Psychological Approach to Explanation and Prevention*. Chippenham: Psychology Press Ltd, Taylor and Francis.

Home Office (2001) *Youth Lifestyle Survey 1998–1999*. London: HMSO.

Hood, R. (1992) *Race and Sentencing*. Oxford: Clarendon Press.

Hovland, C.I., Janis, I.L. and Kelley, H.H. (1953) *Communication and persuasion: psychological studies of opinion change*. New Haven: Yale University Press.

Jackson, J.L., Van Koppen, P.J. and Herbrink, J.C.M. (1993) *Does the service meet the needs?* Leiden, The Netherlands: NSCR.

Jacobs, J. (1962) *The Death and Life of Great American Cities*. New York: Vintage.

Jennings, W.S., Kilkenny, R. and Kohlberg, L. (1983) Moral development theory and practice for youthful and adult offenders. In Laufer, W.S. and Day, J.M. (eds) *Personality Theory, Moral Development, and Criminal Behaviour*. Toronto: Lexington Books.

Joseph, S., Williams, R. and Yule, W. (1997) *Understanding Post-Traumatic Stress*. Chichester: Wiley.

Kidd, R.F. (1985) Impulsive bystanders: Why do they intervene?. In Farrington D.P. and Gunn, J. (eds) *Reactions to Crime: The Public, the Police, Courts and Prisons*. Chichester: Wiley.

Kohlberg, L. (1964) Development of moral character and moral ideology. In Hoffman, M. and Hoffman, L. (eds) *Review of Child Development Research*, vol. 1. New York: Russell Sage Foundation.

Kohnken, G., Milne, R., Memon, A. and Bull, R. (1999) The cognitive interview: a meta analysis. *Psychology, Crime and Law*, 5, 3–28.

Lerner, M.J. and Miller, D.T. (1978) Just world research and the attribution process: looking back and ahead. *Psychological Bulletin*, 85, 1030–51.

Lindsay, R.C. and Wells, G.L. (1985) Improving eye-witness identifications from line-ups: simultaneous versus sequential lineup presentation. *Journal of Applied Psychology*, 70 (3), 556–64.

Loftus, E.F., Loftus, G.R. and Messo, J. (1987) Some facts about weapon focus. *Law and Human Behavior*, 11, 55–62.

Lombroso, C. (1876) *L'Uomo Delinquente*. Milan: Hoepli.

Lupfer, M.B., Cohen, R. and Beranrd, J.L. (1987) The influence of moral reasoning on the decisions of jurors. *Journal of Social Psychology*, 127, 653–57.

Maass, A. and Köhnken, G. (1989) Eye-witness identification: Simulating the weapon effect. *Law and Human Behavior*, 13, 397–408.

MacPherson, Sir William of Cluny (1999) The Stephen Lawrence Inquiry. Cmnd. 4262-1. London. HMSO.

Malpass, R.S. and Devine, P.G. (1981) Guided memory in eye-witness identification. *Journal of Applied Psychology*, 66, 343–50.

McArdle, E. (2003) The order of witnesses is crucial. *Lawyers Weekly USA*, November 2003.

McConville, M., Sanders, A. and Leng, R. (1991) *The Case for the Prosecution*. London: Routledge.

McEwan, J. (1999) Adversarial and inquisitorial proceedings. In Bull, R. and Carson, D. (eds) *Handbook of Psychology in Legal Contexts*. Chichester: Wiley.

Mezey and Taylor (1988). In Brewer, K. (2000) *Psychology and Crime*. Oxford: Heinemann.

Milne, R. and Bull, R. (2003) Interviewing by the police. In Carson, D. and Bull, R. *Handbook of Psychology in Legal Contexts* (2nd edn.) Chichester: Wiley.

Nayak, A. (2003) Through children's eyes: childhood, place and the fear of crime. *Geoforum*, 34 (3), 303–315.

Newman, O. (1972) *Defensible Space: People and Design in the Violent City*. London: Architectural Press.

Novaco, R.W. (1975) *Anger-control: The Development and Evaluation of an Experimental Treatment*. Lexington: Heath.

Olczak, P.V., Kaplan, M.F. and Penrod, S. (1991) Attorney's law psychology and its effectiveness in selecting jurors: Three Empirical Studies. *Journal of Social Behaviour and Personality*, 6, 431–452.

Orne, M. (1984) Hypnotically induced testimony. In Wells, G.L. and Loftus, E.F. (eds) *Eyewitness Testimony: Psychological Perspectives*. New York: Cambridge University Press.

Oxford, T. (1991) Spotting a liar. *Police Review*. 328–29.

Padawer-Singer, A.M. and Barton, A. (1974) The impact of pre-trial publicity on jurors verdicts. In Simon, R.J. (ed.) *The Jury System in America: A Critical Overview*. California: Sage.

Palmer, E.J. and Hollin, C.R. (1998) A comparison of patterns of moral development in young offenders and non-offenders. *Legal and Criminological Psychology*, 3, 225–35.

Pickel, K.L. (1998) Unusualness and threat as possible causes of 'weapon focus'. *Memory*, 6, 277–95.

Piliavin, I.M., Rodin, J. and Piliavin, J.A. (1969) Good samaritanism: an underground phenomenon? *Journal of Personality and Social Psychology*, 13, 289–99.

Raine, A., Buchsbaum, M. and LaCasse, L. (1991) Brain abnormalities in murderers indicated by positron emission tomography. *Biological Psychiatry*, 42, 495–508.

Ressler, R.K., Burgess, A.W. and Douglas J.E. (1998) *Criminal Homicide: Patterns and Motives*. New York: Lexington Books.

Roshier, B. (1989) *Controlling Crime: The Classical Perspective in Criminology*. Milton Keynes: Open University Press.

Rotter, J.B. (1966) Generalised expectancies for internal versus external control of reinforcement. *Psychological Monographs*, 80(1), whole of No. 609.

Saywitz, K., Lamphear, V. and Snyder, L. (1996) Helping children to tell what happened: follow-up study of the narrative elaboration procedure. *Child Maltreatment*, 1, 200–212.

Schachter, S. and Singer, J. (1962) Cognitive, social, and physiological determinants of emotional state. *Psychological Review*, 69, 379–99.

Siegal, L.J. (1986) *Criminology*. St Paul: West Publishing.

Sigall, H. and Ostrove, N. (1975) Beautiful but dangerous: effects of offender attractiveness and nature of the crime on juridic judgment. *Journal of Personality and Social Psychology*, 31, 410–414.

Simmons, J. and Dodd, T. (2003) *Crime in England and Wales 2002/2003*. London: Home Office.

Smith, D.A. and Visher, C.A. (1982) Street level justice: situational determinants of police arrest decisions. *Social Problems*, 29, 167–77.

Spencer, J., Nicholson, G., Flin, R. and Bull., R. (1990) *Child evidence in legal proceedings: An international perspective*. Cambridge: Cambridge University Press.

Sporer, S.L. (1997) The less travelled road to truth: verbal cues in deception detection in accounts of fabricated and self-experienced events. *Applied Cognitive Psychology*, 11, 373–97.

Stephenson, G.M. (1992) *The Psychology of Criminal Justice*. Oxford: Blackwell.

Vennard, J. and Hedderman, C. (1998) Effective treatment with offenders. In Goldblatt, P. and Lewis, C. (eds) Reducing offending: an assessment of research evidence of ways of dealing with offending behaviour. *Home Office Research Study 187*. London: Home Office Research and Statistics Directorate.

Vernis, J.S. and Walker, V. (1970) Policemen and the recall of criminal details. *Journal of Social Psychology*, 81, 217–21.

Vrij, A. (2001) Detecting the liars. *The Psychologist*, 14 (11), 596–98.

Webb, V.J. and Marshall, I.H. (1989) Response to criminal victimisation by older Americans. *Criminal Justice and Behavior*, 16 (2), 239–59.

Wells, G.L., Small, M., Penrod, S.D., Malpass, R.S., Fulero, S.M. and Brimacombe, C.A.E. (1998) Eyewitness identification procedures: recommendations for line-ups and photospreads. *Law and Human Behaviour*, 22, 603–645.

Yarmey, A.D. (2003) Eye-witnesses. In Carson, D. and Bull, R. *Handbook of Psychology in Legal Contexts* (2nd edn.) Chichester: Wiley.

Yochelson, S. and Samenow, S.E. (1976) *The Criminal Personality: A Profile for Change*, vol. 1. New York: Jason Aronsen.

Zimbardo, P.G. (2004) A situationist perspective on the psychology of evil: Understanding how good people are transformed into perpetrators. In Miller, A (ed.), *The Social Psychology of Good and Evil: Understanding our Capacity for Kindness and Cruelty*. New York: Guilford.

INDEX